Corporate Governance and Capital Flows in a Global Economy

GLOBAL OUTLOOK SERIES

A co-publication of the World Economic Forum and Oxford University Press, the Global Outlook Series focuses on issues of significant relevance for the functioning and governance of the world economy. It is designed to provide practitioners, scholars, and students with concise, state-of-the art information on global issues of contemporary interest, with an emphasis on integrating academic scholarship with current interests of scholars and global decision-makers.

Corporate Governance and Capital Flows in a Global Economy
Edited by Peter K. Cornelius and Bruce Kogut

Corporate Governance
and Capital Flows
in a Global Economy

EDITED BY

Peter K. Cornelius, WORLD ECONOMIC FORUM AND

Bruce Kogut, THE WHARTON SCHOOL, UNIVERSITY OF PENNSYLVANIA, AND INSEAD

New York Oxford

OXFORD UNIVERSITY PRESS

2003

OXFORD
UNIVERSITY PRESS

Oxford   New York
Auckland   Bangkok   Buenos Aires   Cape Town   Chennai
Dar es Salaam   Delhi   Hong Kong   Istanbul   Karachi   Kolkata
Kuala Lumpur   Madrid   Melbourne   Mexico City   Mumbai   Nairobi
São Paulo   Shanghai   Taipei   Tokyo   Toronto

Published by Oxford University Press, Inc.
198 Madison Avenue, New York, New York 10016

www.oup.com

Oxford is a registered trademark of Oxford University Press

The term *country* as used in this study does not in all cases refer to the territorial entity
that is a state as understood by international law and practice. The term covers well-defined,
geographically self-contained economic areas that are not states but for which statistical data
are maintained on a separate and independent basis.

Library of Congress Cataloging-in-Publication Data
Corporate governance and capital flows in a global economy /
edited by Peter K. Cornelius and Bruce Kogut.
p. cm. — (Global outlook series ; 1)
Includes bibliographical references.
ISBN 0-19-516705-8; — ISBN 0-19-516171-8 (pbk.)
1. Corporate governance. 2. International business enterprises.
3. Capital movements. I. Cornelius, Peter, 1960– II. Kogut, Bruce Mitchel.
III. Series.
HD2741.C77482 2003
658.4'2—dc21   2003040590

2 4 6 8 9 7 5 3 1

Printed in the United States of America
on acid-free paper

*To our children Paul Konstantin Cornelius,
Emily Johanna Kogut, and Erik Gustav Kogut,
three experts in family governance.*

Foreword

Patrick T. Harker and Gabriel Hawawini

The Wharton School of the University of Pennsylvania and INSEAD are delighted and honored to join the World Economic Forum in presenting this timely and insightful exploration into issues of corporate governance and the impact of governance practices on investments in developing countries. As part of our shared commitment to advancing scholarship and business practice in the global marketplace, this volume presents the work of senior researchers at the world's top academic institutions as well as the work of key policymakers and business leaders.

In recent years, we have witnessed unprecedented changes in the conduct of business. Technological advances, political shifts, and social development have combined to transform companies, industries, and markets in ways unforeseeable just a few decades ago. We are challenged to take full advantage of emerging opportunities, while at the same time confronting the difficulties implicit in superimposing established practices upon divergent cultural milieus. We must also face critical questions of balance between the economic exploitation of developing regions and the economic empowerment of populations heretofore unable to participate fully in the global market. Never before has it been so critical to muster the very best and most experienced thinkers across the widest possible range of disciplines to examine these issues.

When our institutions joined to create the Wharton-INSEAD Alliance in March 2001, our goal was to combine the resources of our faculties and our academic programs to create a global business knowledge network through joint research and educational offerings to students and executives. This collaboration with the World Economic Forum is a natural outgrowth of our alliance. We are proud to contribute the expertise of our professors—along with that of our other valued colleagues rep-resented in these chapters—to promote successful strategies for future market expan-sion and the much-needed economic progress in the developing world.

Patrick T. Harker
Dean and Reliance Professor of Management and Private Enterprise
The Wharton School
The University of Pennsylvania

Gabriel Hawawini
Dean and Henry Grunfeld Chaired Professor of Investment Banking
INSEAD

 # Foreword

Klaus Schwab

Written by top academics and practitioners, this collection of essays is published at a time when confidence in global business has been fundamentally undermined by a series of headline corporate scandals. The scale of these scandals has been unprecedented, and the full extent of the damage they have caused is only beginning to emerge. Equity prices have remained depressed, with the loss in market capitalization on the New York Stock Exchange alone amounting to almost USD 1.5 trillion as of October 31, 2002.

Enron and WorldCom have become synonymous with infectious greed in a corporate world where top managers cook the books, CEOs depart with outrageous severance packages, and shareholders and employees lose their investments, savings, and pensions. These two cases have probably been the most shocking ones, not just because of their sheer magnitude but because they occurred in what has widely been considered the deepest, most transparent, and most secure capital market in the world. As Enron, WorldCom and other cases have painfully shown, financial reporting failures and management wrongdoing are not confined to any particular governance system, or to emerging-market economies where institutions have yet to fully develop. Enron and WorldCom have also shown that the systematic failure to meet expectations can result in a loss of confidence in entire markets no matter where investors are situated or where they invest.

Restoring confidence is the most important task right now. As the Sarbanes-Oxley Act in the United States and the proliferation of governance codes and legal initiatives in several other markets indicate, policy makers understand that this is not "business as usual." The skepticism is deep-seated, and regaining the public's trust will not be easy. Instituting reforms requires, first and foremost, studying why the recent failures were possible and applying the lessons learned from these failures in order to design better framework conditions for investment.

This is what this book is all about. With global financial markets having become more integrated, the book pays particular attention to the role of corporate governance in emerging-market economies and international capital flows. For these countries, the price tag of poor corporate governance seems especially high, as evidenced by the recent crises in Asia. In 1997–1998, the five most heavily affected countries, Indonesia, Korea, Thailand, Malaysia, and the Philippines, lost more than USD 600 billion in market capitalization, or around 60 percent of their combined precrisis gross domestic product. With international investors reassessing the risk profile of their portfolios, total private capital flows to emerging markets are estimated to have fallen in 2002 to levels last seen in the early 1990s.

Access to foreign savings is critical in order to promote economic growth in the developing world. But foreign investors will be willing to invest only if they can be confident that their investments are sufficiently protected. This is increasingly well understood, and in several countries important reforms are already underway. The experience of these countries will provide guidance for other nations and companies as they seek to upgrade their own standards of governance.

It is my sincere hope that this book will make an important contribution to this learning process and help identify best practices to foster financial sector development and sustained economic growth. Its academic rigor and policy relevance makes this volume an outstanding example of our commitment to improve the state of the world. The World Economic Forum is proud to copublish this study with the Wharton School of the University of Pennsylvania and INSEAD, two of the world's leading business schools, and I would like to thank Dean Harker of the Wharton School and Dean Hawawini of INSEAD for their outstanding support of this project. Several of the Forum's members have contributed to this book, showing, as a community, their determination to help restore trust. My particular appreciation goes to the editors, Dr. Peter Cornelius and Professor Bruce Kogut. The collection of essays in this book deserves to be read closely, and I expect it to lend fresh momentum to the debate on corporate governance.

Klaus Schwab
Founder and President, World Economic Forum

 Acknowledgments

This book begins with the observation that there are no best systems of governance, but there are better practices. From this follows our claim: adoption of better practices and understanding how systems work will help increase financial flows to poorer countries.

These chapters are written at a time when international financial markets, in large part, have already been depressed for two years; in the case of the Unites States, the stock markets have not fared worse as an investment since the Great Depression. This dismal performance reflects the hangover of an "irrational exuberance," to recall the words of the US Federal Reserve Chairman, Alan Greenspan, during the height of the bull market. But it also reflects current events, the deep uncertainty over political and military threats, and the scandalous behavior of managers and auditors of blue chip companies in the United States that has shaken investor confidence.

Global uncertainty allows for a moment of reflection for practitioners and academic researchers. The chapters in this book express widely diverse views, personal statements, and even disappointments concerning the behavior of financial-market participants and corporate leaders, and call for considerable change in institutions and a rethinking of what constitutes, in the end, good corporate governance. Written by leading practitioners and researchers, we have not intervened to force a harmony of views; on the contrary, we have sought a reasoned diversity.

Published under the umbrella of the Global Competitiveness Program of the World Economic Forum, this volume is cosponsored by the Reginald H. Jones Center (under a grant from the General Electric Fund) at the Wharton School of the University of Pennsylvania and INSEAD, Fontainebleau, France. We would like to thank these institutions for their support, both financial and moral. We owe a deep thanks to the contributors to this volume who, on rather short notice, produced chapters of depth and novelty.

This project was strongly encouraged by Klaus Schwab and ably supported by a first-rate team at the World Economic Forum, especially Jennifer Blanke and Fiona Paua. Bruce Kogut would like to thank John Paul MacDuffie and Sid Winter, his codirectors of the Jones Center; Landis Gabel and David Schmittlein, academic deans at INSEAD and the Wharton School, respectively; Deans Pat Harker (Wharton School) and Gabriel Hawawini (INSEAD) for their support; and Rachel Barrett for her all-around assistance. The editors would also like to thank Pearl Jusem of DBA Design and Ha Nguyen of HN Design for the layout of this book, and Jackie Knight of DBA Design and Hope Steele of Steele Editorial Services for their editorial support. Finally, thanks to our Oxford editor, Stephen McGroarty, for the rapid production of a book of which we are proud.

CONTENTS

PART II

Corporate Governance, Economic Development, and Cross-Border Capital Flows

PART III

Investors' and Practitioners' Perspectives

Social Corporate Responsibility and the New Learning

 # Contributors

Daron Acemoglu
Department of Economics, Massachusetts
Institute of Technology, USA

Franklin Allen
The Wharton School, University of
Pennsylvania, USA

Erik Berglöf
Stockholm Institute of Transition
Economics (SITE), Stockholm School of
Economics, Sweden

Daniel Berkowitz
Department of Economics, University of
Pittsburgh, USA

Margaret M. Blair
Georgetown University Law Center, and
Brookings Institution, USA

Max Burger-Calderon
Apax Partners, Germany

Steven Carchon
University of Gent, Belgium

Alberto Chong
Research Department, Inter-American
Development Bank, USA

John C. Coffee, Jr.
Columbia Law School, Columbia
University, USA

Peter K. Cornelius
World Economic Forum, Switzerland

William Dale Crist
California Public Employees' Retirement
System (CalPERS), USA

Alexander Dyck
Harvard Business School, Harvard
University, USA

Holly J. Gregory
Weil, Gotshal & Manges LLP, USA;
International Institute for Corporate
Governance, Yale School of Management,
Yale University, USA

Philipp Gusinde
Apax Partners, Germany

Witold J. Henisz
The Wharton School, University of
Pennsylvania, USA

Stefan Hoffmann
Freshfields Bruckhaus Deringer, Germany

Alejandro Izquierdo
Research Department, Inter-American
Development Bank, USA

Simon Johnson
Sloan School of Management,
Massachusetts Institute of Technology,
USA

Michael J. Johnston
Capital Group Companies Inc., USA

Bruce Kogut
The Wharton School, University of
Pennsylvania, USA;
INSEAD, France

Igor Kostikov
Federal Commission for the Securities
Market, Russian Federation

J. Muir Macpherson
McCombs School of Business, University
of Texas at Austin, USA

Alejandro Micco
Research Department, Inter-American
Development Bank, USA

Ira M. Millstein
Weil, Gotshal & Manges LLP, USA;
International Institute for Corporate
Governance, Yale School of Management,
Yale University, USA

Mark Mobius
Templeton Asset Management, Singapore

Anthony Neoh
Hong Kong Bar and China Securities
Regulatory Commission, Hong Kong SAR

Mary O'Sullivan
INSEAD, France

Anete Pajuste
Stockholm Institute of Transition
Economics (SITE), Stockholm School of
Economics, Sweden

Ugo Panizza
Research Department, Inter-American
Development Bank, USA

Michael J. Phillips
Frank Russell Company, USA

Katharina Pistor
Columbia Law School, Columbia
University, USA

Helmut Reisen
OECD Development Centre, Organisation
for Economic Co-operation and
Development, France

Wieslaw Rozlucki
Warsaw Stock Exchange, Poland

Wei-ling Song
Bennett S. LeBow College of Business,
Drexel University, USA

Jonathan Story
INSEAD, France

Lutgart van den Berghe
University of Gent, and Belgian Directors'
Institute, Belgium

Luigi Zingales
Graduate School of Business, University of
Chicago, USA

Corporate Governance
and Capital Flows
in a Global Economy

Chapter 1

Introduction

Corporate Governance and Capital Flows in a Global Economy

Peter K. Cornelius and Bruce Kogut

The most important challenge of the early part of the 21st century is to foster the prospects for improvement in the quality of life of citizens in the poorest countries in the world. Investment is a critical ingredient to meeting this goal. For investment to take place, capital must be borrowed on international markets and invested in poorer countries. The resources of official development agencies are far from sufficient for this task. Over the past decade the private sector has become the primary source of funds for emerging-market economies; only the poorest countries receive the plurality of their funds from official sources. The challenge of addressing the poverty that afflicts billions of people will require the flow of private international capital.

The economic relationship between private sources of finance and low- to medium-income countries has, by any account, been a troubled one. The past 20 years has witnessed several major financial crises embracing not only Latin American countries and transition economies such as Russia, but even the once-named "Asian tigers." Money has flown massively into and out of the most promising of these countries, the upper middle-income countries, and the social and economic consequences have been devastating. Solid firms have become bankrupt, savings have been lost, and unemployment has soared.

There has been a fair amount of debate over the appropriate macroeconomic response to financial crises. This debate is not our concern in this book. We are interested in exploring how improved corporate governance of firms and national systems of governance can serve to provide a more secure environment to encourage capital flows into poor and emerging markets. Since 1989, hundreds of thousands of firms have been created or transformed in the former socialist countries; China is in the midst of a historical transformation toward private enterprises. What are the guidelines for corporate governance at this epochal juncture?

There have been many proposals about how to properly govern a firm. In the past decade, these proposals have increasingly tilted toward the American model as represent-

We would like to thank Mary O'Sullivan for helpful comments on an earlier draft.

ing the appropriate pool of practices that should be applied globally. More recently, there has been renewed interest in European practices, especially financial accounting. For many countries, these practices, if adopted and implemented, would represent a radical improvement in corporate governance, especially for public companies whose shares are traded in stock markets. We fully endorse recommendations to improve corporate governance practices by identifying "best practices" regardless of their national origins.

However, we do not endorse recommendations that favor a single type of a corporate government system. There is frequent confusion between systems of governance and corporate governance practices. This confusion lies at the heart of much mischief; hence, we begin by making a distinction between the two.

> *A system of corporate governance consists of those formal and informal institutions, laws, values, and rules that generate the menu of legal and organizational forms available in a country and which in turn determine the distribution of power— how ownership is assigned, managerial decisions are made and monitored, information is audited and released, and profits and benefits allocated and distributed.*

The definition of a corporate governance system is essentially in the realm of political sociology and economy, as well it should be. Governance is, after all, about the power to control and decide. Countries differ in their cultural and historical backgrounds and political conditions; so, therefore, do corporate governance systems. In this regard, it is not to be forgotten that most companies are not publicly traded. Therefore, a central difference between corporate governance systems in different countries is the variety and relative importance of organizational forms, such as public companies, partnerships, family firms.

However, even if corporate governance systems reflect sociological and political forces in a country's history, the consequences of these systems regarding the performance of firms are surely economic. The link between corporate governance systems and performance is, however, characterized by a complex chain of causality, making it hard to know what practice or what institution is best. Is a unitary board better than a dual board, as we find in Germany? Can such boards work in conjunction with the obligation to have labor represented on boards of large public companies? Are there laws that must be changed?

In part, any comparison across countries is difficult because cultures differ. The classic distinction between equity- and bank-based systems reflects dramatic differences not only in risk preferences, but also in notions of procedural justice. It is best then to take the notion of a *system* seriously and try to understand what the essential elements are and how they cohere. According to proverbial wisdom, northern Europe values, culturally speaking, a reasonably egalitarian society that reveals a preference for lower-risk financing over equity investments. These preferences may be complements, as discussed below, and although cultural in origin, such preferences have economic consequences. Equity and banking systems are not substitutes for one another. The former is better at evaluating investments that require aggregating diverse opinions; banking is more suited for investments in more incremental technologies and industries.[1] One system need not dominate another; they correspond to different national preferences and industrial compositions. Because corporate governance systems have economic consequences, it does not mean that their components are not cultural or political in origin. In fact, it is the political and cultural origins that prevent any easy convergence at the system level.

For a given type of form, however, we have no hesitation in endorsing specific practices as better as others. We offer the following definition of corporate governance as practice:

> *Corporate governance practices are those rules that apply to specific financial markets and organizational forms, and that establish the discretion of parties that possess control rights and the information and mechanisms at their disposal to choose management, propose or confirm major strategic decisions, and to determine the distribution of remuneration and profit.*

For public firms these practices include the determination of the board of directors and its powers and voting rules, protection of minority investors, the publication of audited accounts, covenants restricting managerial actions such as the sale of assets, and the distribution of profits. Such practices will differ among partnerships, limited liability companies, and other organizational forms.

There is no doubt that many firms and many countries have bad governance practices. Economic history is replete with instances where better practices have replaced worse ones. The disaster of mass privatization in Russia recapitulated in many ways the same errors made in stock markets in the 1800s in England and the United States. It is easy to propose with confidence that trades should be registered, shares deposited, asset-stripping without disclosure prohibited, or shareholder meetings announced. These are practices that would have improved the development of capital markets in central and eastern Europe.

In the pages that follow, many of the chapters of this book will propose explanations for why some countries have bad or good practices, or what good practices are. Authors will often agree, but they will also frequently disagree over such issues as whether control rights belong only to owners, whether employees should have a say in governance, or whether governance includes social corporate responsibility. In our view, many of these conflicts reflect a more fundamental difference, one of answering the question: what constitutes a high-performing firm? In our conclusions to this introduction, we will endorse a view that treats a firm as a social community and sees governance as larger than the control rights given to shareholders or direct claimants to residual earnings.

Before turning to a more in-depth look at corporate governance, it is useful to establish the general data on international capital flows. It is the paucity of capital for development that improved corporate governance, as a practice or as a system, can remedy for the better. This is the claim of the book.

INTERNATIONAL CAPITAL FLOWS

The ability of developing countries to attract foreign savings has been limited and international capital flows to emerging-market economies have remained subject to a substantial degree of volatility. While one of the most important manifestations of globalization has been the dramatic increase in international capital flows in the 1990s, developing countries have not fully participated in the increased integration of the international financial markets. In 2001, emerging-market economies are estimated to have attracted gross capital inflows of only about USD 225 billion, or only around 10 percent of total gross capital inflows worldwide (International Monetary Fund [IMF], 2002). On a net basis, emerging markets have actually suffered outflows in the last few years.

The Group of Seven (G7) countries continue to account for the lion's share of global capital flows. According to IMF estimates, total gross inflows to these countries amounted to around USD 2 trillion in 2001, an almost 10-fold increase over the last decade. Gross outflows are estimated at around USD 1.7 trillion in 2001. The major countries' financial systems serve as hubs for gross international capital flows and investment in the sense that they take in gross inflows of capital from abroad, retain some of the flows, and distribute the rest internationally. This hub function is particularly developed in the case of the United States and the United Kingdom, which account for a total of around 60 percent of in- and outflows.

Foreign investors' appetite for US financial assets has remained particularly strong. Several factors explain this. First, the strategic motive to expand internationally has spurred a boom in cross-border mergers and acquisitions and foreign direct investment. Second, central banks have continued to purchase considerable amounts of top-rated US fixed-income securities for transaction purposes. Third, and most important, inflows to the United States have been driven by international investors' perception that US financial assets offer superior investment opportunities. This perception appears to have largely remained intact despite high-profile business failures and corporate governance scandals, including Enron and WorldCom. Many had feared that these scandals, coupled with a sharp slowdown in economic activity in the United States, could result in an abrupt reversal of capital flows, with obvious implications for the US dollar. One reason why such concerns have not (yet) materialized may lie in the fact that on a risk-adjusted basis, US equity and fixed-income markets continued to outperform those in Europe and Japan in the first half of 2002.

Those who had expected that international investors could lose their appetite for US financial assets viewed emerging markets as potential beneficiaries, reflecting a shift in the relative risk balance. Specifically, while investors were prepared to pay a higher premium for US assets partly because of the perceived superiority in the quality of their earnings reporting, Enron was generally expected to trigger a shift away from asset classes with rising risk to assets where risks were already high.

Helmut Reisen (chapter 7) analyzes this issue and concludes that such an outcome depends not only upon comparative risk, but also on wealth effects. Even if emerging markets look less risky (or more accurately, developed markets look more risky!), the dramatic drop in financial wealth severely dampens the resources for investment in general. In fact, a shift to emerging markets has not occurred; private net flows to emerging markets have, in absolute terms, fallen back to their 1992 levels of around USD 120 billion (Institute of International Finance [IIF], 2002). Emerging markets have continued to have their own share of financial crises, and rather than triggering a shift of investment into assets whose risk was already perceived to be high, Enron has led to a general reassessment of investors' risk exposure and a greater appetite for quality, especially that of sovereign debt issued by G7 countries.

According to IIF (2002) estimates, net portfolio investment in emerging-market economies has almost halved, from around USD 20 billion in 1999 to only about USD 10 billion in 2002. By comparison, net portfolio investment peaked at around USD 35 billion in 1996. The decline in cross-border commercial bank lending has been even more dramatic, turning from a net inflow of more than USD 120 billion in 1996 to an estimated net outflow of more than USD 10 billion in 2002. Nonbank lending, mostly bond flows, have also experienced wide swings during the last decade and especially since the 1997–1998 financial crises in Asia, Russia, and Latin America. Foreign direct investment continues to account for the bulk of capital flows to developing countries, although more recently, net flows have also declined, reflecting a slowdown in privatization in many countries. Averaging only about USD 25 billion in the 10 years from 1992 to 2002, net official flows have been insufficient to offset the decrease in net private flows.

Overall, it seems that developing countries' access to foreign savings has remained small. Although financial markets have become increasingly integrated over the last decade, this has not helped much in terms of greater capital accumulation in the developing world. With the notable exception of some Asian countries, domestic savings rates have generally remained low, holding back investment and hence economic development. While we have yet to fully understand the complexities of the development process,[2] it is generally accepted that financial markets play a critical role for economic growth. Well-functioning financial systems help mobilize savings and allocate resources, facilitate the exchange of goods and services, pool and diversify risk, and monitor managers and exert corporate control (e.g., Levine, 1997). This book concentrates on the latter functions.

COMPARATIVE CORPORATE GOVERNANCE

The following chapters focus on two questions: what do we know about international financial flows and corporate governance and can improved corporate governance lead to increased investment flows to developing countries? Some chapters look at one of these two questions; a few look at both.

The contributors to these chapters were chosen so as to provide a variety of perspectives, many of which are often in disagreement. We welcome this diversity, for we do not accept that there is a "best" system. We began this introduction by distinguishing between corporate governance "practices" and "systems" in order to reject "silver bullet theories" that claim one size fits all countries. The literature on corporate governance (much of which is reviewed in this introduction and throughout the book) include pronouncements such as that French law is bad for governance and countries with this type of legal system have more developed capital markets, or that poor countries have a choice between two types of Western systems (of which one is better than the other). It is tempting during a time of great incertitude to play the role of Peter the Great, or Meiji Japan advisers, who look to the West to import new institutions *a la carte*.

More subtle analyses reject silver bullets and claim that importation should be made as a *menu fixe*, because the effectiveness of any one institution will depend upon the effectiveness of another institution. Policies must take into account complementarities, so that they are consistent and efficacious in regard to each other. There is no point, for example, recommending options as part of an executive remuneration if there is no stock market; thus, the policy of executive remuneration and the presence of equity markets are complements. However, this analysis of complementarities often results in the "platinum missile theory" (to continue the metaphor) by which policies are to be accepted as a whole; resident institutions are to be obliterated.

The world consists of a large variety of corporate governance systems, an observation so obvious and so well known among practitioners and in most fields of academic research as to be almost taken for granted. After all, the great economic sociologist Max Weber made his original reputation for his studies on comparative legal systems. This tradition remains very much alive today and it offers an important insight that was first made by Robert K. Merton, the Columbia University sociologist, regarding functional equivalents. The classic story of functional equivalence concerns the finding of the anthropologist Malinowski in the first half of the last century that Freud was wrong regarding the primacy of the father. In the Trobiand Islands, the uncle was the object of psychological ambivalence for the son. But this all made sense, because in this society—according to this contested anthropological account—the father was a distant figure, and the uncle, a central one. The uncle in the Trobiand Island culture was the functional equivalent to the Western father.

It probably is not by chance that the Nobel Prize winner for the development of the mathematics of option pricing, Robert C. Merton, has proposed a functional view of finance.[3] Merton's function view means that although financial systems may differ in the form, they are similar in function. If we blend the two Merton theories together, we have a view of financial systems that consists of many functions (e.g., risk diversification, savings and investment, etcetera) that are provided for in different ways in different countries. In other words, different systems of corporate governance facilitate functionally equivalent roles in societies, such as the development of equity, bank, and private equity markets that diversify and transfer risk among individuals and organizations and that also provide covenants of trust by which consumption is postponed today and money is invested with a future claim against payment.

It is tempting to ask, what is the best system? In our view, there is no answer to this question. Imagine that it would be possible to rank corporate governance systems by an index of national wealth. Even if this ranking were available, the best system would not be obvious. Income per capita is not the only means of comparing countries; countries are also concerned about equity, cultural values, and social norms. Since, to be abstract, countries differ in how they weight and interpret these issues, they will not converge to the same corporate governance system. Within their own system they, and we, may agree, however, that certain practices are better than others given particular forms (the public company, the partnership, the family firm). At the system level, however, determining best practice is more complex.

This recognition of the viability of different systems is not shared by all views of corporate governance. To illustrate the differences in viewpoint and as a way to introduce some of the chapters of this book, we will consider the case of Enron that is discussed at length in chapter 2 by Jack Coffee and which forms the backdrop to many other chapters, such as chapter 22 by Michael Phillips. The Enron scandal—it is no less than that!—consists of a breakdown in governance in a publicly-traded company in the United States. The company—one of the largest in the world and engaged in the complex trading of energy commodity securities and options—failed to report partnership agreements; its top management exited from their equity position while investors and Enron's own employee pension fund bought the defunct stock; and it hid financial losses. Enron's auditor, Arthur Andersen, collapsed due to its fiduciary lapse in auditing and public reporting. This affair represents a weighty failure of corporate governance.

How would proponents of different views come to understand the Enron affair? We consider three overlapping classes of explanation: economic, political, and institutional. Many of the academic chapters fall nicely into one of these three camps; we consider here how many of the chapters contribute to understanding this failure of corporate governance.

The economic view of shareholder versus stakeholder

A dominant view of corporate governance is the primacy of shareholder rights to the residual profits of a firm and, hence, to exercising control of management. This right to control has a clear logic. Since shareholders are the last claimant to profit, they should have the right (as they do the incentive) to monitor management. The argument of Berle and Means, made in the 1930s, is that American firms have highly dispersed shareholders who cannot monitor. However, there are mechanisms by which delegates can be appointed to provide this service. These include the appointment of directors to the board, the right to call shareholder meetings, the requirement of external auditors to verify reports, and covenants that require shareholder votes for certain measures, such as mergers. In fact, these rights are often weaker than stated, but in all, they represent the rights of shareholders to govern the firm.

The Enron scandal reflects, from this view, the peculiar weakness of the American financial system: many owners, but few guards. In this book, Coffee underlines the weakened incentives for "gatekeepers" of auditors and analysts. Most of the board members resigned within six months of the scandal. The larger issue is whether there is a chronic problem in stakeholder oversight. Bowman and Useem (1995) argue that boards are handpicked and not independent. In his contribution to this book, Coffee points to failures in the gatekeeper role. The dilemma is the classic Berle and Means observation: under dispersed ownership, who controls management?

For many countries, this dilemma disappears because shareholdings are concentrated in the hands of a few shareholders. In many stock markets, the capitalization of shares is controlled by a few families or business groups. In such an environment, the problem shifts from the American problem of managers uncontrolled by shareholders to minority investors exploited by large shareholders. From this perspective, it may be true that the Enron scandal is peculiar to the American system. However, the shareholder perspective would nevertheless point to the abuse of minority investors as a critical weakness hindering equity-market development.

The stakeholder theory is the prevailing spirit behind most corporate governance laws in the world, despite its controversial status in the United States and stock market-based economies. Perhaps because of this controversy, the United States in particular has been the thought leader in the debate between shareholder and stakeholder positions, beginning with the important debate between Berle and Dodd in the early 1930s regarding the social responsibility of the firm. The stakeholder theory argues that many entities in society— workers, environmentalists, and community organizations—should have a voice in the governance of a firm. Of course, in many countries this theory is enacted in law, such as the *Mitbestimmung* law in Germany requiring worker representation in supervisory boards of large public corporations. Even in the United States, boards of directors are not liable directly to shareholders, but to the long-term interest of the firm. Boards actively pursue directors who contribute diversity, shorthand for representing different racial and social perspectives.

Since the 1930s, the stakeholder view of the firm has known many reincarnations, including one as a theory of strategic management (Freeman, 1984). Margaret Blair (1995) offers the most sustained development of this approach, which she summarizes in chapter 3 in this book. Her argument begins with the traditional idea that employees embody human capital, some of which is "firm specific" and cannot be transplanted to other firms. As a result, employees are *de facto* investors in the company. It is also in the company's interest to recognize the value of their employees as capital. In the parlance of consulting companies, employees contribute to the "knowledge assets" of the firm.[4]

Mary O'Sullivan (2000), a contributor to this book (chapter 5), noted that this view implies that corporate governance practices influence the capabilities of firms. Since firms are learning organizations, the evolution of competitive advantage is not indifferent to the governance of the firm and the role of workers in this governance.

Firms develop their advantages in reference to competition in their industries and to the institutional demands of their environments (such as labor laws or financial markets). Corporate governance is thus not simply the perspective of top management; it is the framework by which corporations develop their competence and capabilities. Stakeholder involvement guides this development and hence is more than just a monitor or gatekeeper added to the board of directors.

Both the traditional view of stakeholder and the Blair-O'Sullivan version speak directly to the Enron case. Due to the collapse of Enron and Andersen, hundreds of thousands of workers lost their jobs. Many, but far from all, found comparable employment elsewhere. Moreover, Enron's employees lost much of their pension investments, which were heavily invested in Enron stock. The stakeholder perspective would suggest that workers deserved representation in the board (or relevant oversight committees) in order to safeguard their human capital and pension investments.

An analytically interesting issue is O'Sullivan's claim that corporate governance and competitive advantage are tied to each other. The managers of Enron were provided massive incentives to perform—they were awarded stock options and were paid for performance. When Enron moved from a traditional utility company to a broker of sophisticated financial securities, the company experienced a major and incomplete transformation from the staid norms of utility compensation to the compensation policy of an investment bank.

This transformation raises the fundamental question of whether or not the board, auditors, or employee stakeholders had the capability to monitor performance even if the data were available. Did these stakeholders know how to monitor this business? Enron's new businesses relied upon a body of knowledge distant from the traditional competence of the company. Enron top management knew this and sought—perhaps with justification (in their eyes)—to acquire the control and ownership rights to these new businesses through the development of partnerships. It is even possible that these types of partnerships are appropriate control mechanisms for the development of capabilities to manage high-risk investments that are based on expertise rather than on physical assets.

The failure of Enron in the stakeholder view is that it developed two conflicting modalities of corporate governance: the public corporation and the partnership. The company should have been bought out by management who would then bear the risk; the risk should not have been borne by shareholders *and stakeholders* who were inadequately represented and who were increasingly peripheral to the investment banking activities of Enron. We flag, in general, the issue of whether the public company is ever the appropriate corporate governance vehicle of firms competing on the specialized expertise of individuals. The Enron case ultimately points to the inherent conflicts between partnership-oriented competitive advantages housed within public corporations. In this regard, the relative aversion toward public firms in many emerging markets may be an opportunity to develop other organizational forms, such as partnerships, to replace the dominance of the family firm.

There is an economic corollary to the stakeholder and shareholder models: if product markets are competitive, then competition should be sufficient to impose efficient governance on firms. This view, elegantly explained by Allen and Gale (2000), loses some of its force for the Enron case because the new financial markets for trading energy securities and options were highly noncompetitive. Ironically, the successful dominance of Enron in financial markets for energy obscured the incentives and information required for effective monitoring.

Politics

The political approach to corporate governance is probably the closest to the popular belief regarding how firms are organized and how they are controlled. This approach is spread among many camps, so it is useful to distinguish between those who emphasize politics within the firm from those emphasizing politics external to the firm. In a classic study, Cyert and March (1963) proposed that a firm is a "coalition" of interests. In a later formulation of this theme, Cohen, March, and Olsen (1972) considered a "garbage can" model of decision-making, in which solutions seek problems to solve; almost any problem will do. This imagery is not a bad one for the market of ideas and consulting services, but this approach, however interesting, did not propose how governance may or can redress this pathology.

In more elaborate theories, financial economists have also viewed the firm as a political arena in which division heads seek resources partly through misrepresentation. In this view, incentives can rarely be designed to fully align division goals with those of the welfare of the corporation. Consequently, the *ex post* audit is critical to review past decisions. Unfortunately, there is little empirical evidence that firms engage in retrospective evaluation.

The external political approach is more varied. In the United States, Roe (1994) has offered the most sustained analysis by arguing that politics establishes the field in which economics and business may search for corporate governance solutions. He argues that in the United States, populist fears of big business led to Congressional acts—such as an act restricting the taking of sizeable ownership positions in industrial firms by financial institutions—that created the Berle and Means situation of dispersed owners. In other countries, national politics created other outcomes.

The external politics view is essentially shared by Rajan and Zingales (2002), who argue that, contrary to the financial institutional approach (described below), countries change their corporate governance practices over time. They point to the simple evidence that stock markets were far more important for many European economies prior to World War I than they were after World War II. Since institutions (such as types of laws) are believed to be unchanging, these fluctuations indicate the importance of historical fluctuations in the power wielded by interest groups.

This political approach easily fits the popular facts regarding Enron. A political understanding of Enron's internal management awaits more extensive studies, but there is little doubt that Enron pursued a very active lobbying effort. Enron's trading activities grew out of the deregulation of the power market. In this regard, the scandal shares many features with the previous savings and loan debacle in which traditional banks, once partly deregulated, started to invest in complex financial instruments beyond their competence. Enron's competence has been questioned less, but there is no doubt it lobbied for, and benefited from, deregulation. These political efforts included the naming of Wendy Gramm, wife of Senator Phil Gramm, who is an advocate for energy deregulation, to the board. She previously chaired the Commodity Futures Trading Commission that exempted electricity trading operations from oversight by the Commission. About three quarters of all senators and 50 percent of the House members, received Enron contributions. These efforts do not constitute legal violations, but they are the fuel to political fires that alter broader institutions of corporate governance.

Being a political scandal, the Enron case caused a backlash calling for tighter regulation. The Sarbanes-Oxley Act of 2002 was a compromise bill, supported by Republicans and Democrats, designed to strengthen the criminal consequences for top management in cases of misrepresentation of financial results. In addition to requiring the chief executive to sign the audited statements of the company, the law strengthens the power of auditing committees and the regulatory oversight of auditing firms. This law changes, probably incrementally more than radically, corporate governance practices. In this sense, it fits like a glove the political view that corporate governance practice and systems evolve in reference to politicized contexts.

The importance of politics to corporate governance can appear inefficient. To a technocrat who believes that there are universal solutions, the resistance of domestic groups—both business and employee—to change is labeled "politics" and in opposition to efficiency. Of course, this characterization can be true (although sometimes today's technocratic beliefs are tomorrow's witchcraft), but the broader recognition is that both emerging and developed countries will situate governance and control over enterprises in the political context of their countries. This is the point made by Mary O'Sullivan in her chapter in this book. An appropriate policy may be to simply render more transparent the distributional incidence of the benefits and costs to competing alternatives of governance. One suspects that private actors already have an understanding of these benefits.

It is interesting in this regard that Alexander Dyck and Luigi Zingales have contributed chapter 4 to this book summarizing their finding that an active media is a critical factor in monitoring the behavior of firms. Countries with a free and active press have more developed financial markets than those that do not. This result is important for curbing the technocratic preference (to which Confucius and Plato plead guilty) for the enlightened autocrat over the democracy. Whether political dissent is suppressed or conducted in the open, the virtue of an active press is to render politics more transparent. However, experience tells us that it may be hard to convince executives that transparency reported in the media is correlated with accuracy. In fact, Dyck and Zingales argue in their chapter that the media, too, falls prey to a procyclical bias in reporting and, equally disconcerting, business professors are also per-petrators of adding to the bias when bubbles are at hand. That people are averse to raining on a parade is a troubling observation on why corporate governance practices can slip during good times.

Institutions, norms, and society

Politics is invariably bound up with the broader social fabric and institutions of a country. In the past decade, financial economists have observed that firms are organ-ized differently across countries and that within the same form, such as the public com-pany, they differ in governance, such as in the protection of minority investors. This belated recognition has been accompanied by an impressive assembly of data permit-ting cross-country comparisons.

A principal contention of the financial economics literature is the powerful effect of legal systems on financial market development, entrepreneurship, and firms coming to stock markets for the first time.[5] The effect of law on these factors generally points to the inferiority of civil law compared to common law, and in particular, French compared to British law, for market development. These results are verified in many studies published in financial economic journals, and they have earned a riposte: apparently, French law is good for creating better football (soccer) teams; at least it was, until 2002.[6]

The standard conclusion in the law and corporate governance literature consti-tutes what we call a "silver bullet" theory. Common law increases capital market devel-opment and, in some studies, growth. Civil law is bad, especially the French version. The analyses are finer grained than this, entailing an analysis of specific provisions that aid cap-ital market development, such as minority investment protection. The recommendation is clear: adopt and enforce common corporate law and specific provisions.

In large part, these results capture a difference between Anglo-associated coun-tries and the rest of the world, and are open to the charge of confounding law with culture. However, a simpler puzzle is this: why are Continental European countries rich? The objection of Rajan and Zingales is that if legal systems are determinants, why was there more similarity in levels of equity market development 100 years ago than there is now? Even if we accept that equity markets are less developed, are there func-tional equivalents in these markets, such as internal finance, that are channeled through holding companies or even through the state to new opportunities? Have continental European societies succeeded in tempering some culturally-unwanted consequences of capitalism (such as large differences in income and wealth distribution) by favoring nonequity-market finance?

This recent and powerful research on law has, without question, made a funda-mental contribution to the literature by emphasizing the relationship between institu-tions and corporate governance systems. Chapter 6 by Franklin Allen and Wei-ling Song in this book uses this new approach to show that, contrary to the standard intuition, venture capital is used in countries with weak legal enforcement; such capital assumes the role of compensating for institutional weaknesses. Countries with civil law or British law are more apt to have venture-capital markets. Moreover, venture-capital development tends to occur in systems that protect creditors, reinforcing the idea that venture capital is a distinctive type of financing and different from issued equity.

This new approach to law is also used by Alberto Chong, Alejandro Izquierdo, Alejandro Micco, and Ugo Panizza in their chapter on Latin America. They find that better law is not only associated with more capital market development, but also with lower volatility of foreign direct investment. These results suggest that contagion effects (e.g., the effect of the Russian default on Latin American debt premiums) are more potent in legal systems that are perceived as less hospitable for investors.

It is obvious that law is only one part of the claim that institutions influence corporate governance and financial development. In this volume, Daron Acemoglu and Simon Johnson (chapter 13) summarize their work, which uses a clever, if controversial, measure to support a broader claim that institutions do matter. They measure the rate of immigrant deaths in developing countries to indicate the subsequent failure of European institutions to take root, and then show that the countries with high rates of settler mortality in the 1800s are the same ones more likely to be poor today. These results tend to trump the legal law explanation and point to institutions as fairly constant aspects of national landscapes over long periods of time. As a corollary to this look at the history of imperialism, one might surmise that the consequences of the British legal system are spurious and capture instead "cherry picking" among colonies by the United Kingdom, which was the dominant imperial power in the 1800s.

Whatever one makes of the theories discussed in this book, the economic work on institutions is heading in the direction of the sociological literature on the state, politics, and civil society. Padgett and Ansell (1993) provide a detailed and fascinating analysis of the power of the Medici family to govern Florence by simultaneously maintaining their position among the social aristocracy and doing business with the new commercial class. Carruthers (1999) further develops this idea of the interplay of politics, the state, and society by showing how the early English stock market grew on the back of politicized trading that pitted Tories and Whigs. Capital markets developed in England through political networks and the competition for control over colonial trading companies.

This perspective of society, institutions, and business proposes that corporate governance is lodged within the "ties that bind." In this view, the institutions that count are the economic and social ones that consist of thick relationships among business people. Useem (1986) could find no evidence that corporate governance in the United Kingdom is exercised through networks comprising boards of directors and owners, noting instead that control and monitoring are created through "inner circles" of executives sharing a common body of norms about class and proper behavior. In most (if not all) countries, ties among business elites arise from attending elite schools or the military, or from religious or ethnic affiliations or economic class. The origins differ, but the phenomenon is the same: the sharing of values, if not mutual associates, among a class conscious of its existence.

These normative ties may be more encoded in relationships than we realize. Kogut and Walker analyzed Germany as a "small world" whereby firms were tied through having common owners (such as the well-known firms Allianz and Deutsche Bank, but these ties also held for less well-known firms). If they are connected by ownership, German firms have, on average, about five owners in common; this distance is called "five degrees of separation." Kogut and Walker found that firms tied through owners were more likely to buy each other than firms that were not related by ownership.[7] Thus, even though Gorton and Schmid (2000) found no evidence that bank cross-holdings in industry add much value to individual firms, the German corporate ownership ties remain robust, suggesting perhaps that there is social value in the overall system.

This analysis of small worlds has subsequently been applied to other countries, such as Italy and Korea. The results for the United States are worth noting, because they contradict popular and academic belief. Gerry Davis and Mina Yoo studied the United States and found that shareholder dispersion decreased in the 1990s; ownership became more concentrated! A principal explanation is Fidelity and its mutual funds. By sharing analysis across funds, it ended up holding sizeable shares in a core set of companies. Davis, Yoo, and Baker (2002) also looked at board membership, which they found to be similarly concentrated. In reference to Enron, they write:

> Enron and WorldCom have recently been in the news for their perceived failures of corporate governance. President Bush and others have portrayed them as isolated instances—a few bad apples that have not contaminated the whole barrel of corporate America. But while Enron may be an isolated instance of governance gone bad, its board is not especially isolated. Enron's directors served on the boards of 10 other Fortune 1000 companies across the United States, including Compaq, Eli Lilly, Lockheed Martin and Motorola. The directors of those 10 boards, in turn, served on another 49 Fortune 1000 boards. 648 boards were within four degrees of separation from Enron. In human terms, 95 directors had face-to-face contact with Enron directors through their board service, and 482 more directors are only two steps from the Enron board. Among corporate directors, it really is a small world.

It is easy to conclude from this statement that American business displays "crony capitalism." This is not the claim. The prosaic observation is that even in the supposedly most dispersed shareholder economy, ties among owners and directors run fast and thick. Knowing someone, sharing family ties, owning common firms are part of the fundament of economies. In fact, Sweden, an economy known for fairly transparent and honest transactions, puzzled a contributor to this book, Erik Berglöf, and his co-authors, who find that there is very limited protection of minority investors despite a well-developed capital market (Agnblad et al., 2001). They speculate that social ties

may be the glue that holds the pieces together. They may be right, but social ties sometimes holds together saints, and at other times, thieves.

The interesting question is, given such thick ties, why was the trouble at Enron
not caught sooner? Surely it was in the interests of hundreds of investors connected in
this web of relationships to blow the whistle, if they had known. A possible answer is that
these webs work, as Useem suggested, on shared values. If Enron failed, the answer
may well lie in a set of values about the "proper" relationship between a hard day's work
and pay that went awry in the boom stock market of the last decade. In many ways,
the historical suspicion of the stock investor as a "rentier," speculating rather than working, may well have been justified in the breakdown in values and the explosion of expectations regarding what constitutes a successful career.

These are large issues, larger than any single social science discipline, which
cannot be easily answered. They suggest that rapid stock market development should
be regarded as playing with fire in many economies. Economic history is filled with
crashed bubbles that took a generation to overcome the consequential aversion. The
east European economies certainly face this trouble. Building stock markets as subsidiary to broader financial market development is contrary to the financial economics emphasis on the publicly-traded firms. But a lot of evidence in the chapters in this
book—see especially those of Erik Berglöf and Anete Pajuste (chapter 11), and Peter
Cornelius (chapter 10)—point to the primal role played by banks in fostering sound
corporate governance instead of legal and regulatory provisions that are imperfectly
enforced in any event. Banks, as a review by Carlin and Mayer (2000) in a recent volume showed, are often retarding influences on the development of modern financial
systems. For this reason, the entry of foreign banks can play catalyzing roles in the
institutional transformation of emerging-market economies.

GLOBALIZATION AND TRANSFER

What then are we to recommend to developing countries regarding corporate
governance? On the one hand, our answers are very simple. Within a common organizational form, adopt those practices that characterize well-functioning economies. Ira Millstein
and Holly Gregory (chapter 24) offer in this book a body of recommendations of "best
practices" for public companies that are drawn on the US experience. To the lawmakers,
regulators, and investors in developing countries, this advice can be complemented by a call
to make "missions of productivity," as delegates to the United States from France, Germany,
Japan, and other countries did after World War II. Visit stock exchanges, companies of heritage, regulators, and borrow what seems reasonable. If you are not sure when to stop borrowing, then borrow all, including the color of the wall painting. Then view the outcomes
as experiments and be prepared to alter and evolve the mix as wisdom suggests.

Local traditions are, after all, surprisingly resilient. The excellent study of Meiji
Japan by Westney (1987) arrives at a simple conclusion. Japan chose institutions from
the world like dishes on a menu: French police system, British postal system, the German

military (their victory over France in 1871 made the original French choice less attractive). These imports were not imitations, but emulations that were adapted to local traditions. Tokyo and Paris today share a political division by arrondissement, yet few would claim that French and Japanese police systems are the same.

Imported practices and even institutions are never fixed and stable entities, but are adapted to (or ignored in) local conditions. At times, they are also imposed. For this reason, the studies by Berkowitz, Pistor, and Richard (explained in chapter 14 by Pistor and Berkowitz in this book) on the long-term consequences of colonial transplantation, are especially important. They point out that countries of colonial origins with transplanted systems, especially those that were not appropriate to local conditions, have fared worse in terms of growth. While common law systems or, more narrowly, British legal systems, promoted stock market development, such systems hurt overall economic development. A lot more work will be needed to sort out these complex historical relationships, but they surely echo well the recorded experiences of colonial populations resisting the imposition of foreign institutions.

In the parlance of academic studies, countries may resist imported institutions because they clash with the well tuned institutional complementarities that prevail at a given point in time. Such institutional framing has a rigid implication: change one element in an institutional system and overall performance is likely to decay. From this point of view, any importation is bound to be rejected, or else incur damage for local development, if it is incompatible with existing institutions. The tight coupling among institutions implies a "path dependence" tied to the past, from which no country can easily escape.

This characterization of the "conflict" among cultures and the legacy of the past is, in our view, too austere. We prefer a description of the process of importation in a current historical context as conducted in a forum of discourse. The institutional trade among countries becomes an instance to instigate experimentation and public discourse. To varying degrees, this trade, coupled with local institutions, characterizes the painful transformation of the former socialist economies (see Stark, 1996).

Chapter 8 by Bruce Kogut and J. Muir Macpherson in this volume iterates the many paths of investment by which corporate governance practices are transferred: multinational corporations, trade, debt, minority equity, and listings on foreign stock exchanges. The path of penetration is often direct, but is sometimes only affiliated with investments. For example, the expansion of international corporate borrowing in the past three decades occasioned the implantation of subsidiaries by major rating agencies, such as Moody's. Similarly, foreign ownership of banks provide a multiplier effect by subjecting loan decisions and servicing to (presumably) the stringent oversight practices of multinational financial institutions. At a minimum, these investments can also break up local political ties between government, finance, and entrenched interests. The acquisition of First Bank Korea by Newbridge Capital is a case in point. If the many channels of diffusion are considered—multinational investments, foreign bank ownership, international lending and equity listing, privatization—then it is not far-fetched to postulate that many countries are approaching a "tipping point" in their institutions of corporate governance.

Withold Henisz and Jonathan Story (chapter 9) offer in their contribution to this volume a cautionary tale. They take the perspective of the multinational corporation rather than that of the institutional investor and argue, in effect, that corporate governance, narrowly defined, covers only a small portion of the relevant country knowledge required to evaluate an investment opportunity. Discussing at length the case of the global energy sector, they draw upon deep field research to show how risks and opportunities are affected by the overall business system, of which corporate governance practices are but a part. No degree of transfer by the multinational corporation of its practices can resolve these broader institutional challenges.

The chapter by Peter Cornelius and that by Erik Berglöf and Anete Pajuste emphasize the importance of banks to the adjustment process. Cornelius describes in overall terms the extent of capital flows to emerging markets and details the importance of acquisitions of banks to the diffusion of better practices. Berglöf and Pajuste provide a very detailed and impressive account of the current state of governance in central and eastern Europe. Their analysis shows how far many of these economies have come in the past decade and how much remains to be done. Like Cornelius, Berglöf and Pajuste emphasize that the banking sector is the most likely force for governance pressures. Unlike in many countries, the banks in these countries have either been restructured or started anew, or have been taken over by foreign firms. In this regard, banking and financial sectors in central and eastern Europe are in many cases far more international than those of older capitalist countries or emerging markets. Whether these banks desire to, or can, be effective agents for transforming corporate governance systems or individual practices, depends heavily upon local conditions and politics.

This tension between local practices and foreign institutions is clearly felt in practitioners' contributions to this volume. Their comments are anchored in their own experiences as investors responsible for sizeable investment funds, or as directors of stock markets in emerging and middle-income countries. Many of them have been more than students of corporate governance, but have been agents lobbying for, and instigating, institutional changes in corporate governance practices, mostly of publicly-traded firms.

Contributors' comments are made against the backdrop of broad calls for better corporate governance. A major force in this call is the impressive presence of American institutional investors in many countries.[8] Many governments and governmental bodies have commissioned reports, and the International Monetary Fund, World Bank, and Organisation for Economic Co-operation and Development (OECD) have all published recommendations for best practices for corporate governance.[9]

The chapters contributed by those actively engaged in these policy and business debates reflect a consensus that is troubled by recent events. Bill Crist (chapter 16) of the California Public Employees' Retirement System (CalPERS) explains why minority investors should be active investors, even taking roles on the board of directors. He documents the methodology used by the largest pension fund in the world to evaluate the corporate governance practices of firms as a criteria for investment. Mark Mobius (chapter 17) of the Templeton Funds endorses minority shareholder activism, citing positively the policy of CalPERS. He explains that improved governance protecting shareholders holds the keys to more investment in developing markets and he uses, as an example, his own role on the board of the Russian energy giant, Lukoil. Michael Johnston (chapter 15) of the Capital Group states clearly that corporate governance is an important aspect of choosing attractive investment targets by the 35 analysts working in his company on emerging markets. He cites with approval the moves toward fuller disclosure and minority protection in several countries around the world, while noting that the pace is too slow overall. Better governance, in his view, would mean more capital investment in emerging markets.

Max Burger-Calderon and Philipp Gusinde of the venture capital firm, Apax, and Stefan Hoffmann of the law firm, Freshfields Bruckhaus Deringer, provide the perspective on governance for formal private equity investments (chapter 18). They note that these investments consist of three parties (or what they call "tiers"): investors, the private equity company, and the portfolio company. Private equity investments have special properties, since the securities are not publicly traded, regarding exit provisions, dilution, and the transfer of funds between investment vehicles. As in the Allen and Song chapter, they do not see any distinction in the incentives for private equity along the lines of the type of legal system. Of course, countries differ, particularly regarding the US allowance for pension funds to invest in risky and illiquid venture capital projects.

It is not surprising that given the financial muscle of large pension funds and institutional investors and their concern over corporate governance, the three contributions by heads of stock exchanges or regulatory bodies emphasize forcefully their commitment to explicit codes. Chapter 21 by Wieslaw Rozlucki, president of the Warsaw Exchange, is a frank listing of the essential elements of appropriate rules for governance, ranging from minority investor protection to how to conduct board meetings. The contribution of Igor Kostikov (chapter 20), Chairman of the Federal Commission for Securities Market, reveals both the progress and gaps in the corporate governance of Russian firms. Some of the largest firms have adopted international standards regarding transparency of owners, dividends, and financial results, but there is more to be done. The view from China is given by Anthony Neoh (chapter 19), who paints a dynamic picture of a China that is still in-between systems: property rights are not clear, corporate governance is rudimentary, and institutional investors are only starting to appraise the many thousands of firms outside the principal listed firms. He calls for a long-term view in recognition of the fact that far-reaching structural changes are required. These three chapters portray three systems that vary dramatically by their current progress toward achieving world standards in governance.

The area of debate rests not so much on specific practices, but on the scope of corporate governance. Chapter 23 by Lutgart van den Berghe (with Steven Carchon) argues that corporate governance intrinsically concerns corporate social responsibility. Firms are being forced to recognize a "triple bottom line" of financial, environmental, and social performance. Hence, van den Berghe (who is an academic sitting on several corporate boards) concludes, sound corporate governance requires a broader social policy.

Like Bill Crist, Ira Millstein, and Holly Gregory write sympathetically of social corporate responsibility, but view this issue as apart from sound corporate governance. As lead contributors to the OECD report on governance and to the comparative study on European corporate governance codes commissioned by the EU, Millstein and Gregory draw upon a deep reservoir of knowledge and experience regarding both corporate governance systems and governance practices. They argue that although there are many legal systems, there is a core of best practices. Yet, they conclude that business values are the ultimate guarantor of responsible governance.

Michael Phillips (chapter 22) begins with this conclusion, stating that values should be the principal object of attention in understanding corporate governance. He suggests that pure financial return maximization should be replaced by "global responsibility." He dismisses the importance of short-term incentives imposed by markets as constraining what managers can do. Because managers have discretion, their behavior needs to be guided by values. He proposes the creation of a "Global Responsibility Fund" to work with companies to support social programs and to identify societal needs.

These chapters present, in short, the diversity of views found among the academic contributors. These views undoubtedly reflect the great disappointments in accounting and transparency in the United States, Europe, and elsewhere in recent years. But they also pitted two different views of the firm and its governance against one another: one view is that governance is designed to control and monitor, and the other, that governance is the product of policies that foster cooperative social communities. We turn to this more fundamental issue as our conclusion.

CONCLUSION

There are many ways to understand the debate on corporation governance, as we have outlined. Surely, corporate governance is partly about efficiency. But oddly enough, we know little about this. Gompers, Ishii, and Metrick (2003) show that the United States stock market has handsomely rewarded stocks whose public companies have adopted "democratic" governance practices. These studies are rare and are almost entirely focused on publicly traded companies.

We have resisted endorsing one governance system over another. Common sense tells us that what works in Kansas may not work in Beijing. There is good evidence that certain organizational forms, such as the diversified holding company, may be poorly suited to advanced economies and yet fit the circumstances of developing markets (see Khanna and Palepu, 2000). The explanation may be institutional because developing countries lack the institutions of law and financial-market discipline; the holding company plays a role of *functional equivalence* to these institutions. "Same function, but different form" is a simple way to express why international governance systems will not converge, even if practices do so.

Governance, as the word implies, is about power: who gets to exercise it and how it is exercised. It is reasonable for investors in publicly traded companies to press for governance mechanisms that will improve the management of resources. The problem of "who knows best" is a fundamental one in any hierarchy. As much as the board wants management to manage better, management knows more, not only about what the true state of the books may be, but presumably about the business and opportunities. What is true for the board and top management is also true down the hierarchy, whereby division heads will know their business better than top management, and so on.

This problem of the principal agent has led to a popular belief in and burgeoning literature on incentive schemes to get managers to reveal information and to make the right decisions. Justification for the proliferation of stock options as compensation throughout developed countries and even in some developing countries was given as paying managers for their knowledge and for offering an "efficient contract"—that is, if managers should perform badly, they would lose the options and their jobs and would have to seek lower-paid employment. There has been considerable abuse of this system, especially in the United States. US compensation grew to astronomical proportions compared to other countries, options were "repriced" if performance was bad and hence was "out of the money," and control was often lost by the board.

The new wisdom regarding transparency, separation of top management and the board, expensing options, and improving auditing is surely a warranted response and an improvement over past practice. It is indisputable that practices such as capitalizing lease payments (WorldCom) or hiding investments in partnerships (Enron) are wrong. At best, they reflect the human weakness of writing the future to adjust the past and booking expected earnings as current earnings. More likely in some cases, such decisions are also criminal. The adoption of new accounting practices, auditing oversight, and rules for managerial liability makes sense given these abuses.

We endorse these improvements, and yet do not believe that these are cures. For at the heart of the question of corporate governance is a clash between two very different views of what the firm is and how it operates. The first view is that good governance finds incentive-compatible devices to motivate managers to act in the interest of the firm. The functional belief is that the manager cares about effort and reward—get the reward right, and the effort follows. Thus, in the eyes of a former president of the American Financial Association, the poor performance of American firms during the 1980s was due to lax governance that failed to meet international, and especially Japanese, standards of competition (see Jensen, 1993). Management knew what to do, but they were not properly governed.

The second view states that a firm is a community, or a community of communities. The question, from this point of view, would be, who knew what to do in the 1980s in response to international competition? Were the principles of "just in time," "kanban," and "teams" understood by workers or managers? What would a top manager have said? Do what Toyota workers do? One doubts if this would have been effective.

From the point of view of organizational theory, responding to competition is a collective enterprise in which nonmaterial rewards play an important role. These rewards include the identification with the firm, the sharing of knowledge, and the inspiration (as opposed to motivation) to respond to crisis and opportunity.[10] One may judge the predicament of European and American automobile manufacturers as a failure of top management and the board. One can also look at the variation in transformation among these firms as an outcome that is best explained by their organizational properties and the formal and informal mechanisms by which new knowledge is learned and used.

The job of good governance in this organizational view is to create conditions that improve capabilities inside a firm and among all parties contracting with the firm. The financial approach of effort and incentives is very often counterproductive to this end. It suffers from a fundamental problem called the "functional fallacy": if you pay people to do something they will do it, because people do things in order to be rewarded. This is not only bad social science; it also carries the seeds of eventual catastrophe. For once every relationship is monetized into a "nexus of contracts," people indeed do optimize and game the system. The solution has created a worse problem. We doubt if there is any governance mechanism that can prevent the consequences that ensue from fully monetizing the employment relationship.

What can be done, then, in this wider organizational view? Margaret Blair proposes a team approach to governance at the top, but in fact, there is no reason to stop there. For workers and managers, the act of "belonging" creates a desire for better over worse outcomes for their organizations. It is an odd thing that companies spend massively on creating consumer identification with a brand, and yet overlook the fact that workers surely are as well influenced by their identification with the company, the product, and even the brand itself. Do workers care about the economic performance of their companies? Do they care about their company's status in their communities? Or about their company's ethical conduct? And if not, is this not a signal of something seriously wrong about the firm?

By conventional indexes, employee participation in governance has been on the decline in most countries. In this book, Mary O'Sullivan reviews the evidence for work councils and employee participation and concludes that in most wealthy countries, participation is in retreat. Yet there is other evidence. In knowledge-intensive firms such as law practices, consulting, and advertising, partnerships are prevalent and characterized by internal rather than external control. One wonders if the recent experience of investment banks and consulting firms "going public" will result in generating adequate financial rewards to investors or in creating the team-based logics required for effective and efficient production of high-value services. If not (and we expect considerable failure along these lines), reversion to partnerships may be a likely outcome for many of these experiments. Neither is the family firm in retreat; this form of business organization is still dominant in all economies. Based on an assessment of all organizational forms, employee participation in firms is an important feature in an economy.

If the governance of the public firm is to be fixed, there may well be a need to look at the emotional properties of other organizational forms regarding their harnessing of knowledge as a cooperative element, rather than a controlling device, in the production of valued products and services. The power of identity, pride, and loyalty should not be neglected as significant resources in a firm. In this view, we ask less "how does hierarchy control" than "how does the organization" help develop and orchestrate the competence of employees. It would be poor advice to advocate more and better ways to govern by control at the cost of governing through better organization.

We hope that this book contributes not only to dialogue, but to multilateral trade of ideas, practices, and institutions. These are original chapters offering diverse points of view. The topic is controversial; offering an integration of views is not only impossible, it would also impede the required debate. At the end of the day, it may be the quality of this debate that best serves the objective of helping to improve the growth prospects of the world economy. The essays in this book are offered in this spirit.

NOTES

1   Allen and Gale (1999). See Zysman (1983) for an early discussion of the topic.

2   For an empirical assessment of national competitiveness and the ability to achieve sustained economic growth in a large sample of countries, see the World Economic Forum's annual *Global Competitiveness Report*.

3   On functional equivalents, see Merton (1949); on functional finance, Merton (1990); on Trobiand Islands, Malinowski (2001/1927). Robert K. Merton, the sociologist, is the father of Robert C. Merton, the financial economist and Nobel Laureate.

4   Rajan and Zingales (2000) offer a similar perspective on the power of employees and the governance solution of increasing their firm-specific investments.

5   The initial articles of La Porta et al (1997, 1998) established these results that have been canonized in the subsequent literature.

6   See West (2002).

7   Kogut and Walker (2001). An earlier version of their report was summarized in the World Economic Forum publication, *World Links*, published in January 2000.

8   See Plihon and Ponssard (2002) for data regarding European countries.

9   A listing of these reports can be found at http://www.ecgi.org/codes/all_codes.htm.

10 See Kogut and Zander (1996) for a general view; O'Sullivan (2000) develops the relationship between governance and learning in her book. Recent developments in corporate finance show that there is a rapid convergence toward this view, as in Zingales (2000).

REFERENCES

Agnblad, J., E. Berglöf, P. Högfeldt, and J. Svancar. 2001. "Ownership and Control in Sweden: Strong Controlling Owners, Weak Minorities, Social Control," in Barca and Becht (eds.) *The Control of Corporate Europe*, Oxford: Oxford University Press.

Allen, F., and D. Gale. 1999. "Diversity of Opinion and Financing of New Technologies," *Journal of Financial Intermediation* 8, pp. 68–69.

Allen, F., and D. Gale. 2000. "Corporate Governance and Competition." In X. Vives, ed., *Corporate Governance: Theoretical and Empirical Perspectives*. Cambridge: Cambridge University Press.

Berkowitz, D., K. Pistor, and J.-F. Richard. 2003. "The Transplant Effect," *American Journal of Comparative Law* (forthcoming).

Berle, A. A., Jr. 1931. "Corporate Powers as Powers in Trust," *Harvard Law Review* 44, no. 7, pp. 1049–1074.

Blair, M. M. 1995. *Ownership and Control: Rethinking Corporate Governance for the Twenty-First Century*. Washington, DC: Brookings Institution.

Bowman, E. H., and M. Useem. 1995. "The Anomalies of Normal Governance." In E. H. Bowman and B. Kogut, ed., *Redesigning the Firm*. New York: Oxford University Press.

Carlin, W., and C. Mayer. 2000. "How Do Financial Systems Affect Economic Performance?", "Corporate Governance and Competition." In X. Vives, ed., *Corporate Governance: Theoretical and Empirical Perspectives*. Cambridge: Cambridge University Press.

Carruthers, B. G. 1999. *City of Capital: Politics and Markets in the English Financial Revolution*. Princeton: Princeton University Press.

Cohen, M., J. March, and J. Olsen. 1972. "A Garbage Can Model of Organizational Choice," *Administrative Science Quarterly* 17, pp. 1–25.

Cornelius, P., ed. 2003. *The Global Competitiveness Report 2002-2003*. Published for the World Economic Forum, New York: Oxford University Press.

Cyert, R., and J. March. 1963. *A Behavioral Theory of the Firm*. Upper Saddle River, NJ: Prentice Hall.

Dodd, E. M. 1932. "For Whom are Corporate Managers Trustees?" *Harvard Law Review* 45, pp. 1145–1163.

Freeman, R. E. 1984. *Strategic Management: A Stakeholder Approach*. Boston: Pittman.

Gompers, P. A., J. L. Ishii, and A. Metrick. 2003. "Corporate Governance and Equity Prices," *Quarterly Journal of Economics* (forthcoming).

Gorton, G., and F. Schmid. 2000. "Universal Banking and the Performance of German Firms," *Journal of Financial Economics* 58, pp. 29–80.

Institute of International Finance (IIF). 2002. *Capital Flows to Emerging Market Economies*. Washington, DC: Institute of International Finance.

International Monetary Fund (IMF). 2002. *Global Financial Stability Report: Market Developments and Issues*. Washington, DC: International Monetary Fund.

Jensen, M. 1993. "The Modern Industrial Revolution, Exit and the Failure of Internal Control Systems," *Journal of Finance* 48, pp. 831–880.

Khanna, T., and K. Palepu. 2000. "Is Group Affiliation Profitable in Emerging Markets? An Analysis of Diversified Indian Business Groups," *Journal of Finance* 55, pp. 867–891.

Kogut, B., and G. Walker. 2001. "The Small World of Germany and the Durability of National Networks," *American Sociological Review* 66, pp. 317–335.

Kogut, B., and U. Zander. 1996. "What Do Firms Do? Coordination, Identity and Learning," *Organization Science* 7, pp. 502–518.

La Porta, R., F. Lopez-de-Silanes, A. Shleifer, and R. Vishny. 1997. "Legal Determinants of External Finance," *Journal of Finance* 52, pp. 1131–1150.

La Porta, R., F. Lopez-de-Silanes, A. Shleifer, and R. Vishny. 1998. "Law and Finance," *Journal of Political Economy* 106, pp. 1113–1155.

Levine, R. 1997. "Financial Development and Economic Growth: Views and Agenda," *Journal of Economic Literature* 35, pp. 688–726.

Malinowski, B. 2001. (First published 1927). *Sex and Repression in Savage Society*. London: Routledge.

Merton, R. 1949. *Social Theory and Social Structure: Toward the Codification of Theory and Research.* Glencoe, IL: Free Press.

Merton, R. C. 1990. "The Financial System and Economic Performance," *Journal of Financial Services Research* 4, pp. 263–300.

Montesquieu, C. L. 1748. *De l'esprit des lois*. Geneva: Barrilot & Fils.

O'Sullivan, M. 2000. *Contests for Corporate Control. Corporate Governance and Economic Performance in the United States and Germany.* Oxford: Oxford University Press.

Padgett, J. F., and C. K. Ansell. 1993. "Robust Action and the Rise of the Medici, 1400–1434," *American Journal of Sociology* 98, pp. 1259–1319.

Plihon, D., and J.-P. Poussard. 2002. *La Montée en Puissance des Fonds d'Investissement: Quels enJeux pour les Entreprises.* Paris: Le Documentation Francaise.

Rajan, R., and L. Zingales. 2002. "The Great Reversals: The Politics of Financial Development in the 20th Century," NBER Working Paper No. 8178. Cambridge: National Bureau of Economic Research.

Roe, M. 1994. *Strong Managers, Weak Owners: the Political Roots of American Corporate Finance.* Princeton: Princeton University Press.

Stark, D. 1996. "Recombinant Property in East European Capitalism." *American Journal of Sociology* 101, pp. 993–1027.

Teubner, G. 2001. "Legal Irritants: How Unifying Law Ends Up in New Divergences." In P. A. Hall and D. Soskice, eds., *Varieties of Capitalism*. Oxford: Oxford University Press.

Useem, M. 1986. *The Inner Circle: Large Corporations and the Rise of Business Political Activity in the U.S. and U.K.* Oxford: Oxford University Press.

West, M. 2002. *Legal Determinants of World Cup Success.* Online. http://www.wcfia.harvard.edu/seminars/pegroup/worldcup.pdf

Westney, D. E. 1987. *Imitation and Innovation: The Transfer of Western Organizational Patterns to Meiji Japan.* Cambridge: Harvard University Press

Zingales, L. 2000. "In Search of New Foundations," *Journal of Finance* 55, pp. 1623–1653.

Zysman, J. 1983. *Government, Markets and Growth: Financial Systems and the Politics of Industrial Change.* Ithaca, NY: Cornell University Press.

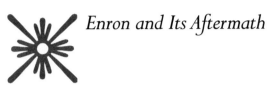 *Enron and Its Aftermath*

Chapter 2

What Caused Enron?
A Capsule of Social and Economic History of the 1990s

John C. Coffee, Jr.

The sudden explosion of corporate accounting scandals and related financial irregularities that burst over the financial markets between late 2001 and the first half of 2002—e.g., Enron, WorldCom, Tyco, Adelphia, and others—raises an obvious question: why now? What explains the sudden concentration of financial scandals at this moment in time? Much commentary has rounded up the usual suspects and blamed the scandals on a decline in business morality, "infectious greed,"[1] and similar subjective trends that cannot be reliably measured. Unfortunately, this approach simply reasons backward: because there has been an increase in scandals, there must have been a decline in business morality. An equally common theme has been to announce that the boards of directors failed in all these cases.[2] This may well have been true, but it does not supply an explanation of why a sudden surge of failures occurred. Nor does it tell us what caused these boards to fail. Were the boards delinquent in ignoring obvious warning signals? Or were they blinded by the gatekeepers and others on whom they necessarily rely? Still a third reaction has been the more cynical response that a wave of recriminations, soul-searching, and scapegoating necessarily follows in the aftermath of any market bubble's collapse, and clearly a large frothy bubble did burst in 2000.[3] As an historical matter, this may be true, but it again does not mean that normative criticisms are not justified.

In contrast to all these responses, this chapter will take a very different approach toward the issue of causation. Without defending any of these boards or applauding the current state of business morality, it will nonetheless suggest that the last year's explosion of financial irregularity was the natural and logical consequence of trends and forces that have been developing for some time. Ironically, some of these developments were themselves well-intentioned reforms, and, even if their reversal might reduce the incidence of fraud, such a policy prescription would also take us back to a world of high inefficiency and limited accountability. The blunt truth is that recent accounting scandals and the broader phenomenon of earnings management are by-products of a system of corporate governance that has indeed made corporate managers more accountable to shareholders and, as a result, extremely responsive to the market. But sensitivity to the market can be a mixed blessing. This observation does not deny that further reforms are needed, but it suggests that a balance has to be struck, because insensitivity to the market is also not the answer.

Although this perspective does not absolve boards of directors from blame, it suggests that the fundamental developments that destabilized our corporate governance system were ones that changed the incentives confronting both senior executives and the corporation's outside gatekeepers. Although the boards, themselves, may well have failed, little reason exists to believe that the behavior of boards changed or deteriorated over recent decades (and some reason exists to believe that board performance has improved). Thus, blaming the board is a myopic theory of causation that leads nowhere, because it cannot explain the sudden surge in irregularities. In contrast, a focus on gatekeepers and managers provides a better perspective for analyzing both what caused these scandals and the likely impact of the recent congressional legislation in the United States (popularly known as the Sarbanes-Oxley Act of 2002) that was passed in their wake. In overview, this chapter will relate changes in corporate regulation and governance over the last two decades to the recent scandals, then focus on the special institution of corporate "gatekeepers" on whom it argues modern corporate governance depends, and finally turn to the Sarbanes-Oxley Act.

THE PRIOR EQUILIBRIUM: AMERICAN CORPORATE GOVERNANCE AS OF 1980

If we turned the clock back 20 odd years to 1980, we would find that the dominant academic commentary of that era articulated a "theory of managerial capitalism" that essentially saw the public corporation as a kind of bloated bureaucracy that maximized sales, growth, and size, but not profits or stock price.[4] Academic writers such as Robin Marris and William Baumol viewed the firms of that era as pursuing an empire-building policy, which "profit-satisficed," rather than profit maximized.[5] The interests of different constituencies were balanced by professional managers, and, at least in much of this literature, no special priority was assigned to the interests of shareholders. Such a management strategy was motivated in large part by the desire of the corporation's managers to increase their own security and perquisites. Conglomerate mergers, for example, achieved these ends by reducing the risk of insolvency, as they placed managers at the top of a diversified (but different) portfolio of businesses that could cross-subsidize each other.[6] Also, with greater size came greater cash income to managers and a reduced risk of corporate control contests or shareholder activism.

Some academic writers in this era—most notably Oliver Williamson—did not view the conglomerate as necessarily inefficient; rather, Williamson argued that internal capital markets could be as efficient as external ones.[7] Still, both sides in this debate concurred that managers were effectively insulated from shareholder demands and could treat shareholders as just one of several constituencies whose interests were to be "balanced." Please note that nothing in this account suggests that a higher morality constrained managers of this era.

This equilibrium was profoundly destabilized during the 1980s by the advent of the hostile takeover. Although hostile takeovers predated the 1980s, it was only during the 1980s, beginning in 1983,[8] that they first began to be financed with junk bonds. Junk bond financing made the conglomerate corporate empires of the prior decade a tempting target for the financial bidder, who could reap high profits doing a "bust-up" takeover. In turn, this gave managements of potential targets a stronger interest in the short-term stock price of their firms than they had had in the past, because, even if takeover defensive tactics might work for a while, a target firm would not be likely to remain independent if its market price remained significantly below its break-up value for a sustained period.

Less noticed at the time, but possibly even more significant from today's perspective, was the change in executive compensation. Leveraged buyout (LBO) firms, such as Kohlberg Kravis Roberts, entered the takeover wars, seeking to buy undervalued companies, often in league with these firms' incumbent management. Alternatively, they sometimes installed new management teams to turn the company around. Either way, the goal of the LBO firms was to create strong incentives that would link management's interest to the firm's stock market value. Thus they compensated senior managers with much greater ownership stakes than had customarily been awarded as stock options. Institutional investors also picked up this theme, encouraging greater use of stock options to compensate both managers and directors. This process accelerated in the 1990s, but it began in the 1980s and was a by-product of the takeover movement.

THE OLD ORDER CHANGETH: THE NEW GOVERNANCE PARADIGM OF THE 1990s

The two principal forces that initially changed American corporate governance over the 1990s have already been identified: the takeover movement and growing use of equity compensation. Other forces that crested during the 1990s—including the heightened activism of institutional investors, a deregulatory movement that sought to dismantle obsolete regulatory provisions, and the media's increasing fascination with the market as the 1990s progressed—reinforced their impact, because in common they all made managers more sensitive to their firm's market price. In so doing, however, these forces also inclined managers to take greater risks to inflate that stock price. The dimensions of this transition are best revealed if we contrast data from the beginning and the end of the 1990s. As of 1990, equity-based compensation for chief executive officers of US public corporations appears to have been only around 5 percent of their total annual compensation, but by 1999, this percentage had risen to an estimated 60 percent.[9] Although the current scale and significance of stock options as a motivator of management will be discussed later, the critical point here is that the 1990s was the decade in which senior executive compensation shifted from being primarily cash-based to being primarily stock-based. With this change, management became focused not simply on the relationship between market price and break-up value (which the advent of the bust-up takeover compelled them to watch), but also on the likely future performance of their firm's stock over the short run. Far more than the hostile takeover, equity compensation induced management to obsess over their firm's day-to-day share price.

Not only did market practices change during the 1990s, but legal changes facilitated both the use of equity compensation and (unintentionally) the ability of managers to bail out at an inflated stock price. Prior to 1991, a senior executive of a publicly held company who exercised a stock option would be required to hold the underlying security for six months in order to satisfy the holding requirements of Section 16(b) of the Securities Exchange Act of 1934. Otherwise, the executive could be made to surrender any gain to the corporation as a "short swing" profit. In 1991, the Securities and Exchange Commission (SEC) reexamined its rules under § 16(b) and broadly deregulated.[10] In particular, the SEC relaxed the holding period requirements under § 16(b) so that the senior executive could tack the holding period of the stock option to the holding period for the underlying shares. Thus, if the stock option had already been held six months or longer, the underlying shares could be sold immediately on exercise of the option. Because qualified stock options usually must be held for several years before they become exercisable, this revision meant that most senior executives were free to sell the underlying stock on the same day they exercised the option. Very quickly, this became the prevailing pattern. Although it was not the intent of these reforms to authorize or encourage bailouts, they made it possible for senior executives with vested options to exploit a temporary price spike in their firm's shares by exercising their options and selling in a single day.

Even prior to the 1990s, earnings management was a pervasive and longstanding practice, but its goal had traditionally been to smooth out fluctuations in income in order to reduce the volatility of the firm's cash flows and present a simple, steadily ascending line from period to period. Thus, techniques such as "cookie jar" reserves were perfected to enable management to save earnings for a "rainy day" by storing "excess" earnings in reserves. If one looks at the SEC's pronouncements on earnings management during the 1990s, however, the nature of this practice appears to have changed. Increasingly, managements appear to have shifted to focusing on techniques for premature revenue recognition, and throughout the 1990s, accounting scandals rose.[11]

At least in part, the increased willingness of managements to recognize income prematurely (in effect, to misappropriate it from future periods) seems linked to another phenomenon: the need to satisfy the forecasts made by those security analysts covering the firm. By the mid 1990s, even a modest shortfall in earnings below the level forecasted could produce a dramatic market penalty, as dissatisfied investors dumped the firm's stock. But before one can rely on management's difficulty in satisfying the analyst's forecast to explain earnings management, a circularity problem must first be faced. At bottom, the security analyst's chief source of information about the company is its senior management. If management feared being unable to meet the analyst's projection, why did management not encourage the analyst to make less aggressive forecasts in the first instance? The most logical answer involves again the growing importance of equity compensation. Aggressive forecasts drove the firm's stock price up and enabled management to sell at an inflated price. Premature revenue recognition then became a means by which managements satisfied aggressive forecasts and sustained high market valuations.

High market valuations were not, however, simply the product of aggressive forecasting. Beginning around 1994 and continuing until 2000, the stock market in the United States entered the longest, most sustained bull market in US history. In such an excited environment, aggressive forecasting produces an assured market reaction. Moreover, the market euphoria that a sustained bull market generates may cause investors, analysts, auditors, and other "gatekeepers" to suspend their usual skepticism.

Accounting scandals have a long history over the last half century,[12] and Enron and related scandals arguably may have an impact roughly comparable to the Savings and Loan (S&L) crisis in the late 1980s (and episode that similarly resulted in Draconian legislation[13]). Both episodes show that the underlying driving force was probably managerial incentives more than any decline in ethics. After the S&L crisis, it was quickly perceived that bank promoters had an excessive incentive to take risk because the government guaranteed their bank's financial obligation to depositors (thus resulting in a classic "moral hazard" problem). In the case of the Enron-era scandals, the impact of stock compensation may have played a similar explanatory role. This explanation leads to a tentative generalization: perverse incentives cause scandals, not declines in ethics. Still, an alternative hypothesis remains plausible: namely, that a market bubble explains (or at least contributes significantly to our understanding of) the failure of those monitors who should have restrained management. Because multiple explanations can account for the pervasive gatekeeper failure that has accompanied the recent financial and accounting scandals, a synthesis seems necessary, and this requires us to focus more closely on what defines and motivates the professional gatekeeper.

THE CHANGING POSITION OF THE GATEKEEPER DURING THE 1990s

Although the term *gatekeeper* is commonly used,[14] its meaning is not self-evident. As used in this article, gatekeepers are reputational intermediaries who provide verification and certification services to investors.[15] These services can consist of verifying a company's financial statements (as the independent auditor does), evaluating the creditworthiness of the company (as the debt rating agency does), assessing the company's business and financial prospects vis-à-vis its rivals (as the securities analyst does), or appraising the fairness of a specific transaction (as the investment banker does in delivering a fairness opinion). Attorneys can also be gatekeepers when they pledge their professional reputations to a transaction (as counsel for the issuer typically does in an initial public offering), but, as later discussed, the more typical role of attorneys serving public corporations is that of the transaction engineer, rather than that of a reputational intermediary.

Characteristically, the professional gatekeeper essentially assesses or vouches for the corporate client's own statements about itself or a specific transaction. This duplication is necessary because the market recognizes that the gatekeeper has a lesser incentive to deceive than does its client and thus regards the gatekeeper's assurance or evaluation as more credible. To be sure, the gatekeeper as watchdog is arguably compromised by the fact that it is typically paid by the party that it is to watch, but its relative credibility stems from the fact that it is in effect pledging a reputational capital that it has built up over many years of performing similar services for numerous clients. In theory, such reputational capital would not be sacrificed for a single client and a modest fee. Nonetheless, here as elsewhere, logic and experience can conflict. Despite the clear logic of the gatekeeper rationale, experience over the 1990s suggests that professional gatekeepers do acquiesce in managerial fraud, even though the apparent reputational losses seem to dwarf the gains to be made from the individual client.[16] The deep question about Enron and related scandals is then not why did some managements engage in fraud? Rather, it is why did the gatekeepers let them?

Initially, obvious reasons can be advanced why gatekeepers should resist fraud and not acquiesce in accounting irregularities. In theory, a gatekeeper has many clients, each of whom pays it a fee that is modest in proportion to the firm's overall revenues. Arthur Andersen had, for example, 2,300 audit clients.[17] On this basis, the firm seemingly had little incentive to risk its considerable reputational capital for any one client. During the 1990s, many courts bought this logic hook, line, and sinker. For example, in *DiLeo v. Ernst & Young*,[18] Judge Easterbrook, writing for the Seventh Circuit, outlined precisely the foregoing theory:

> The complaint does not allege that [the auditor] had anything to gain from any fraud by [its client]. An accountant's greatest asset is its reputation for honesty, closely followed by its reputation for careful work. Fees for two years' audits could not approach the losses [that the auditor] would suffer from a perception that it would muffle a client's fraud. . . . [The auditor's] partners shared none of the gain from any fraud and were exposed to a large fraction of the loss. It would have been irrational for any of them to have joined cause with [the client].[19]

Of course, the modest fees in some of these cases (for example, the audit fee was only USD 90,000 in *Robin v. Arthur Young & Co.*)[20] were far less than the USD 100 million in prospective annual fees from Enron that Arthur Andersen & Co. explicitly foresaw. But does this difference really explain Arthur Andersen's downward spiral? After all, Arthur Andersen earned over USD 9 billion in revenues in 2001.[21]

Once among the most respected of all professional service firms (including law, accounting, and consulting firms), Andersen became involved in a series of now well known securities frauds—e.g., Waste Management, Sunbeam, HBOCMcKesson, The Baptist Foundation, and now Global Crossing—that culminated in its disastrous association with Enron. Those who wish to characterize the recent corporate scandals as simply the work of a "few bad apples" may wish to present Arthur Andersen as an outlier, in effect an "outlaw" firm that masqueraded as honest. This theory, however, simply does not hold water. The available evidence in fact suggests that Andersen was no different than its peers (except possibly less lucky).[22] All in all, the better inference is that something led to a general erosion in the quality of financial reporting during the late 1990s. During this period, earnings restatements, long a proxy for fraud, suddenly soared. To cite only the simplest quantitative measure, the number of earnings restatements by publicly held corporations averaged 49 per year from 1990 to 1997, then increased to 91 in 1998, and finally skyrocketed to 150 and 156, respectively, in 1999 and 2000.[23]

What caused this sudden spike in earning restatements? Because public corporations must fear stock price drops, securities class actions, and SEC investigations in the wake of earnings restatements, it is not plausible to read this sudden increase as the product of a new tolerance for, or indifference to, restatements. Even if some portion of the change might be attributed to a new SEC activism about "earnings management,"[24] which became an SEC priority in 1998,[25] corporate issuers will not voluntarily expose themselves to enormous liability just to please the SEC. Moreover, not only did the number of earnings restatements increase over this period, but so also did the amounts involved.[26] Earnings restatements thus seem an indication that earlier earnings management has gotten out of hand. Accordingly, the spike in earnings restatements in the late 1990s implies that the Big Five firms had earlier acquiesced in aggressive earnings management—and, in particular, premature revenue recognition—that no longer could be sustained. Later it will be suggested that not only did the costs in deferring to the client go down, but the benefits also went up.

For the moment, however, it is more useful to focus on the possibility that this pattern of increased acquiescence by the gatekeeper to its client during the 1990s was not limited to the auditing profession. Securities analysts probably have encountered even greater recent public and congressional skepticism about their objectivity. Again, much of the evidence is anecdotal, but striking. As late as October 2001, 16 out of the 17 securities analysts covering Enron maintained *buy* or *strong buy* recommendations on its stock right up until virtually the moment of its bankruptcy filing.[27] The first brokerage firm to downgrade Enron to a *sell* rating in 2001 was Prudential Securities, which no longer engages in investment banking activities.[28] Revealingly, Prudential is also believed to have the highest proportion of sell ratings among the stocks it evaluates.[29]

Much like auditors, analysts are also *reputational intermediaries*, whose desire to be perceived as credible and objective may often be subordinated to their desire to retain and please investment banking clients. One statistic inevitably comes up in any assessment of analyst objectivity: namely, the curious fact that the ratio of *buy* recommendations to *sell* recommendations has recently been as high as 100 to 1.[30] In truth, this particular statistic may not be as compelling as it initially sounds because there are obvious reasons why *buy* recommendations will normally outnumber *sell* recommendations, even in the absence of conflicts of interest.[31] Yet a related statistic may be more revealing because it underscores the apparent transition that took place in the 1990s. According to a study by Thomson Financial, the ratio of *buy* to *sell* recommendations increased from 6 to 1 in 1991 to 100 to 1 by 2000.[32] Again, it appears that something happened in the 1990s that compromised the independence and objectivity of the gatekeepers on whom our private system of corporate governance depends.[33] Not surprisingly, it also appears that this loss of relative objectivity can harm investors.[34]

EXPLAINING GATEKEEPER FAILURE

It is now time to generalize. The outstanding point is supplied by the fact that none of the watchdogs that should have detected Enron's collapse—auditors, analysts, or debt rating agencies—did so before the penultimate moment. This is the true common denominator in the Enron debacle: the collective failure of the gatekeepers. Why did the watchdogs not bark in the night when it now appears in hindsight that a massive fraud took place? Here two quite different, although complementary, stories can be told. The first will be called the *general deterrence* story and the second, the *bubble* story. The first is essentially economic in its premises and the second, psychological.

The deterrence explanation: The underdeterred gatekeeper

The general deterrence story focuses on the decline in the expected liability costs arising out of acquiescence by auditors in aggressive accounting policies favored by managements. It postulates that, during the 1990s, the risk of auditor liability declined while the benefits of acquiescence increased. Economics 101 teaches us that when the costs go down, while the benefits associated with any activity go up, the output of the activity will increase. Here, the activity that increased was auditor acquiescence.

Prior to the 1990s, auditors faced a very real risk of civil liability, principally from class action litigation.[35] Why did the legal risks go down during the 1990s? The obvious list of reasons would include:

1. the Supreme Court's *Lampf, Pleva* decision in 1991, which significantly shortened the statute of limitations applicable to securities fraud;[36]

2. the Supreme Court's *Central Bank of Denver* decision,[37] which in 1994 eliminated private "aiding and abetting" liability in securities fraud cases;

3. the Private Securities Litigation Reform Act of 1995 (PSLRA), which (a) raised the pleading standards for securities class actions to a level well above that applicable to fraud actions generally; (b) substituted proportionate liability for "joint and

several" liability; (c) restricted the sweep of the Racketeer-Influenced and Corrupt Organizations (RICO) statute so that it could no longer convert securities fraud class actions for compensatory damages into actions for treble damages; and (d) adopted a very protective safe harbor for forward-looking information; and

4. the Securities Litigation Uniform Standards Act of 1998 (SLUSA), which abolished state court class actions alleging securities fraud.[38]

Not only did the threat of private enforcement decline, but the prospect of public enforcement similarly subsided. In particular, there is reason to believe that, from some point in the 1980s until the late 1990s, the SEC shifted its enforcement focus away from actions against the Big Five accounting firms toward other priorities.[39] In any event, the point here is not that any of these changes were necessarily unjustified or excessive,[40] but rather that their collective impact was to reduce appreciably the risk of liability. Auditors were the special beneficiaries of many of these provisions. For example, the pleading rules and the new standard of proportionate liability protected them far more than it did most corporate defendants.[41] Although auditors are still sued today, the settlement value of cases against auditors has gone way down.

Correspondingly, the benefits of acquiescence to auditors rose over this same period, as the Big Five learned during the 1990s how to cross-sell consulting services and to treat the auditing function principally as a portal of entry into a lucrative client. Prior to the mid 1990s, the provision of consulting services to audit clients was infrequent and insubstantial in the aggregate.[42] Yet, according to one recent survey, the typical large public corporation now pays its auditor for consulting services three times what it pays the same auditor for auditing services.[43] Not only did auditing firms see more profit potential in consulting than in auditing, but they began during the 1990s to compete based on a strategy of *low balling*, under which auditing services were offered at rates that were marginal to arguably below cost. The rationale for such a strategy was that the auditing function was essentially a loss leader by which more lucrative services could be marketed.

Appealing as this argument—that the provision of consulting services eroded auditor independence—may seem, it is potentially subject to at least one important rebuttal. Those who defend the propriety of consulting services by auditors respond that the growth of consulting services made little real difference because the audit firm is already conflicted by the fact that the client pays its fees.[44] Put as bluntly as possible, the audit partner of a major client (such as Enron) is always conflicted by the fact that such a partner has virtually a "one-client" practice. Should the partner lose that client for any reason, the partner will probably need to find employment elsewhere. In short, both critics and defenders of the status quo tend to agree that the audit partner is already inevitably compromised by the desire to hold the client. From this premise, a prophylactic rule prohibiting the firm's involvement in consulting would seemingly achieve little.

Even if true in part, this analysis nonetheless misses a key point: namely, the difficulty faced by the client in firing the auditor in the real world. Because of this difficulty, the unintended consequence of combining consulting services with auditing services in one firm is that the union of the two enables the client to threaten the auditing firm more effectively in a "low visibility" way. To illustrate this point, let us suppose, for example, that a client becomes dissatisfied with an auditor who refuses to endorse the aggressive accounting policy favored by its management. Today, the client cannot easily fire the auditor. Firing the auditor is a costly step, inviting potential public embarrassment, public disclosure of the reasons for the auditor's dismissal or resignation, and potential SEC intervention.[45] However, if the auditor also becomes a consultant to the client, the client can then easily terminate the auditor as a consultant (or reduce its use of the firm's consulting services) in retaliation for the auditor's intransigence. This low visibility response requires no disclosure, invites no SEC oversight, and yet disciplines the audit firm so that it would possibly be motivated to replace the intransigent audit partner. In effect, the client can both bribe (or coerce) the auditor in its core professional role by raising (or reducing) its use of consulting services.

Of course, this argument that the client can discipline and threaten the auditor/consultant in ways that it could not discipline the simple auditor is based more on logic than actual case histories. It does fit the available data, however. A recent study by academic accounting experts, based on proxy statements filed during the first half of 2001, finds that those firms that purchased more non-audit services from their auditor (as a percentage of the total fee paid to the audit firm) were more likely to fit the profile of a firm engaging in earnings management.[46]

The irrational market story

Alternatively, Enron's and Arthur Andersen's downfalls can be seen as consequences of a classic bubble that overtook the equity markets in the late 1990s and produced a market euphoria. But what exactly is the connection between a market bubble and gatekeeper failure? Here a hypothesis needs to be advanced that, although plausible, cannot be rigorously proven: in a bubble, gatekeepers become less relevant and hence experience a decline in both their leverage over their client and the value of their reputational capital. That is, in an atmosphere of market euphoria in which stock prices are expected to ascend endlessly and exponentially, investors do not rely on gatekeepers, and managements in turn regard them as more a formality than a necessity. Gatekeepers are critical only when investors are cautious and skeptical and rely on their services, but in a market bubble, caution and skepticism are by definition largely abandoned. Arguably, auditors continue to be used in such an environment more because SEC rules mandate their use (or because no individual firm wished to call attention to itself by becoming the first to dispense with them) than because investors demanded their use. As a result, because gatekeepers have reduced relevance in such an environment, they also have reduced leverage with respect to their clients. Thus, if we assume that the auditor will be largely ignored by euphoric investors, the rational auditor's best competitive strategy (at least for the short term) was to become as acquiescent and low cost as possible.

For the securities analyst, a market bubble presented an even more serious problem: put simply, it was dangerous to be sane in an insane world. During the late 1990s, the securities analyst who prudently predicted reasonable growth and stock appreciation was quickly left in the dust by the investment guru who prophesized a new investment paradigm in which revenues and costs were less important than the number of "hits" on a website. Moreover, as the initial public offering (IPO) market soared in the 1990s, securities analysts became celebrities and valuable assets to their firms;[47] indeed, they became the principal means by which investment banks competed for IPO clients, as the underwriter with the "star" analyst could produce the biggest first-day stock price spike. But as their salaries thus soared, analyst compensation came increasingly from the investment banking side of their firms. Hence, just as in the case of the auditor, the analyst's economic position became increasingly dependent on favoring the interests of persons outside their profession (i.e., consultants in the case of the auditor and investment bankers in the case of the analyst) who had little reason to respect or observe the standards or professional culture within the gatekeeper's profession.[48]

The common denominator linking these examples is that, as auditors increasingly sought consulting income and as analysts increasingly competed to maximize investment banking revenues, the gatekeepers' desire to preserve their reputational capital for the long run was compromised by their ability to obtain additional income from new sources. Additionally, as later discussed, the value of that reputational capital may have declined because investors in a bubble cease to rely on gatekeeping services. Either way, it could have become more profitable for firms to realize the value of their reputational capital by trading on it in the short run than by preserving it forever. Indeed, if it were true that auditing became a loss leader in the 1990s and that securities research was not self-supporting, one cannot logically expect gatekeeping firms to expend resources or decline business opportunities in order to protect reputations that were only marginally profitable.

Toward synthesis

These explanations still do not fully explain why reputational capital built up over decades might be sacrificed (or, more accurately, liquidated) once legal risks decline and/or a bubble develops. Here, additional factors need to be considered.

1. **The Increased Incentive for Short-Term Stock Price Maximization.** The pressure on gatekeepers to acquiesce in earnings management was not constant over time, but rather this pressure grew during the 1990s. As noted earlier, executive compensation shifted during the 1990s from being primarily cash based to being primarily equity based. The clearest measure of this change is the growth

in stock options. Over the last decade, stock options rose from 5 percent of shares outstanding at major US companies to 15 percent—a 300 percent increase.[49] The value of these options rose by an even greater percentage and over a dramatically shorter period: from USD 50 billion in 1997 in the case of the 2,000 largest corporations to USD 162 billion in 2000—an over 300 percent rise in three years.[50] Stock options create an obvious and potentially perverse incentive to engage in short-run, rather than long-term, stock price maximization because executives can exercise their stock options and sell the underlying shares on the same day.[51] Interestingly, this ability was, itself, the product of deregulatory reform in the early 1990s, which relaxed the rules under Section 16(b) of the Securities Exchange Act of 1934 to permit officers and directors to exercise stock options and sell the underlying shares without holding the shares for the previously required six-month period.[52] Thus, if executives inflated the stock price of their company through premature revenue recognition or other classic earnings management techniques, they could quickly bail out in the short term by exercising their options and selling, leaving shareholders to bear the cost of the stock decline when the inflated stock price could not be maintained over subsequent periods. Given these incentives, it becomes rational for corporate executives to use lucrative consulting contracts, or other positive and negative incentives, to induce gatekeepers to engage in conduct that made these executives very rich. The bottom line is then that the growth of stock options resulted in gatekeepers being placed under greater pressure to acquiesce in short-term oriented financial and accounting strategies.

2. **The Absence of Competition.** The Big Five obviously dominated a very concentrated market. Smaller competitors could not expect to develop the international scale or brand names that the Big Five possessed simply by quoting a cheaper price. More importantly, in a market this concentrated, implicit collusion develops easily. Each firm could develop and follow a common competitive strategy in parallel without fear of being undercut by a major competitor. Thus, if each of the Big Five were to prefer a strategy under which it acquiesced to clients at cost of an occasional litigation loss and some public humiliation, it could more easily observe this policy if it knew that it would not be attacked by a holier-than-thou rival stressing its greater reputation for integrity as a competitive strategy. This approach does not require formal collusion but only the expectation that one's competitors would also be willing to accept litigation losses and occasional public humiliation as a cost of doing business.

    Put differently, either in a less concentrated market where several dozen firms competed or in a market with low barriers to entry, it would be predictable that some dissident firm would seek to market itself as distinctive for its integrity. But in a market of five firms (and only four for the future), this is less likely.

3. **Observability.** That a fraud occurs is not necessarily the fault of auditors. If they can respond to any fraud by asserting that they were victimized by a dishonest management, auditors may be able to avoid the permanent loss of reputational capital—particularly so long as their few competitors have no desire to exploit their failures because they are more or less equally vulnerable. In other words, a system of reputational intermediaries works only if fault can be reliably assigned.

4. **Reduced Leverage.** In a bubble environment, clients may depend less on gatekeepers, and so gatekeepers have less leverage. If investors naturally assume that stock prices will rise, they will engage in less scrutiny of financial statements. Moreover, they may want issuers to use aggressive accounting policies in order to fuel earnings growth and higher market valuations. In such an environment, caught between equally greedy management and greedy investors, gatekeepers are more likely to acquiesce because ultimately their reputational capital has diminished value.

5. **Principal/Agent Problems.** Auditing firms have always known that an individual partner could be dominated by a large client and might defer excessively to such a client in a manner that could inflict liability on the firm. Thus, early on, they developed systems of internal monitoring that were far more elaborate than anything that law firms have yet attempted. But within the auditing firm, this internal monitoring function is not all powerful. After all, it is not itself a profit center. With the addition of consulting services as a major profit center, a natural coalition developed between the individual audit partner and the consulting divisions; each had a common interest in checking and overruling the firm's internal audit division when the latter's prudential decisions would prove costly to them. Cementing this marriage was the use of incentive fees. If those providing software consulting services for an audit firm were willing to offer the principal audit partner for a client a fee of 1 percent (or so) of any contract sold to the partner's audit client, few others within the firm might see any reason to object. If software consulting contracts (hypothetically, for USD 50 million) were then sold to the client, the audit partner might now receive more compensation from incentive fees for cross-selling than from auditing and thus had greater reason to value the client's satisfaction above his interest in the firm's reputational capital. More importantly, the audit partner now also had an ally in the consultants, who similarly would want to keep their mutual client satisfied, and together they would form a coalition potentially able to override the protests of their firm's internal audit unit (if it felt that an overly aggressive policy was being followed). Although case histories exactly matching this pattern cannot yet be identified, abundant evidence does exist for the thesis that incentive fees can bias audit decision-making.[53] Interestingly, Enron itself presents a fact pattern in which the audit firm's on-the-scene quality control officer was overruled and replaced.[54]

IMPLICATIONS: EVALUATING CONGRESSIONAL RESPONSE

Does it matter much which of the foregoing two stories—the deterrence story or the bubble story—is deemed more persuasive? Although they are complementary rather than contradictory, their relative plausibility may matter in terms of deciding whether reforms are necessary or desirable. To the extent that one accepts the deterrence story, we may need legal changes aimed at restoring an adequate legal threat. In principle, these changes could either raise the costs or lower the benefits of acquiescence to auditors (or both). To the extent one accepts the bubble story, the problem may be self-correcting. That is, once the bubble bursts, gatekeepers come back into fashion, as investors become skeptics who once again demand assurances that only credible reputational intermediaries can provide.[55]

Viewed historically, the Enron crisis is only one of several modern "accounting crises," extending from the Penn Central crisis in the 1970s to the S&L crisis in the 1980s.[56] But the distinctive difference between the Enron crisis and the crises of the 1970s and the 1980s is that management in the past only had a strong incentive to "cook the books" as their corporation approached insolvency. Only insolvency in an earlier era threatened them with ouster. Today, as the mechanisms of corporate accountability (e.g., takeovers, control contests, institutional activism, and more aggressive boards) have shortened managements' margin for error, the incentive to engage in earnings management and accounting irregularities is more widespread. Put more simply, one may cheat to survive, and survival is more in question in a more competitive world.

Congress's response: The Sarbanes-Oxley Act

Passed almost without dissent, the Public Company Accounting Reform and Investor Protection Act of 2002 (popularly known as the Sarbanes-Oxley Act) essentially addresses the problem of accounting irregularities by taking control of the accounting profession out of the hands of the profession and assigning it to a new body: the Public Company Accounting Oversight Board (the "Board"), which is authorized to regulate the profession, establish auditing standards, and impose professional discipline.[57] Conceptually, this is not a new approach, as the Board's authority largely parallels that of the National Association of Securities Dealers (NASD) over securities brokers and dealers. What is new, however, is explicit recognition of the significance of conflicts of interest, because the Act bars auditors from providing a number of categories of professional services to their audit clients and further authorizes the Board to prohibit additional categories.[58] Thus, if conflicts of interest compromised auditors, the Act responds with an appropriate answer.

But if accounting irregularities were more the product of a lack of general deterrence or the increased incentive of corporate executives to "cook the books" because of the temptations created by stock options, the Act is less clearly responsive to these problems. For example, except in a minor way, the Act does not seek to revise or reverse the PSLRA;[59] nor does it make gatekeepers liable in private litigation to investors where the gatekeeper knowingly aided and abetted a securities fraud. Finally, the Act never addresses stock options or executive compensation, except to the extent that it may require the forfeiture of such compensation to the corporation if the corporation later restates its earnings.[60] In short, the potential benefits from acquiescing in accounting irregularities appear to have been reduced for auditors, but the expected costs remain low because the level of deterrence that they once faced has not been restored.[61]

Prospects for the future

Some critics have regarded the Sarbanes-Oxley Act as more rhetoric than serious reform;[62] others (probably more) view it as a sweeping intrusion into our existing system of corporate governance. This chapter's view is roughly intermediate: the Act is a reasonable, but incomplete, response to serious problems, but with some rough edges that were inevitable given the speed with which it passed and the number of floor amendments. The conflicts of interest affecting auditors are likely to be successfully curtailed by it, but, absent stronger legal threats, there is little reason to believe that accounting firms will take sufficient steps to monitor and control their individual partners, who usually have more than sufficient incentives to deter to their dominant clients. Perhaps alternatives to litigation, such as the mandatory rotation of audit firms, would also work, but the Act stopped short of legislating this remedy as well.[63] Market corrections may mitigate the rate of accounting scandals for the near future, but, given the regularity of accounting scandals over US financial history, it would be rash to predict their disappearance because of Sarbanes-Oxley.

Finally, should the rest of the world expect to catch this American disease of accounting irregularities? Or does their relative immunity to it show the superiority of their own systems of accounting?[64] The best answer here is that the frequency of American accounting scandals has little to do with substantive accounting rules or philosophies and more to do with the structure of share ownership. Dispersed ownership in the United States contrasts with concentrated ownership in Europe and elsewhere. In concentrated ownership systems, a controlling shareholder monitors management and has little incentive to create short-term price spikes or to engage in aggressive earnings management (in part because a controlling shareholder will only sell in a control transaction at a control premium and cannot bail out into the market). Conversely, in dispersed ownership systems, strong executives may be only weakly monitored by their board and do have the incentive to cause price spikes into which they bail out. As a result, even if European accounting systems were inferior, we would still witness fewer accounting scandals abroad.

CONCLUSION

This chapter has sought to explain that Enron is more about gatekeeper failure than board failure. It has also sought to explain when gatekeepers (or *reputational intermediaries*) are likely to fail. Put simply, reputational capital is not an asset that professional services firms will inevitably hoard and protect. Indeed, during a bubble, the value of such capital may itself decline as their clients come to view the gatekeeper's services as superfluous. Logically, as legal exposure to liability declines and as the benefits of acqui-escence in the client's demands increase, gatekeeper failure should correspondingly increase—as it apparently did in the 1990s. Still, all gatekeepers are not alike. Securities analysts never faced any serious prospect of legal liability, even prior to 1990, and dur-ing a bubble the value of their services clearly went up.

Although this chapter has focused on incentives, popular commentary has instead used softer-edged concepts—such as "infectious greed"[65] and a decline in morality—to explain the same phenomena. Yet, there is little evidence that "greed" has ever declined; nor is it clear that there are relevant policy options for addressing either greed or business morality generally. In contrast, focusing on gatekeepers tells us that there are special actors in a system of private corporate governance whose incentives must be regulated.

Reasonable persons can always disagree what reforms are desirable. But the starting point for an intelligent debate is the recognition that the two major, contem-porary crises now facing the securities markets—i.e., the accounting irregularities revealed after the collapse of Enron and the growing controversy over securities ana-lysts, which began with the New York Attorney General's investigation into Merrill, Lynch—involve at bottom the same problem: both are crises motivated by the discov-ery by investors that reputational intermediaries upon whom they relied were con-flicted and seemingly sold their interests short. Neither the law nor the market has yet solved either of these closely related problems.

NOTES

1   Federal Reserve Chairman Alan Greenspan coined this colorful phrase, saying that "An infectious greed seemed to grip much of our business community." See Norris (2002).

2   A special committee of Enron's own board has already concluded that its board failed to mon-itor officers or conflicts of interest adequately. See Powers (2002). A Senate subcommittee has similarly assigned the principal blame to the Enron Board. See US Senate (2001).

3   Although this bubble initially burst in 2000, a further decline occurred in the late spring of 2002 as WorldCom and other crises appear to have further shaken market confidence. The S&P 500 index fell 26 percent between May 21 and July 23, 2002. See Nicholls (forth-coming 2002). Professor Nicholls, however, is skeptical that this market decline was caused by these corporate scandals. In his view, market downturns give rise to a "post-hoc fallacy" that scandals revealed in the wake of a market downturn caused that downturn.

4   See, e.g., Baumol (1995) and Marris (1969); see also Williamson (1963).

5   See Nicholls (2002). Sources cited supra note 3.

6   See Amihud and Lev (1981) and Marcus (1982); see also Coffee (1987).

7   See Williamson (1975; 1981).

8   1983 is the date identified by the Congressional Research Service as the first occasion on which "junk bonds" were used to finance hostile takeovers. See Congressional Research Service (1985).

9   See Altman (2002) (citing data collected by Harvard Business School Professor Brian Hall).

10   See Securities Exchange Act Release No. 34-28869 (Feb. 8, 1991) (adopting revised Rule 16b-3(d), which permits an officer or director to tack the two holding periods).

11   For a brief review of recent accounting scandals, which have been numerous, see Cunningham (2002). For the assertion that management became obsessed with earnings, see Gordon (2002).

12   See Cunningham (2002).

13   The S&L crisis led directly to the Financial Institutions Reform, Recovery and Enforcement Act of 1989 (FIRREA), Pub. L. No. 101-73, 103 Stat. 183 (1989), which imposes high fiduciary standards on directors of thrift and savings and loan institutions. Much as Sarbanes-Oxley has, FIRREA also created a new regulatory body: namely, the Resolution Trust Corporation.

14   The term *gatekeeper* is not simply an academic concept. In Securities Act Release No. 7870 (June 30, 2000), the SEC recently noted that "the federal laws . . . make independent auditors 'gatekeepers' to the public securities markets." 2000 SEC LEXIS 1389.

15   For a fuller, more theoretical consideration of the concept of the gatekeeper, see Kraakman (1984), Kraakman (1986), and Choi (1998).

16   This observation is hardly original with this author. See, for example, Prentice (2000).

17   See Mittelstadt (2002).

18   901 F.2d 624 (7th Cir. 1990); see also *Melder v. Morris* and *Robin v. Arthur Young & Co.* (mere USD 90,000 annual audit fee would have been an "irrational" motive for fraud).

19   See note 18, p. 629.

20   See *Robin v. Arthur Young & Co.*

21   Arthur Andersen's website reports that revenues for 2001 were USD 9.34 billion. See www.andersen.com.

22   Compared with its peers within the Big Five accounting firms, Arthur Andersen appears to have been responsible for less than its proportionate share of earnings restatements. Although it audited 21 percent of Big Five audit clients, it was responsible for only 15 percent of the restatements experienced by the Big Five firms between 1997 and 2001. On this basis, it was arguably slightly more conservative than its peers. See *Newsweek* (2002). In discussions with industry insiders, the only respect in which I have ever heard Andersen characterized as different from its peers in the Big Five was that it marketed itself as a firm in which the audit partner could make the final call on difficult accounting questions without having to secure approval from senior officials within the firm. Although this could translate into a weaker system of internal controls, this hypothesis seems inconsistent with Arthur Andersen's apparently below-average rate of earnings restatements.

23   See Moriarty and Livingston (2001).

24   Accounting firms have sometimes attempted to explain this increase on the basis that the SEC tightened the definition of "materiality" in the late 1990s. This explanation is not very convincing, in part because the principal SEC statement that tightened the definition of materiality—Staff Accounting Bulletin No. 99—was issued in mid 1999, after the number of restatements had already begun to soar in 1998. Also, SAB No. 99 did not truly mandate restatements, but only suggested that a rule of thumb that assumed that amounts under 5 percent were inherently immaterial could not be applied reflexively. See Staff Accounting Bulletin No. 99, 64 F.R. 45150 (August 19, 1999).

25   The SEC's prioritization of earnings management as a principal enforcement target can be approximately dated to SEC Chairman Arthur Levitt's now-famous speech on the subject in 1998. See Levitt (1998).

26   According to Moriarty and Livingston (2001), companies that restated earnings suffered market losses of USD 17.7 billion in 1998, USD 24.2 billion in 1999, and USD 31.2 billion in 2000. Expressed as a percentage of the overall capitalization of the market (which was ascendingly hyperbolically over this period), these losses for 1998 through 2000 came to 0.13 percent, 0.14 percent, and 0.19 percent, respectively, of market capitalization. In short, however expressed, the losses increased over this period.

27   See Torres (2002, p. 6): "In the case of Enron, 16 out of 17 analysts had a buy or a strong buy rating, one had a hold, none had a sell—even as the company stock had lost over half its value and its CEO suddenly resigned." 2002 WL 2011028; see also Partnoy (2002) (similar 16 out of 17 tabulation).

28   See Young (2001).

29   See Young (2001).

30   A study by Thomas Financial/First Call has found that less than 1 percent of the 28,000 stock recommendations issued by brokerage firm analysts during late 1999 and most of 2000 were "sell" recommendations. See Opening Statement of Congressman Kanjorski (2001, p. 1).

31   "Sell-side" analysts are employed by brokerage firms that understandably wish to maximize brokerage transactions. In this light, a "buy" recommendation addresses the entire market and certainly all the firm's customers, while a "sell" recommendation addresses only those customers who own the stock (probably well less than 1 percent) and those with margin accounts who are willing to sell the stock "short." In addition, "sell" recommendations annoy not only the issuer company, but also institutional investors who are afraid that sell recommendations will "spook" retail investors, causing them to panic and sell, while the institution is "locked into" a large position that cannot easily be liquidated.

32   See Kanjorski (2001, p. 1, citing study by First Call).

33   Participants in the industry also report that its professional culture changed dramatically in the late 1990s, particularly as investment banking firms began to hire "star" analysts for their marketing clout. See Morgenson (2002c, at Section 3-1, suggesting major change dates from around 1996).

34   Although the empirical evidence is limited, it suggests that "independent" analysts (i.e., analysts not associated with the underwriter for a particular issuer) behave differently than, and tend to outperform, analysts who are associated with the issuer's underwriter. See Michaely and Womack (1999).

35   As of 1992, Congress was advised that the securities fraud litigation costs for just the six largest accounting firms (then the "Big Six") accounted for USD 783 million, or more than 14 percent of their audit revenues. Potential exposure to loss was in the billions. See US Senate (1993). One major auditing firm, Laventhol & Horwath, did fail and entered bankruptcy as a result of litigation and associated scandals growing out of the savings and loan scandals of the 1980s. See Laventhol & Horwath (2002). The accounting profession's bitter experience with class litigation in the 1980s and 1990s probably explains why it became the strongest and most organized champion of the Private Securities Litigation Reform Act of 1995.

36   *Lampf, Pleva, Lipkind & Petigrow v. Gilbertston* (1991), (creating a federal rule requiring plaintiffs to file within one year of when they should have known of the violation underlying their action, but in no event more than three years after the violation). This one-to-three year period was typically shorter than the previously applicable limitations periods which were determined by analogy to state statutes and often permitted a five or six year delay— if that was the period within which a common law fraud action could be maintained in the particular state).

37   *Central Bank of Denver, N.A. v. First Interstate of Denver, N.A.* 511 U.S. 164 (1994).

38   See Pub. L. No. 105-353, 112 Stat. 3227 (codified in scattered sections of 15 U.S.C.). For an analysis and critique of this statute, see Painter (1998).

39   This point has been orally made to me by several former SEC officials, including Stanley Sporkin, the long-time former head of the Commission's Division of Enforcement. They believe that the SEC's enforcement action against Arthur Andersen, which was resolved in June, 2001, was one of the very few (and perhaps the only) enforcement action brought against a Big Five accounting firm on fraud grounds during the 1990s. See *Securities and Exchange Commission v. Arthur Andersen LLP*, SEC Litigation Release No. 17039, 2001 SEC LEXIS 1159 (June 19, 2001). Although the Commission did bring charges during the 1990s against individual partners in these firms, the Commission appears to have been deterred from bringing suits against the Big Five themselves because such actions were extremely costly in manpower and expense and the defendants could be expected to resist zealously. In contrast, during the 1980s, especially during Mr. Sporkin's tenure as head of the Enforcement Division, the SEC regularly brought enforcement actions against the Big Five.

40   Indeed, this author would continue to support proportionate liability for auditors on fairness grounds and sees no problem with the PSLRA's heightened pleading standards, as they have been interpreted by some courts. See, e.g., *Novak v. Kasaks*, 216 F. 3d 300 (2d Cir.), *cert. denied* 531 U.S. 1012 (2000).

41   At a minimum, plaintiffs today must plead with particularity facts giving rise to a "strong inference of fraud." See, e.g., *Novak v. Kasaks*. At the outset of a case, it may be possible to plead such facts with respect to the management of the corporate defendant (for example, based on insider sales by such persons prior to the public disclosure of the adverse information that caused the stock drop), but it is rarely possible to plead such information with respect to the auditors (who by law cannot own stock in their client). In short, the plaintiff faces a "Catch 22" dilemma in suing the auditor: it cannot plead fraud with particularity until it obtains discovery, and it cannot obtain discovery under the PSLRA until it pleads fraud with particularity.

42   Consulting fees paid by audit clients exploded during the 1990s. According to the Panel on Audit Effectiveness, which was appointed in 1999 by the Public Oversight Board at the

request of the SEC to study audit practices, "audit firms' fees from consulting services for their SEC clients increased from 17% … of audit fees in 1990 to 67% . . . in 1999." See the Panel on Audit Effectiveness, *Report and Recommendations* (Exposure Draft 2000) at p. 102. In 1990, the Panel found that 80 percent of the Big Five firms' SEC clients received no consulting services from their auditors, and only 1 percent of those SEC clients paid consulting fees exceeding their auditing fees to the Big Five. Although the Panel found only marginal changes during the 1990s, later studies have found that consulting fees have become a multiple of the audit fee for large public corporations. See text and note 43.

43   A survey by the *Chicago Tribune* this year finds that the 100 largest corporations in the Chicago area (determined on the basis of market capitalization) paid on average consulting fees to their auditors that were over three times the audit fee paid the same auditor. See Stewart and Countryman (2002). The extreme example in this study was Motorola, which had over a 16:1 ratio between consulting fees and audit fees.

44   For the academic view that "auditor independence" is an impossible quest, in large part because the client pays the auditor's fees, see O'Conner (2002).

45   Item 4 ("Changes in Registrants Certifying Accountant") of Form 8-K requires a "reporting" company to file a Form 8-K within five days after the resignation or dismissal of the issuer's independent accountant or that of the independent accountant for a significant subsidiary of the issuer. The Form 8-K must then provide the elaborate disclosures mandated by Item 304 of Regulation S-K relating to any dispute or disagreement between the auditor and the accountant. See 17 CFR 228.304 ("Changes in and Disagreements With Accountants on Accounting and Financial Disclosure").

46   See Frankel, Johnson, and Nelson (2002). Firms purchasing more non-audit services were found more likely to just meet or beat analysts' forecasts, which is the standard profile of the firm playing "the numbers game."

47   For the view that investment banking firms changed their competitive strategies on or around 1996 and thereafter sought the "popular, high-profile analyst" as a means of acquiring IPO clients, see Morgenson (2002c, at Section 3-1, quoting chief investment officer at Trust Company of the West).

48   This is the essence of the claims made in a recent lawsuit initiated by the New York Attorney General against five chief executive officers of major US corporations. See McGeehan (2002).

49   See Morgenson (2002a); see also Morgenson (2002b).

50   See Morgenson (2002a, citing study by Sanford C. Bernstein & Co.). Thus, if USD 162 billion is the value of all options in these 2,000 companies, aggressive accounting policies that temporarily raise stock prices by as little as ten percent create a potential gain for executives of over USD 16 billion—a substantial incentive.

51   This point has now been made by a variety of commentators who have called for minimum holding periods or other curbs on stock options. These include Henry M. Paulson, Jr., chief executive of Goldman, Sachs, and Senator John McCain of Arizona. See Leonhardt (2002).

52   Rule 16b-3(d) expressly permits an officer or director otherwise subject to the "short-swing" profit provisions of Section 16(b) of the Securities Exchange Act of 1934 to exercise a qualified stock option and sell the underlying shares immediately "if at least six months elapse from the date of the acquisition of the derivative security to the date of disposition of the . . . underlying equity security." See 17 C.F.R. 240.16b-3(d). The SEC comprehensively revised its rules under Section 16(b) in 1991, in part to facilitate the use of stock options as exec-

utive compensation and to "reduce the regulatory burden" under Section 16(b). See Securities Exchange Act Release No. 34-28869 1991 SEC LEXIS 171 (February 8, 1991). A premise of this reform was that "holding derivative securities is functionally equivalent to holding the underlying equity security for purpose of Section 16" (pp. 35–36). Hence, the SEC permitted the tacking of the option holding period with the stock's holding period, thereby enabling officers and directors to exercise options and sell on the same day (if the option had already been held six months).

53   One of the most famous recent accounting scandals involved the Phar-Mor chain of retail stores. There, after the audit partner for Coopers & LyBrand was denied participation in profit sharing because he had insufficiently cross-sold the firm's services, he sold USD 900,000 worth of business in the next year (most of it to Phar-Mor and its affiliates), but then failed to detect USD 985 million in inflated earnings by Phar-Mor over the following three years. See Prentice (2000, p. 184); Bazerman et al. (1997, p. 89).

54   Carl E. Bass, an internal audit partner, warned other Andersen partners in 1999 that Enron's accounting practices were dangerous. David Duncan and Enron executives are alleged to have had Mr. Bass removed from the Enron account within a few weeks after his protest. See Manor and Yates (2002). If nothing else, this evidence suggests that the internal audit function within one Big Five firm could be overcome when the prospective consulting fees were high enough.

55   Federal Reserve Chairman Alan Greenspan has indeed suggested that market corrections will largely solve the problems uncovered in the wake of Enron. See "Remarks by Chairman Alan Greenspan," (available on the Federal Reserve website at www.federalreserve.gov/boarddocs/speeches) Greenspan (2002). In his view, earnings management came to dominate management's agenda, and as a result: "It is not surprising that since 1998 earnings restatements have proliferated. This situation is a far cry from earlier decades when, if my recollection serves me correctly, firms competed on the basis of which one had the most conservative set of books. Short-term stock price values then seemed less of a focus than maintaining unquestioned credit worthiness" (p. 4). He goes on to predict that: "A change in behavior, however, may already be in train" (p. 5). Specifically, he finds that "perceptions of the reliability of firms' financial statements are increasingly reflected in yield spreads of corporate bonds" and that other signs of self-correction are discernible.

56   For an overview of these crises, see Cunningham (2002).

57   Section 101(c) of the Act enumerates broad powers, including the authority to "establish . . . auditing, quality control, ethics, independence, and other standards relating to the preparation of audit reports for issuers. . . ."

58   Section 201 of the Act, which is to be codified as Section 10A(g) of the Securities Exchange Act of 1934, specifies eight types of professional services that the auditor may not perform for an audit client, and also authorizes the Board to prohibit additional services if it determines that they may compromise auditor independence.

59   Section 804 of the Act does extend the statute of limitation for securities fraud suits, thereby reversing a 1991 Supreme Court decision that had shortened the time period. See *Lampf, Pleva, Lipkind & Petigrow v. Gilbertston*.

60   Section 304 of the Act requires the forfeiture of certain bonuses "or other incentive-based or equity-based compensation" and any stock trading profits received by a chief executive officer or chief financial officer of an issuer during the 12-month period following the filing of

an inflated earnings report that is later restated. This does cancel the incentive to inflate earnings and then bail out, but the enforcement methods applicable to this provision are unspecified and the provision applies only if the earnings restatement is the product of "misconduct." Ambiguities abound here.

61   Prior to the 1990s, private litigation was a real (and arguably even excessive) constraining force on auditors. See text and note 35.

62   See Cunningham (2003).

63   Section 204 of the Act does require rotation of the lead partner, at least every five years, but not the audit firm itself.

64   Before it is assumed that Europe is immune to accounting scandals, it should be noted that the Neuer Markt, the high-tech German market for young companies, will be closed in 2003 after a series of financial and accounting scandals tarnished its reputation. See Landler (2002). It was, however, an uncharacteristic European market.

65   Federal Reserve Chairman Alan Greenspan has coined this rhetorical phrase, saying that "An infectious greed seemed to grip much of our business community." See Norris (2002). This article's more cold-blooded approach would say that the rational incentives created by stock options and equity compensation overcame the limited self-regulatory safeguards that the accounting profession had internalized.

REFERENCES

Altman, D. 2002. "How to Tie Pay to Goals, Instead of the Stock Price," *The New York Times*, September 8, Section 3, p. 4.

Amihud, Y., and B. Lev. 1981. "Risk Reduction as a Managerial Motive for Conglomerate Mergers," *Bell Journal of Economics* 12, 605–617.

Baumol, W. 1959. *Business Behavior, Value and Growth*. New York: Macmillan.

Bazerman, M., al. 1997. "The Impossibility of Auditor Independence," *Sloan Management Review* (Summer 1997).

Central Bank of Denver, N.A. v. First Interstate of Denver, N.A., 511 U.S. 164 (1994).

Choi, S. 1998. "Market Lessons for Gatekeepers," *Northwestern University Law Review* 92.

Coffee, J. C. Jr. 1987. "Shareholders Versus Managers: The Strain in the Corporate Web," *Michigan Law Review* 85.

Congressional Research Service. 1985. *The Role of High Yield Bonds in Capital Markets and Corporate Takeovers: Public Policy Implications*, 99th Congress, 1st Session.

Cunningham, L. A. 2002. "Sharing Accounting's Burden: Business Lawyers in Enron's Dark Shadow," *Business Lawyer* 57.

Cunningham, L. A. 2003. "The Sarbanes-Oxley Yawn: Heavy Rhetoric, Light Reform (and It Might Just Work)," *University of Connecticut Law Review* 36 (forthcoming).

Financial Institutions Reform, Recovery and Enforcement Act of 1989 (FIRREA), Pub. L. No. 101-73, 103 Stat. 183.

Frankel, R., M. Johnson, and K. Nelson. 2002. "The Relation Between Auditors' Fees for Non-Audit Services and Earnings Quality," MIT Sloan Working Paper No. 4330-02. Online from Social Sciences Research Network. http://www.ssrn.com at id= 296557.

Gordon, J. N. 2002. "What Enron Means for the Management and Control of the Modern Business Corporation: Some Initial Reactions," *University of Chicago Law Review* 69.

Greenspan, A. 2002. "Remarks by Chairman Alan Greenspan," *Corporate Governance*, the Stern School of Business, New York University, NY, March 26. Online. http://www.federalreserve.gov/boarddocs/speeches.

Kanjorski, P. E., 2001. Opening Statement, House Subcommittee on Capital Markets, Insurance, and Government Sponsored Enterprises, "Hearing on Analyzing the Analysts," June 14.

Kraakman, R. 1984. "Corporate Liability Strategies and the Costs of Legal Controls," *Yale Law Journal* 93.

Kraakman, R. 1986. "Gatekeepers: The Anatomy of a Third-Party Enforcement Strategy," *Journal of Law, Economics and Organization* 2.

Lampf, Pleva, Lipkind & Petigrow v. Gilbertston, 501 U.S. 350, 359-61 (1991).

Landler, M. 2002. "German Technology Stock Market to Be Dissolved," *The New York Times*, September 27, p. W-1.

Laventhol & Horwath. 2002. "What Role Should CPA's Be Playing in Audit Reform?" Partner's Report for CPA Firm Owners, April.

Leonhardt, D. "Corporate Conduct: Compensation: Anger at Executives' Profits Fuels Support for Stock Curb," *The New York Times*, July 9, p. A-1.

Levitt, A. 1998. "The Numbers Game: Remarks at NYU Center for Law and Business" (September 28).

Manor, R., and J. Yates. 2002. "Faceless Andersen Partner in Spotlight's Glare; David Duncan Vital to Federal Probe after Plea," *Chicago Tribune* April 14, p. C-1.

Marcus, A. J. 1982. "Risk Sharing and the Theory of the Firm," *Bell Journal of Economics* 13, pp. 369–378.

Marris, R. 1969. *The Economic Theory of Managerial Capitalism*. London: Macmillan.

McGeehan, P. 2002. "Spitzer Sues Executives of Telecom Companies over 'Ill Gotten' Gains," *The New York Times* October 1, p. C-1.

Melder v. Morris, 27 F.3d 1097, 1103 (5th Cir. 1994)

Michaely, R., and K. Womack. 1999. "Conflict of Interest and the Credibility of Underwriter Analyst Recommendations," *Review of Financial Studies* 12, pp. 653–686.

Mittelstadt, M. 2002. "Andersen Charged with Obstruction, Vows to Fight," *Dallas Morning News*, March 15, p.1.

Morgenson, G. 2002a. "Corporate Conduct: News Analysis; Bush Failed to Stress Need to Rein in Stock Options," *The New York Times*, July 11, p. C-1

Morgenson, G. 2002b. "Market Watch: Time For Accountability at the Corporate Candy Store," *The New York Times*, March 3, p. C-3.

Morgenson, G. 2002c. "Requiem for an Honorable Profession," *The New York Times*, May 5, p. 3-1.

Moriarty, G. B., and P. Livingston. 2001. "Quantitative Measures of the Quality of Financial Reporting," *Financial Executive* (July/August).

Newsweek. 2002. "Periscope: How Arthur Andersen Begs for Business," *Newsweek*, March 18, p. 6.

Nicholls, C. 2002. "The Outside Director: Policeman or 'Policebo'?" (Unpublished Draft).

Norris, F. 2002. "The Markets: Market Place: Yes, He Can Top That," *The New York Times*, July 17, p. A-1.

Novak v. Kasaks, 216 F. 3d 300 (2d Cir.), *cert. denied* 531 U.S. 1012 (2000).

O'Conner, S. 2002. "The Inevitability of Enron and the Impossibility of Auditor Independence under the Current Audit System." (Unpublished Draft).

Painter, R. 1998. "Responding to a False Alarm: Federal Preemption of State Securities Fraud Causes of Action," *Cornell Law Review* 84.

Partnoy, F. 2002. Testimony of Frank Partnoy, Professor of Law, University of San Diego School of Law, Hearings before the United States Senate Committee on Governmental Affairs, January 24, 2002.

Powers, W. C. Jr. et al. 2002. Report of Investigation by the Special Investigative Committee of the Board of Directors of Enron Corp. (Feb. 1, 2002), 2002 WL 198018.

Prentice, R. A. 2000. "The Case of the Irrational Auditor: A Behavioral Insight into Securities Fraud Litigation," *Northwestern University Law Review* 95.

Robin v. Arthur Young & Co., 915 F. 2d 1120, 1127 (7th Cir. 1990).

Securities and Exchange Commission (SEC). 1999. Staff Accounting Bulletin No. 99, 64 F.R. 45150 (August 19, 1999).

Securities and Exchange Commission v. Arthur Andersen LLP, SEC Litigation Release No. 17039, 2001 SEC LEXIS 1159 (June 19, 2001).

Securities Exchange Act Release No. 34-28869 (February 8, 1991). 1991 SEC LEXIS 171.

Securities Exchange Act Release No. 7870 (June 30, 2000). 2000 SEC LEXIS 1389.

Stewart, J. K., and A. Countryman. 2002. "Local Audit Conflicts Add Up: Consulting Deals, Hiring Practices in Question," *Chicago Tribune*, February 24, p. C-1.

Torres, F. 2002. Statement of Frank Torres, Legislative Counsel, Consumers Union, before the United States Senate, Committee on Governmental Affairs, on the Collapse of Enron: The Role Analysts Played and the Conflicts They Face, February 27, 2002.

US Senate. 1993. Private Litigation Under the Federal Securities Laws: Hearings Before the Subcommittee on Securities of the Senate Committee on Banking, Housing and Urban Affairs, 103rd Cong., lst Sess. No. 103-431 (statement of Jake L. Netterville); reprinted in Fed. Sec. L. Rep. (CCH) No. 1696, (January 10, 1996).

US Senate. 2001. Report of the Permanent Subcommittee on Investigations of the Committee of Governmental Affairs, United States Senate, "The Role of the Board of Directors in Enron's Collapse," (Report 107-70) (July 8, 2001).

Williamson, O. 1963. "Managerial Discretion and Business Behavior," *American Economic Review* 53, pp. 1032–1057.

Williamson, O. 1975. *Markets and Hierarchies: Analysis and Antitrust Implications*. New York: Free Press.

Williamson, O. 1981. "The Modern Corporation: Origins, Evolution, Attributes," *Journal of Economic Literature* 19, pp. 1537–1568.

Young, L. 2001. "Independence Day," *Smart Money* XI, p. 28.

Chapter 3

Shareholder Value, Corporate
Governance, and Corporate Performance
A Post-Enron Reassessment of the
Conventional Wisdom

Margaret M. Blair

The first two years of the 21st century have been a sobering time for scholars and policymakers interested in corporate governance. As recently as two years ago, leading corporate scholars were prepared to declare that history was over in the ongoing debate about what corporate governance systems produce the best long-term outcomes for society.[1] Yale law professor Henry Hansmann and Harvard law professor Reinier Kraakman (2000) told us that the evidence was in, and that Anglo-Saxon–style market capitalism and shareholder primacy had proven itself to be the only system that could produce sustained economic growth.[2] These scholars based their empirical claims in part on the apparent success of the "shareholder-oriented model" of corporate governance that they claimed characterized the United States in the 1990s.[3]

Now, in the early fall of 2002, it has become clear that much of the stock market boom that had led to high yields on corporate equities and helped fuel strong economic growth in the United States during the 1990s was little more than a bubble, pumped up by the helium of accounting legerdemain. US stock prices have fallen back to where they were in 1997, wiping out most of the spectacular share-price gains that had led business people and policymakers to talk of a "New Economy;"[4] economic growth in the United States remains soft[5] and wave after wave of financial disclosure scandals are devastating investors and employees of US companies that had led the 1990s boom.

In light of these events, what can we say now about the role of corporate governance in the performance of corporations, and the economies of which they are part?

This chapter will review a number of the elements of what, by the year 2000, had become the conventional wisdom about corporate governance, and consider the evidence for the various assumptions and claims behind that conventional wisdom. Then

Work on this project was supported, in part, by the Georgetown-Sloan Project on Business Institutions. Erin Peters provided valuable research assistance on this project.

it will suggest some alternative ways of interpreting that evidence, and propose the outlines of a new framework for understanding the problem of corporate governance, and for considering how various governance arrangements might help provide the institutional basis of sustainable corporate performance.

THE CONVENTIONAL WISDOM

Throughout the last two decades, economists, finance theorists, corporate legal scholars, and policymakers around the globe have been keenly interested in how corporations are governed, and how they should be governed. How should corporate executives balance pressures from financial markets for high stock returns against the need for long-term investments in innovation, customer and supplier relations, human resources, sustainable environmental performance, and good relations with their communities? How can investors have confidence that managers and directors will pursue the right balance? Are takeovers, for example, good or bad for corporate performance and economic growth? More generally, what institutional arrangements are needed to encourage the right outcome?

At least two broadly defined schools of thought have sought to answer these questions (Blair, 1995). These two views were first framed during the debate that took place in the United States in the 1980s and early 1990s about hostile takeovers and leveraged buyouts. One school argued that US corporations had become fat and lazy because corporate executives were building empires instead of investing only in those projects that added value for shareholders.[6] By this view, hostile takeovers and leveraged buyouts were the mechanisms by which financial markets were trying to impose some financial discipline on corporate executives: they removed executives of poorly performing companies (Palepu, 1986; Morck, Shleifer, and Vishny, 1988a, 1988b, 1989; Martin and McConnell, 1991); they forced their replacements to pay out large amounts of cash flow in the form of debt service (Jensen, 1986, 1988); and they tied the compensation of executives in the reorganized firm to stock price performance through compensation packages loaded with stock and stock options (Jensen, 1986, 1989; Jarrell, Brickley and Netter, 1988; Kaplan and Stein, 1993).

The countervailing view was that the ubiquitous threat of hostile takeovers in the 1980s and other financial pressures forced corporate executives to manage for short-term stock price performance, and prevented them from developing and implementing innovative strategies for long-term growth (Stein, 1989; Twentieth Century Fund, 1992; US GAO, 1993). By this view, financial market pressures for short-term stock price increases helped to explain why US corporations were falling behind foreign competitors in major industries, such as steel, automobiles, consumer electronics, and semiconductors (Dertouzos, Lester, and Solow, 1989). The remedy, according to proponents of this view, was for large financial institutions to take long-term stakes in companies, and provide "patient capital" (Porter, 1992).

From very early in the debate, the financial market discipline view prevailed among most economists and financial and legal scholars. Finance theorists developed a compelling theoretical argument to support this view. They argued that the central problem of corporate governance was a "principal-agent" problem: how to get corporate managers to act as loyal and committed "agents" for the shareholders or "owners" of corporations (Jensen and Meckling, 1976; Fama and Jensen, 1983.). The so-called market for corporate control, through which financial investors could remove poorly performing managers, was viewed as a helpful, even necessary part of the arrangements that reigned in potentially wayward managements. (Jensen, 1986; Shleifer and Vishny, 1988) Advocates of this view produced voluminous evidence that the stock prices of companies rose when they became a target of a hostile takeover, and the fact of higher stock prices was taken as proof that the acquirer expected to manage the companies more efficiently than existing management.[7]

Meanwhile, across the globe, the collapse and breakup of the Soviet Union in the early 1990s seemed to prove that capitalism had won against socialism, lending credibility in general to arguments that markets always allocate resources more efficiently than bureaucracies, and in particular, that financial market discipline was a critical component of good corporate governance. Western advisers rushed to transition countries to tell them that, if they wanted to make their industrial enterprises competitive in world markets, they needed to sell control rights over those enterprises to financial investors, and put in place the institutional supports to create and sustain markets in which the claims and control rights could be traded (see, for example, Black and Kraakman, 1996).

As the 1990s unfolded, the United States pulled out of the recession of 1992 and into the longest peacetime expansion in the country's history. This expansion, led by the dramatic growth in investment in telecommunications, software, biotechnology, and the Internet, seemed to prove that US financial markets, far from being focused only on the short term, were quite capable of directing resources to long-term, innovative ventures, as well as adapting quickly in response to changes in the economic environment. Meanwhile, growth in the Japanese and European economies slowed to a crawl.[8]

All of these developments provided support and vindication for the financial market discipline advocates—so much so, that there seemed little left to debate. In the United States and Britain, all but a handful of scholars and policymakers and a few holdouts in the labor movement adopted the view that the appropriate goal of corporate governance is the maximization of shareholder value, and that the way to achieve this is to give increasing control over corporations to financial investors. By the late

1990s, this view was becoming more and more prominent in Europe and Japan, and in transition and developing countries as well.[9]

This conventional wisdom, that shareholder value should be the single, guiding principle of corporate governance, and that, to support this goal, enhanced investor control and oversight should be encouraged, has a number of assumptions and beliefs behind it, and implications that flow from it, that bear closer examination. The next section subjects these assumptions and implications to careful analysis.

A CLOSER LOOK AT THE SHAREHOLDER VALUE PRINCIPLE

The shareholder value principle of corporate governance incorporates or implies the following set of fundamental beliefs:

- Maximizing value for shareholders is the right social goal for corporations because it is equivalent to maximizing the overall wealth being created by a corporation.

- Financial markets do a good job of assessing the true value of financial securities such as common stock. Hence stock price performance is the best measure of value being created for shareholders.

- Maximizing share value also helps to discipline managers because it involves holding them accountable for a single metric that, in theory, is forward looking. Introducing other metrics would confuse things and make it easier for managers to use their positions to advance their own interests rather than the interests of shareholders.

- Managers and directors will do a better job of maximizing share value if they are given high-powered incentives in the form of compensation packages tied to stock price performance, such as stock options.

- For the full discipline of financial markets to work, outside investors must be free to take control of companies in hostile buyouts, and managers and directors should not be able to entrench themselves by putting up impenetrable barriers to such transactions.

- Except perhaps for a few laws that make it easier for managers to try to deter takeovers, US corporate law generally requires shareholder primacy. And, because it works so well in the United States, other countries should also adopt shareholder primacy regimes.

Let's consider each of these beliefs in turn.

Everyone is better off if share value is maximized

The belief that maximizing share value serves the broader social good because it is equivalent to maximizing the total value created by a corporation derives from a theory of the firm adopted by finance theorists and legal scholars in the 1980s, in which a firm is understood to be a "nexus of contracts."[10] The theory highlights the nature of relationships underlying the firm—that is, among managers, employees, suppliers, customers, creditors, and shareholders. But proponents of the theory argue that the relationships of all of the firm's participants to the firm, except for those of shareholders, are governed by contracts that specify what each party is to do, and what each party should get in return. The shareholders' role is to be the "residual claimant": they are not entitled to a fixed amount, but are to get what is left over after all other participants have received what they are contractually entitled to receive (Easterbrook and Fischel, 1991). If the claims of all other participants are fully protected by contract, according to the logic of this theory, then maximizing what is left over for shareholders is equivalent to maximizing the size of the whole pie.[11]

Strictly speaking, the "nexus of contracts" model of the corporation implies that corporations have no "owners" in the traditional sense of that term, since no one can own the "nexus" through which they all engage with each other. But, shareholder value advocates argue, shareholders act as the residual claimants, and also have certain control rights. So, advocates believe, it is a useful, and not misleading, shorthand expression to call shareholders the "owners." The rhetoric of "ownership," however, subtly redefines corporations in terms of the presumed property rights of one class of participants in the firm, thereby adding a tone of moral superiority to the idea that corporations should be run in the sole interest of shareholders, a tone that is not implied by the nexus of contracts theory alone.

To anyone who has worked for a corporation or observed the ways that corporations can externalize some of their costs onto employees, customers, or the communities where they operate, the idea that maximizing share value is equivalent to maximizing the total social value created by the firm seems obviously wrong. But even from the point of view of the finance theorist who adopts a nexus of contracts perspective, finance theory itself demonstrates conclusively that this idea is wrong. Finance theory teaches us that the value of any claim on a firm is a function of the expected flow of payments to the holder of that claim, and the risk associated with the claim. Will the hoped-for payments actually be made? Will they be as much as the claimant hopes, or will the payments vary in size over time? Will they be made on time? Thus, if holders of one type of claim can shift risk onto holders of other types of claims, the value of the first type of claim will be increased at the expense of the value of the other claims.

Under corporate law, shareholders in US corporations have what is called "limited liability." Limited liability is a legal doctrine that means that the shareholders will not be held personally liable for debts (or tort claims) of the corporation. Thus shareholders always gain if the price of the stock goes up, but their potential losses are limited on the downside. In effect, creditors and other claimants are bearing some of the downside risk—they may be the ones who lose if the firm loses the gamble.

The argument extends to providers of nonfinancial inputs as well. Corporate employees, for example, make investments in specialized knowledge and networks of relationships needed in their jobs as well as in developing a reputation within the firm for working hard. Such investments are specific to the enterprise, and may be worthless to other employers. If the firm does well, the employee hopes to benefit from these specialized investments over the long term as the employee earns promotions and the firm continues to pay salaries, bonuses, and retirement benefits (Blair, 1995).

Hence all investors in corporations share to some degree or other in the risk of the enterprise, and it is often possible to make the holders of one kind of claim (such as stock) better off at the expense of holders of other claims on the firm (such as debt claims), simply by shifting risk. In retrospect, this is what many of the most egregious transactions at Enron were actually about: while they *appeared* to move assets and associated liabilities off of Enron's books, thus reducing the risk borne by Enron investors, in fact, the risk associated with those assets was being retained by Enron through side deals that were not fully reported (Bratton, 2002). So, unbeknownst to most of Enron's investors, Enron's common stock was becoming dramatically more risky during the last two or three years before the firm filed for bankruptcy protection. Substantial risk was also being shifted onto employees and creditors. The increase in risk of the stock, not coincidentally, made Enron stock *options* at least temporarily more valuable.[12] If Enron executives who were taking these gambles with corporate assets had, by chance, won the enormous bets they were placing, they would now be even more dramatically wealthy than they are. As it happens, they overplayed their hands, and when creditors discovered how risky their investments in Enron actually were, they cut off all further credit to Enron, forcing the company into bankruptcy proceedings. In the process, virtually all of the equity value in the company was lost, ultimately making the stock options worthless too.[13]

The fact that shareholders and option holders can often be made better off at the expense of creditors and employees and others with firm-specific investments at risk in the corporation means that, neither in theory nor in practice, is it true that maximizing the value of equity shares is the equivalent of maximizing the overall value created by the firm.[14]

Shareholder primacy advocates often argue, nonetheless, that, in the long run, corporations will have to be fair with their creditors, suppliers, employees, and other "stakeholders" in order to ensure that they will continue to participate in the enterprise (see, for example, Jensen, 2001). In this way, maximizing the "long-run" value of the equity shares will necessarily require that the other stakeholders be compensated according to their expectations, so that in the "long run," it can still be true that maximizing share value is equivalent to maximizing total social value. To whatever extent this argument is correct, it can be reversed: in the long run, regardless of whose interests are considered primary, a corporation will have to provide an adequate return to shareholders and other financial investors or investors will not continue to supply capital to the firm. In theory, then, a corporate goal of maximizing long-run value for, say, employees, would also produce the maximum social value since all other stakeholders will have to be protected to ensure their long-run participation.[15] So this "in the long run" argument fails to make a case that shareholders' interest should be given precedence over other legitimate interests and goals of the corporation.

Stock prices reflect the true underlying value of the stock

The belief that share prices are a good measure of the actual value of a corporation to its shareholders is based on a financial theory known as the "efficient capital markets hypothesis." This theory says that at any point in time, if financial markets are deep and liquid enough, the price for which a share of stock trades is the best available estimate of the true underlying value of the security. Although finance theorists understand that this theory can never be proven,[16] they nonetheless continue to debate the question of how efficient capital markets are. On the one hand, there is evidence that market prices in US stock markets respond very quickly to good or bad news (Fama, 1970). On the other hand, there is also evidence that financial markets as a whole go through periods of boom and bust in which, in retrospect, it becomes clear that stock prices must have deviated substantially from their underlying fundamental value.[17] Some scholars have argued that, in fact, financial markets respond very quickly to information that is easy to interpret, but they respond to complex information only very slowly and imperfectly.[18] And a growing body of empirical work in "behavioral finance" suggests that financial markets overreact, and that they are susceptible to fads and bandwagon thinking that may allow stock prices to get badly out of line with reality before enough investors will act to sell an overpriced stock, or buy an underpriced one, to cause the stock price to move back into line (see, for example, Fama, 1998; Shiller, 2000; and Shleifer, 2000).

The fact that financial markets overreact and do not absorb complex information quickly and correctly means that there is room for corporate insiders to manipulate stock prices by releasing misleading information into the markets. The experience of the last two years certainly suggests that insiders can sometimes cause stock prices to deviate widely from the true underlying value. But even when insiders are not intentionally misleading the market, they will probably have knowledge that other market investors do not have, and therefore have reason to know when a stock's market price is out of line with the underlying reality. That is why US securities law forbids trading on "inside information," although, the lessons of the last two years must surely include the reminder that insiders do sometimes trade on information the market does not yet have.

Managers must have a single metric against which to measure their performance

The argument is commonly advanced that directors and managers must be held accountable for a single metric such as shareholder value, because otherwise they cannot be held accountable at all.[19] In its own way, this argument is an admission that the other rationales for shareholder primacy are bankrupt, but that we should nonetheless use share value to measure the performance of corporate officers and directors because it is simple and easy to apply, while other metrics are complex, subject to manipulation by managers, and inevitably involve tradeoffs that require subjective rather than objective judgment. Here again, the events of the past few years should disabuse all of us of any notion that share price is not a manipulable metric. While it is true that share prices respond to new information, and perhaps even true that over any 5- to 10-year period share prices on deep and liquid markets will tend, on average, to reflect the true underlying value of a corporation (whatever that means), the long run can be quite long relative to the financial health of a given corporation, which can change dramatically in 5 to 10 years. Meanwhile, the damage done in the short-run, while the market is being fooled, can be substantial. The point is not that share price is irrelevant, but that it is overly simplistic— in fact, dangerously so, as I will argue below—to focus too much attention on share price to the exclusion of other measures of corporate and managerial performance.

The importance of high-powered incentives

The belief that managers and directors should be compensated in stock and stock options in order to create high-powered incentives for them to maximize share value follows naturally from the approach of using the economists' model of human behavior to analyze corporate governance questions. Economic analysis is based on a set of assumptions about the way people work in groups. In particular, part of the conventional wisdom has been that directors and managers of companies will always make decisions in ways that serve their own personal interests unless they are either tightly monitored and constrained (which is costly, and raises the question of who will monitor the monitors), or given very strong incentives to manage in the interests of shareholders (e.g., Shleifer and Vishny, 1997). This premise about the way the world works has led to a small industry of compensation consultants who have advised firms to pay corporate executives and directors in stock options, so that they would be highly motivated to get the company's stock price to go up. The problem has been that stock options, as discussed above, create skewed incentives for executives—option holders win big if the stock goes up, but they are not penalized if the stock price goes down. Furthermore, the models used by the compensation consultants often provide that if the stock price goes down, then options should be repriced, or executives should be awarded a large number of additional options (with a lower strike price) so that they will again be well-motivated to get the stock price to go up from wherever it is at the time (Gillan, 2001).

The result has been a veritable orgy of stock option awards to CEOs and other senior managers of US companies. Just 20 years ago, salary, benefits, and performance bonuses typically accounted for 65 percent of CEO compensation, and stock option gains and grants no more than 35 percent (Blair, 1994). Total CEO compensation was also, on average, about 42 times the earnings of the average factory worker.[20] By 2001, total CEO compensation, of which stock option gains and new stock option grants accounted for more than 85 percent,[21] had ballooned to 400 times the earnings of the average worker.[22]

Although stock options do help tie CEO pay to the performance of the stock price, they create other incentives that can be quite perverse. As noted above, stock options are more valuable the more risky the underlying security, so that stock option compensation can encourage CEOs to pursue very risky strategies. This is especially true if the options are "out of the money" (meaning that the current stock price is below the strike price of the options) or just barely "in the money" (meaning that the current stock price is just barely above the strike price of the options). In such situations, the stock option holder stands to win big if a corporate gamble pays off, but can lose little or nothing if the gamble fails.

An additional danger arises from the fact that compensation packages that depend heavily on stock options can encourage corporate executives to play games to try to manipulate the stock price so that their options will be in the money when it is time for the executive to exercise his options. This can encourage executives to focus on stock price, rather than focusing on the underlying fundamentals of the business they are in. Al Dunlap, for example, was given USD 2.5 million three-year options, plus one million shares of restricted stock, when he was hired as CEO at Sunbeam in 1996 (plus an annual salary of USD 1 million) (Hill, 1999, p. 1101), and he handed out large stock option packages to more than 250 of the top Sunbeam executives and managers. In 1997 the company reported sharply increased sales and profits so that in February, 1998, Sunbeam's board gave Dunlap a raise in salary to USD 2 million, and USD 3.75 million more options.[23] But it turned out that those high sales and profits had been achieved by manipulating the accounting—taking an oversized restructuring charge in 1996, for example, and using the surplus to pad income in 1997 (Byrne, 1999). Dunlap was caught and fired, and thus lost the game he was playing.[24] But when faced with potentially huge upside potential and little or no downside financial risk, the incentives to play such games are quite powerful, putting enormous pressure on corporate executives to meet or beat the numbers that Wall Street analysts are predicting.

Another result of stock option-based compensation has been the widespread practice of "earnings management." At its most benign level, earnings management is simply using the flexibility available in the accounting rules to smooth earnings or cash flow numbers. But once the practice is sanctioned, it can lead to egregious abuses and, as the Sunbeam experience indicates, and as we have seen in recent months at WorldCom and other companies, outright fraud.[25]

Stock option compensation can be incredibly seductive. In fact, the temptation it creates to focus solely on stock prices, regardless of how they are achieved, can be so powerful that it appears that during the last few years before Enron filed for bankruptcy, the entire board of directors, including CEO Kenneth Lay, had lost track of what actual business the company was in—what goods and services it was providing for sale to sell to consumers, for example—and came to believe the company was making huge amounts of money in some kind of "New Economy" commodities trading business, although no one seemed to be able to actually explain the business. In reality, it turns out, the trading activity amounted to little more than a massive con game to create the appearance of growing revenues and profits, to try to keep the stock price rising.

The dangers of accounting manipulation extend beyond the companies where executives are actually engaging in such practices. Because many corporations operate in highly competitive industries, manipulation at one company can help to set an unrealistically high performance hurdle at competing companies, which adds to the pressures on corporate executives at those companies to pursue risky strategies, or to also begin manipulating their numbers.[26]

Financial market discipline requires an unfettered market for corporate control

Most proponents of the share value principle also believe that financial market discipline in the form of an active market for corporate control is an important part of any corporate governance system (Manne, 1965; Jensen, 1988; 1993; Scharfstein, 1988; Easterbrook and Fischel, 1991). According to these theorists, an active takeover market should make shareholders better off because it makes it easier for control of corporations to be transferred to those who can manage them best. Early empirical evidence based on what happens to the stock price of firms that become targets seemed consistent with this theory (Jensen and Ruback, 1983). Some of the gains to target company shareholders in hostile takeovers in the 1980s were later explained by the subsequent sell-off of assets in the target firms to other firms in related lines of business (Bhagat, Shleifer, and Vishny, 1990), and some were apparently explained as the transfer of value from workers through layoffs and reductions in wages and benefits (Shleifer and Summers, 1988; Neumark and Sharpe, 1996; and Pontiff, Shleifer, and Weisbach, 1990). But much of the gain remains unexplained, and as the 1980s takeover wave played itself out, many of the transactions that took place toward the end of the decade failed to produce improved performance (Long and Ravenscraft, 1993; Kaplan and Stein, 1993).

But regardless of the source of the gains, one of the implications of the shareholder value principle is the belief that if shareholders could get a higher price for their shares *now* by selling out to a "raider," they ought to be permitted to do so, and the existing board should not be allowed to get in the way. Arguments by existing managers that directors should be allowed to reject hostile takeovers when they believe that shareholders would be even better off later if the firm is not taken over contradict the efficient capital markets hypothesis, so they were never accepted by most finance-oriented scholars.

This faith in the importance of the market for corporate control has led to ongoing debates among corporate legal scholars in the United States about institutional arrangements and response tactics designed to deter takeovers. Shareholder value proponents have been convinced that such arrangements and tactics ought to be bad for shareholders, and by extension, bad for corporate performance and for the economy as a whole.

Two such takeover defenses have been the focus of considerable empirical research in an attempt to determine their impact on corporate performance and shareholder value: "poison pills," which are rights granted to existing shareholders that have the effect of imposing substantial costs on potential acquirers; and "staggered" boards, in which (typically) the term of each board member is three years, and only a third of the board is elected each year.

Early research suggested that poison pills reduce shareholder wealth (Ryngaert, 1988; Malatesta and Walkling, 1988). But subsequent research suggested that poison pills give managers leverage, helping them to negotiate a higher price in the event of a takeover offer, and later empirical studies could no longer find evidence of reduced shareholder value from poison pills (Comment and Schwert, 1995). In fact, Danielson and Karpoff 2002, find evidence that operating performance improves modestly in the five years after a company adopts a pill. Also, it is interesting to note that most young firms adopt poison pills at the time that they go public in an "initial public offering" (IPO) (Daines and Klausner, 1999). Theorists have argued that the original entrepreneurs in a firm can be expected to put governance arrangements in place that will make the firm as valuable as possible to outside investors when they go public, so the fact that most IPO firms have poison pills suggests either that pills do not reduce value to shareholders, or that the protection they provide to management is valuable enough to the original entrepreneurs for other reasons that they are willing to sacrifice some value in the shares they sell to the public.

Most public companies in the United States have staggered or "classified" boards (Bebchuk, Coates, and Subramanian, 2002). The benefits of a staggered board include continuity and stability of the board, as well as a greater independence from management (Koppes, Ganske, and Haag, 1999). But, some scholars argue, staggered boards provide a potent takeover defense—especially when combined with poison pills—because they require an acquirer to wait through at least two election cycles to replace enough members of the board to gain control. Bebchuk, Coates, and Subramanian (2002) provide evidence that the takeover defense provided by staggered boards reduced the returns earned by shareholders of target firms in the late 1990s.[27] Sanjai Bhagat and Richard Jeffris (2002) find conflicting evidence, however. Using a simultaneous equation model that takes into account the interactions among takeover activity, takeover defenses, managerial turnover, and corporate performance, they conclude that a wide variety of so-called "takeover defenses" (including poison pills and staggered boards) are not actually effective at deterring takeover activity in firms where performance has been poor. In other words, takeover activity and managerial turnover are linked to firm performance, regardless of the presence or absence of poison pills or staggered boards (Bhagat and Jeffris, 2002, p. 13)

US law requires shareholder primacy

Since the early 1990s, advisers from US-based multinational financial institutions have been preaching the message of shareholder primacy to transition economy countries looking to reform their economies, and even to other developed countries.[28] One of the reasons has been a belief that US law requires shareholder primacy, and that, since it has worked so well in the United States, other countries should adopt similar legal rules. One of the ironies in the whole international debate about corporate governance, however, is that US corporate law does not actually require shareholder primacy. Rather, US corporate law comes closer to requiring "director primacy"(Blair and Stout, 1999; Bainbridge, 2002).[29] State laws governing the incorporation of firms typically provide that "all corporate powers shall be exercised by or under the authority of, and the business and affairs of the corporation managed by or under the direction of, its board of directors"(Model Business Corporation Act §8.01(b)). Shareholders are allowed to vote each year on a slate of directors nominated, generally, by the existing directors, and they are allowed to vote on certain major transactions (such as a sale of the business or a liquidation). But other than that, shareholders in large, publicly-traded corporations have few formal powers.

Meanwhile, the law regards directors as fiduciaries for the corporation, not agents of shareholders (Clark, 1987). For this reason, courts give directors very wide discretion in the choices they make about a firm's strategy or transactions. Directors can only be held liable for breach of their fiduciary duties if they are grossly negligent in approving corporate actions, or if they engage in transactions that benefit themselves at the expense of the corporation. (See detailed discussion in Blair and Stout, 1999.)

Nonetheless, although corporate law has not changed significantly in recent years to give shareholders more formal power, a few large institutional investors have taken an active role in voicing concerns about the performance of certain corporations, and about corporate governance in general.[30] Because these investors have the ability to sell their shares, as well as to voice their criticisms publicly, thereby putting downward pressure on stock prices, corporate directors and managers have learned to listen when institutional investors speak. Thus, in US companies in which institutional investors hold substantial blocks of shares, those institutional shareholders sometimes exercise considerable clout, making the system look on the surface more like a true shareholder primacy system.

Scholars have debated whether, in this way, the presence of a large institutional shareholder might help to reduce the "agency problem" in corporations, and whether activism by such shareholders might improve corporate performance (Black, 1992; Jacobs, 1991). Early evidence suggested that firm financial performance rises as the holdings of the largest shareholder rise, up to a relatively low point (such as 5 or 10 percent), and then falls as the holdings of the largest shareholder gets larger (Morck, Shleifer, and Vishny, 1988b; Wruck, 1989; and McConnell and Servaes, 1990). One explanation that has been offered for this phenomenon is that, as the holdings of the largest shareholder rise to levels in which he or she can begin to exercise control, that shareholder becomes better able to extract private benefits from his position, sometimes at the expense of the firm as a whole. In any case, empirical studies have been unable to find a consistent, robust, relationship between evidence of large shareholder activism and corporate performance (Black 1992; and Bhagat, Black, and Blair, 1999).

DOES CORPORATE GOVERNANCE, IN FACT, MATTER FOR CORPORATE PERFORMANCE?

As we have already discussed above, it turns out to be hard to find evidence that features of the governance of US corporations that corporate scholars originally thought were important, actually matter very much. The threat of hostile takeover in an active market for corporate control may help to discipline management, but the evidence on whether actual takeovers improve corporate performance is mixed. Institutional arrangements such as staggered boards and poison pills that were put in place to deter takeovers may have little or no actual deterrence effect, or measurable effect on performance,[31] and activism by large-block shareholders does not, so far, seem to produce consistent improvement in corporate performance.

What about board "independence"—the idea that directors should not have close personal, financial, or business relationships with CEOs or other members of the management team that could influence their attitude toward management and perhaps deter them from disciplining management when needed? This idea has become so widely viewed as necessary for good corporate governance that during the summer of 2002, both the New York Stock Exchange and the Nasdaq proposed new rules that would require that firms registered on those exchanges have a majority of independent directors, as well as increase the role that independent directors must play on the boards (NYSE 2002; Nasdaq 2002). Yet, here again, the idea sounds sensible, but the evidence is sparse. Bhagat and Black (2002), among others, find "no convincing empirical evidence that the proportion of independent directors impacts future performance as measured by a variety of stock price and accounting measures."[32]

The bottom line is that researchers have been unable to find strong and consistent evidence that variations in corporate governance arrangements among US companies have much impact one way or the other. Some studies show small effects of some arrangements in some narrow circumstances, but often the results have not held up in other samples. And in any case, the effects tend to be small.

Yet, when corporations around the globe are compared with each other, there are dramatic differences in corporate performance from one country to another (Shleifer and Vishny, 1997). Such differences are apparently related to broad institutional arrangements such as whether the country has an active and efficient financial market, an independent accounting profession, court systems that are uncorrupted and capable of adjudicating complex contractual disputes, and effective securities regulation. Shleifer and Vishny (1997, p. 739), for example, suggest that the essential element for effective corporate governance is some mechanism of "legal protection for the interests of at least some of the investors, so that mechanisms of extensive outside financing can develop." Beyond that, they conclude that the evidence is not even compelling enough to decide whether or not the US system of corporate governance, with widely-traded shares, liquid markets, and reasonably effective securities regulation, is better than the systems in other developed countries in Europe or in Japan, where corporate shares tend to be much more closely held by dominant financial institutions that are actively involved in corporate governance. If it is impossible to decide between systems in developed countries, it is even less realistic to expect to find strong effects of, say, staggered boards, or independent auditing committees, within a given system.

In other words, once a country has in place the basic institutional arrangements to support the use of the corporate legal form (including sophisticated, but uncorrupted courts, reasonably honest trading of financial securities, an independent accounting profession, and effective security markets regulators), and flexibility to custom-design governance arrangements at the level of each firm, it may be that the details of board structure and the degree of management independence versus shareholder involvement, really do not matter very much, at least in a way that we can measure in a broad cross-section of firms. The details of corporate governance are worked out in each company on a case by case basis, and sometimes the arrangements appear to work very well, and sometimes they fail and must be reworked. Economic reasoning, in fact, would predict that institutional arrangements would tend to vary across firms according to what works in each firm. But if each firm has chosen the best approach for that firm, with only random errors, we would not necessarily be able to observe performance differences that vary systematically with the details of governance structures.

Nonetheless, the broadly-defined institutional setting in which corporations act, and the norms and standards supported by those institutions, may matter significantly.[33]

A NEW FRAMEWORK FOR THINKING ABOUT CORPORATE GOVERNANCE

The first three parts of this chapter critiqued the shareholder value principle and argued that structural and institutional details of corporate governance may not have a substantial and consistent impact on corporate performance. So what does matter? Can we say anything of importance about the relationship between corporate governance and corporate performance, beyond the importance of basic legal and institutional infrastructure? I believe we can, and in this section I offer an alternative way to understand the goals and purposes of corporations that I believe can better support sustainable corporate performance. I begin by suggesting that the central problem to be addressed by forming a corporation is what my colleague Professor Lynn Stout and I have elsewhere called the "team production" problem (Blair and Stout, 1999).

A "team production problem" arises any time that a group of individuals agree to work together on a complex production task, in a situation in which it is difficult to agree in advance about what everyone is supposed to contribute, and what everyone can expect to get out of the joint effort.[34] The problem arises because team members will have to make investments in the joint enterprise—by contributing time, effort, money, and/or ideas—that may be sunk in the business and hence not recoverable except by carrying out the enterprise and sharing in the income it generates. Since most team members' investments are, in this sense, enterprise-specific, team members must make themselves vulnerable to each other as they undertake the business venture. Each team member is vulnerable not only because the venture itself is inherently risky, but because any one of the other team members could try to "hold-up" the team by threatening to pull her contributions back out unless she gets a larger share of the proceeds. For individuals who make especially important contributions, the potential threat of being held up by some other team member can be troubling enough that it can prevent individuals from working together as a team in the first place.

When a team is small, very often team members can develop trusting relationships and work out terms on which they will work together as they go, without elaborate corporate governance arrangements or rules. But a large enterprise that involves hundreds or thousands of participants requires some basic institutional arrangements or ground rules to facilitate cooperation among team member. For business enterprises in the developed world, the most common institutional arrangement is to be "incorporated." Incorporation provides a unique solution to the contracting problems in team production. Through the incorporation process, the law creates a separate legal entity that has many of the same rights and powers under the law as a flesh-and-blood person would have.[35] In particular, it can own property, enter into contracts, and be held liable for debts or tort claims. In the typical business corporation, shareholders receive stock in the corporation in exchange for their contribution of financial capital. Executives and employees receive some cash compensation, but they may also receive stock, or options, or promises of deferred compensation, as well as the expectation of future raises and promotions if the enterprise is successful. Suppliers, bondholders, and other creditors also get claims on the corporation, some of which are short-term claims that are rapidly paid off, and others that are more long-term.

But, importantly, while each participant has some kind of claim against the corporation, none of them "owns" the corporation; the corporation is an entity separate from all of its participants. Moreover, by the incorporation process, the corporation itself—not any of its individual participants—becomes the owner of all the assets contributed by the various participants for use in production, as well as of any output from the enterprise (at least until such output is distributed). The fact that the corporation owns the assets used in production means that, in forming the corporation, the team members all give up much of their ability to "hold up" the enterprise. Once they contribute their input, it becomes the property of the corporation and is no longer subject to the control of the contributor. Thus the corporate form of organization can be seen as a legal mechanism that facilitates cooperation among team members by making it easier for team members to credibly commit to each other that they will not hold up the team once production gets under way.

The team production approach to understanding corporations suggests a very different role for directors than the principal-agent approach favored by shareholder primacy advocates. In the principal-agent model, shareholders are seen as the "owners" of corporations,[36] who hire directors to run the corporation for them because they are too busy to do it for themselves. In the team production model, directors are the people who are given the legal responsibility to act for the corporation (since it, obviously, cannot act on its own). By forming a corporation and selecting directors, corporate participants agree to yield ultimate control rights over the corporate enterprise to the board. The effect of this agreement is to tie their hands, so they cannot easily snatch control back and use it to hold up the other participants. Board members, then, are part of the institutional mechanism intended to facilitate trust among all the team members. An important role of directors in this model is to serve as the mediators for the team members, the final arbiters of any disputes that may arise among them over enterprise strategy, or over the division of enterprise output (Blair and Stout, 1999). As such, it is important to the long-term health and prosperity of the enterprise that team members view board members as fair and trustworthy.

Under team production analysis, several features of US corporate law that are inconsistent with shareholder primacy make sense. For example, shareholders may not dictate tactics or policy to directors,[37] or demand dividends.[38] And the law is extremely deferential to the decisions of directors.[39] If this were not true, if directors' decisions could easily be challenged in court, or if directors were subject to the direct command and control of any of the team members, those team members could not credibly commit to the other team members not to attempt a hold up. Hence, as long as directors do not use their positions to steal from the team (the corporation) or otherwise enrich themselves at the expense of the team, and as long as directors exercise a reasonable amount of care in carrying out their duties, courts will not second-guess them.

Team production theory also explains why so few corporate decisions must be put to a vote of shareholders.[40] It also offers an explanation for why directors owe fiduciary duties to the corporation itself, and not directly to shareholders.[41] And it explains why shareholders may not sue directors on their own behalf for violations of directors' fiduciary duties, but must undertake what is called a "derivative" suit.[42] In a derivative suit, the shareholder may seek court permission to act for the corporation as a whole in suing directors for violations of their fiduciary duties and in attempting to collect damages. But she must first convince the court that she, and not the directors, should be entitled to act for the corporation.[43] Moreover, if she wins the suit and directors are required to pay damages, the payments go not to the shareholder who sued but to the corporation (see Clark, 1986, p. 659).

The team production approach suggests that corporate performance must be measured in multiple dimensions, and that no single measure of corporate performance can tell the whole story of how well the corporation is doing. Share price is important, because, even though it is noisy and subject to manipulation, it should at least reflect what one subset of financial investors on any given day think is the value of their claim on the corporation. But it also matters whether the corporation is meeting the expectations of other participants, not to mention whether it is fairly and accurately presenting its financial position to investors. Are bills from suppliers being paid on time? Are the operations and assets acquired in the last merger being well integrated into the company's operations? Are assets, liabilities, and risks to all corporate participants being fairly valued and accurately reported to investors? Are appropriate wages and benefits being paid? Are new technologies being developed and new products being introduced? Are the company's brands being effectively promoted? Are managements' growth plans realistic? Is the company on track to deliver planned growth and profits, and if not, what is the cause of the delay? Are employees being trained and prepared for increased or changing responsibilities? Is there a suitable succession plan in place for the top management team?[44]

The allure of shareholder value is that it is so easy: easy to use to monitor executives, and easy to incorporate in a compensation system. But being simple to understand and easy to measure doesn't make it the right measure of performance, and certainly not the only measure of performance that counts. The ease and simplicity of the share price metric, in fact, is part of what makes it such a dangerous measure to rely upon. Focusing only on share price performance encourages managers, directors, analysts, and investors to be lazy, to take short cuts in developing corporate strategies and plans, and in evaluating how well the firm is doing.[45] Or worse, by sending the message that only financial gain matters, a monomaniacal focus on share value can inadvertently also send the message that personal integrity and trustworthy behavior do not matter. By contrast, the team production approach emphasizes the complexity of the problem of governing and managing a corporation, points to the demanding nature of the job of corporate executives and directors, and signals that directors and other team members are expected to cooperate with each other rather than try to extract gains at each others' expense.

Professor Stout and I have suggested elsewhere (Blair and Stout, 2001b) that one way to understand the job of corporate directors is that they are charged with making the trade-offs that are required to keep a productive team together, to make sure all of the essential members of the team play fairly with each other, share the necessary information with each other, and continue to contribute. In some cases, boards may also be called upon to help team members develop a new strategy or work out a different way to create value for the team.

One common criticism of the team production analysis of corporate governance is that, while it may explain why corporate law *permits* directors to make trade-offs among competing interests instead of compelling them to act only in the interests of shareholders, it does not explain why directors *would bother* to work hard or make decisions for the benefit of the corporation and not just for their own personal benefit. In response, we have argued that the effectiveness of the system ultimately relies on corporate directors being trustworthy (Blair and Stout, 2001a). Although to scholars steeped in the logic of economic and legal reasoning, such a response may seem naive, substantial empirical evidence from cooperative game experiments suggests that human beings are not always the coldly-rational, self-interested creatures that populate economic models. Instead, human beings seem to respond to social and cultural messages. If the social signals tell them that they are expected to trust the other players, and to be trustworthy themselves, and if the economic incentives to break trust or "defect" are not overwhelming, then the vast majority of people will choose to cooperate. Alternatively, if the social signals tell them that the game they are playing (or the social interaction they are involved in) is a competitive one in which they are expected to, say, win as much money as they can, even if doing so is harmful to the group, then that is what most people will do (Blair and Stout, 2001a).

Professor Stout and I further argue that, in practice, legal constraints rarely bind tightly enough to compel people to cooperate, and economic incentives often tilt against cooperation (Blair and Stout, 2001a). So when we observe cooperative, trustworthy behavior in the business world, chances are that this result is driven by strong social norms and expectations of trustworthy behavior in the particular context, rather than by law or economic incentives (Blair and Stout, 2001a and 2001b).

In other words, we believe that trust is the necessary glue that holds long-term business relationships of any kind together.[46] This is true even where an adequate legal and institutional infrastructure is in place, and it is probably especially true where such infrastructure is missing. And, it is clearly true for the relationships among all team members in a corporation, since even where law and institutions are strong, courts nearly always decline to adjudicate disputes between participants in a corporation over the allocation of assignments and rewards.[47] Professor Stout and I argue that it is the special role of corporate directors, in this context, to be people whom the team members feel they can trust, the wise elders, persons of honor and integrity, as well as of wisdom and good judgment. Just as the board as a whole is part of an institutional arrangement to facilitate trust, board members must be seen as the keepers and upholders of the team's trust. If the team members perceive directors to be these things, they will all be more willing to make themselves vulnerable to the other members of the team—to trust—by making necessary enterprise-specific investments.

CONCLUSION

This chapter argues that the notion that the primary, or in extreme versions, the only legitimate goals of corporate management and governance should be to maximize the value of the shareholders' interest in the company is based on a series of elegant and facile, but deeply flawed assumptions about the nature of the relationships among corporate participants, about how financial markets work, about how human beings work together in groups, and about what the law requires. Contrary to these assumptions, shareholders are neither the "owners" of corporations, nor the only claimants with investments at risk; stock prices do not always accurately reflect the true underlying value of equity securities; managers will not necessarily do a better job of running corporations if they focus solely on share value, or if they are heavily incentivized with stock options, or if they are constantly vulnerable to being ousted in a hostile takeover; and corporate law does not require shareholder primacy.

Instead, this chapter suggests that, once the basic institutional framework is in place (rule of law, sophisticated and uncorrupted courts, an independent accounting profession, liquid financial markets and an adequate securities regulation system), the principal element needed to foster wealth-creating productive activity may be a powerful set of cultural norms emphasizing personal and group integrity, cooperative behavior among team members, and responsibility in the team's relationships to the larger communities in which it operates.[48] Organizing productive activities within a corporation provides one mechanism for encouraging cooperative engagement by a number of participants in a complex enterprise, each with different roles to play, and each making contributions that are at risk in the venture. The corporate form facilitates cooperation because it permits the participants to make credible commitments to each other to cooperate, and not to try to hold up the other participants by threatening to prematurely withdraw their contribution. They do so by yielding ultimate control over their contributions and over output from the enterprise to a board of directors.

The team production theory of corporate law points to the central and crucial role played by corporate directors. It also suggests that the norms and standards established for corporate directors and other corporate participants—the mutual expectations of trustworthy behavior—may be at least as important to corporate performance as laws and institutional arrangements.

Of course, there may be "bad apples" in any bushel. Some corporate actors will occasionally betray the trust that other corporate participants have placed in them even if the laws and institutional arrangements are strong, and the cultural messages supportive of trustworthy behavior on the part of corporate executives and board members.[49] But, if corporate leaders are continuously bombarded with messages that shareholder value is the only performance metric that matters, and if corporate directors and officers are compensated in ways that give them high-powered incentives to focus solely on shareholder value, then we should not be surprised to find that those officers and directors are more likely to neglect such niceties as honesty, personal integrity, and commitment to the mutual benefit of all the participants in the corporate enterprise.

The corporate scandals of the last year in the United States have caused even the most strident advocates of the shareholder primacy principle to begin to question the wisdom of a system too focused on share value. Harvard professor Michael Jensen, for example, now argues that the goal of corporations should be "enlightened value maximization" which recognizes that "value maximization is not a vision or a strategy or even a purpose," but only a "scorecard" (Jensen 2001, p. 15). A team production approach to understanding corporations would suggest the same role for shareholder value, with the amendment that shareholder value is only one of a number of score-cards, all of which must be considered in judging overall corporate performance.

NOTES

1 See Hansmann and Kraakman (2001).

2 The "consensus on a shareholder-oriented model of the corporation results in part from the failure of alternative models of the corporation . . . . Since the dominant corporate ideology of shareholder primacy is unlikely to be undone, its success represents the 'end of history' for corporate law" (Hansmann and Kraakman, 2001). Professors Hansmann and Kraakman were not the only prominent specialists to believe that the market capitalism and share-holder primacy outperformed all other approaches to corporate governance. During the last few years of the 1990s and continuing at least to the fall of 2002, the World Bank has spon-sored a series of training seminars in various developing and transition countries to preach the benefits of American-style corporate governance arrangements. The World Bank web site notes that "the activities of the Bank in corporate governance focus on the rights of share-holders, the equitable treatment of shareholders, the treatment of stakeholders, disclosure and transparency and the duties of board members." As of September 2002, the Bank had pro-duced assessments of corporate governance practices in 15 countries, including Brazil, India, Turkey, Poland, the Philippines, and Georgia, and has, in partnership with the Organisation for European Co-operation and Development (OECD), organized regional "roundtables" on corporations to promote best practice. See http://www.worldbank.org/privatesector/cg/index.htm (accessed on Sept. 12, 2002).

3 "A simple comparison across countries adhering to different models—at least in very recent years—lends credence to the view that adherence to the standard model [the 'shareholder-oriented' model] promotes better economic outcomes. The developed common law juris-dictions have performed well in comparison to the principal East Asian and continental European countries, which are less in alignment with the standard model. The principal examples include, of course, the strong performance of the American economy in compar-ison with the weaker economic performance of the German, Japanese, and French economies" (Hansmann and Kraakman 2000, p. 12).

4 The return on a very broad-based market index, the Wilshire 5000, averaged a modest 8.36 percent return per year from 1995 through 2002. See *S&P US Indices*. Rev. Sept. 16, 2002. Online. Available at http://www.spglobal.com/June2002(USA).pdf.

5 See, e.g., J. E. Hilsenrath, "Growth in Productivity Slows; Forecasts for Economy Worsens," *Wall Street Journal*, Aug. 12, 2002, p. A2. See also J. M. Barry, "Economy Still Soft, Greenspan Warns; Fed Chief Cited Subdued Sectors," *Washington Post*, Dec. 20, 2002, p. E-1.

6 Shleifer and Vishny (1997, p. 746) summarize evidence that corporations made bad diversifica-tion decisions in the 1960s, 1970s, and 1980s, and in general paid too much for acquisitions.

7 Jensen and Ruback (1983) summarizes the early evidence. See Stout (1990) for an argu-ment that the premia paid for acquired companies is not necessarily evidence that the acquirer expects to do a better job of managing the company.

8 Real (inflation adjusted) Gross Domestic Product (GDP) grew at 1.1 percent per year in

the last decade in Japan, at 1.99 percent per year in Europe, and at 3.3 percent per year in the United States. (Calculated from Organisation for Economic Co-operation and Development [OECD]. 2002. *Annual National Accounts: Comparative Tables Based on Exchange Rates and PPPs*. Rev. Sept. 16, 2002. Online. http://cs4hq.oecd.org/oecd/selected_view.asp?tableId= 561&viewname=ANAPart2.)

9   See, e.g., OECD (1998, p. 27), in which the Business Sector Advisory Group on Corporate Governance stated that "most industrialized societies" recognize that the "generation of long-term economic profit to enhance shareholder value" is the corporation's primary objective. The *Principles of Corporate Governance*, adopted by the OECD in 1999 (OECD, 1999), took a somewhat attenuated shareholder primacy perspective, emphasizing shareholder rights, but also noting that "the competitiveness and ultimate success of a corporation is the result of team-work that embodies contributions from a range of different resource providers . . .," and that "it is, therefore, in the long-term interest of corporations to foster wealth-creating co-opera-tion among stakeholders" (OECD 1999, p. 33). See also Lazonick and O'Sullivan (2002).

10   The phrase is usually attributed to Jensen and Meckling (1976, p. 310), who argued that organizations "are simply legal fictions which serve as a nexus for a set of contracting rela-tionships among individuals."

11   Yale professor Shyam Sunder (2001) notes that conventional accounting measures calculate the value created by corporations solely in terms of the value left over after other participants in the enterprise have been paid. He provides a fascinating discussion of the possibility of measuring the value created by the firm from the vantage point of participants other than shareholders.

12   Options, which are "derivative" securities that give the holder the right to buy the underly-ing security at a fixed price until some expiration date, become more valuable the more risky the underlying stock is because, like stockholders who have limited liability, option holders capture all the potential gain from gambles, but do not bear the downside risk.

13   But not before quite a few senior executives had managed to exercise their options and sell their stock, thus locking in their gains and leaving other stockholders and corporate claimants holding a greatly depleted bag.

14   See Blair and Stout (2001b) for an expanded explanation, based on options theory, of why maximizing value for shareholders is not equivalent to maximizing the total value created by the corporation.

15   Sunder (2001) notes that, since markets for financial capital are among the most liquid and efficient in the world, shareholder returns should, on average at least, always be equal to the opportunity cost of capital, and there should be no excess returns. By contrast, suppli-ers of other resources used in the corporation often provide specialized or unique inputs that might be able to demand a premium. From this point of view, one would expect that the only wealth being created by the firm would generally be captured by other participants, and not by the providers of financial capital. Sunder makes this point to call attention to the arbitrariness of measuring the value of a firm by looking only at its value to shareholders.

16   To prove that a market-determined price accurately reflects the true value of the security would require some independent way to measure the "true value." Hence any test of how close stock prices are to their true value is simultaneously and unavoidably a test of whether the model being used to measure the "true value" is a good model. If the market price varies from the price predicted by the model, we can never tell whether the problem is that the model is wrong, or the problem is that the market is not efficient in determining the price.

17 See, e.g., Shiller (2000), Stout (1990), and Stout (1997). Were stock prices in US financial markets overvalued in the early months of 2000 when the Dow peaked at more than 11,000, for example? Are they undervalued now? Is it conceivable that the fundamentals actually changed so much between the spring of 2000 and the summer of 2002 and that stock prices were accurate at both times?

18 Stout (2000) reviews the empirical evidence that complex information is incorporated into stock prices only slowly and incompletely.

19 Shareholder primacy advocate Michael Jensen (2001, p. 5) attacks "stakeholder theory," which he views as the only alternative to shareholder primacy, on the grounds that "it is logically impossible to maximize in more than one dimension at the same time," and that "stakeholder theory … leaves boards of directors and executives in firms with no principled criterion for problem solving" (p. 11). See also Monks and Minow (1995, p. 25). Of course this is only an issue if one feels compelled to describe corporate goals in terms of "maximization." Economists prefer the language of maximization because mathematical models can be used to describe a decision-making process based on maximization. But most organization theorists believe that in practice, no one knows what it means to "maximize" business goals, so that managers operate instead by setting challenging goals and trying to at least reach them. See Cyert and March (1963), on "satisficing."

20 See G. Ip. "New York Fed President Chides CEOs on Hefty Compensation: McDonough Urges Officials to Cut Their Pay, Citing Years of Outsized Gains," *Wall Street Journal*, Sept. 12, 2002, p. A-2.

21 Calculated from data in G. Strauss. "Why Are These CEOs Smiling? Must Be Payday; Analysis Shows That Top Executives Rarely Felt Shareholders' Financial Pain Last Year," *USA Today*, March 25.

22 See Ip, supra note 20.

23 "Dunlap Wants Stock Options Re-priced," *Palm Beach Post*, April 7.

24 Fraud charges were brought against Dunlap by the Securities and Exchange Commission (SEC), and numerous shareholders filed lawsuits after the accounting manipulations were revealed and Sunbeam's share price collapsed in 1998. These charges were finally settled in early September, 2002, when Dunlap agreed to pay out USD 15 million to settle the shareholder suits, and $500,000 to settle the fraud charges. Dunlap was also permanently banned by the SEC from ever serving as an official of a public company. See M. Schroeder, "Dunlap Settles Fraud Charges with the SEC," *Wall Street Journal*, Sept. 5, 2002, p. C-1.

25 Even shareholder primacy advocate Michael Jensen and his colleagues have come around to the view that corporate managers should not pursue short-term shareholder value maximization, noting that "an overvalued stock can be as damaging to the long-run health of a company as an undervalued stock," and warning of the dangers of the earnings expectations game. See Fuller and Jensen (2001). This concession, it should be noted, seriously undermines arguments Jensen and others made in the 1980s justifying hostile takeovers on the grounds that they offered shareholders of target firms an immediate gain on their investment.

26 Executives at companies that were competing with WorldCom reported such pressures to the *New York Times*. "Our performance did not quite compare and we were blaming ourselves," said Sprint chief executive William T. Esrey. See S. Schiesel, "Trying to Catch WorldCom Mirage," *New York Times*, June 30, 2002, Sect. 3, p. 1.

27 Stout (2002) notes that even if Bebchuk, Coates, and Subramanian are correct that the combination of staggered boards and poison pills reduces the returns to shareholders of companies that become takeover targets, this does not imply that the presence of takeover defenses in a firm are bad for shareholders. The problem is that Bebchuk et al. measure only the effect of the takeover defenses *ex post*, once the firm has become a takeover target, and they fail to measure the potential *ex ante* benefits to the firm and its shareholders from having the defenses in place. Takeover defenses may enhance a firm's ability to attract human capital and other resources, for example, precisely because they make the firm less likely to be taken over and broken up. See discussion below of the importance of "team production" in corporations.

28 See cites supra, note 3.

29 Bainbridge (2002) coined the phrase "director primacy."

30 For a summary of the efforts of TIAA-CREF to improve corporate governance, see Biggs (2002). For a summary of the corporate governance activities of CalPERS, see CalPERS web site at www.calpers-governance.org/forumhome.asp. See also the web sites of the Council of Institutional Investors, at www.cii.org/corp_governance.htm, and of the International Corporate Governance Network at www.icgn.org, and the chapter by W. D. Crist, chapter 16 in this volume. For an example of relatively intrusive engagement by an institutional shareholder in corporate governance, see B. Orwall, "Forum to Allow Disney Investors to Air Grievances," *Wall Street Journal*, Sept. 12, 2002, p. A-6, noting that Providence Capital of New York was planning to host a meeting of institutional investors for the purpose of finding out their views on the corporate governance practices at Walt Disney Co.

31 Coates (1999, Abstract) notes that "two decades of empirical research on poison pills and other takeover defenses does not support the belief—common among legal academics—that defenses reduce firm value."

32 MacAvoy and Millstein (1999) argue that nominal independence of board members may not by itself bear any strong relationship to whether a board is active and independent in its action. They construct a measure of board independence based on a survey of board practices (including such things as whether nonmanagement directors meet independently of management on a regular basis), and find that evidence of independent board action is positively correlated with a measure of performance that is a variation on Economic Value Added (EVA). See Rappaport (1986) for an explanation and discussion of the concept of and method of measuring EVA.

33 Professor Bernard Black has suggested that corporate governance details may be very important in settings where courts aren't functioning, regulation is corrupt, and there are no institutions in place that can prevent theft of corporate resources by insiders. For example, he compares the performance of 21 major Russian corporations that have publicly-traded securities with their rankings on an index of their corporate governance practices. He finds that all of the companies trade at a huge discount relative to their Western counterparts, but that companies with good corporate governance practices are discounted much less than companies with poor governance practices. The most well-governed company in the sample, telephone company Vimpelcom, trades at a discount of about 50 percent relative to comparable companies in Europe and the United States, while the worst-governed company, Yuganskneftegas, an oil company, trades at 100th of 1 percent of its estimated potential value in the west.

34 It is virtually impossible to draft and enforce complete contracts, fully specifying the terms of the long-term relationships among the team members, without introducing perverse

incentives into the relationship. If team members agree in advance that they are going to split the proceeds evenly, for example, then everyone will have an incentive to shirk, since they will get the same share of the output no matter how hard they work. But if they do not agree to a distribution rule in advance, the team could easily fall apart as they argue with each other over the proceeds.

35 See, e.g., Del. Code Ann. tit. 8, §106.

36 Recall the discussion above, however, in which I argue that such designation is not accurate legally, but is at best a convenient, if misleading, metaphor.

37 See, e.g., *Auer v. Dressel*, 118 N.E. 2d 590, 593 (NY 1954), holding that directors have no obligation to respond to a shareholder resolution demanding reinstatement of a dismissed officer.

38 See, e.g., *Kamin v. American Express Co.*, 86 Misc.2d 809, 383 N.Y.S.2d 807 (1976), aff'd on opinion below, 54 A.D.2d 654, 387 N.Y.S.2d 993 (1st Dept. 1976) noting that whether or not to pay a dividend is "exclusively a matter of business judgment for the Board of Directors".

39 The "business judgment rule" is a doctrine adopted by the courts which says that the courts should presume that "in making a business decision the directors of a corporation acted on an informed basis, in good faith and in the honest belief that the action taken was in the best interests of the company" (Aronson v. Lewis, 473 A.2d 805, 812 [Del. 1984]).

40 Shareholders must be given a chance to vote for directors, but existing directors nearly always nominate the slate to be voted on. Shareholders must also be given a chance to vote on certain fundamental corporate changes such as a sale of all or substantially all of the assets of the firm, or a merger in which the company will cease to be an independent firm. See discussion of shareholder voting rights in Blair and Stout (1999, pp. 309–315). And, under proposed new stock exchange rules, shareholders must be given a chance to vote on stock option-based compensation plans. See NYSE 2002; Nasdaq 2002. These are the only decisions that must be subjected to shareholder vote by law, although incorporators may specify in the corporate charter that a vote of shareholders is required for other decisions.

41 See Restatement (Second) of Agency § 14C cmt.a (1958), stating that directors owe duties to "the corporation itself rather than to the shareholders individually or collectively". Some case law describes directors' fiduciary duties as running to the corporation and its shareholders, but extensive case law authorizing directors to consider nonshareholder interests in deciding what is best for the corporation makes it clear that directors' duties are not limited to shareholders but are owed to the corporation generally. Blair and Stout (1999, note 105).

42 See discussion of rules of derivative suits in Blair and Stout (1999, pp. 292–297).

43 This requires a showing that directors have a conflict of interest that is so substantial that it would influence their judgment in deciding whether to pursue the case.

44 Most management literature addresses corporate performance in a multidimensional way, and even economic analysis of firm performance from the perspective of industrial organization theory (as opposed to finance theory) uses a multidimensional approach. Scherer and Ross (1990, pp. 4–5), for example, suggest that corporate performance should be evaluated on the basis of "production and allocative efficiency, progress, full employment [and] equity."

45 Business consultant Allan Kennedy has argued that many companies in the last two decades have been "mortgaging their future in pursuing shareholder value to the exclusion of other stakeholders—employees, governments, communities, suppliers, and customers." See "The

End of Shareholder Value," interview with Kennedy by Jane Christophersen, published in *Shareholder Value Magazine*, July/Aug. 2001, p. 38. See also Kennedy (2000).

46   Tirole (1986, p. 208) notes that "it is widely recognized by sociologists that without the countless acts of cooperation that take place everyday between members, most organizations would break down."

47   Williamson (1985, p. 249) notes that courts refuse to get involved in disputes between divisions of a corporation over transfer prices or the allocation of a bonus pool, referring to matters such as these as within the "zone of acceptance," in which participants of the corporation must accept the decision of the internal hierarchical decision-making process of the corporation.

48   Former Chancellor of the Delaware Court William T. Allen has emphasized the importance of factors such as "reputation, pride, fellowship, and self-respect" in determining how active and effective corporate directors are in guiding a corporation toward strong overall performance. See Allen (1993, p. 11).

49   Sally (1995) finds evidence that the cooperation rate in social dilemma games can be made to vary from as low as 5 percent to as high as 95 percent, depending upon a variety of contextual variables and social signals. While dramatizing the importance of social and cultural context in eliciting cooperative behavior, this finding also confirms that there will be some "bad apples" no matter what, which may explain why law and institutions also matter.

REFERENCES

Allen, W. T. 1993. "Corporate Governance: The Internal Environment." Unpublished memorandum to 1993 Fifth Tulane Corporate Law Institute.

Bainbridge, S. M. 2002. "Director Primacy: The Means and Ends of Corporate Governance," UCLA School of Law Research Paper No. 02–06. Los Angeles, CA: University of California Los Angeles.

Bebchuk, L. A., J. C. Coates IV, and G. Subramanian. 2002. "The Powerful Antitakeover Force of Staggered Boards: Theory, Evidence, and Policy," Stanford Law Review 54, pp. 887–951.

Bhagat, S., and B. Black. 2002. "The Non-Correlation Between Board Independence and Long-Term Firm Performance," Journal of Corporation Law 27, pp. 231–273.

Bhagat, S., and R. H. Jefferis, Jr. 2002. *The Econometrics of Corporate Governance Studies.* Cambridge, MA: MIT Press.

Bhagat, S., B. Black, and M. Blair. Forthcoming. "Relational Investing and Firm Performance," Journal of Financial Research.

Bhagat, S., A. Shleifer, and R. Vishny. 1990. "Hostile Takeover in the 1980s: The Return to Corporate Specialization," *Brooking Papers on Economic Activity: Microeconomics,* pp. 1–72.

Biggs, J. H. 2002. "Corporate Failure and Corporate Governance," TIAA-CREF Participant Aug., pp. 2–3.

Black, B. S. 1992. "The Value of Institutional Investor Monitoring: The Empirical Evidence," UCLA Law Review 39, pp. 895–939.

Black, B., and R. Kraakman. 1996. "A Self-Enforcing Model of Corporate Law," Harvard Law Review 109, pp. 1911–1981.

Blair, M. M. 1994. "CEO Pay: Why Such a Contentious Issue?" Brookings Review 12, pp. 23–37.

Blair, M. M. 1995. *Ownership and Control: Rethinking Corporate Governance for the Twenty-first Century*. Washington, D.C: Brookings Institution Press.

Blair, M. M., and L. A. Stout. 1999. "A Team Production Theory of Corporate Law," Virginia Law Review 85, pp. 247–328.

Blair, M. M., and L. A. Stout. 2001a. "Trust, Trustworthiness, and the Behavioral Foundations of Corporate Law," University of Pennsylvania Law Review 149, pp. 1735–1810.

Blair, M. M., and L. A. Stout. 2001b. "Director Accountability and the Mediating Role of the Corporate Board," Washington University Law Quarterly 79, pp. 403–447.

Bratton, W. 2002. "Enron and the Dark Side of Shareholder Value," Tulane Law Review 76, pp. 1275–1362.

Byrne, J. A. 1999. "Chainsaw: He Anointed Himself America's Best CEO," Business Week Oct. 18, 1999, pp. 128–149.

Chert, R. M., and J. March. 1963. *A Behavioral Theory of the Firm*. Englewood Cliffs, NJ: Prentice-Hall.

Clark, R. C. 1986. *Corporate Law*. Boston: Little, Brown and Co.

Clark, R. C. 1987. "Agency Costs Versus Fiduciary Duties." In J. W. Pratt and R. J. Zeckhauser, eds., Principals and Agents: The Structure of Business. Cambridge, MA: Harvard Business School Press.

Coates, J. C. IV. 1999. "The Contestability of Corporate Control: A Critique of the Scientific Evidence on Takeover Defenses," OCL Discussion Paper No. 265. Cambridge, MA: Harvard University John M. Olin Center for Law, Economics, and Business.

Coates, J. C. IV. 2001. "Explaining Variation in Takeover Defenses," California Law Review 89, pp. 1301–1389.

Comment, R., and W. Schwert. 1995. "Poison or Placebo? Evidence on the Deterrence and Wealth Effects of Modern Antitakeover Measures," Journal of Financial Economics 39, pp. 3–43.

Cyert, R. M., and J. G. March. 1963. *A Behavioral Theory of the Firm*. Englewood Cliffs, NJ: Prentice-Hall.

Daines, R., and M. Klausner. 2001. "Do IPO Charters Maximize Firm Value? Antitakeover Protection in IPOs," Journal of Law, Economics, and Organization 17, pp. 83–118.

Danielson, M. G., and J. M. Karpoff. 2002. "Do Pills Poison Operating Performance?" Working Paper. Online. http://papers.ssrn.com/abstract=304647.

Dertouzos, M., R. Lester, R. Solow, and the MIT Commission on Industrial Productivity. 1989. *Made in America: Regaining the Productive Edge*. Cambridge, MA: MIT Press.

Easterbrook, F., and D. Fischel. 1991. *The Economic Structure of Corporate Law*. Cambridge, MA: Harvard University Press.

Fama, E. F. 1970. "Efficient Capital Markets: A Review of Theory and Empirical Work," Journal of Finance 25, pp. 383–423

Fama, E. F. 1998. "Market Efficiency, Long-Term Returns, and Behavioral Finance," Journal of Financial Economics 49, pp. 238–306.

Fama, E. F., and M. C. Jensen. 1983. "Separation of Ownership and Control," Journal of Law and Economics 26, pp. 301–325.

Fuller, J., and M. C. Jensen. 2001. "Just Say No to Wall Street," TSB Working Paper No. 02–01. Hanover, NH: Amos Tuck School of Business at Dartmouth College.

Gillan, S. L. 2001. "Option-Based Compensation: Panacea or Pandora's Box?" Journal of Applied Corporate Finance 14, pp. 115–128.

Hansmann, H., and R. Kraakman. 2001. "The End of History for Corporate Law," Georgetown University Law Review 89, pp. 439–468.

Hill, J. G. 1999. "Deconstructing Sunbeam—Contemporary Issues in Corporate Governance," University of Cincinnati Law Review 67, pp. 1099–1127.

Jacobs, M. T. 1991. Short-Term America: The Causes and Consequences of Our Business Myopia. Cambridge, MA: Harvard Business School Press.

Jarrell, G. A., J. A. Brickley, and J. M. Netter. 1988. "The Market For Corporate Control: The Empirical Evidence Since 1980," Journal of Economic Perspectives 2, pp. 49–68.

Jensen, M. C. 1986. "Agency Costs of Free Cash Flow, Corporate Finance, and Takeovers," American Economic Review 76, pp. 323–329.

Jensen, M. C. 1988. "Takeovers: Their Causes and Consequences," Journal of Economic Perspectives 2, pp. 21–48.

Jensen, M. C. 1989. "Eclipse of the Public Corporation," Harvard Business Review 67, pp. 61–74.

Jensen, M. C. 1993. "The Modern Industrial Revolution, Exit, and the Failure of Internal Control Systems," Journal of Finance 48, pp. 831–880.

Jensen, M. C. 2001. "Value Maximization, Stakeholder Theory, and the Corporate Objective Function," TBS Working Paper No. 01-09. Hanover, NH: Amos Tuck School of Business at Dartmouth College.

Jensen, M. C., and W. H. Meckling. 1976. "Theory of the Firm: Managerial Behavior, Agency Costs and Ownership Structure," Journal of Financial Economics 3, pp. 305–360.

Jensen, M. C., and R. S. Ruback. 1983. "The Market for Corporate Control: The Scientific Evidence," Journal of Financial Economics 11, pp. 5–50.

Kaplan, S., and J. Stein. 1993. "The Evolution of Buy out Pricing and Financial Structure in the 1980s," Quarterly Journal of Economics 108, pp. 313–357.

Kennedy, A. 2000. The End of Shareholder Value: Corporations at the Crossroads. Cambridge, MA: Perseus Publishing.

Koppes, R. H., L. G. Ganske, and C. T. Haag. 1999. "Corporate Governance Out of Focus: The Debate Over Classified Boards," Business Law 54, pp. 1023–1055.

Lazonick, W., and Mary O'Sullivan. 2002. "Maximizing Shareholder Value: A New Ideology for Corporate Governance." In W. Lazonick and M. O'Sullivan, eds., Corporate Governance and Sustainable Prosperity. New York: Palgrave.

Long, W. F., and D. J. Ravenscraft. 1993. "Decade of Debt: Lessons from LBOs in the 1980s." In M. M. Blair, ed., The Deal Decade: What Takeovers and Leveraged Buyouts Mean for Corporate Governance. washington, DC: Brookings Institution Press.

MacAvoy, P., and I. M. Millstein. 1999. "The Active Board of Directors and Its Effect on the Performance of the Large Publicly Traded Corporation," Journal of Applied Corporate Finance 11, pp. 8–20.

Malatesta, P., and R. Walkling. 1988. "Poison Pill Securities: Stockholder Wealth, Profitability, and Ownership Structure," Journal of Financial Economics 20, pp. 347–376.

Manne, H. 1965. "Mergers and the Market for Corporate Control," Journal of Political Economy 75, pp. 110–126.

Martin, K., and J. McConnell. 1991. "Corporate Performance, Corporate Takeovers, and Management Turnover," Journal of Finance 46, pp. 671–688.

McConnell, J., and H. Servaes. 1990. "Additional Evidence on Equity Ownership and Corporate Value," Journal of Financial Economics 27, pp. 595–612.

Monks, R. A. G., and N. Minow. 1995. Corporate Governance. Cambridge: Blackwell Business.

Morck, Randall, Andrei Shleifer, and Robert Vishny. 1988a. "Characteristics of Targets of Hostile and Friendly Takeovers." In A. Auerbach, ed., Corporate Takeovers: Causes and Consequences. Chicago: University of Chicago Press.

Morck, R., A. Shleifer, and R. Vishny. 1988b. "Management Ownership and Market Valuation: An Empirical Analysis," Journal of Financial Economics 20, pp. 293–315.

Morck, R., A. Shleifer, and R. Vishny. 1989. "Alternative Mechanisms of Corporate Control," American Economic Review 79, pp. 842–852.

National Association of Securities Dealers Automated Quotation (Nasdaq). 2002. Summary of Nasdaq Corporate Governance Proposals As of September 13, 2002. Rev. Sept. 16, 2002. Online. http://www.nasdaqnews.com/about/corpgov/CorpGovProp0913.pdf.

Neumark, D., and S. A. Sharpe. 1996. "Rents and Quasi Rents in the Wage Structure: Evidence from Hostile Takeovers," Industrial Relations 35, pp. 145–179.

New York Stock Exchange (NYSE). 2002. Corporate Governance Proposals Reflecting Recommendations from the NYSE Corporate Accountability and Listing Standards Committee As Approved by the New York Stock Exchange Board of Directors," August 1, 2002. Rev. Sept. 12, 2002. Online. http://www.nyse. com/about/report.html.

Organisation for Economic Co-operation and Development (OECD). 1998. Corporate Governance: Improving Competitiveness and Access to Capital in Global Markets: A Report to the OECD by the Business Sector Advisory Group on Corporate Governance. Paris: Organisation for Economic Co-operation and Development.

Organisation for Economic Co-operation and Development (OECD). 1999. Principles of Corporate Governance. Paris: Organisation for Economic Co-operation and Development.

Palepu, K. 1986. "Predicting Takeover Targets: A Methodological and Empirical Analysis," Journal of Accounting and Economics 8, pp. 3–35.

Pontiff, J., A. Shleifer, and M. S. Weisbach. 1990. "Reversions of Excess Pension Assets after Takeovers," Rand Journal of Economics 21, pp. 600–613

Porter, M. E. 1992. Capital Choices: Changing the Way America Invests in Industry. Washington, DC: Council on Competitiveness and Harvard Business School.

Rappaport, A. 1986. Creating Shareholder Value: The New Standard for Business Performance. New York: Free Press.

Ryngaert, M. 1988. "The Effect of Poison Pill Securities on Shareholder Wealth," Journal of Financial Economics 20, pp. 377–417.

Sally, D. 1995. "Conversation and Cooperation in Social Dilemmas: A Meta-Analysis of Experiments from 1958 to 1992," Rationality and Society 7, pp. 58–93.

Scharfstein, D. 1988. "The Disciplinary Role of Takeovers," Review of Economic Studies 55, pp. 185–199.

Scherer, F.M., and D. Ross. 1990. *Industrial Market Structure and Economic Performance, 3rd edition*. Boston: Houghton Mifflin.

Shiller, R. 2000. *Irrational Exuberance*. Princeton, NJ: Princeton University Press.

Shleifer, A. 2000. *Inefficient Markets: An Introduction to Behavioral Finance*. Oxford: Oxford University Press.

Shleifer, A., and L. H. Summers. 1988. "Breach of Trust in Hostile Takeovers." In A. J. Auerbach, ed., Corporate Takeovers: Causes and Consequences. Chicago: University of Chicago Press.

Shleifer, A., and R. W. Vishny. 1988. "Value Maximization and the Acquisition Process," Journal of Economic Perspectives 2, pp. 7–20.

Shleifer, A., and R. W. Vishny. 1997. "A Survey of Corporate Governance," Journal of Finance 52, pp. 737–783.

Stein, J. 1989. "Takeover Threats and Managerial Myopia," Journal of Political Economy 96, pp. 61–80.

Stout, L. A. 1990. "Are Takeover Premiums Really Premiums? Market Price, Fair Value, and Corporate Law," Yale Law Journal 99, pp. 1235–1296.

Stout, L. A. 1997. "How Efficient Markets Undervalue Stocks: CAPM and ECMH Under Conditions of Uncertainty and Disagreement," Cardozo Law Review 19, pp. 475–492.

Stout, L. A. 2000. "Stock Prices and Social Wealth," HLS Discussion Paper No. 301. Cambridge, MA: Harvard Law School.

Stout, L. A. 2002. "Do Antitakeover Provisions Decrease Shareholder Wealth? The Ex Post/Ex Ante Measurement Problem," Stanford Law Review 55, pp. 845–861.

Sunder, S. 2001. "Value of the Firm: Who Gets the Goodies?" ICF Working Paper No. 02-15. New Haven, CT: International Center for Finance at the Yale School of Management.

Tirole, J. 1986. "Hierarchies and Bureaucracies: On the Role of Collusion in Organizations," Journal of Law, Economics, and Organization 2, pp. 181–214.

Twentieth Century Fund. 1992. Report of the Task Force on Market Speculation and Corporate Governance. New York: Twentieth Century Fund Press.

United States General Accounting Office (US GAO). 1993. "Competitiveness Issues: The Business Environment in the United States, Japan, and Germany," GAO/GGD-93-124. Washington, DC: United States General Accounting Office.

Williamson, O. E. 1985. *The Economic Institutions of Capitalism: Firms, Markets, Relational Contracting*. New York: Free Press.

Wruck, K. 1989. "Equity Ownership Concentration and Firm Value," Journal of Financial Economics 23, pp. 3–28.

Chapter 4

The Bubble and the Media

Alexander Dyck and Luigi Zingales

> Nothing but a newspaper can drop the same thought into a thousand minds at the same moment. A newspaper is an adviser that does not require to be sought, but that comes of its own accord and talks to you briefly every day of the common weal, without distracting you from your private affairs.
>
> De Toqueville, *Democracy in America*, Vol II, Section II, Chapter VI

A growing body of literature (e.g., La Porta et al., 1997) compares corporate governance systems across countries by comparing the set of rules and regulations in these countries. Almost invariably the United States comes atop of such rankings. In fact, the United States is often considered the champion of the shareholders' value model and the example other countries should follow. At least, this was true until recent corporate scandals and the ensuing bankruptcy of corporate giants such as Enron and WorldCom. How could the billions in transactions between Enron and its subsidiaries be hidden? How could the false accounting charges of WorldCom not be revealed by internal and external auditors? Is the system fundamentally flawed? Or does it simply lack appropriate legal and regulatory instruments?

In this chapter we advance a different explanation. While transparency can and should be improved, we do not think that the lack of proper rules is the fundamental problem. Many of the improprieties could have been discovered even under the current disclosure system. Why, then, were they not discovered?

To answer this question we delve deeper into the economics of information collection and dissemination. A simple, but thus far ignored, point is that the incentives

We thank Mark Bradshaw, Bruce Kogut, David Moss, Forest Reinhardt and Julio Rotemberg for helpful discussions. We also gratefully acknowledge financial support from the Division of Research, Harvard Business School, the Center for Research on Security Prices and the George Stigler Center at the University of Chicago.

to uncover negative information are much smaller during stock market booms, especially those periods of stock market euphoria often labeled as bubbles. The reasoning goes as follows. The primary source of information collection and aggregation in any financial markets is clearly the speculators. After all, one of the advantages of having a stock market is that it motivates people to collect information, because they can personally gain from that information. During a phase of stock market euphoria, however, the incentives to collect negative information are very limited. In order to profit from negative news a speculator has to take a short position. Short positions, however, are very dangerous during a phase of euphoria. Waiting for the bad news to appear and be incorporated into prices, a speculator has to factor in a great deal of what De Long et al. (1990) calls noise trader risk: the risk of the public becoming even more enthusiastic about the stock and driving the price up. Hence, during stock market bubbles short sellers are unlikely to search for negative information.

Even if speculators have little incentive to uncover bad information, why don't other sources reveal them? The problems with equity analysts are well known and are discussed in the chapter by John Coffee in this volume. The question we focus upon here is, why don't the media have an incentive to uncover bad news? After all, journalists do not have to take the risk of short selling a stock. Furthermore, they seem to have a career-concern reason to uncover negative news. A scoop will enhance their reputation, increasing their lifetime earnings. And at first glance there appear to be few conflicting incentives.

This reasoning, however, is too simplistic. It ignores the subtle incentives behind information production, collection, and dissemination. In this paper we focus on this aspect. We argue that both the production of information by the company and the dissemination of this information by the media is seriously affected during a stock market bubble.

In a stock market bubble, prices are driven above their fundamental values. But astronomical multiples can be reconciled with standard valuation formulas only thanks to inflated expectations about future growth. In fact, stock market bubbles are generally associated with talk about a "new era." As a consequence, during a bubble investors (and thus companies) pay much more attention to their growth forecast and thus to news about it. Illustrative accounting studies (e.g., Bradshaw and Sloan, 2002) reveal that the responsiveness of stock prices to earnings increased more than threefold during the latest period of euphoria of the 1990s. Companies' incentives to spin news positively and to aggressively challenge bad news are therefore greatest during a bubble. Unfortunately, during a period of high valuation journalists are also particularly willing to buy into that positive spin.

We argue that a positive spin in corporate reporting arises as a result of a quid pro quo relationship between companies and journalists. An important asset in a journalist's professional portfolio is the privileged sources of information he or she has access to. After all, the Watergate scandal would have never exploded were it not for a "deep throat" tipping Woodward and Bernstein in the right direction. One former journalist described the situation to us thus, "When I started I thought the client was the public, but I soon learned that in practice my client is the source."[1] But how do journalists maintain access to these sources? How do they reward them?

We distinguish between two possibilities. One is that the informed insider has an interest in the diffusion of information per se. For example, in the Watergate case, Richard Nixon's adversaries had political reasons to leak information. They did not need to be rewarded: the diffusion of information was their own reward. The second scenario is a quid pro quo between the source and the journalist. The source repeatedly reveals valuable information to the journalist in exchange for a positive spin on the news being revealed. The first case is more frequent in environments, like the political one, where there are open conflicts of interest. This is relatively rare in the case of corporations, with the exception of contested takeovers or internal fights to succeed a failing CEO. In general, however, all corporate insiders have a strong vested interest in a higher stock price and, hence, in leaking only positive news. For companies, then, the quid pro quo scenario appears more likely. The distortionary effects of this quid pro quo have been recognized by the Securities and Exchange Commission (SEC) when it forced equal access to companies' conference calls.

Since companies' valuation are particularly sensitive to news during stock market bubbles, corporate insiders will be particularly careful in selecting their privileged journalist sources during these periods. Stated differently, during good times insiders have an extra incentive to get the good news out and to limit bad news. On the other side, journalists will find it particularly valuable to be in the good graces of insiders of a glamorous stock. Hence, they will be particularly careful portraying such stocks in a positive way, for fear of losing a valuable source in the future.

Such incentives change in a downturn. First of all, companies might have an interest in revealing bad information when other companies are not doing so well; this type of cycle is emphasized in Rajan (1994). Second, during a downturn the valuation of a stock depends more on its liquidation value, than on its future growth, making it less sensitive to news. A point, again, that seems to be borne out in accounting studies on the responsiveness of stock prices to earnings. Finally, in downturns conflicts inside a company are more likely to arise, leading to leaks in information. Hence, production of negative information becomes more abundant (possibly excessively abundant) during a market downturn.

We provide some indirect evidence of cyclicality in business reporting consistent with our quid pro quo hypothesis by looking at the composition of Harvard Business School cases, which are a widely used source of information about businesses. There are two types of Harvard cases: field cases, which benefit from access to companies' internal data sources, and so-called library cases, which are compiled using only public sources. Field cases are based in part on private information provided by the company to the Harvard professor who is writing the case. The explicit quid pro quo for this access is that the case needs to be approved by the company before being released.

We expect greater use of field-based cases during expansionary periods. Companies are expected to be more willing to share the data when the picture the case writer will portray is a positive one, that is, during expansionary phases of the business cycle. In downturns, companies are less willing to share their information because the picture the case writer will portray is likely to be more negative.

We find this pattern of cyclicality to be true. As suggested by the raw data presented in Figure 4.1, in years with strong market returns, such as those we have seen from 1995–2000, there is a high reliance on field-based cases. Market downturns, such as those in 1991, 1995, and 2001, dramatically reverse such trends—in 2001 alone, for example, we see a 62 percent increase in public-source cases. We document this more systematically in the text. While indirect, this evidence suggests a relationship between the type of information used in business coverage and stock market performance.

Can this cyclical bias in reporting explain dramatic failures in corporate governance such as Enron? We think so. In previous research (Dyck and Zingales, 2002), we have shown that the media play a fundamental role in any corporate governance system by imposing large reputational costs on managers and directors of firms that behave against societal norms. That the media has this power, however, does not imply they use it efficiently or effectively. In fact, in this chapter we argue that they do not. This cyclical bias in reporting weakens the outside monitoring of companies during booms, creating the scope for egregious abuses such as Enron.

FIGURE 4.1   **Are Incentives in Uncovering Bad News Anticyclical? The Proportion of Field-based HBS Cases and Market Returns (1986–2001)**

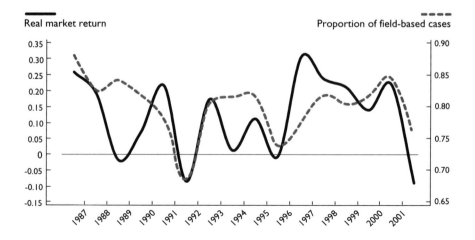

Thus far, we have treated the bubble as an exogenous phenomenon. There is, however, a possible feedback loop between the reluctance of the media to release bad information and a stock market euphoria. To be sustained (at least temporarily), stock market euphoria needs to involve a large segment of the investing population. But where do these people gather information to form their opinions on stock prices? The media, of course. Thus, a reluctance by the media to diffuse negative information may fuel investors' biased expectations, sustaining the bubble a little bit longer. In fact, one can easily conceive of a scenario in which a period of sustained increases in stock prices due to changes in the fundamentals decimates the number of short sellers, leaving the market dependent on the media to form a correct opinion. But the media have few incentives to portray any other than a positive perspective, fueling the bubble. In fact, all of the bubbles followed periods of sharp increase in stock prices due to fundamental reasons (Garber, 2000).

The idea that outside monitoring is reduced during an asset bubble is not new. More than a century ago, Walter Bagehot (1873) wrote: "The good times too of high price almost always engender much fraud. All people are most credulous when they are most happy; and when much money has just been made, when some people are really making it, when most people think they are making it, there is a happy opportunity for ingenious mendacity." Bagehot's view figures prominently in the accounts of euphorias and panics offered by Galbraith (1979),[2] Kindleberger (1989, p. 90),[3] Shiller (2000), and Coffee (this volume). These authors, however, assume that investors are completely irrational, or that they at least become so during moments of euphoria. In contrast, our argument does not rely on investors being irrational. Most importantly, we focus on the crucial channel through which euphoria and panics are spread: the media. We show that in reporting corporate news, media tend to be biased and this bias is accentuated during booms.

The rest of the chapter proceeds as follows. The first section uses the Enron example to illustrate that much of the failure in corporate governance could have been uncovered if the media had chosen to pursue this information actively, and that they deliberately chose not to. The second section gives an analysis of the incentives behind the production, revelation, and dissemination of companies' information. The third section provides some empirical evidence of the cyclicality of news spinning by looking at the composition of Harvard Business School cases. In the fourth section we discuss the implication of this cyclicality for corporate governance. Conclusions follow.

AN ILLUSTRATION OF THE ARGUMENT: ENRON AND THE MEDIA

It is interesting to analyze the role played by the media in the demise of Enron. On the one hand, a deputy managing editor of the *Wall Street Journal* boasted that "without the stories that Smith and Emshwiller [two *Wall Street Journal* reporters] wrote, Enron would have gotten on fine. There is no evidence that it would have collapsed."[4]

On the other hand, Sherman (2002) notes that "to excavate back issues of magazines like *Forbes, Fortune, Worth, Business 2.0,* and *Red Herring* is to enter a parallel universe of cheerleading and obsequiousness, a universe where applause obliterated skepticism." Are the media the savior or are they part of the problem?

To answer this question let's look at some facts, as reported by Sherman (2002). The first inquiry into Enron's accounting came from an article by Jonathan Weil, then a reporter for the Texas edition of the *Wall Street Journal.* In a July 2000 piece, Weil writes "what many investors may not realize is that much of these companies' recent profits constitute unrealized, noncash gains. Frequently, these profits depend on assumptions and estimates about future market factors, the details of which the companies do not provide, and which time may prove wrong." Weil's piece was never published in the national edition of the *Wall Street Journal,* but it appeared on the Dow Jones newswire, where it attracted the attention of James Chanos, a hedge-fund manager, who began to scrutinize the company's financial statements. There he discovered cagey references to "related party" transactions involving Enron's senior officers and massive insider selling. It was enough to induce him to sell short the stock in November 2000. Short sellers, however, only profit when the negative information becomes public. Thus, Chanos tipped off a reporter at Fortune, Bethany McLean, who in March published a story entitled "Is Enron Overpriced?," in which she questioned how, exactly, Enron made its money. Another short seller tipped off Peter Eavis, of TheStreet.com, who in an article on May 9, 2001, started to mention shady "related entities."

Yet, it took Skilling's surprise resignation in August for three *Wall Street Journal* reporters (Friedland, Smith, and Emshwiller) to start an investigation of Enron's financial statements. They quickly realized that "things weren't adding up at Enron" (Sherman, 2002). Most importantly, "sources close to Enron began to furnish the *Journal* with documents" (Sherman 2002).

But it was only after Enron announced a USD 618 million third-quarter loss that the *Wall Street Journal* (October 2001) identified the link between earnings and the shady partnerships. The *Journal* was able to link Enron's reduction in shareholder equity to the CFO's mysterious partnerships. Only at this point did other media and the SEC start to investigate.

This brief account of Enron's demise illustrates several important points about the role of the media. First, while many transactions were concealed, there was enough public information available to raise serious doubt about the credibility of Enron's earnings. As the former editor of the *Financial Times,* Richard Lambert, stated: "the Annual Report for 2000 should have raised all kind of questions about the group's cash flow…about the length and complexity of the footnotes to the account, often a warning that things are not what they appear."[5] This opinion was reiterated by the CEO of Pearson, the group owning the Financial Times, in a recent interview to the *Royal Society of Arts Journal*: "sometimes I do think that the business press—and I include the FT in this—has not worked hard enough to ferret out these stories."

The second important lesson is that the media as a whole, instead of scrutinizing Enron's accounts, acted as cheerleader all the way to the end. According to Jonathan Weil of the *Wall Street Journal*, financial journalists "outsourced their critical thinking skills to Wall Street analysts, who are not independent and, by definition, were employed to do nothing but spin positive company news in order to sell stock. There was hardly a Wall Street analyst covering the stock whose firm was not getting sprinkled with cash in some form or another by Enron." The day before Jeffrey Skilling resigned, *Business 2.0* featured his photo on the cover with the titles "The Revolution LIVES." In its September 2001 issue, *Red Herring* insisted: "Forget about Microsoft. America's most successful, revered, feared—and even hated—company is no longer a band of millionaire geeks from Redmond, Washington, but a cabal of cowboy/traders from Houston: Enron."[6]

The third point is that such behavior is not an accident, but the result of reporters' incentives. Any attempt to report negative information or simply to question the existing optimistic consensus incurs constant harassment from the target company. One UBS PaineWebber analyst was fired three hours after issuing a warning about financial deterioration at Enron, followed by a retraction of the negative statement and UBS PaineWebber's issuance of an optimistic outlook on Enron's future.[7] During an investor conference call, a caller who criticized Enron's delays in releasing financial information was labeled an "asshole" by Skilling.[8] Similarly, *Fortune*'s journalist McLean was labeled "unethical" by Skilling, who hung up on her. Furthermore, the chairman of Enron, Ken Lay, called *Fortune*'s managing editor Rik Kirkland, implying that McLean's piece should be cut.[9]

The last important point is that the incentives to report bad information about a company change dramatically as the company's stock price deteriorates. One could simply appeal to the journalists' herding mentality, but we think there is more to it than that. As Sherman's (2002) account of the Enron story demonstrates, as the stock price falls, journalists start to have access to more negative information. Short sellers start feeding them and so do company's insiders, who hope to benefit from a turnaround of the company. These sources were not available when the stock price was booming. When a company's fortunes deteriorate not only do journalists have access to more negative news, they also have less reasons to hide them. The possibility of a demise of the company reduces the value of an ongoing relationship, increasing a journalists' willingness to report negative information.

The economics of media reporting is, therefore, not as straightforward as economic models implicitly assume. Thus, to understand the effect of a stock market bubble on the quality and type of media reporting, we need to closely study the incentives to generate, reveal, and disseminate information. This is the task to which we now turn.

MEDIA INCENTIVES AND GOVERNANCE

The economics of media coverage

To understand the economics behind news media we need to start appreciating their role. The main role of news media is to filter and aggregate information, repackaging it with some entertainment value. For example, the dry and prolix prose of police reports is transformed into a thrilling story about the latest murders. As in any other markets, the type of information produced and its quantity depend on supply and demand considerations. While these considerations are similar across topics, some issues are unique to corporate news. Since this is the area in which we are interested, we will confine our reasoning to this case.

The positive externality of media for corporate governance

The presence of an active press can increase expected penalties for improper behavior through at least two channels. In the conventional reputation story (e.g., Fama, 1980), managers' wages in the future depend on shareholders' and future employers' beliefs about whether the managers will attend to their interests in those situations where they cannot be monitored. Managers, however, care about their reputation not only vis-à-vis future employers, but also vis-à-vis society at large. Commenting on the recent legal reforms in US corporate governance, Robert Mills, managing director of UBS Warburg, recently argued that for him a tougher punishment than the threat of jail time would be explaining to his son the story about it in the *Wall Street Journal*.[10]

The strength of reputation as a corrective device, however, depends upon the extent to which information about past behavior is disseminated. As the opening quote from De Toqueville suggests, and as we develop in Dyck and Zingales (2002a), the media play a pivotal role in communicating information about managers to the public. For instance, in Dyck and Zingales (forthcoming) we show that the diffusion of information by the press affects the amount of corporate value that insiders appropriate for themselves, the so-called private benefits of control. Across 39 countries, a higher rate of diffusion by the press is associated with lower private benefits of control, and this influence persisted even controlling for differences in laws and legal regimes.[11] This evidence is consistent with many statements by executives. As William Browder, managing director of Hermitage Capital, the largest public equity fund in Russia claims, "The court of public opinion is much more effective than the Russian legal system and much fairer."[12]

The economics of information production

Arguing that the media has a positive externality for corporate governance does not imply that the news media will provide the optimal amount of coverage to address all governance problems. To answer the question of why the optimal coverage is not likely to be provided, we need to focus on the incentives to uncover bad information. Consider, first, the supply side. Collecting information about companies is very costly.

Digging through annual reports, questioning the validity of different accounting practices, and so on requires both time and expertise. Most importantly, it is a very risky activity. Without a lead, a random investigation will turn out to be fruitless most of the time. Unless he or she uncovers a major fraud, a journalist who spends a lot of time digging through annual reports has little to show for it. According to Sherman (2002), it took two months for Jonathan Weil to prepare the Enron article, and this article did not even make it to the national edition of the *Journal*.

A much easier (and safer) alternative for a journalist is to rely on companies' press releases. In fact, the stated goal of these releases is precisely to help journalists quickly absorb a great quantity of facts. Of course, these releases are not unbiased: they try to spin the story in the direction that is most favorable to the company. While expert reporters can easily see through the spin, a complete undoing of the built-in bias requires time and effort. Whether the market will adequately compensate journalists for this time and effort depends upon the structure of the demand for information, a question we will return to soon.

From a reporter's point of view the real downside of relying on press releases is the lack of any competitive edge. A reporter wants to differentiate his or her product, wants to report critical information before other reporters. What constitutes critical information, however, depends upon what other reporters write. It is a game similar to Keynes' famous beauty contest, where everybody tries to guess what everybody else prefers. In this game the real competitive edge is personal contacts. Sources inside or very close to the company that will tip on major coming news ahead of the rest of the crowd.

These contacts are extremely valuable for reporters, who cultivate them actively. But they do not come for free. News sources generally have a reason to leak information. They want to scare off a competitor, reassure shareholders, prevent a board coup, and so on. In the political arena, it is the fierce competition between opposing parties with different agendas that generate a relatively unbiased set of information sources. But in the corporate world, such competition is lacking. Except for short sellers, all informed parties have a vested interest in a high stock valuation: managers, who hold stock options; employees, whose jobs depend on the company doing well and whose retirement accounts depend on its stock doing well; and analysts, whose fortunes are very often linked to the success of the stock they analyze. If all the sources have an interest in a positive spin, the news coming from them will be clearly biased.

Once again, a reporter could potentially undo this bias, but in addition to the problems discussed above, he or she faces an additional constraint: the need to reward sources. And since all these sources have a vested interest in a high stock price, the way to reward them is to spin the story in a positive direction. The last thing reporters want to do is develop a reputation for writing negative articles—they will find it extremely difficult to develop and maintain their own sources and they will face constant harassment in doing their job (as happened to the journalists writing about Enron). A possible remedy for a media outlet is not to disclose the name of writers (as the *Economist* does). Hiding their identity makes it easier for reporters to write negative stories about companies. But even this device is imperfect. Most companies know which journalists are assigned to their case and they can easily infer who is writing. Hence, it is impossible to remove completely reporters' positive bias toward the companies they cover.

Thus far, we have also argued that producing negative news is much more costly than producing positive news about a company. This does not necessarily mean that in equilibrium less bad news will be produced—it depends on the price attached to one type of news versus the other. Will negative news be rewarded more than positive news? Will the premium be sufficient to reward the additional costs negative news involves?

We doubt that. While a scoop benefits a reporter, the benefits she receives are not different if the scoop reveals bad information or good information about a company. The costs the reporter receives, however, do depend on the type of scoop. In fact, negative scoops are more dangerous, because in some countries they expose a reporter to the risk of being sued for defamation by the company. Even if the article is correct, the cost of the trial can easily break a reporter both emotionally and financially. By contrast, no such a risk exists for a positive scoop. Even if the scoop turns out to be false, the reporter is not sued by the myriads of investors who bought the stock on the basis of the false scoop. Hence, positive scoops are more rewarding for a reporter than negative ones.

But even if negative scoops were rewarded more, the incentives to seek such a scoop could remain excessively low. The risk involved in a negative scoop is such that a risk-averse reporter might not seek one even in the presence of a premium.

Cyclicality in the media's bias

Thus far, we have simply described how the economics of information production lead the media to report, on average, a positive image of a company. We have said nothing about possible variations in the magnitude of this bias over time. Now we will argue that this pro-company bias is stronger during a boom and weaker, to the point of being reversed, during a downturn.

The first reason for the bias discussed is the cyclicality in the availability of different sources of information. As argued above, speculators are the primary source of information collection and aggregation in any financial market because they can personally gain from that information. During a phase of stock market euphoria, however, the incentives to collect negative information are very limited because of the dangers of noise trader risk: the risk of the public becoming even more enthusiastic about the stock and driving the price up. During the dot-com frenzy Lamont and Thaler (2001) document deviations from the fundamental value of more than 30 percent even when it was possible to perfectly hedge a short position (as in the case of Palm Pilot and

3Com). One can only imagine what happens when such a perfect hedge does not exist. Hence, during stock market bubbles short sellers are unlikely to search for negative information or to tip off the media. Similarly, no insiders want to rock the boat when the company is doing well and it trades at high multiples. As Sherman's (2002) account describes, Enron insiders started to leak internal information only after the resignation of Skilling. Before, nobody dared to.

The second reason for this cyclicality is the asymmetry in the value of the quid pro quo relationship over the business cycle. When a company is doing well it has a lot of positive news to leak to the media. Hence, antagonizing a successful company with a negative report can be very costly for a journalist. The "uncooperative" reporter will be denied access to companies' data, a loss to the reporter of a valuable source of privileged information. By contrast, in a downturn a company will have very little information it wants to share with reporters. Therefore, antagonizing it with a negative report and being cut off from access to company data will not be so costly. If, in addition, the company is on the verge of bankruptcy, the scope of the quid pro quo relationship with reporters is reduced and the temptation for the reporter to deviate and report bad information increases.

The third reason why negative reports about companies are anticyclical is that the effort companies put into preventing them is procyclical. During a boom phase, a lot of the value of a stock depends on a company's prospects for future growth. And these prospects are highly influenced by the information released by the media. In contrast, in a market downturn, the value of a stock is more driven by the value of its asset in place, which is more tangible and thus less affected by any story reported in the media. Hence, the effort companies might devote to spinning news for the press is going to be much more intense during a boom phase than during a downturn.[13]

Similarly, it is more costly for a reporter to antagonize a company when he or she is the only one doing it, than when many others are doing so. Questioning the integrity of a company's numbers when the company is doing well is very dangerous. A single pundit or reporter can be easily harassed or even sued, since the company can hope, with this strategy, to prevent others from following the first's example. But when a company is openly questioned by multiple sources, the aggressive strategy becomes self defeating and each reporter runs little risk of being harassed or sued. This asymmetry can, by itself, generate a herding behavior among reporters.

Illustrative of the strong forces to suppress "bad" information is the reception that Alan Greenspan received for the rather mild criticism he offered on December 6, 1996 when he asked, "How do we know when irrational exuberance has unduly inflated asset values, which then become subject to unexpected and prolonged contractions...?"[14] Immediately, he was criticized as being not only out of touch with the economy, but for jeopardizing the economic boom. That Greenspan, one of the most independent of market commentators and who had a well established reputation, was subject to severe criticism hints at the ferocity with which bad news is greeted by those with less independence and reputation, such as the equity analysts and newspaper reporters described above in the Enron example.

This phenomenon is not unique to the 1990s. Paul Warburg (a banker) and Roger Babson (a statistician) were exposed to public condemnation for their early criticism of speculation in 1929 (Galbraith, 1990). Galbraith himself received death threats for his mild criticism of the speculative buildup in 1955: "The postman each morning staggered in with a load of letters condemning my comments, the most extreme threatening what the CIA was later to call executive action, the mildest saying that prayers were being offered for my richly deserved demise" (Galbraith 1990, p. 9). And in 1986 the *New York Times* refused to publish an article it commissioned him to write when he concluded that a crash was inevitable.

A more elaborate version of such bias coming from the consumers of business news is suggested by Mullanaithan and Shleifer (2002). They assume that readers believe more articles that confirm prior articles, while they discount the others. With such behavior it pays for reporters to follow the herd. During boom periods, they will accentuate positive news, while in downturns they will emphasize negative ones. While this behavior is sufficient to generate cyclicality in media reporting, it cannot fully account for some of the evidence we will discuss later.

Extensions

In all the above discussions we have implicitly assumed that individual reporters have full discretion in their choices. In fact, which topics are investigated and how much time is dedicated to single investigations is decided in part by media headquarters. Much of the analysis, however, carries through at that level as well. In fact, at that level the pressure to please companies can be even more severe, since companies' advertising is a major source of revenue.

We have also ignored the possibility of outright corruption, where companies pay reporters or newspapers to spin their versions of the facts and/or suppress bad information. We have done so because in the United States (but not necessarily in other countries) this is extremely rare. Kindleberger (1990), under the heading, "venal journalism," cites numerous examples of the press being bought by speculators during the South Sea Bubble in the United Kingdom and on the Continent in the 19th century, but suggests that the United States has been much less open to such problems.

This is not to say that there have been no charges. Journalist Phillip Longman (2002, p. 19) contends that in the US, "business publications, especially those celebrating the boom, were growing fat from dot-com ads…at any publication, there is, of course, a tension between the need to please advertisers and the need to please readers. … at business publications in the 1990s, it [this tension] was resolved in a manner that favored advertisers—and worse, advertisers, who, it has turned out, were selling shoddy products." In the case of Enron, questions have been raised about the conflicts many journalists faced as a result of direct or indirect payments from Enron through speeches and positions on Enron's advisory board. Josh Lipton (2002) reports Andrew Sullivan's challenge to journalists: "Exactly how many pundits have been on Enron's payroll? How many of them have disclosed that fact in their relevant publications? How much was each paid?" In this respect, conflicts may be at least as severe for academics writing about business issues, through their multiple contacts with companies through consulting engagements and board and advisory positions.

Of course, allowing for that possibility will only strengthen our reasoning, both in terms of the average bias and in terms of its time series variation. Companies will have both more resources with which to bribe and more benefits from a positive spin in a boom than in a downturn, hence they will end up bribing reporters more.

EMPIRICAL EVIDENCE ON THE "SPIN" OF BUSINESS COVERAGE AND STOCK MARKET CYCLES

What evidence is there that companies try to spin information to make their performance look stronger? And what evidence is there that the media is more inclined to take or exaggerate this spin during booms than downturns?

Companies spinning information

Existing research on press releases of company financial information shows efforts by companies to spin. It is often the case when companies reveal information that they also reveal information from a previous year to facilitate comparisons. Reflective of strategic spinning of information, Schrand and Walther (2000) report that companies systematically tilt these comparisons to make current performance look stronger. They are much more likely to remind readers of extenuating reasons for strong performance in previous years than to remind readers of extenuating circumstances for poor information.

Bradshaw and Sloan (2002) provide complementary evidence based on what firms define and emphasize in their press releases surrounding mandatory filing of earnings. The traditional definition of earnings is that required by generally accepted accounting principles (GAAP). But there are alternatives, variously called pro forma earnings, operating earnings, or, most commonly, "street earnings."[15] These alternatives are suspect, at least according to the chief accountant of the SEC, as the Wall Street Journal reported: "Mr Turner said it appears as if some companies are intentionally trying to 'spin investors' by issuing news releases highlighting pro forma earnings, which tend to omit items that would reduce reported earnings. Mr Turner jokingly called such earnings figures 'everything but the bad stuff.' "[16]

Bradshaw and Sloan (2002) report that looking at the average of all US equities, street earnings have exceeded GAAP earnings every year since 1987. And again, consistent with spinning, companies have been in the lead in defining and emphasizing these earnings, with the typical press release announcement emphasizing street earnings earlier than GAAP earnings when this interpretation would put the company in a better light. In 1998–1999, for instance, a buoyant market, this spin was put on the numbers 43.5 percent of the time.[17]

Business coverage open to spin and stock market cycles

Now we turn to evidence that business coverage is more open to spin in boom times than downturns. Our empirical evidence comes from another source of business information—case studies prepared by professors at Harvard Business School. This is not the traditional business press; in fact the business school has as a disclaimer on all cases: "Cases are not intended to serve as endorsements, sources of primary data, or illustrations of effective or ineffective management." Nonetheless, the case studies are an important source of information on business: Harvard Business School case studies are sold all over the world, they form the basis of the curriculum at many business schools, and they are used as sources in many news articles.

We focus our analysis on the two most common types of Harvard cases: field cases, which benefit from access to companies' internal data sources, and the so-called library cases, which are compiled using only public sources. Field cases are the most typical type of case study. They are based in part on private information provided by the company to the Harvard professor who is writing the case. The explicit quid pro quo is that field cases require approval by the company before release. In fact, the most objective way of classifying a case study as a field or library case is whether the case writer has felt compelled to get a "green card" for the case; that is, a green document that a company representative has to sign to release the case study that contains private information.

That field cases, which are subject to company approval, might be more influenced by the companies involved than are cases from public sources, is illustrated by the following episode. "I learned that Enron was upset with my public-source case on the conflict surrounding the company's investment in India," recalls Harvard Business School professor Louis Wells. "After the second time the case was taught, someone from the administration approached me, told me of the company's concerns, and asked if anything could be done about it. Another faculty member was, I was told, writing a field-based case on the same subject. It was suggested that I might consider teaching the more rich field case, if it fit my teaching objectives. Meanwhile, I sent my public-source case to Enron for comment. In the end, I removed the public-source case from the system and adopted a shortened version of the field case, which was indeed richer in information and enabled me to accomplish the original teaching objectives."[18]

The advantage of looking at Harvard Business School cases is that it is possible to identify when the quid pro quo takes place. By looking at the composition of case studies over time we can see if the proportion open to spin is influenced by the market. If our hypothesis about cyclical behavior is correct, we expect greater use of field-based cases during expansionary periods. When the case to be written is meant to portray a positive image of the company (i.e., during expansionary phases of the business cycle), the implicit price to be paid for access to privileged information is lower. Hence, companies will be more willing to share their information and Harvard Business School professors will be more willing to engage in the quid pro quo with a company. As one of the authors attests, during the recent stock market boom there were more unsolicited offers by companies to support case studies than in the period before the boom. In downturns, unsolicited proposals for case studies are fewer; companies are less willing to share their information as the picture the case writer will portray is likely to be more negative.[19]

Our test of the theory is a simple one: does the proportion of field-based cases move positively with the stock market? Empirically, we regress the proportion of field-based cases against a measure of market returns (and a time trend to account for any changes in the approach to collecting information about companies over time at Harvard Business School). To test this we collected data from Harvard Business School on the number of field and library cases published each year since 1970. With this information, we calculated the proportion of field-based cases in any year.

The summary statistics of our sample are provided in Table 4.1. The typical case study is field-based, with the average proportion of field-based cases equal to 82 percent with significant variation, from 69 to 94 percent. Visual inspection of the data also shows a trend to reduced reliance on field cases over these 30 years, so we will account for this possibility in our empirical analysis. The remainder of the table simply summarizes well-known trends in real market returns and in real GDP over this time period, with an average real market return of 4.9 percent and an average increase in real GDP of 3.1 percent. As the Business School has grown, so has the number of case studies, with an increase over time from 56 case studies in 1971 to 406 case studies in 2001.

TABLE 4.1 **Summary Statistics**

VARIABLE	MEAN	MEDIAN	STANDARD DEVIATION	MIN.	MAX.	NUMBER OF OBS.
Percentage of field-based cases	0.816	0.816	0.052	0.686	0.935	31
Real market return	0.049	0.070	0.17	-0.367	0.35	31
Real GDP growth	0.031	0.035	0.022	-0.020	-0.073	31
Number of Harvard Business School cases	245	276	108	56	406	31

Table 4.2 confirms what was suggested by Figure 4.1—business coverage that relies on sources prone to spin is cyclical. The positive and significant coefficients on market returns in columns 1 and 3 show that over the whole sample (1971–2001) and, particularly, in the latter half of the sample (1986–2001), field-based cases are sensitive to market returns. The results suggest that a one standard deviation improvement in market return brings forth a 1.6 percent increase in field-based cases in general, and that this sensitivity is increasing, with an estimated 3.3 percentage point increase in field-based cases for a one standard deviation increase in market returns during the mid-1980s and 1990s. The effect of stock market downturns appears particularly important. As an illustration, in the stock market downturn of 2001, field-based cases account for just 75 percent of all cases, a full 10 percent drop from the good times of 2000. The same was true in the last significant market downturn in 1991, where field cases accounted for just 68 percent of all cases, while two years earlier in better times they accounted for 82 percent.

TABLE 4.2   Is There a Cyclical "Spin" in Business Coverage?

The dependent variable is the percentage of Harvard Business School case studies that are field-based by publication year (1971–2001). This is defined as the ratio of the number of field-based case studies (field-based cases require written approval from firms before use) to the total number of field-based and library cases (library cases do not require firm approval before use) in a given publication year. (Source: Harvard Business School Publishing.) In column 1 and 2 we regress the percentage of field-based case studies against the real market return and real GDP growth respectively using the whole sample period of 1971–2001 and including controls for a time trend and a constant. In columns 3 and 4 we repeat this analysis restricting ourselves to 1986–2001, the second half of our sample period. The real market return is the percentage change in end of year Dow Jones index less the percentage change in the Consumer price index in that year. (Sources: Dow Jones, Economic Report of the President.) Real GDP growth is the percentage change in real GDP. (Source: Economic Report of the President.) A positive coefficient on real market return and/or real GDP growth indicates a sensitivity of use of field-based cases to market and macroeconomic performance.

INDEPENDENT VARIABLES	DEPENDENT VARIABLE: PERCENTAGE OF FIELD-BASED CASE STUDIES BY PUBLICATION YEAR			
	(1)	(2)	(3)	(4)
Real market return	0.095* (0.054)		0.193** (0.083)	
Real GDP growth		0.775* (0.394)		2.52*** (0.538)
Time trend	-0.003*** (0.001)	-0.002** (0.001)	-0.002 (0.002)	-0.002 (0.002)
Constant	6.75*** (2.05)	5.13*** (1.86)	5.06 (4.40)	5.30 (3.19)
Years covered	1971–2001	1971–2001	1986–2001	1986–2001
Number of years	31	31	16	16
Adjusted R-squared	0.18	0.20	0.22	0.59

Notes: * denotes significant at 10%, ** denotes significant at 5%, *** denotes significant at 1%.

Columns 2 and 4 show that the sensitivity is not only to market returns, but also to the state of the macroeconomy, and that again, the sensitivity is highest in the latter half of the period. Our regression estimates suggest that over the whole sample period (the latter half) a one standard deviation change in the economy brings forth a 1.7 percent (5.5 percent) increase in field-based cases.

Does this matter?

Now that we have (hopefully) convinced the reader that media are biased in their reporting and that this pro-company bias is stronger during booms than during recessions, we can ask the more fundamental question: does it matter?

In a frictionless world, where speculators are free to short a stock and they are not afraid to do so, this media bias will have no serious consequence on prices. Speculators have no bias in one direction or the other and hence they will force prices to their fundamental values.

In the real world, however, short sales are not as easy as long positions. Hence speculators find it more difficult to correct overvaluations than undervaluations. As a result, overvaluations can persist. Unfortunately, the described bias in media reporting does nothing to reduce this problem. In fact, it exacerbates it. When the force of speculation is crippled by short-sell constraints, the media, instead of convincing the public-at-large that the prices are above fundamentals, will tend to feed the exuberance. In other words, while the media are probably not responsible for the rise of bubbles, they clearly play a part in sustaining them.

Even if this cyclicality in media does not affect prices, however, it does have important effects on corporate governance. As we show in Dyck and Zingales (forthcoming), the pressure exerted by the media is an important component of a good corporate governance system. When such pressure weakens, abuses are inevitable. "The press blithely accepted Enron as the epitome of a new, post-deregulation corporate model," stated *Business Week* in an unusual *mea culpa*, "when it should have been much more aggressive in probing the company's opaque partnerships, off balance sheet maneuvers, and soaring leverage." Unfortunately, our analysis suggests that this is not an occasional lapse, but a systematic problem that emerges during stock market booms.

That media's incentives to uncover negative information are weakened during booms does not mean media play no role in corporate governance. As the Enron episode illustrates, the press still played an important role in stopping abuses at Enron, and has played a very important role in imposing penalties long before any legal penalties are introduced. The point we want to stress here is that during booms the monitoring provided by the media is less than that provided during normal or bad times. The fact that the weakening of media's incentives to uncover bad news could lead to such egregious behavior such as Enron emphasizes the importance of the media. After all, the quality of the legal system did not change over the stock market cycle. For what other reason should corporate behavior have changed?

What can be done?

If this problem is indeed so severe, what can be done to attenuate it? Our analysis of media incentives suggests one possible solution. The reason why reporters engage in quid pro quo relationships with companies is to reduce the cost of collecting information. Thus, the higher this cost is, the stronger these relationships will be. After all, the percentage of public information cases is higher in accounting and finance (where case writers have access to better public sources) than in entrepreneurship and strategy, where public sources are lacking. Thus, to weaken these ties between reporters and companies, enhanced corporate disclosure can be useful. Our analysis suggests, however, that the presence of the information in the public domain is not sufficient; the cost of gathering is also very important. The higher this cost, the bigger will be the incentive for a journalist to skip this cost and rely on direct company sources. Consider, for instance, the accounting treatment of stock options. Many have argued that disclosure in the footnotes is sufficient (i.e., what is required under current accounting provisions), since sophisticated investors can calculate the implied costs of options and restate financials. Our perspective suggests otherwise. This indirect form of disclosure raises the costs for journalists to use this information to uncover or communicate corporate misdeeds.

CONCLUSION

In this chapter we advance a new explanation for the severe lapses in corporate governance experienced by US companies in the last few years. This explanation focuses on the role of the media, an ignored, but we think important, institution in determining governance outcomes. We argue that during stock market booms the healthy pressure exerted by the press on companies is weakened, because reporters find it more convenient to buy into companies' spin. We provide some indirect evidence of this effect by looking at the percentage of Harvard Business School cases that are field-based, that is, that rely on companies' internal sources. Consistent with our quid pro quo theory, this percentage increases during booms and drops during recessions.

We suggest that greater availability of ready-to-use public information can reduce reporters' incentive to enter into quid pro quo relationships, maintaining greater independence of the press even during booms.

NOTES

1   Jonathan West, interview with author, November 17, 2002.

2   "In good times, people are relaxed, trusting and money is plentiful. ... under these circumstances the rate of embezzlement grows, the rate of discovery falls off, and *bezzle* increases rapidly."

3   "In a boom, fortunes are made, individuals wax greedy and swindlers come forward to exploit that greed."

4   Quoted in Sherman (2002).

5   Quoted in: Johnson, R. 2002. "City Scribblers Smarting Over Questions of Competence," *The Daily Telegraph,* Friday, October 11, p. 18.

6   All quotes in this paragraph are from Sherman (2002).

7   Based on documents revealed by Representative Waxman of California in the House Government Reform Committee and reported in: R. Oppel Jr, 2002. "The Man Who Paid the Price for Sizing up Enron," *The New York Times* March 27, p. C-1.

8   Smith, R., and J. Emshwiller. 2001. "Enron Prepares to Become Easier to Read," *Wall Street Journal* August 28, p. C-1.

9   Quoted in Sherman (2002).

10 Wharton, *Institutional Investors as a Force for Change*, Rev. November 12, 2002. Online. http://knowledge.wharton.upenn.edu/articles.cfm?catid=1&articleid=655&homepage=yes.

11 In this chapter we use differences across countries in the diffusion of the press to identify the impact of the press. Because the press cannot be important if their reports are not read, diffusion is clearly a rough indicator of media importance, but one of the few available in a large cross-section of countries.

12 See Dyck (2002).

13 On the other hand, a CEO facing a downturn might be particularly interested in protecting his public image.

14 Remarks by Chairman Alan Greenspan at the Annual Dinner and Francis Boyer Lecture of the American Enterprise Institute for Public Policy Research, Washington, DC, December 5, 1996. Greenspan, A. *The Challenge of Central Banking in a Democratic Society.* Rev. September 30, 2002. Online. http://www.federalreserve.gov/boarddocs/speeches/1996/19961205.htm.

15 Bradshaw and Sloan (2002, p. 45) report that these definitions exclude supposed nonrecurring items such as restructuring charges, merger and acquisition costs, goodwill amortization, certain results of subsidiaries, stock-based compensation costs, and even, in the case of Amazon, interest expense on long-term debt.

16 *Wall Street Journal.* 2001. "SEC Probes 4 Firms For Possible Abuses Of Pro-Forma Results," June 19, p. C-18.

17 Based (in each period) on a random sample of 200 earnings press releases where the street numbers exceeded the GAAP numbers.

18 Louis Wells, in an interview with the author, November 15, 2002.

19 The Mullanaithan and Shleifer (2002) herding theory does not predict any push from the supply side. Hence, this episode, as well as Enron's sharing of data sources in exchange for a better spin of the case, is only consistent with the quid pro quo theory.

REFERENCES

Bagehot, W. 1873. *Lombard Street: A Description of the Money Market*. Foreword P. L. Bernstein. 1999. Reprint, New York: John Wiley & Sons.

Bradshaw, M., and R. Sloan. 2002. "GAAP versus The Street: An Empirical Assessment of Two Alternative Definitions of Earnings," *Journal of Accounting Research* 40, pp. 41–66.

De Long, J. B., A. Shleifer A, L. H. Summers, and R. J. Waldman. 1990. "Noise Trader Risk in Financial Markets," *Journal of Political Economy* 98, pp. 703–738.

Dyck, A. 2002. "The Hermitage Fund: Media and Corporate Governance in Russia." Harvard Business School Case Study 2-703-010. Cambridge, MA: Harvard Business School.

Dyck, A., and L. Zingales. 2002. "The Corporate Governance Role of the Media." In *The Right to Tell: The Role of Mass Media in Economic Development*. Washington, DC: World Bank.

Dyck, A., and L. Zingales. 2003. "Private Benefits of Control: An International Comparison," *Journal of Finance* (forthcoming).

Galbraith, J. K. 1979. *The Great Crash of 1929*. Boston: Houghton Mifflin.

Galbraith, J. K. 1990. *A Short History of Financial Euphoria*. New York: Viking Press.

Garber, P. M. 2000. *Famous First Bubbles: The Fundamentals of Early Manias*. Cambridge, MA: MIT Press.

Kindleberger, C. 1989. *Manias, Panics and Crashes: A History of Financial Crises*. New York: Basic Books.

La Porta, R., F. Lopez-de-Silanes, A. Shleifer, and R. Vishny. 1997. "Legal Determinants of External Finance," *Journal of Finance* 52, pp. 1131–1150.

Lamont, O., and R. Thaler. 2001. "Can the Market Add and Subtract? Mispricing in Tech Stock Carve-Outs," NBER Working Paper 8302. Cambridge, MA: National Bureau of Economic Research.

Lipton, J. 2002. "Ethics: Enron's Helpers," *Columbia Journalism Review* 40. Online. http://www.cjr/year/02/2/liptonenron.asp.

Longman, P. 2002. "Bad Press," *Washington Monthly* 43, p. 19.

Mullanathan, S., and A. Shleifer. 2002. "Media Bias," NBER Working Paper No. 9295. Cambridge, MA: National Bureau of Economic Research.

Rajan, R. G. 1994. "Why Bank Credit Policies Fluctuate: A Theory and Some Evidence," *Quarterly Journal of Economics* 109, pp. 399–441.

Schrand, C., and B. Walther. 2000. "Strategic Benchmarks in Earnings Announcements: The Selective Disclosure of Prior-Period Earnings Components," *The Accounting Review* 75, pp. 151–177.

Sherman, Scott. 2002. "Enron: Uncovering the Uncovered Story," *Columbia Journalism Review* 40, pp. 22–29.

Shiller, R. 2000. *Irrational Exuberance*. New York: Broadway Books.

Expanding the Purview of Governance:
Employees and Early Investors

Chapter 5

 Employees and Corporate Governance

Mary O'Sullivan

Corporate governance is concerned with the institutions that influence how control over resource allocation is exercised in business corporations: who exercises control, what allocation decisions they make, and who benefits from these decisions. What do we mean when we speak of employee representation in corporate governance? In this chapter, I view employees as having a role in corporate governance when they have some voice in decision-making processes that affect how resources within the corporate enterprise are allocated. Moreover, I am concerned only with situations in which employees' influence over corporate activity is institutionalized, whether through formal requirements, informal norms, or both, so that employees' role in governance is not at the discretion of any other group in the economy (such as shareholders). The means through which employees may exert such influence are quite varied, but they include representation on boards, works councils, and, in some cases, enterprise unions.

There are other, more indirect, ways in which employees may influence how and to what ends control is exercised in the corporate economy. Employee ownership is one possible mechanism for doing so—employees may derive a beneficial interest from being shareholders in the corporate economy even if, as commentators on employee ownership emphasize, share ownership does not necessarily imply any form of control over corporate activity. Employees may also exert an indirect influence on corporate control through collective bargaining; to the extent that they are successful in wage negotiations, employees can shape the distribution of the benefits from corporate activity. Finally, there may be attempts to protect employees from the adverse effects of corporate actions, such as layoffs, through regulation that places constraints on the extent to and the conditions under which corporations can rationalize operations.

I begin this chapter by asking what is at stake when we consider the role of employees in corporate governance? Over the last two decades, the general tendency

I would like to express my thanks to Bruce Kogut, Bill Lazonick, and Jonas Pontusson for their insightful comments on earlier versions of this chapter.

in the academic literature on corporate governance has been to treat the structure of corporate control as an economic phenomenon. A shareholder perspective on corporate governance has largely dominated that debate, but even as it has come under attack in recent years from theories that emphasize the role of stakeholders, especially employees, in corporate governance, the discussion continues to be preoccupied with issues of economic efficiency (for exceptions, see Jacoby, 2000; Charny, 1999; Pistor, 1999; Roe, 1999; Jackson, 2001).

If one seeks to understand the reality of employees' roles in actual systems of corporate governance, however, it is an analysis of power, rather than one of efficiency, that seems crucial. At the beginning of the 21st century, across the advanced economies, there was a wide variation in employees' roles in systems of corporate governance. In the United Kingdom and the United States, employees had a negligible institutionalized role in the control of corporate activity. Continental Europe, in contrast, remained distinctive for its continued commitment to industrial democracy, encased in law and collective bargaining agreements. Japan had a system of corporate governance that gave employees a much less formal, but still important, influence over corporate decisions, a role that has endured despite the past decade of economic stagnation. These different national patterns largely reflect the legacy of past struggles over the distribution and exercise of corporate power in these countries.

For most economically-advanced countries, employee representation, in enterprises, where it exists, was instituted in the aftermath of World War II. Important elements of the business class in aggressor and occupied countries were discredited through their wartime collaboration with German and Japanese military powers, and the political left was legitimated through its pivotal role in resistance. This historical juncture led to massive institutional changes that shaped the contours of power in the corporate economy in the postwar period, and that exert influence to this day. Any argument that purports to take the subject seriously, therefore, must grapple with the politics of employees' role in corporate governance, a point I illustrate in this chapter using the cases of Germany and the United States (for a comparison of Germany and Japan, see Jackson, 2001, pp. 121–170).

So, politics matters, but how does it matter? Understanding how politics influenced corporate governance, by analyzing the roles of critical junctures, of agency and contingency, of structural features of politics, is necessary for understanding why employees developed or did not develop an institutionalized role in corporate governance in certain countries at particular times. To emphasize the inextricable role of politics in shaping the role of employees in corporate governance, however, is not to deny that economic factors play an important role. On the contrary, I emphasize that the real intellectual challenge in this area is to understand how economic forces interact with politics to shape the possibilities and problems of employees' role in corporate governance. Political arrangements that affect the structure of corporate control may exert an important influence on the structure and dynamics of economic activity. Influence can also go in the other direction as characteristics of the economy shape political ideologies, interests, and action.

Given how far we need to go to understand the politics and economics of employees' role in corporate governance in the past, we can really only speculate about the relevance of the role of employees in corporate governance today and in the future. However, it is difficult to avoid such speculation, given the important political and economic developments that have occurred since existing systems of employee representation were put in place. Will the role of employees in corporate governance be a major issue in the 21st century? Should it? Will institutionalized systems of employee representation in corporate governance fade away for lack of political support? Given the transformations that have occurred in the global economy, would we be better off without them? Is employee representation in corporate governance incompatible with the demands placed on enterprises by technological and market change?

In the conclusion to this chapter, I suggest that there are certainly signs that declining union power in the advanced industrial economies may be undermining the strength of existing institutions of employee representation where they do exist. Looking forward, moreover, there are good reasons to be doubtful that organized labor will be committed and able to augment their capacity to contest the control exercised by employers in the corporate economy. However, and notwithstanding the pervasive corporate rhetoric of employee empowerment, employers' willingness and ability to create substitutes for institutionalized systems of employee representation seem modest at best.

There is little comfort in this analysis for the rest of us. As concerns about the legitimacy and viability of the distribution and exercise of power in the corporate economy have grown, especially in the last few years, the prospects for any concerted and sustained commitment to contest the way in which that power is used and abused seem more limited than ever. Certainly, looking to shareholders or nongovernmental organizations seems far from a panacea for controlling the "princes of industry."

WHAT IS REALLY AT STAKE?

There are a variety of perspectives from which questions of corporate governance can be formulated and addressed, but it has been economic analysis that has largely dominated contemporary discussions of the subject in the academic literature. This is hardly a surprise. Economic analysis is focused on resource allocation: what is to be produced, how it is to be produced, and for whom it is to be produced. Contemporary debates about corporate governance stem, in part, from the recognition by economists of the centrality of corporate enterprises for allocating resources in the economy. From an economic perspective, the central issues to be addressed with respect to corporate governance are the relationship between institutions of corporate governance and the economic performance of corporate enterprises (O'Sullivan, 2000).

Until recently, most economic analyses of corporate governance paid little attention to the question of whether employees ought to have an institutionalized role in these systems. In the 1980s and 1990s, discussions of corporate governance were dominated by an argument that claimed that shareholder interests should be taken as the primary objective for those who run the corporation. From this perspective, the crucial governance institutions that affected economic performance were those that influenced the relationship between managers and shareholders. Employee representation was at best seen as irrelevant to good corporate governance and at worst, as a barrier to it.

That has recently changed. The shareholder theory of corporate governance has been confronted directly on the territory that it carved out for itself—that is, the economics of corporate governance. Of particular importance are arguments for stakeholder governance that are built on an analysis of the role of firm-specific investments in human assets in the success of the enterprise and the prosperity of the economy. Common to these perspectives is a rejection, from an economic perspective, of the maximization of shareholder value and an emphasis on the importance of employees' role (and the role of other stakeholders) in systems of corporate governance (see Blair, 1995; Blair and Stout, 1999; Rajan and Zingales, 1998; Roberts and Van den Steen, 2000; for an approach based on the economics of innovation rather than human capital theory, see O'Sullivan, 2000).

The central concern of this recent research is with what works from an economic perspective in terms of the role of employees and other stakeholders in corporate governance. Implicitly, and in some cases, explicitly, these arguments suggest that the role of employees in actual systems of corporate governance would be a function of economic factors. In other words, employee representation would somehow be chosen in the areas of economic activity in which it is productive.

In moving from this perspective to the reality of employee representation in corporate governance, there is really only one option: to analyze the implications for economic efficiency of alternative approaches to employee representation. Indeed, there is now extensive literature focusing on exactly this issue by addressing questions such as whether or not codetermination is good or bad for economic performance in Germany (see, for example, Sadowski et al., 2000). The analytical and methodological challenges of doing this work are substantial, but there is a much more fundamental problem associated with addressing employee representation in corporate governance as if representation were primarily about economic efficiency. Such an approach abstracts from the fact that in dealing with corporate governance we are essentially dealing with structural features of corporate economies that are inextricably linked to the distribution of power in our societies. In reality, variety and change in employees' role in corporate governance seems to be much more a creature of political conflict and change than economic functionality.

In the discussion that follows I develop this point using an abbreviated historical comparison of the evolution of corporate governance in Germany and the United

States. These two countries differ dramatically in terms of the institutionalized power of employees to influence corporate decision-making. These contemporary differences have much to do with the political crises that presented themselves in the two countries and the ways in which they were resolved.

THE POLITICS OF EMPLOYEES' ROLE IN CORPORATE GOVERNANCE

The compromise on industrial democracy in Germany

The system of corporate governance that was established in the Federal Republic of Germany after World War II and that persists in a unified Germany to this day has become famous (and, in some circles, infamous) for the institutional support that it provides for employee involvement in the decision-making process in German enterprises. Codetermination (*Mitbestimmung*) is typically defined in contemporary discussions of corporate governance in Germany as consisting of two key elements: employee representation on the supervisory board of corporate enterprises, and on works councils that operate at the level of plants and enterprises.

The current system of codetermination was formally put in place in the early 1950s by the government of the Federal Republic Germany (FRG), but the system has deeper historical origins that were marked by intense political struggle. Works councils have existed in Germany since at least the late 19th century, but in these early years they were established and run at the discretion of individual employers and provided little opportunity for workers to really contest employer control over the enterprise. It was not until World War I that works councils were systematically established in the German economy to elicit the cooperation of the country's powerful unions in the wartime production effort.

In the chaos that followed the collapse of the Reich, works councils became the target of a revolutionary movement in Germany as militants established "soviet" councils to take over German industry. Concerned about the possibility of losing control to the radical elements in the labor movement, employers were willing to cede considerable ground to reformist unions. For their part, these unions saw an alliance with employers as a way of containing the militant threat to their own position. In November 1918, employers and unions signed the Stinnes-Legien Agreement, which gave them joint responsibility for determining wages, hours, and working conditions in industry. In addition, the agreement established works councils (*Arbeiterausschüsse*) to facilitate negotiations between workers and management on social issues related to production (Thelen, 1991, p. 67).

However, the consensus on the merits of works councils did not hold for long. In 1920, the German Employers' Association challenged the Works Council Act that was put before the Reichstag, but the law passed despite their opposition (Thelen, 1991, p. 69). However, as employers regained their prewar strength during the 1920s they became more resistant to the demands of their workers. In some cases, they even resisted the institution of works councils in their plants (Thelen, 1991, pp. 66–71).

As the 1920s unfolded and the prevailing climate became increasingly hostile to employee demands, the reformist unions searched for new ways of understanding their position in the Weimar Republic and how they might ameliorate it in the future. These unions were struggling for a third option that might serve as a viable alternative to capitalism and communism. In 1928, the Socialist Trade Union Federation, the ADGB (*Allgemeiner Deutsche Gewerkschaftsbund*), laid out a vision of economic democracy (*Wirtschaftsdemokratie*) at the enterprise, local, regional, and national levels that involved joint decision-making by employers and employee representatives (works councils and unions) (for the intellectual background to this vision, see Beal, 1955; Markovits 1986, p. 67).

When the Nazis took power they dissolved the unions and thus put an end to these aspirations. However, when German labor leaders returned from exile after the defeat of the Nazis, they placed economic democracy at the heart of their political platform. The German unions "demanded full-fledged labor participation on a basis of parity in virtually every aspect of the German economy. This included labor input 'from below' (i.e., at the shop-floor and plant level), 'in the middle' (in the company boardrooms) and 'from above' (via national as well as state-level economic planning agencies which were to guide—if not totally control and/or own—the major segments of the German economy)" (Markovits, 1986, p. 66). These objectives were enshrined in the Munich Programme agreed to by the German Federation of Unions (*Deutscher Gewerkschaftsbund*; DGB) at its first congress on October 13, 1949.

By that time important developments that were to affect the unions' capacity to achieve their demands had already taken place. In the immediate aftermath of World War II, a number of experiments in codetermination came into operation. As early as 1947, union representatives had attained parity representation on the supervisory board of virtually all companies in the coal, iron, and steel industries; the appointment of a union-approved labor director; and the establishment of works councils with considerable powers within the plants. Works councils had also sprung up in many other parts of the economy, as employees organized themselves to get production going again.

Employees achieved these advances in a context in which many German employers found themselves discredited given their collaboration with, or profiteering under, the Nazis. Employee representation, in many cases, was won in exchange for the cooperation of some of these discredited employers in resisting the Allies' intended dismantlement of German industry. In other cases, workers struck to wring codetermination from employers (Markovits, 1986, p. 68).

Codetermination did not, however, experience a smooth transition from Allied to German law in the newly constituted FRG. Immediately after the war, in reaction to the abuse of concentrated power to which, as evidenced during the Nazi period, uncontested managerial control could lead, there had been considerable support for transforming the German system of corporate governance to give employees greater influence.

However, the onset of the Cold War and the perceived importance of the West German economy as a bulwark against the power of the Soviets led to a decline in the commitment to this path. Moreover, with the defeat of the Social Democrats by the Christian Democratic Union (CDU) in the FRG's first elections in 1949 there was a shift to the right in German politics. Finally, employers themselves became more able and willing to resist fundamental changes in corporate governance.

The unions began negotiating with employers in January 1950 to extend the parity codetermination that had been achieved in coal, iron, and steel to the rest of the economy. The employers, however, refused to make any concessions on labor representation within the enterprise. As the political climate changed and with the end of Allied dismantlement of industrial assets in May 1950, even the gains that had already been won in the coal, iron, and steel industry now seemed, as Markovits put it, "a bothersome interference with the managerial prerogatives over the most fundamental aspects of a capitalist order, the rights and responsibilities connected with the ownership of private property" (Markovits, 1986, p. 77). In November 1950, when a leak from the economics ministry revealed that the government was working on a plan to eliminate *Montanbestimmung* (codetermination in the coal and steel industries), it looked as if employers might achieve the rehabilitation of managerial prerogative that they sought.

However, they had not reckoned with the power of the unions to mobilize resistance to such a move. Strike votes revealed overwhelming support among employees for the legal institution of *Montanbestimmung* in the FRG and the Chancellor, Konrad Adenauer, agreed to support the union position. As a result, the Codetermination Act was passed in 1951. It mandated parity worker representation on the supervisory boards of enterprises in the coal, iron, and steel industries *(Montanmitbestimmung)*. It also provided that the labor director in these companies—a member of the management board—could not be appointed against the wishes of the employee representatives.

If the unions managed to win this battle, only one year later they lost the war with respect to the extension of codetermination to the rest of the German economy. When the Works Constitution Act *(Betriebsverfassungsgesetz)* was passed in 1952, it regulated employee representation on the supervisory boards of companies in industries other than the *Montan* industries as well as plant-level representation. It did so in ways that fell so far short of the aspirations of the German labor movement at the time that it was described by the DGB as "a dark moment for democratic development in the Federal Republic" (Markovits, 1986, p. 77).

Enterprises with more than 500 employees were obligated by the Works Constitution Act of 1952 *(Betriebsverfassungsgesetz)* to reserve only one third of the supervisory board seats for employee representatives. The formation of works councils *(Betriebsräte)* was also mandated by the act. Councils were to be elected by all blue-collar and white-collar workers in a plant and were designed to give employees the right to participate in and receive information about the management of the shop floor. Specifically, the 1952 Act gave works councils important codetermination rights over issues such as working hours, piecework rates and bonuses, working conditions, and transfers and dismissals. The act also gave works councils rights to information about personnel planning, financial decisions, and major strategic changes (Müller-Jentsch, 1986, 1995).

The Works Constitution Act was seen as an important setback by German unions, in part because it denied employees parity representation in the German economy other than in the *Montan* industries. However, controversy about the Act largely focused on the fact that works councils were granted exclusive domain over labor representation at the plant level and made formally independent of the unions. Intended by the employers and their political supporters to serve as a counterweight to the political power of the unions, works councils were to cooperate with management to promote the welfare of the company and they were forbidden by law to be involved in strikes. Fearing that labor representation in the FRG would be transformed into a system of "yellow" or pro-enterprise unions that would ultimately undermine labor's political power, German unions stridently opposed the introduction of works councils in the form conceived of in the 1952 Act (Markovits, 1986; Müller-Jentsch, 1995). However, the Act passed despite their opposition.

The unions continued to have a somewhat ambiguous relationship with the works councils through the 1950s and into the early 1960s, but from an early stage the majority of works councilors in the FRG were union representatives (Thelen, 1991, p. 80; Müller-Jentsch, 1995). When the Sozialdemokratische Partei Deutschlands (SPD) finally managed to win a role in government in the late 1960s and the time looked right for reopening the discussion of codetermination, unions took an increased interest in the mechanisms that already existed in plants and enterprises. Moreover, a renewed emphasis on works councils proved politically attractive for another reason—it allowed unions to deal with growing demands for greater democracy within their own organizations (Thelen, 1991, pp. 96–100).

The Codetermination Act of 1972 mandated that all companies with more than 2,000 employees increase employee representation on their supervisory boards from one third to one half of the seats. The position of chairman of the board was required by law to be filled by a shareholder representative; in the event of a tied vote he was granted a double vote. Thus the law continued to tilt the balance of control of the supervisory board in favor of employers. Companies with more than 500 and less than 2,000 employees continued to allocate one third of their supervisory board seats to worker representatives. Many German employers were hostile to the Codetermination Act of 1976 and they challenged it in the Federal Constitutional Court on the grounds that it violated private property rights. The employers' case was, however, overturned.

The institutionalization of employee representation in corporate governance in Germany is fundamentally a story of political crisis. Particularly crucial was the chaotic aftermath of the two World Wars that the Germans waged and lost, as well as the less cataclysmic social crisis of 1968. It is only by understanding these critical junctures that the contemporary position that German employees occupy in the structure of corporate control can be understood.

Of course, the position of German employees is constrained in many ways. The control over resources that labor representatives exercise through their participation on supervisory boards is limited by the restricted role that the board as a whole plays in corporate decision-making. Indeed, there have been suggestions that employers have limited the powers of the supervisory board with a view to further controlling the influence of employees (Gerum et al., 1988). As far as works councils are concerned, their rights are strong with respect to social and personnel matters but weak when it comes to financial and strategic issues (Müller-Jentsch, 1986, 1995). Moreover, the power of the works councils to promote the interests of employees is proscribed by the statutory ban on strikes to enforce workplace demands and the fact that labor representatives, union members or otherwise, are legally bound to act in a manner that promotes the overall health of the enterprise (Müller-Jentsch, 1986, 1995).

Notwithstanding these restrictions, the German system of corporate governance provides more institutional support for the employee's voice in corporate decision-making than in any country in the world. It is true that in other continental European countries there are mechanisms of governance that support a role for employees in corporate resource allocation. In most cases, the origin of these mechanisms bear a close resemblance to that of the German system. However, in all cases, other European systems are much more modest than the German system in what they contemplate in terms of employee involvement.

Whereas many other continental European countries provide for some type of board representation for employees, in no other country does it extend to more than one third of all board seats (Schulten et al., 1998). Works councils, or institutions that resemble them, are also common in Europe, but in most cases, they have rights to consultation and information only, and even then, primarily with respect to social and personnel issues. Besides Germany, works councils have important rights to codetermination primarily in Austria and the Netherlands.

The protection of managerial prerogative in the United States

In the United States, in contrast, there has been no institutionalization of employee representation in corporate governance. While the country was involved in both world wars, it never faced a situation of social and economic chaos in the postwar periods. Nevertheless, these wars, especially World War I, did prompt serious discussions of employee representation in the United States. Moreover, the United States faced its own acute crisis in the form of the Great Depression, and this crisis had decisive implications for the possibilities for employee representation in the US economy, implications which turned out to be quite different, however, from what we have seen in Germany.

As for Germany, World War I proved to be a watershed in the US history of employee representation. In an attempt to encourage the participation of workers in the war effort, the National War Labor Board encouraged the establishment of shop committees—representative bodies voted into office by all employees in a shop or plant—to negotiate with management on matters pertaining to the workplace. Particular attention was focused on firms where labor conflict threatened to disrupt wartime production (Brody, 2001, p. 359).

When the war was over, some employers maintained plant-level representation for employees, mainly with the intention of stifling unionization attempts. There were companies that took a broader view of employee representation, however, seeing it as part of an integrated approach to labor management. This has been described as "welfare capitalism" (Jacoby, 1985, 1997; Lazonick, 1990, ch. 8). While other companies cut back benefit programs to nonmanagerial employees as labor unrest faded, some of these companies maintained, and even strengthened, their programs. Nevertheless, most of the schemes that were put in place in the late teens and 1920s were rather modest in what they contemplated for employee involvement. As Rogers put it: "with the exception of a small number of plans that provided more or less extensive participation rights, including representation on plant committees, representation on boards of directors, and participation in profits and stock ownership or collective bargaining, however, most of these plans gave workers no real power in decision making" (Rogers, 1995, p. 390).

With the Great Depression, the limitations of corporate commitments to workers were thrown into stark relief. The Depression resulted in massive declines in sales, capacity utilization, and employment, especially for the large manufacturing enterprises that sold in the durables markets (Chandler, 1970, pp. 23, 36). The major industrial corporations sought to keep their managerial organizations intact, with the brunt of the massive cutbacks in employment falling on production workers, especially those in mass-production industries who were classified as "semi-skilled." By 1933 production employment in US manufacturing had fallen to 31 percent and wages and salaries to 48.6 percent of their 1929 levels (Chandler, 1970, p. 36).

The economic hardship experienced by workers, as measured by the availability of work, reached a high point in 1933 as the unemployment rate reached 24.9 percent of the labor force, compared with only 3.2 percent in 1929. But high levels of unemployment, although they declined from this peak, persisted for the rest of the 1930s. It was not until 1941, thanks to the wartime economy, that unemployment fell below 10 percent of the labor force (Chandler, 1970, pp. 5–6).

When, during the 1930s, even the most dominant industrial corporations failed to provide shop-floor workers with stable and remunerative jobs, many of these employees turned to industrial unionism to provide them with some control over their futures. Backed by New Deal legislation that protected the rights of workers to organize unions and engage in collective bargaining, shop-floor employees in American manufacturing built powerful mass-production unions that would become a major force in ensuring them employment security and high wages in the post-World War II expansion.

New Deal legislation also had decisive implications for the future of employee representation plans. The National Labor Relations Act (the Wagner Act), passed in 1935, prohibited employer domination of labor organizations, which were defined to include any body that represented employees in negotiations with management over conditions of work. US employers adopted an attitude of outright hostility to employee representation schemes that gave employees more discretion, especially when they saw such schemes as providing unions with an opportunity to interfere with their control over the production process. For example, in attempting to explain the violent reaction by General Motors (GM) management to the United Auto Workers (UAW) strike of 1936–1937, Alfred Sloan later wrote that "what made the prospect [of unionism] seem especially grim in those early years was the persistent union attempt to invade basic management prerogatives. Our rights to determine production schedules, to set work standards and to discipline workers were all suddenly called into question" (Sloan, 1964, p. 406). If, by the mid-1930s, corporate managers finally had to accept that they were required by law to bargain with labor unions in good faith, they took pains to ensure that managerial prerogatives were recognized as beyond the scope of collective bargaining.

As unions became more powerful, discussions among employers of the importance of managerial prerogative and its protection became quite anxious. In 1933, 11.6 percent of the nonagricultural labor force was organized into trade unions; by 1955 the unionization rate had risen dramatically to 33.2 percent. Unions made particularly strong gains during the war years; their membership increased from 26.9 percent in 1940 to 35.5 percent in 1945 (US Bureau of the Census, 1976, p. 178). Moreover, during this period, collective bargaining procedures were institutionalized in key sectors of the US economy, including the automobile, steel, and rubber sectors. The war also provided the impetus for a new wave of employee representation plans, this time in the form of joint management-labor committees, in order to facilitate the war production effort by maintaining labor peace.

Even under conditions of wartime production, however, managerial authority over the production process was not really compromised to any significant degree by collective bargaining or labor-management committees. Nevertheless, as the war ended, many corporate managers spoke of the need to reestablish their unilateral control over corporate activities, control that they claimed had been undermined by labor interests during the war. With the end of the war in sight, unions also began to concern themselves with the preservation and extension of their strength.

"Respectable" unions were not seen as the only threat to management control. A wildcat strike wave from 1942 to 1945 caused serious disruptions across a number of leading industrial sectors, reflecting a surge of shop-floor unrest aimed, not only at managers, but also at union leaders. The union leadership then proved that it had not forgotten how to strike when, during the postwar bargaining rounds of 1946, 1947, and 1948, unions and management fought for advantage. For many, even most, unionists, their increased activism was designed to increase their leverage in negotiating wages and working conditions rather than a signal of their desire to participate in corporate decisions about the allocation of corporate resources. But there were union leaders who wanted to go beyond the field of personnel policy in their negotiations with corporate management (Harris, 1982, pp. 67–74).

One of these union leaders was Walter Reuther of the UAW. He took over as head of the UAW General Motors Department in 1939, and aroused the suspicion and ire of GM management when in 1940 he announced his "500 Planes a Day" plan to produce military planes without disrupting civilian production. What became known as the Reuther Plan generated interest and respect in many quarters but Charles Wilson, the president of GM, was less impressed by Reuther's experiment in "counterplanning from the shop floor up" (Lichtenstein, 1995, p. 162):

> Everyone admits that Reuther is smart but this is none of his business....If Reuther wants to become part of management, GM will be happy to hire him. But so long as he remains Vice-President of the Union, he has no right to talk as if he were Vice-President of a company.
>
> (Janeway, *Struggle for Survival,* New York, Weybright and Talley, 1951, p. 231, cited in Lichtenstein, 1995, p. 166)

When, in the first postwar bargaining round, Reuther attempted to link wage increases to GM's capacity to pay, calling on the company to open its books so that all could see that they could afford higher wages without raising prices to consumers, GM management took it as further evidence of Reuther's desire to violate their rights to control the businesses they ran and they fought back with vehemence. The UAW struck to achieve their demands, but was unsuccessful on all issues related to managerial prerogative:

> Reuther lost on all of the "economic" issues of the strike. He had to move much further from his initial wage demand than GM did from its first wage offer, and he failed utterly in his attempt to introduce corporate pricing policy as a proper subject for bargaining or arbitration. The sovereign power of corporate management to make investment and pricing policy—"the very heart of management judgment and discretion in private industry"—was protected absolutely. GM did not even have to disclose any of the confidential information on which forecasts and decisions were based.
>
> (Harris, 1982, p. 140)

GM was well satisfied with the settlement it won not only for its implications for the economic performance of the company, but also because of the agreement's broader significance:

The corporation had made its point, on behalf of the entire business community, that basic management rights were not negotiable. The scope of collective bargaining had been narrowly confined to wages, hours, and working conditions, and even there the corporation's power to take an initiative in instituting was adequately broad.
(Harris, 1982, p. 143)

Most subsequent collective bargaining agreements followed the lead set by the 1945 UAW-GM contract in incorporating a "right-to-manage" clause. From that time on, industrial unions did not, in general, challenge the principle of management's right to control the development and utilization of the enterprise's productive capabilities. An internal battle was fought over the appropriate agenda for organized labor, but it ended in defeat for the left wing of the US labor movement. The conservative elements of the movement took control and pursued a bargaining strategy that was focused on winning job security, wage increases, and fringe benefits for their members (Lichtenstein, 1982; Schatz, 1983).

The case of the United States also underlines the importance of political crises and their resolution in shaping long-term patterns of employee representation in corporate governance. The demands of wartime production led to experiments with employee representation that provided some opening for a limited contestation of corporate control. However, after these wars, life returned to normal in the United States, a condition that proved a lot more difficult to achieve in Germany, other parts of continental Europe, and Japan, and the US employer opposition to challenges to managerial prerogative became a formidable barrier to institutionalized forms of employee representation.

Notwithstanding this opposition, the US case is notable for the concerted attempts by employers, albeit a small minority of them, to initiate their own employee-representation plans as a substitute for institutionalized plans. Historians have speculated about what the prospects for these plans would have been if the crisis of the Great Depression had not occurred. Some scholars have argued that these employer-initiated plans would have survived and expanded from where they were in the 1920s (Brody, 1980; Kaufman, 2000; Moriguchi, 2000); others see them as an inherently unstable form of governance given the modesty of what they contemplated in terms of participation for employees (Rogers, 1995, p. 392). In any event, the way in which the crisis of labor relations was resolved in the wake of the Great Depression meant that the possibility of continuing with the experience of the 1920s was not available by the late 1930s. Furthermore, employers' fervent resistance to any other form of employee representation was successful, and managerial prerogative remained sacrosanct in the US economy.

HOW DID POLITICS INFLUENCE EMPLOYEE REPRESENTATION?

The history of corporate control in the 20th century underlines the fact that openings for fundamental reform of any type in systems of corporate governance occur infrequently. As far as the role of employees in these systems is concerned, the discussion of Germany and the United States underlines the centrality of political crisis and struggle in giving rise to, or obstructing, an institutionalized role for them in corporate governance. Of course, to say simply that "politics matters" does not help us to understand why certain developments occurred or why they were sustained. In what follows, I suggest, albeit tentatively, different ways in which we might understand the characteristics of the political processes that gave rise to, or blocked, employee representation in corporate governance in different places and at different times.

It is not easy to make any sort of general statement about the actual crises themselves. Indeed, the possibility that each of these crises was *sui generis* or contingent should always be kept in mind as a palliative to academics' wont to see order where none existed. Nevertheless, it does seem that something that makes some general sense can be said about the events that opened up debate on employees' role in corporate governance, even if the comments are neither universal nor comprehensive. Discussions of employees' role in corporate governance have typically taken place when serious questions have been posed about the legitimacy of employer power in the workplace or its effectiveness for achieving societal objectives. Over the course of the 20th century, one can identify four types of circumstances in which this has occurred.

First, serious questions have been raised when employers have been perceived to use their power in ways that advance their own interests at the expense of societal interests. American employers, for example, were seen in this light during the Great Depression. In his presidential acceptance speech in 1932, Franklin Delano Roosevelt laid out his view of what had brought on the Depression, and it was a view that laid responsibility firmly on the shoulders of those who controlled corporate investment decisions; everyone else was portrayed as a victim of their misuse of power.

In the years before 1929 we know that this country had completed a vast cycle of building and inflation....Now it is worth remembering and the cold figures of finance prove it that during that time there was little or no drop in prices...although these same figures proved that the cost of production fell very greatly; corporate profit resulting from this period was enormous...the consumer was forgotten...the worker was forgotten...and the stockholder was forgotten.

(Tugwell, 1968, p. 256).

Second, the legitimacy of employer power has also been challenged, at least in the 20th century, when employers were deemed to have used their power in ways that actively embraced or passively promoted nonliberal values. In the last century, wars

served as the critical catalysts here. World War II, in particular, created a crisis of legitimacy for employers in parts of continental Europe and Japan because of their active or
passive support for militaristic states. Profound suspicion of the merits of systems of corporate governance that provided only modest checks on employer power, was the
immediate result.

Third, since in liberal democracies employers have typically defended the legitimacy of their power in terms of the sanctity of private property, that power has been
called into question when the link between private property and employer power was
weakened. The recognition that a separation between ownership and control had
occurred prompted a famous debate in the United States on the economic, political
and societal implications of the separation (Berle and Means, 1932, p. 356). The implications of a separation of ownership and control in the corporate economy for employer
legitimacy have also been discussed, at various times, in most of the other advanced
industrial economies.

Finally, societal demands for less authoritarian practices within the workplace
have several times led to a concerted attack on employer authority in the enterprise.
The best example here is the social crisis of 1968 in Europe, and the events that led up
to and followed it, which prompted major debates not only about power in the workplace but about many forms of control and their exercise in society. Wars, too, have
often led to a rise in societal expectations with regard to democracy in the workplace,
not least because works councils have often been put in place during these times to
encourage maximum production; in the postwar period, raised expectations often led
to direct attacks on employer power.

A role for employees in corporate governance has only been seriously considered when profound questions have been raised about the legitimacy or effectiveness
of employer power. However, calls for employees to be more involved in corporate
decision-making have not always followed from such questioning. Critics of the institution and exercise of control in the enterprise sector have often looked to other forms
of countervailing power, rather than a transformation of corporate governance, to contest employer control. By the end of World War II in Britain, for example, the ideological commitment by unions and the Labour Party to the nationalization of industry was
much greater than the commitment to employee involvement in the control of industry (Dahl, 1947). Similarly, in Sweden, at least until the early 1970s, much more emphasis was placed on centralized collective bargaining than on industrial democracy as a
countervailing force to employer power (Pontusson, 1992, pp. 161–185). Furthermore,
challenges to the legitimacy of employer power have also been met by ideological
responses from those who exercise control, responses that have often been effective in
staving off more radical criticisms (see, for example, Bendix, 1974).

Even when an employee role in the governance of the corporate sector became
a real possibility, it was typically only successful when the challenge to employer power
was serious enough to constitute a crisis. It seems clear that we cannot understand

the actual evolution of employee representation without an analysis of the character-istics of these "critical junctures" that called into question the legitimacy or effective-ness of the existing balance of power. However, emphasis on the importance of these crises, the process through which they were resolved and their immediate outcomes should not to be taken to imply that patterns of employee representation in corpo-rate governance across country and over time are reducible to these exceptional devel-opments. The way in which these crises were resolved was often surprising due, on the one hand, to the role played by contingent factors and, on the other hand, to the influ-ence of individuals. Furthermore, and in quite a different vein, structural characteris-tics of political life exerted an important influence on patterns of employee represen-tation in corporate governance.

One can identify these patterns in the way in which political actors in different times and places understood the opportunities that critical junctures presented, what they wanted to achieve in the chaos that resulted as well as their capacity to organize themselves to act to achieve their objectives. Furthermore, just because compromises were made in the wake of these crises did not imply that they would actually influence how control was exercised in the corporate economy. Much depended on how differ-ent actors took advantage of, as well as extended and made practically relevant, the compromises that were actually put in place in the wake of critical junctures; once again, the structural characteristics of politics would seem to have played an important role in shaping these developments. In short, as Karl Marx put it in *The Eighteenth Brumaire of Louis Napoleon*: "Men make their own history, but they do not make it as they please; they do not make it under self-selected circumstances, but under circum-stances existing already, given and transmitted from the past."

Scholars have pointed to different types of structural characteristics of politics—characteristics of the nation state, labor movement, and employer class—that may be relevant to understanding patterns of employee representation in corporate governance across countries and over time. Political characteristics of nation states have been given particular prominence in these discussions. Especially common is an argument that dis-tinguishes between the United States and many continental European countries in terms of organized labor's influence in government, and that relates unions' differential role in this regard to patterns of employee representation in corporate governance (see, for example, Rogers, 1995, p. 394; for an alternative approach, see Jackson, 2001). As Jacoby (2000) points out, however, there are some problems with the argument, notably in its consistency with important cases such as the United Kingdom.

There is also much to be learned from attempts to relate employee represen-tation in corporate governance to the strength, ideologies, interests, and organization of unions across countries (see, for example, Huber Stephens and Stephens, 1982). As I have already noted, we certainly cannot assume that unions are necessarily commit-ted to industrial democracy. Moreover, the level of their commitment to workplace representation can change over time.

In a similar way, it may be productive to link the politics of the employer class to the institutionalization or otherwise of employee representation in the corporate sector. This line of inquiry has proven fruitful for political scientists analyzing the rise and evolution of the welfare state as well as certain characteristics of labor markets (Swenson, 1991; Pontusson and Swenson, 1996), and there may also be mileage in the approach for understanding employee representation. Certainly, employers have played a crucial role in influencing the politics of employee representation over time and across countries. What is less clear, however, is whether there are interesting differences in employer attitudes with regard to institutionalized employee representation in corporate decision-making.

The historical record does suggest the prominence, if not unanimity, among employers of an attitude of hostility to any institutionalized role for employees in corporate governance. It is possible that this perception is wrong and that there has been variation across countries and over time in employers' willingness to experiment with giving employees a voice in corporate decisions. Particularly interesting is the question of whether employers learn how to appreciate the benefits of employees' role in corporate governance, as some commentators suggest German employers have, once they have to put up with it. However, it may well be that the unified expression of hostility by employers is real and reflects employers' feeling of the fundamental importance of the issue of managerial prerogative.

THE POLITICAL ECONOMY OF CORPORATE GOVERNANCE

The discussion until now has emphasized the point that analyses of corporate governance that do not deal with the politics of corporate governance are of limited value for understanding the challenges and possibilities of employees' role in corporate governance. However, the importance of political processes for shaping that role does not imply that economic analysis is of no use for understanding the characteristics and implications of the involvement of employees in corporate governance. The real challenge is to understand how political and economic forces interact to shape the possibilities for corporate governance and employees' role within it.

Political arrangements that affect the structure of corporate control may exert an important influence on economic outcomes by facilitating or constraining what is feasible and attractive in terms of economic organization and activity. When employees do not have an institutionalized voice in corporate governance, employers may well forego opportunities for value generation that rely on employees' investing more time and effort than market-based incentives alone would bring forth. In this way, employers' efforts to preserve their own autonomy of action may penalize the rest of society.

A different version of the same argument is more commonly voiced these days. One often hears the claim that an active voice for employees in corporate governance places limits on economic activity by restricting the range of managerial actions that are possible, notably by inhibiting actions such as layoffs that are deemed to be contrary to employees' interests even if they are necessary for economic efficiency. Once again, the vested interests of one group may become pitted against the welfare of the rest.

The above argument is certainly plausible, but it demands a certain critical scrutiny before it is accepted as a general statement. On the one hand, it is not necessarily true that employee representatives will resist actions that affect them adversely if they are deemed to be in the overall interest of the enterprise's survival; to the contrary, one of the economic benefits that Freeman and Lazear associate with works councils is that "councils with rights to information reduce economic inefficiencies by moderating worker demands during tough times" (Freeman and Lazear, 1995, p. 28). In the extensive process of restructuring that has been underway in the German enterprise sector recently, we do see that employers have often been able to win considerable concessions by decentralizing negotiations to the enterprise and plant levels.

In addition, the assumption that liberty of managerial action translates into superior economic performance is a facile one. Managers, like most of us, come in all different shapes and sizes. Some of them are able and motivated by objectives that are tightly linked to the success of the organizations for which they work; many are not, something that was made all too clear recently by the ignominious record of some corporate leaders. Requiring these managers to defend their positions to the ones who they manage and to take seriously employee-initiated solutions to enterprise problems may well make a fruitful contribution to enterprise performance.

In other words, political institutions should not only be seen as constraints on economic opportunities; they can also facilitate such opportunities. This point is increasingly recognized in economics, as part of an institutional turn in the discipline, although it is typically made with reference to legal protections for financial investors. A similar logic can be applied to investments by employees, and indeed it is exactly this point that is the central one in the new theoretical literature on corporate governance that emphasizes the importance of stakeholders' other than financial investors.

It should be emphasized here that in analyzing the relationship between politics and economics, the task is made analytically and empirically complex by the fact that it is difficult to isolate the effects of the presence or absence of institutions of employee representation on economic performance. How employee representation interacts with other institutional elements of a system of corporate governance, such as the structure of financial control, and with broader characteristics of the economic system, such as the institutions that support skill formation, needs to be taken into account. One stream of academic analysis that attempts to capture the influence of political arrangements on economic possibilities using such a systemic approach has been developed by political scientists and economists on "varieties of capitalism." The central point of the approach is that different institutional formations, of which employee representation is one element, facilitate various types of economic possibilities while constraining others. It is difficult to say which of these systems generates superior economic performance—different institutional formations result in strengths in certain types of economic activity and weaknesses in others, but different varieties of capitalism can be associated with overall economic success (see, for example, Albert, 1991; Kogut, 1993; Amable et al., 1997; Hall and Soskice, 2001).

If politics can shape economic possibilities, the structure of an economy as well as its developmental trajectory will undoubtedly influence, even if they are unlikely to determine, the ideologies, interests, and capacity for action of political actors. The argument is, perhaps, most easily illustrated for organized labor. As we have seen, there is evidence of considerable differences between union movements in different countries and at different times in their attitudes to employee representation. It is possible that these attitudes are shaped by cultural and social factors. It is also fruitful, however, to analyze the extent to which these variations reflect differences in the characteristics of the workforce that these unions represent and, in turn, the structure of economic activity within enterprises, across sectors and over time. To be more specific, the role that employees actually occupy in the productive process may exert an important influence on their ideology with respect to employee representation, their interest in achieving it, and their capacity to organize themselves to fight for it. And, over time, structural economic change is likely to lead to important changes in working class politics with respect to employee representation in corporate governance.

IS THE ROLE OF EMPLOYEES IN CORPORATE GOVERNANCE RELEVANT TODAY?

What is the relevance today of these discussions of the political economy of the role of employees in corporate governance? Arguably, given the limits of our understanding of the subject even as we look at it in retrospect, we are in a rather weak intellectual position to reflect on its future. Yet, contemporary debates on corporate governance are happening now, possibilities for reform of existing systems that can be created today may not be available tomorrow, and it is too easy to sit on the fence while all of this passes by.

The scope for organized labor to become a renewed source of countervailing power for employer control in structures of corporate governance seems to be rather modest. Recent political and economic trends seem to have diminished the power of unions and arguably their commitment to extending existing systems of employee representation in the enterprise sector. It does not seem, however, that employers, if left to their own devices, can be relied on to develop viable alternatives to employee representation; rather, they seem to be conforming to their historical practice of introducing only limited involvement of employees in corporate decision-making.

Unions and employee representation in corporate governance

A central theme that runs through comparative historical accounts of corporate governance is the importance of the strength, ideology, and interests of trade unions for the emergence of institutionalized systems of employee representation. Moreover, the support of unions seems to play an important role in supporting the effectiveness of these systems once they have come into existence. In thinking about the future role of employees in governance—both the likely persistence of existing institutions that support such a role as well as the prospects for their extension—the decline in union density in the private sector over the last 20 years in most of the advanced industrial economies would seem to be an ominous trend.

Organized labour plays an important role in institutionalized systems of employee representation in corporate governance in countries where they exist. The vast majority of works council representatives in continental European countries are union members. One would expect, therefore, that to the extent that unions decline their diminishing strength would also be reflected in the composition of employee representatives within the workplace. If we look at the results of works councils elections in Germany and France, we do see important increases in the percentage of the vote accounted for by nonunion councilors at the expense of union members in recent decades, although, it should be noted that for France, that trend would seem to have reversed itself in the 1990s, with unions clawing back some of their losses.

Union decline would seem to have significance, not only for the composition of works councils, but also for the influence and effectiveness of these bodies. A recent study of works councils (*comités d'entreprises*) in France drew a sharp distinction between union-affiliated and nonunion councils:

> Union-affiliated works councils were much more able to make use of all the possibilities of intervention at their disposal, whether intervention towards the employer, particularly concerning economic issues, or in matters concerning social and cultural activities. Non-unionised works councils appeared more fragile, more dependent on the employer and less confident towards the workers themselves.
>
> (Dufour, 1998)

A survey of German works councilors also reveals the importance of union support for works councils, with a majority of councilors expressing a desire for more support in the future (Schulten, 2001). The implications of these findings are that a decline in union representation will have negative implications for the capacity of works councils to undertake their activities effectively.

If there are good reasons to suppose that union strength and weakness will have implications for existing forms of employee representation in corporate governance, the relation between them is more complex than might appear at first glance. Participation rates in voting for employee representatives at the level of the workplace and the enterprise are typically much higher than union density rates (Boeri et al., 2001, p. 82). In other words, employees display higher levels of commitment to these institutions than to unions; there are, therefore, dangers associated with simple extrapolations from union density to the strength of institutions of employee representation in corporate activity.

These extrapolations may be misleading for another reason. As we have seen, at different times and in different places unions have displayed quite varied levels of commitment to employee representation in corporate governance for achieving their objectives. The strength of unions, as measured by density, tells us little about the importance that unions ascribe to these institutions. It is possible that, even as unions have declined, their interests in, and commitment to, using and advancing employee rights to participate in the enterprise may have increased, especially in countries in which workplace rights are strong and therefore worth defending.

However, unions can only support and defend these rights where they already have a membership base. Perhaps the biggest threat to existing systems of employee representation in countries where they are established is the changing composition of the workforce that has made economic activities in which unions have traditionally been weak increasingly important relative to parts of the economy that have been strongholds for union representation. These changes in workforce composition have occurred as a result of sectoral shifts, for example, from manufacturing to services. Occupational change has also been an important factor, with a shift from manual to nonmanual jobs as well as a growing professionalization of the workforce. Finally, changes in the importance of particular types of firms, for example, an increase in the relative importance of small firms, have also been emphasized as important in explaining union decline.

These trends do seem to be relevant in accounting for changes in the coverage of institutions of employee representation as well. In the case of Germany, for example, there has been a noticeable decline in the coverage of codetermination. In 1998, the Commission on Codetermination, funded by the Bertelsmann Foundation and the Hans-Böckler Foundation (Bertelsmann Stiftung and Hans-Böckler-Stiftung, 1998), reported evidence that showed an important drop in the percentage of employees in the private sector that were represented by a supervisory board and/or a works council. Between the mid-1980s and the mid-1990s, the percentage of employees represented by a supervisory board and a works council fell from 30.5 to 24.5 percent, and the percentage represented by a works council only dropped from 18.9 to 15.0 percent. Particularly striking was the fact that, by the mid-1990s, more than 60 percent of all private-sector employees worked in environments where the institutions of codetermination were entirely absent (*mitbestimmungsfreie Zone*). Declining coverage of codetermination is typically attributed to many of the same factors that are invoked to explain union decline, notably the increasing role of small enterprises where the institutions of codetermination have traditionally been weak, as well as structural change in the Germany economy that has favored sectors, especially the service industries, in which traditional forms of worker representation works councils as well as unions have failed to establish a strong foothold (Hassel, 1989, p. 489).

Whether the decline in the coverage of institutions that support employee representation in governance is inevitable is harder to say. As far as employee representation in the enterprise is concerned, we also see some political initiatives to make employee organization easier. In Germany, for example, a major overhaul of the Works Constitution Act in June 2001 was a direct response to the findings and recommendations of the Commission on Codetermination. Of particular importance was the fact that it simplified the procedures for the election of works councils, a move that is predicted to increase the prevalence of these councils in small- and medium-sized enterprises (Behrens, 2001).

Even when these reforms take place, however, they tend to focus more on defending what is there than with expanding employee rights to participate in workplace decisions. Behrens draws attention to this fact by contrasting the recent reform to the Works Constitution Act with the last major reform in 1972: "In 1972, the left-wing government and the unions jointly sought to bring democracy and participation to the shop floor and thus planned to improve the quality of representation. Today, however, it is a major goal of the new works council reform to keep co-determination from deteriorating" (Behrens, 2001).

The real question for the future is whether the labor movement will have the interest and impetus to extend what is there already. It is in fact very hard to see where such an initiative would come from either today or in the near future. That conclusion, moreover, does not seem to depend on assuming that union decline will continue. Even if unions manage to revitalize themselves by appealing to new members in sectors where they have previously been poorly represented—and there are signs of success in this regard—it is not clear that employee representation will have the kind of appeal that it needs to be a rallying force across sectors, occupations, and firms. The realities of, and possibilities for, workplace control may simply be too diverse across all of these different contexts for it to be used in this way and, as a result, bread-and-butter issues may be a much more effective base for union organizing in areas where union strength has thus far been weak.

Employers and employee representation in corporate governance

Employers and their representative associations often argue that the notion of an institutionalized voice for employees in corporate governance is outdated. Current institutions are seen as the legacy of a past that was fundamentally different from the present in terms of relations between employers and employees. The future may well have a role for employee representation in corporate decision-making, but, it is often claimed, that role needs to be a flexible one that can be adapted to the exigencies of particular enterprises operating in rapidly-changing competitive and technological environments. From this perspective, institutionalized systems of employee representation in corporate governance are too rigid. Employee representation in the workplace and the enterprise must be, to a much greater extent, at the discretion of employers.

This ideology is translated into action in different ways. Some commentators emphasize the importance of employers' use of the "iron fist," a strategy of hard-line opposition to challenges to their managerial prerogatives. Others point to employers' use of the "velvet glove," a softer approach that offers employees alternatives to institutionalized systems of representation for having an influence on corporate decisions. To the extent that these strategies of "suppression" and "substitution" are effective, they are likely to make mechanisms for employee representation that are autonomous of employer discretion more difficult to institute than before.

Certainly, it does appear that employers' willingness to confront the power of unions in the workplace and, at least in some countries, even to undermine their existence, has increased in recent years (for the US case, see Human Rights Watch, 2000). To the extent that employers' strategies are successful, they are likely to have a negative indirect effect on institutions of employee representation, given the latter's dependence on union support for their effectiveness. That employers are displaying increased resistance to unions does not, however, imply that they are directly trying to undermine institutionalized forms of workplace representation. In countries where employee representation is strong, employers are typically quite cautious about expressing outright opposition to it if, for no other reason, than to avoid the backlash that it might generate. In addition, employers may well see these representative bodies in a more favorable light than unions. They may even regard a relative increase in the influence of employee representation at the enterprise level as a way of undermining or preempting union influence.

Where the hostility of employers typically manifests itself, however, is in reaction to attempts to augment institutional support for employee voice in corporate governance. The implacable opposition of the European employers' organization, Union of Industrial and Employers' Confederations of Europe (UNICE), to the European Works Council directive is a case in point. The president of UNICE portrayed the directive as "an extremely expensive and damaging measure" and claimed that it would undermine the competitive position of enterprises operating in Europe "by seriously delaying companies' freedom to take vital decisions in good time" (quoted by Knutsen, 1997, pp. 297–298). Similarly, German employers, in reaction to the recent reform of the legal framework for works councils, have recently voiced vociferous opposition.

Besides greater employer use of tough tactics, one can also identify attempts to undermine institutionalized forms of employee representation through substitution. Certainly, there is a widespread, even pervasive, use of the rhetoric of employee involvement in enterprises today. However, as far as the reality of what employers have done to really change employees' role in corporate decision-making, the picture is much less clear-cut.

Most of what we know about the contemporary use by employers of employee involvement comes from studies of "high-performance workplaces." Surveys show that there has been considerable diffusion of "innovative work practices" such as quality circles, job rotation, teams, and total quality management in the advanced industrial economies. However, many companies—in some countries, a majority of them—have not adopted any of these practices and most of the adopters employ these practices in a piecemeal way, notwithstanding evidence that the practices work effectively only when used systemically. As far as the employee representation dimension is concerned, moreover, empirical evidence suggests that the level of employee involvement is extremely modest even in companies that adopt these practices (see, for example, Appelbaum et al., 2000; Osterman, 2000; Coriat, 2002).

To describe the trends that we see in employer strategies toward employee participation does not, of course, tell us how they might affect economic performance. It is plausible, as employers contend, that institutionalized forms of employee representation in the workplace are too rigid in an increasingly competitive environment. Where you come down on this debate is largely a function of how much flexibility you think enterprises need to be competitive and, more precisely, what type of flexibility they need.

There is an ongoing debate in the academic literature on the implications of intensified competition, and the technological and market change that it implies, for organizational flexibility. What has emerged from this discussion is the importance of distinguishing between two different types of organizational flexibility: the functional flexibility that comes from "enhancing employees' ability to perform a variety of jobs and participate in decision-making", and the numerical flexibility that operates by "reducing costs by limiting workers' involvement in the organisation" (Kalleberg, 2001). In terms of empirical evidence, we actually know very little about how these two organizational strategies affect enterprise performance. If anything, there is more evidence on performance enhancements associated with functional flexibility than numerical flexibility. There is, in fact, a small but important body of literature on the negative effects of downsizing on organizational performance that suggests that emphasis on numerical flexibility may actually undermine the possibilities for performance improvement offered by functional flexibility. Nevertheless, when employers talk about the potential rigidities of employee involvement, they often speak as if maintaining numerical flexibility was clearly a criterion for doing good business. At least in public policy discussions, that position should be treated with some skepticism while we lack the evidence to be sure of this position.

CONCLUSION

Will employee representation in corporate governance be a major political issue in the future? Is there enough employee representation in the corporate sector today and will it be adequate for the future? Will employees get as much representation as they want and will society get as much as it needs?

I have argued that it is difficult to see the source of political momentum for an enhanced role for employees in corporate governance in the future. That does not imply, however, that this augurs well for employees or society. Indeed, I have suggested that some of the economic arguments that have been used by employers to contest an institutionalized role for employees in corporations depend on assumptions about what intensified competition implies for organizational change, and that such assumptions are open to question. From a political perspective, moreover, it is clear that questions about the legitimacy and effectiveness of employer control have not gone away. It is perhaps too much to say that we may be on the verge of a crisis in this regard, although a few more scandals on the scale of what we have already seen may well tip that balance.

Yet even if a political opening for serious change in corporate governance were to appear, even if a noticeable shift in the balance of power over the allocation of corporate resources was to be contemplated (as it might be in such a crisis), it is not at all clear that such a shift would involve an increased role for employees in corporate governance. In dealing with the fallout from what has already happened, what is striking is the absence of discussion of an enhanced role for employees in averting future scandals.

Most commentators are looking either to an augmented role for shareholders and/or to nongovernmental organizations in the system of corporate governance in order to prevent a recurrence of what we have seen. There are, in fact, serious limits to such "solutions" to any crisis of corporate legitimacy and effectiveness. The scope to develop countervailing power on the basis of these groups is rather weak. In theory, shareholders have an interest in contesting unbridled managerial control, but in practice, shareholders' willingness and ability to organize themselves to effect change seem to be extremely modest. As far as nongovernmental organizations are concerned, their commitment to sustained involvement with the corporate sector to effect change would seem to be limited by the very fact that they are not interest groups; moreover, and as with shareholders, we may also question whether they know enough about the activities of particular corporations to contest how control is exercised within them.

In short, when we analyze the abilities and incentives of these groups to transform corporate governance, there is clearly nothing approaching a panacea to the problems that we confront today. Arguably, from the perspective of their abilities and incentives to influence corporate activity, employees represent a much more promising basis for corporate governance reform than shareholders and nongovernmental organizations. However, contemporary political trends pose a major obstacle to their playing a more important role in corporate governance in advanced industrial economies. If history repeats itself, the only way we will get around this obstacle is if the crisis in confidence in the legitimacy or efficacy of employers' control over the corporate sector gets much more serious. How uplifting it would be if, in contrast, we could learn enough from history to make some new mistakes in the field of employee representation, rather than slavishly repeating old mistakes.

REFERENCES

Albert, M. 1991. *Capitalisme contre Capitalisme*. Paris: Seuil.

Amable, B., R. Barre, and R. Boyer. 1997. "Les systemes d'innovation à l'ere de la globalisation," Paris: Economica.

Appelbaum, E., T. Bailey, P. Berg, and A. Kalleberg. 2000. *Manufacturing Advantage: Why High-Performance Work Systems Pay Off*. Ithaca, NY: Cornell University Press.

Beal, E. 1955. "Origins of Codetermination," *Industrial and Labor Relations Review* 8, pp. 483–498.

Behrens, M. 2001. *Works Constitution Act Reform Adopted*. European Industrial Relation Observatory On-line. http://www.eiro.eurofound.ie/2001/07/feature/DE0107234F.html.

Bendix, R. 1974. *Work and Authority in Industry: Ideologies of Management in the Course of Industrialization*. Berkeley, CA: University of California Press.

Berle, A., and G. Means. 1932. *The Modern Corporation and Private Property*. New York: Macmillan.

Bertelsmann Stiftung, and Hans-Böckler-Stiftung, eds. 1998. *Mitbestimmung und neue Unternehmenskulturen: Bilanz und Perspektiven. Bericht der Kommission Mitbestimmung*. Gütersloh: Bertelsmann Stiftung.

Blair, M. 1995. *Ownership and Control: Rethinking Corporate Governance for the Twenty-First Century*. Washington, DC: Brookings Institution.

Blair, M., and M. Roe, eds. 1999. *Employees and Corporate Governance*. Washington, DC: Brookings Institution.

Blair, M., and L. Stout. 1999. "A Team Production Theory of Corporate Law," *Virginia Law Review* 85, pp. 247–328.

Boeri, T., A. Brugiavini, and L. Calmfors. 2001. *The Role of Unions in the Twenty-First Century*. Oxford: Oxford University Press.

Brody, D. 1980. "The Rise and Decline of Welfare Capitalism." In D. Brody, ed., *Workers in Industrial America: Essays on the Twentieth Century*. New York: Oxford University Press.

Brody, D. 2001. "Why No Shop Committees in America: A Narrative History," *Industrial Relations* 40, pp. 356–376.

Chandler, L. 1970. *America's Greatest Depression, 1929–1941*. New York: Harper & Row.

Charny, D. 1999. "Workers and Corporate Governance: The Role of Political Culture." In M. Blair and M. Roe, eds., *Employees and Corporate Governance*. Washington, DC: Brookings Institution.

Coriat, B. 2002. "Employee Participation and Organisational Change in European Firms," CEPN-IIDE Working Paper. Paris: Centre d'Economie de l'Université Paris Nord and International/ Intercultural Development of Education.

Dahl, R. 1947. "Workers' Control of Industry and the British Labor Party," *American Political Science Review* 41, pp. 875–900.

Dufour, C. 1998. *Works Council Survey Reveals Major Differences in Practice*. European Industrial Relations Observatory On-line. http://www.eiro.eurofound.ie/1998/04/Feature/FR9804101F.html

Freeman, R., and E. Lazear. 1995. "An Economic Analysis of Works Councils." In J. Rogers and W. Streeck, eds., *Works Councils: Consultation, Representation, and Cooperation in Industrial Relations*. Chicago: University of Chicago Press.

Gerum, E., H. Steinmann, and W. Fees. 1988. *Der Mitbestimmte Aufsichtsrat: Eine Empirische Untersuchung*. Stuttgart: C. E. Poeschel.

Hall, P., and D. Soskice. 2001. *Varieties of Capitalism: The Institutional Foundations of Comparative Advantage*. Oxford: Oxford University Press.

Harris, H. J. 1982. *The Right to Manage: Industrial Relations Policies of American Business in the 1940s*. Madison, WI: University of Wisconsin Press.

Hassel, A. 1999. "The Erosion of the German System of Industrial Relations," *British Journal of Industrial Relations* 37, pp. 483–505.

Huber Stephens, E., and J. Stephens. 1982. "The Labor Movement, Political Power, and Workers' Participation in Western Europe," *Political Power and Social Theory* 3, pp. 215–249.

Human Rights Watch. 2000. *Unfair Advantage: Workers' Freedom of Association in the United States under International Human Rights Standards*. Washington, DC: Human Rights Watch.

Jackson, G. 2001. "The Origins of Nonliberal Corporate Governance in Germany and Japan." In W. Streeck and K. Yamamura, eds., *The Origins of Nonliberal Capitalism: Germany and Japan in Comparison*. Ithaca, NY: Cornell University Press.

Jacoby, S. 1985. *Employing Bureaucracy: Managers, Unions, and the Transformation of Work in American Industry, 1900–1945*. New York: Columbia University Press.

Jacoby, S. 1997. *Modern Manors: Welfare Capitalism since the New Deal*. Princeton, NJ: Princeton University Press.

Jacoby, S. 2000. "Corporate Governance in Comparative Perspective: Prospects for Convergence," *Comparative Labor Law and Policy Journal* 22, pp. 5–32.

Kalleberg, A. 2001. "Organizing Flexibility: The Flexible Firm in a New Century," *British Journal of Industrial Relations* 39, pp. 479–504.

Kaufman, B. 2000. "The Case for the Company Union," *Labor History* 41, pp. 321–350.

Knutsen, P. 1997. "Corporatist Tendencies in the Euro-Polity: The EU Directive of 22 September 1994, on European Works Councils," *Economic and Industrial Democracy* 18, pp. 289–323

Kogut, B. 1993. *Country Competitiveness: Technology and the Organization of Work*. Oxford: Oxford University Press.

Lazonick, W. 1990. *Competitive Advantage on the Shop Floor*. Cambridge, MA: Harvard University Press.

Lichtenstein, N. 1995. *The Most Dangerous Man in Detroit: Walter Reuther and the Fate of American Labor*. New York: Basic Books.

Markovits, A. 1986. *The Politics of the West German Trade Unions: Strategies of Class and Interest Representation in Growth and Crisis*. Cambridge: Cambridge University Press.

Moriguchi, C. 2000. "The Evolution of Employment Relations in U.S. and Japanese Manufacturing Firms, 1900–1960: A Comparative Historical and Institutional Analysis," NBER Working Paper 7939. Cambridge, MA: National Bureau of Economic Research.

Müller-Jentsch, W. 1986. *Soziologie der industriellen Beziehungen: Eine Einführung*. Frankfurt: Campus-Verlag.

Müller-Jentsch, W. 1995. "Germany: From Collective Voice to Co-Management." In J. Rogers and W. Streeck, eds., *Works Councils: Consultation, Representation, and Cooperation in Industrial Relations*. Chicago: University of Chicago Press.

O'Sullivan, M. 2000. *Contests for Corporate Control: Corporate Governance and Economic Performance in the United States and Germany*. Oxford: Oxford University Press.

Osterman, P. 2000. "Work Reorganization in an Era of Restructuring: Trends in Diffusion and Effects on Employee Welfare," *Industrial and Labor Relations Review* 53, pp. 179–196.

Pistor, K. 1999. "Codetermination: A Sociopolitical Model with Governance Externalities." In M. Blair and M. Roe, eds., *Employees and Corporate Governance*. Washington, DC: Brookings Institution.

Pontusson, J. 1992. *The Limits of Social Democracy: Investment Politics in Sweden*. Ithaca, NY: Cornell University Press.

Pontusson, J., and P. Swenson. 1996. "Labor Markets, Production Strategies, and Wage Bargaining Institutions: The Swedish Employer Offensive in Comparative Perspective," *Comparative Political Studies* 29, pp. 223–250.

Rajan, R., and L. Zingales. 1998. "Power in a Theory of the Firm," *Quarterly Journal of Economics* 108, pp. 387–432.

Roberts, J., and E. Van den Steen. 2000. "Shareholder Interests, Human Capital and Corporate Governance," GSB Research Paper No. 1631. Stanford, CA: Stanford University.

Roe, M. 1999. "Codetermination and German Securities Markets." In M. Blair and M. Roe, eds., *Employees and Corporate Governance*. Washington, DC: Brookings Institution.

Rogers, J. 1995. "United States: Lessons from Abroad and Home." In J. Rogers and W. Streeck, eds., *Works Councils: Consultation, Representation, and Cooperation in Industrial Relations*. Chicago: University of Chicago Press.

Rogers, J., and W. Streeck, eds. 1995. *Works Councils: Consultation, Representation, and Cooperation in Industrial Relations*. Chicago: University of Chicago Press.

Sadowski, D., J. Junkes, and S. Lindenthal. 2000. "The German Model of Corporate and Labor Governance," *Comparative Labor Law and Policy Journal* 22, pp. 33–66.

Schatz, R. 1983. *The Electrical Workers: A History of Labour at General Electric and Westinghouse, 1923–60*. Champaign, IL: University of Illinois Press.

Schulten, T. 2001. *Survey Examines Industrial Relations at Establishment Level in 1999/2000*. European Industrial Relations Observatory On-line. http://www.eiro.eurofound.ie/2001/02/Feature/DE0102208F.html

Schulten, T., S. Zagelmeyer, and M. Carley, 1998. *Board-level Employee Representation*. European Industrial Relations Observatory On-Line. http://www.eiro.eurofound.ie/1998/09/study/TN9809201S.html

Sloan, A. 1964. *My Years with General Motors*. New York: Doubleday.

Swenson, P. 1991. "Bringing Capital Back In, or Social Democracy Reconsidered: Employer Power, Cross-class Alliances and Centralization of Industrial Relations in Denmark and Sweden," *World Politics* 43, pp. 513–544.

Thelen, K. 1991. *Union of Parts: Labor Politics in Postwar West Germany*. Ithaca, NY: Cornell University Press.

Tugwell, R. 1968. *The Brains Trust*. New York: Viking Press.

Vincent, C. 2002. *Research Examines Employee Representation*. European Industrial Relations Observatory On-Line. http://www.eiro.eurofound.ie/2002/01/Feature/FR0201111F.html

US Bureau of the Census. 1976. *The Statistical History of the United States: From Colonial Times to the Present*. New York: Basic Books.

Chapter 6

Venture Capital and Corporate Governance

Franklin Allen and Wei-ling Song

In the United States, venture capital has been particularly important in many new industries at the initial stage. It accounts for about two thirds of the private-sector external equity financing of high-technology firms (see Freear and Wetzel, 1994). Venture capital differs from standard forms of financing in that there is a much greater involvement of the providers of funds than is the case with other forms of lending (such as bank loans) in an attempt to avoid the problems arising from asymmetric information. Lenders are also concerned about resolving the uncertainty of cash flows. The absence of collateral means they cannot simply leave the entrepreneurs to their own devices—they must ensure that resources are not squandered if they are to try and earn a return on their investment. They provide finance in stages to ensure that option value is maximized. As Kaplan and Strömberg (2002) have documented, these characteristics of venture capital mean that the contractual arrangements for venture capital are much more complex than for most types of finance. Typically they involve both sides receiving part of the upside potential of the project—in other words, they have equity-type characteristics.

Venture capitalists typically provide finance for a limited period of time. If a firm is successful, its needs for capital rapidly outstrip the capacity of limited partnerships that are the usual providers of venture capital in the United States. An important exit mechanism for venture capitalists is an initial public offering (IPO) of the company. Even though IPOs are costly in a number of ways, they often represent the best means for initial investors to obtain a return. Another common exit mechanism is outright sale of the startup to a large firm.

The venture capital industry has prospered most in the United States and the vast majority of the academic literature has been concerned with the United States. In a cross-country study of venture capital, Jeng and Wells (2000)—using data from 1986 to 1995 for 21 countries—document that venture capital is less important in other countries than it is in the United States. Their main finding is that the existence of an active IPO market is the most important determinant of the importance of venture capital in a country. This is consistent with the finding of Black and Gilson (1998) in a comparison of the United States and Germany, that the primary reason venture capital is relatively successful in the United States is the active IPO market that exists there.

As the next section documents, it took some time before a widely used contractual and institutional framework for venture capital became established in the United States. This framework, together with the complexity of the contract forms and the staging of finance, suggests that corporate governance is a crucial component of venture capital. In this chapter we consider the relationship between venture capital and corporate governance using data on venture capital from 33 countries during the 1990s. Whereas Jeng and Wells (2000) included only 4 Asian countries, our data set includes 16. The data we use to measure corporate governance come from La Porta et al. (1998). Our main findings are as follows.

First, corporate governance plays a different role in venture capital than it does in the public equity and bond markets. The variable measuring law and order is *negatively* related to the importance of venture capital finance. In other words, countries with less law and order have a higher degree of venture capital. This is in marked contrast to the findings of La Porta et al. (1997) with regard to the public markets, where the opposite relationship holds, indicating that explicit contracts are not as important as the conventional wisdom suggests. In fact, implicit relationships appear to provide a good substitute, allowing venture capital to fill the gap for the public markets. More in line with conventional wisdom, creditor rights are significant in determining the amount of venture capital in the market.

Second, the allocation of investment across different stages of finance and different industries depends more on macroeconomic factors than on corporate governance variables.

Third, in Low-GDP countries, venture capital is more important for low-technology industries than for high technology industries.

Fourth, venture capital boomed and became significant in many countries during the stock market boom or "bubble" of the late 1990s.

Finally, a comparison of Asian and European venture capital shows that in Asia there was more investment in early-stage projects, while in Europe there was more investment in late-stage projects. In Europe there was also more investment in medical and biotechnology industries.

In the next section, we document the way in which venture capital developed and operates in the United States. The following section describes the data and variables we use; then we investigate the role of corporate governance in determining the importance of venture capital across countries, and the final section concludes.

VENTURE CAPITAL IN THE UNITED STATES

Many high-technology companies in the United States have initially been funded with venture capital.[1] Although venture capital has been used for over 50 years, it is only in the last 20 years or so that it has become a significant source of funds for new companies. American Research and Development (ARD), which was founded in 1946, was the first modern US venture capital firm. It was a publicly traded, closed-end investment company. Initially, ARD was not particularly successful; it did not attract institutional investors in the way that its founders had hoped. Eventually it was profitable but not spectacularly so, providing investors with a 15.8 percent annual return over its 25 years as an independent firm, compared with 12.8 percent on the Dow Jones over the same period. A large proportion of this return came from a USD 70,000 investment in Digital Equipment Corporation; without it, the return to investors would have been only 7.4 percent.

Private venture capital companies were established to manage the investments of wealthy individuals, but because of ARD's lack of success, there were no publicly traded venture capital firms founded until Small Business Investment Companies (SBICs) were established under the Small Business Investment Act of 1958. These are tax-advantaged corporations licensed by the Small Business Administration (SBA) to provide professionally managed capital to risky companies. One of the main advantages that SBICs had was access to low-cost SBA loans. The SBIC program suffered from a number of difficulties, including a lack of institutional investors and investment managers who were not the most talented. Despite these problems, SBICs did succeed in channeling many more funds to startup companies than ARD had done.

In the late 1970s, there were a number of important changes that allowed venture capital to start growing dramatically. The first was a change in the US Labor Department's interpretation of the "prudent man" provision of the Employee Retirement Income Security Act (ERISA). This had traditionally been interpreted as ruling out investments in new companies or venture capital funds. However, in 1978 a proposal was made to allow such investments, provided the entire portfolio was not endangered; this proposal was adopted the following year.

The second change was the reduction in maximum capital gains tax rates, from 49.5 percent to 28 percent in 1978 and to 20 percent in 1981.

The third important change was the start of the widespread use of limited partnerships as the investment form. Prior to the 1980s, only a small fraction of venture capital investments were structured in this way. During the 1980s and 1990s, however, over 80 percent of the capital committed to venture capital was in this form.

The limited partnership form has a number of advantages. Among these advantages is the fact that the partnership's income is not subject to the corporate income tax. When a partnership distributes securities, they are not taxed until they are sold. To qualify for these and other advantages several conditions must be met:

- A fund's life must have a predetermined finite lifetime.

- The transfer of limited partnership units is restricted so they cannot be easily bought and sold.

- It is not possible to withdraw from the partnership before the termination date.

- In order to preserve their limited liability, limited partners cannot participate in the day-to-day management of the fund.

The typical life of funds is ten years, with extensions from one to three years allowed. The fourth limitation means that the venture capitalists that run the fund are general partners and bear unlimited liability. The funds usually do not borrow or engage in activities that expose them to large liabilities, however, so this is not an important restriction.

An important aspect of venture capital contracts is the way in which the venture capitalists are compensated. There are typically two components to this: a fixed fee and share of the profits. The fixed component is usually between 1.5 percent and 3 percent of net asset value, and the other component is around 20 percent of the profits.

Venture capital investment involves a number of stages.[2] Venture capitalists may provide funds for all or some of these stages. The basic document governing the relationship between the venture capital firm and the company in which they are investing is the *stock-purchase agreement*. This specifies the amount and timing of the investment in the company. Usually, the amount invested grows through time. At each stage the amount invested is expected to carry the firm through until the next stage. By staging the financing in this way, the venture capitalists can maximize the option value of the investment by making sure the correct continuation decision is made.

The form of security that is usually used in venture capital investments is *convertible preferred stock*. The important parameters for these are:

- the conversion price, which can be contingent on firm performance;

- liquidation preferences, including a description of the events that trigger liquidation; and

- dividend rate, payment terms, and voting rights (typically on an as-if-converted basis).

The convertible preferred typically does not pay a dividend on a current basis, but at the discretion of the board of directors. Sometimes the dividends accrue and are not paid in cash, but the liquidation preference entitles the holders to the face value and the accrued dividends.

The agreements between venture capitalists and the firm typically have a number of other components. Venture capitalists can usually call for the redemption of the preferred stock. They also often have preemptive rights and rights of first refusal if new stock is issued. Key employees are often required to execute employment contracts with noncompetition clauses. Employees in startups accept low salaries in return for some kind of equity interest, and the vesting of shares is often laid out in the agreements. Finally, the agreements usually specify extensive access to information such as monthly financial statements, frequent operating statements, and the right to inspect at will.

The evidence in this section suggests that venture capital requires a quite specific contractual and institutional framework to become a significant means of funding. The complexity of the contractual forms and the role of stage financing also suggest that corporate governance is an important factor in venture capital, at least in the United States. We next go on to consider the importance of corporate governance in other countries.

DATA AND VARIABLES

Sample selection

Venture capital information on 33 countries during the decade of the 1990s is obtained from the *2001 Yearbook of National Venture Capital Association* (NVCA) for the United States, *The 2002 Guide to Venture Capital in Asia* (*Asian Venture Capital Journal*, or AVCJ) for Asian countries, and various *Yearbooks* of the European Private Equity and Venture Capital Association (EVCA) for European countries.[3] Because the focus of this chapter is on the relationship between corporate governance and venture capital, we use the list of countries in La Porta et al. (1998), which provides governance information on 49 countries, as the starting point. We then match this list with venture capital information available to us. This screening produces a sample that contains 32 countries. We add China and obtain governance information from Allen, Qian, and Qian (2002). All other macro indicators were downloaded from the World Bank online database except Taiwan, which is obtained from the National Statistics Bureau of Executive Yuan of the Republic of China. Legal origin information for each country is also obtained from La Porta et al. (1998). China is not classified based on legal origin.

Because of information availability, we left out Canada and all South American and African countries. Among these countries, only Canada has average real GDP per capita (measured in constant 1995 US dollars) above USD 10,000 during the 1990s. The remainder all have GDP per capital of less than USD 10,000. They are likely to have fewer venture capital activities than more-developed countries. Although many developing countries are left out in our study, we still retain 8 developing countries in Asia in our sample, which we classified as the *Low-GDP group*. Among the remaining countries, 12 having GDP per capita above USD 25,000 are defined as the *High-GDP group*; this group comprises the United States, Japan, and 10 European countries. The rest of the countries considered are the 13 countries in the *Mid-GDP group*, which includes some European countries, Israel, New Zealand, Australia, and the 4 newly industrialized "little dragons" in Asia: Hong Kong, Singapore, South Korea, and Taiwan.

Variables and descriptive statistics

There is no standardized format for reporting information among the three trade associations: AVCJ, EVCA, and NVCA. Therefore, a detailed description of variable definition is necessary to ensure consistency and to facilitate interpretation of the results.

Three proxies are employed to examine the level of venture capital activities. They are venture capital investment portfolio (VCIP), annual new funds raised, and total annual disbursements.[4] Most of the countries have information on VCIP from 1993 to 2000; the information on the remaining two variables are available from 1994 to 2000. We also examine the growth rates of venture capital activities. However, none of the independent variables in this study could explain the growth rates across countries; thus, we do not report the results.

Venture capital investment portfolio for Asian countries is the cumulative total of existing investments less any divestments made as defined by AVCJ. That for European countries is the "Portfolio at Cost" on December 31 reported by EVCA. NVCA does not report VCIP, thus, "Capital under Management" is used as the proxy for VCIP for the United States. Note that capital under management includes total capital available for investment plus cumulative investment portfolio currently held. As will be discussed later, the venture capital information from NVCA is not directly comparable with that from the other two trade associations in many ways. In addition, economically, the venture capital industry in the United States has a much longer history and is more developed than others. As a robustness check, all the analyses were repeated without US data. The findings are essentially unchanged and thus are not reported.

Table 6.1 reports VCIP in 1993 and 2000 in two measures: in constant 1995 US dollars in millions and as a percentage of GDP. Geometric average growth rates for both measures during this period are also reported. The last column shows the average real GDP per capita in 1995 US dollars during 1991 to 2000, which is used to classify countries' economic development into High-GDP, Mid-GDP, and Low-GDP groups. From Panels A and B of Table 6.1, one can see that most of the Asian countries started with few venture capital activities in 1993 but European countries had higher levels in place. However, both regions grew dramatically during the 1990s with an average growth rate of 33 percent for Asia and that of 24 percent for Europe (Column 6 of Panel D, % GDP based). These two numbers are insignificantly different due to big variation among countries in each region. The average growth rate for the United States is also 24 percent.

TABLE 6.1   **Level and Growth of Venture Capital Investment Portfolio by Country**

COUNTRY	VCIP IN 1993 (USD)	VCIP IN 2000 (USD)	%CAGR (USD)	VCIP IN 1993 (% GDP)	VCIP IN 2000 (% GDP)	%CAGR (%GDP)	GDPPC (USD)
PANEL A. Asia							
Australia	1,268	2,650	11	0.37	0.58	7	21,159
China	429	4,051	38	0.08	0.39	26	602
Hong Kong SAR	—	9,027	24	—	5.48	20	22,145
India	111	1,618	47	0.04	0.35	38	388
Indonesia	41	161	22	0.02	0.08	18	982
Israel	—	4,614	50	—	4.34	44	15,672
Japan	7,359	11,420	6	0.14	0.20	5	42,776
Malaysia	91	549	29	0.12	0.49	22	4,213
New Zealand	1	309	117	0.00	0.46	111	16,189
Pakistan	0	11	122	0.00	0.02	115	494
Philippines	30	221	33	0.04	0.25	28	1,100
Singapore	859	4,484	27	1.24	3.95	18	23,392
South Korea	1,629	7,312	24	0.39	1.18	17	10,768
Sri Lanka	14	45	18	0.12	0.27	12	731
Taiwan	505	3,525	32	0.22	1.29	29	11,893
Thailand	80	447	28	0.06	0.26	24	2,652
PANEL B. Europe							
Austria	14	317	56	0.01	0.12	52	29,831
Belgium	1,072	2,776	15	0.41	0.88	11	27,759
Denmark	208	681	18	0.13	0.33	15	34,853
Finland	100	1,045	40	0.08	0.63	33	26,813
France	5,533	19,818	20	0.37	1.13	17	27,363
Germany	4,313	15,132	20	0.18	0.56	17	30,406
Greece	—	309	96	—	0.22	90	11,665
Ireland	263	630	13	0.46	0.60	4	19,972
Italy	1,727	6,327	20	0.17	0.53	18	19,324
Netherlands	1,811	7,420	22	0.46	1.51	18	27,635
Norway	203	919	24	0.15	0.54	20	34,139
Portugal	251	428	8	0.25	0.33	4	11,239
Spain	661	2,784	23	0.12	0.40	19	15,491
Sweden	545	4,843	37	0.24	1.75	32	27,785
Switzerland	367	1,641	24	0.12	0.49	22	44,593
United Kingdom	10,787	33,078	17	1.03	2.56	14	19,489
PANEL C. North America							
United States	32,969	192,164	29	0.48	2.13	24	28,441

continued

TABLE 6.1 **Level and Growth of Venture Capital Investment Portfolio by Country**
(continued)

SUBGROUP	VCIP IN 1993 (USD)	VCIP IN 2000 (USD)	%CAGR (USD)	VCIP IN 1993 (% GDP)	VCIP IN 2000 (% GDP)	%CAGR (%GDP)	GDPPC (USD)
PANEL D. Average (Number of Observations) by Subgroup and t-test for Differences between Subgroup							
Asia	886.9	3,152.7	39	0.2	1.2	33	10,947.2
	(14)	(16)	(16)	(14)	(16)	(16)	(16)
Europe	1,857.0	6,134.3	28	0.3	0.8	24	25,522.2
	(15)	(16)	(16)	(15)	(16)	(16)	(16)
Asia vs. European	−1.04	−1.22	1.10	−0.7	0.95	0.94	−3.88***
High-GDP	4,541.3	21,514.6	26	0.2	0.9	22	31,866.1
	(12)	(12)	(12)	(12)	(12)	(12)	(12)
Mid-GDP	1,795.1	5,806.0	36	0.4	1.7	30	16,799.8
	(10)	(13)	(13)	(10)	(13)	(13)	(13)
Low-GDP	99.4	887.7	42	0.1	0.3	36	1,395.2
	(8)	(8)	(8)	(8)	(8)	(8)	(8)
High-GDP vs. Mid-GDP	0.89	1.03	−0.94	−1.53[a]	−1.51[a]	−0.79	7.1***
High-GDP vs. Low-GDP	1.34[a]	1.07	−1.53[a]	2.95***	2.53**	1.27	13.77***
Mid-GDP vs. Low-GDP	1.48[a]	1.58[a]	−0.43	2.54**	2.22**	−0.35	9.48***
English legal origin	4,222.1	19,202.0	41	0.4	1.7	35	13,456.7
	(11)	(13)	(13)	(11)	(13)	(13)	(13)
French legal origin	1,390.6	4471.6	29	0.2	0.6	25	15,838.8
	(8)	(9)	(9)	(8)	(9)	(9)	(9)
German legal origin	2,088.2	6,199.7	27	0.2	0.6	24	28,377.7
	(6)	(6)	(6)	(6)	(6)	(6)	(6)
Scandinavian legal origin	264.2	1,871.8	3	0.2	0.8	25	30,897.4
	(4)	(4)	(4)	(4)	(4)	(4)	(4)
English vs. French	0.78	0.83	0.85	0.79	1.66[a]	0.7	−0.53
English vs. German	0.44	0.58	0.88	0.99	1.3	0.7	−3.21**
English vs. Scandinavian	0.77	0.64	0.59	0.93	0.87	0.52	−3.72***
French vs. German	−0.77	−0.64	0.15	0.64	−0.18	0.1	−1.94*
French vs. Scandinavian	1.21	0.78	−0.07	0.87	−0.69	−0.01	−4.6***
German vs. Scandinavian	1.41[a]	1.52[a]	−0.29	0.36	−0.48	−0.14	−0.33

Venture capital investment portfolio (VCIP) for Asian countries is the cumulative total of existing investments less any divestments made as defined by Asian Venture Capital Journal (AVCJ). That for European countries is the "Portfolio at Cost" on December 31 reported by European Private Equity & Venture Capital Association (EVCA). National Venture Capital Association (NVCA) does not report VCIP, thus "Capital under Management" is used as the proxy for VCIP for the United States. The unit for the first two columns is millions in constant 1995 US dollars. "%CAGR" is the geometric annual growth rate in percentage for VCIP in real US dollars and in percent of GDP over 1993–2000. The "Number of Observations" for growth rate calculation is 7, except those for Hong Kong, Israel, and Greece, which are 4, 3, and 5, respectively. GDPPC is average GDP per capita during 1991–2000 in constant 1995 US dollars. The "High-GDP" group contains countries having average GDP per capita greater than or equal to USD 25,000. The "Mid-GDP" group includes countries having average GDP per capita less than USD 25,000 and greater than or equal to USD 10,000. The "Low-GDP" group includes those with GDP per capita less than USD 10,000. "Legal origin" identifies the country's Company Law or Commercial Code origin as classified by La Porta et al. (1998). There is no legal origin classification for China.

[a] indicates significance at the 10-percent level for a one-tailed test.

*, **, *** indicate significance at the 10-, 5-, and 1-percent level, respectively, for a two-tailed test.

—— indicates data not available.

In general, the growth rates of venture capital do not differ among groups with different GDP per capita, but the levels of venture capital differ, in particular, when the level is standardized by GDP regardless of time period. The Mid-GDP group has the highest level of venture capital (as a percentage of GDP), followed by the High-GDP group and then the Low-GDP group. In terms of dollar measure (constant 1995 US dollars), there is no difference between the High-GDP and the Mid-GDP groups in both 1993 and 2000. The Mid-GDP group has marginally significant higher VCIP in dollar measure than the Low-GDP group in both 1993 and 2000. There are little differences among legal origin subgroups.

In Table 6.2, new funds raised are the total capital raised during 2000 and are given as a percentage of GDP. Similarly, total annual disbursements are the amounts invested in portfolio companies. For Asian and European countries, the numbers include both venture capital and buyouts. Although the figures of Asia are larger than those of Europe, these numbers are not significantly different. For the United States, only venture capital is included because NVCA reports allocation information based on capital committed to venture capital. The venture capital funds raised in the United States were USD 92.9 billion in 2000. Including the capital committed to buyouts, mezzanine, and other private capital, total private equity capital in the United States summed to USD 167.65 billion in 2000, which is a huge number compared with that of any other country in 2000. Both the High- and Mid-GDP groups raise (invest) significantly larger amounts of funds than the Low-GDP group in 2000. In general, there is little difference between groups with different legal origins. Most of the differences are not significant, and those that are significant are so only at the 10 percent level for a one-tailed test.

TABLE 6.2 **Venture Capital Funds, Sources, and Disbursements in 2000 by Region and by Country**

Country	% GDP New Funds Raised	% GDP Total Annual Disbursements	DOMESTIC Sources (%)	DOMESTIC Uses (%)	SAME REGION Sources (%)	SAME REGION Uses (%)	OUTSIDE REGION Sources (%)	OUTSIDE REGION Uses (%)
PANEL A. Asia								
Australia	0.28	0.17	81	96	4	2	15	2
China	0.19	0.08	56	81	17	17	27	2
Hong Kong SAR	1.94	1.49	9	13	20	84	71	3
India	0.26	0.19	10	92	21	5	69	3
Indonesia	0.00	0.02	52	100	14	0	34	0
Israel	3.41	2.77	72	89	2	0	26	11
Japan	0.10	0.05	76	82	4	7	20	11
Malaysia	0.19	0.12	46	89	26	10	28	1
New Zealand	0.30	0.20	90	89	10	11	0	0
Pakistan	0.01	0.01	87	100	0	0	13	0
Philippines	0.12	0.11	35	86	22	13	43	1
Singapore	1.98	1.40	30	16	31	67	39	17
South Korea	0.43	0.60	68	94	8	3	24	3
Sri Lanka	0.04	0.07	62	100	8	0	30	0
Taiwan	0.52	0.37	82	78	6	9	12	13
Thailand	0.25	0.07	23	91	15	8	62	1
PANEL B. Europe								
Austria	0.11	0.08	92	88	9	12	0	0
Belgium	0.26	0.23	100	56	0	15	0	30
Denmark	0.40	0.16	99	69	1	23	0	8
Finland	0.42	0.29	83	70	14	25	4	5
France	0.44	0.38	58	88	22	7	21	4
Germany	0.30	0.23	79	82	11	9	9	9
Greece	0.25	0.16	66	31	3	64	31	5
Ireland	0.19	0.22	83	78	11	22	6	0
Italy	0.24	0.25	47	77	40	13	13	10
Netherlands	0.67	0.48	53	51	35	37	12	12
Norway	0.23	0.17	100	87	0	8	0	5
Portugal	0.08	0.16	100	93	0	7	0	0
Spain	0.32	0.19	57	97	31	2	12	1
Sweden	1.27	0.93	35	60	40	40	25	0
Switzerland	0.25	0.24	76	25	6	69	18	6
United Kingdom	1.12	0.86	37	69	17	24	46	8
PANEL C. North America								
United States	0.94	1.05	—	—	—	—	—	—

continued

TABLE 6.2 **Venture Capital Funds, Sources, and Disbursements in 2000 by Region and by Country (continued)**

Country	% GDP		DOMESTIC		SAME REGION		OUTSIDE REGION	
	New Funds Raised	Total Annual Disbursements	Sources (%)	Uses (%)	Sources (%)	Uses (%)	Sources (%)	Uses (%)
PANEL D. Average (Number of Observations) by Subgroup and t-test for Differences between Subgroup								
Asian (n = 16)	0.6	0.5	55	81	13	15	32	4
Europe (n = 16)	0.4	0.3	73	70	15	24	12	7
Asia vs. European	0.86	0.83	−2.03*	1.3	−0.43	−1.12	3.22***	−0.97
High-GDP (n = 12)	0.4	0.4	77	69	13	23	10	8
Mid-GDP (n = 13)	0.9	0.7	63	71	14	24	23	6
Low-GDP (n = 8)	0.1	0.1	46	92	15	7	38	1
High-GDP vs. Mid-GDP	−1.31	−1.33^a	1.43^a	−0.16	−0.24	−0.08	−1.91**	0.91
High-GDP vs. Low-GDP	2.45**	2.39**	2.98***	−3.18***	−0.48	2.27**	−4.29***	2.48**
Mid-GDP vs. Low-GDP	2*	2.14**	1.48^a	−1.97*	−0.27	1.64^a	−1.75*	2.28**
English legal origin (n = 13)	0.8	0.7	52	77	14	19	34	4
French legal origin (n = 9)	0.3	0.2	63	75	18	18	18	7
German legal origin (n = 6)	0.3	0.2	76	76	9	18	16	6
Scandinavian legal origin (n = 4)	0.6	0.4	79	71	14	24	7	5
English vs. French	1.64^a	1.58^a	−0.88	0.12	−0.87	0.16	1.68^a	−0.98
English vs. German	1.29	1.15	−1.69^a	0.27	1.28	−0.02	1.64^a	−1.36^a
English vs. Scandinavian	0.48	0.63	−1.27	0.46	−0.12	−0.43	1.82*	−0.36
French vs. German	−0.2	−0.48	−1.64^a	0.04	1.77^a	−0.05	0.68	−0.01
French vs. Scandinavian	−1.75^a	−1.22	−1.07	0.3	0.51	−0.57	1.3	0.5
German vs. Scandinavian	−1.44^a	−0.69	−0.02	0.25	−0.83	−0.42	1.0	0.87

"New Funds Raised" (total annual disbursements) are total capital raised (invested) during 2000 as a percentage of GDP. For Asian and European countries, the numbers include both venture capital and buyouts. For the United States, only venture capital is included. "Same Region" indicates the percentage of funds raised (sources) or disbursements (uses) in the same continent. "Outside Region" indicates region outside the home continent. The last 6 columns (% "Sources" and "Uses") do not contain US data because, by the definition of NVCA, it provides US only for domestic activities. Thus we do not have information on foreign funding sources and investment for the United States. The numbers of observations for the means of "High-GDP" and "English legal origin" groups are 12 and 13, respectively. The "High-GDP" group contains countries having average GDP per capita during 1991–2000 greater than or equal to USD 25,000. The "Mid-GDP" group includes countries having average GDP per capita less than USD 25,000 and greater than or equal to USD 10,000. The "Low-GDP" group includes those with GDP per capita less than USD 10,000. "Legal origin" identifies the country's Company Law or Commercial Code origin as classified by La Porta et al. (1998). There is no legal origin classification for China.

^{a} indicates significance at the 10-percent level for a one-tailed test.

*, **, *** indicate significance at the 10-, 5-, and 1-percent level, respectively, for a two-tailed test.

— indicates data not available.

FIGURE 6.1 **New Funds Raised as a Percentage of GDP during 1994 through 2000 by Region**

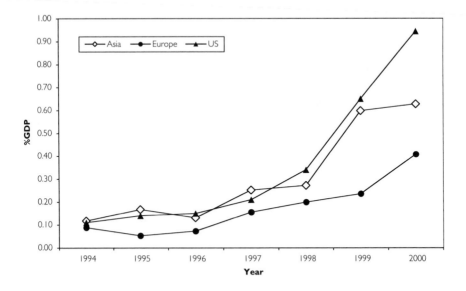

Figures 6.1 and 6.2 provide the time-series information on new funds raised as a percentage of GDP each year from 1994 to 2000 by region and by GDP per capita level, respectively. It can be seen from Figure 6.1 that the United States has a higher level of new funds raised near the end of the 1990s compared with the average figures for Asia and Europe. Before 1997, there are few differences among different regions. After 1997, however, venture capital activities pick up in all regions with different levels. Figure 6.2 demonstrates similar trends. Since 1997, the Mid-GDP group has the highest new funds raised as a percentage of GDP, followed by the High-GDP group, then by the Low GDP group.

Table 6.2 also reports the funding sources and allocations (uses) of funds in 2000 by region. The "Same Region" column indicates the percentage of funds raised (sources) or disbursements (uses) in the same continent but outside the home country. The "Outside Region" column indicates the percentage of funds raised—sources or disbursements (uses)—outside the home continent. The last six columns (% Sources and Uses) do not contain US data because the NVCA provides only US domestic activities. Thus, we do not have information on foreign funding sources and investments for the United States.

Europe tends to have a higher percentage of funds provided by domestic investors, but Asia has a higher percentage of funds that come from outside the continent. There is no difference in disbursements in region between Asia and Europe. In

FIGURE 6.2 **New Funds Raised as a Percentage of GDP during 1994 through 2000 by GDP per Capita Level**

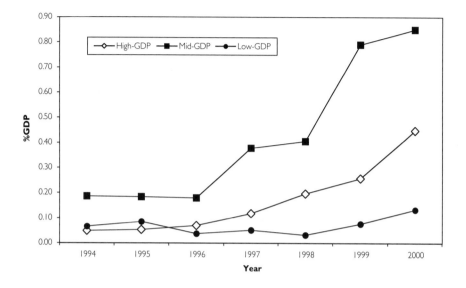

terms of funding sources, the High-GDP group has the highest percentage provided by domestic investors, followed by the Mid-GDP group. The Low-GDP group has the highest percentage of funds provided by investors outside its home continent. The reverse is true for disbursements of funds. The Low-GDP group invests a higher percentage of funds domestically than both the High- and Mid-GDP groups. Both the High- and Mid-GDP groups invest a higher percentage of funds in other countries in their home continents and outside the home continents.

Table 6.3 reports the allocations of funds by stage and by industry. The "Early" stage column includes seed and startup investments. The "Later" stage includes mezzanine, buyout and turnaround for Asia; that for Europe includes replacement capital and buyout; that for the United States contains buyout/acquisition and other later stage firms funded by venture capital, which does not include funds raised specifically for buyouts and mezzanine and other private equity. "High-Tech" includes computer-related, electronics, information technology, and telecommunications industries for Asia as defined by AVCJ. That for Europe includes communications, computer-related, and other electronic-related industries as defined by EVCA. That for the United States includes online specific, communications, computer software and services, semiconductor and other electronics, and computer-hardware industries as defined by the NVCA. "Med-Tech" includes medical, health-related, and biotechnology industries. "Non-Tech" comprises the remaining industries.

TABLE 6.3 **Venture Capital Disbursements in 2000 by Stage and by Industry**

Country	BY STAGE (%)			BY INDUSTRY (%)		
	Early	Expansion	Later	High-Tech	Med-Tech	Non-Tech
PANEL A. Asia						
Australia	16	53	31	26	7	67
China	43	43	14	30	7	63
Hong Kong SAR	26	35	39	37	6	57
India	49	42	9	53	6	42
Indonesia	9	63	28	39	3	58
Israel	51	36	13	66	9	25
Japan	19	44	37	36	2	63
Malaysia	30	48	22	47	3	50
New Zealand	29	57	14	50	8	43
Pakistan	80	20	0	17	3	80
Philippines	19	63	18	44	0	56
Singapore	30	44	26	53	9	38
South Korea	28	38	34	41	1	57
Sri Lanka	53	37	10	33	2	66
Taiwan	33	42	25	65	6	30
Thailand	17	48	35	31	3	67
PANEL B. Europe						
Austria	37	54	9	43	8	49
Belgium	47	46	7	47	9	43
Denmark	13	46	41	26	29	45
Finland	35	29	36	39	17	44
France	22	36	43	44	6	50
Germany	35	45	20	37	16	47
Greece	5	57	39	60	0	40
Ireland	50	45	5	81	6	13
Italy	18	33	49	28	3	69
Netherlands	19	55	26	32	6	62
Norway	35	63	2	43	5	53
Portugal	17	57	26	34	1	66
Spain	18	51	32	29	6	65
Sweden	10	15	76	19	8	73
Switzerland	9	20	71	16	5	79
United Kingdom	12	34	54	23	15	62
PANEL C. North America						
United States	23	54	23	85	7	8

TABLE 6.3 **Venture Capital Disbursements in 2000 by Stage and by Industry (continued)**

	BY STAGE (%)			BY INDUSTRY (%)		
Subgroup	Early	Expansion	Later	High-Tech	Med-Tech	Non-Tech
PANEL D. Average (Number of Observations) by Subgroup and t-test for Differences between Subgroup						
Asian (n = 16)	33	45	22	42	5	54
Europe (n = 16)	24	43	33	38	9	54
Asia vs. European	1.65[a]	0.41	−1.8*	0.77	−2.04**	−0.01
High-GDP (n = 12)	25	42	33	39	10	51
Mid-GDP (n = 13)	26	45	30	46	6	49
Low-GDP (n = 8)	38	46	17	37	3	60
High-GDP vs. Mid-GDP	−0.05	−0.5	0.36	−0.94	1.62[a]	0.4
High-GDP vs. Low-GDP	−1.53[a]	−0.5	1.74*	0.31	2.36**	−1.2
Mid-GDP vs. Low-GDP	−1.48[a]	−0.17	2.19**	1.25	1.66[a]	−1.6[a]
English legal origin (n = 13)	36	43	22	46	6	47
French legal origin (n = 9)	19	51	30	40	4	57
German legal origin (n = 6)	29	41	30	38	6	56
Scandinavian legal origin (n = 4)	23	38	39	32	15	54
English vs. French	2.28**	−1.85**	−1.31	0.84	1.81**	−1.16
English vs. German	1.06	0.39	−1.3	0.68	0.08	−0.67
English vs. Scandinavian	1.2	0.57	−1.53[a]	1.31	−2.46**	−0.56
French vs. German	−1.27	1.78**	−0.34	0.03	−1.16	0.34
French vs. Scandinavian	−0.54	1.46[a]	−0.76	1.34	−2.88**	0.39
German vs. Scandinavian	0.46	0.22	−0.36	0.89	−1.65[a]	0.03

The "Early" stage includes seed and startup investments. The "Later" stage includes mezzanine, buyout, and turnaround for Asia. The "Later" stage for Europe includes replacement capital and buyout; that for the United States contains buyout/acquisition and other later stages funded by venture capital, which does not include funds raised specifically for buyouts, mezzanine, and other private equity. "High-Tech" includes computer-related, electronics, information technology, and telecommunications industries for Asia as defined by AVCJ. That for Europe includes communications, computer-related, and other electronic-related industries as defined by EVCA. That for the United States includes online specific, communications, computer software and services, semiconductor and other electronics, and computer hardware industries as defined by NVCA. "Med-Tech" includes medical, health-related, and biotechnology industries. "Non-Tech" comprises the remaining industries. The "High-GDP" group contains countries having average GDP per capita during 1991–2000 greater than or equal to USD 25,000. The "Mid-GDP" group includes countries having average GDP per capita less than USD 25,000 and greater than or equal to USD 10,000. The "Low-GDP" group includes those with GDP per capita less than USD 10,000. "Legal origin" identifies the country's Company Law or Commercial Code origin as classified by La Porta et al. (1998). There is no legal origin classification for China.

[a] indicates significance at the 10-percent level for a one-tailed test.

*, **, *** indicate significance at the 10-, 5-, and 1-percent level, respectively, for a two-tailed test.

—— indicates data not available.

Panel D of Table 6.3 shows that Asia tends to invest a higher percentage of funds at an early stage, while Europe invests a higher proportion at a later stage. Europe tends to invest more in the medical and biotechnology industry than Asia does. The Low-GPD group allocates a significantly higher percentage of funds at the early stage than both the High- and Mid-GDP groups and in Non-Tech industry than the Mid-GDP group. Such results could be driven by the fact that Low-GDP countries have less-developed stock markets, which discourage later-stage investments. As Jeng and Wells (2000) have shown, IPOs have no effect on early-stage investment but they are a significant factor that determines later-stage investments. In addition, Non-Tech industry is not as risky as High-Tech industry and does not require highly skilled workers, which may explain higher investments in the Non-Tech sector by the Low-GDP group. The High-GDP group allocates a higher percentage of funds to the medical and biotechnology industry, followed by the Mid-GDP group, then by the Low-GDP group.

The English legal origin group does not differ from the German and Scandinavian legal origin groups in early-stage investment, but invests more in the early stage than the French legal origin group, which has the weakest legal protections of investors investing more in the expansion stage than all others. The Scandinavian legal origin group invests the highest percentage in the medical and biotechnology industry.

THE ROLE OF CORPORATE GOVERNANCE

Links between law, financial development, and economic growth

Direct governance structures between investors and venture capitalists, on the one hand, and venture capitalists and portfolio companies, on the other hand, are not available. Therefore, in order to understand the links between these two groups, we resort to analyzing the relationships between venture capitalism and governance with the level of venture capital activities and the extent of investor protection and contract enforcement across countries. The validity of this approach is supported by La Porta et al. (2000). It contends that empirical evidence that links investor protection to more valuable stock markets, higher IPO rates (see, for example, La Porta et al., 1997), and insider ownership of cash flows and corporate valuation (see, for example, Gorton and Schmid, 2000), thus reflecting strong investor protection, is associated with effective corporate governance. Himmelberg, Hubbard, and Love (2000) and Wurgler (2000) also provide evidence of links between investor protection and efficient allocation of capital. Therefore, in this study, we use investor protection and law enforcement to proxy the effectiveness of governance and examine its role on venture capital activities across countries.

La Porta et al. (1998) provide various measures of investor protection and enforcement, such as shareholder rights, creditor rights, efficiency of judicial system, rule of law, corruption, accounting standards, and so on.[5] However, among those proxies, we find that two variables— creditor rights and rule of law—have explanatory power on the levels of venture capital activities across countries.

Creditor rights is an index aggregating four measures indicating creditor protection: the index ranges from 0 to 4. These four measures include "no automatic stay on assets," "secured creditors first paid," "restrictions for going into reorganization," and "management does not stay in reorganization." *Rule of law* assesses the law-and-order tradition in the country. The numbers range from 0 to 10, with lower scores for less tradition of law and order. Both creditor rights and rule of law information are obtained from La Porta et al. (1998) for all countries considered except for China, which is from Allen, Qian, and Qian (2002).

Besides the governance variables, we also control for the level of economic development, past real economic growth, and the development of the stock market.[6] Dummy variables indicating whether a country is in Asia and a country's legal origin are also included. Economic growth, financial development, governance, and investor protection are correlated as suggested by many empirical studies.[7] The proxy for the level of economic development is average real GDP per capita in 1995 US dollars during 1991 to 2000. Both continuous measure (Log of GDP per capita) and dummy variable specification that indicate a high or middle level of GDP per capita are employed in the regressions. Our findings are robust to both specifications; therefore, in most of the regressions, only one set of results is provided.

Past real economic growth is a four-year average GDP growth rate based on constant 1995 US dollars prior to the year that dependent variables are measured. For example, where VCIP in 2000 is the dependent variable, the four-year average for economic growth covers 1996 to 1999. The development of the stock market—that is, the market capitalization as a percentage of GDP—is defined similarly. The control of market capitalization is crucial during our sample period for several reasons. First, it is documented that IPOs are an important exit method employed by venture capitalists (see Jeng and Wells, 2000; Black and Gilson, 1998).[8] A well-developed stock market implies a better channel of exit. Second, the development of the stock market may indicate the country's future economic condition and thus may signal an investment opportunity to venture capitalists. In addition, the development of a stock market in a country could be the result of integrated legal and governance structures as La Porta et al. (1997) suggest. Finally, Johnson et al. (2000) link the measures of corporate governance with the declines of stock markets in emerging countries during the 1997–1998 Asian financial crisis. In aggregate, these reasons suggest that stock market development could affect venture capital investment in a country. However, stock market development also contains information overlapping with the measures of governance. These discussions indicate the complexity of interpretation of regression results.

Determinants of venture capital activities

Table 6.4 reports the determinants of venture capital activities across countries. "VCIP 2000" measures the cumulative venture capital investment as a percentage of GDP at the end of 2000. The results of Model (1) show that creditor rights are a significant determinant of the level of venture capital across countries rather than shareholder rights (not reported). Venture capitalists tend to invest in counties with *less* tradition of law and order. It can be argued these findings are consistent with the nature and role of venture capital. Venture capital claims often more closely resemble creditor claims than equity claims. Therefore, creditor protection is more important for venture capital activities. The negative relation of VCIP with rule of law is perhaps more surprising. What this suggests is that relationships are more important in many countries than contracts. As a result, venture capital investments become more important in countries where the rule of law is less established.[9]

The level of economic development (measured by GDP per capita) is positively related to the level of venture capital investments. Past real GDP growth does not affect the level of venture capital investments, but the size of market capitalization (as a percent of GDP) does positively affect it. As discussed above, the significant positive coefficient on market capitalization is consistent with several explanations. It may indicate any one or all of the following: an easier channel for venture capital exit, a better economic outlook for the country, or a more developed financial infrastructure as a result of better investor protection aggregated from various governance measures. The last explanation works in the direction of not finding significant results for governance measures.

The German legal origin group, which includes bank-centered Germany and Japan, has a lower level of venture capital activities than the English legal origin group. As a robustness check, Model (2) uses a more continuous measure of economic development (Log of GDP per capita) than Model (1), which uses High-GDP and Mid-GDP dummy variables. As Table 6.4 indicates, the results are robust. Both new funds raised and total annual disbursements are the sums of 4 years (1997–2000) numbers measured as a percentage of GDP. The findings are essentially the same as those of VCIP 2000.[10]

We further examine the allocations in different stages and in industries. Although governance affects the level of venture capital activities, it does not influence the allocations to different stages of investments and industries except in the medical and biotechnology industries, as Table 6.5 shows. Higher past real GDP growth encourages more early-stage investment. Larger market capitalization as a percentage of GDP encourages more later-stage investment since the exit channel becomes more important for the later stage. Better creditor protection is associated with a higher percentage of funds allocated to the medical and biotechnology industry. Higher GDP per capita and past real GDP growth are associated with higher allocation to High-Tech industry. The reverse is true for Non-Tech industry.

TABLE 6.4 **Determinants of the Level of Venture Capital Activities across Countries**

Independent Variable	VCIP IN 2000 (1)		VCIP IN 2000 (2)		NEW FUNDS RAISED		TOTAL ANNUAL DISBURSEMENTS	
	Estimate	t-stat	Estimate	t-stat	Estimate	t-stat	Estimate	t-stat
Creditor rights	0.34	2.65***	0.37	2.44***	0.41	2.15**	0.22	1.91*
Rule of law	−0.36	−3.56***	−0.34	−2.64***	−0.64	−3.72***	−0.45	−4.34***
High-GDP (indicator variable)	4.14	5.37***	—	—	7.18	5.31***	4.96	6.15***
Mid-GDP (indicator variable)	3.12	6.15***	—	—	5.60	6.45***	3.70	7.15***
Ln (GDP per capita)	—	—	0.98	4.28***	—	—	—	—
Lag real GDP growth	0.03	0.35	0.10	1.21	0.12	1.09	0.12	1.76*
Lag market capitalization/GDP*100	0.01	5.12***	0.01	3.39***	0.02	4.50***	0.01	3.63***
Asia (indicator variable)	0.91	2.31***	0.59	1.32	0.66	0.96	0.21	0.51
French origin (indicator variable)	−0.30	−0.71	−0.04	−0.08	−0.48	−0.78	−0.35	−0.97
German origin (indicator variable)	−1.57	−3.72***	−1.10	−2.36***	−2.20	−3.29***	−1.38	−3.46***
Scandinavian origin (indicator variable)	−0.70	−1.40	−0.34	−0.61	−0.56	−0.68	−0.70	−1.44
Intercept	−0.69	−0.70	−7.41	−4.06***	−0.77	−0.58	−0.05	−0.07
Adjusted R^2	0.74		0.62		0.71		0.70	
Number of observations	33		33		33		33	

Venture capital investment portfolio (VCIP) for Asian countries is the cumulative total of existing investments less any divestments made as defined by Asian Venture Capital Journal (AVCJ). That for European countries is the "Portfolio at Cost" on December 31 reported by European Private Equity & Venture Capital Association (EVCA). The National Venture Capital Association (NVCA) does not report VCIP, thus "Capital under Management" is used as the proxy for VCIP for the United States. The number is standardized by GDP. "New Funds Raised" ("Total Annual Disbursements") are total capital raised (invested) from 1997 to 2000 as a percentage of GDP. For Asian and European countries, the numbers include both venture capital and buyouts. For the United States, only venture capital is included. The "High-GDP" group contains countries having average GDP per capita during 1991–2000 greater than or equal to USD 25,000. The "Mid-GDP" group includes countries having average GDP per capita less than USD 25,000 and greater than or equal to USD 10,000. The "Low-GDP" group includes those with GDP per capita less than USD 10,000. "Creditor rights" is an index aggregating four measures indicating creditor protection: the index ranges from 0 to 4. "Rule of law" assesses the law-and-order tradition in the country. The number ranges from 0 to 10, with lower scores for less tradition of law and order. Both creditor rights and rule of law information are obtained from La Porta et al. (1998) for all countries except for China, which is from Allen, Qian, and Qian (2002). "Legal origin" identifies the country's Company Law or Commercial Code origin as classified by La Porta et al. (1998). There is no legal origin classification for China. Lag variables are 4-year average prior to the dependent variables' time period.

*, **, *** indicate significance at the 10-, 5-, and 1-percent level, respectively, for a two-tailed test.

TABLE 6.5 **Determinants of Venture Capital Stage and Industry Disbursements across Countries**

	DISBURSEMENT BY STAGE						DISBURSEMENT BY INDUSTRY					
	Early		Expansion		Later		High-tech		Med-tech		Non-tech	
Independent Variable	Estimate	t-stat	Estimate	t-stat	Estimate	t-stat	Estimate	t-stat	Estimate	t-stat	Estimate	t-stat
Creditor rights	3.16	1.23	0.03	0.01	−3.20	−1.13	−0.52	−0.18	1.79	2.00*	−1.27	−0.42
Rule of law	−1.27	−0.58	2.57	1.32	−1.31	−0.54	−2.52	−0.99	0.63	0.83	1.89	0.73
Ln (GDP per capita)	−0.16	−0.04	−0.14	−0.04	0.31	0.07	8.84	1.96*	0.27	0.20	−9.10	−1.97*
Lag real GDP growth	2.70	1.87*	0.58	0.46	−3.28	−2.08**	3.66	2.20**	0.28	0.56	−3.94	−2.32**
Lag market capitalization/GDP*100	−0.08	−1.84*	−0.07	−1.79*	0.15	3.12***	−0.04	−0.77	−0.01	−0.43	0.05	0.88
Asia (indicator variable)	−5.50	−0.73	10.00	1.50	−4.50	−0.55	3.41	0.39	−3.09	−1.18	−0.31	−0.04
French origin (indicator variable)	−12.87	−1.50	11.45	1.51	1.38	0.15	−2.97	−0.30	−2.15	−0.72	5.12	0.51
German origin (indicator variable)	−2.92	−0.37	−3.50	−0.50	6.43	0.74	−7.96	−0.87	−1.09	−0.40	9.05	0.97
Scandinavian origin (indicator variable)	−8.39	−0.89	−4.54	−0.54	12.97	1.25	−15.66	−1.43	5.25	1.60	10.41	0.93
Intercept	37.39	1.20	22.40	0.81	40.18	1.18	−27.02	−0.75	−3.61	−0.33	130.63	3.56***
Adjusted R^2	0.31		0.04		0.32		0.1		0.33		0.1	
Number of Observations	33		33		33		33		33		33	

The dependent variable is the percentage of funding allocated to each corresponding category. The "Early" stage includes seed and startup investments. The "Later" stage includes mezzanine, buyout, and turnaround for Asia. That for Europe includes replacement capital and buyout. That for the United States contains buyout/acquisition and other later stages funded by venture capital, which does not include funds raised specifically for buyouts and mezzanine and other private equity. "High-Tech" includes computer-related, electronics, information technology, and telecommunications industries for Asia as defined by AVCJ. That for Europe includes communications, computer-related, and other electronic-related industries as defined by EVCA. That for the United States includes online specific, communications, computer software and services, semiconductor and other electronics, and computer-hardware industries as defined by NVCA. "Med-Tech" includes medical, health-related, and biotechnology industries. "Non-Tech" comprises the remaining industries. "Creditor rights" is an index aggregating four measures indicating creditor protection: the index ranges from 0 to 4. "Rule of law" assesses the law-and-order tradition in the country. The number ranges from 0 to 10, with lower scores for less tradition of law and order. Both creditor rights and rule of law information are obtained from La Porta et al. (1998) for all countries except China, which is from Allen, Qian, and Qian (2002). "Legal origin" identifies the country's Company Law or Commercial Code origin as classified by La Porta et al. (1998). There is no legal origin classification for China. Lag variables are 4-year average prior to the dependent variables' time period.

*, **, *** indicate significance at the 10-, 5-, and 1-percent level, respectively, for a two-tailed test.

CONCLUSION

Venture capital is a special funding source that has fueled the development of many big companies in the technology sector in recent years both in the United States and internationally. In this chapter, we examine the venture capital activities around the world in the 1990s and link such activities with corporate governance across countries. We build upon the recent empirical evidence on the links among law and external public financing and extend the financing menu to private equity funding such as venture capital.

Although the venture capital industry in the United States started in 1946, this special funding source did not play a significant role in the economy until the 1980s, the decade in which many other countries started their venture capital industries or further developed the industries from their initial start. The dramatic boom of this industry, however, did not occur until the decade of the 1990s, not only in the United States but also in Asia and in Europe, regardless of the level of GDP per capita and legal origin. All groups experienced impressive average growth rates above 20 percent, while some are close to 40 percent during the period 1993 to 2000.

The prosperity of the venture capital industry in the 1990s raises an empirical question: does the level and growth of venture capital investments in different countries depend on corporate governance? Venture capital tends to invest in firms that are younger, more intangible, and riskier but have higher expected payoffs. Such investment objectives demand financial contracting between venture capitalists and venture firms resort to equity or equity-related claims but with the flavor and control of credit holders. Our findings show that venture capitalists seek to invest in countries with better creditor protection rather than shareholder protection, which is more relevant for publicly traded firms. It highlights the main difference between private and public equity in terms of the natures of their claims.

Despite the conventional wisdom that contracts play an important function in venture capital, we find a negative relation between the rule of law and venture capital. This suggests that relationships can substitute for contracts with this type of financing. Our findings contrast with those of La Porta et al. (1997), who find that the size of other funding sources, both debt and public equity, is larger in countries with more tradition of rule and order. This indicates that venture capital can substitute for debt and equity financing in the public markets. Thus we provide some evidence on the unique role of venture capital in the economy in contrast to other financing means.

We do not find any links between governance and venture capital allocations except for the role of creditor rights in the medical and biotechnology industry. It appears that governance matters for the level of venture capital activities across countries, but does not affect allocations. Instead, fundamental economic conditions and the development of capital markets affect the industry and stage allocations, respectively.

In the United States, venture capital is primarily associated with high-technology industries. Our findings indicate this is true in other countries that have high and medium GDP levels. However, in Low-GDP countries venture capital is more often used for low-tech industries.

Finally, a comparison of the Asian and European venture capital industries indicates important differences. In Asia there is more investment in early-stage projects, while in Europe there is more investment in late-stage projects. Also, in Europe there is more investment in medical and biotechnology industries.

NOTES

1   This section draws on Fenn, Liang, and Prowse (1997); Sahlman (1990); and Wright and Robbie (1998).

2   See Table 2 on p. 479 of Sahlman (1990) for a description of these.

3   AVCJ reports Australia, New Zealand, and Israel as Asian countries, so we also classify them as belonging to the Asian group.

4   In the venture capital industry, investments made to portfolio (venture) companies are referred to as *disbursements*, so they are not confused with investments made by investors who provide capital to the venture capital funds.

5   Shareholder rights are also antidirector rights in La Porta et al. (1998).

6   We also include market capitalization growth; however, this variable is rarely significant in the regressions. Thus we drop this variable in our analysis.

7   See Beck, Levine, and Loayza (2000); Beck and Levine (2002); Levine and Zervos (1998); Rajan and Zingales (1998); and Demirguc-Kunt and Maksimovic (2002).

8   See Barry et al. (1990) for the role of venture capitalists during IPOs.

9   The results are not driven by collinearity between creditor rights and rule of law. We use alternative model specifications that drop each variable in turn. The findings are more significant.

10   We use the data of last four years in the 1990s because, as Figures 6.1 and 6.2 indicate, the venture capital activities started to show variation across countries since 1997.

REFERENCES

Allen, F., J. Qian, and M. Qian. 2002. "Law, Finance, and Economic Growth in China," Unpublished Working Paper. University of Pennsylvania and Boston College.

Barry, C. B. et al. 1990. "The Role of Venture Capital in the Creation of Public Companies: Evidence from the Going-public Process," *Journal of Financial Economics* 27, pp. 447–471.

Beck, T., and R. Levine. 2002. "Industry Growth and Capital Allocation: Does Having a Market- or Bank-based System Matter?" *Journal of Financial Economics* 64, pp. 147–180.

Beck, T., R. Levine, and N. Loayza. 2000. "Finance and the Sources of Growth," *Journal of Financial Economics* 58, pp. 261–300.

Black, B. S., and R. J. Gilson. 1998. "Venture Capital and the Structure of Capital Markets: Bank versus Stock Markets," *Journal of Financial Economics* 47, pp. 243–277.

Demirguc-Kunt, A., and V. Maksimovic. 2002. "Funding Growth in Bank-based and Market-based Financial Systems: Evidence from Firm-level Data," *Journal of Financial Economics* 65, pp. 337–363.

Fenn, G. W., N. Liang, and S. Prowse. 1997. "The Private Equity Market: An Overview," *Financial Markets, Institutions & Instruments* 6, pp. 1–105.

Freear, J., and W. E. Wetzel, Jr. 1994. "Who Bankrolls High-tech Entrepreneurs?" *Journal of Business Venturing* 5, pp. 77–89.

Gorton, G., and F. A. Schmid. 2000. "Universal Banking and the Performance of German Firms," *Journal of Financial Economics* 58, pp. 29–80.

Himmelberg, C. P., R. G. Hubbard, and I. Love. 2000. "Investor Protection, Ownership, and Investment: Some Cross-country Empirical Evidence." Unpublished Working Paper. Columbia University.

Jeng, L. A., and P. C. Wells. 2000. "The Determinants of Venture Capital Funding: Evidence across Countries," *Journal of Corporate Finance* 6, pp. 241–289.

Johnson, S., P. Boone, A. Breach, and E. Friedman. 2000. "Corporate Governance in the Asian Financial Crisis," *Journal of Financial Economics* 58, pp. 141–186.

Kaplan, S. N., and P. Strömberg. 2003. "Financial Contracting Theory Meets the Real World: An Empirical Analysis of Venture Capital Contracts," *Review of Economic Studies* (forthcoming).

La Porta, R., F. Lopez-de-Silanes, A. Shleifer, and R. Vishny. 1997. "Legal Determinants of External Finance," *Journal of Finance* 52, pp. 1131–1150.

La Porta, R., F. Lopez-de-Silanes, A. Shleifer, and R. Vishny. 1998. "Law and Finance," *Journal of Political Economy* 106, pp. 1113–1155.

La Porta, R., F. Lopez-de-Silanes, A. Shleifer, and R. Vishny. 2000. "Investor Protection and Corporate Governance," *Journal of Financial Economics* 58, pp. 3–27.

Levine, R., and S. Zervos. 1998. "Stock Markets, Banks, and Economic Growth," *The American Economic Review* 88, pp. 537–558.

Rajan, R. G. and L. Zingales. 1998. "Financial Dependence and Growth," *The American Economic Review* 88, pp. 559–586.

Sahlman, W. A. 1990. "The Structure and Governance of Venture-Capital Organizations," *Journal of Financial Economics* 27, pp. 473–521.

Wright, M., and K. Robbie. 1998. "Venture Capital and Private Equity: A Review and Synthesis," *Journal of Business Finance and Accounting* 25, pp. 521–569.

Wurgler, J. 2000. "Financial Markets and the Allocation of Capital," *Journal of Financial Economics* 58, pp. 187–214.

Capital Flows and Multinational Corporations

Chapter 7

Prospects for Emerging-Market Flows Amid Investor Concerns about Corporate Governance

Helmut Reisen

While investor concerns have in the past focused on corporate governance practices in emerging markets, these concerns have now been redirected to the United States and other developed countries that are the core of the world financial system. During the 1990s, US and other countries' economic performance had suggested that capital-market driven corporate governance generated higher productivity growth, finance for entrepreneurs, and dynamic competition.[1] The problem of asymmetric information, the unique knowledge possessed by management, and the principal-agent dilemma, that minority shareholders must rely on somebody else to act in their interest, seemed solved by the concept of shareholder value and stock-related incentives for managers. With corporate governance pegged to and measured by share prices, there were massive incentives to raise these prices at any cost.[2] The string of scandals publicized almost daily, especially in the United States—accounting irregularities, colluding auditors, distorted incentives for investment analysts, to name a few (for more, see Bank of England, 2002)—had, by mid-2002, finally raised the risk premium on corporate equity and debt in developed countries. The scandals also underlined liquidity risk faced by companies with debt downgraded to the sub-investment level or that may be subject to collateral calls (see Figure 7.1).

This chapter assesses the impact of higher-risk developed-country corporate assets on the prospects for and composition of private capital flows to emerging-market economies. Because investors have been paying a higher premium (in terms of higher price-earnings ratios and lower interest rates) for US assets partly because of the perceived superiority in the quality of their earnings reporting, one could expect a shift away from asset classes with rising risk to assets where risks were already high—

The author is grateful to Peter Cornelius (World Economic Forum), Alexander C. Lehmann (International Monetary Fund) and Sebastian Schich (Organisation for Economic Co-operation and Development [OECD]) for helpful comments on a prior draft. The views expressed in the paper are the author's alone, and should be attributed neither to the OECD nor to the OECD Development Centre.

FIGURE 7.1 **S&P 500 Composite Price Index (LHS) and High Yield Co Spreads (RHS)
April–July 2002, Daily Data**

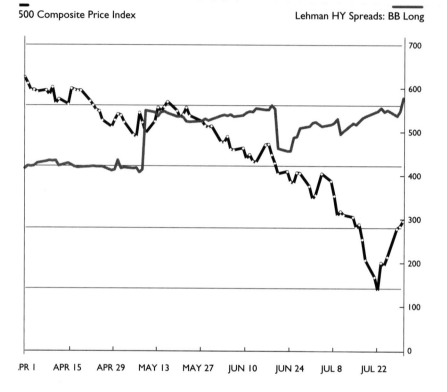

emerging-market debt and equity, for example. Such a shift, according to the nascent theory of capital-flow composition, would also impact on the mix of flows: lower foreign direct investment (FDI) flows to emerging markets as relative capital cost start to balance, compensated by higher portfolio debt and equity flows to emerging markets.

Higher flows to emerging markets, however, can be impeded by the negative repercussion of lower asset prices in the developed markets on the real economy as well as by the rise in global risk aversion that would hit all peripheral asset classes, including emerging markets, disproportionately. Risk aversion would affect emerging markets via the debt dynamics triggered by a double-dip recession and by global risk aversion, with potential solvency problems for two core emerging market economies, Brazil and Turkey. Apart from event risk, there is also regulatory and policy risk (Basel II, private-sector involvement, international bailouts) hanging over prospects for emerging-market flows.

These issues will be discussed in turn. The chapter will first develop a litera-ture-based framework for the determinants of the magnitude and mix of emerging-market flows; the relative role of corporate governance under asymmetric informa-tion will be highlighted. Then, two global scenarios (cyclical recovery versus structur-al slump in the wake of the information technology [IT] boom) will be discussed, includ-ing the implications of changes in important flow determinants such as raw material prices, chip prices, the US dollar, and the absorptive capacity of developed countries. Finally, the chapter weighs the prospects for emerging-market flows, with a focus on the shifts in relative capital cost that occurred between April 1 and July 30, 2002, the date the Sarbanes-Oxley Act[3] was signed into law in the United States. It appears that corporations in emerging markets have not benefited from a general portfolio shift as a result of a lower perception of corporate standards in developed markets. However, rising risk aversion has not generally translated into higher capital cost for emerging markets, pointing to investors' ability to differentiate between low- and high-quality credits in the emerging-market sphere.

DETERMINANTS OF EMERGING-MARKET FLOWS

After the Brady Plan helped solve the Latin American debt crisis of the 1980s and Asian capital markets opened up to foreign investors, the first half of the 1990s saw emerging markets receiving massive inflows of private capital. This rise has been mir-rored by an effort in the literature to explain the determinants of emerging-market capital flows. An early concern was whether the new flows were driven by push (i.e., global) or by pull (domestic) factors. With the majority of emerging markets on a sub-investment grade rating, their assets are credit rationed, hence the importance of glob-al factors that determine the overall supply of global funds to the emerging-market asset class. The relative importance of external or domestic factors in driving capital flows also has important implications for policy. If capital flows were driven largely by domestic factors, developing countries could attract a steady and predictable flow of foreign capital and could minimize cycles by adopting sound macroeconomic and finan-cial policies. However, as capital mobility to emerging markets remains limited, devel-oping countries are vulnerable to unexpected external shocks even if they maintain prudent policies.

Research suggests that both external and domestic factors contribute to capi-tal flows, but their relative importance appears to vary over time. Most research assumed a loosely-specified framework of push and pull factors and estimated a reduced-form equation that had elements of both. Calvo, Leiderman, and Reinhart (1993) found that cyclical declines in US interest rates and asset returns were correlated with increases in proxies for capital inflows (foreign reserve accumulation and real exchange rate appreciation) to Latin America in the early 1990s, suggesting that external factors were the primary determinant of capital inflows to developing countries in that period.

Fernandez-Arias (1996) studied a broader sample of emerging markets (1989 to 1993) and estimated that global interest rates accounted for nearly 90 percent of the increase in portfolio investment flows for the "average" emerging market. Milesi-Ferretti and Razin (1998) present a broader perspective in their study of sudden reversals in capital inflows in 86 countries from 1971 to 1992; they found that both external and domestic factors, particularly those affecting the sustainability of external borrowing, play a role in explaining sudden reversals of capital inflows (as measured by an increase in the current account of a recipient country). External factors that increase the likelihood of capital flow reversals include worsening terms of trade (the ratio of export to import prices), high US interest rates, and low official transfers to the developing country. Among the domestic factors likely to be associated with a reversal in capital inflows are larger current account deficits, a smaller ratio of exports plus imports to gross domestic product (GDP), lower foreign reserves, and a smaller proportion of concessional debt.

Different types of flows are not determined in a uniform way, as they belong to different asset classes and are handled by different actors. Despite the remarkable rise of private cross-border capital flows over the past decade, the composition of these flows remains ill-explained; there is considerable potential return from studies conducted in this area. A model recently advanced by Hull and Tesar (2000) predicts that firms with good credit risks will prefer to raise capital through the bond market, that medium-risk firms unable to tap the bond market will rely on bank loans and/or equity, and that firms with poor credit ratings rely on equity finance. The basic assumptions that underlie these predictions are that bondholders have priority claims over shareholders; that equity finance includes a risk premium to account for "lemon" firms (which are assumed to be indistinguishable to prospective investors); and that bank finance comes with the flexibility of restructuring and the possibility of information-sharing between the firm and the bank, but entails a monitoring cost reflected by the intermediation spread. The Hull and Tesar (2000) theory can be restated for a discussion of cross-border trade thus: countries populated with high-growth firms and characterized by a relatively high degree of corporate transparency will show a pecking order of bonds, then bank loans, and finally, equity investment in their capital account. This pattern should hold for most Organisation for Economic Co-operation and Development (OECD) countries. For developing countries, by contrast, we should observe a higher degree of FDI finance, which minimizes information risks relative to other capital flows.

Razin, Sadka, and Yuen (1995) use the cost-of-financing argument to explain different forms of capital flows, finding "greenfield" FDI to be least costly, followed by debt flows and then by portfolio equity flows. FDI is less costly because participation in the management reduces the asymmetric information problem. Chen and Khan (1997) derive their results from the inefficiency of the domestic financial market in the recipient country; this inefficiency model is based on the asymmetry of the information available to outside investors who rely on information from the domestic financial market and from insiders of firms. The Chen and Khan (1997) analysis allows predictions to be made about the mix of flows, based on a host country's growth potential and financial market development. Countries where growth potential dominates the degree of financial-market development will receive more FDI than portfolio-equity flows; countries with suitable parameter values for both growth potential and financial markets will see relatively more equity inflows. The Chen-Khan model allows for sudden reversals of capital flows for economies experiencing changes either in perceived growth potential or financial-market integrity, or changes in both.[4]

FDI flows are generally held to be driven by longer-term considerations. The fact that FDI displays little reversibility and even acts as the predominant form of foreign savings to liquidity-constrained developing countries during financial crises, has been explained by their sunk-cost nature (Sarno and Taylor, 1999) and by the absence of asymmetric information between borrowers and lenders that plagues other forms of capital flows and that generates herd effects (Razin, Sadka, and Yuen, 1999). As more and more countries compete to attract FDI—through, for example, the liberalization of FDI policies, privatization and promotion programs, including the granting of incentives—their regulatory frameworks for FDI are becoming similar. As a result, the appeal of any particular host country to potential investors is increasingly determined by factors other than FDI regimes. These include the nature of its macroeconomic environment, the size and growth of its market, the quality of its physical infrastructure, and the skill composition of its human resources (United Nations Conference on Trade and Development, 2000).

Changes in relative capital cost for companies based in industrial versus developing countries may go a long way to explain the recent rise in global mergers and acquisitions, and the resulting rise of FDI to emerging markets (Reisen, 2001a). Corporate capital cost is the sum of equity cost and debt cost weighted by the relative share of equity and debt in total capital invested in the company. Equity cost is the sum of real risk-free interest rates, expected inflation (or devaluation, if expressed in dollars), and the equity-risk premium that investors require in order to buy and hold a stock; the premium is determined, among other factors, by the stock's volatility. Debt costs are the sum of real risk-free interest rates, expected inflation or devaluation,[5] the corporate bond yield spread over risk-free assets, and the country's sovereign yield spread over US treasuries.

The tremendous stock market boom in Europe and the United States during the late 1990s, particularly in the technology, media, and telecommunication industries, lowered equity costs for such (listed) companies; the introduction of the euro created a vibrant and liquid debt market and caused a lowering of debt costs, especially for European companies. While the drop in capital costs in industrial countries stimulated global expansion plans—and with hindsight, excessive expansion in some cases—

potential acquisition targets in developing countries were hit by rising capital cost in the wake of repeated financial crises. Rising sovereign risk spreads on emerging-market bonds, credit starvation (hence prohibitive debt costs) as local banking systems collapsed, nominal exchange-rate depreciations, and a rising equity-risk premium for emerging markets all contributed to higher capital cost in emerging markets. This turned emerging-market–based companies into attractively priced acquisition targets. It follows from the above analysis that the recent rise in FDI flows was of a temporary nature, and could probably not have continued at those levels despite the ongoing trend toward globalized production structures.

The global investor base for emerging-market equities includes dedicated funds, global funds that track regional or global equity indexes, and "crossover" investors in search of high absolute returns. As for equities, investor decisions are mainly driven by risk-adjusted returns and the potential benefits of portfolio diversification, which in turn are based on the degree of correlation of emerging-market equities with developed stock markets. Differences with respect to the exposure to country-specific shocks, the stage of economic and demographic maturity and the (lack of) harmonization of economic policies would suggest that the diversification gains will not disappear quickly.

Meanwhile, the wave of mergers and acquisitions has hollowed out emerging stock markets. This has strongly reduced their liquidity, and as illiquid markets are more volatile than liquid markets, investors require a higher risk premium before they invest in them. Some stock markets are now so small in terms of market capitalization and turnover that they have faded away from institutional investors' radar screens, despite low prospective valuation levels. Until the mid-1990s, emerging-market assets delivered superior returns to investors, but they have since suffered from a series of financial crises. The poor performance of emerging-equity markets since the post-Mexican crisis period has often been attributed to weak local banking systems, lack of transparency, and poor corporate governance practices. This has prompted the current international effort to codify best practices and to disseminate them widely. Institutional investors are starting to pay attention to standards and codes. In early 2002, the California Public Employees' Retirement System (CalPERS), the biggest public pension plan in the United States with an investment portfolio of USD 151 billion, decided to adopt a new model for investing in emerging markets. Market liquidity and volatility, market regulation and investor protection, capital market openness, settlement proficiency, and transaction costs account for 50 percent of their criteria. Political stability, financial transparency, and labor standards account for the remaining 50 percent. Only 13 emerging markets have been defined as "permissible"[6] (Reisen, 2002a).

Country-specific investment criteria may provide a catalyst for changes in governance, openness, and transparency practices. The authorities of countries that are on the radar screens of institutional investors and that are close to making it onto the list of investable countries may be enticed to carry out "final steps," for example, in bank regulation or market openness, to push themselves into the investable-market league.

A recent investor opinion survey (McKinsey, 2002) finds that most institutional investors are prepared to pay a premium (in terms of higher price-earnings ratios) for companies exhibiting high governance standards, with the premium rising the less high standards were assumed to be the case. Premiums averaged 12 to 14 percent in North America and western Europe, 20 to 25 percent in Asia and Latin America, and more than 30 percent in eastern Europe and Africa. Strengthening the quality of accounting procedures was listed by investors as the greatest concern.

A recent Bank for International Settlements paper analyzed the determinants of international bank lending to the largest countries in Asia and Latin America through a framework based on "push" and "pull" factors (Jeanneau and Micu, 2002). The results show that both types of factors determine international bank lending. However, the Jeanneau and Micu (2002) assessment differs from assessments in the literature from the early 1990s in that aggregate lending to emerging-market countries appears to have been procyclical to growth in lending countries, rather than countercyclical. Moreover, the sharp increase in short-term lending during the early 1990s seems to have been largely a pull phenomenon. There is also evidence that fixed-rate regimes encouraged international bank lending, and that there were bandwagon and contagion effects.

As shown in Table 7.1, bank lending to emerging markets has collapsed since the 1998 financial crises. While demand for bank loans by emerging-market economies has lessened as these economies realized their vulnerability to massive reversals of bank loans, the major reason for the decline in loans is the regulatory risk that banks now face under the evolving global financial architecture. While the Group of Seven (G7) countries, in response to the 1998 Russian crisis, have been trying to exorcise moral hazard in international bank lending through stricter rules on crisis lending and greater private-sector involvement in crisis resolution, international banks' risk aversion toward emerging-market lending has been on the rise. Regulatory risk, therefore, will strongly shape the future of bank lending to poor countries.

International banks' increasing rate of ownership of subsidiaries in developing countries has resulted in significant increases in lending in local currency. Apart from the liberalization of financial services, the series of financial crises in emerging markets has

TABLE 7.1 **International Banks' Involvement with Developing Countries**

	JUNE 1998 (USD bn)	DEC 2000 (USD bn)	% CHANGE (at annual rate)
Loans outstanding	924	739	-8.8
Other assets[a]	110	155	14.7
Loans by subsidiaries in local currency	248	435	25.2

[a]Includes holding of debt securities, some derivative positions, and equities.

Source: BIS consolidated banking statistics, from Griffith-Jones (2002)

significantly reduced the entry costs for foreign banks, not only because of currency devaluations, but because crises led to an erosion of the net worth of banks. From the perspective of international banks, lending through subsidiaries has the advantage of allowing better credit screening from lending officers located in specific emerging economies. However, the main advantages for the bank is avoiding currency mismatches and, thus, exchange-rate risk (Griffith-Jones, 2002).

Brady bonds (resulting from the transformation of bank credit claims into bonds in countries suffering from a debt overhang in the late 1980s and early 1990s) established the basis for the development of an emerging bond market, but failed to build safeguards to avoid widespread collapse such as happened in the Russian crisis of 1998. To investors, emerging-market bond spreads (over G7 government bonds) offer potential return enhancement and diversification benefits in fixed-income portfolios. To emerging-market borrowers, bond spreads determine the capital cost at which they can tap world financial markets. Yield spreads on bonds (of the same currency and maturity) are, above all, a borrower-specific proxy for the probability of default, and to a lesser extent, used for recovery rates in case of default and for trading illiquidity. Global liquidity, the related investor appetite for risk, and raw material prices have also been shown to affect spread movements of emerging-market bonds. Emerging-market dollar bond spreads have been extremely volatile as the underlying assets are illiquid, defaultable instruments, as well as time-series short. This presents formidable challenges for quantifying credit risk.

The influence of credit ratings on the terms (and magnitude) at which developing countries can tap world bond markets has become primordial over the last decade. Since the bond markets are effectively unregulated, credit-rating agencies have become the markets' de facto regulators. Indeed, unlike industrial countries, for which capital market access is usually taken for granted, sovereign ratings play a critical role for developing countries as their access to capital markets is precarious and variable.

Sovereign spreads and ratings are jointly determined by qualitative and quantitative factors. Measures of economic and financial performance are used in the quantitative assessment while political developments, especially those that bear on fiscal flexibility, form the core of the qualitative evaluation. On average, around three quarters of the variance in sovereign rating notches can be explained by indicators of debt burden (debt service/exports, public sector borrowing/GDP, external debt/GDP, domestic debt/GDP); investment (domestic credit growth, investment/GNP, capital investment growth); balance of payments flexibility (exports/GDP, export growth); economic strength (per capita GDP, real GDP growth, consumer price inflation, unemployment, FDI/GDP, reserves/GDP); and liquidity (short-term debt/exports, short-term debt/reserves, reserves/imports, short-term debt/reserves). Note that some of these rating determinants, such as GDP growth and credit growth, are to a certain degree endogenous to capital inflows (Reisen, 2002b).

Global credit cycles have been shown to have an important impact on the volatility of default rates. Global and regional contagion of financial crises can also lead to considerable deviations of spreads from underlying credit fundamentals. During the period 1970 to 1999, one-year default rates for speculative-grade issuers in *Moody's Global Database* oscillated between roughly 1 percent in tranquil times and 10 percent in crisis years. Spreads on sub-investment bonds move disproportionately to the underlying credit risk— they push to extreme levels during crisis episodes and in the immediate aftermath of a crisis, unlike investment-grade bond spreads, which move much less. The subsequent potential to reap high benefits from investing in distressed assets is often exploited when risk-free returns are low and investor appetite for risk high. The link between industrial-country interest rates and emerging-market bond spreads is not straightforward, however. To the extent that lower industrial-country rates lead to greater capital flows to emerging-market countries, lower rates cause increases in exposure to emerging-market borrowers that can in turn cause spreads to rise, offsetting the higher appetite for risk that normally results from lower rates.

Emerging-market bond spreads reflect not only credit risk, but also varying degrees of risk aversion by global investors. In a recent study, Kumar and Persaud (2001) find a close correlation between their risk appetite index and emerging markets bond index (EMBI)+ spreads; the correlation is quite close in times of systemic crises (such as the second half of 1998), with the risk appetite index leading the turning point in EMBI+ spreads.

POTENTIAL EFFECTS OF THE CRISIS IN CORPORATE GOVERNANCE ON FLOWS

On April 22, 2002, the Institute of International Finance (IIF) (2002a), assuming a gradual improvement of global economic conditions, still saw "signs of recovery in private capital flows" to the 29 emerging-market economies it currently covers.[7] The Institute forecast that net private capital flows to these economies would pick up, moving from USD 132 billion in 2001 to USD 160 billion in 2002. However, only a quarter later, the IIF (2002b) revised downwards its forecasts (Table 7.2), express-

TABLE 7.2 **Institute of International Finance Forecasts for Emerging-Market Flows, USD bn**

	2000	2001	2002F
Private flows, net	187.6	126.0	122.9
Direct equity, net	135.3	134.6	113.2
Portfolio equity, net	14.4	11.1	10.5
Bank credit, net	-0.3	-26.4	-10.7
Bonds, net[a]	38.2	6.7	9.9

[a]includes other nonbank private creditors

Source: Institute for International Finance, *Capital Flows to Emerging Market Economies*, September 18, 2002

ing concerns both about the pace of global recovery and the fallout of the US corporate confidence crisis on emerging-market flows. Private-market economists currently hold one of two views on the state of global economic affairs.

One view is that the global economy follows a *cyclical* pattern: the United States is coming out of recession and clawing itself back to a potential output path (which is 3.5 percent) despite current governance problems, the outfall from the attacks on the World Trade Center and the enormous uncertainties associated with a possible war in Iraq, and the negative wealth effect on consumption arising from the strong fall in stock markets. Supported by continuing productivity growth, which keeps inflation in check and the Federal Reserve on hold, equity levels will gradually come back to normal, with the Dow in the 9,500 to 10,500 range. Dollar strength would be revived, while government bond prices would suffer.

The other view, to which economists are increasingly subscribing, is that of a *structural (boom-bust)* pattern. According to this view, the US economy is digesting the massive information technology boom of the late 1990s, triggering, first, FDI flows into the US information technology industry, then portfolio equity inflows, then purchases of US credit instruments. The US dollar appreciated, as net inflows exceeded a current account deficit worth 4.5 percent of GDP. US household savings fell to zero. Now—in the bust phase—we witness net capital outflows from the United States, and equity prices are being driven down back to fundamentals, which see the Dow in the 7,500 to 8,500 range and the US dollar in the range of USD 1.15 to EUR 1.20. Corporate and household balance sheets are being repaired, with less corporate borrowings and higher household savings. This adjustment exerts a dampening effect on economic activity, with expected 0 percent growth during the next quarters and a significant risk of outright recession. Real estate has softened the bust so far, but for how long? Moreover, Japan stays in deflation, with little hope for reform, and a stronger euro will be detrimental to Europe's only source of growth—exports. Morgan Stanley's Stephen Roach, who has long stressed the post-bubble risks, places a 60 to 65 percent on such a scenario, implying a double-dip recession in the United States.

Meanwhile, as analyzed by Graham, Litan, and Sukhtankar (2002), the less than sanguine global outlook is further darkened by a series of US financial scandals, which have discredited the initial belief that the Enron fraud was an isolated event. While investor concerns about corporate practices have led to a strongly increased risk premium on US corporate assets during the second quarter 2002 (see below), corporate governance standards in emerging markets have been perceived as improved by global institutional investors (McKinsey, 2002).[8]

Even before the US accounting scandals broke, evidence presented in Table 7.3 indicate that blue-chip Asian companies now seem to keep more transparent accounts than their US counterparts, while investors have been paying a premium (in terms of higher price-earnings ratios) for US stocks partly because of the perceived superiority in the quality of their earnings reporting. Last year, the gap between pro forma earnings, which exclude many expenses (such as stock options),[9] and actual earnings, reported

TABLE 7.3 **Accounting Transparency in Top US and Asian Companies, 2001**

	NASDAQ TOP FIVE [1]	S&P 500 TOP FIVE [2]	ASIA TOP FIVE [3]
GAAP p/e ratio	159	37	8
Pro forma p/e ratio	52	31	9
Earnings gap, in %	-206	-19	+3

[1] Microsoft, Cisco Systems, Intel Corp., Dell Computer Corp., Oracle Corp

[2] General Electric Co., Exxon Mobile Corp., Microsoft, Wal-Mart Stores Inc. Intel Corp

[3] China Mobile Ltd, Taiwan Semiconductor Manufacturing Co., Hutchison Whampoa Ltd, PetroChina Corp., Cheung Kong (Holdings) Ltd.

Source: Credit Lyonnais Securities Asia; SmartStockInvestor.com

according to generally accepted accounting principles (GAAP), was considerable in blue-chip US firms, while the gap was even mildly negative in the top Asian firms.

It would be simplistic, however, to conclude that the changed perception of corporate governance standards in the United States relative to standards in emerging markets would lead to a portfolio shift from asset classes with rising risk (i.e., US equity and corporate debt) to assets where the perceived risk was already high but slightly falling (i.e., emerging-market debt and equity). If this was the case, portfolio flows to emerging markets could be expected to rise, while FDI would be dampened by rising capital cost in the United States and other developed home countries. The main channels through which the perspectives on capitals flows to the emerging markets can be affected by the fallout from the US corporate crisis are:

- the impact of rising capital cost on investment demand in developed countries;

- the wealth effect of tumbling equity markets (and possibly other asset values) on consumer demand in the developed countries;

- higher credit and liquidity risk, notably resulting from a lower or no growth scenario;

- higher risk aversion of global investors; and

- a lower US dollar against major key currencies.

The current situation of rising uncertainty will give way to one where risk premia will stabilize; therefore, any forecast at this stage must be preliminary. It would seem, however, that most financial-market adjustments occurred between early April, when a series of scandals based in fraudulent corporate practices were released, and July 2002, when the US administration and the US Securities and Exchange Commission began corrective measures. The effect of lower investor confidence in corporate governance standards, however, can hardly be isolated. Apart from the market sentiment that the odds for a US double-dip recession had risen, political uncertainties surrounding two emerging-market heavyweights, Brazil and Turkey, intensified amid exploding debt dynamics. On the other hand, double-dip concerns and emerging-market debt concerns were, to a certain degree, endogenous to the higher risk aversion in that resulted from the US corporate scandals. Table 7.4 provides the key parameters for that period.

Capital cost increased quite strongly in the United States from early April through the end of July despite the drop in risk-free interest rates. Equity cost for S&P 500 firms increased from 6.5 percent to 7.6 percent, thanks to a rise in the equity risk premium (the difference of the sum of dividend yield plus expected dividend growth minus the inflation-adjusted risk-free interest rate) from 1 to 3 percent.[10] Corporate debt cost rose from 9.6 to 10.3 percent on high-yield corporate debt (BB rated) as the rise in spreads exceeded the drop in risk-free interest rates; high-grade corporate debt (AA rated), by contrast, experienced a slight drop in interest rates, from 7.1 to 6.7 percent, despite rising spreads as the yield on risk-free US Treasury bonds (10-year maturity) tumbled 5.4 to 4.6 during the observation period. The monthly US portfolio flow monitor provided by Mellon Financial did not indicate a net portfolio outflow during the period from April to July 2002, as foreign demand for US government bonds outweighed the rise in portfolio equity outflows. Overall, data suggest private-sector outflows from the United States during that period; in those four months, the US dollar weakened against other key currencies—against the yen, for example, the greenback lost about 10 percent (Table 7.4).

When the S&P 500 dropped more than 20 percent during the same four month period—from 1,147 to 902—it may have intensified the negative wealth already

TABLE 7.4 **Key Determinants of US Capital Cost, April 2002 versus July 2002**

	APRIL 1, 2002	JULY 31, 2002
US Treasury 10-year yield, % p.a.	5.43	4.58
US CPI inflation, expected, % p.a.	1.4	1.7
High-grade corporate spread, basis points (AA rated)	167	213
High-yield corporate spread, basis points (BB rated)	416	567
S&P 500, at open	1147	902
S&P 500 dividend yield, %	1.38	1.88
US GDP growth 2002, % p.a. consensus forecast	2.30	2.30
Dividend growth, % p.a.	3.70	4.00
Equity risk premium, %	1.05	3.00
USD/Yen	132	120

Source: Primark Datastream

weighing on consumption from a two-year bear market. Private US consumption had withstood large stock market wealth losses during 2000 and 2001 because monetary policy helped to produce a very robust housing market. But by mid-2002, there were signs that the housing market had reached a peak while wealth losses in the equity market had been increasing.[11] Graham, Litan, and Sukhtankar (2002) adopted the estimate used by the US Federal Reserve Board, which suggests that over a period of 12 months an extra dollar of stock market wealth increases spending by an average of 3.5 cents. The Federal model assumes that investment would fall 0.8 percent per year in response to a 20 percent decline in stock market wealth (ignoring any feedback effects). This calibration yields an estimate that if the S&P 500 index stays roughly at levels reached on July 19, 2002—that is, 850—the confidence crisis will lower US GDP by USD 35 billion (about 0.35 percent) in the first year of the base case scenario.

From the data presented in Tables 7.5 and 7.6, it seems that capital cost in emerging markets reacted to the US corporate crisis quite differently during April and July 2002. Least affected was emerging Asia, where sovereign spreads rose by about 100 basis points, somewhat less than the 150 basis point rise recorded for high-yield corporations in the United States during the same period. Asian stock market values dropped by 10 percent, but less than the S&P 500 (minus 21 percent). Emerging Europe saw its sovereign spreads rise by more than 220 basis points over that period, but this rise must be partly attributed to rising doubts about the speed of European Union enlargement and political uncertainties in Turkey; stock markets fell somewhat less than did the S&P 500. Latin America saw its capital cost shoot up during April and July 2002, as investor confidence was hit by the presidential elections looming in Brazil and most Latin American borrowers were shut out of capital markets.

For the immediate effects of deteriorated perceptions of US corporate standards, it would seem that any portfolio shift out of US corporate assets did not produce a net benefit to emerging-market assets. Higher US capital cost, lower growth

TABLE 7.5 Emerging-Market Sovereign Bond Spreads, April 2002 versus July 2002
—Spreads in Basis Points Over 10-Year US Treasury Bonds

	APRIL 1, 2002	JULY 31, 2002
Emerging Asia	363	470
Emerging America	510	1158
Emerging Europe	481	707

Source: Lehman Brothers

TABLE 7.6 **Emerging-Market Stock Market Indices, April 2002 versus July 2002**
—MSCI USD Price Indices Rebased

	APRIL 1, 2002	JULY 31, 2002
Emerging Asia	100	90.2
Emerging America	100	65.3
Emerging Europe	100	85.0

Source: Morgan Stanley

prospects as a result of lower prospective consumption and, possibly, lower corporate investment in the United States and other developed countries, as well as higher risk aversion by global investors, have also contributed to increased capital cost in emerging markets.

How does this all add up for the prospective capital supply to emerging markets in the short term? We can only speculate, and in doing so explicitly focus on the potential intermediate impact of (relatively) lowered confidence in corporate governance standards in the major home countries. The most important determinants to observe thus are lowered growth prospects resulting from a negative wealth effect and a drop in investment, the change in corporate capital cost and in risk aversion, and price effects on products that prominently shape emerging markets' terms of trade. Regarding the latter, while prices of computer chips have tumbled, raw material prices stayed fairly even from early April through the end of July 2002.

FDI from developed countries will remain the most important form of inflows to emerging markets, but will stay constrained by lowered recovery prospects, higher capital cost, and tightened bank credit in the developed world. These factors impact, above all, on mergers and acquisitions and on greenfield investment by companies that either carry lower ratings or are dependent on bank credit; new direct investments in raw materials should be less affected. Lower growth prospects in the developed world translate into lower exports from developing countries and a decreased ability to service foreign debt. But the FDI outlook is not entirely bleak: very big emerging markets, such as China and India, command a growing consumer base and virtually unlimited supply of labor, and are less dependent on world markets than small open economies. These countries should remain attractive FDI hosts. Smaller Asian economies may once again benefit from Japanese FDI inflows, stimulated by a stronger yen relative to the US dollar. Moreover, where financial crises and tumbling ratings have brought US dollar asset prices to very low levels, as they recently did in Argentina and Brazil, mergers and acquisitions may be stimulated despite higher corporate capital costs in the United States and other developed countries.

Apart from policy risk (discussed below), bond finance for emerging markets is set to be burdened by projected rating downgrades over upgrades, and an outlook for credit quality that remains tilted toward the negative (Standard & Poor's, 2002). However, Table 7.7 reveals strong regional divergence. During the second quarter of 2002, the credit ratio—the ratio of downgrades per upgrade—stood at a fairly balanced 13:11 in Asia and at 7:4 in the eastern Europe/Middle East/Africa (EEMEA) region, but showed a strongly negative reading of 16:2 in Latin America. Should the global recovery materialize, EEMEA and Asian bonds would benefit from higher corporate profitability, better macroeconomic prospects, and an improved rating outlook. If, on the other hand, equity-market sentiment in the developed countries stays depressed, bond market access would be hampered by emerging-market borrowers, particularly for those borrowers looking to tap dollar- or euro-dominated debt markets.

Latin America still remains most vulnerable to the risk of further rating downgrades, following a significant spread widening in the period from April to July 2002 (Figure 7.2) associated with considerable uncertainties in the run-up to the October 2002 elections. The number of issuers with negative outlooks by mid-2002 has been highest in Latin America. At the opposite end, the EEMEA region is best placed to benefit from potential upgrades with the highest share of bond issuers under positive rating outlook; notably, the recent sovereign upgrade of Russia has provided positive market sentiment. To a lesser extent, this sentiment holds for Asia as well, where a number of banks have recently been put on a positive rating outlook. It is noteworthy that the ratings of some corporate issuers recently improved, thanks to the fact that the emerging-market issuer was acquired by better-rated companies from developed countries. In this way, past FDI flows can also improve future bond flows to emerging markets.

In principle, a relative deterioration of perceived developed-country corporate governance standards relative to emerging markets should benefit the equity flows to the latter. Moreover, simple valuation measures such as price-earnings ratios and price-to-book ratios might suggest that emerging-market equities are considerably cheaper than those in developed countries (International Monetary Fund [IMF], 2002). Relative valuation measures, such as the equity risk premium (the premium required by investors

TABLE 7.7 **S&P Rating Changes, 2002 Second Quarter**
—Number of Bond Issuers

| | SOVEREIGN | | CORPORATE | |
	Down	Up	Down	Up
Asia/Pacific	2	0	11	11
Eastern Europe/Middle East/Africa	4	2	3	2
Latin America	1	0	15	2

Source: Standard & Poor's, Global Credit Market Trends, Second Quarter 2002

FIGURE 7.2 **Lehman Emerging Market Sovereign Bond Spreads, April-July 2002 versus 10-Year US Treasury Bills**

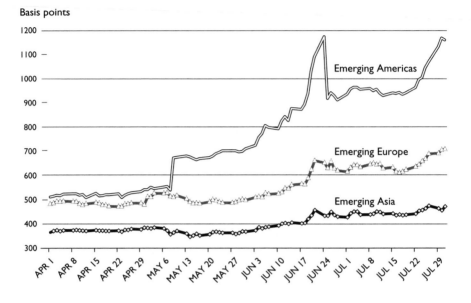

to hold the riskier asset class equities rather than bonds), by contrast, suggest that emerging-market stocks are not unequivocally cheap. Table 7.8 provides two snapshots of the current equity risk premium in three emerging-market regions.

The first computes the equity risk premium by subtracting local real government bond yields (10-year maturity) from the sum of dividend yield and assumed earnings growth. The calculation finds the equity risk premium actually very low (hovering above 1 percent only) compared to the current equity risk premium in developed stock markets. Hence, emerging-market equities should be unattractive relative to emerging-market bonds at the moment, at least for local investors. This suggests that only if and when sovereign risk premia embedded in emerging-market bond yields have declined to levels considerably lower than those witnessed by mid-2002, should emerging-market equity valuations become attractive.

The second snapshot (Table 7.8, numbers in parentheses) calculates the equity risk premium from a global investor perspective by comparing it to the real 10-year US Treasury yield. This procedure generates a better perspective for emerging-market equity flows. Asian markets appear particularly attractive, while the calibration yields the least favorable outlook for Latin America, partly because of assumed depressed earnings growth. Note, however, that the emerging-market equity risk premium has been

TABLE 7.8 **Real Bond Yields and Equity Risk Premia**
—in Percent, 2002 Latest

	EMERGING ASIA	EMERGING EUROPE	EMERGING LATIN AMERICA
Dividend yield	1.6	2.0	3.7
+ Dividend growth, % p.a.	5.9	3.0	0.7
- Real bond yield region	5.9	3.3	3.4
(- Real bond yield US)	(2.9)	(2.9)	(2.9)
= Equity risk premium region	1.6	1.7	1.0
(= Equity risk premium global)	(4.6)	(2.1)	(1.5)

Note: dividend growth equals GDP forecasts

Source: Datastream

negative over the period 1990 to 2001, the return on the International Finance Corporation Investable Composite being almost two percentage points lower on average than that from holding the 10-year US Treasury bond. Seen from this angle, therefore, emerging-equity markets might well attract some foreign money, because valuation measures have improved.[12]

As for bank credit flows to emerging markets, the corporate confidence crisis in the developed world generates a short-term perspective of severe lending constraints, although the mid-term outlook may have improved recently due to important policy changes. Higher default risk, notably in sub-investment–grade corporate borrowers and Latin American borrowers, has burdened US and European (especially Spanish) banks as reflected in depressed banking sector stock prices. Recent Bank for International Settlements data indicate that banks have continued to retrench aggressively from Latin America, while borrowers from other emerging markets maintained favorable access to the syndicated loan market during the second quarter of 2002. While there was a pronounced global slowdown in credit growth during in the first half of 2002, aggregate lending to emerging markets, with the exception of Latin America, was little affected.

On a longer-term perspective, the outlook for bank credit flows has improved recently, with a USD 30 billion IMF package provided to Brazil in August 2002, complete with November 2001 amendments to the initial Basel Capital Accord proposals by the Basel Committee on Banking Supervision (Basel II). The decision to offer such a large package to Brazil has been interpreted by market observers as a major U-turn in an official policy that had increasingly emphasized the moral-hazard cost of large bailouts, and as representing a break with the tradition of supporting large aid programs only for countries with US military bases or a common border (Hale, 2002). Just as the decision *not* to bailout Russia in 1998 had triggered a retrenchment of bank credit to emerging markets, it is therefore foreseeable that the Brazil support might help restore bankers' sentiment in the longer term if (and it is a big "if") Brazil's unpleasant debt dynamics (Williamson, 2002) can be improved by currency appreciation, restoration of growth, and lower interest spreads.

Basel II has been drafted from a supervisory perspective with the particular aim that banks carry capital charges that are better aligned with underlying credit risk than they did under Basel I, the 1988 Basel Accord. But how might Basel II affect the supply of private finance to developing countries? Initial analyses (Reisen, 2001b) fed the concern that Basel II would raise capital cost and the volatility of credit supply to sub-investment–grade borrowers, namely, the bulk of the developing and emerging markets.[13] In an analysis for the OECD Development Centre, Weder and Wedow (2002) explore the consequences of Basel II for international capital flows to emerging markets. The paper shows that the magnitude of the effects depends critically on a number of assumptions, including: the mapping of risk weights to ratings, assumptions about required return on capital, assumptions about competition and diversion effects, and the assumption that minimum capital requirements are binding constraints. Overall, the results suggest that Basel II—taking into account the "potential modifications" of November 2001—will have only a moderate impact on international capital flows. The November calibration yields a much less dramatic increase in regulatory capital requirements than the January 2001 proposals. This is a result of the assumption of a lower asset correlation for higher risks. While Basel II will not be implemented before 2006, lending behavior might already be impacted, with the November 2001 modifications providing relief for the regulatory capital required on bank lending to most emerging markets compared to the initial January 2001 proposals.

SUMMING UP

Investor perceptions of corporate governance have moved to the forefront of influences on financial markets; the drop in confidence in corporate governance standards in developed countries has resulted in higher corporate capital cost. While corporate governance practices in Asia and eastern Europe have lately been perceived as slightly improved, this catch-up has failed to produce a tangible portfolio shift toward emerging-market assets. Unlike in the early 1990s, the drop of investment returns in developed markets has failed to "push" capital flows to the emerging markets.

The major channels through which capital flows have been prospected here are changes in absolute and relative capital (debt and equity) cost, the wealth effect resulting from asset markets, changes in credit risk, and changes in risk aversion. The immediate effects of deteriorated perceptions of US corporate standards—higher capital cost; lower growth prospects as a result of lower prospective consumption, and, possibly, lower corporate investment in the United States and other developed countries; and higher risk aversion by global investors—have also contributed to increased capital cost in emerging markets.

As for the prospective capital supply to emerging markets over the short- to medium-term, FDI will remain constrained by lowered recovery prospects, higher capital cost, and tightened bank credit in the developed world. Bond finance for emerging markets is set to be burdened by an overhang of rating downgrades over upgrades, and an outlook for credit quality that remains tilted toward the negative. Should, however, a global recovery materialize, European and Asian bonds stand to benefit most from higher corporate profitability, better macroeconomic prospects, and an improved rating outlook. While simple valuation measures (the price-earnings and price-to-book ratios) suggest that emerging-market equities are considerably cheaper than those in developed markets, a relative valuation measure (the equity-risk premium) would suggest that emerging-market stocks are not unequivocally cheap. Only if sovereign risk premia embedded in emerging-market bond yields have declined to levels considerably lower than those witnessed by mid-2002, will emerging-market equity flows pick up again.

NOTES

1   The exuberance of the late 1990s also managed to overwhelm seasoned economists. The late Rudi Dornbusch wrote in June 1998 in the *Wall Street Journal*: "The US economy likely will not see a recession for years to come. We don't want one, we don't need one, and, as we have the tools to keep the current expansion going, we don't have one. This expansion will run forever."

2   Curiously, the debate on corporate governance has focused on shareholder value, while neglecting the impact of corporate governance on corporate bond prices.

3   The Sarbanes-Oxley Act represents a response to the series of accounting irregularities that have shaken the confidence of investors in US corporate financial markets. The act aims at ensuring the provision of timely and reliable information, improving the accountability of corporate officers, and promoting the independence of auditors.

4   However, theory and evidence presented in a recent paper by Shang-Jin Wei (2000) for the OECD Development Centre seems to contradict the predictions of the information-asymmetry approach presented above, including those by Hull and Tesar, if you accept that local information and corruption problems are correlated. Wei presents strong empirical evidence that countries with high corruption indexes have a relatively low share of FDI in their capital imports while bank and portfolio flows are unaffected by corruption levels in the host country. International direct investors are more likely to have repeated interactions with local officials (for permits, taxes, health inspections, and so forth) than foreign banks or portfolio investors, raising the need to pay bribes and deal with extortion by local bureaucrats. Second, direct investment involves greater sunk cost than bank loans or portfolio investment. This puts direct investors in a weaker bargaining position than investors in more

liquid assets. This *ex post* disadvantage of FDI would make international direct investors more cautious than international portfolio investors *ex ante* to raise their claims on a host country with low standards of corporate governance.

5 Goldberg and Klein (1998) find that a depreciation in the domestic real exchange rate relative to the yen increases direct investment from Japan to Asia, while the depreciation relative to the yen "crowds out" direct investment from the United States to Asia. No relationship is found between the real exchange rate and direct investment to Latin America.

6 Of these, curiously, Argentina (currently rated by Moody's and other agencies as being in "selective default") scores best according to the investment criteria.

7 The IIF assumed that "despite Argentina's deepening crisis, and concerns over corporate profits and the quality of financial reporting in the United States, market perceptions of risk have abated" (IIF, 2002). On September 18, the IIF had turned more pessimistic, as can be seen from Table 7.2.

8 From 2000 to 2002, the premium investors would pay for a well-governed company fell from 24 to 27 percent to 20 to 25 percent in east Asia, on average by three percentage points. Obviously, investors are equally concerned about the quality of the national corporate governance framework they operate in (see, for example, Oman, 2001).

9 According to Professor Jeremy Siegel of Wharton, a new, more conservative definition of core earnings proposed by Standard & Poor's produces profits 17 percent below those in conventionally-reported accounts. Options expenses accounted for most of the difference as the net effect of other adjustments (such as pension fund gains) offset each other.

10 A recent survey among institutional investors reported in the *Financial Times* found that most still found the US stock market to be overvalued until the equity premium reverted to the historical average of about 3.5 percent (a level which would imply a further drop of almost 20 percent with other parameters constant).

11 The Michigan survey of consumer confidence indicated a sharp fall during early July 2002. It noted: "although interviews conducted in late July were not as negative as earlier in the month, the loss in confidence for the month as a whole was still substantial. The July decline reversed all the gains recorded during the past six months, with *widespread concerns among consumers about the potential economic impact from the accounting scandals and declines in stock prices*" (Hale, 2002).

12 Another potential benefit of emerging-equity markets resides in their contribution to global portfolio diversification, but this benefit has receded over the last five years as the correlation between changes in the Nasdaq index and emerging-market equity prices has increased. It is not known to what extent the US corporate governance problem might bring that correlation down again and thus restore potential diversification benefits. Recent indications of a reduction in US investment home bias via an upward shift in American Depository Receipts investment will further co-integrate capital markets, importing foreign market volatility to the United States and extending the influence of US market events to foreign stock markets.

13 Under the draft proposals, the rigid capital ratio of 8 percent introduced in the 1988 Basel Accord will be maintained; new is how the risk weights to the capital ratio would be determined. The Committee is proposing two main approaches to the calculation of risk weights: a "standardized" and an "internal ratings-based" approach. One major change compared to

the 1988 Basel Accord is that for sovereign and bank exposures, membership in the OECD will no longer provide the benchmark for risk weights. Risk weights determine the banks' loan supply and funding costs, because banks have to acquire a corresponding amount of capital relative to their risk-weighted assets. A 20 percent risk weight for a given borrower, for example, implies that the bank has to acquire USD 1.60 for every USD 100 in loans.

REFERENCES

Bank of England. 2002. *Financial Stability Review*. London: Bank of England.

Calvo, G., L. Leidermann, and C. Reinhart. 1993. "Capital Inflows and Real Exchange Rate Appreciation in Latin America," *IMF Staff Papers* 40, pp. 108–151.

Chen, Z., and M. Khan. 1997. "Patterns of Capital Flows to Emerging Markets: A Theoretical Perspective," IMF Working Paper WP 97/13. Washington, DC: International Monetary Fund.

Fernandez-Arias, E. 1996. "The New Wave of Private Capital Inflows: Push or Pull?" *Journal of Development Economics* 48, pp. 389–418.

Graham, C, R. Litan, and S. Sukhtankar. 2002. "Cooking the Books: The Cost to the Economy," Brookings Policy Brief No. 106. Washington DC: Brookings Institution.

Griffith-Jones, S. 2002. "Capital Flows to Developing Countries: Does the Emperor Have Clothes?" Unpublished Draft, Institute of Development Studies, Sussex, Brighton, UK.

Goldberg, L., and M. Klein. 1998. "Foreign Direct Investment, Trade, and Real Exchange Rate Linkages in Developing Countries." In R. Glick, ed., *Managing Capital Flows and Exchange Rates: Perspectives from the Pacific Basin*. Cambridge: Cambridge University Press.

Hale, D. 2002. "Will Falling Equity Prices Produce a Double Dip in the US Economy?" Unpublished Paper, Zurich Financial Services, Chicago.

Hull, L., and L. Tesar. 2001. "The Structure of International Capital Flows." In H. Siebert, ed., *The World's New Financial Landscape: Challenges for Economic Policy*. Berlin and Heidelberg: Springer.

Jeanneau, S., and M. Micu. 2002. "Determinants of International Bank Lending to Emerging Market Countries," BIS Working Papers No. 112. Basel: Bank for International Settlements.

Institute of International Finance (IIF). 2002a. *Capital Flows to Emerging Market Economies*, Washington, DC: Institute of International Finance (April).

Institute of International Finance (IIF). 2002b. *Capital Flows to Emerging Market Economies*, Washington, DC: Institute of International Finance (September).

International Monetary Fund (IMF). 2002. *Global Financial Stability Report: Market Developments and Issues*. Washington, DC: International Monetary Fund.

Kumar, M. S., and A. Persaud. 2001. "Pure Contagion and Investors' Shifting Risk Appetite: Analytical Issues and Empirical Evidence," IMF Working Paper WP/01/134. Washington, DC: International Monetary Fund.

McKinsey & Company. 2002. *Global Investor Opinion Survey 2002*. McKinsey & Company.

Milesi-Ferretti, G. M., and A. Razin. 1998. "Current Account Reversals and Currency Crises: Empirical Regularities," NBER Working Paper No. 6620. Cambridge, MA: National Bureau of Economic Research.

Oman, C. 2001. "Corporate Governance and National Development," OECD Development Centre Technical Paper No. 180. Paris: Organisation for Economic Co-operation and Development.

Razin, A., E. Sadka, and L.-W. Yuen. 1995. "A Pecking Order Theory of Capital Inflows and International Tax Principles," IMF Working Paper WP/96/26. Washington, DC: International Monetary Fund.

Reisen, H. 2001a. "Comment on R. Hausmann and E. Fernandez-Arias 'Foreign Direct Investment: Good Cholesterol?'" In J. Braga de Macedo and E. Iglesias, eds., *Foreign Direct Investment Versus Other Flows to Latin America*. OECD Development Centre Seminars. Paris: Organisation for Economic Co-operation and Development.

Reisen, H. 2001b. "Will Basel II Contribute to Convergence in International Capital Flows?" Paper presented at the 29th Economics Conference, Oesterreichische Nationalbank.

Reisen, H. 2002a. "Standards, Codes and Pension Flows," WIDER Angle, No. 1/2002. Helsinki: World Institute for Development Economics Research.

Reisen, H. 2002b. "Ratings Since the Asian Crisis." In R. French-Davis and S. Griffith-Jones, eds., *Capital Flows to Emerging Markets Since the Asian Crisis*. Helsinki: United Nations University, World Institute for Development Economics Research.

Sarno, L., and M. P. Taylor. 1999. "Moral Hazard, Asset Price Bubbles, Capital Flows, and the East Asian Crisis: The First Tests," *Journal of International Money and Finance* 18, pp. 637–657.

United Nations Conference on Trade and Development (UNCTAD). 2000. *World Investment Report*. Geneva: United Nations Conference on Trade and Development.

Weder, B., and M. Wedow. 2002. "Will Basel II Affect Capital Flows to Emerging Markets?" OECD Development Centre Technical Paper No. 199. Paris: Organisation for Economic Co-operation and Development.

Wei, S.-J. 2000. "Corruption, Composition of Capital Flows and Currency Crises," OECD Development Centre Technical Paper No. 165. Paris: Organisation for Economic Co-operation and Development.

Williamson, J. 2002. "Is Brazil Next?" IIE Policy Brief PB 02-7. Washington DC: Institute for International Economics.

Chapter 8

Direct Investment and Corporate Governance
Will Multinational Corporations "Tip" Countries Toward Institutional Change?

Bruce Kogut and J. Muir Macpherson

This chapter addresses the following question: can multinational corporations serve to improve the growth prospects of developing countries by improving institutions of corporate governance? This is a challenging question that we parse into two smaller questions: first, what do we know about foreign direct investment (FDI) and its effects on growth?; second, in what ways can FDI improve the institutions of corporate governance in a country?

FDI (and its major conduit, mergers and acquisitions) plays a significant role in domestic capital formation and, hence, in domestic capital markets. The statistical evidence, in general, indicates that multinational corporations can provide more than capital; they can increase the productivity of local operations and generate positive "externalities" in some countries, insofar as their operations also improve the performance of competitors and suppliers.

However, the evidence for multinational corporations conveying knowledge and better practice to countries is, in the aggregate, weak. Multinational corporations' most direct contribution to countries is the provision of capital that is more stable than portfolio investments. Because mergers and acquisitions grew remarkably as a share of FDI in recent years and because FDI flows are themselves volatile, direct investment *flows* for developing countries are also volatile, but far less so than portfolio flows. As a *stock*, direct investment is stickier than portfolio investments and hence has less dramatic direct effects on the volatility of the real economy.

The effects on corporate governance practices and systems of corporate governance are harder to detect, but the raw data, however simple, suggest that the cumulative channels of diffusion can well constitute a "tipping point" for many countries. (For a distinction between corporate governance and governance systems, see the introductory chapter of this volume.) First, the absolute stock of direct investment in most

We would like to thank Kedar Phadke for his research assistance, and the financial support of the Reginald H. Jones Center of the Wharton School, INSEAD, and the World Economic Forum.

countries has risen dramatically over the past 20 years. In countries where governance is poor, foreign ownership offers the benefit of lower-cost capital, since the foreign firm has in all probability a better governance policy and is domiciled in a country with better corporate governance systems. The more difficult question to answer is whether or not this foreign firm will become a causal agent for instigating better governance practices in the host country. A foreign firm may also care about governance practices in a country insofar that it depends upon local partners, extends credit to local suppliers, or views the development of mature financial markets as important to its strategies. We doubt that these motivations are likely to lead to much pressure to improve local governance systems. We note that such incentives also exist for portfolio investors who are minority shareholders, or who hold the bonds of foreign companies in numerically more companies and hence are stronger forces for effecting changes in host-country corporate governance systems.

New investment channels also add to the pressure for corporate governance reform. One of the more interesting phenomena of the past decade has been the issuing of stock by firms on foreign stock exchanges, principally American. This trend has both positive and negative consequences, but it points to the many ways in which governance practices are flowing between countries, often via the investments of multinational corporations but also by the foreign equity listing of domestic companies. Unfortunately, most companies cannot meet the listing requirements in major markets. The bond markets, however, are more accessible to firms and our data show that these may be more important, both as a source of capital and foreign corporate governance monitoring, for a broader array of developing-country firms. We demonstrate the importance of international debt financing and the global expansion of foreign banks and rating services by reviewing the evidence, given in Table 8.5, that emerging countries have crossed a "tipping point" in their development of corporate governance practices. It is the broad presence of foreign minority investors, international lending, and foreign bank investments that point most impressively to the global channels by which better corporate governance practices are diffused.

STATISTICAL OVERVIEW

A statistical description of the distribution of FDI provides, contrary to the reasonable readers' expectations, a rather fascinating perspective on the global economy. In the following tables, we use the data that consider FDI as reported in World Bank and International Monetary Fund (IMF) tabulations. Few countries report "retained earnings" by foreign subsidiaries, even though this source has, in some years, frequently dominated other types of direct investment (such as acquisitions).

FDIs are investments by firms domiciled in one country that purchase significant equity positions in existing enterprises or establish new business entities in another country. Thus, it is investments made by firms (or in some cases individual entrepreneurs) that own and control assets in another country. By and large, it is useful to think of these firms as multinational corporations, though this definition includes very large firms to small and medium-size firms operating in only two countries.

Direct investment is not the same thing as portfolio and short-term investments. Direct investment can entail the transfer of technologies and management skills and is strongly linked to rights over managerial decisions. For purposes of statistical accounting, direct investment is defined in reference to a critical percentage of ownership. For the United States, direct investment is 10 percent or more ownership of the capital of a foreign firm. Equity shares above this amount constitute "ownership control." This definition has changed over time and varies by country, but the spirit of the arbitrary cut point is to identify ownership control.

Portfolio investments are defined as equity purchases that do not constitute ownership and consist of small equity investments (small being less than the critical cutoff for direct investment), bonds, and long-term bank loans. A third category of capital flows consist of short-term debt flows, though due to the difficulty of sorting out short- and long-term flows, portfolio is often used to denote these flows as well. Portfolio investments are clearly not always passive investments, and the investment activity described in many chapters in this volume (see the chapter by Bill Christ, for example) are expressions of the effort to influence capital allocation decisions that are usually associated with ownership control.

Table 8.1 provides the aggregate totals over 20 years (1980 to 2000) by region and income level. To standardize these numbers, FDI and portfolio flows are also

TABLE 8.1 **Foreign Investment by Income and Region (in Percent), 1980–2000***

	INWARD FDI	OUTWARD FDI	INWARD PORTFOLIO	OUTWARD PORTFOLIO
INCOME				
High Income	7.9	9.7	13.7	12.1
Upper middle income	10.3	1.5	6.9	1.4
Lower middle income	7.0	1.1	2.0	1.0
Low income	3.9	0.7	1.1	0.2
REGION				
East Asia & Pacific	3.7	3.3	5.2	6.1
Europe & Central Asia	10.7	14.5	18.8	19.1
Latin America & Caribbean	9.7	1.5	7.9	1.3
Middle East & North Africa	5.0	1.7	1.0	3.7
North America	9.1	7.8	12.9	6.0
South Asia	1.8	0.0	1.3	-0.1
Sub-Saharan Africa	5.8	2.7	6.0	2.8

* Figures as a percentage of gross fixed capital formation

Sources: Inward FDI: World Bank, *World Development Indicators 2002*; Outward FDI: Ibid; Inward Portfolio: IMF, *International Financial Statistics Online*; Outward Portfolio: Ibid

divided by fixed capital formation representing domestic nonfinancial investment (FCF). FDI is a composite of financial investments (incurred through acquisitions or purchases of equity) and real investment (incurred through the building of plants or real estate acquisitions, etcetera). Nevertheless, the ratio of FDI to investment provides a sense of the importance of foreign investment to total domestic capital formation and thus to one of the key engines of growth.

A striking observation from Table 8.1 is the importance of FDI in domestic capital formation. Since the study by Feldstein and Horioka (1980), it has been widely noted that the principal source for domestic investment is, by far, domestic savings. This remained true up through the 1990s; by the end of the last decade, FDI had grown quickly, especially through merger and acquisition activity, but capital formation remains fundamentally dominated by local savings.

The other observation from Table 8.1 is that foreign investment plays a relatively minor role in poor countries, which already suffer from low levels of domestic investment. FDI's share of fixed capital formation in low-income countries is half what it is in high-income countries. Portfolio investment is more paltry still, with flows only one tenth of that destined for developed countries, even considering the smaller size of their economies. While portfolio investment is nearly twice direct investment in developed countries, it is less than a third of FDI in low-income countries. As a result, what little foreign investment does flow to low-income countries comes in the form of direct investment. The developing countries that attract the most foreign investment, particularly FDI, are those that already have the highest incomes. Thus, foreign investment in developing countries is inversely related to development needs, both in terms of absolute size of flows and size relative to domestic capital investment (see Figure 8.1).

FIGURE 8.1 **Share of Inward FDI by Income 1980–2000**

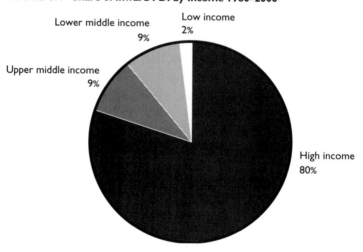

Source: World Bank, *World Development Indicators 2002*

Table 8.1 does not, however, provide a good view of how the distribution of direct investment has changed over time. This overview is provided in the following graphs.

Figures 2a and 2b show the breakdown by two types of financial flows, inward direct investment and portfolio investment. The direct investment figures show that this source of investment was fairly stable for developing countries in the 1990s, falling off for all countries in 2001 due to recessionary forces in developed countries. (See the discussion in Chapter 7 by Reisen.) After a promising rise in the mid-1990s, portfolio investment in developing countries plummeted after 1997. In part, this shift during the 1990s reflects the drying up of investment flows in response to financial crises, first the Mexican, then the Asian, and more recently the Russian and, currently, the Argentine, all followed by flights to more security in high-income country capital markets. It also shows the impact of the technology bubble that pulled investment into leading markets. The combination leads to the dramatic surge of portfolio investment away from developing economies.

FIGURE 8.2a **Inward FDI to Fixed Capital Formation Ratio**

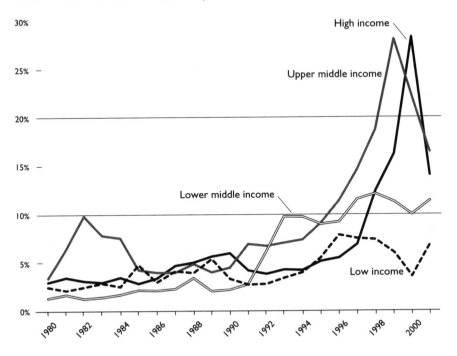

Source: World Bank, *World Development Indicators 2002; UNCTAD, World Investment Report 2002*

FIGURE 8.2b   **Inward Portfolio Investment to Fixed Capital Formation Ratio**

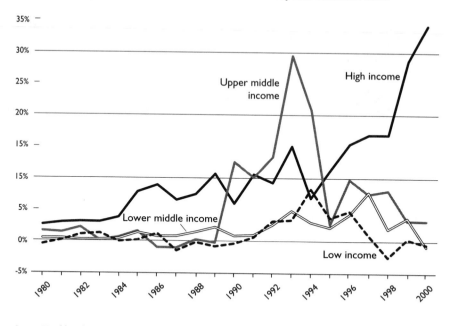

Source: World Bank, *World Development Indicators 2002*

MULTINATIONAL CORPORATIONS AND KNOWLEDGE

It is important to note that the above data underestimates direct investment flows, though better data would not change our conclusion that poor countries are capital poor. FDI need not, in fact, require any foreign capital flow at all. A firm can borrow locally and use the funds to acquire a company or set up a subsidiary. It can trade technology, or any intangible asset (such as a brand) against equity. While almost all cross-national studies (including those resulting in data we showed above) are forced to use balance of payment figures on direct investment as a capital flow (because of a lack of an alternative means of computation), it is important to emphasize that the distinguishing features of direct investment is control, on the one hand and, invariably, transfer of knowledge on the other hand. Cross-border control is often not unique to direct investment, for even small shares of investment in equity through pension funds or bank and debt lending can be large enough in value to cause minority investors to seek to monitor and control managerial behavior.[1]

As an alternative definition to that given earlier, we can define FDI as an organizational vehicle by which knowledge is transferred and its use controlled and facilitated across national borders by multinational corporations. We include in this definition the possibility that the knowledge transferred consists of better corporate governance practices. This definition claims too much in some cases, for firms can invest overseas for other reasons: to arbitrage tax regimes, hurt competitors, extend a monopoly position, or to benefit from cheap sources of labor and natural resources. All these reasons do not necessarily involve a transfer of knowledge and they form the basis, sometimes with reason, for the mistrust of multinational corporations that is surprisingly well-spread through the world.

Economic studies on the multinational corporation have been oddly locked into a framework in which direct investment is seen as a flow from one country into another. Business studies take the multinational corporation as the principal unit of interest and observe that the multinational corporation, as an organization that spans borders, can also locate overseas in order to tap into local knowledge and to transfer research results and better practices between different national sites. It can also organize multinational production by coordinating different organizational forms of subcontractors with subsidiaries; the final product represents the outcome of globally disbursed suppliers, and only some may be directly owned. The multinational corporation is then a network through which not only capital and product flows, but also technology and organizing practices. It is hard to understand the large volumes of investment by foreign firms in the very expensive Silicon Valley, without the perspective that FDI exploits the transfer of knowledge *between* countries, not just simply from the home to foreign country.

FDI, even when it is motivated by the sourcing of production as opposed to ideas, is not simply drawn to the lowest-cost labor site. Many multinational corporations do not "know" how to make use of unskilled labor; their production processes are too capital-intensive and their management systems are designed for certain skill levels. The long-standing complaint over the use of "inappropriate technologies" is naïve on this score. Firms transfer what they know. Multinational corporations are intensive in the use of knowledge and skilled labor. It is not surprising that many countries with expensive labor draw in foreign investment; as long as their productivity compensates for the disadvantage, they offer proximate markets and they do not pose problems of political or institutional risk. Thus, countries such as Germany drew in FDI despite high wages, until the relative productivity of labor deteriorated in recent years. There is no simple link between wages and direct investment.[2]

Yet, despite these observations, there is considerable controversy in the social science literature on the positive effects of FDI, be it on productivity, growth, or corporate governance. These studies probably represent one of the widest divides between what a business audience would expect (FDI improves the productivity of a country) and what the economic studies find (FDI does not clearly improve a country's development prospects). We review these studies briefly, but their upshot can be summarized here: first, knowledge flows to a country by many channels, hence direct investment is often redundant; second, countries and industries differ, so why should we expect consistent results?

EVIDENCE OF RESEARCH AND DEVELOPMENT SPILLOVERS

There is little doubt that knowledge diffuses across borders. There is, nevertheless, only weak evidence that multinational investments act in the aggregate to channel research and development spillovers. An appropriate image of this process is that a multinational corporation consists of a bunch of pipes that conduct knowledge between various countries; the receptor countries invariably adapt the knowledge, which may then be transmitted to other countries. FDI can create international spillovers either by transferring knowledge into the host country, or from the host to other countries.

How would such spillovers occur? In part, they would occur through vertical relationships in which technology-intensive inputs are used as intermediary goods. In turn, these inputs may require downstream manufacturers to invest in ways to adapt and improve the imported technologies, or the inputs may serve to stimulate innovations. Trade would seem as well suited as direct investment for this kind of spillover. FDI might stimulate spillovers by transferring innovative capacity into a country. This capacity might diffuse locally through the movement of personnel or through developing relationships with local institutes and other firms.

Economic studies have focused largely on industry and country aggregates to identify spillovers in research and development (R&D). The first studies looked at whether firms enter a country in order to source R&D and evidence was found for this behavior for developed countries (Cantwell, 1989; Kogut and Chang, 1991). To address the issue of spillovers, Coe and Helpman (1995) and Coe, Helpman, and Hoffmaister (1997) looked at the cross-national effects of R&D expenditures focusing on trade. They found that these links exist, but their intensity varied across national pairs. US expenditures have a different effect on Brazil than do Japanese expenditures, for example. Though these authors did not note the corollary of their findings, these results point to the presence of a global infrastructure, or network, that channels knowledge differentially among national economies.

Lichtenberg and van Pottelsberghe (1998) amended the Coe and Helpman results, confirming that trade openness is correlated with foreign R&D spillovers. In a later article, they find that FDI transfers R&D but in only one direction: the multinational corporation appears to transfer technology back to its home country when investing in more advanced countries (Lichtenberg and van Pottelsberghe, 2001). This confirms more strongly than previous studies the evidence for sourcing of technology.

Increasingly, we also have studies that trace patent citations, showing how foreign and domestic firms build upon each other's research and how this knowledge is transferred with mixed success to laboratories outside a region. These studies allow a more detailed view of R&D activities. They make the following inference: if a patent attributed to a firm, say in Palo Alto, cites another patent attributed to a Palo Alto firm, then the knowledge can be said to spillover from one firm to the next. Controls are used to filter out such influences as the economic importance of a region. This method was pioneered by Jaffee, Trachtenberg, and Henderson (1991), and has been used in a number of studies.

The method also allows for inferences regarding the role of multinational corporations. Almeida (1996) tracked citations made by foreign multinational corporations in the American semiconductor industry. He found that their local subsidiaries contributed to local knowledge (their patents were cited more than foreign firms without local subsidiaries), indicating spillovers. Song, Almeida, and Wu (2001) determined that Taiwan and Korean engineers that patented in the United States continued to build upon these specific patents after emigrating back to their home countries. These results point strongly to the importance of international labor markets and provide the most direct evidence for research spillovers.

These above patent results are restricted to a few countries and to one activity (patents in design) in one industry. Studies just on regions within the United States show that spillovers vary by location—Silicon Valley, for example, has a far higher rate of spillovers than Boston (Silicon Valley has a intraregional mobility rate among important patentors that is eight times that of Route 128), and some regions have no spillovers at all; and that spillovers are higher among smaller firms and can be traced to the intraregional mobility of patent holders (Almeida and Kogut, 1997, 1999). Knowledge thus does not simply spill, but because of its tacit nature, its diffusion depends upon, for example, the movement of people in the context of specific institutional settings. If this is true for regions within the United States, how much more so should it be true for international diffusion!

TRANSFERRING BEST PRACTICES AND PRODUCTION SPILLOVERS

There is widespread evidence that FDI creates spillovers to other firms and it also seeks to benefit from such spillovers. While the evidence for spillovers is often hard to capture in macroeconomic data—and when captured, the results are confusing and inconsistent—there are many quantitative studies at the plant level that document the productivity effects of adopting new practices. Thus, we expect productivity to rise if better plants replace worse plants, but this does not constitute spillover.

The academic business literature consists of many studies that indicate improved performance due to the transfer or imitation of better practice. The most famous of these studies are the international motor vehicle studies that established two points: one, that there are large productivity differences among firms and countries in the 1980s and two, that these differences are attributable to managerial practices (see Womack et al., 1991). The subsequent studies, particularly those of John Paul MacDuffie (1995), indicated the importance of understanding practices as "bundles," or to use more current parlance, as "complementarities" regarding the choice of managerial, organizational, and technical dimensions.

These kinds of detailed studies, both quantitative and qualitative, suggest that FDI can be the source of several productivity improvements:

- competition encourages imitation and also eliminates poorly performing firms;

- firms share common infrastructure built by foreign multinationals, from better roads and ports to improvements in suppliers and logistics;

- workers and managers are trained and move to new positions with domestic firms.

In other words, spillovers can be horizontal (competing firms improve), or they can be vertical (suppliers or buyers improve).

Although these sources of gains seem obvious, statistical studies on spillovers in production are more mixed than might be the a priori expectation. For example, Aitken and Harrison (1999) show that (at least in Venezuela) even FDI can hurt domestic productivity. Since FDI is attracted to the more productive industries, there is a selection bias that falsely suggests a positive relation between FDI and productivity. When the analysis controls for industry, FDI lowers productivity, presumably because competitors must operate smaller plants. These results recall the inability of Blömstrom (1986) to tell if their positive finding of spillovers in Mexican manufacturing was in fact the result of spillovers or if it was a survival bias, meaning that bad firms are eliminated. The Aitken and Harrison paper does not rule out this other explanation.

However, the analysis by Blalock and Gertler for Indonesia shows considerable evidence for spillovers to suppliers and also to other competitors (Blalock and Gertler, 2002a, 2002b). The generation of externalities depends upon whether domestic firms are capable of making use of the technology. This finding suggests that the presence of spillovers depends on factors than will vary by country and industry.

Blömstrom (1999) provides an extensive and critical review of the studies on productivity spillovers. It suffices then to quote his conclusion verbatim: "It seems clear from these studies that host country and host industry characteristics determine the impact of FDI, and that systematic differences between countries and industries should therefore be expected. There is strong evidence pointing to the potential for significant spillovers benefits from FDI, but also ample evidence indicating that spillovers do not occur automatically" (p. 176). From this, we conclude that, in general, direct investment will not necessarily generate spillovers for a country.

FOREIGN DIRECT INVESTMENT AND GROWTH

It may be expected that capturing spillovers among plants and firms by a statistical analysis is a hard thing to do, a bit like trying to separate out the ingredients of a stew. But surely such effects should show up at the macroeconomic level, even if we don't quite know where they come from. If the spillover is to lower prices, then consumers gain and more should be consumed, and the usual welfare calculation suggests society is better off; this should show up in growth and productivity. If the spillover is to lower costs, then growth and productivity gains are again generated. Similarly, if the spillover is to improve local corporate governance practices, these effects should also be picked up in growth rates.

However, foreign capital might also have a neutral and even potentially negative effect. These effects have nothing to do with the possibility that foreign firms are sometimes not good citizens, a fact for which there are sufficient historical examples. After all, even the US government charged Japanese firms with systematically avoiding the payment of taxes. These neutral or negative effects can be purely economic in origin, even if their consequences are mediated by social and political variables. Consider the case of European electronics, in which foreign competition eroded European revenue that could have been used to support a broad-based innovative effort. Even in high-tech Europe, there was concern that knowledge was embodied in imported intermediate goods, and hence not transferred locally. There is good reason to doubt the wisdom of government subsidies to uncompetitive industries, but we can also recognize the danger that resources are "sticky" and are not easily transported to new industries. A more challenging thesis is that FDI may break up traditional relations among business, government, and labor.[3] This impact may be all for the better, but clearly the inroads of globalization are not seen as neutral by either business or labor in many countries.

Given this and the earlier discussion, it is not surprising that the evidence is very mixed. The sociology literature provides the forum for the most active and fruitful debates, since unlike economists, sociologists are not generally disposed to think of multinational corporations or FDI as good. This rather interesting debate resulted in an important article by De Soysa and Oneal (1999). They make two observations. First, FDI increases per capita income, but only if a country has an educated population. Second, the contribution to growth from a dollar of FDI to an economy is higher than that of a domestic dollar.

It is odd that the sociological literature has converged on a positive relationship, while the economics literature is still divided. Empirical analyses at the country level have shown that the FDI to GDP ratio has a positive and significant association with GDP per capita growth (Blömstrom et al., 1992; Balasubramanyam et al., 1996). Borensztein, de Gregorio, and Lee (1998) found FDI to be positive, but that there was a negative effect for the poorest countries. Carkovic and Levine (2002) find no positive relationship for FDI and growth. They conclude:

> After resolving many of the statistical problems plaguing past macroeconomic studies and confirming our results using two new databases on international capital flows, we find that FDI inflows do not exert an independent influence on economic growth. Thus, while sound economic policies may spur both growth and FDI, the results are inconsistent with the view the FDI exerts a positive impact on growth that is independent of other growth determinants.

(Carkovic and Levine, 2002, p. 13)

Thus, we may have discovered a rare astrological constellation, with sociology finding a positive effect of FDI, and economics finding no direct effect on the growth rates of countries.

SUMMARY

How should we understand these results? We propose the following:

1. Direct investment is a capital contribution and this is its primary contribution to domestic growth;

2. Knowledge flows to countries in many forms, through vertical and contractual supply channels, the mobility of students and workers, the market for technology, and direct investment; these may be partial, if not complete, substitutes for each other on average;

3. Multinational corporations transfer better practices, but they also may generate negative externalities that cancel the gains in the aggregate;

4. The gains realized depend upon the type of knowledge (tacit, machine embodied, managerial), the industry, and the characteristics of the country.

The second point deserves attention, because there is interesting evidence that speaks to it. Knowledge can be diffused by many means. A new product innovation is, in part, simply an idea, and ideas in this form are public goods, easy to copy by those who know how to do it. Of course, they may not know how to do it, and in this case, they will need to learn how to imitate it, or improve it. Trade partners may pass on the information, capital equipment can be purchased in markets, and patents and know how can be bought in the market place or acquired by collaboration. As a result, evidence that multinational corporations diffuse knowledge does not mean that such knowledge can't diffuse by other means.

In looking at market and cooperative transactions for research and development in Belgium, Veugelers and Cassiman (1999) found that FDI creates an externality, but only if a country does not have alternative channels to the international market. For those countries with strong trade ties, multinational corporations do not bring extra benefits. (Here we throw up a cautionary flag: 20 to 40 percent of world trade is "within" multinational corporations, that is between two entities in different countries with some ownership between them). Studies by Kogut and Zander (1993) and Almeida, Song, and Grant (2002) show that though firms may be better at transferring tacit knowledge, markets still serve to broker knowledge. Indeed, Rogers (2002) finds that mobility of students (independent of local educational institutes) contributes to growth; the reverse brain drain is an alternative channel of the diffusion of (some kinds of) knowledge.

An interesting case is Bangalore, India, for it represents a region in a poor country that has successfully developed a high technology software industry that serves the global market. How important are investments by multinational corporations to Bangalore? We might think that trade in knowledge, such as software, would be prone to informational hazards where the buyer could not easily verify the quality. In such cases, goes one theory, we can expect to find multinational corporations. Bannerjee and Duflo (2000) argue that the software industry of Bangalore has, in effect, substituted for the multinational by creating verifiable reputations that support contractual agreements. Of course, this substitution is hardly enough. The region also benefited from international labor mobility, local institutes of technology, shared infrastructure, and cooperative government policies. Multinational corporations did not play a major role in investing in these sites until the regional already was on a high-growth trajectory. A simple calculation might show that direct investment and growth are correlated, but the point made by Carkovic and Levine (2002) is that direct investment is drawn to growth and knowledge flows to growth regions by whatever channels are made available: contracts, mobility, direct investment, human education. When all these factors are present as in the Bangalore case, then why should direct investment appear as a direct contributor?

In other words, direct investment is helpful when other institutions are in place, including proactive government policies. It is asking too much of direct investment that it should do the heavy lifting alone. The objectives of the state do matter.

The objectives and policies of private actors have an important role to play as well. Direct investment is part of the strategy of multinational corporations that sometimes choose to transfer knowledge, but at other times, may seek to prevent such international spillovers. Chung and Alcacer (2002) describe how foreign companies investing in the United States come with different motives that influence their choice of location and behavior. Technological laggards take steps to absorb spillovers from their more advanced competitors while technological leaders limit spillovers to preserve their advantage. The benefits to the local economy depend partly upon the objectives of the foreign firm.

Governments at least implicitly understand these motives. In differing historically in their openness to direct investment, they are often following implicitly different theories of how knowledge diffuses in their context of their national conditions. The United Nations Conference on Trade and Development (UNCTAD) publishes a simple index that lists countries by their actual and potential inward investment positions (UNCTAD, 2002). Singapore shows the greatest realization of direct investment flows; Korea and Taiwan are relatively modest recipients. All three countries have grown strongly in both traditional and high technology sectors. Clearly, international knowledge transfers have occurred despite the low penetration of multinational corporations in Korea and Taiwan.

A NEW CASE FOR DIRECT INVESTMENT: VOLATILITY

We should conclude from the above discussion that policies toward direct investment are important. The very poorest countries should welcome investment and, as a second-order condition, knowledge flows. Indeed, there is another reason why poor countries should invite direct investment: it is a more stable source of finance and, following significant financial crises, less likely to vacate a country than portfolio flows.

The importance of volatility has been flagged by Dani Rodrik (1997) in his nuanced critique of globalization. He makes the common sense point that nevertheless seems to have escaped treatment in the economic policy literature, that people care about the volatility of their income and consumption. Globalization, especially in countries with inadequate financial market development, can increase volatility if investment leaves a country too quickly. Even for advanced countries, speculative bubbles and financial runs are possible consequences of information imperfections in markets (recent experience supports this contention). Clearly, given the incompleteness and imperfection of financial markets in emerging markets, we can expect volatile capital movements.

Volatility is an easy number to estimate. Lipsey (1999) provides two kinds of estimates. The first is simply counting the number of times net capital flows switch signs; he finds that direct investment has an average duration of 4.29 years and portfolio of 3.26 years for the period 1980 to 1995. A second measure is the coefficient of variation, which is the standard deviation divided by the mean. He found that direct investment fluctuated slightly less for most regions, though slightly more for the United States.

It may be of more interest to recalculate these figures using a different methodology and aggregation. We calculate the means and variances for a longer period of time (1980 to 2001) using an auto-regressive integrated moving average model (which is a rolling three-year average in our application). This method avoids the problem that countries with a high growth in direct investment from the start to the end of a 21-year period will show a high volatility. To focus comparatively on poor countries, we show their aggregation for different income categories.

Table 8.2 reports the aggregation by income categories, using as a weight the share of a country's GDP out of total GDP in each category. Two things can immediately be seen: the first is that the volatility of direct investment is nearly identical across all income groups, and the second is that portfolio flow volatility rises dramatically as income declines. For wealthy countries, direct investment volatility is not substantially different from portfolio. For the middle- to lower-income countries, direct investment is dramatically less volatile. So not only is FDI a higher volume flow for developing countries (as shown in Table 8.1), but it may also be a higher *quality* flow (as shown in Table 8.2).

TABLE 8.2 **GDP-weighted Investment Coefficient of Variation, 1980–2000**

INCOME	INWARD FDI	INWARD PORTFOLIO
High Income	0.32	0.46
Upper middle income	0.32	1.23
Lower middle income	0.33	1.43
Low income	0.23	5.23

Sources: Inward FDI: World Bank, *World Development Indicators 2002;* Inward Portfolio: IMF, *International Financial Statistics Online*

Aggregating data into income groups underestimates volatility because of a portfolio diversification effect; country movements are not perfectly correlated in each category. In Appendix 1, we show the data at the country level. There are a number of countries that have missing data (our "prior" is that these countries would tend to be very volatile in their capital flows). Still, the list has the majority of countries in the world and is interesting because it shows just how volatile portfolio flows are for some countries. Note also that a number of wealthy countries have volatile direct-investment flows, while the portfolio estimates indicate that poorer countries are uniquely the most volatile. If we look at magnitudes, we have to count down to country number 29—to Somalia—on the portfolio list to find portfolio volatility estimates that are less than the highest direct-investment volatility estimate.

We do not know very much about the factors that influence direct-investment volatility. It is important to remember that direct investment mostly consists of retained earnings, especially in countries that have large existing stocks of foreign company investments. Therefore, an important question is, when do flows become negative by repatriating investment or shutting down operations? In a rare study of such decisions in developing countries, Song (2002) looked at the decisions of Japanese electronic firms to shutdown, switch operations to another country, or upgrade technological capabilities in response to deteriorating relative-cost competitiveness in the Asian Tiger countries. One of the most important factors was the degree to which these plants are integrated into the local economy through vertical supply chains. If we recall that some studies find positive effects and others negative effects of direct investment, Song's plant-level observations are particularly interesting. It is likely that direct investment is not only less volatile if foreign plants participate in local supply chains, but that their effect on local spillover is also likely to be greater.

The controversial decision of foreign sporting shoe manufacturers to switch from sourcing from Korea to Indonesia and elsewhere in Asia had an immediate impact on employment. Yet, these operations (run by local Korean contractors) were minimally integrated with the wider Korean economy, and the employment was picked up (at that time) by other industries. Understanding the micro details of direct investment would no doubt clarify the puzzle of why the productivity benefits do not show up in the aggregate numbers.

THE NEWEST CASE FOR DIRECT INVESTMENT: CORPORATE GOVERNANCE

The latest case being made for direct investment is that multinational corporations benefit corporate governance. This argument, as we stated at the outset of our analysis of this issue, confuses corporate governance and corporate governance systems. It is reasonable to believe that, on average, public foreign firms from developed countries are better governed than public firms in developing countries. Financial markets are more developed and, hence, firms are more regulated. (This is ironical, because in financial economics up to recent years, regulations were viewed as a hindrance to market forces that punished illicit behavior through reputational consequences.)

It should be remembered that in all countries, most firms are privately held. It is less obvious, though possibly true, that a privately-held firm in a rich country can be expected to be better governed than one in a poor country. There are no studies; this is speculation. The real comparison, then, is with governance between publicly-held firms. We are no longer comparing governance systems, but rather governance among a form common to many countries, the publicly-incorporated and publicly-traded corporation.

Direct investment might influence corporate governance through two mechanisms. By setting up plants and operations, it forces local firms to compete more effectively, including for capital. Thus, domestic firms will be forced by competition to adopt improved governance practices to lower their capital costs. While this argument seems reasonable (and there is some passing evidence for it), competition by trade, or, for that matter, competition in general, seems to be an adequate substitute. Here we have returned to the fundamental argument that the best governance is product-market competition.

The second influence is that the foreign firm takes over a poorly governed domestic firm. The studies of Dyck and Zingales (forthcoming), among others, indicate that poor governance qua poor protection for minority investors results in a higher cost of capital. Because dominant investors appropriate "private benefits," the value of stock shares is depressed. An acquisition would seem to be promoted in this case.

While this makes *prima facie* sense, the logic by which this occurs is not transparent. The dilemma is, however, obvious. Poor governance means that more efficient buyers may not prevail in making a purchase of an underperforming firm. The owners of the domestic firm would have to be willing to sell, which they are less likely to do if they earn more by private benefits than by being acquired. Of course, it may be that given that the overall system provides poor governance, the multinational corporation can arrange side payments. These payments should not be illegal, and they can be akin to golden parachutes used in developed countries. Obviously, there is also the potential for illegal payments and abuse. We do not endorse the claim that corruption is a necessary evil. The evidence is that corruption debilitates economic growth, in addition to being immoral.

This implication becomes clearer in working out the algebra for how much premium would have to be paid by an acquiring firm for a company that provides private benefits to a dominant shareholder. Simple algebra suggests that small but controlling shares of the total value of a firm can pose large obstacles to a takeover. Let S be the total value of shares and α the proportion of shares owned by the dominant shareholder; let PB be the value of private benefits. The basic arithmetic suggests that the dominant shareholder's investment is worth: α S + PB. The existing value of firm to all equity holders is α S + PB + (1- α) S. The buyer will have to pay a premium to the dominant shareholder equal at least to PB in order to create an incentive to sell. The important point to note is that in the absence of side payments, the premium is paid to all existing (dominant and minority) investors, assuming a UK type of provision assuring a uniform price. Thus, the buyer must pay at least $(1/\alpha)$ [PB] over the current value of the shares to equity holders. (Some countries, such as the UK, mandate the same price for all shareholders; in many other countries, prices will vary.) *There is then a multiplier effect* (i.e., $(1/\alpha)$) *that can dramatically increase the acquisition premium.*

This multiplier effect is especially pronounced if dominant shareholders can extract high private benefits with a low proportion of shares. In other words, an acquisition in this environment would have to promise substantial efficiency gains or strategic value to justify the share price. Alternatively, these environments also imply strong motivations to provide side payments to dominant shareholders rather than make large premium payments to minority investors. Obviously, these side payments may take the form of corruption.

For completeness, we have to ask whether the multinational buyer would eliminate private benefits for itself after the acquisition. Perhaps the benefits accrue to local management and not to headquarters. The subsidiary, after all, is still located in the same country and system as before. Is there sufficient oversight of these activities from foreign management? There are many scandals concerning foreign subsidiaries failing to report correctly. There is no science for determining profits and performance in conditions of exchange rate variability, inflation, and political turmoil. Ultimately, control in large multinationals is maintained by the quality of managerial personnel who care about their reputations. They also may maintain a local board of directors for oversight, an expensive and otherwise puzzling practice by multinational corporations. We may understand this governance as similar to the law and economics of efficient wages, in which small chances of being caught can only be offset by losing the promise of a salary in excess of the norm. (The judge who fined and sentenced the financier Michael Milken for insider trading said that the penalty must be large—since the gains are so tempting and the chances of being caught so low, how else can the law deter white-collar crime?) Multinational corporations do pay premium wages and salaries, and losing such a plum job is a probable loss to managers and workers compared to alternatives. However, a more prosaic practice is the imposition of "modern human resource management," in which managers and directors are selected for their adherence to values for integrity. We should not forget that "good values attract good managers" is an implicit contract in well-functioning organizations.

No matter how we judge whether multinational corporations will eliminate private benefits, what is clear is that the amount of direct investment by mergers and acquisitions is astronomical. Table 8.3 reports figures for the amount of cross-border acquisitions by income group and Figure 8.3 gives shares of outward acquisition activity by country. The United Kingdom and the United States dominate international merger and acquisition flows, but continental European transactions are also large. For developing countries, mergers and acquisitions compose a considerable portion of foreign investment. The figure indicates 113 percent of direct investment is mergers and acquisitions from 1987 to 2001. While puzzling, it should be remembered that our direct investment data are balance of payment flows. This percentage is a simple reminder that investment can be made by equity swaps, local borrowing, and technology transfers, none of which enter into the balance of payments.

Merger and acquisition data reveal that a few big deals make up the large proportion of the value of total transactions. Will foreign acquisitions then bring corporate governance to the host country? These transactions bring better governance practices, but it also useful to remember that this governance is not a single system. Rather,

TABLE 8.3 **Cross-Border Mergers and Acquisitions**

Income	1990–1995		1996–2001		1990–1995		1996–2001	
	Outward M&A*	M&A/FCF (%)	Outward M&A*	M&A/FCF (%)	Inward M&A*	M&A/FCF (%)	Inward M&A*	M&A/FCF (%)
High Income	619,995	2.5	3,339,170	13.3	243,681	1.6	1,165,330	8.2
Upper middle income	17,293	1.0	61,771	2.5	36,641	2.5	211,132	9.2
Lower middle income	9,974	0.4	38,675	1.1	14,738	0.9	58,938	2.0
Low income	15,565	1.6	41,817	3.8	32,702	4.0	94,038	9.5

*Constant 1995 USD (millions)

Sources: M&A: UNCTAD, *World Investment Report, 2002*; Fixed Capital Formation: *World Bank,World Development Indicators 2002*

FIGURE 8.3   **Outward M&A by Value 1990–2001**

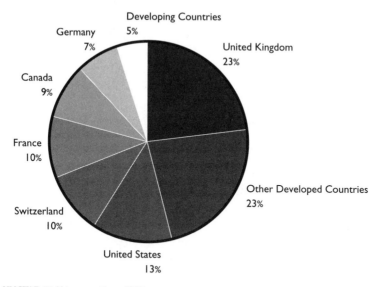

Source: UNCTAD, *World Investment Report 2002*

it is a cacophony of systems: Anglo, German, Japanese, Swedish, French, Swiss, Dutch. Mergers and acquisitions are related to complex trade ties between countries and, hence, the influences from national systems are many (Macpherson, 2003). These systems may share a common body of practices regarding protection of minority investors, but they do not offer an integrated solution to governance. This, in theory, has a potential benefit: institutional designers may analyze the national varieties of foreign firms operating in their country as "natural experiments" from which they may infer what practices suit local conditions. We return to this potential in the conclusions.

There is another reason why the lessons taught by acquisitions may not be effective: the acquisitions are often not central targets in a country. Most countries have ownership clubs, in which cross-holdings are held among industrial and financial firms. Even in the dispersed shareholder market of the United States, the structures consist of "small worlds." (See the introductory chapter regarding Enron.) Kogut and Walker (2001) conducted a simple study of Germany to illustrate the implications. They showed that German corporate ties make up many small worlds and that acquisitions tend to reinforce these worlds, rather than break them up. In fact, if we take an ownership tie between a firm and reassign it randomly to other firms, we can see that it would take a tidal wave of foreign acquisitions to break up the German system.[4]

A CASE FOR A TIPPING POINT

Foreign acquisitions by themselves, in other words, are not likely to break up most national clubs or diffuse corporate governance practices. For diffusion to occur, there must be channels by which practices are learned, either by competitive imitation or by self-regulation or state regulation. We could imagine an island of firms with better practices that then "infect" other firms. It is possible that some countries have attained such tipping points through foreign acquisitions. This depends on their numerical frequency and their potential to "infect."

While we should remain skeptical that acquisitions will be numerically significant enough to "tip" a country, it is part of a larger trend that collectively might make a difference. Consider the many channels by which corporate governance may infect a country: privatization, acquisition of banks, minority investment, and inverse equity listings. Let's take each of these in turn.

The 1990s witnessed a spectacular explosion of privatizations that represented unusual times for foreign firms to alter historical relationships. Brune, Garrett, and Kogut (2003) estimate that between 1985 and 1999, USD 1.3 trillion of assets were privatized (not including mass privatizations), representing 7.6 percent of the world GDP for 1985. Relative to their GDPs, the world's largest five privatizers were Belize, Bolivia, Cape Verde, Guyana, and Portugal, each of which privatized more than one third of their 1985 GDPs. In certain countries, privatizations have been dominated by foreign buyers, but they are not in the aggregate a significant source of FDI. During the 1990s, the World Bank estimates that developing countries raised more than USD 320 billion from privatization sales, USD 140 billion of it from foreign sources.[5] As large as these figures are, they still accounted for less than 1 percent of FDI into these countries during the same period.

Privatization and acquisition of financial institutions, because of their role in providing debt and monitoring other local firms, might have an importance outside the sheer values given by our acquisition and privatization figures. The hope would be that banks would be acquired by banks from countries with stricter governance standards and thus improve not only their own governance but also that of the companies to which they provide credit. World Bank data show that between 1990 and 1999, 36 developing countries sold 180 banks for USD 26 billion.[6] The largest bank privatizations occurred in Mexico, Poland, and India, but almost all of these sales were to local investors; foreign investors were often banks from other developing countries or from banking havens. Finally, most banks were only partially privatized, leaving large government stakes. As a result, the prospects of transferring stricter governance standards to developing countries through this channel seem discouraging.

Figures on the value of bank acquisitions are difficult to come by because many of the details are negotiated privately. The data on transaction counts, however, are more promising for governance. They show that of the more than 2,600 acquisitions of majority or minority stakes in developing-country banks, 2,160 were made by firms in developed countries and only 450 were made by developing-country firms. While there may be other consequences of the concentration of financial services in high-income countries, we can hope that one may be the improvement of corporate governance standards, both at the banks themselves and at the firms to which they offer credit. We return to the role of foreign banks below.

OTHER TYPES OF FOREIGN INVESTMENT

For all of the reasons discussed above, corporate governance in developing countries is unlikely to be improved by majority-owned foreign investment, whether it takes place via acquisition or greenfield investment. Competition for portfolio-equity investment might provide discipline on companies with poor corporate governance, but many developing-country capital markets function poorly and are not very deep. Morck, Yeung, and Yu (2000) demonstrate that even many developed-country stock markets are highly synchronous and reflect little firm-specific information; most of the price movements reflect country, not firm, risk. In this environment, it is very difficult for an informed investor to profit from trading on differences in corporate governance since prices will not reflect this information.

Furthermore, the focus on improving protection for minority shareholders is in some sense misplaced since most companies are privately held, especially in countries that do not have Anglo-American capital markets. Here again, we distinguish between corporate governance systems and practices. English-speaking countries collectively have a stock market capitalization to GDP ratio of 140 percent, nearly double the rest of the OECD countries' 75 percent. Developing countries come in at only 33 percent.[7]

Strengthening shareholder protections will, over the long term, improve the functioning of domestic capital markets but will have little immediate effect on the majority of existing companies that are not listed on any exchange. The role of capital markets in reforming corporate governance will have to come from avenues accessible to privately-held firms, such as private minority-equity investments and bank debt.

Many of the transactions recorded as FDI take the form of minority investments in existing foreign companies. Since anything more than a 10 percent stake in a company is recorded as FDI, there are many investments that are too large to be passive portfolio investments but too small to constitute a controlling interest. Often, these investments are made to cement another deal between a multinational corporation and a local firm. Since they neither require the company to be listed nor require local owners to give up control, such investments are still available to private companies with high private benefits of control, a description that would apply to many firms in developing countries.

Before making such an investment, a multinational corporation has to perform due diligence examination of available local partners, including the suitability of their corporate governance. Since this type of transaction provides foreign capital and a valuable long-term business relationship, we would expect local companies to compete for them. Competition for these relationships could lead firms to improve firm practices, including corporate governance. After the deal is made, the multinational corporation has the information and incentive to play a monitoring role that may also serve to curb abuses and improve governance practices. Furthermore, these transactions are large enough to be effective and numerous enough to play a role in altering the prevailing quality of corporate governance practices in a country.

Larger than all the other foreign investment flows discussed so far are loans from foreign banks to private enterprise in developing countries. These can take the form of foreign currency credit from an overseas bank or local currency credit from the local affiliate of a foreign-owned bank. Foreign currency loans to developing countries has grown from USD 140 billion in 1990 to nearly USD 400 billion in 2002.[8] These flows have not grown as fast as foreign direct investment, but they are still two to three times larger. They represent an increase from 4 to 6 percent of GDP.

More significantly, the penetration of foreign-owned banks into the domestic markets of many developing countries has increased substantially over the past twelve years. The liberalization of financial services has allowed foreign banks to increase their reported local claims almost 20-fold, from USD 24 billion to USD 450 billion, and from 1 percent to 7 percent of total developing-country GDP.[9] This explosive growth may account for the slower growth of cross-border claims, since banks are able to enter and serve many developing-country markets with local affiliates. Banks now do more business in developing countries through local operations in local currencies than they do through foreign currencies and foreign transactions. (See the chapter by Peter Cornelius.)

In both cross-border transactions and local transactions, the growth of foreign banking has been most rapid in the highest-income developing countries. In 1990, foreign banks actually had larger operations in the poorest countries than they had in middle-income countries. While foreign banking operations in poor countries have grown modestly, in the more advanced developing countries they have grown explosively and are now much larger than those in poor countries.

The expansion of international corporate borrowing—that is, funds raised either overseas or by loans from local banks owned by foreign investors—over the past three years has occasioned the establishment of subsidiaries by major rating agencies. Numerically, these investments are minor, but they can have a major political and economic impact on local firms who confront public and published evaluations of their creditworthiness. In Figure 8.4, we show the diffusion of the expansion of Moody's rating services to foreign markets. (Unfortunately, we were unable to acquire these data from other financial rating services.) Moody's provides primarily the service of rating the riskiness of a company in terms of its ability to make payments on its debt. It does not rate the equity attractiveness of a company. An

FIGURE 8.4 **Countries Covered by Moody's**

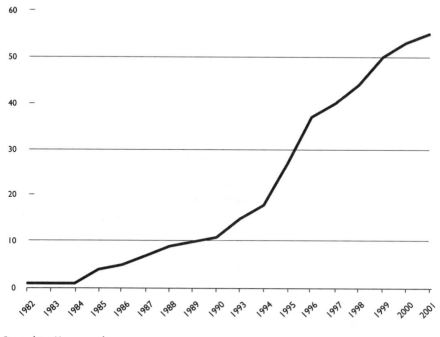

Source: http://www.moodyseurope.com

interesting observation is that Moody's was present in more countries in the 1930s than in the 1980s. (Recall the massive lending made by the United States as a consequence of World War I.) In the 1990s, Moody's expanded around the globe, including to emerging markets. It is this multinational expansion of institutional guardians into developing markets that may generate some of the most powerful effects of direct investment.

COMPANIES GOING TO FOREIGN CAPITAL MARKETS

As we discussed earlier, direct investment sometimes goes to a country to source knowledge; this is called inverse direct investment. Another form of this flow is inverse-equity flows. Developing countries are, to a significant extent, approaching developed-country capital markets rather than merely waiting for capital to come to them. This pattern is the parallel to what Mira Wilkins (1988) called the "freestanding firm" that came to emerging markets 100 years ago. This firm was headquartered in a developed country, where its stock was listed, but all of its activities was located overseas (e.g., tin mining in Malaysia). Wilkins' contention is that entrepreneurs could not list in local financial markets because they were not developed; developed markets permitted sufficient liquidity and bonding (investors knew each other) to support equity financing.

From a governance perspective, the current inverse-equity listing means that companies from developing countries can choose their own stock markets. Tapping developed-country capital markets requires conforming to developed-country governance standards. Companies can therefore appear to choose to "import" a stricter governance system if their own system is insufficient.[10] Table 8.4 shows the money raised in overseas capital markets by firms from countries in different income groups. While the amount of money raised declines sharply with income, its importance as a source of investment is actually much higher for developing countries than it is for developed ones. Despite the publicity around foreign listings through American Depository Receipts (ADR) and Global Depository Receipts (GDR) shares, Table 8.4 shows that the number of firms able to take advantage of this technique is relatively limited.[11] The table also shows that the vast majority of money raised overseas is raised in the form of bonds. Most companies are private, especially in the developing world, and they therefore do not have access to equity markets in any country.

Firms that list on foreign exchanges must meet their disclosure and other governance requirements. Since these tend to be stronger or better enforced than those of developing-country financial markets, firms have the opportunity to subject themselves to tighter oversight in exchange for a potentially lower capital cost. To the extent that foreign listing does spread governance standards, it is the US model that is being globalized, since more than 96 percent of overseas equity was raised in the United States from 1990 to 2000.[12]

TABLE 8.4 **Sources of Overseas Investment 1990–2000**

INCOME	M&A SALES*	M&A/FDI (%)	EQUITY ISSUED OVERSEAS*	OVERSEAS EQUITY/ PORTFOLIO (%)	BONDS ISSUED OVERSEAS*	OVERSEAS BONDS/ PORTFOLIO (%)
High income	1,409,011	26	108,637	2	1,471,363	21
Upper middle income	247,773	43	15,347	5	94,653	32
Lower middle income	73,676	13	5,106	8	33,794	51
Low income	126,741	114	1,308	6	7,962	34

*constant millions 1995 USD

Sources: M&A Sales: UNCTAD, *World Investment Report 2002;* M&A/FDI: World Bank, *World Development Indicators 2002;* Equity Issued Overseas: Thomson Financial, SDC Platinum database; Overseas Equity/Portfolio: IMF, *International Financial Statistics Online;* Bonds Issued Overseas: Thomson Financial, SDC Platinum database; Overseas Bonds/Portfolio: IMF, *International Financial Statistics Online*

Still, we caution again against inferences that are too strong. The benefits of foreign listings presume that corporate governance improves. In a rare study, Davis and Marquis (forthcoming) looked at the board of directors of companies listed on foreign exchanges and concluded that boards remained largely national in their composition. Davis and Marquis (forthcoming) conclude: "On average, the foreign firms we studied organize their boards in the same ways as their domestic counterparts. Few make their financial statements available electronically to (potential) investors. They typically attract few equity analysts and receive very little interest from institutional investors (a median of under 2 percent)." In short, the value of a foreign listing is partly the signal it sends about quality rather than that of enforcement. A foreign listing does not mean convergence to a global corporate governance standard. More important, a foreign listing reveals a selection bias: those owners who enjoy private benefits will be less likely to list overseas. Hence, it is unclear what net change will be transmitted by these listings.

It will be interesting to see whether the trend to list overseas complements FDI or becomes a substitute for it. A recent study by Alfaro, Chanda, Kalemli-Ozcan, and Sayek (2002) find that there are "complementary" benefits of FDI when there is adequate domestic financial development. We hesitate to endorse yet another study on direct investment spillover, except to raise two points. It makes sense that spillovers may require a financial sector to finance operations that are complementary to "new ideas," but it is not at all obvious that spillovers require an equity market. Second, with the massive trend toward listings on international equity markets servicing the needs of the larger international companies, most countries will not develop liquid stock markets. The future of the many exchanges in central Europe are in doubt, and those in eastern Europe have never developed and perhaps never will (see Claessen, Djankov, and Klingebiel, 2000). Financial history shows that almost all regional stock exchanges do not survive. After all, the United States is reported to have had more than 200 exchanges in the 1800s, and even Russia had a dozen in the heady days of voucher trading (Michie, 1987; Spicer, 1998). The role of domestic capital markets for development especially for smaller countries is, in a single word, complex.

CONCLUSION

In Table 8.5, we attach estimates of the importance of the sources of FDI, privatization, acquisitions of banks, minority investments, and inverse equity listings. These are not exclusive categories, so there is no sense in adding up the columns. In short, most countries in the world are heavily infected by pressures for higher corporate governance practices, especially regarding publicly-traded and large companies. Whether countries "tip" in changing their overall corporate governance systems will vary by case. Some countries may have systems that work well for their culture and stage of development; others may resist change because political interests prefer the status quo. But there is no doubt in the data. By the year 2000, the highways by which the

TABLE 8.5   **Sources of Foreign Investment and Governance Contagion (in Percent)***

	INWARD FDI		INWARD PORTFOLIO		M&A SALES		CROSS-BORDER LOANS		FOREIGN AFFILIATE LOANS		FUNDS RAISED OVERSEAS		PRIVATIZED ASSETS	
INCOME	1990	2000	1990	2000	1990	2000	1990	2000	1990	2000	1990	2000	1990	1999
Upper middle income	5.0	16.1	8.7	2.9	4.2	11.1	32.2	45.1	3.6	71.4	0.33	1.12	5.26	7.06
Lower middle income	2.0	9.4	0.2	-0.8	0.1	1.4	11.4	14.7	1.6	8.2	0.23	0.18	0.03	1.12
Low income	1.7	3.2	-0.1	-0.4	1.5	11.6	24.6	28.0	8.1	15.4	0.01	0.08	0.07	1.97

* Figures as a percentage of Fixed Capital Formation

Sources: Inward FDI: World Bank, *World Development Indicators 2002*, Inward Portfolio: IMF, *International Financial Statistics Online*; M&A Sales: UNCTAD, *World Investment Report 2002*; Cross-border Loans: Bank of International Settlements, *Consolidated International Banking Statistics* (various); Foreign Affiliate Loans: Bank of International Settlements, *Consolidated International Banking Statistics* (various); Funds Raised Overseas: Thomson Financial, SDC Platinum database; Privatized Assets: Brune, Garrett, and Kogut (2003)

"infection" of better corporate governance travels were no longer dirt roads: they were well-paved, with traffic passing in both directions (we would like to believe).

There is some evidence that these channels create what can be called a self-reinforcing process. Perotti and Oijen (2001) argue, with evidence, that privatization leads to an improved foreign perception of a country, and that these improvements lead to more rapid financial-market development. Policies can make an institutional difference, if they signal broad and credible commitments to economic change.

For some, multinational corporations represent a lighthouse of better practice. The evidence for these effects is very mixed. As we saw, the aggregate data do not consistently show that direct investment adds to the productivity or growth of countries. Overall, globalization brings benefits, but these benefits are not uniquely and decisively tied to investments by multinational corporations at a time when knowledge can flow by many channels.

It is hard to make the case that multinational corporations will choose to be agents for institutional changes in world corporate governance. The argument that multinational corporations will lobby for changes in institutions of corporate change is far from settled, in evidence or in logic. After all, the incentives for such lobbying cut in both directions for a foreign firm. The history of the multinational corporation reverberates with clangs of criticisms—sometimes of unquestionable foundation—concerning its power and business practices. Foreign firms have been implicated in scandals; they have engaged in practices to influence local politics by questionable means and have even unsettled governments. The worst of this history might be largely behind us, but the residues are certainly still poignant.[13]

Because of their history, from time to time there is a call for regulation of multinational corporations. The OECD, among other institutions, has written up a code of behavior; countries, notably the United States, have passed laws forbidding foreign corruption (often in response to salient cases). We have asked in the above analysis if multinational corporations will lobby for better corporate governance. We do not judge this possibility to be an important element in creating better corporate governance. Neither do we conclude that foreign listings by domestic firms—what we have called inverse-equity listings—will be very influential.

Instead, we argue that minority investors, portfolio investors, and banks have played and can play the most important governance role in a country, because better corporate governance lies in their interest and together they hold investments in many companies. Foreign control of banks is potentially powerful (and hence politically sensitive), for banks care about payments to service loans and the managerial practices of their clients. Foreign ownership brings a degree of political independence as well as the concern to meet the demands of shareholders. Through their loan portfolios, banks occupy "multiplier" positions in an economy.

We have cautioned frequently against inferring too much from selected studies. Countries are living societies that balance many elements: cultural, political, equity, and wealth. Given a particular form, such as the public company, there are worse and better corporate governance practices. Regarding corporate governance *systems*, we advise against blanket recommendations. Here the multinational corporation can play an important role as a body of natural experiments, in which foreign governance practices are mixed with local practices and values (Kogut, 1995). It is this variety and experimentation that represents an opportunity for government, business, and citizens to re-think the national institutions of corporate governance.

NOTES

1   The IMF and OECD emphasize a "lasting interest" to define direct investment, but this deletion of control appears to be pragmatic rather than theoretical; it is easier to classify a minority investment as "lasting" and to avoid the semantics of what amount of equity constitutes "control." For the purposes of the IMF (which is concerned about financial stability), this definition is adequate, and it may also be adequate for understanding the motives behind why minority shareholders with small, but still important, holdings (such as pension fund investments) may care about governance.

2   This issue is different from the question of how FDI affects wages. Here the evidence shows overwhelming that multinational corporations pay higher wages. For an excellent review, see Lipsey (2002). The debate is over whether trade or direct investment affects the wages of the home country, that is, do multinational corporations "export jobs" and hence lower home wages.

3   See Amsden (1989) for a discussion of Korea and Shapiro (1994) who both analyze the impact of FDI on a country's political and economic fabric.

4   *World Link*, the World Economic Forum publication, summarized an early version of this work in 1999. See Kogut and Walker (2001) for the full study.

5   World Bank Group's Privatization Transaction Database (1990–1999) compiled by the Development Economics Group of the World Bank.

6   Ibid.

7   World Bank (2002). It is unfortunate to attribute the low capitalization of emerging markets to poor governance. We are again dealing with different corporate governance *systems* where there are many private firms. We have little data on their governance properties compared to family-owned firms in rich countries.

8   Data are from the Bank of International Settlements, Consolidated International Banking Statements. The increase in the value of loans is not matched by a similar increase in loans as a fraction of GDP because of GDP growth during this period.

9   Ibid.

10 See Coffee (2002) for an initial discussion.

11 With ADR, a foreign firm deposits its share in a bank, and the bank creates dollar-denominated shares sold. GDR works on the same basis but outside the United States.

12 Our calculations are based on data from the Thomson Financial SDC Platinum database.

13 See Mira Wilkin's history of American Business Abroad, especially the early history of the Vanderbilts in Nicaragua (Wilkins, 1970). Edith Penrose provided a memorable analysis of the oil industry, called the "seven sisters" (Penrose, 1968).

REFERENCES

Aitken, B., and A. Harrison. 1999. "Do Domestic Firms Benefit from Direct Foreign Investment? Evidence from Venezuela," *American Economic Review* 89, pp. 605–618.

Alfaro, L., A. Chanda, S. Kalemli-Ozcan, and S. Sayek. 2002. "FDI and Economic Growth: The Role of Local Financial Markets," HBS Working Paper No. 01-083. Cambridge, MA: Harvard Business School.

Almeida, P. 1996. "Knowledge Sourcing By Foreign Multinationals: Patent Citation Analysis in the US Semiconductor Industry," *Strategic Management Journal* 17, Winter, pp. 155–165.

Almeida, P., and B. Kogut. 1997. "The Exploration of Technological Diversity and the Geographic Localization of Innovation," *Small Business Economics* 9, pp. 21–31.

Almeida, P., and B. Kogut. 1999. "Localization of Knowledge and the Mobility of Engineers in Regional Networks," *Management Science* 45, pp. 905–917.

Almeida, P., J. Song, and R. M. Grant. 2002. "Are Firms Superior to Alliances and Markets? An Empirical Test of Cross-Border Knowledge Building," *Organization Science* 13, pp. 147–161.

Amsden, A. 1989. *Asia's New Giant: South Korea and Late Industrialization.* New York: Oxford University Press.

Balasubramanyam, V., D. Sapsford, and M. Salisu. 1996. "Foreign Direct Investment and Growth in EP and IS Countries," *Economic Journal* 106, pp. 92–105.

Bank of International Settlements (BIS). 1990–2002. Consolidated International Banking Statistics. Basel: Bank of International Settlements.

Bannerjee, A., and E. Duflo. 2000. "Reputation Effects and the Limits of Contracting: A Study of the Indian Software Industry," *Quarterly Journal of Economics* 115, pp. 989–1017.

Blömstrom, M. 1986. "Foreign Investment and Productive Efficiency: The Case of Mexico," *Journal of Industrial Economics* 15, pp. 97–110.

Blomström, M. 1999. *The Economics of International Investment Incentives*. Paris: Organisation for Economic Co-operation and Development.

Blömstrom , M., R. Lipsey, and D. Konan. 1992. "What Explains Developing Country Growth?" NBER Working Paper No. 4132. Cambridge, MA: National Bureau of Economic Research.

Blalock, G., and P. Gertler. 2002a. "Technology Diffusion from Foreign Direct Investment through Supply Chains." Unpublished Paper. Department of Applied Economics and Management, Cornell University, Ithaca, NY.

Blalock, G., and P. Gertler. 2002b. "Firm Capabilities and Technology Adoption: Evidence from Foreign Direct Investment in Indonesia." Unpublished Paper., Department of Applied Economics and Management, Cornell University, Ithaca, NY.

Borensztein, E., J. De Gregorio, and J. W. Lee. 1998. "How Does Foreign Direct Investment Affect Economic Growth?" *Journal of International Economics* 45, pp. 115–135.

Brune, N., G. Garrett, and B. Kogut. 2003. "The Global Spread of Privatization: The Role of International Financial Institutions," Reginald H. Jones Center Working Paper No. 1. Philadelphia, PA: Wharton School of the University of Pennsylvania.

Cantwell, J. 1989. *Technological Innovation and Multinational Corporations*. Oxford: Basil Blackwell.

Carkovic, M., and R. Levine. 2002. "Does Foreign Direct Investment Accelerate Economic Growth?" UM Working Paper, Department of Economics. Minneapolis, MN: University of Minnesota.

Chung, W., and Juan Alcacer. Forthcoming. "Heterogeneous Investment Motives and Location Choice of Foreign Direct Investment in the United States," *Management Science*.

Claessens, S., S. Djankov, and D. Klingebiel. 2000. "Stock Markets in Transition Economies," WBFS Discussion Paper No. 5. Washington, DC: World Bank.

Coe, D., and E. Helpman. 1995. "International R&D Spillovers," *European Economic Review* 39, pp. 859–887.

Coe, D., E. Helpman, and A. W. Hoffmaister. 1997. "North-South R&D Spillovers," *Economic Journal* 107, pp. 134–149.

Coffee, J. 2002. "Competition Among Securities Markets: A Path Dependent Perspective," Columbia Law and Economics Working Paper No. 192. New York: Columbia Law School.

Davis, G., and C. Marquis. Forthcoming. "The Globalization of Stock Markets and Convergence in Corporate Governance." In R. Swedberg and V. Nee, eds., *The Economic Sociology of Capitalism*. Cambridge: Cambridge University Press.

De Soysa, I., and J. R. Oneal. 1999. "Boon or Bane? Reassessing the Effects of Foreign Capital on Economic Growth," *American Sociological Review* 64, 766–782.

Dyck, A., and I. Zingales. 2003. "Why Are Private Benefits of Control So Large in Certain Countries and What Effects Does This Have on Their Financial Development?" *Journal of Finance* (forthcoming).

Feldstein, M., and C. Horioka. 1980. "Domestic Saving and International Capital Flows," *Economic Journal* 90, pp. 314–329.

International Monetary Fund (IMF). 2002. *International Financial Statistics Online*. http://ifs.apdi.net/imf.

Jaffe, A., M. Trajtenberg, and R. Henderson. 1991. "Geographical Localisation of Knowledge Spillovers as Evidenced by Patent Citations," *Quarterly Journal of Economics* 108, pp. 577–599.

Kogut, B. 1995. "Foreign Direct Investment, Experimentation, and Governance in Transition Economies." In C. Gray, R. Frydman, and A. Rapacynski, eds., *Corporate Governance in Central and Eastern Europe*. Budapest: World Bank and Central European University.

Kogut, B., and S. J. Chang. 1991. "Technological Capabilities and Japanese Foreign Direct Investment in The United States," *Review of Economics and Statistics* 73, pp. 401–413.

Kogut, B., and U. Zander. 1993. "Knowledge of the Firm and the Evolutionary Theory of the Multinational Corporation," *Journal of International Business Studies* 24, pp. 625–646.

Kogut, B., and G. Walker. 2001. "The Small World of Germany and the Durability of National Networks," *American Sociological Review* 66, pp. 317–335.

Lichtenberg, F., and B. van Pottelsberghe de la Potterie. 1998. "International R&D Spillovers: A Comment," *European Economic Review* 42, pp. 1483–1491.

Lichtenberg, F., and B. van Pottelsberghe de la Potterie. 2001. "Does Foreign Direct Investment Transfer Technology Across Borders?" *The Review of Economics and Statistics* 83, pp. 490–497.

Lipsey, R. 1999. "The Role of Foreign Direct Investment in International Capital Flows." In M. Feldstein, ed., *International Capital Flows*. Cambridge, MA: National Bureau of Economic Research.

Lipsey, R. 2002. "Home and Host Country Effects of FDI," Presented at the ISIT Conference on Challenges to Globalization, Lindingo, Sweden, May 24–25.

MacDuffie, J. P. 1995. "Human Resource Bundles and Manufacturing Performance: Organizational Logic and Flexible Production Systems in the World Auto Industry," *Industrial and Labor Relations Review* 48, pp. 197–221.

Macpherson, J. M. 2003. "Global Trade Networks, Knowledge Flows, and the Returns to Cross-Border Acquisitions." Unpublished PhD Dissertation, Wharton School, University of Pennsylvania.

Michie, R. C. 1987. *The London and New York Stock Exchanges, 1850–1914*. London: Allen and Unwin.

Morck, R., B. Yeung, and W. Yu. 2000. "The Information Content of Stock Markets: Why Do Emerging Markets Have Synchronous Stock Price Movements?" *Journal of Financial Economics* 58, pp. 215–260.

Pack, H. 1987. *Productivity, Technology, and Industrial Development*. New York: Oxford University Press.

Penrose, E. 1968. *The Large International Firm in Developing Countries*. London: Allen and Unwin.

Perotti, E., and P. van Oijen. 2001. "Privatization, Market Development and Political Risk in Emerging Economies," *Journal of International Money and Finance* 20, pp. 43–69.

Rodrik, D. 1997. *Has Globalization Gone Too Far?* Washington, DC: Institute for International Economics.

Rogers, M. 2002. "Absorptive Capability and Economic Growth: How Do Countries Catch-Up?" Online. http://users/ox.ac.uk/~manc0346/absorptive.pdf.

Shapiro, H. 1994. *Engines of Growth: The State and Transnational Auto Companies in Brazil*. Cambridge: Cambridge University Press.

Song, J. 2002. "Firm Capabilities and Technology Ladders: Sequential Foreign Direct Investments of Japanese Electronics Firms in East Asia," *Strategic Management Journal* 23, pp. 191–210.

Song, J., P. Almeida, and G. Wu. 2001. "Mobility Of Engineers and Cross-Border Knowledge Building: The Technological Catching-Up Case of Korean and Taiwanese Semiconductor Firms." In H. Chesbrough and R. Burgelman, eds., *Research in Technology and Innovation Management*. New York: Elsevier.

Spicer, A. 1998. "Institutions and the Social Construction of Organizational Form: The Development of Russian Mutual Funds, 1992–1997." PhD Dissertation, Wharton School, University of Pennsylvania.

Thomson Financial Services Company. 2002. Securities Data Company Platinum Database. New York: Thomson Financial Services Company.

United Nations Conference on Trade and Development (UNCTAD). 2002. *World Investment Report 2002: Transnational Corporations and Export Competitiveness*. New York: United Nations Conference on Trade and Development.

Veugelers, R., and B. Cassiman. 1999. "Importance of International Linkages for Local Know-How Flows: Some Econometric Evidence from Belgium," CEPR Discussion Paper No. 2337. London: Centre for Economic Policy Research.

World Bank. 2002. World Development Indicators (CD-ROM). Washington, DC: World Bank.

Wilkins, M. 1970. *The Emergence of Multinational Enterprise: American Business Abroad from the Colonial Era to 1914*. Cambridge, MA: Harvard University Press.

Wilkins, M. 1988. "The Free-Standing Company, 1870-1914: An Important Type of British Foreign Direct Investment," *Economic History Review* 41, pp. 259–282.

Womack, J., D. Jones, and D. Roos. 1991. *The Machine That Changed the World*. New York: HarperCollins.

APPENDIX 8.1 **Coefficient of Variation for Inward Investment Flows 1980–2000**

COUNTRY	PORTFOLIO	FDI	COUNTRY	PORTFOLIO	FDI
Albania		0.33	Djibouti		0.23
Algeria		0.94	Dominica	2.00	0.54
Angola		0.28	Dominican Republic	0.13	0.40
Antigua and Barbuda	1.97	0.20	Ecuador	1.03	0.07
Argentina	1.42	0.69	Egypt	2.14	0.22
Armenia	7.92		El Salvador	5.55	2.08
Aruba	0.68	0.66	Equatorial Guinea		0.37
Australia	0.37	0.24	Estonia	1.15	0.37
Austria	0.27	0.52	Ethiopia		
Azerbaijan		0.19	Fiji		0.27
Bahamas	0.06	0.43	Finland	0.34	0.82
Bahrain	0.61	0.88	France	0.50	0.18
Bangladesh	18.67	0.41	Gabon	1.11	0.41
Barbados	1.07	0.22	Gambia		0.38
Belarus	1.52	0.74	Georgia		0.40
Belgium	0.34	0.30	Germany	0.54	0.47
Belize	0.44	0.26	Ghana		0.34
Benin	0.45	0.34	Greece		0.07
Bolivia	0.82	0.17	Grenada	1.77	0.16
Bosnia			Guatemala	7.80	0.50
Botswana	2.87	0.22	Guinea		0.36
Brazil	1.13	0.18	Guyana	1.02	0.41
Bulgaria	2.84	0.20	Haiti		0.20
Burkina Faso		0.42	Honduras		0.25
Burundi		0.43	Hong Kong SAR	0.71	0.29
Cambodia			Hungary	0.61	0.43
Cameroon		0.40	Iceland	0.45	0.35
Canada	0.41	0.28	India	0.85	0.15
Cape Verde		0.64	Indonesia	3.20	0.24
Central African Republic	0.60		Iran		0.38
Chad		0.60	Ireland	0.57	0.33
Chile	1.08	0.49	Israel	0.59	0.18
China	1.05	0.08	Italy	0.30	0.38
Colombia	0.49	0.39	Jamaica	0.22	0.20
Comoros		0.53	Japan	0.67	0.63
Congo, DR		0.34	Jordan		0.47
Costa Rica	0.53	0.13	Kazakhstan	0.88	0.12
Cote d'Ivoire	0.41	0.24	Kenya	2.35	0.40
Croatia	0.67	0.28	Kiribati		0.22
Cyprus	0.69	0.18	South Korea	0.45	0.23
Czech Republic	0.37	0.30	Kuwait	1.03	1.03
Denmark	1.55	0.42	Kyrgyz Republic	21.40	0.40

APPENDIX 8.1 **Coefficient of Variation for Inward Investment Flows 1980–2000**

COUNTRY	PORTFOLIO	FDI	COUNTRY	PORTFOLIO	FDI
Lao PDR		0.27	Saudi Arabia		0.75
Latvia	1.55	0.21	Senegal	5.06	0.84
Lesotho		0.45	Seychelles	2.17	0.19
Liberia		0.40	Sierra Leone		1.14
Libya		0.58	Singapore	1.83	0.26
Lithuania	0.97	0.41	Slovak Republic	0.60	0.36
Macedonia, FYR	0.94	0.72	Slovenia	0.82	0.24
Madagascar		0.32	Solomon Islands		0.82
Malawi	0.79		Somalia		2.19
Malaysia	1.83	0.16	South Africa	0.59	1.15
Maldives		0.11	Spain	1.18	0.21
Mali		0.73	Sri Lanka	0.37	0.58
Mauritania	0.29	0.60	St. Kitts and Nevis	2.44	0.22
Malta	9.04	0.38	St. Lucia	1.68	0.19
Mauritius	76.72	0.56	St. Vincent	3.04	0.32
Mexico	1.01	0.16	Sudan		0.45
Moldova	10.84	0.41	Suriname	10.20	1.39
Mongolia		0.22	Swaziland	1.55	0.51
Morocco	1.43	0.71	Sweden	0.88	0.91
Mozambique		0.60	Switzerland	0.52	0.15
Myanmar			Syrian Arab Republic		0.35
Namibia	0.47	0.23	Tanzania		0.07
Nepal		0.46	Thailand	0.82	0.24
Netherlands	0.80	0.31	Togo	0.39	0.26
Netherlands Antilles	3.02	0.51	Tonga	0.78	0.20
New Zealand	3.40	0.25	Trinidad and Tobago		0.20
Nicaragua			Tunisia	0.46	0.34
Niger		0.78	Turkey	1.83	0.15
Nigeria	15.48	0.45	Turkmenistan		
Norway	0.61	0.17	Uganda		0.07
Oman	1.80	0.22	Ukraine	47.83	0.17
Pakistan	1.92	0.21	United Kingdom	0.32	0.22
Panama	0.36		United States	0.22	0.12
Papua New Guinea	0.32	0.59	Uruguay	0.51	0.13
Paraguay	23.95	0.49	Vanuatu		0.14
Peru	1.11	0.54	Venezuela	2.65	0.40
Philippines	1.51	0.46	Vietnam		0.14
Poland	0.58	0.08	Yemen		
Portugal	0.86	1.91	Zambia	1.91	0.43
Romania	7.86	0.43	Zimbabwe		0.22
Russian Federation	2.26	0.30			
Rwanda		0.21			

Chapter 9

Corporate Risk Assessment and Business Strategy

A Prime Task for Senior Management

Witold J. Henisz and Jonathan Story

How can we make corporate strategy in such a volatile world economy? Answering this question requires us to look at a much broader canvas than we do when we consider business strategy conventionally. Conventional business strategy divides conveniently into three parts, like Caesar's description of Gaul: what's going on inside the corporation; what is happening in terms of competition in the firm's markets; and, by deduction, what both inquiries hold for the firm's future. The recent pressure for improved corporate governance is but one example of this approach, which no doubt has the advantage of bringing management to focus on essentials—but in a world undergoing complex transformation, it is an approach that we believe is—to say the least—inadequate. What's going on inside the corporation and in the firm's markets is certainly a major driver of business strategy, but an excessive emphasis on these components could lead senior management to be the victims of external events that they have failed to anticipate. For example, in a consideration of the impact of governance on international capital flows, it would be remiss to not consider the impact of governance at the global and country levels as well as corporate governance.

Corporate strategies have to be elaborated, and opportunities and risks have to be assessed in full recognition of the external environment in which they take place. Environmental uncertainty is not easily described or encapsulated as a risk parameter in a simple accounting formula, but rather interacts with corporate strategy in global, national, and industrial contexts. The best measure of a country's risk level is of little use if managers do not appreciate its strategic implications and limitations. Pierre Wack of Royal Dutch Shell Petroleum explained it best when he implored managers to recognize that forecasts are typically wrong when you need them most (Wack, 1985). Wack argues that uncertainty should not be merely measured but accepted and planned for.

Throughout our analysis we focus on four dimensions that together form the playing field on which firms struggle to measure and manage uncertainty:

- Politics is not just what politicians do, but embraces all undertakings where the wills of two or more people are harnessed to a particular task (de Jouvenel, 1957). This extensive definition avoids the trap of state-centrism, without going so far as to assert that states or the state system are obsolete. States are concerned primarily to ensure that business conditions within their own jurisdictions are sufficiently attractive to foster wealth-creating activities and to attract inward investment by multinational corporations. Yet their powers are shared with other players, which operate alongside— and often in disregard of—states. Given this dispersion of authority, many traditional functions of the state to provide for their citizens are no longer discharged at all.

- Markets are indispensable people-centered knowledge and information systems. They price all factors of production—land, labor, capital, and technology—through the interplay of supply and demand. The price mechanism serves as a self-regulating system, which coordinates the activities of millions and serves as an exploratory device for new needs and technologies (Brittan, 1995). The driving force behind this self-regulating system is the entrepreneur, not government.

- Ideologies provide all-embracing explanations of purpose in collective human activities. Nationalists demand self-determination, liberals proclaim the need for an efficient global economy, techno-optimists see the cure for human problems in universal access, or religious zealots call for people to follow the path to salvation. The world, in short, continues to be driven forward by forces that interplay in kaleidoscopic ways to challenge old ways and stimulate a myriad of responses.

- Geopolitics is another driving force. Here states take center place, with the United States in a league of its own, by all measures of power capability (Nye, 1991). What the United States does is more important to the rest of the world, to put it briefly, than what the rest of the world does is to the United States. The other pole is Europe: hugely wealthy, with a potential global currency, a worldwide corporate reach, and a key emporium for the transition economies, Africa, and the Mid-East.

We begin by summarizing the extant literature on political risk and capital flows, which has gradually evolved beyond treating risk as a country-level black box to incorporate interdependencies and contingencies in risk analysis that touch on each of the four dimensions that we highlight above. Our framework for country risk analysis extends this tendency and develops a more complete depiction of the risks and opportunities faced by managers. We emphasize the heterogeneity that exists within country risk across various industries, firms, and even projects. We include three detailed applications of the broader governance framework that we provide.

RISK AND CAPITAL FLOWS

Surveys of multinational managers repeatedly highlight the centrality of the policy environment for international investment decisions (Kobrin et al., 1980; Root, 1968). A survey of 3,951 firms in 74 countries found that corruption and judicial unpredictability were the second and third most serious obstacles to doing business, following only taxation (Pfeffermann and Kisunki, 1999). A similar survey of the largest global multinational corporations found that nonconventional risks such as corruption, crony capitalism, and political risk cost firms USD 24 billion in lost revenue in 1998 alone, leading 84 percent of subsidiaries in emerging markets to fall short of their financial targets and an 8 to 10 percent diminution in total corporate returns (Merchant International Group, 1999). Another recent report estimated the economic significance of governance broadly defined and found that in countries with "opaque" governance (i.e., China, Russia, Indonesia, Turkey, South Korea, Romania, and the Czech Republic), investors contemplating entry faced the equivalent of an increase in corporate income taxes of 33 to 46 percent relative to the costs of entering a country with stronger governance (i.e., the United States or Chile) (Wei and Hall, 2001). In a similar analysis of portfolio flows, countries were penalized by 900 to 1,316 basis points. Countries with poorer governance also accumulated more debt relative to foreign direct investment (FDI) and more foreign currency–denominated debt pointing to a potential correlation between governance and the likelihood of financial crises (Wei and Wu, 2001; Johnson et al., 1998; chapter 13, this volume).

Despite the strong survey-based evidence regarding the importance of governance, the literature linking specific measures of governance to actual capital flows has historically yielded only mixed support for a strong causal link between the two variables. Researchers struggled with the multifaceted nature of risk and the difficulty of capturing the true environment faced by managers using any single metric. Improved data and analytical techniques have allowed for an evolution from the simple correlations between measures of sociopolitical instability and capital inflows, which were the focus of much of the early empirical work,[1] to more complete models that include various contingencies.

Politically unstable or repressive regimes might still receive high capital inflows from their allies in the Cold War or in the aftermath of an International Monetary Fund (IMF) or World Bank financing arrangement (Schneider and Frey, 1985). Rapidly growing countries implementing credible host country reforms that enjoyed the support of relatively homogenous polities, given an absence of serious interest groups or bureaucratic divisions, might also receive greater inflows than suggested by an accounting of their sociopolitical characteristics (Gastanaga, Nugent, and Pashamova, 1998). Even country-level environments lacking these safeguards could still attract investors able to protect their own investments by using the credible threat of exit provided by an extensive international subsidiary network (Janeba, 2001) or a nonreplicable and/or rapidly depreciating technology (Oxley, 1999).

Although such surveys and broad quantitative studies are useful for supporting the notion that governance matters and hint at the complexities in ascertaining precisely how, neither the surveys nor the studies provide substantial assistance to managers seeking to avoid the risks and seize the opportunities provided by cross-national differences in governance. The development of such a strategic framework requires an assessment of the global, national, industrial, and firm-level effects of governance. This is what we attempt to fashion here.

THE DYNAMICS OF GLOBAL GOVERNANCE

Trying to predict global trends is hazardous, but it is unavoidable if we are competing in world markets. The assumptions we make about where the future may lead us have therefore to be spelled out as clearly as possible. One set has the world converging on western political norms, on western economic policy, and on a market-driven process of world integration. Convergence on western political norms is evident in the contagion of political transition toward representative forms of government. The spread of market-friendly policies attests to convergence in economic policy approaches. Consumer tastes tend to become more alike as living conditions rise for all. Ultimately, a global public interest is best served, this view holds, by international organizations, governments, and nongovernmental organizations working together for the good of "the international community" (Kaul, Gruberg, and Stern, 1999). Overall, the vision is of a radiant future for humankind. Investors can be confident that their international expansions will eventually be integrated into this global system, and they should seek advantage in that future system by developing a global upstream and downstream network and the experience necessary to manage such a complex system.

An alternative set of assumptions focuses more on the choices that people make as individuals or collectively. In such a highly political world, the same factors that are seen by many as contributing to convergence become sources of divergence. Political actors of any stripe may not heed the call of economists and sacrifice the livelihoods of the comparatively disadvantaged on the altar of free trade. Markets are embedded in social and political institutions, and do not exist independently of the rules and institutions that establish them. In this view, as the world becomes a smaller place, frictions between peoples from different civilizations rise. National governments project their own demands into international institutions, so that the system of global governance under construction is a negotiated construct, which reflects the institutional arrangements—national, regional, or global—from which they emerged. Overall, giving salience to discretion in human affairs points to diversity and divergence rather than to linearity, integration, and convergence. There is no dissolvent to the tensions afflicting the world; quite the contrary, globalization is a stimulus. Investors should therefore expand abroad to seize the advantage provided by these different institutional structures, prices, cultures of management, and networks of international governance in full recognition of the complexities involved in doing business "over there."

Each one of these stories of the world's future holds kernels of insight. Their true force only comes to light if they are presented as complementary opposites: a diversity of state institutions in a non-homogeneous world, penetrated and shaped by systems of economic coordination, operating powerfully to create a more homogeneous world civilization; alongside aspirations to create a system of global governance out of the world's existing institutional framework as the counterpart to a world of relentless competition between peoples, states, corporations, or currencies.

Our point is that, together, these two sets describe a dialectical process of change at the level of markets, societies, and cultures in which firms and governments are co-participants. Corporations are, however, leading this revolutionary process. This process is dialectical, not in Marx's sense of class against class, but in the sense that it offers the world's population a prospect for convergence on common norms of governance, incomes, and life expectations. But it is only a prospect, and a fragile one at that, because the irreversible road toward a still illusive world civilization is paved also with unprecedented challenges of adaptation. These challenges may take a variety of forms—from political backlashes to protect cherished traditions, to changes of regime or unexpected exchange rate contagions. The implication for risk analysis as an intermediary variable between capital flows and various levels of governance is that we cannot reasonably assume that the two interact in readily predictable ways. This means that investors must simultaneously integrate their global operations and beware that backlash is built into the process of global integration, currently underway. So let us move on to the next stage, and discuss how an investor may assess a specific country's prospects along the dimensions of politics, markets, culture, and geopolitics.

COMPARING DIFFERENT BUSINESS CONDITIONS IN DISTINCT TERRITORIES

If, based on our expectations regarding global convergence or divergence, we decide to invest time and money abroad, we have to instruct ourselves about the way the countries we choose to operate in function. We must avoid the temptation of taking an easy way out of inevitable complexity by opting for a mood of "optimism" or "pessimism" about such-and-such a territory. Examining the world as it is for the investor is a pre-requisite for sound business practice. Consider, for instance, the advice on offer in the years 1993–1997, whereby corruption in Indonesia was said to have moderated substantially, bureaucratic efficiency and government quality to have improved, and the likelihood of government renegotiation or contract expropriation to have waned. Such assessments by Political Risk Services and other rating agencies track the recent experience of investors, not the probability that such experiences will continue, as investors discovered to their cost in 1998.

As a step toward presenting the complex linkages between global dynamics and country-level factors, we turn here to the notion of a *national business system*, which we simply define as holding three key, related components (Whitley, 1999). First come the *state institutions* dealing with financial markets structures and labor market regulations. Most emerging market countries have bank-based financial systems, while their financial markets have traditionally been used to allocate financial resources authoritatively for use by state corporations (France) or private *chaebols* (Korea). Labor market regulations are the product of national social contracts, the details of which can make all the difference as to whether an investment goes ahead or not. The second component of a business system relates to the coordination of economic activities between stakeholders. This yields a spectrum of types from loose coordination among firms, as in the United Kingdom, through highly hierarchical and authoritative structure of business interest representation, such as in Austria and Germany, or state-centered business representation as in China or France. The third component relates to the way firm policy is made—its governance—and the organizational attributes that enable firms to transform its *resources* into outputs using the skills and knowledge of their employees in codified or tacit routines. This touches on the level of workforce skills in the short term, the development of collective competences in the medium term, and, in the long-run, the dynamic capability of innovation (Nelson and Winter, 1982; Teece, Pisano, and Shuen, 1997).

Let us return to our four driving forces: politics, markets, ideology, and geopolitics, now using them to link the global dynamics we highlighted above to the concept of business system as a way into accenting the strategic implications of each of our four forces for international investors.

Politics

International diplomacy now regularly associates state institutions with corporations and nongovernmental organizations. Corporations negotiate the terms of their investments and the distribution of its rents around the world with other firms, through direct discussions with governments, and more indirectly through government channels. These channels may be bi-lateral, for instance China pressuring France to desist from arms sales to Taiwan by depriving French corporations of mainland contracts. They may be multi-lateral, such as EU negotiations for enlargement to incorporate the candidate countries of central-eastern Europe. Or they may focus on global trade negotiations in the World Trade Organization (WTO) on patent policies and nontariff barriers. Corporations thus establish transnational networks of alliances and enter bilateral bargains with states, where control over outcomes is negotiated. This is the "new diplomacy" (Stopford and Strange, 1991) between states and corporations, which overlays and differs from the bi- or multilateral diplomacy of states. It has considerable significance for corporations, which have become—whether they like it or not—political players in what many people around the world consider to be a nascent world polity. The three strategic implications of the entrance of multinational corporations into international diplomacy are:

1. Managers, like politicians before them, should assess their relative bargaining power in negotiations with governments, multilateral bodies, and nongovernmental organizations (Fagre and Wells, 1982; Kobrin, 1987; Vernon, 1977).

2. Managers must negotiate with foresight. The outcome of a negotiation depends not only on the terms of the final agreement but also on the credibility that such terms will in fact be realized.

3. Corporations are responsible not only to shareholders, but should also expect to be held accountable for their actions to a wider world community.

Markets

The global economic structure may be simply summarized: 80 percent of global income is enjoyed by 16 percent of the world's population. The rest, in short, depend on the West for access to its markets, for its technologies, and to attract inward investment. The global structure is built on inherited inequalities, and these are reflected in international economic relations. International economic relations between one state and world markets may be traced through flows of goods and services, investments, and capital movements. The structures of national economies and their specializations and competences result from natural endowments, and even more so from past policies. Relative prices for goods and services within the national economy relate to relative prices on world markets through the balance of payments and the foreign exchange rate of the national currency with regard to other currencies trading on world markets. Over the past decade, developing country governments have sought to overturn the status quo distribution of income and wealth by attracting foreign investors willing to fund their domestic transformation. Investors should recognize that, despite the large potential for mutual gain, the interests of the developing country governments thus differ markedly for their own goal of profit maximization: the division of rents as between the host country and the parent company is and will remain a source of tension.

Ideology

There exists a battle of cultures in world time and local time. World time is an analogy for fast travel, instant communications, and a networked economy. Its essence is ahistorical, as the past is interesting only insofar as it provides clues to the future.

World time tends to speak English with an American accent. Local time is an analogy for the provincial reality of most people's experience, and stretches far beyond the life of individuals into mythologized pasts that populate the many mental landscapes of the world's peoples, with holy places, ruins, and legends. It is bound by history and geography. At the heart of the world's present condition is this juxtaposition of the two categories of time. Consider the crucial matter of ownership (Mason and Encarnation, 1994): one rendering of an open world economy is the requirement for equal access to markets for corporate assets. But most countries have cross-shareholdings to exclude foreigners. In Malaysia, one explanation for Prime Minister Mahathir's decision in August 1998 to lock foreign investors into the Kuala Lumpur market was the pre-emption of a fire sale of Malay properties to Chinese entrepreneurs, following a prospective collapse of the ringit. According to this perspective, Mahathir gave priority to preserving ethnic harmony over IMF prescriptions for prompt market adjustments to market disequilibria. Similar examples may be multiplied around the world. The conflict between world time and local time enhances the conflict between host country governments and investors over the distribution of rents.

Geopolitics

Geopolitics now encompasses the desire of all states to maintain a degree of autonomy not only from foreign states but also from foreign corporations, markets, and ideologies. This search for autonomy induces states to act as a "megaforce" (Austin, 1990) in the markets through control over financial flows, licenses, procurement, labor or tariffs, quotas, and foreign exchange. A side effect is the growth in political markets, as corporate managers have to bid for favors from public officials. As often as not, states tend to trace an invisible barrier around their national assets in order to retain a degree of autonomy from traditional foes (Vernon, 1971; 1977). As often as not these are neighbors. Consider for instance, the Republic of Korea's limits on foreign ownership, ostensibly applying to foreigners in general. Their prime target is Japan, Korea's former colonizer. Thus the investor is but one player in a wider political and economic battle for rents and power that may involve the home country government as well as other perceived foes. Full awareness of the dimensions of this conflict is essential for maximizing an investor's own share of the final returns.

BUSINESS SYSTEMS AND INDUSTRY ANALYSIS

Beyond this assessment of global dynamics and national context, investors must also examine industry-specific risks and opportunities. Many of the elements described above will vary or have a differential weight across industries. Beginning with the state institutions that govern the access to the factors of production, policies that enhance the availability of skilled labor or ISO-certified suppliers in the domestic economy may be of paramount concern for investors in many manufacturing sectors but of little note to firms in natural resource extraction, construction, textiles, and other sectors employing primarily unskilled labor.

Investors should similarly examine those policies that promote investment in a sector, particularly where they are differentially applied within that sector either across geographic regions or classes of producers. These may include direct investment incentives such as tax holidays, infrastructure guarantees, and regulatory concessions, or they may be found in the country's general taxation and regulatory system. At one level, preferential treatment clearly signals a government's desire for international investment and a more favorable investment climate. Such preferences, however, may be removed or reversed in the future, requiring a careful analysis of the credibility of the policy regime in the light of the country's position in the state system and the global economy, the structure of its national political institutions, and the preferences of other influential actors in the polity over the time horizon of the relevant policies. Less favorable policies may actually be preferred if they are perceived by investors as more stable.

More generally, and invoking elements of ideology, investors should examine the extent to which their target sector has historically been in the domain of state ownership or state operation. Do societal values favor private participation in the sector and the associated pursuit of profits, or does the polity place a greater weight on public interests such as equity and security? Privatizations or the opening of sectors with heavy historic government involvement signal both a need for private investment and a deviation from historic norms of state control. The fact that governments need foreign entry offers the potential to craft favorable economic incentives or structure a regulatory system that safeguards investors against future policy shifts. Investors, however, should not exploit such bargaining power to its fullest extent in every case. Such shifts in the role of the state are, in rare instances, the result of local innovation (e.g., Chile in the 1970s or 1980s), in which case such investor encouragement may be helpful in moving to a new equilibrium more rapidly. More commonly, however, these shifts are externally imposed (e.g., by the IMF, the World Bank, or a current macroeconomic crisis), in which case demands for changes in policy or institutional design that are inconsistent with broader societal values may engender a backlash. The extent of such a backlash—our dialectical process in action—will vary not only in the way that the polity perceives the sector but will also be a function of the country's position in the international state system and global economy and its national political structures, which may moderate government incentives to renege upon, alter, or reinterpret commitments made to investors (Henisz and Zelner, 2002).

The coordination of economic activity among stakeholders in the existing supply chain is equally deserving of analysis. Do existing suppliers and customers welcome the new investment, or are they closely tied to existing competitors who perceive entry as a competitive threat? In the latter case, less-developed business systems that a new investment can help advance may be preferable to their more-developed but less welcoming counterparts.

Even when national business systems appear *prima facie* equivalent or comparable, industries may still differ substantially based on differences in their mean levels of governance, resources, or capabilities. An extreme contrast of such variation comes from the comparison of the resources involved in the construction of a multimillion dollar manufacturing facility versus the provision of consulting services. In the former case, the factory, once built, can not easily be disassembled or transformed to another use. Governments, suppliers, customers, and competitors thus have substantial leverage over investors in *ex post* bargaining, making any structural checks on policy discretion particularly valuable. By contrast, consultants can be put on the next plane out of a country should the terms of an agreement change. Some country-specific human capital may be difficult to redeploy, but it is the nature of the industry to emphasize redeployable human capital rather than knowledge that is context-specific. The ability of governments, suppliers, customers, and competitors to alter agreements is minimized by the threat of exit. The legal regime, political structure, and other country-level factors that make reneging, alteration, or reinterpretation of policy commitments difficult become less relevant in risk analysis. Thus the nature of the transaction undertaken in the host country is as important as the nature of the state system in ascertaining the level of political risk faced by the investor (Henisz, 2000; Henisz and Williamson, 1999).

FIRM-LEVEL ANALYSIS

Substantial variation exists in risk profiles even within a given industry. Two firms considering an investment in an identical project may govern that investment in ways that offer substantially different levels of risk or safeguards against a given level of risk. Firms differ in the factors of production under their control, the routines they employ to transform those factors into outputs, and the dynamic capabilities that lead to the development of those routines over time. Because of these differences, the same country- and industry-level environment may have a very different impact across firms. We consider the impact of varying each of these three firm-level characteristics.

One common safeguard against risk is the partnership with a well-connected local firm or the development of a close relationship with host country government officials. Firms, however, differ in their ability to manage these relationships (Lorenzoni and Lipparini, 1999; Anand and Khanna, 2000). Differences in the choice of governance or in its effectiveness may lead firms in the same country and industry to face substantially different risk profiles if the host country government perceives that reneging, altering, or reinterpreting an agreement with a subsidiary that includes a well-connected local partner and multinational working closely together involves lower political net benefits than a similar policy change imposed upon a solely foreign venture. As ventures that involve local partners are more familiar with local factor-markets, culture, politics, and other host country characteristics, joint ventures typically source and hire more from the domestic economy than do their purely foreign-owned counterparts. The loss to local firms, employees, and other constituents of the host country government is therefore likely to be greater when governments renege upon joint ventures as opposed to a wholly owned foreign subsidiary (Henisz, 2000). Of course, such dependence may turn into a handicap if regime change leads to a change in the definition of a well-connected firm.

Even two firms with the same governance structure and the same effectiveness in managing that internal relationship may face different risk profiles based on their capabilities in managing their external relationships. Such capabilities may develop through skill in forging personal ties and developing trust, or they may involve the deployment of other firm resources to support or influence the relationship. For example, some firms may use their ties to a powerful external political constituency (e.g., the United States in Latin America or France in West Africa) (Nigh, 1985), to prominent actors in the global economy such as rating agencies or international financial institutions, or to prominent actors in the domestic political system. Such linkages provide a voice that may restrain inimical policy changes or even lead to favorable policy outcomes. Once again, such dependence may turn into a handicap if bilateral relations between the host and home country sour or if the host country regime changes, making previously beneficial ties an encumbrance.

Another form of safeguard that similarly poses risks to investors is the strategic use of technology that is of great potential value to local actors. Firms are justifiably worried about the reverse engineering of their technology and the devaluation of their research and development expenses. Such concerns are particularly acute in countries with poor protection for intellectual property or weak legal regimes (Mansfield, 1994). One strategy in the face of such risk is to avoid countries where such technological expropriation is likely to occur (Henisz and Macher, 2002). Another strategy is to develop mechanisms for protecting the technology and preventing its diffusion to potential competitors (Oxley, 1999). Two firms in the same industry that differ in their reliance on legal regimes and intellectual property protection versus governance, trade secrets, modular technology, or rapidly depreciating technology may perceive very different risks in a host country environment. Investors should be aware, however, of the limits of such technological hedges—especially in the face of rapidly evolving technological change or strong social preferences regarding the widespread availability of the underlying technology.

A firm's own past experiences in the home country or other countries may also provide it with an advantage in assessing the nature of local risks and the best mechanisms for managing such risks. A diversity of international operations may also provide more leverage in bargaining with the host country government as such diversity makes the firm less dependent upon its local operations, making the threat of exit more plausible. By contrast, firms with little prior experience and highly focused international operations have greater difficulty in recognizing patterns of behavior, identifying plausible safeguards, and threatening to exit (Henisz and Delios, 2001).

APPLICATIONS

We have summarized evidence at the global, national, industrial, and firm-level that investors should examine in order to grasp fully the risks and opportunities that they face in their international investments. Though we have offered several isolated motivating examples, our framework has been largely abstract and subject to the criticism of list making. We want to demonstrate the relevance of our framework by applying it to three prominent cases. These applications highlight the extent to which investor analysis of country risk incorporates multiple levels of information, thereby requiring a careful mating of country-level information to firm-specific knowledge. By applying our framework to these cases we see the real tradeoffs with which senior management must grapple in designing their international strategies. First, we examine the limits in the scope of third-party intervention as determined by pressures for national sovereignty and national champions through the lens of a trade dispute between Bombardier and Embraer. Next, we show that the superficially puzzling decisions by Intel to locate a fabrication facility in a small isolated market that offered few tax concessions without the aid of a local partner is in fact consistent with a richer analysis of the risks and opportunities faced by Intel's site-selection team. Finally, the experience of independent power producers in east Asia demonstrates the sensitivity in entry strategies to the structure of state institutions, the importance of those strategies for performance, and the feedback risks inherent in even the best-designed risk mitigation strategies.

Globalization and national sovereignty: The potential and limits of the WTO

The increasing scale and scope of global trade introduces multilateral political institutions as legitimate and actors in global diplomacy. Prominent among such entities and the sole such actor to have the power to sanction its members (albeit with an extremely lengthy appellate process) is the WTO. Supporters and critics alike have emphasized the loss of sovereignty experienced by national governments who are now limited in their ability to unilaterally increase protection of certain industries or, alternatively, who are restricted from responding to legitimate environmental, health, and social demands of their polity. The increased profile of the WTO attests to the heightened convergence of the global economy and the increased role of market-based forces over their political and social counterparts. Firms with international disputes that fall within the jurisdiction of the WTO cannot, however, count on a rapid or rule-based resolution of these disputes even in areas that are explicitly within its realm of authority, particularly when they run afoul of strong pressures for national sovereignty and prestige.

One prominent example of the limits of WTO authority comes from the aerospace sector, where an ongoing dispute between Canada's Bombardier and Brazil's Embraer demonstrates the continued strength of national sovereignty particularly in industrial sectors that trigger strong nationalist sentiment. Despite requests in 1996 by the Canadian government for an investigation of the export subsidy offered by the Brazilian government to Embraer and a counterclaim by Brazil into various subsidies by the Canadian government to Bombardier, the case remains unresolved. Both national governments have been found to be in violation of the WTO rules, but their proposed remedies to their violations have been found insufficient, leading to further claims and appeals in their six-year-old dispute. Although the WTO has authorized sanctions, those penalties take the form only of allowed increases on tariffs from the other country on unrelated products. Neither government is willing to allow its national champion manufacturer to lose sales on account of subsidies provided by their counterpart. As a result, the governments continue to pursue bilateral negotiations under the threat of WTO-authorized penalties in an attempt to avoid a full-scale trade war. The fact that both nations are WTO members has in all likelihood prevented such an escalation from developing earlier, but it has proved far from a panacea to continued political pressures to defend national champions.

The location of this dispute in a high-profile industry such as aerospace is no coincidence. Politicians are loathe to sacrifice concentrated (in geography and time) local jobs or corporate revenue for the benefit of diffuse consumer welfare, but their desires are only further enhanced when the affected sector strikes an emotional chord with voters who perceive it as a symbol of national independence or national pride. Even better for local managers if they can point to actual or potential spillover benefits from their industry to buyers, suppliers, workers, or other associated parties. Clearly, aerospace falls in such a category, thereby enhancing the probability that a government will ignore or delay demands for compliance with WTO rulings. Firms in industries that at home or abroad are characterized by such national pressures for policy intervention should be realistic regarding the extent of redress that multilateral organizations are likely to provide. More generally, the scope and timing of WTO intervention will be a function of industrial characteristics that predispose the host or home-country governments to intervention.

National business systems and technological hedges: Intel's decision to locate in Costa Rica

Intel's decision to locate fabrication and manufacturing facilities abroad demonstrates the conflict and mutuality between the scenarios of global convergence and divergence, the importance of national business systems, and the role of firm-level technology in hedging against political risks. The initial list of countries considered—Argentina, Brazil, Chile, China, Costa Rica, India, Indonesia, Korea, Mexico, Puerto Rico, Singapore, Taiwan, and Thailand—was subsequently shortened to Brazil, Chile,

Costa Rica, and Mexico. The planned factory would import the vast majority of its components and export 100 percent of its output, demonstrating the increased integration of the global market economy even for a firm at the technological frontier and in need of highly skilled workers. Were the world economy to truly converge into a single market, however, site selection would be irrelevant as political, economic, and cultural characteristics would be identical (Ghemawat, 2001). Instead, nations remain distinct entities in each of these three dimensions, competing with each other for the possibility of hosting Intel's USD 500 million plant and the 2,000 jobs that it will bring to the local economy directly, plus the additional jobs that could follow if other high-technology firms follow Intel's lead. This process of competition among states for an investment of this size substantially aided Intel in securing a larger share of the rents than would be possible for a smaller investor with less potential spillover benefits (Gourlay, 2001).

Thus Intel began a complex series of site visits to the countries on its short list and evaluated the prospects for profitability of their new facility. Each government saw potential economic and political benefits to securing the facility and offered policy concessions that further enhanced relative inequalities in factor costs that spurred Intel to consider foreign locations for the facility. Electricity costs and supply reliability; airlift capacity and access to major markets; labor quality, costs, and flexibility (including a strong desire to have a non-unionized workforce); and taxes all factored into the decision calculus and posed some disadvantages for each country: Brazil (unionized and costly labor as well as security costs), Chile (distance from markets and costly skilled labor), Mexico (unionized labor), and Costa Rica (supply of skilled labor, electricity costs, and transportation infrastructure). More generally, the larger role of the state in the Brazilian economy and, even in the case of free-market Chile, the existence of capital controls on portfolio investment gave rise to concerns regarding the long-term prospects for repatriation of capital to the United States (Nelson, 1999).

Intel was careful, however, to emphasize variables other than the terms of the deal. Intel also went to great lengths to assess the local culture, surveying "local residents, financial power brokers, business leaders, old-money families and politicians . . . to uncover attitudes and perceptions within [the] community that may differ from what chamber of commerce promoters are telling the company." The vice-president of Intel International summarizes this component of their site selection strategy as a desire "to be aligned with the local community." The prospects for economic and political stability featured prominently in Costa Rica's success, as well as its long heritage of democracy, a broad market-based economy, and its membership in the WTO and the Caribbean Basin Initiative of the United States. "Intel didn't want to strike a 'deal' on tax incentives with one politician, only to find that the next leader to take office might rescind it" (Gourlay, 2001).

Turning to industry-specific factors, Costa Rica had singled out high technology as a priority sector for attracting foreign direct investment as it slowly lost competitiveness in textiles to other lower labor cost economies. According to the president of Costa Rica, Jose Maria Figueres,

> We wanted to incorporate Costa Rica into the global economy in an intelligent way. Globalization was more than simply opening the country to foreign trade. We needed a national strategy not based on cheap labor or the exploitation of natural resources. We wanted to compete based on productivity, efficiency and technology. . . . many textile firms had [left] the country and the government received severe criticism for not trying to sustain the maquila industry . . . [but] the foreign investment attraction strategy had changed. We wanted to attract industries with higher value-added, that would allow Costa Ricans to increase their standard of living.
> (excerpted from Nelson, 1999, p. 5)

Brazil, in contrast, saw little need to bargain with Intel as they already had billions of dollars of foreign direct investment inflows including a high-technology cluster around the domestic aerospace firm Embraer, while Chile offered few concessions due to their free-market ideology. Intel also stressed that the concessions it secured should be generally available to all firms making investment of equal size so that it could not be singled out as a recipient of special treatment and a target of populist backlash. Mexican concessions to work around legal requirements for unionization actually served as a detriment to that country's prospects (Spar, 1998). The limited scope of high-technology investment in Costa Rica ironically served as an advantage for that nation, as Intel had its own global supply network, could use its first-mover (Acer had a telephone call center in Costa Rica but few other high-technology firms had located within the country) advantage to secure larger concessions without competing against other large entrenched, particularly domestic, competitors for either concessions or crucial factors of production such as skilled labor.

Finally, turning to firm-specific factors, Intel—given its size, prominence, and technological sophistication—had no need to partner with a local firm to secure these gains. They did rely on a well-developed internal routine for site selection to secure the best possible terms and their stability over time. The rapid generational change in the industry gave further incentives to the Costa Rican government and local players not to renege, alter, or reinterpret any agreements with Intel as all parties wanted Intel's initial investment to expand in subsequent product generations.

With the aid of this analysis, each of the initially puzzling decisions seems prescient. Given the intermediate stage of global linkages that characterize the world economy, the decision to locate in a small, relatively isolated market still allowed for global market access and increased Intel's bargaining power with the host country government. The national business system was a prime consideration in the site selection process, but current policies were given secondary weight to the credibility of those policies as influenced by the relatively democratic political structure and the availability of similar terms to other large-scale investors. Finally, Intel was able to eschew a local partner despite local market uncertainties due to its strong and rapidly evolving position of technological leadership. Technology and reputation thus replaced relationships as the source of Intel's ongoing leverage with the Costa Rican government.

The importance of state structures and the limits of governance in politically salient industries: Independent power production in Southeast Asia

A third case that highlights the need to consider multiple levels of analysis in international investment is the contrast between the experiences of private power investors in three Southeast Asian countries after the Asian crisis. Here, the nature of the service to be sold (electricity) dictates mostly domestic production rather than international trade, so the role of globalization is limited to the dramatic (30-fold) increase in international investment in the sector, leading to a potential convergence of market structure and market players across national markets. In global terms, this increase in investment seemed justified by the huge demand for energy in emerging markets relative to the slower growth in energy consumption forecast in developed countries. The four markets that we consider—Thailand, the Philippines, Malaysia, and Indonesia—each experienced a drastic negative economic shock leading to a political reevaluation of the contingent division of rents. Specifically, contracts between the governments and investors that largely left non-construction risks in the hands of the public sector were renegotiated when the economy unexpectedly contracted, raising questions about the fairness of contractual terms that suddenly increased public but not private liabilities at a time of severe local hardship. These questions were particularly acute due to the immaturity of the formal institutional structures supporting private ownership in the electricity sector. The extent of the renegotiations experienced by investors after the crisis was strongly influenced by the structure of national political institutions. The contrast between the survival of firms in Malaysia and Indonesia, the two countries with the least credible policymaking structures, also demonstrates the limits of even the best designed firm-level risk mitigation strategies.

Compare, first, the treatment of investors in Thailand and the Philippines with that of investors in Indonesia and Malaysia following the 1997 financial crisis as a function of their respective state institutions. At the time of the crisis, the 393-seat lower house of the Thai legislature was divided among 10 parties. This heterogeneity of partisan affiliations ensured that any new policy proposal or change in the status quo policy required the approval of multiple parties with their own competing interests.

Similarly, the Philippine post-crisis government faced a razor-thin majority that relied on the support of independents and other allies in both chambers, as the controlling party held 110 of 221 seats in the lower legislative chamber and 10 seats in the 22-seat senate.

The institutions in Malaysia and Indonesia looked quite different. The prime minister of Malaysia at the time of the crisis, Dr. Mahathir, had been in power since 1982, and his party, United Malays National Organization, had been in power since Malaysia gained its independence in 1965. Moreover, several of the ostensible opposition parties in the Parliament had been created by the United Malays National Organization and voted with it as members of the National Front Coalition. The situation in Indonesia was even more clear-cut: President Suharto was elected by a People's Consultative Assembly to which he had appointed 575 of 1,000 members, and his Golkar Party controlled no less than 64 percent of the remaining elected members, who constituted the lower legislative chamber. In neither country was the judiciary considered truly independent.

Investors in Thailand and the Philippines, with their stronger institutional safeguards, fared relatively well following the crisis. In Thailand, investors had assumed the exchange rate risk under their original power purchase agreements (PPAs), but the Thai government actually chose to assume a larger fraction of the costs of the currency depreciation than it had to under the contracts. Similarly, in the Philippines, the government chose to absorb the costs of demand shortfalls by honoring its contractual commitments to various independent power producers (IPPs), despite the fact that this meant mothballing several state-owned generating facilities and procuring electricity at prices that were sometimes substantially higher than the state-owned enterprise's (SOE's) internal generation cost. Later, after absorbing substantial losses as a result of this policy, the government did exert pressure on IPPs to accept reduced contractual commitments, but it was just pressure—not fiat.

Electricity investors in Malaysia and Indonesia experienced much less favorable treatment once the financial crisis began. In 1997, the Malaysian government announced the suspension of its largest IPP contract (the 2,400 Bakun hydroelectric project). The SOE asked for assistance from the remaining IPPs to help meet its growing financial obligations to them; requested that the government place on hold all new IPP projects, including those with government approval and signed PPAs; and called for a 90-day deferment for payments to IPPs along with a 12 percent reduction in existing PPA payments. In Indonesia, the government announced in September 1997 that it would postpone or review infrastructure projects worth a total of more than RUP 50 trillion (USD 6 billion), leading to the postponement of 13 projects and the review of 6 more (out of a total of 26). In March 1998, the SOE sent a letter to its IPPs informing them that ". . . in light of the current monetary crisis . . . payment for purchase of geothermal steam and electric energy . . . will be in rupiah with an exchange rate of US $1 = 2,450 rupiah." The actual exchange rate at the time was RUP 10,000/USD 1.

Consider next the outcome of investors who adopted the widely recommended governance mechanism of taking on a local (i.e., host country) partner with privileged political access in the cases of Malaysia and Indonesia. The differential success of investors in these two countries following the 1997 Southeast Asian financial crisis illustrates the potential for a political backlash. Because the formal institutional supports for private infrastructure investment in these countries were so weak, as discussed above, investors were forced (often literally) to rely on informal networks, including members of the ruling government, as contractual supports. Electricity investors in Malaysia who were closely linked to the Mahathir government through local partners benefited from these ties somewhat following the 1997 crisis. For example, despite widespread doubts regarding its economic viability, the largest IPP in Malaysia (the Bakun hydroelectric project) continues to resurrect itself, due in no small part to the friendship between its chairman Ting Pek Khiing and the prime minister. In Indonesia, however, the same type of partnering practice ultimately backfired and magnified investors' exposure when a political transition occurred. In May 1998, after the 38-year reign of President Suharto, Suharto's vice president and close friend B. J. Habibe replaced him in office. Habibe and a series of subsequent presidents undertook a high-profile campaign against the corruption, cronyism, and nepotism ("KKN" in local parlance) that had characterized the Suharto regime. The Indonesian state audit agency subsequently reported that it had "found indications of corruption, collusion and nepotism in all 27 [private power] contracts" and thus had legal standing to terminate these agreements. The very partners that foreign investors had chosen to protect themselves from political risk thus became substantial liabilities in investors' relationships with the new government after a political transition.

Two lessons emerge from the experience of investors in the independent power sector in Southeast Asia. First, the structure of a country's political institutions—specifically, the extent to which checks and balances across or within various government bodies influences the feasibility of policy change—influences the entry strategy and performance of international investors. Where checks and balances are more binding (e.g., Thailand), investors are able to rely more strongly upon contractual and legal safeguards to protect themselves against any subsequent policy shifts. Furthermore, the eventual negative impact of a given negative shock or policy shift will be moderated more by this political structure than by a more concentrated political regime. Investors in countries that lack checks and balances (e.g., Malaysia and Indonesia) are forced to rely more heavily upon informal relationships and well-connected local partners. Not only do these safeguards provide less cover in times of crisis, but also the identity of the preferred local partner may shift suddenly in the case of regime change, leading to strong negative feedback effects for the *ex ante* best feasible strategy.

CONCLUSION

Let us conclude with a number of simple points. First, risk for corporations operating around the world is a multi-level construct. We suggest four levels—the global state and market system, the peculiar features and setting of our relevant states, an industry-specific analysis, and firm-specific characteristics—that we can look at through four different lenses. This approach poses the fundamental economic question of "who gets what?" and the cultural question of "who are We as opposed to who are They?" It also considers the complex diplomacy of interdependence in a semi-integrated world, and the geopolitical question that raises matters of organizational autonomy and political efforts to escape the constraints of vicinity. Researchers and managers are both beginning to incorporate some of these levels and questions into their analyses, but the gap between best practice, mean practice, and analysis appears to be widening, making the exposition of a conceptual framework such as we have attempted here particularly beneficial.

Second, corporate governance is one important piece in a complex puzzle, but it needs to be seen in broader context. Elites exist, as we know, and are always going to calculate and negotiate their perceived interests as best they can, whether or not we call them enlightened leaders of nations at one moment or crony capitalists the next. As Barry Eichengreen has pointed out in his discussion on the Asian crisis, economic policy is framed in a politicized environment both internationally and locally (Eichengreen, 1999). We have to be careful not to project our often-unexpressed cultural preferences, for instance, for a clear separation between the domains of public power and the private sphere at the expense of a more difficult and challenging assessment of the multiple factors that play together in any situation. We have to develop the mental fitness to work through such complexity so as to be able to arrive on the other side, as it were, where we can begin to assess the possible implications, the likely futures that we face.

Third, as our case study applications illustrate, risk management involves complex tradeoffs. Multilateral institutions may constrain national political entities but not equally in all industries. Site location decisions involve complex tradeoffs between global, national, industrial, and firm-specific factors that must be evaluated in a dynamic context. Finally, political structures or the lack thereof provide strong cues as to appropriate risk mitigation strategies, but these strategies—and any others designed to offset political risk—give rise to a set of associated costs and secondary risks that must be appropriately factored in the manager's cost-benefit calculus.

Finally, we can try to put numbers to our risk assessment exercise. But they are no more than subjective values which we attach to our judgments. As highlighted by our three applications, the context-specific nature of the risks involved highlights the virtue of a rich framework that includes global, national, industrial, and firm-level factors. The vice of being over orderly and structured in combining these various dimensions is to miss out on the extra-ordinary capacity of the six billion human beings presently living on this planet to make it an exciting and unpredictable place in which to do business. Risk management is nevertheless a valid, indeed an inescapable, activity for senior management. It is inescapable because the future is where business risk and reward lie. It is valid because cross-functional teams of senior management familiar with industry-, firm-, and project-level characteristics working with country experts familiar with national political and social characteristics can together answer the following three questions:

1. Where in this complex multi-level system are the risks and opportunities that can have an impact on our profitability?

2. How can we influence the key decision-making bodies to minimize the probability of an adverse policy or maximize the probability of a favorable policy in a cost-effective manner?

3. How can we manage the residual risk and uncertainties to improve our competitive position relative to our competitors?

Answering these questions is not a job that senior managers can credibly delegate to gurus and number-crunchers. If ever there is an activity for senior management, this is it.

NOTE
1   For a review of this earlier work, see Kobrin (1979).

REFERENCES

Anand, B., and T. Khanna. 2000. "Do Firms Learn to Create Value? The Case of Alliances," *Strategic Management Journal* 21, pp. 295–315.

Austin, J. E. 1990. *Managing in Developing Countries: Strategic Analysis and Operating Techniques*. New York: Free Press.

Brittan, S. 1995. *Capitalism with a Human Face*. Northampton, MA: Edward Elgar.

de Jouvenel, B. 1957. *Sovereignty: An Inquiry into the Political Good*. Chicago: University of Chicago Press.

Eichengreen, B. 1999. *Toward a New International Financial Architecture: A Practical Post-Asia Agenda*. Washington, DC: Institute for International Economics.

Fagre, N., and L. T. Wells. 1982. "Bargaining Power of Multinational and Host Governments," *Journal of International Business Studies* 13, pp. 9–23.

Gastanaga, V. M., J. B. Nugent, and B. Pashamova. 1998. "Host Country Reforms and FDI Inflows: How Much Difference Do They Make?" *World Development* 26, pp. 1299–1314.

Ghemawat, P. 2001. "The Cross-Border Integration of Markets and International Business." Harvard Business School Competition & Strategy Working Paper Series, 5701. Boston, MA: Harvard Business School.

Gourlay, P. R. 2001. "Setting Sites," *US Business Review Online*, November.

Henisz, W. J. 2000. "The Institutional Environment for Multinational Investment," *Journal of Law, Economics and Organization* 16, pp. 334–364.

Henisz, W. 2002. *Politics and International Investment: Measuring Risks and Protecting Profits.* Northampton, MA: Edward Elgar.

Henisz, W. J., and A. Delios. 2001. "Uncertainty, Imitation, and Plant Location: Japanese Multinational Corporations, 1990–1996." *Administrative Science Quarterly* 46, pp. 443–475.

Henisz, W. J., and J. T. Macher. 2002. "Technology, Experience and Politics: Plant Locations in the Global Semiconductor Industry, 1995–2000." Online.www.umich.edu/~cibe/faculty/macher.pdf

Henisz, W. J., and O. E. Williamson. 1999. "Comparative Economic Organization—Within and Between Countries," *Business and Politics* 1, pp. 261–277.

Henisz, W. J., and B. A. Zelner. 2002. "Values, Institutions and the Dynamics of Bargaining Power: Managing to Keep the Lights on (and the Profits Flowing)." Online. www-management.wharton.upenn.edu/henisz/papers/hz_mklo.pdf.

Janeba, E. 2001. "Attracting FDI in a Politically Risky World," NBER Working Paper No. 8400. Cambridge, MA: National Bureau of Economic Research.

Johnson, S., et al. 1998. "Corporate Governance in the Asian Financial Crisis," Stockholm Institute of Transition Economics Working Paper No. 137. Stockholm: Stockholm Institute of Transition Economics.

Kaul. I., I. Gruberg, and M. A. Stern, eds. 1999. *Global Public Goods: International Cooperation in the 21st Century*. New York: Oxford University Press.

Kobrin, S. J. 1979. "Political Risk: A Review and Reconsideration," *Journal of International Business Studies* 10, pp. 67–80.

Kobrin, S. J. 1987. "Testing the Bargaining Hypothesis in the Manufacturing Sector in Developing Countries," *International Organization* 41, pp. 609–638.

Kobrin, S. J., et al. 1980. "The Assessment and Evaluation of Noneconomic Environments by American Firms: A Preliminary Report," *Journal of International Business Studies* 11, pp. 32–47.

Lorenzoni, G., and A. Lipparini. 1999. "The Leveraging of Interfirm Relationships as a Distinctive Organizational Capability: A Longitudinal Study," *Strategic Management Journal* 20, pp. 317–338.

Mansfield, E. 1994. "Intellectual Property Protection, Foreign Direct Investment and Technology Transfer," International Finance Corporation Discussion Paper. Washington, DC: The World Bank.

Mason, M., and D. Encarnation, eds. 1994. *Does Ownership Matter? Japanese Multinationals in Europe*. Oxford: Clarendon Press.

Merchant International Group. 1999. *The Intelligence Gap*. London: Merchant International Group.

Nelson, R. 1999. "Intel's Site Selection Decision in Latin America," Thunderbird Case A06-99-0016.

Nelson, R. R., and S. G. Winter. 1982. *An Evolutionary Theory of Economic Change*. Cambridge, MA: Belknap Press.

Nigh, D. 1985. "The Effects of Political Events on United States Direct Foreign Investment: A Pooled Time-series Cross-sectional Analysis," *Journal of International Business Studies* 16, pp. 1–17.

Nye, J. S. 1991. *Bound to Lead: The Changing Nature of American Power*. New York: Basic Books.

Oxley, J. E. 1999. "Institutional Environment and the Mechanisms of Governance: The Impact of Intellectual Property Protection on the Structure of Inter-firm Alliances," *Journal of Economic Behavior and Organization* 38, pp. 283–310.

Pfeffermann, G., and G. Kisunko. 1999. "Perceived Obstacles to Doing Business: Worldwide Survey Results." Unpublished Paper.

Root, F. R. 1968. "Attitudes of American Executives Towards Foreign Governments and Investment Opportunities," *Economics and Business Bulletin* 20 (January), pp. 14–23.

Schneider, F., and B. S. Frey. 1985. "Economic and Political Determinants of Foreign Direct Investment," *World Development* 13, pp. 161–175.

Spar, D. 1998. "Whale in a Swimming Pool," IFC Impact, Summer. Online. http://www.ifc.org/publications/pubs/impact_summer98/impsm98.htm.

Stopford, J., and S. Strange. 1991. *Rival States, Rival Firms: Competition for World Market Shares*. New York: Cambridge University Press.

Teece, D. J., G. Pisano, and A. Shuen. 1997. "Dynamic Capabilities and Strategic Management," *Strategic Management Journal* 18, pp. 509–533.

Vernon, R. 1971. *Sovereignty at Bay: The Multinational Spread of U.S. Enterprises*. New York: Basic Books.

Vernon, R. 1977. *The Strain on National Objectives: The Developing Countries, Storm over the Multinationals: The Real Issues*. Cambridge, MA: Harvard University Press.

Wack, P. 1985. "Scenarios: Uncharted Waters Ahead," *Harvard Business Review* (September-October), pp. 72–89.

Wei, S.-J., and T. W. Hall. 2001. *Investigating the Costs of Opacity: Deterred Foreign Direct Investment*. PriceWaterhouseCoopers Report. Online. http://www.opacityindex.com/scripts/dow_download.pl

Wei, S.-J., and Y. Wu 2001. "Negative Alchemy? Corruption, Composition of Capital Flows and Currency Crises," NBER Working Paper No. 8187. Cambridge, MA: National Bureau of Economic Research.

Whitley, R. 1999. *Divergent Capitalisms: The Social Structuring and Change of Business Systems*. New York: Oxford University Press.

Role of Foreign Banks in Governance

Chapter 10

Foreign Bank Ownership and Corporate Governance in Emerging-Market Economies

Peter K. Cornelius

Traditionally, efficient corporate governance is seen as being best achieved by enabling stockholders to exercise control. According to this view, the objective of introducing good corporate governance should be addressed by promoting the development of well-functioning securities markets, breeding active and influential stockholders, and legislating corporate laws that would assure stockholders a controlling position on corporate boards.

In the literature, following the Berle and Means (1932) tradition, the widely held firm is used as the standard assumption underlying the corporate governance problem—that is, weak, dispersed shareholders have to deal with self-interested management. In practice, however, most firms have a dominant owner. Moreover, this dominant shareholder, frequently a family or the state, is very often involved in the management of the firm. The closely held firm is much more typical in many industrialized countries, and even more so in developing countries and transition economies. Furthermore, although the number of listed companies has increased considerably in recent years, the overwhelming majority of firms in emerging-market economies has remained unlisted. The Standard & Poor's Investable Country Index currently includes only 30 markets with around 1,200 stocks, and many markets have remained relatively illiquid. In addition, few countries have put in place a regulatory framework foreign investors would regard as appropriate, an important reason why the California Public Employees' Retirement System (CalPERS), for example, limits the universe of permissible markets to only 14.[1] In the absence of broad and deep equity markets, insider control—the de facto or *de jure* capture of controlling rights by managers and the strong representation of their interests in corporate strategic decision-making—has remained a particularly serious issue in many emerging market economies. Against this background, alternative external monitoring mechanisms have been sought. One candidate that could implement such a mechanism, it has been argued, is banks. The proponents of this approach typically point to the postwar high-growth performance of both the German and Japanese economies, where banks maintained continuous relationships with corporate clients and occupied unique positions in corporate governance. As Aoki and Kim (1995, xiv) emphasize, there are phenomena in both economies that seem to suggest that bank monitoring might be consistent with, and even complementary to, a certain degree of insider control.[2]

The problem is, of course, that such an approach would require a sufficiently strong banking system, a prerequisite few emerging market countries fulfill. Many countries have suffered severe banking crises in recent years (Kaminsky and Reinhart, 1999), casting serious doubts as to whether domestic banking institutions could help raise corporate governance standards.

Could foreign banks instead play an increasingly important role in this regard? As a matter of fact, foreign participation in retail and investment banking in emerging-market economies has grown substantially in the second half of the 1990s. The increase has been particularly pronounced in central and eastern Europe, where in some countries foreign control rose eightfold. As a result, the ratio of assets of banks where foreigners own the majority of total equity to total bank assets has reached, in some cases, more than 50 percent. In Asia and Latin America, the increase in foreign participation has been less dramatic, but still very significant.

This trend is likely to continue. In January 2000, member governments of the World Trade Organization (WTO) started a new round of negotiations to promote the progressive liberalization of trade in services. The negotiations build upon the General Agreement on Trade in Services (GATS), which, as the first and only set of multilateral rules covering international trade in services, came into force in January 1995. Four years later, in March 1999, the Financial Services Agreement (FSA) became effective. Providing the basis for the current round of negotiations, this agreement represents the legal framework for cross-border trade and market access in financial services and a mechanism for dispute settlement.

In examining whether foreign banks could help improve corporate governance in emerging-market economies, this chapter is organized as follows: first is a discussion about the role of banks in corporate governance from a conceptual point of view. Then follows a review of the recent surge in foreign bank ownership in developing countries and transition economies. The next section examines what drives banks to expand abroad and what they do once they arrive in a foreign market. A discussion of the banks' role in upgrading corporate governance and reviewing the empirical evidence that begins to emerge as follows. Then, finally, there is a conclusion.

THE MARKET FOR CORPORATE CONTROL AND THE ROLE OF BANKS

There are substantial cross-country differences in the ownership of firms. As far as the Organisation for Economic Co-operation and Development countries are concerned, bank ownership of corporate equity continues to play a particularly important role in Japan and, to a somewhat lesser degree, in Germany (La Porta et al., 1999). In the United States, by contrast, banks play virtually no role. Individuals are the most important owners of corporate equity, followed by pension funds and nonfinancial corporations.

Important differences between the United States on the one hand and Germany and Japan on the other also exist with regard to merger and acquisition transactions. One reason why merger activity has remained substantially greater in the United States over the last decade is explained by the comparatively larger number of companies listed on the US stock market. But the observation that the market for corporate control in the United States has been considerably more active remains intact even if one normalizes the dollar value of mergers and acquisitions by the stock market capitalization. This finding is consistent with a substantial gap between the number of hostile takeovers in the United States, Germany, and Japan.

Since US banks typically own no equity in firms, they are infrequently represented on the board. Their main role in corporate governance is through their role as lenders, and their main tool appears to be covenants they insert in the loan contract and the maturity they set for the loan (Dittus and Prowse, 1996, p. 28). In firms that file for bankruptcy or restructure their debt privately, bank lenders with debt outstanding to the firm frequently receive significant blocks of voting stock, appoint their representatives to the board of directors, and insert restrictive covenants in the companies' restructured lending agreements to give them more say in the firm's investment and financing policies.

By comparison, German banks take a much more active part in corporate governance.[3] Their significance does not stem from the control of external sources of finance, however, a key channel of influence in Japan. Rather, the main governance tool of German banks is based on proxy votes through which they monitor and exert control, as well as on a pyramid structure of holding companies and representation on the supervisory board (Franks and Mayer, 2001; and Kogut and Walker, 2001). In some cases, banks continue to hold considerable stakes directly in firms, but this is rather rare.

In Japan, by contrast, banks represent important shareholders themselves, as evidenced by the substantial balance sheet problems that emerged in the wake of the sharp decline in equity prices over the last decade. For larger companies, one bank typically serves as the company's main financial institution, maintaining close ties to the company in cash management and credit operations. Debt-to-equity ratios continue to be high by international standards, representing an important barrier to outside takeovers. Banks do not normally interfere in company management in Japan, but if a company does get into trouble, the bank usually steps in and, if necessary, replaces the existing management, normally from incumbent personnel. Aoki (1990) thus describes Japanese companies as subject to the dual control of internal managers and external bankers.

As Stiglitz (1985) pointed out, allowing large equity- and debt-holders of the firm to be the same agents, thereby restricting firms' sources of external finance to few investors, may have a number of potential advantages. For example, banks may play a particularly effective monitoring role, with the agency problems of debt finance being potentially reduced. Some empirical support for this hypothesis was found by Cable (1985) in a study on Germany; in this study, profitability among large firms was positively related to the proportion of equity voting rights controlled by the three largest banks and by bank representation on the board of directors. Further, as Walter (2000) has argued, a bank can exercise greater control over the riskiness of projects chosen by the firm, especially if it is shareholder of that firm.

Moreover, German firms with tighter bank ties were found to be less sensitive to liquidity constraints in their investment decisions than firms with looser ties (Gorton and Schmid, 2000). This seems to suggest that bank ties are important in reducing the information and agency problems associated with external finance and governance. On the other hand, Edwards and Fischer (1994) found bank control of voting rights in Germany to be only weakly correlated to the number of bank representatives on the supervisory board. Conversely, they found little evidence for the hypothesis that bank representation on the supervisory board is positively correlated with greater borrowing from banks. While the empirical evidence thus continues to be inconclusive, Dittus and Prowse (1996) interpret the different findings that "...banks play an important corporate governance role *only in those firms that are widely held and that do not enjoy the benefits of large shareholder monitoring*" (italics original).

Allowing banks to own equity can result in conflicts of interest, however. One potential problem, for instance, involves the risk of banks making unsound loans to firms in which they have an equity stake. Conversely, especially if the equity holding is large, there may be a risk that the bank influences the firm to take out loans at premium rates. Furthermore, investing in equity and debt may amplify the risk of bank failure, although some (e.g., Saunders and Walter, 1994) have argued that there are potential risk reduction gains from expanding the permissible asset class for bank investments. Other conflicts of interest may arise from the fiduciary responsibilities of a bank and its role as an investment banker; the bank's interest in completing a merger and acquisition transaction versus its obligation to a target company that is or has been a client; and the bank's responsibilities to the asset holders versus the profitability of stuffing or churning investment portfolios (Walter, 2000, p. 119).

In order to perform their monitoring function, banks do not need to own shares, however. Berglöf and von Thadden (2000, p. 284) argue that banks' most important source of influence is typically their role as concentrated creditors. This role appears especially critical at relatively early stages of economic development, when the general lack of information on borrowers and underdeveloped legal systems to enforce contracts hamper suppliers of long-term financial instruments, such as equities and bonds, in evaluating risk and reward. In these circumstances, banks seem best suited to solve the asymmetric information problem by evaluating and monitoring private loans (Levine, 2000; and Dobson and Hufbauer, 2001).

Banks do not even have to pursue their monitoring role actively. Rather, they (as well as other creditors) can take a passive approach, depending on collateral for security. While in the passive mode the bank's credit analysis focuses primarily on the value of the security rather than the operations of the firm; in practice, even fully secured lending generally includes some degree of active monitoring.

In general, creditors are assumed to be more risk-averse than equity holders because they do not share in upside gains. In times of financial distress, creditor monitoring might therefore be more appropriate (Aghion and Bolton, 1992). Short-term creditors have more control levers at their disposal and tend to exert the strongest control. Short-term credit is refinanced more often and hence provides more opportunities for creditors to review investment decisions, adjust interest rates to account for risk, or refuse to roll over or grant additional loans altogether. Moreover, given that short-term credit is often secured by short-term assets, foreclosure on these assets is relatively easy. Longer-term credit is less flexible because of the typically thinner market for long-term assets. This makes long-term creditors weaker and less credible monitors. On the other hand, long-term credit tends to carry a relatively smaller danger of premature liquidation of potentially viable debtor firms (Baer and Gray, 1995, p. 70).

Effective debt monitoring requires an appropriate legal and institutional framework. Active monitoring by creditors requires debt contracts to be sufficiently flexible. Moreover, there needs to be adequate availability of information from reliable accounting and sufficient disclosure requirements as well as workable frameworks for reorganization and liquidation. Passive monitoring, by contrast, requires efficient property markets, which in turn require clear legal definition and enforcement of property rights (both existent and contingent), low-cost information (through property and collateral registries), and asset markets of sufficient size and depth.

According to LaPorta et al. (1997), the degree of creditor protection can generally be perceived as a function of the following factors: (1) there is no automatic stay (secured creditors are able to gain possession of their security once the reorganization petition has been approved); (2) secured creditors are paid first; (3) there are restrictions on going into reorganization; (4) management is required to leave in reorganization; and (5) legal reserve requirements. In practice, however, things may be more complex, and the strict legal application of creditor protection might lead to suboptimal outcomes (Berglöf and von Thadden, 2000, p. 287). Debtor-creditor law may be too hard or too soft on management or controlling owners, and it may favor inefficient liquidation (when continuation would be optimal) or inefficient continuation (when liquidation would be optimal). Moreover, while conflicts typically arise between creditors in cases of bankruptcy, there may be much earlier conflicts if different creditors have different lending experiences and intervention capacities. Creditors will therefore seek to influence a firm in distress in different ways and with different objectives. As a result, the one-dimensional goal of maximizing creditor protection may provide little guidance for the design of corporate law.

Furthermore, there may be an important gap between the existence of laws— "law on the books"—and their actual enforcement, potentially retarding financial sector development (Pistor, Raiser, and Gelfer, 2000). Therefore, the quality of laws can only be a crude proxy for the effectiveness of legal systems. Instead, it has been argued, it is the effective enforcement of laws rather than the quality of laws that provides a better predictor of economic growth. As a matter of fact, Klapper and Claessens (2002) find a considerable degree of variation across 37 countries with regard to the use of bankruptcy laws (correcting for financial development and macroeconomic shocks). In countries where creditor rights are strong and the judicial system efficient, bankruptcy laws are generally more frequently used—that is, creditors are more likely to undertake the costs of bankruptcy if they are able to effectively use the courts in the case of default.

To some extent at least, weak legal systems and lax enforcement can be compensated for by good corporate governance practices at the firm level. Using data on firm-level corporate governance rankings across 14 emerging markets, Klapper and Love (2002) study the degree of variation in firm-level governance standards within countries and find that these standards tend to matter more in economies with weak legal environments. Overall, however, their findings suggest that the average firm-level governance is lower in countries with weaker legal systems.

As the following discussion shows, however, the last few years have seen a substantial increase not only in foreign bank participation in emerging-market economies but indeed also in lending in domestic currency to households and firms by foreign-owned banks. This surge appears particularly worth noting, given that creditor protection and the enforcement of laws in many countries are found to be subpar.

FOREIGN BANK OWNERSHIP: EMPIRICAL EVIDENCE

In the second half of the 1990s, the presence of foreign-owned banks in developing and transition economies increased dramatically. According to International Monetary Fund (IMF) staff estimates, foreign control of the domestic banking system has been particularly pronounced in central and eastern Europe, where in several countries 50 percent or more of the total equity of the banks, valued by their total assets, were owned by foreign institutions (Table 10.1). Holding more than half of total equity typically ensures effective control of a bank. However, in order to prevent hostile takeovers, a smaller percentage, a threshold many analysts put at 40 percent, will generally suffice. In some cases, this percentage can make a substantial difference. In

Hungary, for example, the 40-percent threshold puts more than 80 percent of the banking system under foreign control, whereas under the 50-percent rule foreign banks controlled only around 57 percent of the banking system at end-1999.

No matter where one draws the line, however, foreign control has risen substantially between 1994 and 1999 in transition economies. One important factor has been the privatization of state-owned banks following severe banking crises in several countries. As Berglöf and Bolton (2002) argue, it was actually not until foreign banks were allowed to acquire strategic stakes in the domestic banking sector that private ownership took a firm hold in the banking sector of most countries. Initially, the divesture was concentrated on smaller and medium-sized banks, but more recently the privatization of large banks has gathered momentum. Hungary took the lead in the privatization, and with foreign banks allowed to participate, foreign control (taking 50 percent as a threshold) already amounted to around 20 percent in 1994.[4]

TABLE 10.1 **Foreign Bank Ownership in Selected Emerging Markets[a] (in Percentage)**

	FOREIGN CONTROL, End-1994[b]	FOREIGN CONTROL, End-1999[b]	FOREIGN CONTROL, End-1999[c]	FOREIGN PARTICIPATION, End-1999
CENTRAL EUROPE				
Czech Republic	5.8	49.3	50.7	47.3
Hungary	19.8	56.6	80.4	59.5
Poland	2.1	52.8	52.8	36.3
LATIN AMERICA				
Argentina	17.9	48.6	48.6	41.7
Brazil	8.4	16.8	17.7	18.2
Chile	16.3	53.6	53.6	48.4
Colombia	6.2	17.8	17.8	16.2
Mexico	1.0	18.8	18.8	18.6
Peru	6.7	33.4	33.4	33.2
Venezuela	0.3	41.9	43.9	34.7
ASIA				
Korea	0.8	4.3	16.2	11.2
Malaysia[d]	6.8	11.5	11.5	14.4
Thailand	0.5	5.6	5.6	6.0

[a] Based on data from Fitch IBCA's BankScope Database

[b] Ratio of assets of banks where foreigners own more than 50 percent of total equity to total bank assets

[c] Same as in note b, but at 40 percent level

[d] Figures include finance companies and merchant banks that are majority-owned by Malaysian interests; foreign participation in the commercial banking sector is significantly higher (estimated by the IMF at around 23 percent)

Source: IMF (2000, p. 153)

An alternative measure that is often used is the degree of foreign participation defined as the ratio of the sum across all banks of the assets of each bank multiplied by the percentage of equity held by foreigners to total bank assets. This measure presents a similar picture, although it might be argued that the control of banks may not be directly or exclusively related to the proportion of a bank's equity held by a particular owner. While more recent cross-country data is not available, it can be assumed that foreign bank ownership in central and eastern Europe has continued in the current decade—measured either in terms of foreign participation or of foreign control.

Generally speaking, this also applies to Latin America, where foreign bank ownership had also risen substantially in the second half of the 1990s. While at end-1994 the percentage of the banking system controlled by foreign institutions (50 percent threshold) averaged only 7.5 percent for the countries shown in Table 10.1, this percentage rose to 25 percent by the end of the decade. Since then, however, foreign ownership has expanded further. The dismantling of restrictions vis-à-vis foreign institutions has no doubt played an important role, as evidenced by the takeover bid of Bancomer by BBVA shortly after the Mexican Congress had lifted the historical restriction on buying the country's largest banks. With Banca Serfin, the third largest Mexican bank, also sold in the first half of 2000, the share of assets under foreign control is estimated to have risen to about 40 percent in Mexico (IMF, 2000, p. 154). The relatively smallest share of foreign control is found in Brazil, and this is explained in part by the large share of bank assets under government control and the existence of three large, well-capitalized private banks. Nevertheless, during the period that is considered here, foreign control of Brazilian banks has doubled.

In Asia, finally, foreign banks have played a comparatively smaller role, reflecting in part official policies that have limited entry. Given that these limitations have applied especially to local retail banking markets, foreign participation has generally been biased toward corporate banking. In several countries, the restrictions have put limits on both the number of foreign banks that could enter the market and the number of branches they could establish within the market. However, many Asian countries have liberalized access to the domestic banking market after the financial turmoil of 1997 and 1998. Thailand, for example, where the last foreign bank license was issued in 1978, increased the limit of foreign ownership from the precrisis level of 25 percent to the current level of 100 percent. The dismantling of restrictions has led to a noticeable increase in foreign bank ownership; this level has remained below that in other regions, however.

A particularly interesting case is Malaysia, where in the late 1950s foreign banks controlled more than 90 percent of assets. The authorities encouraged the setting up of new domestic banks and at the same time progressively restricted the activities of foreign banks, however, and by end-1999 the latter's share was estimated to have fallen to less than 25 percent (see Table 10.1, footnote d). Under the GATS, Malaysia has committed to relaxing entry requirements, and anticipating greater competition, the authorities have begun to encourage small banks to merge, fostering the consolidation of the banking industry. Since the start of the Asian financial crisis, the number of domestic financial institutions has dropped from 54 to just 10 by mid-2002.

The dramatic increase in foreign bank ownership has contributed to a substantial decline in cross-border commercial bank lending—there was a net outflow of an estimated USD 11 billion in 2002, compared to a net inflow of USD 124 billion in 1996. According to the Institute of International Finance (2002), commercial banks are taking a more direct role in domestic markets by investing in local operations and lending in domestic currency. In just one decade (between 1992 and 2001), domestic currency lending to emerging-market economies by banks that report to the Bank for International Settlements recorded a 15-fold increase. At the end of the second quarter of 2002 local claims of foreign-owned banks vis-à-vis domestic clients in local currencies amounted to almost USD 525 billion, or about 40 percent of total claims (Table 10.2).

There is reason to assume that the surge in foreign bank participation will actually continue and that it may even gather momentum in countries where foreign ownership has remained relatively low. One key factor will be the continuous dismantling of barriers to access to the domestic banking sector in many countries under the FSA of the GATS. The FSA came into effect on March 1, 1999, and since that time it has provided the legal framework for cross-border trade and market access in financial services and a mechanism for dispute settlement. It covers by far the largest share of trade in services, which is estimated at almost USD 1.5 trillion annually, or around 20 percent of total cross-border trade. When it became effective, the FSA was widely regarded as an important step toward more open and efficient financial systems (Cornelius, 2000). Indeed,

TABLE 10.2 **Consolidated Bank Claims, International and Local, at end-June 2002**

	TOTAL FOREIGN CLAIMS	LOCAL CLAIMS IN LOCAL CURRENCY	INTERNATIONAL CLAIMS
Developing Countries	1,333.3	524.8	809.0
Africa & Middle East	152.7	33.1	119.6
Asia & Pacific	395.3	140.5	254.8
Europe	293.4	103.6	189.8
Latin America	491.9	247.2	244.7
Developed Countries	10,073.4	2,836.0	7,237.4

Source: Bank for International Settlements, BIS Consolidated Banking Statistics for the Second Quarter of 2002, Table 1.

many hailed the agreement as a major success, given the "strategic" importance of the financial sector, and the risk that several countries could have backtracked on previous commitments in light of the financial turmoil in Asia, Russia, and Brazil at that time (Moore, 2000). Encouraged by this success, member governments of the WTO began a new round of negotiations in January 2000 to promote the further progressive liberalization of trade in services. Box 1 provides a brief overview of the agreement.

BOX I **The GATS and Financial Services Trade**

Rather than represent a liberalization agreement itself, the GATS provides only a framework for liberalization of trade in services.[5] In so doing, it is based on three pillars. First of all, it includes a framework agreement, which contains general provisions covering all sectors (i.e., financial services, telecommunications, and information technology). Second, special annexes and other agreements, such as the Understanding on Financial Services, contain provisions focusing specifically on the sector concerned. The third pillar, finally, consists of scheduled commitments on market access, national treatment, and other commitments. Regarding this last point, the GATS defines trade in financial services, like in other services, in terms of four modes of supply:[6]

1. cross-border supply, not requiring the physical movement of consumers or suppliers (e.g., consumers or financial institutions in one country are permitted to take a loan or purchase securities from a foreign bank);

2. consumption abroad, whereby consumers are allowed to purchase financial services while travelling abroad (e.g., a resident in one country crosses the border and opens a bank account in a foreign country);

3. commercial presence, or permanent establishment of service-providing entities in the territory of the consumer (e.g., a country allows the establishment of foreign banks in its territory);

4. movement of natural persons who supply financial services in the territory of a foreign country (e.g., a bank opens a subsidiary abroad and is allowed to send personnel to that country).

The GATS rules are based on the same general principles as trade in goods, that is, most-favored nation treatment (MFN) (Article II) and transparency (Article III). There are important limitations, however, which renders the GATS rules weaker than those of the General Agreement on Tariffs and Trade (GATT). For example, national treatment is not an automatic, but negotiable, right. Exemptions to the MFN obligation in specific sectors are permitted, provided that the measures are listed in the list of MFN exemptions and that such obligations, in principle, should not extend beyond 10 years. Specific obligations regarding market access and national treatment (Articles XVI and XVII, respectively) are based on a positive list or bottom-up approach, that is, they apply only to services that are inscribed in the Schedules of Commitments of countries where specific commitments are listed in the form of limitations or measures applicable. Such limitations are listed for each of the four modes of supply and may be either cross-sectional or sector-specific.

Clearly this approach is less liberal than the negative-list or top-down approach employed in the North American Free Trade Agreement and OECD agreements, where all sectors are covered unless specifically excluded.

Moreover, the Annex on Financial Services recognizes that countries may take measures for prudential reasons, including for the protection of investors and depositors, and for preserving the integrity and stability of the financial system. While such measures shall not be used as a means to circumvent a country's commitments or obligations under the GATS, they do not need to be inscribed in the Schedules of Specific Commitments, whether or not they are in conformity with any other provisions of the Agreement. However, there is no definition of prudential rules, and as Sorsa (1997) argues, the broad prudential carve-out in the GATS can imply very broad departures from the basic principles of the Agreement. Potentially, the measures can permit discrimination among countries, for example, on the basis of capital adequacy ratios or national treatment.

However, even in the absence of such measures, the GATS may not be sufficient to ensure foreign suppliers' market access. While Article XVII requires that foreign suppliers must receive treatment "no less favorable" than national suppliers, in some cases better-than-national treatment may actually be necessary for foreign institutions to be able to compete. For instance, a regulator in a member country that prohibits universal banking could preclude such services from branches of a bank from a member state that allows universal banking. While during the negotiations general agreement emerged that each country must have the right to regulate its financial industry in order to ensure stability, there will thus always be a potential that these policies form barriers to market access. Removing all potential barriers to market access therefore requires harmonizing regulatory policies, a process for which the GATS, however, does not provide an adequate framework.

Recognizing that financial instability and external imbalances may be closely intertwined, the GATS also allows members to introduce temporary restrictions in the event of serious balance of payments problems—subject to consultations with WTO members (Article XII). However, as Sorsa (1997) argues, the role of the WTO Committee on Balance of Payments Restrictions appears vague, given that the IMF independently approves restrictions on current account payments that fall under its IMF jurisdiction. As a matter of fact, if a particular restriction on payments and transfers is approved by the IMF, the Balance of Payments Committee's role may be limited to approving what the IMF has already done under its mandate.

Capital account restrictions are also subject to approval by the WTO Committee on Balance of Payments Restrictions, but only to the extent that they affect international transfers and payments for transactions relating to specific commitments under the agreement. Suppose, for instance, a mode 1 country experienced large capital inflows and imposed restrictions in response to mounting concerns about the exchange rate and sudden reversals of flows. In practice, however, the potential role of the Committee seems rather limited, given that at present relatively few countries have made commitments under mode 1, reflecting fears that a more liberal trade policy could seriously undermine financial stability.

WHAT DO FOREIGN BANKS DO?

Several studies, which have recently been summarized by Clarke et al. (2001), have found a positive and significant correlation between the flow of bank foreign direct investment (FDI) and the extent of integration between home and host countries through trade flows and/or nonfinancial FDI. This finding has usually been interpreted as suggesting that banks follow their customers abroad. However, considerable caution is warranted, as a positive correlation between banking FDI and nonfinancial FDI does not necessarily imply that foreign banks are providing financial services primarily, or exclusively, to the affiliates of clients from their home countries. As Clarke et al. (2001) point out, co-location does not necessarily imply a high level of interaction between banks and nonfinancial firms from the same home country. Interestingly, finding a causal link between bank FDI and nonfinancial FDI is particularly difficult in the case of developing countries (Miller and Parkhe, 1998). In fact, causation might run in the other direction. With developing host countries offering substantial profit opportunities in the supply of financial services, foreign banking might precede and perhaps pull entry of nonfinancial sector firms.

Other studies have focused on the extent to which profitable opportunities attract foreign banks. Typically, these studies find that host-country GDP per capita and inflation are negatively associated with foreign bank presence, while host-country stock-market capitalization has a positive relation, suggesting that foreign banks are more likely to enter host countries with better prospects for growth. Moreover, several studies reviewed in Clarke et al. (2001) find greater foreign presence where local banks have higher average costs, lower net interest margins, and higher cash flows (suggesting a low degree of efficiency of using capital), and where the average bank size is comparatively small. These factors are believed to play a particularly important role in developing countries as opposed to industrialized countries.

Studying what attracts foreign banks requires controlling for host country regulations on foreign entry. Studies that address this issue specifically typically find that foreign banks prefer countries with fewer regulatory restrictions on banking activity. With financial services trade progressively liberalized under the FSA, however, the importance of this factor may diminish over time.

As Kono and Schuknecht (1998) argue, dismantling barriers to access often goes hand in hand with the liberalization of the domestic financial services sector. Highly regulated financial markets often feature interest rate controls and credit ceilings for individual institutions. Moreover, lending interventions by governments channel resources into priority sectors for the financing of government deficits. Distortions can be particularly severe if such interventions require cross-subsidization from other lending, possibly resulting in credit rationing and shortages in otherwise profitable sectors. To the extent that financial market liberalization is accompanied, or driven, by the opening of the domestic market to foreign bank participation, the potential benefits can be considerable. Under mode 3 (commercial presence, see Box 1), as Kono and Schuknecht (1998) argue, there are strong incentives for countries that open their banking systems to foreign competition (commercial presence) to increase market transparency, improve bank supervision, and ensure that banks upgrade their risk management systems (Table 10.3). By contrast, under mode 1, such incentives are much weaker. At the same time, mode 1 liberalization is more likely to result in larger capital flows, with a possible bias toward short-term flows potentially leading to greater volatility.

Large banks are usually more apt to expand abroad. While several studies find a position correlation between the size of banks and their degree of internationalization, it appears that foreign entrants tend to be relatively more efficient than domestic competitors in developing countries. Moreover, foreign banks seem to suffer from fewer

TABLE 10.3 **Effects of Financial Services Commitments on Capital Flows and the Financial System, as Affected by the Mode of Supply and the Range of Instruments**

	BY MODE OF SUPPLY		BY RANGE OF INSTRUMENTS WHICH CAN BE SUPPLIED	
	Mode 1	Mode 3	Narrow[a]	Broad
CAPACITY-BUILDING				
Improved transparency/Information	Weak	Strong	Weak	Strong
Incentive to improve regulation/supervision	Weak	Strong	Weak	Strong
Infrastructure/market development	Weak	Strong	Weak	Strong
Risk management	Weak	Strong	Weak	Strong
CAPITAL FLOWS				
More capital flows	Yes	Limited	[b]	[b]
Bias toward short-term lending	Strong	Weak	Possibly Strong	Weak
Increased volatility	Strong	Weak	Possibly Strong	Weak
EFFICIENCY/LOCAL BENEFITS				
More competition/efficiency	Strong	Strong	Weak	Strong
Skills/technology transfer	Weak	Strong	Weak	Strong
Local employment creation	Weak	Strong	Weak	Strong

[a] Commitments exclude or limit provision of important instruments/allow only lending and deposit-taking.

[b] Depends on the instrument and mode of supply permitted, and market conditions.

Source: Kono and Schuknecht (1998)

nonperforming loans. In addition to size and efficiency considerations, however, home country factors may have pushed banks into expanding abroad. One example is Spanish banks, which have invested heavily in Latin America in response to financial deregulation in Spain and increased competition brought about by the European Monetary Union.

Once foreign banks enter the market, domestic banks generally find it difficult to protect their profits. Using an 80-country sample of both developed and developing countries, Claessens, Demirguc-Kunt, and Huizinga (forthcoming) find that foreign banks reduce the profitability of domestic banks. Noninterest income and overall expenses of domestic banks are found to be negatively affected by foreign entry, an observation the authors interpret as implying that foreign bank entry leads to greater efficiency in the domestic banking system. Studies on individual countries, moreover, found evidence that foreign entry tended to be associated with lower intermediation spreads, reduced nonfinancial costs, and improved loan quality for the banking sector overall.

The positive impact stemming from lowering barriers to entry and allowing participation of foreigners in domestic banking markets is found to have at least partly offset any adverse effects on competition intensity brought about by consolidation in the banking sector. Gelos and Roldós (2002) find that while the number of banks has fallen in most emerging markets during the period 1994 to 2000, this decline has not systematically resulted in an increase in concentration measured by the share in total deposits of the largest banks and by Hirshman-Herfindahl indexes. According to their analysis, government-led restructuring processes in Asian countries have generally resulted in a reduction in the number of banks. However, the degree of concentration remained relatively stable, because larger, and previously protected banks tended to lose market shares to the more dynamic medium-sized banks. As Rajan and Zingales (1998) argue, initially the protection of banks had typically taken the form of maximum rates of deposits, whereas more recently explicit or implicit guarantees and barriers to entry were used to increase the banks' franchise value. In central and eastern Europe, a reduction of the number of banks has even been associated with a lower concentration. Moreover, as Bonin and Ábel (2000) argue, the credible threat of competition from foreign banks has disciplined domestic banks in individual transition economies and led to an improvement in the quality of their portfolios. To the extent that there are contestable market conditions, the actual degree of competition might actually be even higher than the standard summary statistics suggest.

While foreign bank participation is normally not confined to the wholesale market, foreign institutions do not compete with domestic banks in all sectors equally. One sector where foreign participation typically leads to increased competition is manufacturing. By contrast, foreign banks are less likely to be involved in consumer lending. In general, foreign banks appear to allocate greater shares of their lending portfolios to commercial and industrial loans, suggesting that such loans may be comparatively more important in the markets for loans to large companies. To what extent foreign competition may have forced some small domestic banks to exit the market, resulting in a decline in the supply of credit to informationally opaque small businesses, remains an open question, however. While some studies seem to have found some empirical support for this hypothesis, others—controlling for other factors affecting lending to small and medium-sized enterprises—provide evidence that large foreign banks might actually have lent relatively more to this market segment than large domestic banks.

Further support for the view that foreign bank participation might actually improve firms' access to credit is provided by Clarke, Cull, and Soledad Martinez Peria (2002), who have surveyed more than 4,000 enterprises in 38 developing and transition economies. Examining borrowers' perceptions regarding interest rates and access to long-term credit, they find a positive association with the presence of foreign banks. Enterprises in countries with high levels of foreign bank penetration tended to rate interest rates and access to long-term loans as lesser constraints on enterprise operations and growth than enterprises in countries with lower levels of foreign penetration. These findings are consistent with the view that the potential advantages of foreign entry—improved sector efficiency, new credit scoring technologies, and domestic banks seeking new market niches—may outweigh the potential tendency of foreign banks to eschew lending to small and medium-sized enterprises. Against this background, the following section discusses the relationship between foreign bank participation and corporate governance.

FOREIGN BANKS AND CORPORATE GOVERNANCE

Who owns firms in emerging-market economies? Unfortunately, there is little consistent information, but from the limited data we do have, it appears that in these economies financial institutions have relatively little control over firms. La Porta et al. (1999) report that in Argentina, only 5 percent of the large publicly-traded firms are controlled by financial institutions, with a cut-off rate set at 20 percent. As far as medium-sized enterprises in Argentina are concerned, financial institutions were found to play virtually no role. This applies also to Korea and Mexico, two other emerging markets included in the study, regardless of the firm size.

In contrast, La Porta et al. (1999) found substantial influence by families. In Argentina, 65 percent of the sample of large publicly traded firms are reported to be controlled by families, again employing a cut-off rate of 20 percent. In Mexico, all firms in the sample were found to be controlled by families. In Korea, the ratio is significantly smaller, but at an estimated 20 percent, is still significant. La Porta et al. (1999) also examine how many of the 20 largest firms a controlling family controls. On average, the answer ranges from 1.05 in Mexico to 1.33 in Korea, with Argentina representing the middle rank at 1.18. In the latter, a member of the controlling family was found to be part of management in almost two thirds of the cases; in Mexico, this occurred in 95 percent of the cases.

Korea stands out in terms of the importance of widely held stock, especially with regard to large, but also medium-sized publicly traded firms. Considering the 20 largest companies, this share accounts for 55 percent and 30 percent, respectively. In Argentina, the state and other corporations represent important shareholders of large publicly traded firms, with each accounting for 15 percent of all shareholders. Overall, however, the La Porta et al. (1999) findings suggest that families represent the most important group of shareholders in the countries included in the study, whereas banks play virtually no role. Often, family control is enhanced through pyramid structures, cross-shareholdings, and deviations from one share, one vote, rules. Although there is little systematic cross-country evidence for a larger sample of countries, other studies (e.g., Berglöf and von Thadden, 2000) claim that the observed pattern is rather typical for developing nations and transition economies.

While banks in emerging markets currently play, if any, only a minor role as shareholders, the question arises whether a greater role would be useful, the idea being for them to become more involved in corporate governance. This question has attracted considerable attention, especially in the context of the transformation process in central and eastern Europe (e.g., Aoki and Kim, 1995). Those who advocate a greater involvement have typically pointed to the experience in Germany and Japan. Compared with other potential players, such as investment funds, banks have been seen as particularly well placed to mitigate the severe information problems between managers and any potential owners (Dittus and Prowse, 1996). To the degree that firms require new loans or the rollover of existing ones, banks, it has been argued, can and do request privileged access to internal information about the firm. In particular in the case of large clients, banks are likely to know the enterprise managers and their capacities fairly well. Finally, banks' monitoring capabilities are enhanced if they require firms to hold their deposit accounts with the main lending bank.

There are also a number of important arguments against a larger role for banks in corporate governance. First of all, banks have other functions to fulfill that might be even more important than corporate control, an issue that is particularly relevant given the limited availability of resources. In transition economies and developing countries at an early stage of development, banks often represent the predominant source of external finance, and are almost always the only provider of financial instruments and the only supplier of payment services. The quality of these functions may be poor, but as long as the banks are the only game in town, their role is essential. Second, banks in many developing countries, and especially transition economies, suffer from a severe lack of expertise and human capital in evaluating and monitoring firms.

Third, while bank-based corporate governance systems may be quite effective for economies with many growth opportunities, as economies mature opportunities in existing firms tend to decline and excess positive cash flow may develop. In such an environment, Claessens and Glaessner (1997) argue, bank-based systems typically have a hard time disciplining managers.

Fourth, it has been argued that state ownership of banks undermines the potential role of banks as shareholder activists. In an analysis of 92 countries, La Porta, Lopez-de-Silanes, and Shleifer (2002) found that government ownership has remained large and pervasive. They also found that government ownership tends to be higher in countries with low levels of per capita income, backward financial systems, interventionist governments, and poor protection of property rights. Moreover, as Booth et al. (2001) argue, extensive government ownership can seriously complicate the distinction between bank and market-based financing. According to their analysis, government-directed credit programs to preferred sectors, along with controls on the prices in security markets, can be expected to have a significant impact on corporate financing patterns. Finally, it has been argued that the persistence of expectations of future bailouts, weak bank supervision, and the lack of competition in many countries can seriously undermine banks' incentives to use corporate control powers to maximize firm value.[7]

As argued above, however, banks do not necessarily need to hold shares as a tool to exert control on management. They may also play a key role through their lending operations, either actively (credit decisions and cash management functions) or passively (secured lending). *Ex ante*, they play an important role in screening good and bad enterprise projects, and through the threat of bankruptcy, they exercise contingent control over firms (Aghion and Bolton, 1992). Of course, where banks are weak, undercapitalized, and subject to government intervention in terms of directed lending, one should not expect them to help strengthen corporate governance. Furthermore, Johnson et al. (2000) provide ample examples where banks themselves were at the core of governance scandals during the financial crises in Asia and Russia in 1997 and 1998. In several cases, collapses of banks were associated with complete expropriation by bank managers, whereas creditors and minority shareholders got nothing.

Well-governed banks are a necessary condition for exerting control on borrowers and for helping improve governance. Banks can be expected to play their part only if they have a sound loan portfolio. Otherwise, there is the danger of creditor passivity, since filing for bankruptcy may reveal the weak financial situation of the bank (Mitchell, 1993; Roland, 1995). A sound loan portfolio requires that banks possess the necessary skills to monitor and manage risk. Moreover, reliable information is vital. In order for lending operations to be viable, the lender must have access to information on the borrower and the capacity to act on that information (Baer and Gray,

1996, p. 77). Creditor protection and the enforcement of laws are also critically important. Finally, from a macroeconomic standpoint, debt can be expected to be an efficient controlling device only if the banks' lending operations are large enough.

Foreign-owned banks are less likely to be subject to government interventions and may therefore be considered as superior candidates. Moreover, they tend to be better endowed with human capital and possess the necessary skills to monitor and manage credit risk. Interestingly, it appears that the surge in foreign bank ownership has not been confined to countries where creditor rights are comparatively high. In Argentina, Peru, and Venezuela, for instance, foreign control ranges from around one third to almost 50 percent, although the protection of creditors is perceived to be rather poor (La Porta et al., 1997).

In fact, foreign banks might actually help protect creditor rights in these countries. More generally, it has been argued (Gerschenkon, 1962; Rajan and Zingales, 1998) that when accounting rules and regulatory and contractual enforcement institutions are still weak, banks might be better placed to ensure creditor protection. In countries that lack such institutions, small investors are deterred from investing in the stock market for fear of being exploited by inside traders and unscrupulous stock price manipulators. Small investors might therefore feel that their savings are better protected in deposit or savings accounts at banks, which are generally subject to some form of supervision by the state (Berglöf and Bolton, 2002).

As we have seen before, the increase in foreign bank ownership has been associated with a substantial rise in the share of lending by foreign banks in domestic currency, which at least partly has come at the expense of cross-border lending in foreign currency. Moreover, domestic credit to households and enterprises in most emerging market countries has continued to grow as a percentage of GDP over the last decade (Table 10.4). However, retained profits have typically remained the most important source of investment.

Thus, debt provided by foreign banks (and more generally, the banking system) has probably played a rather limited role as an effective controlling device so far. Interestingly, however, foreign banks seem to be attracted to markets where corporate boards are perceived to work comparatively well. The empirical link between creditor rights and foreign bank ownership seems rather weak; however, based on data from the World Economic Forum's Executive Opinion Survey 2001 (Porter et al., 2002, question 10.17), there appears to be a positive correlation between foreign bank ownership and the degree to which corporate boards are perceived to be controlled by outside shareholders as opposed to management (Figure 10.1; 1=corporate boards in your country are controlled by management, 7=by powerful outside shareholders).

TABLE 10.4 **Domestic Credit to the Private Sector in Selected Countries**

	DOMESTIC CREDIT TO PRIVATE SECTOR (% GDP), 1990	DOMESTIC CREDIT TO PRIVATE SECTOR (% GDP), 2000
Czech Republic	N/A	49.7
Hungary	46.6	30.9
Poland	3.1	26.0
Argentina	15.6	23.8
Brazil	38.9	37.6
Chile	47.2	68.0
Colombia	30.8	27.7
Mexico	17.5	13.2
Peru	11.8	25.9
Venezuela	25.4	12.1
Korea	65.5	101.9
Malaysia	69.4	135.5
Thailand	83.4	108.8

Source: The World Bank (2002)

That foreign banks (and the banking system more generally) have probably played only a limited role in corporate governance, does not necessarily mean that this role will remain limited. As Berglöf and Pajuste in this volume argue with regard to central and eastern Europe, "in the medium-run there is some hope that large commercial banks will start to play a more active role in financing and monitoring companies." To the extent that commercial banks will eventually become more active, one may expect foreign institutions not only to be part of that trend, but to actually play a lead role. In some regions, notably Asia and Latin America, lending in local currency has already risen significantly, both in absolute terms and as a percentage of total domestic credit. With foreign bank ownership having increased dramatically in central and eastern Europe, it can be expected that local claims in local currency will also rise markedly over the next few years.[8] However, with the role of external finance supplied by commercial, and especially foreign, banks anticipated to become more important, these institutions can be expected to provide greater leverage on management.

But for debt to become an important controlling device and for foreign banks to play a lead role, further development is needed in several areas. First of all, the quality of information needs to be improved in many developing countries and transition economies. The financial and cost accounting systems of firms must be developed, asset values inventoried, and changes in asset holdings documented. To the extent that there are information asymmetries, it may be costly or impossible for outsiders to fund the growth of a firm with either debt or equity (Diamond, 1991).

FIGURE 10.1   **Foreign Bank Ownership and Board Control in Selected Emerging Markets**

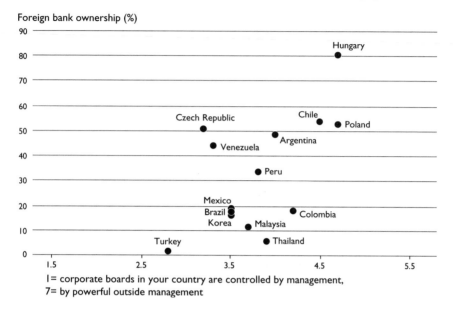

Foreign bank ownership (%)

1 = corporate boards in your country are controlled by management,
7 = by powerful outside management

Second, there needs to be an appropriate legal framework for debt collection. Liquidation and collateral laws are critical. The latter is particularly important from the viewpoint of passive monitoring. In many countries, there is a broad range of problems. In some, the definition of property that can be used as collateral appears too narrow; real property can be used as a mortgage, but liens on movable property can be limited by the legal requirement that they be possessory, that is, the property subject to the lien must be physically in the possession of the lender. Moreover, the registration of liens is sometimes inadequate, and secured creditors in some countries come far down in priority—below procedural costs, payments to employees, taxes, and rents on government properties. Furthermore, the process of execution of liens is often fraught with serious problems that need to be addressed if debt is to play a more important role as a controlling device. Creditors oftentimes must go to court (or arbitration) to get a decision that the loan is indeed due, and this can take months.[9] And once a decision is made and the creditor gains execution on a lien, the market for many assets is thin.

While the first two factors—information and legal framework—play an equally important role for both domestic and foreign banks, for the former a third condition appears essential: there must be appropriate incentives for creditors (Baer and Gray, p. 78ff). Incentives can be seriously undermined, for example, if banks themselves are not allowed to fail, but are repeatedly recapitalized. If laws and norms on fiduciary responsibility are weak and information on banks' financial status is scant, managers may not feel much pressure to implement credit policies and to force turnarounds on delinquent borrowers. Arguably, foreign banks appear much less likely to be recapitalized by foreign governments, so they have a strong incentive to collect debt. Given the sheer number of banking crises in emerging-market economies over the past few decades and the cost of bank consolidation in these cases—ranging from as much as 41 percent of GDP to 55 percent of GDP in Chile (1981 to 1985) and Argentina (1980 to 1982) respectively—this may indeed be an important factor explaining why foreign banks may play a leading role in a corporate governance framework where debt becomes an important controlling device.

CONCLUSION

This chapter has been motivated by two observations: first, in most developing countries and transition economies, well-functioning stock markets are still lacking. In the absence of such markets, the *de facto* or *de jure* capture of controlling rights by insiders has remained a serious problem. Second, many emerging-market economies have enjoyed a tremendous increase in foreign bank ownership in the last few years, and to the extent that market access will be further liberalized under the FSA and the GATS, the ratio of foreign participation looks set to increase further.

Against this background, we have discussed the role of debt as a control device in emerging-market economies and, more specifically, the potential role of foreign-owned banks. The following findings emerge from our analysis.

First, foreign banks do not necessarily follow their clients who invest abroad. While in many cases a co-location is found, there is little evidence that foreign banks are providing financial services primarily, or exclusively, to the affiliates of clients from their home countries.

Second, foreign banks typically increase competition and often lead to greater efficiency, as signaled by lower intermediation spreads, reduced nonfinancial costs, and improved loan quality. While foreign bank participation is normally not confined to the wholesale market, they appear to allocate greater shares of their lending portfolios to commercial and industry loans.

Third, foreign bank participation might actually improve firms' access to credit. By contrast, the evidence remains mixed as to whether foreign competition may have forced small domestic banks to exit the market, resulting in a decline in the supply of credit to informationally opaque small businesses.

Fourth, banks in emerging-market countries have been found to play only a minor, if any, role as shareholders. To the extent that banks, and foreign banks more specifically, are to play a greater role in upgrading corporate governance, this has to be based on their lending operations.

Fifth, in several regions, notably in Asia and Latin America, foreign banks' local claims in local currency has risen significantly over the past decade, representing a significant share of their total foreign claims (including international claims arising from cross-border operations).

Sixth, while foreign banks usually have more advanced skills and techniques to monitor and manage credit risk and are less likely to be subject to government interventions, their role in terms of exerting pressure on management has remained limited.

Seventh, for banks to play a more important role, improvements in a number of areas need to be made, chief among them the availability of reliable information and an appropriate framework for debt collection.

Finally, while reliable information and appropriate debt collection are equally important for domestic and foreign banks, foreign banks might have an important advantage to the extent that they are less likely to lack incentives to collect debt. The lack of creditor incentives resulting from repeated recapitalizations of domestic banks can indeed be serious. Taking into account the dramatic increase in foreign bank ownership, the increased participation in the supply of domestic credit, and strong incentives to collect debt, foreign banks may be expected to play a leading role toward a corporate governance framework where debt becomes an important control device. Foreign bank participation, however, will not lead to sustained improvements, unless further progress is made in providing better information and an adequate framework for debt collection.

NOTES

1 See http://www.calpers.ca.gov/invest/emergingmkt/emergingmkt.htm.

2 More recently, the role of banks in Germany, but especially in Japan, have been viewed more critically.

3 A comprehensive comparison of the US versus German systems is provided by O'Sullivan (2000). The important question whether the Anglo-Saxon and the German (and other) corporate governance systems are converging is addressed in detail by van den Berghe (2002).

4 Of the 29 foreign-owned commercial banks operating in Hungary, 21 are greenfield projects and eight are privatized banks (Szapáry, 2001, p. 19).

5 A detailed discussion of the history of the GATS and the structure of its provisions can be found in Kono et al. (1997) and Dobson and Jacquet (1998).

6 Note that the exact definition of the transactions limits the scope of the agreement. For example, while mode 2 requires the authorities of country A to permit its residents to open a bank account in country B, the GATS does not require the authorities of country B to allow foreigners to make deposits in its banks.

7 It has also been claimed that in transition economies, the relationships banks might have established with firms in the pre-reform period could make it harder for them to engage in radical downsizing and restructuring than it would be for other investors with no such links (Dittus and Prowse, 1996, p. 58).

8   As Szapáry (2001) argues in the case of Hungary, borrowing from the banking system has remained low so far since many companies operating in Hungary are owned by multinational firms that borrow from their mother companies or from banks abroad.

9   An interesting anecdote in this context is Hungary, which adopted a devastatingly effective bankruptcy law. The law had an automatic trigger that more or less overnight forced much of Hungary's industry into court-led bankruptcy procedures. The sheer number of cases paralyzed Hungary's courts. Hungary had to water down its new bankruptcy law and remove the automatic trigger (Berglöf and Bolton, 2002, p. 84).

REFERENCES

Aghion, P., and P. Bolton. 1992. "An 'Incomplete Contract' Approach to Bankruptcy and the Financial Structure of the Firm," *Review of Economic Studies* 59, pp. 473–494.

Aoki, M. 1990. "Towards an Economic Model of the Japanese Firm," *Journal of Economic Literature* 28, pp. 1–27.

Aoki, M., and H.-K. Kim. 1995. "Controlling Insider Control: Issues of Corporate Governance in Transition Economies." In M. Aoki and H.-K. Kim, eds., *Corporate Governance in Transitional Economies. Insider Control and the Role of Banks.* Washington, DC: World Bank.

Baer, H. L., and C. W. Gray. 1996. "Debt as a Control Device in Transitional Economies: The Experience s of Hungary and Poland." In R. Frydman, C. W. Gray, and A. Rapaczynski, eds., *Corporate Governance in Central Europe and Russia: Volume 1. Banks, Funds, and Foreign Investors.* Budapest: Central European University Press.

Berglöf, E. 1995. "Corporate Governance in Transition Economies: The Theory and Its Policy Implications." In M. Aoki and H.-K. Kim, eds., *Corporate Governance in Transitional Economies: Insider Control and the Role of Banks.* Washington, DC: World Bank.

Berglöf, E., and E.-L. von Thadden. 2000. "The Changing Corporate Governance Paradigm: Implications for Developing and Transition Economies." In S. S. Cohen and G. Boyd, eds., *Corporate Governance and Globalization: Long Range Planning Issues.* Cheltenham: Edward Elgar.

Berglöf, E., and P. Bolton. 2002. "The Great Divide and Beyond: Financial Architecture in Transition," *Journal of Economic Perspectives* 16, pp. 77–100.

Berglöf, E., and A. Pajuste. 2003. "Corporate Governance in Central and Eastern Europe." In P. Cornelius and B. Kogut, eds., *Corporate Governance and Capital Flows in a Global Economy.* New York: Oxford University Press.

Berle, A., and G. Means. 1932. *The Modern Corporation and Private Property.* New York: MacMillan.

Bonin, J. P., and I. Ábel. 2000. "Retail Banking in Hungary: A Foreign Affair?" WDI Working Paper No. 356. Ann Arbor, MI: William Davidson Institute at the University of Michigan Business School.

Booth, L., V. Aivazian, A. Demirgüç-Kunt, and V. Maksimovic. 2001. "Capital Structures in Developing Countries," *The Journal of Finance* 56, pp. 87–130.

Cable, J. 1985. "Capital Market Information and Industrial Performance: The Role of West German Banks," *The Economic Journal* 95, pp. 118–132.

Claessens, S., and T. Glaessner. 1997. *Are Financial Sector Weaknesses Undermining the East Asian Miracle?* Washington, DC: World Bank.

Claessens, S., A. Demirgüç-Kunt, and H. Huizinga. 2003. "How Does Foreign Entry Affect the Domestic Banking Market," *Journal of Banking and Finance* (forthcoming).

Clarke, G., R. Cull, M. Soledad Martinez Peria, and S. M Sánchez. 2001. "Foreign Bank Entry: Experience, Implications for Developing Countries, and Agenda for Further Research," WB Policy Research Working Paper No. 2698. Washington, DC: World Bank.

Clarke, G., R. Cull, and M. Soledad Martinez Peria. 2002. "Does Foreign Bank Penetration Reduce Access to Credit in Developing Countries? Evidence from Asking Borrowers," Paper presented at Financial Globalization: A Blessing or a Curse? joint conference, Center for Financial Studies at Johann Wolfgang Goethe University, George Washington University, and World Bank, Washington, DC, May 30.

Cornelius, P. K. 2000. "Trade in Financial Services, Capital Flows, and the Value-at-Risk of Countries," *The World Economy* 26, pp. 649–672.

Diamond, D. W. 1991. "Debt Maturity Structure and Liquidity Risk," *Quarterly Journal of Economics* 106, pp. 709–737.

Dittus, P., and S. Prowse. 1996. "Corporate Control in Central Europe and Russia: Should Banks Own Shares?" In R. Frydman, C. W. Gray, and A. Rapaczynski, eds., *Corporate Governance in Central Europe and Russia. Volume 1. Banks, Funds, and Foreign Investors.* 2 vols. Budapest: Central European University Press.

Dobson, W., and P. Jaquet. 1998. *Financial Services Liberalization in the WTO.* Washington, DC: Institute for International Economics.

Dobson, W., and G. C. Hufbauer. 2001. *World Capital Markets. Challenge to the G-10.* Washington, DC: Institute for International Economics.

Edwards, J., and K. Fischer. 1994. *Banks, Finance and Investment in Germany*. Cambridge: Cambridge University Press.

Franks, J., and C. Mayer. 2001. "Ownership and Control of German Corporations," *Review of Financial Studies* 14, pp. 943–977.

Gelos, G. R., and J. Roldós. 2002. *Consolidation and Market Structure in Emerging Markets Banking Systems.* Online: http://www.worldbank.org/research/conferences/financial_globalization/consolidation2.pdf.

Gerschekron, A. 1962. *Economic Backwardness in Historical Perspective. A Book of Essays*. Cambridge, MA: Harvard University Press.

Gorton, G., and F. A. Schmid. 2000. "Universal Banking and the Performance of German Firms," *Journal of Financial Economics* 58, pp. 29–80.

Institute of International Finance (IFF). 2002. *Capital Flows to Emerging Market Economies.* Online. http://www.iif.com/data/public/cf_0102.pdf.

International Monetary Fund (IMF). 2000. *International Capital Markets.* Washington, DC: International Monetary Fund.

Johnson, S., P. Boone, A. Breach, and E. Friedman. 2000. "Corporate Governance in the Asian Financial Crisis," *Journal of Financial Economics* 58, pp. 141–186.

Kaminsky, G. L., and C. M. Reinhart. 1999. "The Twin Crises: The Causes of Banking and Balance-of-Payments Problems," *The American Economic Review* 89, pp. 473–500.

Klapper, L. F., and S. Claessens. 2002. *Bankruptcy Around the World: Explanations of Its Relative Use*. Online. http://www1.worldbank.org/publicsector/legal/Bankruptcy.pdf.

Klapper, L. F., and I. Love. 2002. "Corporate Governance, Investor Protection, and Performance in Emerging Markets," WB Policy Research Working Paper No. 2818. Washington, DC: World Bank.

Kogut, B., and G. Walker. 2001. "The Small World of Germany and the Durabilitiy of National Networks," *American Sociology Review* 66, pp. 317–355.

Kono, M., and L. Schuknecht. 1998. "Financial Services Trade, Capital Flows, and Financial Stability," WTO Staff Working Paper ERAD 98–12. Geneva: World Trade Organization.

Kono, M., P. Low, M. Luanga, et al. 1997. "Opening Markets in Financial Services and the Role of the GATS." Special Studies. Geneva: World Trade Organization.

La Porta, R., F. Lopez-de-Silanes, A. Shleifer, and R. Vishny. 1997. "Legal Determinants of External Finance," *Journal of Finance* 52, pp. 1131–1150.

La Porta, R., F. Lopez-de-Silanes, A. Shleifer, and R. Vishny. 1999. "Corporate Ownership Around the World," *Journal of Finance* 54, pp. 471–517.

La Porta, R., F. Lopez-de-Silanes, and A. Shleifer. 2002. "Government Ownership of Banks," *Journal of Finance* 57, pp. 265–301.

Levine, R. 2000. "Bank-Based or Market-Based Financial Systems: Which Is Better?" WDI Working Paper No. 442. Ann Arbor, MI: William Davidson Institute at the University of Michigan Business School.

Mitchell, J. 1993. "Creditor Passivity and Bankruptcy. Implications for Bankruptcy Reform." In C. Mayer and X. Vives, eds., *Capital Markets and Financial Intermediation*. Cambridge: Cambridge University Press.

Miller, S.R., and A. Parkhe. 1998. "Patterns in the Expansion of U.S. Banks' Foreign Operations," *Journal of International Business Studies* 29, pp. 359–390.

Moore, M. 2000. "Financial Services and the WTO," BIS Review 73/2000, pp. 1–2.

Organisation for Economic Co-operation and Development (OECD). 1998. *Corporate Governance: Improving Competitiveness and Access to Capital in Global Markets*. Paris: Organisation for Economic Co-operation and Development.

O'Sullivan, M. 2000. *Contests for Corporate Control: Corporate Governance in the United States and Germany*. Oxford: Oxford University Press.

Pistor, K., M. Raiser, and S. Gelfer. 2000. "Law and Finance in Transition Economies," *The Economics of Transition* 8, pp. 325–368.

Porter, M.E., J.D. Sachs, P.K. Cornelius, J.W. McArthur, and K. Schwab. 2002. *The Global Competitiveness Report 2001–2002*. New York: Oxford University Press.

Rajan, R. G., and L. Zingales. 1998. "Which Capitalism? Lessons from the East Asian Crisis," *Journal of Applied Corporate Finance* 11, pp. 40–48.

Roland, G. 1995. "Political Economy Issues of Ownership Transformation in Eastern Europe." In M. Aoki and H.-K. Kim, eds., *Corporate Governance in Transitional Economies. Insider Control and the Role of Banks*. Washington, DC: World Bank.

Saunders, A., and I. Walter. 1994. *Universal Banking in the United States: What Could We Gain? What Could We Lose?* New York: Oxford University Press.

Sorsa, P. 1997. "The GATS Agreement on Financial Services—A Modest Start to Multilateral Liberalization," IMF Working Paper WP/97/55. Washington, DC: International Monetary Fund.

Stiglitz, J. E. 1985. "Credit Markets and the Control of Capital," *Journal of Money, Credit, and Banking* 17, pp. 133–152.

Szapáry, G. "Banking Sector Reform in Hungary: Lessons Learned, Current Trends and Prospects," NHB Working Paper 2001/5. National Bank of Hungary. Online. http://www.mnb.hu.

World Bank. 2002. *World Development Indicators.* Washington, DC: World Bank.

Van den Berghe, L. 2002. Corporate Governance in a Globalising World: Convergence or Divergence? A European Perspective. Boston, MA: Kluwer Academic Publishers.

Walter, I. 2000. "Capital Markets and Control of Enterprises in the Global Economy." In S. S. Cohen and G. Boyd, eds., *Corporate Governance and Globalization: Long Range Planning Issues.* Cheltenham: Edward Elgar.

Chapter 11

Emerging Owners, Eclipsing Markets?
Corporate Governance in Central and Eastern Europe

Erik Berglöf and Anete Pajuste

The countries in central and eastern Europe have pursued remarkably different policies and followed strikingly different trajectories. Despite these differences, the structures of their financial systems are rapidly converging. The contours of post-socialist capitalism are emerging, and the specific challenges of corporate governance are becoming clearer. The purpose of this chapter is to characterize the main features of the corporate governance challenge facing the countries of central and eastern Europe, and to suggest the thrust of policy intervention.

New comparable data on ownership and control and financing patterns shows that the emerging capitalist systems share many features.[1] Although the extent of remaining government ownership differs from one country to another, private ownership dominates everywhere. Ownership and control are becoming increasingly concentrated, with the emergence of corporate groupings and significant foreign owners in most countries. As firms grow in size, ownership and control are separated primarily by the use of a pyramid structure. As on the rest of the European continent, firms often have a second large shareholder. Most firms in central and eastern Europe are still owner-managed, but professional management is becoming more common. However, even in firms with professional managers, controlling shareholders play a critical role. Moreover, for better or for worse, large shareholders are also playing, and will most likely continue to play, a role beyond their immediate mandate and influencing the course of politics, in particular by shaping the rules pertaining to corporate governance and financial sector development.

The emerging ownership and control structures have important implications for corporate governance. In owner-managed firms, the fundamental tradeoff is between providing incentives to entrepreneurship and protecting minority investors. The data and rich anecdotal evidence from these countries suggest that strengthening minority protection is of paramount importance in combating fraud and bringing down financing costs. The main concern of this policy priority is that protection of minorities in incumbents in takeovers may discourage strategic investors and badly needed restructuring in these countries. The mandatory bid rule (MBR) requiring owners with large controlling stakes to buy out remaining shareholders also forces firms to delist, thus undermining the sustainability of these fledgling stock markets.

As controlling owners gradually distance themselves from day-to-day management in favor of professional managers, the nature of the corporate governance problem changes. Managers must be monitored, and only controlling owners have sufficient incentive to perform this task. Even in these firms, the main corporate governance conflict remains the conflict between controlling owners and minority investors. But the key tradeoff is between providing controlling owners with incentives to monitor and protecting minority investors. Once the worst forms of fraud have been contained, excessive emphasis on minority protection would reinforce the informational advantage of the management.

The importance of monitoring by the large shareholder is reinforced by the weakness of other mechanisms for corporate governance. With strongly concentrated ownership and control, hostile takeovers and proxy fights are largely ineffective as disciplining devices. Similarly, boards of directors cannot be expected to play an independent role, and the role of executive compensation schemes is more limited in companies controlled by a single shareholder. Moreover, litigation is unlikely to be a successful, or reliable, mechanism in environments of weak legal enforcement, and large commercial banks have yet to become deeply involved in financing the corporate sector.

The current weakness of these supplementary mechanisms, however, does not imply that efforts should not be made to develop them. In the medium term there is some hope that increasing the involvement of commercial banks will provide some monitoring. Over time, improved financing opportunities can increase competition in the market for corporate control and help improve contestability. As the legal environments improve, in particular with respect to enforcement, there is some hope that litigation could also become a mechanism contributing to better corporate governance.

The regulatory response to the emerging ownership and control structures has largely been determined by the process of accession to the European Union. Regulators have emulated existing institutions in current member states and to some extent anticipated possible regulation at the EU level. As a result, the central and eastern European (CEE) countries have adopted regulations that on paper are stronger minority protection than that of most EU countries. However, in implementing existing regulation, efforts are made to maintain the incentive for active controlling shareholders. For example, the interpretation of the MBR appears to be very lax in several countries, leaving more possibilities for a control premium and facilitating block trades.

We start the next section by describing some current features of the institutional environment of the countries in central and eastern Europe. The following section documents the strong concentration of ownership and control in listed firms, and also identifies some differences in patterns across countries. Next we attempt to define main features of the corporate governance problem(s) facing the countries of central and eastern Europe, and discuss the implications for the regulatory tradeoffs they are facing; the conclusion follows.

THE INSTITUTIONAL BACKDROP

The emerging financial architecture

Financial sector transition from a planned economy to a market-oriented economy involved transforming a single institution responsible for monetary policy and commercial banking, the so-called monobank, into a decentralized financial system integrated into a market economy. After an initial phase of similar measures to break up the monobank and to deal with the heritage of central planning, the countries of central and eastern Europe chose very different policies and followed different trajectories of financial development. A "Great Divide" opened up between those countries that managed to establish a sound institutional foundation, resist pressures to bailout firms, and enforce contracts, and those that did not. Interestingly, the countries that made it to the "right" side of the divide have managed to combine fiscal and monetary responsibility with the enforcement of contracts (Berglöf and Bolton, 2002).

The more successful countries in central and eastern Europe followed very different financial development policies. Procedures for restructuring bad loans, privatization strategies for enterprises and banks, policy toward foreign entry in the banking sector, regulatory barriers to entry of new banks, and policies toward stock market development all differed markedly. In particular, countries in transition opted for very different strategies for privatizing state-owned enterprises. For example, Hungary started privatization early and followed a case-by-case sales method, while the Czech Republic opted for a mass voucher privatization scheme. Poland was slow in implementing mass privatization, but in the meantime a large number of individual firms were privatized through management buyouts and liquidation schemes.

Development paths also differed markedly. Table 11.1 shows the development of domestic credit to the private sector as a share of GDP. This standard but very poor measure indicates that only in Estonia, Poland, Slovakia, and Slovenia did credit expand relatively steadily. The Czech Republic had a very high stock of credit early on, but this reflected the mass privatization of enterprises and extensive bad loans rather than financial development. After several banking crises during the first half of the 1990s, credit in the Czech Republic dropped from 45 percent of GDP in 1990 to 25 percent in 1994. Since then, its level of credit has expanded in step with economic growth. Similarly, Latvia and Lithuania also recovered after initial banking crises.

TABLE II.I **Domestic Credit to Households and Enterprises Over GDP (in Percent)**

COUNTRY	1993	1994	1995	1996	1997	1998	1999
Czech Republic	—	51.8	55.3	55.5	60.0	61.5	56.1
Estonia	7.3	11.1	12.5	15.1	20.0	24.4	26.4
Hungary	28.7	24.7	22.3	20.8	21.4	22.7	23.4
Latvia	—	14.7	11.8	7.0	8.5	12.3	15.7
Lithuania	—	13.4	14.0	11.5	9.4	10.6	12.3
Poland	10.2	10.5	10.7	13.0	15.6	17.4	20.6
Slovenia	—	23.1	27.5	28.8	28.6	32.8	35.9
Bulgaria	4.1	3.1	10.6	19.0	15.6	11.4	13.2
Romania	—	—	—	—	8.3	9.0	9.1
Russia	—	6.8	7.9	7.0	7.7	10.6	10.2
Slovak Republic	—	25.8	24.3	28.4	36.1	41.7	39.8
Ukraine	1.1	1.1	1.5	1.3	1.8	4.8	7.6

Source: IMF, *International Financial Statistics*

In other countries, the link between finance and growth is even weaker. Bulgaria experienced rapid growth in credit in the mid 1990s and then a drastic fall in the late 1990s, but its economy declined or showed moderate growth over this time period. In Russia, financial markets developed rapidly and credit to households and enterprises increased somewhat in the late 1990s, while the economy continued to stagnate. The financial crisis in August 1998 had little long-term impact on real growth. Ukraine, and many other countries that were formerly part of the Soviet Union, did not see any financial development of note.

The financial sectors of these countries have converged. They are now strongly dominated by mainly foreign-controlled banks lending primarily to governments and other financial institutions. Banks provide some working capital finance to the corporate sector, but so far they have played a limited role in financing investments. Investment finance comes almost exclusively from retained earnings, and most external finance comes through foreign direct investment. The difference between lending and borrowing rates have declined significantly in level and volatility in most countries of central and eastern Europe, but they remain high by the standards of developed market economies. Important weaknesses in the institutional environment, particularly in the enforcement of laws and regulations, have yet to be addressed. The process of accession to the European Union is providing useful pressure to bring this process forward.

The emergence—and eclipse—of stock markets

Countries established stock exchanges at different points of the transition process. Slovenia, Hungary, Bulgaria,[2] Poland, and Russia opened their stock markets very early (1990–1991), and the Czech Republic, Slovakia, and Lithuania followed in 1993. Trading on the Latvian and Romanian stock exchanges started in mid 1995; Estonia did not open up its stock exchange until spring 1996.

The countries followed very different policies toward stock market development in the early stages of transition (Claessens, Djankov, and Klingebiel, 2000). This variation can to a large extent be explained by differences in the privatization policies pursued in the countries. Most of the listed companies are privatized firms rather than new start-ups. Table 11.2 shows the development of number of shares in the stock markets.

Among the countries in the region we can distinguish three approaches.[3] In Bulgaria, the Czech and Slovak Republics, Lithuania, and Romania listing was mandatory after mass privatization. The stock exchanges in these countries are characterized by an initial rapid increase in the number of listed companies and then a gradual, in some countries steeper, decrease. In the early phases very few shares were actively traded, and once the markets became more established illiquid shares have been de-listed as a result of more stringent regulation (e.g., minimum capital and liquidity requirement).

The other group of countries—Estonia, Hungary, Latvia, Poland,[4] and Slovenia—chose to start with a small number of listed shares, which increased as the markets developed. The shares listed were usually voluntary initial public offerings. The third group of countries—Russia and Ukraine—combined both of the previous methods: i.e., some voluntary offerings and some mandatory listing of minority packages of the privatized enterprises.

TABLE 11.2 **Number of Listed Securities (All Markets)**

	1994	1995	1996	1997	1998	1999	2000	2001
Bulgaria	16	26	15	15	998	828	506	392
Czech Republic	1,028	1,716	1,670	320	304	195	151	102
Estonia	0	0	19	31	29	24	21	17
Hungary	40	42	45	49	55	66	60	56
Latvia	0	17	34	51	68	67	63	63
Lithuania	183	351	460	667	1,365	1,250	1,188	902
Poland	44	65	83	143	198	221	225	230
Romania (BSE)	0	9	17	75	126	127	114	65
Romania[a]	0	9	17	5,542	6,072	5,643	5,496	5,149
Russia	72	170	73	208	237	207	249	—
Slovak Republic	521	850	970	918	833	830	866	888
Slovenia	—	—	—	85	92	134	154	156
Ukraine	—	—	—	—	125	125	139	—

Notes: — indicates data not available. *All markets* refers to all equity markets – official and free market.

[a] Bucharest Stock Exchange (BSE) and RASDAQ

Sources: Home pages of national stock exchanges; International Finance Corporation *Emerging Markets Database*

The development of market capitalization also reflects the chosen privatization method. In countries that followed more gradual privatization, equity market capitalization increased slowly (e.g., Poland, Hungary), while in countries with rapid mass privatization, market capitalization jumped to very high levels and then decreased due to de-listing of illiquid shares (e.g., the Czech Republic).

By the end of 2000, stock market capitalization was the highest in Russia (see Table 11.3), followed by Poland, Hungary, and the Czech Republic. The rest of the stock markets in the region are negligible, partly due to the small size of the country (Estonia, Latvia, Lithuania, and Slovenia) or poor regulatory framework (Bulgaria, Romania, Slovak Republic, and Ukraine). Nonetheless, even the largest stock exchanges in transition economies are relatively small on a world scale. (See the comparison with other world markets in Table 11.3.) It is interesting to note that the market capitalization figures for the frontrunners in transition countries are similar to those of Portugal and Greece (the newest members of the EU) in the mid 1990s.

TABLE 11.3 **Equity Market (Including Free Markets) Capitalization at the End of Period (Millions of US Dollars)**

	1995	1996	1997	1998	1999	2000	2001
Bulgaria	61	7	2	992	706	617	—
Czech Republic	9,186	14,248	12,786	12,045	12,956	11,391	9,191
Estonia	—	728	1,139	492	1,795	1,733	1,473
Hungary	2,399	5,273	14,975	14,028	16,433	11,926	10,210
Latvia	10	151	337	688	880	590	687
Lithuania	380	1,253	2,173	2,959	3,177	3,052	2,626
Poland	4,564	8,390	12,135	20,461	29,882	31,399	25,933
Romania (BSE)	100	61	632	357	317	366	1,228
Romania[a]	100	61	2,137	1,152	1,313	1,172	2,301
Russia	15,863	37,230	128,207	20,598	72,205	38,922	—
Slovak Republic	5,354	5,770	5,292	4,117	3,568	3,268	3,458
Slovenia	312	891	1,625	2,450	2,880	3,101	3,387
Ukraine	—	—	3,667	570	1,121	1,881	—
Greece	17,060	24,178	34,168	79,992	204,213	110,839	83,481
Portugal	18,362	24,660	38,954	62,954	66,488	60,681	46,337
Spain	197,788	242,779	290,383	402,180	431,668	504,219	468,203
United Kingdom	1,407,737	1,740,246	1,996,225	2,374,273	2,933,280	2,576,992	2,164,716
United States	6,857,622	8,484,433	11,308,779	13,451,352	16,635,114	15,104,037	13,766,261
Germany	577,365	670,997	825,233	1,093,962	1,432,190	1,270,243	1,071,749

Notes: — indicates data not available.

[a] Bucharest Stock Exchange (BSE) and RASDAQ

Sources: Homepages of national stock exchanges; International Finance Corporation *Emerging Markets Database*; International Federation of Stock Exchanges

The stock markets are also small relative to the size of the economies (Table 11.4 shows the ratio of market capitalization to GDP, a ratio widely used in cross-country studies to proxy for stock market development). In four countries—the Czech Republic, Estonia, Hungary, and Lithuania[5]—the market capitalization to GDP is above 20 percent. This level compares with that of Greece and Portugal in the mid 1990s and is slightly below the respective figure in Germany. Bulgaria, Romania, and Ukraine, on the other hand, have very low (below 10 percent) market capitalization to GDP ratios.

The downward sloping tendency in capitalization figures after 1999 has several explanations. First, the overall stock market downturn in the world has affected most transition markets adversely. Second, stricter listing requirements (e.g., the minimum capital requirement, information disclosure and transparency) have forced many companies to de-list. The low number of initial public offerings (IPOs)[6] and the many voluntary de-listings suggest that the costs of listing outweigh the benefits. Listed companies have to provide much more information on a regular basis than unlisted ones, and are

TABLE 11.4 **Equity Market Capitalization to GDP at the End of Period (in Percent)**

	1995	1996	1997	1998	1999	2000	2001	AVERAGE (98–00)
Bulgaria	0.47	0.07	0.02	7.79	5.45	4.90	—	6.05
Czech Republic	17.65	24.68	24.17	21.16	23.57	22.17	16.20	22.30
Estonia	—	16.68	24.64	9.40	34.50	33.19	26.62	25.70
Hungary	5.37	11.67	32.79	29.82	34.22	25.62	19.67	29.89
Latvia	0.22	2.94	5.98	11.30	13.21	8.25	9.10	10.92
Lithuania	6.31	15.88	22.67	27.53	29.79	27.04	21.90	28.12
Poland	3.59	5.83	8.42	12.85	19.27	19.92	14.71	17.35
Romania (RSE)	0.28	0.17	1.79	0.85	0.89	0.99	3.09	0.91
Romania[a]	0.28	0.17	6.06	2.74	3.69	3.18	5.79	3.20
Russia	4.69	8.89	29.41	7.29	37.29	14.99	—	19.86
Slovak Republic	27.96	28.13	25.11	18.72	17.66	16.60	16.90	17.66
Slovenia	1.66	4.72	8.93	12.51	14.35	17.11	18.11	14.66
Ukraine	—	—	7.31	1.36	3.64	6.02	—	3.67
Greece	14.51	19.44	28.18	65.90	163.62	99.02	71.70	109.51
Portugal	17.12	22.00	36.63	56.04	57.84	57.08	42.16	56.99
Spain	33.86	39.81	51.71	68.40	71.55	89.63	80.40	76.53
United Kingdom	107.41	119.34	131.98	141.53	164.68	180.29	152.23	162.17
United States	93.45	109.46	137.26	154.63	181.76	152.98	136.54	163.12
Germany	13.44	20.95	27.55	29.48	36.83	31.11	57.78	32.47

Notes: — indicates data not available.

[a] Bucharest Stock Exchange (BSE) and RASDAQ

subject to more stringent supervision and scrutiny by the public. Third, ownership is becoming increasingly concentrated, and as most of the countries have introduced mandatory bid rules,[7] owners passing a certain threshold must offer to buy the entire firm. As a result they must leave the stock exchange, because one of the listing requirements is that a certain minimum of shares (e.g., 25 percent) must be in public circulation. We will return to how the regulatory authorities have tried to mitigate the negative effects of the mandatory bid rule through lax enforcement.

From "law-on-the-books" to enforcement

Investor protection in corporate law and securities markets regulation differ considerably across countries. Pistor (2000) provides a standardized comparison of "law-on-the-books" using an aggregated variable, stock market integrity, which covers conflict of interest rules, independence of shareholder registers, insider trading rules, mandatory disclosure thresholds, state control of capital market supervision agency, and the independence of capital market supervision (Table 11.5). For comparison, the cumulative shareholder rights index (called the *anti-directors index* in La Porta et al., 1997) is provided for our sample countries, as well as four legal origin groups and the world average for 49 countries in the La Porta et al. sample.

TABLE 11.5 **Investor Protection**

	STOCK MARKET INTEGRITY (Pistor, 2000)				CUMULATIVE SHAREHOLDER RIGHTS ("anti-director index" in La Porta et al, 1997)			
	1992	1994	1996	1998	1992	1994	1996	1998
Bulgaria	1	1	5	5	4	4	4	4
Czech Republic	3	3	4	5	2	2	3	3
Estonia	0	2	4	4	2	2	3.75	3.75
Hungary	3	3	3	5	2.5	2.5	2.5	3
Latvia	1	1	1	1	3.5	3.5	3.5	3.5
Lithuania	2	1	1	1	2.5	3.75	3.75	3.75
Poland	4	4	4	4	3	3	3	3
Romania	1	1	1	1	3	3	3	3
Russia	2	3	3	3	2	2.5	5.5	5.5
Slovak Republic	0	2	2	2	2.5	2.5	2.5	2.5
Slovenia	0	3	3	3	0	2.5	2.5	2.5
Ukraine	1	1	1	1	2.5	2.5	2.5	2.5
Average	**1.50**	**2.08**	**2.67**	**2.92**	**2.46**	**2.81**	**3.29**	**3.33**
Common law	—	—	—	—	—	—	4	—
French civil law	—	—	—	—	—	—	2.33	—
German civil law	—	—	—	—	—	—	2.33	—
Scandinavian civil law	—	—	—	—	—	—	3	—
World Average (49)	—	—	—	—	—	—	3	—

Sources: Pistor (2000); La Porta et al. (1997)

These two variables do not provide an idea on how these laws are actually implemented, supervised, and enforced. The European Bank for Reconstruction and Development (EBRD) evaluation of commercial law and financial regulations extensiveness and effectiveness attempts to capture these aspects. Table 11.6, for the years 1998 and 2000, shows that enforcement (effectiveness) is lagging behind the extensiveness. Enforcement of financial regulations was particularly behind, but at the same time it also improved the most in period from 1998 to 2000.

The court system is still not working efficiently and is characterized by high level of corruption. The World Bank Business Environment and Enterprise Performance Survey (BEEPS) study shows that companies have rather little trust in the judiciary system (Table 11.7). We observe that, for example, the Central Bank has considerably higher rating than the courts. The evaluation of fairness, honesty, and enforceability in legal systems is rather poor. The shaded countries—the Czech Republic, Latvia, Lithuania, (and Russia and Ukraine)—have lower than average evaluation in all categories (except the quality of the Central Bank for Latvia). This shows that companies in these five countries are more pessimistic (as compared with their counterparts in other sample countries) about the overall efficiency, fairness, honesty, and enforceability of the legal system in particular countries.

TABLE 11.6 **Law on Books versus Enforcement**

	Commercial Law Extensiveness (Law on Books)		Commercial Law Extensiveness (Enforcement)		Financial Regulations Extensiveness (Law on Books)		Financial Regulations Extensiveness (Enforcement)	
	1998	2000	1998	2000	1998	2000	1998	2000
Bulgaria	4	4	4	3.7	4	3	3	2.3
Czech Republic	4	3	4	3.3	3.3	4	2.7	2.7
Estonia	3	3.7	4	3.3	3.3	4	2.7	2.7
Hungary	4	4	4	3.7	4	4	4	4
Latvia	3.3	4	2	3.7	3.3	3	2.3	3
Lithuania	4	4	3	3.3	2.7	4	2	3.7
Poland	4	3.7	4	4	4	4	3	4
Romania	4	3.3	4	3.7	3	4	2.7	3
Russia	3.7	3.7	2.3	3	3	3	2	2.7
Slovak Republic	3	3	2	3	3	3	2	2.7
Slovenia	3	4	3	3.7	3.3	4	2.7	4
Ukraine	2	3.3	2	2	2	3	1.7	2.3
Average	**3.50**	**3.64**	**3.19**	**3.37**	**3.24**	**3.58**	**2.57**	**3.09**

Note: The variable ranges from 1, 1+, 2– . . . to 4–, 4, 4+. The numbers in this table are constructed as follows: e.g., 3+ is 3.3, 4– is 3.7, and round numbers remain intact.

Source: EBRD *Transition Report* (2000).

TABLE 11.7 **Evaluation of Quality and Efficiency of Legal System**

	COMPANIES' RATING OF THE OVERALL QUALITY AND EFFICIENCY OF ... (from 1 = very good to 6 = very bad; "don't knows" excluded)		EVALUATION OF COUNTRY'S LEGAL SYSTEM, associations with the following descriptions (from 1 = always to 6 = never; "don't knows" excluded)		
	Judiciary/Courts	Central Bank	Fair and Impartial	Honest/ Uncorrupted	Able to Enforce Decisions
Bulgaria	3.34	2.83	3.94	4.23	2.43
Czech Republic	4.13	3.26	3.97	4.17	3.69
Estonia	3.43	2.45	3.06	3.05	3.09
Hungary	3.52	2.77	2.94	2.76	3.37
Latvia	3.84	2.48	3.90	3.96	4.34
Lithuania	3.87	2.95	4.19	4.40	3.49
Poland	3.75	2.33	3.50	3.52	3.81
Romania	3.63	3.07	3.52	3.88	3.29
Russia	3.84	4.23	4.40	4.57	4.35
Slovak Republic	3.74	2.90	3.62	3.86	3.12
Slovenia	4.00	2.05	2.94	2.98	2.58
Ukraine	3.77	3.18	4.24	4.54	4.01
Average	3.74	2.87	3.69	3.83	3.46

Source: World Bank, BEEPS survey (http://info.worldbank.org/governance/beeps/)

Kaufmann et al. (2002) aggregate the governance indicators constructed by different international institutions, databases, and consulting firms, and compile country measures for regulatory quality, rule of law, and control of corruption (see Table 11.8). The 2000/2001 data show that in all the three categories Romania, Russia, and Ukraine score the lowest, while the Czech Republic, Estonia, Hungary, and Slovenia score the highest. Table 11.8 shows that the average regulatory quality, rule of law, and control of corruption in transition economies is well below the averages in developed markets. However, there is huge variation within the sample countries—the best-performing transition countries score higher than or close to Greece (e.g., in 2000/2001 Estonia outperforms Greece in all three categories).

The 10 CEE countries can roughly be classified into four groups in terms of their approach to enforcement of investor protection and securities markets regulations. The first group, Poland and Hungary, has chosen strict regulatory mechanisms aimed at investor protection from management and large blockholder fraud. These two countries have also put considerable effort into enforcement mechanisms, often the most deficient part of the legal framework in transition economies. Comparing these two countries, Hungary has weaker regulation than Poland, but its stock market performance is boosted by the specific choice of privatization method, and it relies heavily on sales of controlling stakes to foreigners. This method has increased foreign con-

TABLE 11.8 **Aggregate Governance Indicators**

	REGULATORY QUALITY		RULE OF LAW		CONTROL OF CORRUPTION	
	2000/2001	1997/1998	2000/2001	1997/1998	2000/2001	1997/1998
Bulgaria	0.16	0.52	0.02	−0.15	−0.16	−0.56
Czech Republic	0.54	0.57	0.64	0.54	0.31	0.38
Estonia	1.09	0.74	0.78	0.51	0.73	0.59
Hungary	0.88	0.85	0.76	0.71	0.65	0.61
Latvia	0.3	0.51	0.36	0.15	−0.03	−0.26
Lithuania	0.3	0.09	0.29	0.18	0.2	0.03
Poland	0.41	0.56	0.55	0.54	0.43	0.49
Romania	−0.28	0.2	−0.02	−0.09	−0.51	−0.46
Russia	−1.4	−0.3	−0.87	−0.72	−1.01	−0.62
Slovak Republic	0.27	0.28	0.36	0.13	0.23	0.03
Slovenia	0.52	0.53	0.89	0.83	1.09	1.02
Ukraine	−1.05	−0.72	−0.63	−0.71	−0.9	−0.89
Average for TE	**0.15**	**0.32**	**0.26**	**0.16**	**0.09**	**0.03**
Greece	0.71	0.6	0.62	0.5	0.73	0.82
Portugal	0.81	0.89	0.94	1.08	1.21	1.22
Spain	1.08	0.86	1.12	1.03	1.45	1.21
Average	**0.87**	**0.78**	**0.89**	**0.87**	**1.13**	**1.08**
United Kingdom	1.32	1.21	1.61	1.69	1.86	1.71
United States	1.19	1.14	1.58	1.25	1.45	1.41
Germany	1.08	0.89	1.57	1.48	1.38	1.62
Average	**1.20**	**1.08**	**1.59**	**1.47**	**1.56**	**1.58**

Sources: Kaufmann, Kraay, and Zoido-Lobaton (2002); aggregated governance indicators

trol of local companies and helped generate interest in these stocks, bringing more liquidity to the market.

The three Baltic States and Romania early on implemented rather strict security market regulations. But the capacity of the capital market regulators to exercise their regulatory function fully has been limited, largely due to the lack of clear legal responsibilities, resources, and experience. A weak factor in Estonia and Latvia is disclosure and transparency of information, for example, on the voting power of controlling owners, concerted action (voting agreements, corporate linkages), as well as sometimes the true identity of the owner (if it is an offshore entity). Lithuania has gone a step further in terms of information disclosure. As mentioned by Olsson (2001), the information on block holdings, structure of the blocks, and concerted action is easily available in that country.

The Czech and Slovak Republics did not pay proper attention to the regulatory framework, and have seen fraud, tunneling of resources, and significant stagnation in the local stock markets. The Czech securities law did not require much disclosure (shares could change hands off exchange at less than market price); there was no single clearing and settlement facility; supervision of intermediaries was very lax; and minority shareholders had almost no say against any expropriation and fraud by company managers and Investment Privatization Funds working in concert with managers. The situation has improved with the adoption of the once-again-revised Commercial Code (as of 1 January 2001). The Slovakian case is similar; but more stringent regulations have come in force only as of 1 January 2002. Bulgaria started with a completely unregulated securities market. The situation was slightly improved with the 1995 Law on Securities, Stock Exchanges and Investment Companies, though the law was ambiguous in terms of the definition of "related party," and it did not impose any mandatory bid thresholds (Tchipev, 2001). The legislation regarding disclosure and definition of related parties improved with the Law on Public Offering and Securities (2000).

Slovenia stands out in this discussion. The Slovenian method of privatization granted large numbers of shares to employees, former employees, and state-controlled public funds. Besides, Slovenian law provides employees with substantial corporate governance rights, including the right to representation on boards. Privatization has also proceeded more slowly, leaving substantial ownership stakes in the hands of the government. The large presence of government control (in form of state-controlled funds) in Slovenian privatized corporations is a major obstacle to "normal" capital market development in Slovenia. Large state interest has also protected the capital markets from foreigners. For example, only in January 1999 were foreign banks allowed to establish branches in Slovenia, and only in July 1999 were branches and subsidiaries of foreign securities firms allowed to enter the market. As a result, even though the level of institutional and technical development of the stock market in Slovenia is quite advanced, the local market remains segmented from the world market due to capital market restrictions and a "semi-socialistic" corporate governance structure (employee and state control).

INCREASINGLY CONCENTRATED OWNERSHIP AND CONTROL

The emergence of stock markets and the improvement of disclosure requirements for public companies facilitate the study of ownership and control patterns of companies. The information on identity and stake of owners above a certain threshold should, in principle, be publicly available. In this section we present results of a joint effort of a group of researchers carried out under the supervision of the European Corporate Governance Network. The data cover companies in 10 CEE countries and relate them to comparable information for western European companies. We also provide some illustrative examples.

Ownership and control in listed companies

After a decade of transition, certain corporate governance patterns have emerged. As can be seen from Table 11.9 and Figure 11.1, ownership is becoming increasingly concentrated, often exceeding continental European levels. In all countries but Slovenia with its peculiar half-finished privatization, the median largest stake was 40 per cent or larger (e.g., median voting power of the largest owner in 1999 was 56 percent in Belgium, 54 percent in Austria, 52 percent in Italy but only 39 percent in Holland and 33 percent in Sweden).[8] These numbers are likely to be understated. Reporting standards in transition countries are still lagging behind. Even though formal requirements for the disclosure of voting blocks (investors voting in concert) exist, in reality many owners hide behind offshore entities (i.e., the ownership is undisclosed) or act together without disclosing it (based on unofficial agreements).

FIGURE 11.1 **Dynamics of Ownership Concentration**

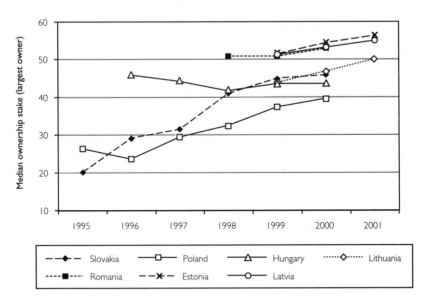

Note: Figure 11.1 shows the median ownership stake of the largest shareholder in seven CEE countries from 1995 to 2001.

Source: ACE Project *Corporate Governance and Disclosure in the Accession Process* (Contract No. 97-8042-R): Poland (Tamowicz, Dzierzanowski); the Baltic States (Olsson, Pajuste, Alasheyeva); the Czech Republic and Slovakia (Brzica, Olsson, Fidrmucova); Hungary and Romania (Earle, Kaznovsky, Kucsera, Telegdy); and Slovenia (Gregoric, Prasnikar, Ribnikar)

TABLE 11.9 **Ownership Stakes of Three Largest Shareholders (2000/2001)**

	YEAR	LARGEST OWNER		SECOND LARGEST OWNER		THIRD LARGEST OWNER		SAMPLE SIZE	COMMENT
		Mean	Median	Mean	Median	Mean	Median		
Bulgaria	2000	59.5	**58.1**	12.7	**10.1**	5.5	**0.0**	104	Direct shareholdings.
Czech Republic	2000	61.1	**52.6**	26.1	**25.3**	13.8	**13.8**	57	Block data.
Estonia	2000	56.2	**54.4**	9.3	**6.7**	4.2	**0.0**	21	Direct shareholdings. Block: 5% of cash flow (= voting) rights.
Hungary	2000	46.2	**43.7**	20.2	**19.5**	10.4	**10.3**	63	Direct ownership. Ultimate ownership and voting rights available only from July 2001. Block: 5% of cash flow rights.
Latvia	2001	57.9	**55.0**	11.1	**7.9**	3.3	**0.0**	60	Direct shareholdings. Block: 5% of cash flow (= voting) rights.
Lithuania	2001	54.2	**49.9**	10.4	**9.9**	5.4	**6.0**	45	Direct shareholdings. Block: 5% of cash flow (= voting) rights.
Poland	2000	44.6	**39.5**	15.6	**10.4**	9.4	**5.0**	210	Voting block data.
Romania	2000	53.4	**53.0**	16.5	**16.0**	9.2	**8.0**	115	Ultimate blockholding (direct and indirect voting stakes have to be disclosed). Information is on voting rights. Compliance though is questionable. Block: more than 5% of votes.
Slovak Republic	2000	51.6	**45.9**	—	—	—	—	28	Listed companies (Tier 1 and 2)
Slovenia	2000	27.4	**22.3**	13.4	**12.1**	9.2	**9.5**	136	Based on analysis of ownership stakes (assumed, votes = equity). Generally, firms are not obliged to report voting blocks.
Average	—	51.2	**47.4**	15.0	**13.1**	7.8	**5.8**	—	

Sources: ACE Project *Corporate Governance and Disclosure in the Accession Process* (Contract No. 97-8042-R): Poland (Tamowicz, Dzierzanowski); the Baltic States (Olsson, Pajuste, Alasheyeva); the Czech and Slovak Republics (Brzica, Olsson, Fidrmucova); Hungary and Romania (Earle, Kaznovsky, Kucsera, Telegdy); Slovenia (Gregoric, Prasnikar, Ribnikar)

Figure 11.2 presents the cumulative distribution of the size of the control stake held by the largest shareholder in nine countries. These percentile plots are compared with the EU countries included in Barca and Becht (2001).[9] A caveat applies here. One should keep in mind the potential bias due to different data availability in the sample countries: for example, Poland's plots may look less concentrated than Bulgaria's because in Poland the ultimate voting blocks were traced while the Bulgarian sample includes direct shareholdings. Nevertheless, we make our best attempt to compare the ownership distribution in these countries. Again, several groups of countries can be identified.

FIGURE 11.2   **Percentile Plots, Group 1: Similar to Austria, Belgium, Italy, and Sweden**

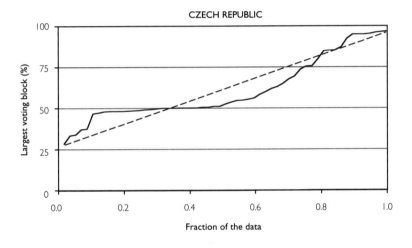

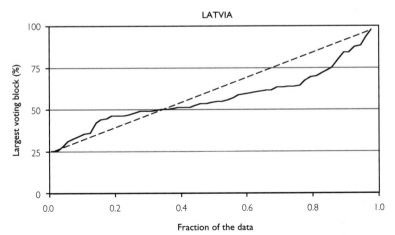

FIGURE 11.2 **Percentile Plots, Group 1: Similar to Austria, Belgium, Italy, and Sweden (continued)**

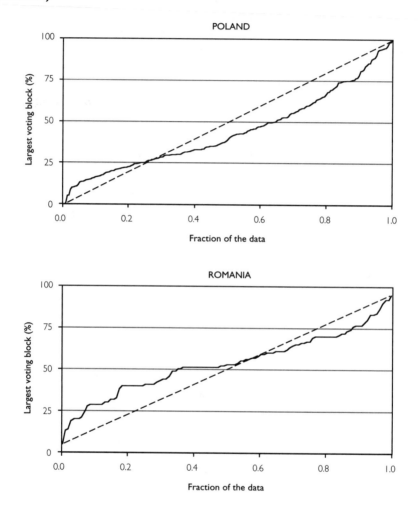

Source: ACE Project *Corporate Governance and Disclosure in the Accession Process* (Contract No. 97-8042-R): Poland (Tamowicz, Dzierzanowski); the Baltic States (Olsson, Pajuste, Alasheyeva); the Czech Republic and Slovakia (Brzica, Olsson, Fidrmucova); Hungary and Romania (Earle, Kaznovsky, Kucsera, Telegdy); and Slovenia (Gregoric, Prasnikar, Ribnikar)

The first group is comprised of the Czech Republic, Latvia, Poland, and Romania, and, in general, resembles the cumulative distributions of Austria, Belgium, Italy, and Sweden. The thresholds of ownership clustering, though, are different. In the Czech Republic, Latvia, and Romania, there is a clear clustering around the 50 percent level, and one half or more of the companies have the largest owner in the 49–70 percent control range. In Poland, there is no clear clustering around any control level, and the concentration level is lower—only in around 35 percent of firms does the largest owner have more than 50 percent of votes. The clustering around 50 percent level can be explained by the mandatory takeover bid threshold, which stands at 50 percent in Latvia and Romania, and until recently also in the Czech Republic (now the threshold is two thirds of the voting capital). The mandatory takeover bid threshold in Poland is also 50 percent, but it has been raised from its previous 33 percent. The lower concentration in Poland can thus reflect slow adjustment to the new mandatory takeover bid threshold (i.e., the owners are not rushing to increase their stakes once the 33 percent threshold is lifted).

The second group, comprised of Estonia, Hungary, and Lithuania, is close to the Netherlands and Spain (distribution below the 45° line). In Hungary, we observe clustering around the 25 percent and 50 percent levels, while in Lithuania it is around the 50 percent level. Generally, the Estonian and Lithuanian distributions are close to uniform density with a slight bias downward. The clustering around the 25 percent level in Hungary can be again explained by the mandatory takeover bid threshold. In Hungary, if there is no other shareholder owning at least 10 percent of the voting rights, the mandatory bid threshold decreases to 25 percent (down from the standard 33 percent + 1 vote). Until July 2001, Hungarian legislation required that the bidder who intended to acquire 33 percent + 1 share (calculated as percent of equity) had to make a mandatory bid for 50 percent + 1 share (Earle et al., 2001). This explains the clustering around the 50 percent level in Hungary. Since July 2001 the threshold remains 33 percent + 1 share (although it is calculated as a percent of voting power), but the bidder has to make the mandatory bid for all voting shares.

FIGURE 11.2 **Percentile Plots, Group 2: Similar to the Netherlands and Spain**

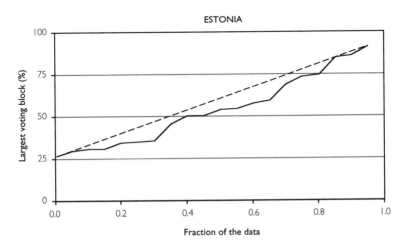

FIGURE 11.2   **Percentile Plots, Group 2: Similar to the Netherlands and Spain (continued)**

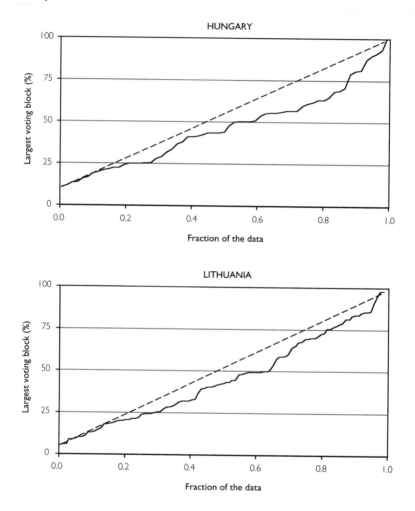

Source: ACE Project *Corporate Governance and Disclosure in the Accession Process* (Contract No. 97-8042-R): Poland (Tamowicz, Dzierzanowski); the Baltic States (Olsson, Pajuste, Alasheyeva); the Czech Republic and Slovakia (Brzica, Olsson, Fidrmucova); Hungary and Romania (Earle, Kaznovsky, Kucsera, Telegdy); and Slovenia (Gregoric, Prasnikar, Ribnikar)

Bulgaria is the only country with a distribution above the 45° line (as in Germany), that is, a private control bias. Again, this may be due to the fact that only direct shareholdings are reported in Bulgaria (as compared with ultimate blocks). Finally, Slovenia stands out with rather dispersed ownership (similar to that of the United Kingdom), which is a result of the specific privatization method carried out in Slovenia (where employee ownership funds are controlled by managers).

FIGURE 11.2 **Percentile Plots, Group 3: Similar to Germany**

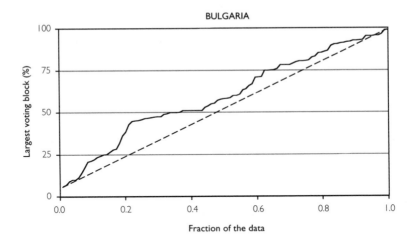

Source: ACE Project *Corporate Governance and Disclosure in the Accession Process* (Contract No. 97-8042-R): Poland (Tamowicz, Dzierzanowski); the Baltic States (Olsson, Pajuste, Alasheyeva); the Czech Republic and Slovakia (Brzica, Olsson, Fidrmucova); Hungary and Romania (Earle, Kaznovsky, Kucsera, Telegdy); and Slovenia (Gregoric, Prasnikar, Ribnikar)

FIGURE 11.2 **Percentile Plots, Group 4: Similar to the United Kingdom**

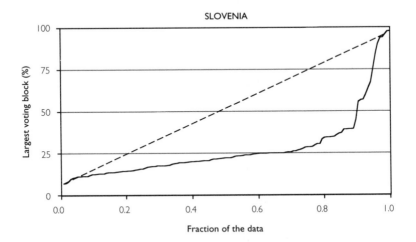

Source: ACE Project *Corporate Governance and Disclosure in the Accession Process* (Contract No. 97-8042-R): Poland (Tamowicz, Dzierzanowski); the Baltic States (Olsson, Pajuste, Alasheyeva); the Czech Republic and Slovakia (Brzica, Olsson, Fidrmucova); Hungary and Romania (Earle, Kaznovsky, Kucsera, Telegdy); and Slovenia (Gregoric, Prasnikar, Ribnikar)

What explains the observed increase in the concentration of ownership and control in transition economies? In part, the increasing concentration could be fictitious, simply reflecting more stringent supervision of disclosure requirements forcing earlier actual owners to disclose their holdings. Nowadays the option of hiding behind private unlisted companies is limited. In most countries market regulators can access the information on ownership of unlisted companies and trace any indirect holdings of main shareholders.

There are, however, reasons to believe that ownership is indeed becoming increasingly concentrated. Poor minority shareholder protection, combined with easier access to bank financing, allow the largest shareholders to buy out minorities to avoid the hassle with regulators. Minority shareholders are also in many cases eager to sell their shares, recognizing that they have little voice in companies' policies (regarding such things as dividends, calling extraordinary shareholder meetings, or appointing independent auditors). Moreover, internal funds and bank loans often suffice to finance companies' growth.

The gradual sellout of state-owned shares is another factor that should have increased ownership concentration. Current majority owners have exploited inside knowledge and contacts to acquire state-owned shares at substantial discounts. Although a large fraction of ownership still remains under state control, individuals or families control the largest stake in most of the countries.

Who controls and how?

Unfortunately, the information on the use of mechanisms for the separation of ownership and control and information on linkages between owners is still poor. This section provides some scattered information, along with examples, of who controls and how they control corporations in central and eastern Europe.

The EU accession countries have followed the EU directives on ownership disclosure. As a result, the requirements for mandatory disclosure of large block holdings have improved substantially during the last couple of years. Definitions of *corporate groups* and *related parties* have become more precise. The lowest notification thresholds have decreased. In 1998, according to Pistor et al. (2000) data, only three sample countries (Bulgaria, the Czech Republic, and Hungary) had the mandatory disclosure threshold at 10 percent of voting rights. The rest of the countries had either higher thresholds or no block ownership disclosure requirements at all. By 2002, most of the countries had adopted the 5 percent mandatory block holding disclosure threshold (see Table 11.10).

TABLE 11.10 **Legal Provisions Governing Selected Investor Protection Issues (2002)**

	MANDATORY ONE SHARE – ONE VOTE	MANDATORY TAKEOVER BID (Threshold)	MANDATORY DISCLOSURE OF LARGER BLOCKS (Lowest Notification Threshold)
Bulgaria	YES	50%, 90%	5% (for official market), 10% (for unofficial market)
	Nonvoting preference shares allowed, but they must carry preferential dividend treatment. A preference share shall be entitled to vote when its dividends have been in arrears for one year and are not paid during the following year together with that year's dividends. (Law on Commerce, Art. 182)	(Law on Public Offering of Securities, Art. 149)	(Law on Public Offering of Securities, Art. 145)
Czech Republic	NO	2/3, 3/4	5%
	Nonvoting preference shares allowed up to 50% of the capital. (Commercial Code § 159) Shares with different nominal values (different votes) allowed; limitations can be set in the Articles of Association; voting caps allowed (Commercial Code § 180).	(Commercial Code § 186)	(Commercial Code § 183)
Estonia	YES	50%	10%
	The same as in Bulgaria. (Commercial Code § 237)	(Securities Market Act, Art 166)	(Securities Market Act, Art 185)
Hungary	NO	33%+1	5%
	Preference shares with respect to voting rights allowed. They can carry voting rights that amount to a maximum of 10 times the nominal value of the share. May also grant a right of veto. (Act CXLIV of 1997 on Companies, Sec. 185; "Business Law in Hungary," p. 224)	If there is no shareholder owning at least 10% of the voting right, the mandatory bid threshold decreases to 25%. (Earle et al., 2001; Rule in effect from July 2001)	(BSE Listing Rules, 18.1.1.6)

continued

TABLE 11.10 **Legal Provisions Governing Selected Investor Protection Issues (2002) (continued)**

	MANDATORY ONE SHARE – ONE VOTE	MANDATORY TAKEOVER BID (Threshold)	MANDATORY DISCLOSURE OF LARGER BLOCKS (Lowest Notification Threshold)
Latvia	NO Issue of ordinary shares with no voting rights or limited voting rights is allowed. Shares without voting rights shall not exceed 40% of the equity capital. (Law on Joint Stock Companies, Art. 23.3)	50%, 75% (Law on Securities, Art. 65)	5% (main list) 10% (other public firms) (Olsson, 2001)
Lithuania	YES The bylaws may deprive some of the shares of stock of the right to vote. If all the voting stock is of the same par value, each share of stock shall have one vote at the meetings of the stockholders. (Law on Stock Corporations, Art. 15; from July 1990)	50% (Resolution Concerning Rules of Tender Offer)	10% (Resolution Concerning Rules on Disclosure)
Poland	NO Shares with preferential voting rights are allowed. They must be registered (as opposed to bearer shares). No preference share shall carry more than five votes. (Company Law, Art. 357; Legal Aspects of Doing Business in Poland)	50% (Law on Public Trading in Securities, Art. 154)	5% (Olsson, 2001)
Romania	YES	50%, 75% (Gov Emergency Ordinance 28, of March 2002)	5% (Olsson, 2001)
Russia	YES/ NO (Law on Joint Stock Companies, Art. 32)	30% (Law on Joint Stock Companies, Art. 80)	20% (Law on Securities, Art. 30)

	MANDATORY ONE SHARE – ONE VOTE	MANDATORY TAKEOVER BID (Threshold)	MANDATORY DISCLOSURE OF LARGER BLOCKS (Lowest Notification Threshold)
Slovak Republic	NO (Olsson et al., 2001)	...	5% (Securities Act; Commercial Code)
Slovenia	YES The same as in Bulgaria. (Companies Act)	25% If the bidder acquires less than 45% and wants after a year to acquire additional shares, he has to make a bid again. Once the 45% threshold is passed, additional shares can be acquired without a bid. (Gregoric, 2002)	5% (Gregoric et al., 2001; Takeover Act, Art. 64)
Ukraine	YES/NO Nonvoting preference shares allowed. (Frishberg et al., 1994)	...	...

Notes: 1 Law on Business Companies (Art. 67) establishes general one share – one vote rule (except the first general meeting where each shareholder has one vote no matter how many shares held). However, the company's contract or statute can limit the number of votes of shareholders owning more than one share, and thus voting rights can be weighted in specific cases in favor of certain shareholders (i.e., this rule ties voting rights to the specific shareholder rather than to the share.

2 For common shares there is a strict one share – one vote rule. However, Art. 32 of the Law on Joint Stock Companies provides a broad range of flexibility in structuring the rights of preferred shares, including the ability to establish different types of preferred shares with different rights. This flexibility, according to Black, Kraakman, and Tarassova (1998), can potentially allow companies to evade the one common share – one vote principle. The company's charter can give voting rights to preferred shareholders, including voting rights equal or superior to those of common shares. But at the same time the law does not require that common shares always have lower priority than preferred shares for receipts of dividends. The preferred shareholders gain the right to vote if dividends have not been paid only in case if the amount of dividends to be paid is specified in the *company's charter*.

Many of the companies currently listed on the stock exchanges in central and eastern Europe are a result of privatization efforts, whether through mass privatization programs (e.g., the Czech Republic, Romania, and Bulgaria), sales to strategic investors (e.g., Poland, Hungary, and Latvia), or employee and management buyouts (e.g., Slovenia and Romania). Irrespective of privatization method used, the privatization of formerly state-owned enterprises gave privileges to managers. As Pistor (2000) argues, incumbents who held *de facto* control rights had an advantage over outsiders with only weak rights to protect them. Using inside knowledge and political connections, many managers have become major shareholders by employing smart schemes of leveraged buyouts, buying up employee shares at discounted prices, or using other (even purely fraudulent) schemes. As a result, one of the stylized facts in transition countries is strong insider ownership and control. Given weak legislative power to protect outside investors, such companies are highly unattractive to foreign and domestic minority investors.

Poland provides a rich set of illustrative examples. Many enterprises, later listed on the stock exchange, were privatized through management and employee buyouts. For example, Agros, a large former state-owned food processing company, was controlled by TIGA, a privatization vehicle set up by employees and managers of former state-owned enterprise (see Figure 11.3). Through preferred shares (one share – five votes) TIGA controlled 81.4 percent of Agros Holding's votes, while its share of cash flows was only 47.5 percent. In fact, full control of Agros should be assigned to Zofia Gaber (the company's director before privatization and then the president of the management board). She was also the largest owner of TIGA with 18.5 percent voting stock and chairwoman of TIGA supervisory board (Tamowicz and Dzierzanowski, 2001).

FIGURE 11.3 **The Case of Agros**

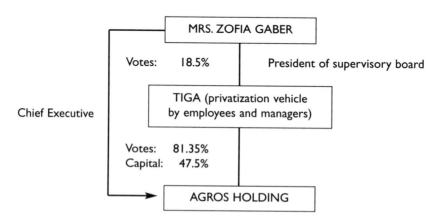

Source: Tamowicz and Dzierzanowski (2001).

At the other end of the spectrum we find a *strong outsider* category: foreign strategic (controlling) investors with low trust in local management. Sensitized by frequent reports on managerial fraud and entrenchment in emerging markets, foreign strategic owners come with their own management or closely supervise the day-to-day operations of local management. Although potentially weakening managerial incentives and entrepreneurial spirit, as well as wasting scarce managerial time on report writing, foreign investors appear to have contributed significantly to corporate restructuring in these countries (Djankov and Murrell, 2002).

The instruments for separating ownership and control are relatively widely used. *Dual-class shares* (preferred shares) are quite common, but low-voting shares are typically preference shares (see Table 11.10).[10] *Pyramidal structures* are widely used in the sample countries (e.g., see Figure 11.4), mainly for two reasons: to limit the equity investment and sometimes to hide true ownership. In most of the sample countries, the identity of the ultimate owner is still undisclosed due to the laxity in regulation or enforcement of disclosure. *Crossholdings* are also observed. In some countries, companies can hold their own stock. For example, in Poland, since January 2001, any corporation is allowed to buy up to 10 percent of its own shares to "defend against direct, significant damage to a company" (Tamowicz and Dzierzanowski, 2001). Recently more countries have introduced rules allowing companies, in exceptional cases, to repurchase their own stock (e.g., if that is approved by the General Meeting, if it is with the purpose to reduce the share capital, etc.)—normally, this is not more than 10 percent of the company capital. In the original formulations of securities laws in the sample countries, most often such an action was prohibited.

In addition, many corporate charters contain arrangements specifically designed to defend companies against takeovers. *Voting caps* are used in, among other countries, Slovenia and Poland. In Poland, there are some examples of a provision that is close to the voting cap, but in general such takeover defense is not utilized. *Special shareholder agreements* or *golden shares* are a common way to secure preferential rights when an outside bid has been launched. In the process of privatization, strategic investors may have been granted preferential rights in form of shareholder agreement. The following example illustrates the special shareholder rights agreements.

Ventspils Nafta (VN) is the second largest (by market capitalization) company listed on the Riga Stock Exchange. Its main business activities are transshipment and storage of oil products. The two largest shareholders of VN are Latvijas Naftas Tranzits (LNT) (48 percent)—a company owned by a group of related persons and entities including off-shores (see Figure 11.4)—and the State (43.5 percent). The remaining State shares will be privatized, but the process is very slow due to highly politicized games around it. At the first round of privatization, LNT was granted special preferential rights, namely that it has veto power to any significant decision (e.g., strategy, dividend policy, or block transfer of shares). Moreover, 5 percent of the company capital is

reserved for LNT. As a result, there is a very little chance that (in the remaining privatization stage) a major shareholder will emerge without an agreement with or approval
of LNT.

FIGURE 11.4   **The Case of VENTSPILS NAFTA**

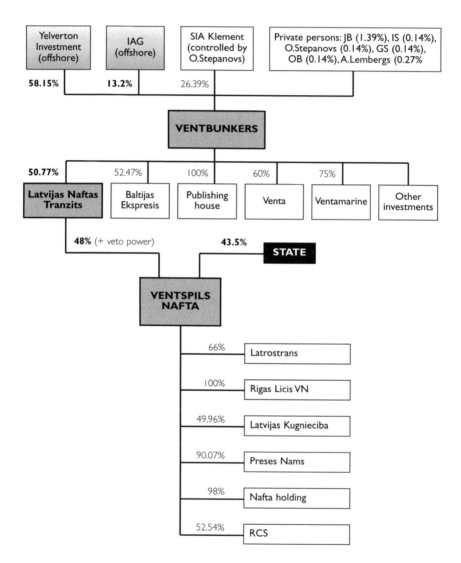

Sources: Newspaper *Diena* (21.08.2002) based on information in Lursoft and annual reports of companies.

Mandatory bid rule and de-listings

The regulatory frameworks have adjusted only in part to the emerging ownership and control structures, and some of the legislation imposed through the EU accession is directly counterproductive. This is particularly true for the mandatory bid rule (MBR), which requires an owner who reaches a certain threshold of control to buy out the other shareholders at the same price that he bought his controlling block. This rule makes takeovers prohibitively expensive and effectively closes down the trade in control blocks. Since 1998, more countries have introduced the mandatory bid rule (Pistor et al., 2000). Meanwhile, one of the few countries that had the MBR before 1997—Poland—raised the threshold from 33 percent to 50 percent, reflecting the pressure of consolidation trend and need for slowing the withdrawal of companies from the market (Tamowicz and Dzierzanowski, 2001). Now in most of the sample countries, mandatory share buy-back threshold is set at 50 percent of voting rights (see Table 11.10).[11] How can it happen, then, that listed firms continue to be majority and supermajority held (largest owner having above 75 percent of the voting power) and there is no share buy-back triggered? We claim that this reflects intentionally weak enforcement.

We will use Bulgaria, Estonia, Latvia, and Romania as illustrative examples. In Bulgaria there are two mandatory bid thresholds: 50 percent and 90 percent.[12] The 50 percent threshold requires everybody who reaches the level of the voting rights in the general assembly to offer a bid or to dispose the excessive shares within 14 days of acquisition. This requirement also applies to the holdings of some "connected persons" (Tchipev, 2001). Nevertheless, the largest shareholder in Bulgaria (according to Tchipev's 2001 study) holds, on average, 59.5 percent of votes. The most likely reason for this phenomenon in Bulgaria is the loose reference to "connected persons." Even though the suggestions of the EU Large Holdings Directive on the accumulation of voting blocks is taken into account in other legislative acts in Bulgaria, the mandatory buy-back rule still refers to "connected persons"—entities directly controlled by the shareholder or those voting in concert according to agreement.

The Latvian Law on Securities (Article 65) stipulates that a person who directly or indirectly acquires the stock of a public company in excess of one half or three quarters of the total quantity of votes shall offer to repurchase the stock belonging to other shareholders. The repurchase offer shall be made also by investors who have voted in favor of the question on withdrawal of stock from public circulation. Accumulation of voting rights is explicitly stated in Article 65, including the voting rights that are acquired by a third person in his or her own name but on assignment of an investor. By law, if the court can prove that two persons were acting in concert without formal agreement, and did not implement the mandatory share buy-back, they would be penalized (the penalty would include not being able to exercise the voting power above the 50 percent threshold).

The Latvian problem lies in enforcement and corruption of the court system. There has been a case when the Financial and Capital Markets Commission (FCMC, the main securities market regulator in Latvia) accused a company listed on the main list (the first tier) for violating the mandatory share buy-back rule. The company, confectionary producer Staburadze, was 43 percent owned by the entity controlled by an Icelandic investor. At some point, two other Icelandic investors acquired shares totaling an additional 8.5 percent and 6.5 percent. The three Icelandic investors were thought to be clearly related (e.g., being business partners in some entities in Iceland). Moreover, Iceland is not a significant foreign investor particularly favoring Latvia (either for reasons of their similar size or for some other reason). Nevertheless, when the case was brought to the court, the FCMC was proved to be wrong: the three Icelandic investors were *not* related. The only sanction the FCMC could impose was to remove the company from the main list to the free (unregulated) market, thus dampening even more the chances of protecting remaining minority shareholders in Staburadze.

In Estonia, the problem seems to be a very loose definition of the *mandatory share buy-back rule*. By law, the mandatory tender offer has to be made if a dominant position is acquired (a *dominant position* is defined as having 50 percent or more of the voting rights). At the same time, the law provides numerous exceptions to this rule. Securities Market Act (Paragraph 173) stipulates that the authority (Inspectorate) has the right to grant exception (six cases) to the requirement of mandatory tender offer if, for example, "the company acquired a dominant position over the target issuer from a company belonging to the same group with the latter and after acquiring the dominant position the company continues to belong to the same group" or "a dominant position was acquired as a result of reducing the share capital of the target issuer." Also the Listing Committee can make exceptions regarding the free float requirement. For example, shares held by a person who has an interest in more than 5 percent of the shares of the issuer are not regarded as being in public hands *unless* the Listing Committee determines that such a person can, for the purposes of this condition, be included in the public.

Finally, in Romania (as in Estonia) there are explicit exceptions to the mandatory tender offer (with the threshold at 50 percent and 75 percent of voting power). The Romanian Government Emergency Ordinance 28 (March 13, 2002) on "Securities, Financial Investment Services and Regulated Markets" (Article 135) stipulates that mandatory public offering is not triggered if the control or majority position has been obtained as a result of an *excepted transaction* or *unintentionally*. The excepted transactions include, among others, acquisition of majority position within the privatization process; unintentional acquisition is, for example, the result of a decrease in share capital, a conversion of bonds into shares, or a merger or succession.

We suggest that the vagueness of the law (in Bulgaria, Estonia, and Romania) and the poor enforcement of the mandatory share buy-back regulation (in Latvia), at least in part, are deliberate. Given the concentration of ownership, most companies would be forced to de-list under a strict enforcement of the rule. Also, such a rule would essentially close down the market for hostile takeovers and eliminate any possibility of controlling owners to capitalize the control rent.

DEFINING THE CORPORATE GOVERNANCE PROBLEM

The corporate governance system provides a set of mechanisms designed to control the fundamental agency problem between management and shareholders. These mechanisms include large shareholder monitoring, markets for takeovers, proxy fights, board intervention, litigation, bank monitoring, and executive compensation schemes (Becht et al., 2002). The mechanisms are supplemented by the checks on behavior provided by general norms, business ethics, and media. The relative importance of these mechanisms depends on the ownership and control structure in the individual firm (which in turn shapes the agency problem) and the broader environment in which the firm operates. The scope for hostile takeovers and proxy fights, for example, depends on the stake of the controlling owner and the general institutional environment, which influences an outside investor's chances of exercising any rights.

The corporate governance problem in central and eastern Europe is shaped by increasingly concentrated control structures, typically with the controlling owner actively involved in the management of the firm. Mechanisms for separating ownership and control are widely used. The financial architecture is still embryonic, but the dominant feature is the strong presence of predominantly foreign-controlled banks. These financial institutions are only marginally engaged in financing corporate investment. Although the legal and general institutional environment has improved tremendously over the last decade, important issues of enforcement remain. Lawmakers and regulators will have to design policies with this reality in mind.

Most of the world has never been through the dispersion of shareholdings; as we have suggested, CEE countries are unlikely to go through it any time soon. Given that a class of professional managers yet has to emerge, and that management in any case cannot be expected to be independent in heavily concentrated ownership structures, the main conflict in these firms will be between controlling shareholders and minority investors. It is in this perspective that we have to revisit some key tradeoffs in the regulation of corporate governance: between managerial initiative and investor protection, between the interests of large blockholders and those of minority investors, and between minority investor protection and the market for corporate control.

Before discussing these tradeoffs it is useful to address the perennial issue of the appropriate balance between "shareholder value" and considerations for other stakeholders, which will also remain important given the heritage in the CEE countries. In some CEE countries, a heritage of employee ownership and a strong role for unions and local community interests are features of corporate decision-making. In other countries, unions are much weaker than they are in western Europe. There are no simple recipes for how to strike the right balance, but the particular stakeholder tradition inherited from socialist times and the early phases of transition will most likely leave sediment in corporate governance for years to come. Many stakeholders matter to the success of a corporation, and much of the managerial challenge lies in balancing these different interests. There are important advantages to relatively simple measures of corporate performance, however, and shareholders are more likely to agree on such objectives. Shareholders are also the only stakeholder group that does not have a collective exit option (as long as the firm is a going concern); any shareholder who wants to leave the firm has to find a buyer for his share.

The classic corporate governance conflict is between management and shareholders. Early contributors to the corporate governance literature in the United States worried about the increasing dispersion of shareholdings and the increasing discretion of managers (Berle and Means, 1932). Much of the regulatory response in the United States has been about trying to trade off the benefits of increased discretion for managerial incentives against the protection of shareholders. With too much protection, managers would have little incentive or room to use their initiative to improve the performance of the firm; with too little protection, investors would not contribute sufficient funds or would demand very high interest (Burkart, Gromb, and Panunzi, 1997). As we have argued, this is unlikely to be the key tradeoff in CEE economies in the foreseeable future. Managers cannot be expected to play the same independent role in a company controlled by a large owner as they can play in the corporation with dispersed shareholders. To the extent that management has been separated from ownership, the main issue in CEE economies is excessive intervention in management by the controlling shareholder, not by the minority investor.

The main conflict is thus between the controlling shareholders and minority investors. Only controlling shareholders have sufficient incentive to monitor management, but they may also be able to extract private benefits, even at the expense of minority investors. As we have seen, many countries allow various mechanisms for separating control from ownership, such as through dual class shares or pyramiding, in order to encourage monitoring. But these mechanisms also increase the incentives to dilute the claims of other shareholders. In environments with weak institutions, like most transition countries, regulation alone will not be sufficient to constrain management; thus there is an increased need for stronger corporate governance.

Regulatory measures could be designed to promote takeovers by shifting the takeover premium to the bidder (e.g., the so-called breakthrough rule proposed by a recent expert group appointed by the Commission). Although such measures have desirable features in terms of promoting hostile takeovers, they may also undermine the incentive to hold controlling blocks, and thus weaken shareholder monitoring of management (Berglöf and Burkart, 2002). With strongly concentrated ownership and control, markets for takeovers and proxy fights are likely to be ineffective in any case.

Moreover, although takeovers may help corporate governance, they also suffer from their own agency problems. In the transition countries, we should not expect too much from the market for corporate control as a disciplining device.

Large blockholders and the market for corporate control are not the only mechanisms available for disciplining managers. Other devices include shareholder litigation and proxy fights, but these are unlikely to be effective or reliable in the transition environment with its weak courts and concentrated shareholdings. Boards of directors cannot be expected to play an independent role in companies controlled by a single shareholder. Executive compensation schemes are yet another way to align the incentives of management with those of the firm. However, as the Enron experience suggests, this is a highly imperfect mechanism, particularly in transition environments where input numbers are highly volatile and even more subject to manipulation by managers than they are in developed market economies.

The corporate governance systems will have to rely on active involvement and monitoring by large blockholders for the foreseeable future, even after the emergence of a class of professional managers. With the possible exception of what can be achieved through executive compensation schemes, none of the other mechanisms are likely to provide significant leverage on management any time soon. In the medium term there is some hope that large commercial banks will start to play a more active role in financing and monitoring companies, but this has not happened yet.

Moreover, experience from transition countries suggests that controlling shareholders (strategic investors) are critical to the successful restructuring of privatized firms. Foreign direct investment, where (by definition) investors take controlling positions, has been particularly important. Some countries have seen considerable inflows of portfolio (minority) capital, but these flows are more volatile than FDI and very sensitive to investor protection. There are, however, also examples of portfolio investors, such as the Hermitage Fund in Russia, that have successfully specialized in investing in severely discounted shares and then pushing for improved overall minority protection to raise the value of their shares.

Minority protection is important to attract outside capital, but it may reduce the disciplinary role of the market for corporate control. In particular, the mandatory bid rule requiring that any control premium is shared equally among the controlling owner and minority shareholders could seriously reduce the probability of a hostile offer. When ownership is dispersed, no control premium is paid and the mandatory bid rule essentially has no effect. But when ownership is concentrated, this rule—intended to protect minority investors against diluting takeovers—unfortunately increases the cost of a takeover, potentially even increasing that cost enough to make the minority shareholders worse off.

Sales of large blocks are desirable, even critical, to successful corporate restructuring in these countries, but the MBR essentially closes down the market for block trades. Moreover, since an MBR reduces the likelihood that a bid will be made in the first place, it entrenches the incumbent controlling owner and diminishes any disciplining role that the market for corporate control may have. Given that transition countries will have concentrated ownership for the foreseeable future, the MBR, at least not in its strict form (which leaves no control premium), does not seem to be part of an optimal regulatory environment. Several of the countries in central and eastern Europe seem, however, to have found ways to mitigate the effects of these, largely externally imposed, rules.

In constraining controlling owners and managers, lawmakers can intervene or rely on self-regulation among the concerned parties. Both methods have costs and benefits, and the tradeoff between them has been accentuated by the recent flurry of voluntary corporate governance codes. Self-regulation probably has greater legitimacy among those constrained by the rules, and this method is very flexible in a rapidly changing technological environment where government rules easily become obsolete. Government regulation has more bite and probably broader legitimacy in the rest of society. Unfortunately, self-regulation is unlikely to be effective in weak transition environments, but the enforcement of government regulation is also more unreliable. Nevertheless, government regulation is necessary to convince large, particularly foreign, investors to commit substantial amounts of capital. Self-regulation is also unlikely to work unless there is government regulation as a strong credible threat in case compliance breaks down. The focus of regulation should be on reducing the scope for fraud that exploits minority shareholders.

The numerous corporate governance codes that exist in CEE countries have served other purposes. They have been quite useful in promoting debate and thus fostered awareness of the underlying issues. They have also allowed some degree of commitment to good behavior. There should be some cost to breaking a well-specified code rather than some general ethical rule. Perhaps most importantly, the codes serve as useful reference points in bargaining on boards of directors and between controlling shareholders and minority investors. Managers and controlling owners will have to motivate when they deviate from the standard, thus shifting status quo in the discussion. Historically, codes were a first step toward binding regulation—compare, for example, the US experience (Coffee, 2001). Government regulation can be challenged in courts and thus promotes court development. Under both forms of regulation, independent media play an important role in bringing out abuses and supporting enforcement. In many of the CEE countries, investigative business journalism is still in its infancy.

In spite of tremendous institutional differences, corporate governance codes around the world—across developed, transition, and developing countries—are remarkably similar. This observation suggests either that there are considerable costs of deviating from these codes, and also that the codes are not (at least not yet) very effective. It also highlights yet another tradeoff, that between harmonization and self-definition of corporate governance problem. Codes are easy to import, even easier than recommendations and binding regulations from governments, but they are much harder to enforce if they do not come out of self-definition. Simple emulation will not foster such a process, and it may in fact even be counterproductive to corporate governance reform when rules are not adjusted to local conditions. We argue that self-definition is, in fact, part of the solution to the problem of enforcement. When legislators and enforcing agencies have been part of the genesis of the rules, they are more likely to continue develop and enforce the rules. Just as in the individual firm, imported codes can serve as a useful reference point in the national regulatory process; any deviations would have to be explicitly motivated by local conditions.

CONCLUSION

Recent scandals like those of Enron and WorldCom have shown that the externalities imposed by governance failures in individual companies reflect on the entire financial system in a country, such as the United States, with highly developed institutions. The emerging capitalist systems face similar but far more difficult challenges. In an increasingly global financial system, these fledgling regulatory environments are competing for international savings. But the ability to attract foreign capital, both FDI and portfolio investment, is only one important consideration in the design of a financial system—the system must also generate domestic savings. In this system, corporate governance is critical. We have outlined the many difficult tradeoffs involved in corporate governance reform in central and eastern Europe. Our main message is that ownership and control is and will remain concentrated for the foreseeable future, and regulatory intervention should focus on eliminating outright fraud while maintaining the incentives for entrepreneurship and large shareholder monitoring. In particular, there is a strong need to make the emerging control structures and what controlling owners do more transparent.

Regulators must recognize that large blockholders are an important feature of the corporate governance system once ownership and management separate. Controlling shareholders are a second-best response to weak legal institutions. Efforts to get rid of large holdings would lead to more managerial discretion in an environment where there are very few other disciplining mechanisms and where sediments of a specific stakeholder culture may obfuscate corporate goals. Moreover, such attempts would not go unanswered. They would most likely lead to further de-listings and increased opaqueness. The market for corporate control is critical to promote transfers of controlling blocks, but given the current high concentration of ownership, these transactions are unlikely to take place against the desire of the controlling shareholders and managers. Strict enforcement of mandatory bid rules would essentially shut down the market for corporate control and further entrench incumbent management and controlling owner.

Empowering (minority) shareholders is still important, since it promotes liquidity in stock markets, which, in turn, provide capital and valuable information for corporate governance and restructuring. Corporate governance codes are useful, but more binding legislation is necessary. Perhaps the single most important objective is to increase transparency, not only about ownership and control structures, but also about what managers and controlling owners do—in particular, how they reward each other. In this regard the countries of central and eastern Europe have an opportunity to leapfrog the developed markets on the European continent where transparency is still wanting. Even strengthening the legal recourse of minority investors could eventually help promote good corporate governance. In the longer term, the combined effects of these mechanisms can also help improve contestability of control, critical in disciplining controlling shareholders and managers and giving new owners and management teams an opportunity to bring about much-needed restructuring.

NOTES

1   We draw on data collected within the European Corporate Governance Network for all the accession countries in central and eastern Europe. These data follow the blueprint set up by a similar data exercise for western Europe and reported in Barca and Becht (2001). We provide detailed and comparable information on the size of controlling blocks in individual firms in most countries. The data are supplemented with indicators of the legal and general institutional environment, including enforcement variables, and specific information on rules relevant to corporate governance.

2   In Bulgaria, during 1992–1994, there were about 20 regional stock exchanges, which merged by the end of 1995. The Bulgarian Stock Exchange remained the only operational stock exchange in the country.

3   See Claessens, Djankov, and Klingebiel (2000) for more detailed discussion of privatization methods in relation to stock market development in transition economies.

4   Poland had some mandatory listings of mass-privatized companies and National Investment Funds. See Claessens, Djankov, and Klingebiel (2000) and references therein.

5   If free market shares were excluded from the market capitalization figure in Lithuania, the market capitalization to GDP would be about half the value stated in Table 11.4.

6   Most of the countries in the sample still have not had a single IPO. Poland had, in total, 47 IPOs by the end of 2000, which is by far the largest number among CEE countries.

7   A *bid rule* is an obligation to offer to buy back shares from minority shareholders once a certain threshold is passed. For example, in Hungary this threshold is 33 percent + 1 share (calculated as percent of voting power), in Latvia, it is 50 percent.

8   See Barca and Becht (2001).

9   The 45° line reflects a uniform density of firms by voting blocks. A distribution above the 45° line reflects concentrated ownership (large voting blocks, or private control bias; and a distribution below the 45° line indicates more dispersed voting control (management or market control bias).

10   Some sample countries have a legal provision stating that common (ordinary) shares carry a strict one share – one vote provision, but almost all countries allow for issuance of preferred shares that can be without voting rights. As in Russia and Lithuania, the flexibility in setting the rights for preferred shareholders in the company bylaws practically allows companies to escape the one share – one vote principle. Hungary, Poland and Latvia are examples where the law clearly provides that the superior voting right shares are allowed. There are some restrictions – in Poland, no preference share shall carry more than five votes, in Hungary – no more than ten votes, and in Latvia the non-voting shares shall not exceed 40 percent of the company capital. Bulgaria, Estonia and Slovenia can be classified as having one share – one vote, because the non-voting preferred shares have strict requirements that set their preferential status to dividends, as well as prescribe an automatic gain of voting power in one year from the time when dividends have not been distributed. The other cases are rather ambiguous.

11   Moreover, voting rights are explicitly defined (e.g., the aggregate voting rights of a person, the company controlled by this person, and a third party, who is committed, on basis of agreement, to carry out joint policies).

12   The 90 percent threshold is optional. It provides the right for the shareholder to make a bid, but it is mandatory in a sense that without this bid it is not possible to unregister the company from the register of public companies. See Tchipev (2001).

REFERENCES

Barca, F., and M. Becht. 2001. *The Control of Corporate Europe*. Oxford: Oxford University Press.

Becht et al. 2002. *Report to the Commission from ECGN/EAST BEEPS Study, 1999*. World Bank. Online. info.worldbank.org/governance.beeps/.

Berglöf, E., and P. Bolton. 2002. "The Great Divide and Beyond—Financial Architecture in Transition," *Journal of Economic Perspectives* 16, pp. 77–100.

Berglöf, E., and M. Burkart. 2003. " 'Break-Through' in European Takeover Regulation." *Economic Policy* (forthcoming).

Berglöf, E., and E.-L. von Thadden. 2000. *The Changing Corporate Governance Paradigm: Implications for Transition and Developing Countries*. In S. S. Cohen, and G. Boyds, eds. *Corporate Governance and Globalization: Long-Range Planning Issues*. Cheltenham: Edward Elgar.

Berle, A., and G. Means. 1932. *The Modern Corporation and Private Property*. New York: Harcourt, Brace & World.

Black, B. S., R. Kraakman, and A. S. Tarassova. 1998. *Guide to the Russian Law on Joint Stock Companies*. Boston: Kluwer.

Bohinc, R., and S. M. Bainbridge. 2000. "Corporate Governance in Post-Privatized Slovenia," SSRN Electronic journal. Online. http://www.ssrn.com.

Burkart, M., D. Gromb, and F. Panunzi. 1997. "Large Shareholders, Monitoring, and the Value of the Firm," *Quarterly Journal of Economics* 112, pp. 693–728.

Claessens, S., S. Djankov, and D. Klingebiel. 2000. "Stock Markets in Transition Economies," The World Bank, Financial Sector Discussion Paper No. 5. Washington, DC: World Bank.

Claessens, S., D. Klingebiel, and S. L. Schmuckler. 2002. "Explaining the Migration of Stocks from Exchanges in Emerging Economies to International Centers," Unpublished Working Paper.

Coffee, J. 2001. "Do Norms Matter? A Cross-country Examination of Private Benefits of Control." Unpublished Paper, Columbia University Law School.

Djankov, S., and P. Murrell. 2002. "Enterprise Restructuring in Transition: A Quantitative Survey," CEPR Discussion Paper No. 3319. London: Centre for Economic Policy Research.

Earle, J. et al. 2001. "Corporate Control in Romania." Unpublished Manuscript, part of the ACE Project *Corporate Governance and Disclosure in the Accession Process* (ACE Project, Contract No. 97-8042-R).

Earle, J., C. Kucsera, and A. Telegdy. 2001. "Corporate Control in Hungary." Unpublished Manuscript, part of the ACE Project *Corporate Governance and Disclosure in the Accession Process* (ACE Project, Contract No. 97-8042-R).

European Bank for Reconstruction and Development (EBRD). 2002. *Transition Report*. London: European Bank for Reconstruction and Development.

Frishberg A., M. Rabij, and A. Loufer. 1994. *Practical Guide to Ukrainian Corporate and Foreign Investment Legislation*. Boston: Kluwer.

Gregoric, A., J. Prasnikar, and I. Ribnikar. 2001. "Corporate Governance in Transitional Economies: The Case of Slovenia." Unpublished Paper, University of Ljubljana.

Johnson, S., J. McMillan, and C. Woodruff. 1999. "Contract Enforcement in Transition," EBRD Working Paper No. 45. London: European Bank for Reconstruction and Development.

Kaufmann, D., A. Kraay, and P. Zoido-Lobaton. 2002. "Governance Matters II: Updated Indicators for 2000/01," World Bank Policy Research Working Paper. Washington, DC: World Bank.

La Porta, R., F. Lopez-de Silanes, A. Shleifer, and R. Vishny. 1997. "Legal Determinants of External Finance," *Journal of Finance* 52, pp. 1131–1150.

La Porta, R., F. Lopez-de Silanes, A. Shleifer, and R. Vishny. 1998. "Law and Finance," *Journal of Political Economy* 106, pp. 1113–1155.

Olsson, M. 2001. "Adopting the Acquis Communautaire in Central and Eastern Europe: A Report on the Transposition and Implementation of the So-Called Large Holdings Directive (88/672/EEC)." Unpublished Paper, European Corporate Governance Network.

Olsson, M. et al. 2001. "A Survey of Corporate Governance and Disclosure Rules in the Slovak and Czech Republics." Unpublished Manuscript, part of the ACE Project *Corporate Governance and Disclosure in the Accession Process* (ACE Project, Contract No. 97-8042-R).

Pistor, K. 2000. *Patterns of Legal Change: Shareholder and Creditor Rights in Transition Economies*. London: European Bank for Reconstruction and Development.

Pistor, K., M. Raiser, and S. Gelfer. 2000. "Law and Finance in Transition Economies," *SSRN Electronic Journal*. Online. http://www.ssrn.com.

Tamowicz, P., and M. Dzierzanowski. 2001. *Ownership and Control of Polish Corporations*. Gdansk: Gdansk Institute for Market Economics.

Tchipev, P. 2001. "Ownership Structure and Corporate Control in Bulgaria," Paper presented at the First Meeting on the South East Europe Corporate Governance Roundtable, Bucharest, Romania, September 20–21, 2001.

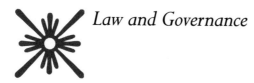 *Law and Governance*

Chapter 12

Corporate Governance and Private Capital Flows to Latin America

Alberto Chong, Alejandro Izquierdo, Alejandro Micco, and Ugo Panizza

Following the debt crisis of the 1980s, Latin America was subject to a surge in private capital flows in the early 1990s. Net private capital flowing to the seven biggest Latin American economies representing about 90 percent of total net flows to the region for the period 1990–2001 not only quadrupled but exceeded official flows by five times.[1] The obvious question is, why? In fact, to some extent, capital inflows were due to two factors: external developments mainly in the United States and the introduction of Brady bonds.

Evidence on the importance of external factors has been provided recently. For instance, Chuhan, Claessens, and Mamingi (1993) show that equity flows seem to be more sensitive to external factors than bond flows, and that bond flows are generally more sensitive to a country's credit rating than equity flows. Similarly, Calvo, Leiderman, and Reinhart (1993) show that external factors play a significant role in determining capital flows and real exchange rate behavior. Fernandez-Arias (1995) emphasized the effects of international interest rates on countries' creditworthiness. The effect of lower interest rates comprises an additional, indirect channel for improvement that may increase capital flow both directly and indirectly.

Along with external factors, the Brady bonds that were introduced following the debt crisis was a crucial institution that became a corporate governance enabler, helping to smooth out asymmetric information problems between countries and private-sector agents. In fact, Brady bonds provided the political governance context that influenced the expected returns to investing and contributed to evening out the payoffs between insiders and outsiders. It helped to develop capital markets as well as to influence the type of capital flows coming to the region and enabling the introduction of Latin American assets in high-risk portfolios. This in turn made it profitable to invest in acquiring information about Latin American markets, thus raising investor interest in the region.

Comments by Peter Cornelius are acknowledged. We would like to thank Virgilio Galdo and Cesar Serra for helpful research assistance. The views expressed in this document are those of the authors and do not necessarily reflect those of the Inter-American Development Bank. The usual disclaimer applies.

The role of external factors and, in particular, the experience with Brady bonds illustrates a simple but powerful principle: well-functioning markets cannot survive without well-defined rules. In fact, the Latin American experience in recent years underscores a third element that should be taken into account when exploring the determinants of private capital flows or foreign direct investment flows. Not only are external factors and political governance elements important, but the corporate governance context is also significant. Although foreign interest rates may affect the performance of Latin American economies, and, while institutions such as the Brady exchange exist, the efficiency of the judiciary or the rule of law may affect the flow of private capital, a frequently overlooked element is the role of corporate rules that may enable capital inflows.

The key issue is that effective corporate governance institutions improve information flows, allow more complete contracts, and avoid moral hazard and adverse selection problems. Insiders will have an incentive to provide information about good investment projects, but they also will have an incentive to withhold information when investment projects go bad or when they have been diverting promised returns. Investors know that bad information is covered up and act accordingly, raising the returns required or refusing to invest at all. In contrast, where information flows to outsiders are timely, accurate, and credible, diversions are more difficult to hide and resources are more likely to be matched with promising investment projects. To ensure that resources are always being targeted to their most efficient uses, investors need to be able to punish insiders explicitly or implicitly. Effective governance institutions play a role in making insiders accountable. Such accountability mechanisms are enhanced when investors have clearly defined powers, the ability to coordinate their actions, and low-cost mechanisms for resolving disputes with insiders (Dyck, 2001).

In this context, the purpose of this chapter is to investigate how corporate governance affects the volatility of private capital flows to Latin America and how corporate governance elements can limit the volatility of private capital flows to developing countries. Although the relationship between governance and amount and composition of capital flows is fairly limited, there are some related studies. For instance, Klapper and Love (2002) use a corporate governance index and provide firm level evidence on corporate governance practices across emerging markets. The idea of their research is to achieve a greater understanding of the environment under which corporate governance matters more. Their empirical tests show that better corporate governance is highly correlated with better operating performance and market valuation. They also provide evidence showing that firm-level corporate governance provisions matter more in countries with weak legal environments. These results suggest that well-governed firms benefit more in bad corporate governance environments, and that firms can partially compensate for ineffective laws and enforcement by establishing good corporate governance and providing credible investor protection. On the other hand, Johnson et al. (2000) argue that weak corporate governance had an important effect on stock market performance and currency depreciation during the Asian crisis of 1997–1998. These authors explain that in the presence of weak corporate governance, stealing by managers may increase when the expected rate return of investment falls. If this is true, for a given negative shock to investors' confidence, countries with poor corporate governance will experience more theft and hence larger capital outflows, stock market collapses, and currency crises.

The chapter is organized as follows: the next section describes the evolution of capital flows to Latin America in the 1990s and shows that capital flows to the region have been highly volatile and sensitive to external factors by focusing on the destructive power of sudden stops in capital flows. The third section puts the issues of political governance and corporate governance in context and describes various governance indicators in Latin America. The main finding of this section is that corporate governance in Latin America compares poorly with corporate governance in both industrial countries and other developing countries. The following section provides empirical evidence on the idea that, although external factors and political governance are important in the determination of capital flows in developing countries, corporate governance reduces the influence of such external factors on capital flows. The conclusion follows.

RECENT EVOLUTION OF CAPITAL FLOWS IN LATIN AMERICA

As described above, after the debt crisis of the 1980s, Latin America was subject to a surge in private capital flows. Indeed, these flows, which were negligible by 1990 (on average 0.1 percent of GDP for the seven biggest Latin American economies [LAC7]), turned into an important feature of macroeconomic developments in the region. At their peak in 1997, they represented on average 3.5 percent of GDP for the LAC7 region, and, for some countries such as Chile, as much as 8.7 percent of GDP in 1997.

These flows were also quite volatile, however. The observed surge in capital flows during the early 1990s was partially offset in 1995 with the emergence of the Mexican crisis, where the refusal of bondholders to roll over short-term government bonds created a liquidity crisis. This event revealed the fact that liquidity crises could also affect sovereign bonds or sovereign debt. Although in the short run several Latin American countries were stressed by the loss of access to capital markets, increasing bond spreads, and, for countries such as Argentina, massive withdrawals of bank deposits, this was a short-lived event. This brevity can be partly attributed to the immediate reaction of the official sector, which set up a significant rescue package. Mexico recovered and financial contagion died out. Private capital flows resumed in 1996, reached their peak in 1997, and remained high during 1998. Indeed, the East Asian crisis starting in 1997 did not substantially affect capital flow behavior to Latin America

FIGURE 12.1   **LAC7 Countries: Private and Official Net Capital Flows (1990–2001)**

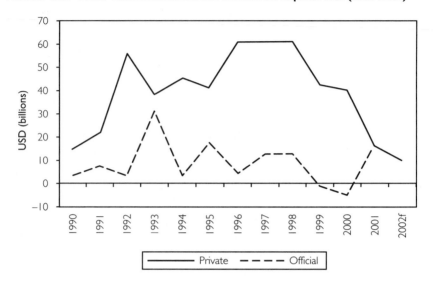

Note: F indicates forecast.
Source: IMF, *World Economic Outlook 2002*

(see Figure 12.1). Although bond spreads increased in late 1997 by about 200 basis points, most of this increase was reversed by early 1998.

What really hit the region was the Russian crisis of August 1998. This crisis represents a milestone in the development of emerging capital markets. As previously described, the massive capital inflows that set sail to Latin America in the early 1990s, financing high growth rates and large current account deficits, came to a sudden standstill following Russia's partial foreign debt repudiation (Calvo, Izquierdo, and Talvi, 2002). It was hard to imagine how a crisis in a country with little if any financial or trading ties to Latin America could have such profound effects on the region. This puzzle cast serious doubt on traditional explanations (based on current account and fiscal deficits) for financial crises and led analysts to focus on the intrinsic behavior of capital markets. Thus it was argued that prevailing rules for capital market transactions may have been responsible for the spread of shocks from one country to other regions (Calvo, 1999). The high leverage of financial intermediaries in margin operations led to a liquidity crunch when Russian bond prices collapsed, which in turn forced massive sales of emerging market assets, including Latin American paper. Interestingly, although the shock facing the Latin American economies came from developments at the center of financial markets, it was not higher risk-free international interest rates that hit Latin American countries. Still, the effect of this new type of external shock was devastating for the region.

Bond spreads, as measured by the EMBI+ index,[2] displayed a dramatic increase following the Russian crisis. On average, spreads increased by more by 660 basis points during 1999. Although they have decreased since then, spreads exhibit a substantial gap compared with pre-crisis levels, exceeding 270 basis points on average for 2002. This gap was higher for 2000 and 2001 (307 basis points and 393 basis points, respectively; see Table 12.1). Higher spreads were accompanied by a large reduction in private capital inflows, which almost halved between 1998 and 1999, from USD 59.6 billion to USD 35.3 billion. Since 1998, there has been a steady decline in these flows, reaching by 2001 lower levels than those observed in 1991 (see Figure 12.1).

A key difference with the early 1990s period is that risk-free world interest rates currently stand at very low levels, yet capital inflows are far from returning to the region as they did before. Instead, the capital flow standstill has been quite prolonged after the Russian crisis. Perhaps new information indicating that a standstill in the capital account can materialize for rather exogenous reasons and can generate such drastic effects on government sustainability[3] may reduce the appetite for holding assets of countries that may be subject to big swings in the real exchange rate, and which are highly dollarized in their liabilities. Several Latin American assets may have been categorized as a riskier asset class in investors' portfolios, reducing their appeal to investors. This may have brought the capital account to a persistent halt.

The fact that the root of this phenomenon lay in Russia's crisis indicates that the capital inflow slowdown contained a large unexpected component. To the extent that the slowdown in capital flows was unexpected, it forced countries to a drastic adjustment of their current account deficits to accommodate the shortage of external credit. Starting in the fourth quarter of 1998, the largest Latin American countries showed a steady decline in their current account deficits, which eventually reached a zero balance by the end of 2000. This adjustment of the current account was, on average, equivalent to 5 percentage points of GDP for the seven largest economies of the region (Calvo, Izquierdo, and Talvi, 2002).

TABLE 12.1 **Difference in Bond Spreads with Minimum Pre-Crisis Levels (in Basis Points)**

	1999	2000	2001	2002
EMBI +	662	307	393	284
EMBI + w/o Argentina	771	329	273	173

Note: Values are yearly averages.
Source: JP Morgan Chase

Such drastic changes in capital flow behavior could not go unnoticed in terms of economic activity. Calvo and Reinhart (2000) illustrate the destructive power of sudden stops in capital flows, and show that when access to international capital markets is closed (something that occurs with distressing frequency in Latin America) the collapse in economic activity is dramatic. Fernández-Arias and Panizza (2002) show that there is a close correlation between private net flows and growth, and they discuss how the volatility of these net flows is associated with the high growth volatility of Latin American countries. Figure 12.2 highlights that it is in particular non-foreign direct investment (non-FDI) flows that are strongly correlated with the growth process of Latin American countries.

In order to assess the relevance of capital flow volatility in Latin American emerging markets relative to other emerging and developed countries, we compared the size of net capital outflows and their share in financial credit to the private sector for the period 1990–2001. Given that capital flow reversals are typically associated with reduced or no rollover of existing credit lines, the size of these reversals relative to the credit stock is a relevant measure in terms of stress experienced by borrowers. This could be important from a corporate governance perspective, because at high stress levels it may be very difficult to comply with existing (noncontingent) contracts. Given this context, corporate governance institutions may be key in explaining the risk involved in keeping or bringing additional capital to distressed economies.

FIGURE 12.2 **LAC7 Business Cycle and Capital Flows**

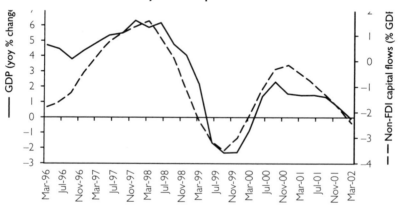

Note: LAC7 includes Argentina, Brazil, Chile, Colombia, Mexico, Peru, and Venezuela
Sources: Corresponding Central Banks; IMF, *International Financial Statistics*, and authors' calculations

Figure 12.3 shows the median percentage capital flow reversal for each country in the sample vis-à-vis the median of capital flow reversals as a share of private sector credit. It highlights two important characteristics, where *reversal* is defined as a negative percentage change in capital flows. First, reversals in capital flows can be high in percentage terms both for emerging and developed economies.[4] Second, however, even when percentage reversals are high, they are small in terms of financial depth for developed economies. The opposite holds true for emerging countries, particularly Latin American economies, where reversals are high both in percentage terms and as a share of credit. With a few exceptions, this measure of capital flow reversals as a share of credit broadly separates countries into cases of small-size reversals, consisting mostly of Organisation for Economic Co-operation and Development (OECD) countries, and cases of larger-size reversals, mainly composed of non-OECD countries. Indeed, when we rank countries from highest to lowest in terms of this measure, all the largest seven Latin American countries fall within the first 40 percent of the sample, indicating that the effects of volatile capital flows are quite relevant in explaining stress in terms of access to credit.[5]

This fact points toward the relevance of corporate governance issues for Latin American countries. To the extent that informational problems become more relevant during reversals, better corporate governance should limit the impact of external conditions on capital flows. Another characteristic of private capital flows that may be relevant from a corporate governance perspective is their composition by type of financing into

FIGURE 12.3   **Capital Flow Reversals (Median Over the Period 1990–2001, Log Scale)**

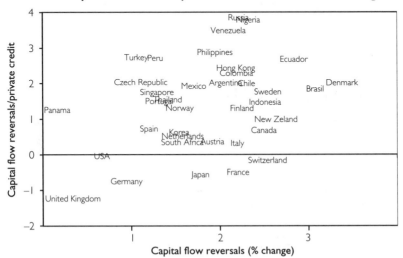

Sources: IMF, *International Financial Statistics* and authors' calculations

foreign direct investment (FDI), equity liabilities, debt liabilities and other flows. Figure 12.4 depicts the share of each type of flow into total private flows. During the early 1990s debt liabilities dominated as the main source of capital flows. This situation was reversed in 1995, as foreign direct investment flows became predominant, and remained the main source of financing from there on. Indeed, this may be a good sign in terms of reducing volatility, given that de-trended FDI flows in Latin America have been less volatile than non-FDI flows.[6] On average, foreign direct investment flows represented 88 percent of total private net flows to the largest seven Latin American countries, whereas debt liabilities represented on average about 40 percent. By contrast, equity liabilities represented a relatively small share of the total all throughout the 1990–2001 period, on average less than 20 percent. This may indicate that investors prefer to have control of the assets they purchase, as is the case of foreign direct investment, or engage in fixed-income contracts, thus avoiding becoming minor shareholders in investment projects, as is the case of equity flows.

POLITICAL GOVERNANCE, CORPORATE GOVERNANCE, AND CAPITAL FLOWS

The role of political governance on capital flows has been widely studied in recent years. For instance, Wheeler and Mody (1992) find no correlation between corruption and FDI, and Fernández-Arias and Hausmann (2001) find that the share of FDI as a share of total capital flows is negatively correlated with a set of indexes measuring

FIGURE 12.4 **LAC7 Countries: Composition of Private Capital Flows (1990–2001)**

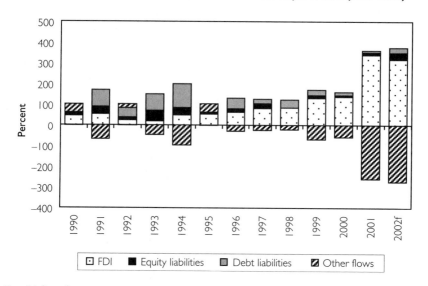

Note: F indicates forecast.
Source: IMF, *World Economic Outlook 2002*

rule of law or creditor rights. Hines (1995), however, finds that US outward FDI is negatively correlated with the level of corruption in the host country; Wei (2000) finds that this finding extends to outward FDI for 12 OECD countries. Wei and Wu (2001) find that, although corruption in the host country is bad for both bank loans and FDI, it is more harmful for FDI. These researchers conclude that a high level of corruption tends to increase the share of bank loans and reduce the share of FDI.

This link between corruption and the flow of FDI, however, is only part of the story, as the role of corporate governance should also be taken into account. In fact, there is a close interaction between the institutions of political and corporate governance, as reflected in the roles of the legislative and the judiciary in the extent to which distributional cartels exert their power, and in the importance of monitoring. It has been argued that it is impossible to move to an essentially rules-based system of governance in the corporate sphere without doing likewise in the political sphere. In fact, it has been claimed that political governance and corporate governance are inseparable (Oman, 2001).

The crucial question is how can corporate governance be linked with capital flows? Johnson et al. (2000) provide a compelling rationale for why better corporate governance may limit the impact of external shocks. In their model, the benefits that managers receive from stealing are inversely correlated with the rate of return of invested resources, and the cost of stealing is positively correlated with corporate governance levels. Therefore, for a given level of corporate governance, a negative shock that reduces the rate of return will lead to increased stealing, and for a given shock, better corporate governance will reduce stealing. Given that foreign investors internalize managers' behavior, both the magnitude of the shock and the level of corporate governance will affect their investment decision. It should be pointed out that, although Johnson et al.'s (2000) paradigm neatly applies to portfolio flows, its application might be extended to include FDI flows. In this latter case, expropriation by managers can be easily substituted with expropriation by politicians who, in periods of economic crisis, may have an incentive to extract more resources from foreign-owned firms.

Our objective is to provide empirical evidence on the extent to which corporate governance plays a role in limiting the way capital flows respond to external shocks. We look at both FDI and portfolios flows and, additional to the use of political governance indicators, we also employ such corporate governance measures.

In empirical terms there is no single paradigm on corporate governance that works in all countries and all companies. Indeed, there exist many different codes of best practices that take into account different legislation, board structures, and business practices in individual countries. However, there are standards that can apply across a broad range of legal, political, and economic environments. In particular, we can provide a basic description of corporate governance in Latin America by focusing on four key categories: creditor rights; shareholder rights; two indexes of procedural formalism of dispute resolution (check collection and tenant eviction); and accounting standards.

Creditor rights are defined as the ability of creditors to use the legal system to force debtors to meet their credit commitments. Creditor rights are an important determinant of credit availability and are closely related with good corporate governance. Measuring creditor rights, however, is not a simple task because most countries have in place both reorganization and liquidation procedures that are used with varying frequency and that confer different levels of protection to different types of creditors. In fact, as creditors do not have homogenous claims against a given debtor, provisions that favor some creditors may hurt others. To deal with these issues, La Porta et al. (1999) score creditor rights in both reorganization and liquidation procedures and then add up the scores to create an aggregate index.[7] Table 12.2 describes corporate governance in various regions of the world and shows that, on average, Latin American countries offer little legal protection to creditors not only when compared with advanced countries but also when compared with developing countries as a whole. Although this is partly explained by the fact that most Latin American countries have a legal system based on French civil law (it is well-known that French Civil law tends to provide less protection to creditors than common law or German and Scandinavian civil law), it should be pointed out that Latin America compares poorly even with other French civil-law countries. La Porta and Lopez-de-Silanes (1998) show that Latin American countries are less likely to place restrictions for going into reorganization, have no-automatic-stay policies, pay secured creditors first, and prevent management from remaining in office.

Shareholder rights measure how strongly the corporate law protects minority shareholders against the expropriation of managers or dominant shareholders. This is important because shareholders have residual rights over the cash flows of the firm.

TABLE 12.2 **Corporate Governance Measures around the World**

CORPORATE GOVERNANCE	LAC	REST OF WORLD	DEVELOPING COUNTRIES	INDUSTRIAL COUNTRIES
Rights of creditors	1.00	2.51	2.11	1.80
Rights of shareholders (Anti-director rights)	2.26	3.11	2.72	3.00
Accounting standards	46.25	64.54	55.10	66.20
Eviction of tenant (rescaled)	4.30	3.58	3.85	3.34
Check collection (rescaled)	4.33	3.43	3.77	3.13

Sources: La Porta et al. (1997), Galindo and Micco (2001), and Djankov et al. (2002)

Therefore, the protection of their rights affects the investors' incentives to invest in equities, and this investment is a key determinant of capital market development. In the case of small shareholders, the right to vote is the main source of control over the resources of the firm. Thus, voting rights and the rights that enhance voting mechanisms are the crucial features of the rights of small shareholders. In this context, an adequate way to build an index of shareholder rights (or "anti-director rights") is to assign a positive score to all the provisions that make voting easier.[8] Table 12.2 shows that, as in the case of creditor rights, average shareholder rights in Latin America are well below the averages for industrial countries, the rest of the world, and even the developing countries as a whole. La Porta and Lopez-de-Silanes (1998) argue that this is mostly due to the fact that the legal system adopted by most Latin American countries is based on French civil law. They point out that, although the incidence of one-share-one-vote rules, cumulative voting for directors, and preemptive rights are not very different between Latin America and other regions, other crucial measures are quite different and typically are more disadvantageous for civil-law Latin American countries. In fact, common-law countries more frequently allow shareholders to exercise vote by mail, which is not the case in most countries in the region. Similarly, no common-law country blocks shares before shareholders' meetings, and most of them do have oppressed minority mechanisms in place, both of which are quite uncommon in Latin America.

The *formalism index* measures substantive and procedural statutory intervention in judicial cases at lower-level civil trial courts. Djankov et al. (2002) show that high levels of procedural formalism are associated with longer judicial proceedings and less fairness in judicial decision. We therefore expect judicial formalism to be associated with poor contract enforcement and poor corporate governance.[9] Table 12.2 shows again that average formalism indexes in Latin America are well below the averages for industrial countries, the rest of the world, and even the developing countries as a whole.

Finally, as recent developments in the United States may attest, accounting standards are central to corporate governance. Without reliable accounting standards it is extremely difficult to assess management performance. Similarly, with poor accounting standards, cash flows may be very difficult to verify and this may reduce the menu of financial contracts available to investors and total credit in the economy (La Porta and Lopez-de-Silanes, 1998). As in the case of creditor rights and shareholder rights, Table 12.2 shows that Latin America has lower accounting standards than industrial countries and the whole set of developing countries.[10] The poor accounting standards that characterize Latin American countries underscore and amplify the severity of the corporate governance problem in the region.

SOME EMPIRICAL EVIDENCE

The methodology used to estimate the impact of corporate governance on capital flows volatility follows Galindo and Micco (2001) and focuses on the estimation of the following equation:

$$FLOWS_{i,t} = \alpha + \beta SHOCK_{i,t} + \gamma(GOV_i * SHOCK_{i,t}) + v_i + \tau_t + \epsilon_{i,t} \qquad (1)$$

where $FLOWS_{i,t}$ measures capital flows to country i in period t, $SHOCK_{i,t}$ is an external shock to country i in period t, GOV_i is a governance indicator for country i, v_i is a country-fixed effect, τ_i is a time-fixed effect, and $\epsilon_{i,t}$ is the error term. If governance plays a role in attenuating the effect of external shocks on capital flows, we expect β and γ to have opposite signs. We introduce country-fixed effects to control for country-specific factors that may affect the level of capital flows, and use time dummies to control for international shocks to capital flows that are common to all countries. Therefore, time dummies control for the surge of capital flows in the early 1990s and the international financial crises of the late 1990s.[11]

In estimating Equation (1), we use annual data for up to 36 developing and emerging market countries for the 1990–2000 period.[12] We use two measures of capital flows, Foreign Direct Investment and Portfolio Flows (bonds and equities). In both cases, we normalize flows by average gross domestic product. In particular, our dependent variable is $(FLOWSi,t)/(\overline{GDP_i})$, where $\overline{GDP_i}$ is country i's average gross domestic product over the 1990–2000 period (for details see Appendix 12.1). We use average gross domestic product rather than current gross domestic product in order to isolate changes in capital flows from changes in gross domestic product.[13] We also use two types of external shocks: a real shock and a nominal shock. A *real shock* is an exogenous demand shock, expressed as the weighted average of the real growth rates of country i's trading partners. As weights, we use total exports to each trading partner divided by country i's GDP. Additionally, a *nominal shock* is defined as $(\overline{EDEBT_i} / \overline{GDP_i})$ $(i_{US,t} - i_{US,t-1})$, where $\overline{EDEBT_i}$ is country i's external debt over the 1990–2000 period and $\overline{GDP_i}$ is country i's average GDP over the 1990–2000 period. As before, we use averages to isolate the effect of interest rate shocks.[14] The nominal shock measures the increase in external debt service due to a change in the foreign interest rate, and this is expressed as the change in the US interest rate multiplied by average external debt expressed as a ratio to average GDP. In fact, Fernández-Arias (1995) provides a rationale of why such shocks are important for capital flows. We expect a positive correlation between real shocks and capital flows and a negative correlation between nominal shocks and capital flows. As measures of political governance, we use the Kaufmann, Kraay, and Zoido-Lobaton (1999) indexes of Rule of Law (ROL) and Effectiveness of the Judiciary (EJ), and as measures of corporate governance we use the La Porta et al. (1997) indexes of Shareholder Rights (SR) and Creditor Rights (CR).[15] We multiply SR and CR by ROL and construct two indexes aimed at measuring effective shareholder rights (EFFSR) and effective creditor rights (EFFCR), correspondingly. We also use the Djankov et al. (2002) indexes of procedural formalism of dispute resolution (TEN indicates procedure formalism in evicting a tenant and CHECK measures procedural formalism in the collection of a check). Appendix 12.2 reports summary statistics for the data used in the empirical analysis.

We start by analyzing how real shocks affect FDI flows (see Table 12.3). As expected, we always find a positive relationship between real external shocks and FDI flows. This implies that positive shocks lead to more FDI and negative shocks to less FDI—in other words, FDI flows are cyclical and amplify external demand shocks. The first two columns of the Table 12.3 show that countries with better political governance (measured by Rule of Law and Efficiency of the judiciary) tend to exhibit a lower correlation between real external shocks and FDI flows. In the cases of Rule of Law, for instance, a one standard deviation increase in governance reduces the sensitivity of FDI flows to external shocks by more than 20 percent (column 1) and the results for effectiveness of the judiciary are basically identical.[16] We find that creditor rights are even more important than political governance. The point estimates indicate that a one standard deviation increase in creditor rights reduces the sensitivity of FDI to external shocks by approximately 40 percent. At the same time, we find no impact of shareholder rights on the sensitivity of FDI to external shock. This last result is not surprising, because with FDIs foreign investors acquire part of the control of the firm and therefore their decision should not be affected by an index that measures the protection of insiders. In fact, we expected shareholder rights to be an important determinant of portfolio equity flows but not FDI.

When we include both political and corporate governance indexes in the same regression (columns 5 and 6), we find that in some cases (for instance, column 5) they are not individually significant, but a Wald test shows that they are jointly significant at 5 percent. Finally, if we combine corporate governance with political governance into an index of effective creditor rights, we find that such an index plays an important role in limiting the cyclical nature of FDI flows (columns 7 and 8). Columns 9 and 10 test the role of procedural formalism. Again, we find FDI in countries with lower levels of procedural formalism (measured by higher values of our rescaled index) tend to have smaller responses to external demand shocks. We conclude that both political and corporate governance seem to play an important role in limiting the cyclical nature of FDI flows to developing countries.

Next we tested whether nominal shocks had an effect on FDI flows to developing countries, but found no correlation between the two variables. We also found no correlation between real shocks and portfolio flows to developing countries.[17] However, we did find a significant correlation between portfolio flows and nominal shocks and, as expected, we find that increases in the US rate lead to lower portfolio flows to developing countries (see the first row of Table 12.4). The first four columns of Table 12.4

TABLE 12.3 **Real Shocks and Foreign Direct Investment Flows**

	(1)	(2)	(3)	(4)	(5)	(6)	(7)	(8)	(9)	(10)
	fdi_r	fdi_r	fdi_r	fdi_r	fdi_r	fdi_r	fdi_r	fdi_r	fdi_r	fdi_r
Real Shock	1.606 (0.772)[b]	3.400 (1.325)[b]	2.332 (0.860)[c]	0.156 (0.618)	3.054 (1.007)[c]	3.987 (1.371)[c]	1.740 (0.956)[a]	1.439 (1.497)	3.085 (0.886)[c]	1.555 (0.650)[b]
RSH_ROL	-1.185 (0.101)[a]	—	—	—	-1.185 (0.135)	—	0.243 (0.251)	—	—	—
RSH_EJ	—	-0.341 (0.139)[b]	—	—	—	-0.150 (.0169)	—	-0.250 (0.230)	—	—
RSH_CR	—	—	-0.547 (0.222)[b]	—	-0.360 (0.260)	-0.616 (0.274)[b]	—	—	—	—
RSH_EFFCR	—	—	—	—	—	—	-0.112 (0.048)[b]	-0.119 (0.036)[c]	—	—
RSH_SR	—	—	—	0.022 (0.157)	—	—	—	—	—	—
RSH_CHEK	—	—	—	—	—	—	—	—	—	-0.366 (0.171)[b]
RSH_TEN	—	—	—	—	—	—	—	—	-1.062 (0.321)[c]	—
CONST.	0.006 (0.004)[a]	0.005 (0.004)	0.005 (0.004)	0.007 (0.004)[b]	0.004 (0.004)	0.003 (0.004)	0.003 (0.004)	0.003 (0.004)	0.005 (0.004)	0.006 (0.004)[a]
N.OBS	360	300	350	360	350	290	350	290	360	360
N. COUNTRIES	36	30	35	36	35	29	35	29	36	36
R^2	0.32	0.31	0.33	0.31	0.33	0.32	0.34	0.34	0.34	0.32

Standard errors in parentheses   [a] significant at 10%   [b] significant at 5%   [c] significant at 1%

Source: Authors' calculations

also show that better political or corporate governance reduces the response of port-folio flows to external nominal shocks. It should be pointed out, however, that the results are either insignificant (as in the case of creditor rights) or only marginally sta-tistically significant. As expected, we now find that shareholder rights are more impor-tant than creditor rights. When we include both political and corporate governance indicators in the same regression (columns 5–8) we find that all the coefficients have the same sign but that they are rarely statistically significant. Again, tests on the differ-ence between coefficients show that political and corporate governance are jointly sig-nificant. Columns 9–12 show that effective creditor rights and effective shareholder rights play significant roles in limiting how portfolio flows respond to external nomi-nal shocks. This supports our previous finding that both political and corporate gover-nance are important in limiting how capital flows to developing countries respond to external factors.[18] The last two columns of the table, however, show that there is no significant correlation between portfolio flows and the interaction between nominal shocks and procedural formalism.

Following the work of Calvo, Leiderman, and Reinhart (1993), many authors have shown the importance of external factors in determining capital flows to devel-oping and emerging market countries. The purpose of this section was to test whether better corporate governance may play a role in limiting the impact of external factors.[19] It is fair to conclude that real external shocks are important determinants of FDI flows and external interest rate shocks are important determinants of portfolio flows. Furthermore, we find evidence for the hypothesis that better corporate governance reduces the sensitivity of capital flows to these external shocks. This is an important result because the growth experience of most developing countries is stunted by their high levels of volatility, and the cyclical behavior of capital flows contributes to these high levels of volatility (Inter-American Development Bank, 1995). The main message of this section is that, by improving corporate governance, developing countries can limit the cyclical behavior of capital flows and hence limit the volatility of their economies.

CONCLUSION

According to recent research, external factors and political governance consid-erations are key determinants of capital flows in Latin America. We postulate that cor-porate governance is a crucial determinant as well. In fact, in this chapter we look at the relationship between corporate governance and private capital flows to Latin American countries, in particular FDI and portfolio flows. We show that capital flows to Latin America tend to be highly volatile and influenced by external factors. Additionally, although we show that the region exhibits low levels of political governance, we also show that there are relative and absolute low levels of corporate governance, as measured by indexes of creditor rights, shareholder rights, and accounting standards. In this con-text, we pursue the idea that better corporate governance can help to limit the impact

TABLE 12.4 Nominal Shocks and Portfolio Flows

	(1) pp_r	(2) pp_r	(3) pp_r	(4) pp_r	(5) pp_r	(6) pp_r	(7) pp_r	(8) pp_r	(9) pp_r	(10) pp_r	(11) pp_r	(12) pp_r	(13) pp_r	(14) pp_r
IRSH	-1.364 (0.528)b	-2.734 (1.091)b	-1.286 (0.575)b	-1.031 (0.464)b	-1.631 (0.612)c	-3.184 (1.202)c	-1.681 (0.561)c	-2.955 (1.110)c	-1.431 (0.557)b	-3.244 (1.126)c	-0.818 (0.549)	-2.300 (1.083)b	-0.838 (0.840)	-0.690 (0.747)
IR_ROL	0.236 (0.113)b	—	—	—	0.199 (0.122)	—	0.231 (0.113)b	—	0.058 (0.145)	—	-0.003 (0.136)	—	—	—
IR_EJ	—	0.241 (0.132)a	—	—	—	0.192 (0.153)	—	0.233 (0.132)a	—	0.192 (0.152)	—	0.166 (0.132)	—	—
IR_CR	—	—	0.145 (0.135)	—	0.093 (0.138)	0.195 (0.169)	—	—	—	—	—	—	—	—
IR_EFFCR	—	—	—	—	—	—	—	—	0.063 (0.033)a	0.084 (0.033)b	—	—	—	—
IR_SR	—	—	—	0.289 (0.172)a	—	—	0.280 (0.171)	0.236 (0.220)	—	—	—	—	—	—
IR_EFFSR	—	—	—	—	—	—	—	—	—	—	0.105 (0.034)c	0.108 (0.035)c	—	—
IR_CHECK	—	—	—	—	—	—	—	—	—	—	—	—	—	0.161 (0.232)
IR_TEN	—	—	—	—	—	—	—	—	—	—	—	—	0.208 (0.269)	—
CONST.	0.007 (0.006)	0.005 (0.007)	0.001 (0.006)	0.007 (0.006)	0.003 (0.006)	0.000 (0.007)	0.007 (0.006)	0.004 (0.007)	0.003 (0.006)	0.002 (0.007)	0.007 (0.005)	0.001 (0.007)	0.012 (0.005)b	0.012 (0.005)b
N. OBS.	360	300	350	360	350	290	360	300	350	290	360	300	288	288
N. COUNTRIES	36	30	35	36	35	29	36	30	35	29	36	30	36	36
R^2	0.06	0.08	0.06	0.06	0.07	0.08	0.07	0.08	0.08	0.10	0.09	0.11	0.02	0.02

Standard errors in parentheses   a significant at 10%   b significant at 5%   c significant at 1%

The dependent variable is portfolio flows (bonds and equities) normalized by average gross domestic product over the 1990–2000 period.

of external shocks on capital flows to developing countries in general, and Latin America in particular. In fact, we find that real external shocks are important determinants of FDI flows and external interest rate shocks are important determinants of portfolio flows. Furthermore, we also find evidence for the fact that better governance reduces the sensitivity of capital flows to these external shocks. As explained above, this is relevant given that the performance of emerging markets, such as those of Latin American countries, is typically stunted by high levels of volatility and the cyclical behavior of capital flows. Improving corporate governance can limit the cyclical behavior of capital flows and hence limit the volatility of these economies.

Although one may conclude that the results of this chapter yield the simple policy prescription that, by improving governance, Latin American countries can limit capital flow volatility, things are not as easy as they seem. There is, in fact, evidence that corporate governance and political governance tend to be affected by historically predetermined factors (such as the origin of the legal code) and, hence, cannot easily be improved. On a more optimistic note, there is some evidence that by adopting better governance standards, individual firms can improve their performance even in countries characterized by a poor political governance environment. These findings seem to indicate that, in order to limit capital flows' sensitivity to external shocks, countries in the region should, besides addressing political governance issues, provide incentives for better corporate governance as well.

NOTES

1   Flows increased from USD 14.7 billion in 1990 to USD 61.7 billion at their peak in 1997.

2   EMBI stands for the well-known Emerging Markets Bond Index and is produced by JP Morgan.

3   This is because of either debt revaluation effects or the emergence of contingent liabilities.

4   For example, the median percentage change for outflow periods can be high in industrialized countries such as Canada or Switzerland, even higher than in many emerging markets.

5   Although the size of these reversals is large in terms of credit to the private sector, this does not necessarily indicate that they were caused by supply shocks. Barajas and Steiner (2001) suggest that the evolution of deposits is by far the dominant factor in credit slowdowns. Credit risk and regulation factors have also played a crucial role, indicating reduced willingness to lend. For instance, in Colombia, where capital inflows were intermediated through the domestic financial system, there is a high correlation between capital flows and credit. There is no systematic evidence for a large set of countries on *credit crunches* (defined as scenarios where credit demand exceeds credit supply); Barajas and Steiner (2001) suggest that this was also the case in Peru. Mody and Taylor (2002) also find support for capital flow crunches in the recent Mexican and Brazilian experiences.

6   The standard deviation of the cyclical component of an index of FDI flows (de-trended by a Hodrick-Prescott filter) is six times smaller than that of an index of de-trended non-FDI flows for the period 1970–2001.

7   Specifically, *creditor rights* are defined as an index formed by adding 1 when (1) the country imposes restrictions, such as creditors' consent or minimum dividends to file for reorganization; (2) secured creditors are able to gain possession of their security once the reorganization petition has been approved; (3) secured creditors are ranked first in the distribution of the proceeds that result from the disposition of the assets of a bankrupt firm; and (4) the debtor does not retain the administration of its property pending the resolution of the reorganization. The resulting index thus ranges from 0 to 4.

8   *Shareholder rights* are defined by aggregating anti-director rights measures into an index. The index is formed by adding 1 when: the country allows shareholders to mail their proxy vote to the firm; shareholders are not required to deposit their shares prior to the general shareholders' meeting; cumulative voting or proportional representation of minorities in the board of directors is allowed; an oppressed minorities mechanism is in place; the minimum percentage of share capital that entitles a shareholder to call for an extraordinary shareholders' meeting is less than or equal to 10 (sample median); or shareholders have preemptive rights that can only be waived by a shareholders' vote. The index ranges from 0 to 6.

9   In particular, we consider two specific formalism indexes: eviction of tenants and check collection. They are calculated by adding up the following indexes: (1) professionals versus laymen, (2) written versus oral elements, (3) legal justification, (4) statutory regulation of evidence, (5) control of superior review, (6) engagement formalities, and (7) independent procedural actions. We rescale the index to range from 0 to 7, where a higher value indicates lower procedural formalism.

10   Examining and rating companies' 1990 annual reports on their inclusion or omission of 90 items creates the index of accounting standards. These items fall into seven categories (general information, income statements, balance sheets, funds flow statement, accounting standards, stock data, and special items). A minimum of three companies in each country was studied. The companies represent a cross-section of various industry groups where industrial companies numbered 70 percent while financial companies represented the remaining 30 percent.

11   Notice that time dummies are correlated with external shock and dropping them improves the results discussed below.

12   The countries in the sample are Argentina, Bolivia, Brazil, Chile, Hong Kong SAR, Colombia, Costa Rica, Dominican Republic, Ecuador, Egypt, El Salvador, Guatemala, Honduras, India, Indonesia, Israel, Jamaica, Jordan, Kenya, Malaysia, Mexico, Nigeria, Pakistan, Panama, Paraguay, Peru, Philippines, Singapore, South Africa, Sri Lanka, Thailand, Trinidad and Tobago, Turkey, Uruguay, Venezuela, and Zimbabwe.

13   Our capital flow data are from the IMF's *World Economic Outlook* database.

14   It should be noted that the weights do not add up to one but are based on export shares to GDP. Trade and GDP growth data are from the World Bank's World Development Indicators.

15   Rather than the original, we use the updated version built by Galindo and Micco (2001).

16   It should be pointed out that there are some outliers in the regression. In particular, dropping Singapore somewhat weakens the results discussed above.

17   We do not report the specific results because they are not informative.

18   It should be pointed out that the results of the regressions of Table 12.4 are partly affected by an important outlier (Hong Kong SAR). If Hong Kong SAR is dropped from the sample, some of the coefficients become statistically insignificant and decrease in magnitude.

19   Although our results may not be extremely robust, it should also pointed out that we control for a host of factors (included in time and country dummies) that tend to be highly collinear with our variables of interest and hence capture part of their effects. When we drop time dummies, we obtain much stronger results.

REFERENCES

Barajas, A., and R. Steiner. 2002. "Credit Stagnation in Latin America," IMF Working Paper No. WP/02/53. Washington, D.C.: International Monetary Fund.

Calvo, G. A. 1999. "Contagion in Emerging Markets: When Wall Street is a Carrier." Unpublished Manuscript, University of Maryland.

Calvo, G., A. Izquierdo, and E. Talvi. 2002. "Sudden Stops and the Real Exchange Rate: Argentina's Lesson," IADB Working Paper No. 469. Washington, D.C.: Inter-American Development Bank.

Calvo, G., L. Leiderman, and C. Reinhart. 1993. "Capital Inflows and Real Exchange Rate Appreciation in Latin America: The Role of External Factors." *International Monetary Fund Staff Papers* 40, pp. 108–151.

Calvo, G., and C. Reinhart. 2000. "When Capital Inflows Suddenly Stop: Consequences and Policy Options." In P. B. Kenen and A. K. Swoboda, eds., *Reforming the International Monetary and Financial System*. Washington, D.C.: International Monetary Fund.

Chong, A., and F. Lopez-de-Silanes. 2003. *Costs and Benefits of Privatization in Latin America*. Washington, D.C.: Inter-American Development Bank (forthcoming).

Chuhan, P., S. Claessens, and N. Mamingi. 1993. "Equity and Bond Flows to Asia and Latin America: The Role of Global Factors and Country Factors," World Bank Policy Research Working Paper No. 1160. Washington, D.C.: World Bank.

Djankov, S. et al. 2003. "The Practice of Justice," *Quarterly Journal of Economics* (forthcoming).

Dyck, A. 2001. "Privatization and Corporate Governance: Principles, Evidence, and Future Challenges," *World Bank Research Observer* 16, no. 1, pp. 59–84.

Fernández-Arias, E. 1995. "The New Wave of Private Capital Inflows: Push or Pull?" *Journal of Development Economics* 48, pp. 386–418.

Fernández-Arias, E., and R. Hausmann. 2001. "Foreign Direct Investments: Good Cholesterol?" In J. Braga de Macedo and E. Iglesias, eds., *Foreign Direct Investments Versus Other Flows to Latin America*. Paris: Organisation for Economic Co-operation and Development.

Fernández-Arias, E., and U. Panizza. 2002. "Capital Flows to Latin America: New Issues and Old Concerns." In S. Kay and E. McQuerry, eds., *Domestic Finance and Global Capital in Latin America*. Atlanta, GA: Latin America Research Group, Federal Reserve Bank of Atlanta.

Galindo, A., and A. Micco. 2001. "Creditor Protection and Financial Cycles," IADB Research Department Working Paper No. 443. Washington, D.C.: Inter-American Development Bank.

Gompers, P., J. Ishii, and A. Metrick. 2003. "Corporate Governance and Equity Prices," *Quarterly Journal of Economics* (forthcoming).

Hines, J. 1995. "Forbidden Payments: Foreign Bribery and American Business after 1977," NBER Working Paper No. 5266. Cambridge, MA: National Bureau of Economic Research.

Inter-American Development Bank (IADB). 1995. *Economic and Social Progress in Latin America: Overcoming Volatility*. Baltimore: The Johns Hopkins University Press.

International Monetary Fund (IMF). 2001. *International Financial Statistics* (CD-ROM). Washington, D.C.: International Monetary Fund.

International Monetary Fund (IMF). 2002. *World Economic Outlook* (CD-ROM). Washington, D.C.: International Monetary Fund.

Johnson, S., P. Boone, A. Breach, and E. Friedman. 2000. "Corporate Governance in the Asian Financial Crisis," *Journal of Financial Economics* 58, pp. 141–186.

Kaufmann, D., A. Kraay, and P. Zoido-Lobaton. 1999. "Aggregating Governance Indicators." Unpublished Paper, Development Research Group, World Bank.

Klapper, L., and I. Love. 2002. "Corporate Governance, Investor Protection, and Performance in Emerging Markets." Unpublished Paper, Development Research Group, World Bank.

La Porta, R., and F. Lopez-de-Silanes. 1998. "Capital Markets and Legal Institutions." In S. Burki, and G. Perry, eds., *Beyond the Washington Consensus: Institutions Matter*. Washington, D.C.: World Bank.

La Porta, R., F. Lopez-de-Silanes, A. Shleifer, and R. Vishny. 1997. "Legal Determinants of External Finance," *Journal of Finance* 52, pp. 1131–1150.

La Porta, R., F. Lopez-de-Silanes, A. Shleifer, and R. Vishny. 1999. "Corporate Ownership Around the World," *Journal of Finance* 54, pp. 471–517.

La Porta, R. F. Lopez-de-Silanes, and G. Zamarripa. 2003. "Related Lending," *Quarterly Journal of Economics* (forthcoming).

Mitton, T. 2002. "A Cross-Firm Analysis of the Impact of Corporate Governance on the East Asian Financial Crisis," *Journal of Financial Economics* 64, pp. 215–241.

Mody, A., and M. P. Taylor. 2002. "International Capital Crunches: The Time-Varying Role of Informational Asymmetries," IMF Working Paper No. WP/02/43. Washington, D.C.: International Monetary Fund.

Oman, C. 2001. "Corporate Governance and National Development," OECD Development Centre Technical Paper No. 180. Paris: Organisation for Economic Co-operation and Development.

Panizza, U. 2001. "Electoral Rules, Political Systems, and Institutional Quality," *Economics and Politics* 13, pp. 311–342.

Shleifer, A., and R. Vishny. 1997. "A Survey of Corporate Governance," *Journal of Finance* 52, pp. 737–783.

Tirole, J. 2001. "Corporate Governance," *Econometrica* 69, pp. 1–35.

Wheeler, D., and A. Mody. 1992. "International Investment Location Decisions: The Case of U.S. Firms," *Journal of International Economics* 33, pp. 57–76.

Wei, S.-J. 2000. "How Taxing Is Corruption on International Investors?" *Review of Economics and Statistics* 82, pp. 1–11.

Wei, S.-J., and Y. Wu (2001) "Negative Alchemy? Corruption, Composition of Capital Flows, and Currency Crises," NBER Working Paper No. 8187. Cambridge, MA: National Bureau of Economic Research.

World Bank. 2001. *World Development Indicators* (CD-ROM). Washington, D.C.: World Bank.

APPENDIX 12.1 **Description of Variables**

VARIABLE	DESCRIPTION
FDI	Annual foreign direct investment for the 1990–2000 period normalized by average gross domestic product over the period 1990–2000. Source: IMF's *World Economic Outlook*.
Portfolio Flows	Annual portfolio flows for the 1990–2000 period normalized by average gross domestic product over the period 1990–2000. Source: IMF's *World Economic Outlook*.
Real Shock	Exogenous demand shock, expressed as the weighted average of the real growth rates of country i's trading partners. As weights, we use total exports to each trading partner divided by country i's GDP. Source: World Bank's *World Development Indicators*.
Nominal Shock	The nominal shock is expressed as the change in the US interest rate multiplied by average external debt expressed as a ratio to average GDP. Source: World Bank's *World Development Indicators*.
Rule of Law	Assessment of the law and order tradition in the country produced by the country-risk rating agency *International Country Risk*. Scale from 0 to 10, with lower scores for less tradition of law and order. Source: Kaufmann, Kraay, and Zoido-Lobaton (1999).
Effectiveness of Judicial System	Assessment of the "efficiency and integrity of the legal environment as it affects business, particularly foreign firms" produced by the country-risk rating agency International Country Risk. Scale from 0 to 10, with lower scores indicating lower efficiency levels. Source: Kaufmann, Kraay, and Zoido-Lobaton (1999).
Shareholder Rights	*Shareholder rights* are defined by aggregating anti-director rights measure into an index. The index is formed by added 1 when: the country allows shareholders to mail their proxy votes to the firm; shareholders are not required to deposit their shares prior to the general shareholders' meeting; cumulative voting or proportional representation of minorities in the board of directors is allowed; an oppressed minorities mechanism is in place; the minimum percentage of share capital that entitles a shareholder to call for an extraordinary shareholders' meeting in less than or equal to 10 (sample median); or shareholders have preemptive rights that can be waived only by a shareholder's vote. The index ranges from 0 to 6. Sources: La Porta et al. (1997); Galindo and Micco (2001).
Effectiveness of Shareholder Rights	Shareholder rights index multiplied by the rule of law rating.
Creditor Rights	*Creditor rights* are defined as an index formed by adding 1 when (1) the country imposes restrictions, such as creditors' consent or minimum dividends to file for reorganization; (2) secured creditors are able to gain possession of their security once the reorganization petition has been approved; (3) secured creditors are ranked first in the distribution of the proceeds that result from the disposition of the assets of a bankrupt firm; and (4) the debtor does not retain the administration of its property pending the resolution of the reorganization. The resulting index thus ranges from 0 to 4. Sources: La Porta et al. (1997); Galindo and Micco (2001).
Effectiveness of Creditor Rights	Creditor rights index multiplied by rule of law rating.

VARIABLE	DESCRIPTION
Formalism Index	This index measures substantive and procedural statutory intervention in judicial cases at lower-level civil trial courts, and it is formed by adding up the following indexes: (1) professional versus laymen, (2) written versus oral elements, (3) legal justification, (4) statutory regulation and evidence, (5) control of superior review, (6) engagement formalities, and (7) independent procedural actions. We rescale the original index so that a higher value indicates lower procedural formalism. Source: Djankov et al. (2002).
Accounting Standards	This index was created by examining and rating companies' 1990 annual reports on their inclusion or omission of 90 items. These items fall into seven categories: general information, income statements, balance sheets, funds flow statements, accounting standards, stock data, and special items. The index ranges from 0 to 100. Source: La Porta et al. (1997).

APPENDIX 12.2 **Summary Statistics**

VARIABLE NAME	OBS	MEAN	STD. DEV.	MIN	MAX
FDI	360	0.021	0.028	−0.022	0.182
Portfolio Flows	360	0.005	0.026	−0.137	0.256
Real Shock	360	0.008	0.013	−0.025	0.074
Nominal Shock	324	−0.001	0.008	−0.035	0.033
Rule of Law	36	4.458	1.956	1.320	8.570
Effectiveness of the Judicial System	30	6.741	1.803	2.500	10.000
Shareholder Rights	36	2.722	1.386	1.000	5.000
Effectiveness Shareholder Rights	36	12.921	10.328	1.320	41.100
Creditor Rights	35	2.114	1.530	0.000	4.000
Effectiveness Creditor Rights	35	10.344	9.216	0.000	34.280
Accounting Standards	47	60.795	13.566	24.000	83.000
Eviction of Tenant (rescaled)	36	1.800	0.975	0.000	3.77
Check Collection (rescaled)	36	2.080	1.346	0.000	5.28

Chapter 13

Institutions, Corporate Governance, and Crises

Daron Acemoglu and Simon Johnson

The prevailing view among economists, international policymakers, and business people is that economic crises are largely the result of mismanaged macroeconomic policies. The International Monetary Fund (IMF), for example, focuses its attention on persuading countries to change these macroeconomic policies. Edwards (1989) analyzes the 34 IMF programs with high conditionality between 1983 and 1985, and provides a breakdown of the typical requirements. Four of the five most common conditions required by the IMF are: control of credit to public sector, control of monetary aggregates, devaluation, and control of public expenditures.

This focus on macroeconomic policies makes perfect sense if macroeconomic policies are the root causes of economic crises. But if macroeconomic policies are themselves the outcome of a deeper and more political process, then the situation is more complicated. It may not be the case that distortionary macroeconomic policies are chosen because politicians believe that high inflation or overvalued exchange rates are good for economic performance. Instead, distortionary policies may reflect underlying institutional problems in these countries—weak protection of investors' property rights, weak rule of law, and weak constraints placed on politicians and business elites. If it is the case that institutional factors are the problem, then it may be hard to change macroeconomic policies effectively because, for example, any improvement in one policy may be offset by a worsening in another policy as long as the underlying institutional problems remain unresolved.

How, exactly, could "institutions" affect economic outcomes? The most likely channels through which institutions affect economic outcomes, are institutions' influence on investment decisions. Three issues influencing investment decisions seem particularly important. The first issue is the level of protection of the property rights of entrepreneurs with the most significant investment opportunities. This primarily entails protecting all entrepreneurs, including big business, against the government. Second, the level of protection of the property rights of a broad segment of society. This involves protecting small entrepreneurs and small investors against the government, elite groups with political power, and big business. Third, prevention of elites from blocking new entry into lucrative lines of business. This requires protecting small or potential businesses against incumbents, who may be very large or just medium-sized and well established with comfortable profits and some political power. The first channel emphasizes the importance of preventing the state (and the elite that may control the state) from expropriating major investors; this is the issue that often gets the most attention. However, the second and third channels are also important for growth, and here the legal protection of investors and the corporate governance of firms play a key role. If corporate governance is weak, because outside investors have few legal rights, for example, it is very hard for new firms to raise capital—thus effectively blocking entry—and, because they have few rights, minority shareholders can be expropriated at will by entrepreneurs. All three "channels" from institutions to investment generally matter for growth.

In addition, as we explain below, there is a strong causal relationship between the historically-determined component of contemporary institutions and volatility (as well as the severity of economic crises and economic growth)—countries that inherited weak (i.e., more "extractive") institutions from European colonial powers are much more likely to experience high volatility and severe economic crises (Acemoglu et al., 2002; Acemoglu, Johnson, and Robinson, forthcoming). Societies with weak institutions for historical reasons have experienced substantially more output volatility and more severe output, exchange rate, banking, and political crises over the past 30 years. This relationship between institutions and volatility has been evident in every decade from at least 1970. In addition, corporate governance may matter for the severity of crises in middle-income countries. On this point we have less data, but evidence from the Asian financial crisis of 1997–1998 suggests that this effect is present to some extent. In particular, crises may be more severe when investors become concerned about being expropriated by the government and other private parties. Companies that adopt stronger firm-specific corporate governance measures can protect themselves to some extent. But it is hard for any company to escape the effects of country-level institutions.

Not only do the data indicate a strong role for institutions, but, once we control properly for institutions, there is *no* systematic role for macroeconomic policies. However, these findings do not imply that macroeconomic policies do not matter. Instead, in equilibrium, macroeconomic policies change only to the extent allowed by institutions. If this is the case, not only is it very difficult for the IMF to change policies effectively, but macroeconomic policies may not generally be useful tools for achieving better economic outcomes. In our view, there are deeper institutional causes leading to economic instability, and these institutional causes lead to bad macroeconomic outcomes via a variety of mediating channels. If we are correct, then distortionary macroeconomic policies are one of the channels that determine macro volatility, but such policies are but one channel. In other words, macroeconomic policies are part of the "tools" that groups in power use to enrich themselves and remain in power. But such policies are only one of many possible tools, and a variety of complex factors, which we do not currently understand, determine which of these tools are used in various circumstances. An interesting possibility—highly relevant to the IMF—implied by this perspective is a "seesaw" effect; that is, preventing the use of a specific macro distortion will not necessarily cure economic instability problems, since underlying institutional problems may manifest themselves in the use of some other tools by politicians and elites to achieve their objectives.

This chapter expands on these points in five sections. First we explain the relationship between institutions and growth. Next is a discussion about using the historical origins of institutions as a way to identify the causal link from institutions to economic growth. This is followed by a summary of the evidence on the link between institutions and economic instability in general, and then a discussion of the importance of corporate governance for crises. The chapter is wrapped up with a discussion of the implications for policymakers and corporate leaders.

INSTITUTIONS AND GROWTH

There are many alternative definitions of institutions. We focus on the cluster of "private property" institutions that: (1) protect major private sector investors, (2) protect the property rights of a broad segment of society, and (3) prevent elites from blocking new entry. These can be contrasted with "extractive institutions," that is, institutions that do not constrain business and political elites. Extractive institutions will typically have a political component—for example, allowing a small elite group to hold all the reins of power—but more broadly, they also allow the elite in power to act in an arbitrary manner with respect to other members of society (e.g., their outside minority shareholders).

This cluster makes sense if you consider the decisions made every day by actual or potential entrepreneurs and investors. An individual asks: should I invest and, if yes, then how much? The answer obviously depends, in part, on the risks. In many countries, a major danger is that the government or some powerful individual will expropriate the benefits of this investment. Elites and politicians are "constrained" if they are not able to expropriate resources easily from others.

Given this definition of private property versus extractive institutions, how can we demonstrate that it is related to economic outcomes, such as income per capita? Figures 13.1 and 13.2 display the simple correlation between alternative measures of institutions and income (measured throughout this chapter as GDP per capita, in purchasing power parity terms). Figure 13.1 measures institutions in terms of the protection for entrepreneurs' property rights. This is the result of assessments

FIGURE 13.1 **Log Income Per Capita in 1995 versus Perceived Protection Against Expropriation Risk, 1985–1995**

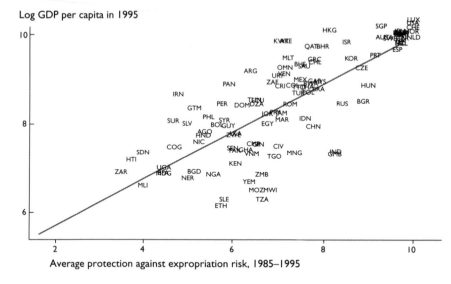

by Political Risk Services between 1985 and 1995, as compiled by Knack and Keefer (1995). Note that we use an average to smooth out any year-to-year fluctuations because we are interested in the long-term relationship. Figure 13.2 measures institutions using expert assessments of the constraints placed on the executive; this is an index constructed by Ted Gurr and refined by a number of political scientists (see Gurr, 1997, for details). In this index, a low score indicates very little constraint and a high score indicates a great deal of constraint (e.g., the United States gets a score of 7). In both cases there is clearly a strong correlation between institutions and the level of income per capita. A similar correlation is present for all other measures of institutions that we have seen.

There is a long-standing idea that constraining institutions have a first-order effect on long-run economic development. Douglass North received a Nobel Prize in part for articulating this idea clearly (see, among others, North and Thomas, 1973; Jones, 1981; North, 1981; Olson, 1982). Recent empirical work has confirmed a strong correlation between institutions and economic/financial development (e.g., Knack and Keefer, 1995; Mauro, 1995; La Porta et al., 1998; Hall and Jones, 1999; Johnson, McMillan, and Woodruff, 2002). But how much of this correlation is due to real causation between institutions and long-run growth?

A correlation does not generally tell us much about causation. Prosperity definitely affects institutions. For example, richer countries may "buy" better institutions. This also happens in the reverse, so just looking at simple correlations is not

FIGURE 13.2 **Log Income Per Capita in 1995 versus Average Constraint on Executive (1950, 1960, 1970)**

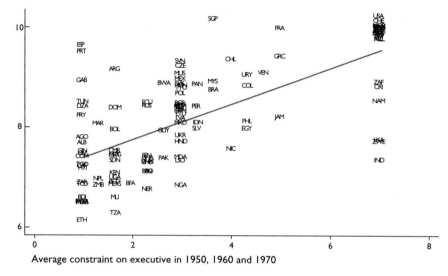

Log GDP per capita in 1995

Average constraint on executive in 1950, 1960 and 1970

enough. In addition, there may be important omitted causal factors—most geographic explanations of income differences between countries, for example, turn out to be flawed precisely because they fail to consider the role of institutions (see Acemoglu, Johnson, and Robinson, 2001, for further discussion). In assessing institutions, in turn, we need a method that accounts for potential "missing" explanatory variables.

One appealing approach is to go back in history and look carefully at how institutions developed in order to isolate a source of variation in institutions that is not contaminated by reverse causation or by other variables that may affect outcomes. In the next section we look at "exogenous" differences in institutions, that is, what happens when institutions are imposed on a country by forces from outside the country, compared to institution-selection being based on a country's economic prospects.

THE ORIGINS OF INSTITUTIONS

One way to isolate the exogenous component of institutions is by focusing on countries that were colonized by European powers. This is an attractive sample to use for understanding the role of institutions in economic development, since the intervention of Europeans, setting up very different institutions in various parts of the globe, is the closest we have to a natural social experiment in the creation of institutions. In addition to telling us something about the effects of colonization, the experience of these countries can inform us about the likely general effects of institutions.

Acemoglu, Johnson, and Robinson (2001) documented that European colonization strategies had radically different implications for economic development. Places prospered when Europeans set up institutions protecting private property rights, enforcing the rule of law, and placing tight constraints on politicians and powerful elites. In contrast, areas stagnated or grew only slowly when Europeans established new—or took over existing—extractive institutions.

What determined where the Europeans were willing to settle? One key factor was the disease environment, that is, how vulnerable the Europeans were to locally prevalent diseases. Where the disease environment was favorable for European settlement, Europeans migrated in large numbers and developed institutions very similar to, or even substantially better than, institutions in Europe. These settler colonies, such as the United States, Canada, Australia, and New Zealand, have grown steadily over the past 200 years, taking good advantage of the opportunity to industrialize. In many other colonies, for example, in sub-Saharan Africa, south Asia, and Central America, Europeans faced high or very high mortality rates (up to 50 percent mortality per year in some places) and settlement was not feasible (see the appendix for a summary of sources for the mortality data). In these areas, the colonizers were much more likely to develop extractive institutions, used mostly to exploit the native population for the benefit of a few rich Europeans. These institutions have persisted through to today. After independence, the beneficiaries of extraction changed and the form of extraction evolved over time, but countries such as Zaire (formerly, Belgian Congo) that had rapacious rule under colonialism have clearly continued to have extractive institutions. These institutions have proved incompatible with sustained and rapid growth.

According to this view, there is a strong causal link between past settlements and income today. Figure 13.3 shows a strong relationship between Europeans as a percent of the population in 1900 among former colonies, and income per capita today. We document, in Acemoglu, Johnson, and Robinson (2001), that this relationship exists because European settlements led to better institutions. Figures 13.4 and 13.5 support this idea by showing that institutions today are better where European settler mortality was lower 200 to 400 years ago. Places where Europeans faced much higher mortality rates are significantly poorer today.

Note that this link absolutely does not imply predestination. In fact, our regressions of institutions today on settler mortality indicate that only about 25 percent of the variation in institutions can be explained by this historical factor. Nevertheless, this 25 percent is enough to provide effective econometric "identification;" that is, it allows us to see the effect of institutions on income per capita (and on other outcomes). Less technically, we can say that there is a tendency for countries with weak colonial-era institutions to have weak institutions today, and although weaknesses can persist, such persistence is definitely not predetermined.

FIGURE 13.3   **Log Income Per Capita in 1995 versus European Settlers as Percent of Population in 1900**

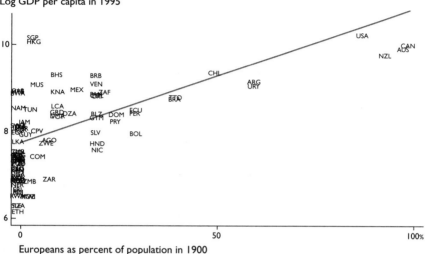

FIGURE 13.4   **Perceived Protection Against Expropriation Risk, 1985–95 versus Log Settler Mortality**

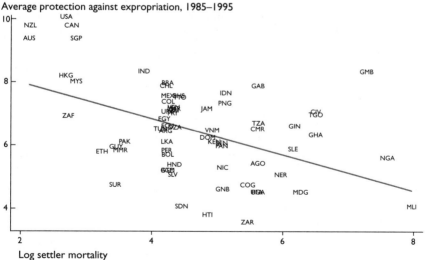

FIGURE 13.5 **Average Constraint on Executive (1950, 1960, 1970) versus Log Settler Mortality**

Average constraint on executive 1950, 1960, 1970

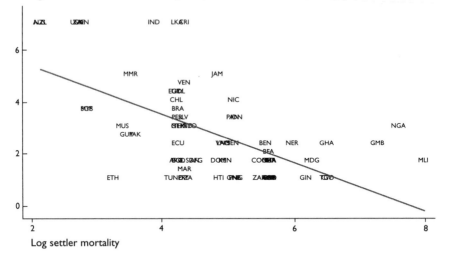

Log settler mortality

Much of the divergence in income per capita among the former colonies took place between 1750 and 1850, when countries with good institutions took advantage of industrialization and modernization opportunities, and those with extractive institutions failed to do so (see Acemoglu, Johnson, and Robinson, 2002). This pattern is true not just for former colonies, but for all countries. No country became relatively rich in the 19th century with "bad" institutions. The countries that became relatively rich by 1914 are, with very few exceptions, the countries that are relatively rich today. Former colonies allow us to examine carefully the relationship between historically-determined institutions and growth, but the relationship we find for these countries in all likelihood holds much more generally.

Returning to the source of variation in institutions, note that malaria and yellow fever caused the majority of European deaths during the early colonization period. Although these diseases were fatal to Europeans who had no immunity, the diseases had much less effect on indigenous adults who had developed various types of immunities. These diseases are therefore unlikely to be the reason that many countries in Africa and Asia are poor today (Figure 13.6). More generally, when we measure the effect of institutions correctly, there is no evidence that the large income differences between former colonies are due to geography, religion, or culture (for a more detailed analysis, see Acemoglu, Johnson, and Robinson, 2001).

There are other examples of differences in economic outcomes due to exogenous differences in institutions. For example, in the 1930s, the level of per capita

FIGURE 13.6 **Log Income per Capita in 1995 versus Log Settler Mortality**

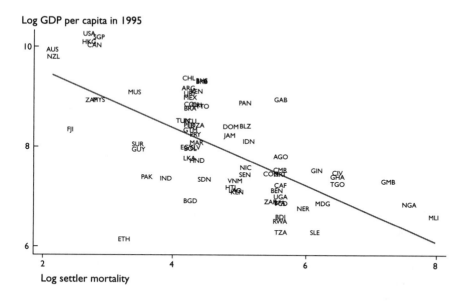

Log GDP per capita in 1995

Log settler mortality

income was roughly similar throughout what was to become North and South Korea; if anything, there was more industry to the north of the 38th parallel. North Korea was captured by the Soviet Union in the dying days of World War II, and a communist regime was imposed. The divergence in per capita income since that time has been remarkable, particularly with South Korea growing rapidly since the 1960s. Again, the evidence suggests that institutions do have a first-order impact on economic prosperity.

Of course, other factors must contribute at least partially to income per capita differences across countries. For example, an increasingly influential view is that many countries, especially those in Africa and South Asia, are poor largely because their populations are unhealthy (Gallup and Sachs, 2000). Bloom and Sachs (1998) argue that poor health conditions in Africa explain a substantial part of the difference between African growth rates and the average growth rates of other countries. More generally, Gallup, Sachs, and Mellinger (1999, p. 5) write, "tropical regions are hindered in development relative to temperate regions, probably because of higher disease burdens and limitations on agricultural productivity." However, once we control for institutions, these variables are no longer significant in cross-country regressions (see Acemoglu, Johnson, and Robinson, 2001). Based on the evidence to date, institutions are by far the most important explanation for cross-country long-term income growth.

INSTITUTIONS AND INSTABILITY

Institutions influence economic development. Do they also affect economic and political stability? Theoretically, a society where elites and politicians are effectively constrained should experience less infighting between various groups trying to take control of the state. If this is the case, the country is likely to pursue more sustainable policies (see Acemoglu et al., 2002, for a formal model of this reasoning). In this view, the cluster of institutions protecting property rights may determine whether there will be significant swings in the political and social environment leading to crises, and whether politicians will be induced to pursue unsustainable policies in order to remain in power in the face of deep social cleavages.

The problem with assessing the effect of institutions on stability is, again, that it is difficult to determine cause and effect and there may be other, "omitted," variables that may be driving everything. Do weaker institutions cause more instability or do more unstable countries have trouble developing strong institutions? Is there an omitted explanation, for example the importance of geographic variables such as latitude, temperature, or disease environment? Just as with income per capita, we can use the historically-determined component of institutions to sort out causation.

Looking only at former colonies, there is a surprisingly strong relationship between European settler mortality rates and various measures of instability and crises over the past 30 to 40 years. This relationship holds for a wide variety of crisis measures, such as overall volatility (standard deviation of growth), severity of crises (worst output drop), largest real exchange rate depreciation, banking crises, and political crises. The relationship also holds for a range of time periods, such as 1970 to 1997, or 1960 to 1997, or 1980 to 1997.

Figure 13.7 shows the relationship between the volatility of output from 1970 to 1997 and European settler mortality. Countries that had higher settler mortality historically have more unstable output levels today. Figure 13.8 plots the size of the largest output drop against log settler mortality. Again, countries with higher settler mortality experienced larger output drops over the last 30 years. Figure 13.9 shows that if we look only at the largest real exchange rate depreciation (a measure of the biggest exchange rate crisis), there is a similar relationship.

The relationship between institutions and instability generally holds if we control for macroeconomic policies. The weak institutions-instability link is still present if we also control for obvious shocks, such as movements in the terms of trade (the ratio of export to import prices). The same relationship holds if we restrict the sample to countries with greater than median world income or to former British colonies.

Institutions shaped by differential European settlement patterns appear to affect instability. In other words, not only did societies that inherited extractive institutions from their colonial past fail to take advantage of development opportunities

FIGURE 13.7 **Volatility of Output Against Log Settler Mortality**

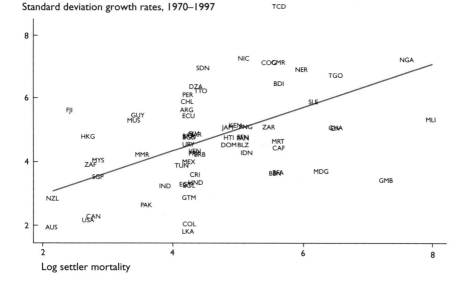

FIGURE 13.8 **Worst Output Drop Against Log Settler Mortality**

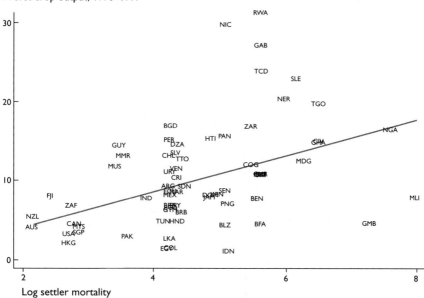

FIGURE 13.9 **Largest Real Exchange Rate Depreciation Against Log Settler Mortality**

Largest real exchange rate devaluation, 1970–1999

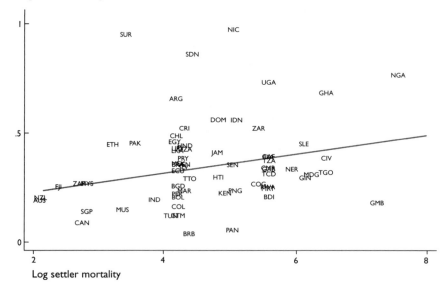

over the long run, but their recent medium-run experience has been characterized by frequent crises and substantial instability. Again, colonialism casts a long shadow; this is interesting in itself, and also helps us to identify the causal effect of institutions on stability.

The Asian crisis of 1997–1998 is an interesting and important recent case that confirms that institutions affect stability. While there is no agreement among economists about the relative importance of the current account, reserves, foreign debt, monetary policy, and fiscal policy for emerging markets in 1997–1998, there is widespread agreement that macroeconomic policies are important in particular instances. However, as Johnson et al. (2000) show, these variables do not have simple or direct effects in determining the extent of the crisis across emerging market countries in 1997–1998. This does not mean that macroeconomic factors were not important in the Asian crisis, but it does suggest that we should look more deeply at the underlying institutional issues. When we do this, institutions turn out to be a robust explanatory variable for the severity of the crisis across all emerging markets open to capital flows.

More generally, macroeconomic policies themselves may be largely an outcome of institutions. Looking at all former colonies, Acemoglu et al. (2002) show that institutions determine macroeconomic policies such as inflation and government spending. Distortionary macroeconomic policies are not typically chosen because politicians believe that budget deficits or other distortions are good for economic performance. More likely, these policies themselves are the result of deeper problems with institutions. Once we control for the effect of institutions on economic outcomes in this manner, standard macroeconomic variables, often blamed for economic crises and volatility, play a relatively minor role.

Overall, these results suggest that there is a first-order effect of institutions on economic and political instability. In short, institutional weaknesses not only cause slow growth over long periods of time (50 to 100 years), but are also associated with higher volatility and instability over shorter time periods (20 to 40 years). Why would there be such a relationship between institutions and instability? The most likely explanation is that institutionally-weak societies are unable to deal with their own economic and political shocks, and this leads to instability. Countries with weak institutions are more likely to suffer major "state failures" (as defined by the State Failures Taskforce, 1998). The problem is that these societies do not effectively constrain politicians—or the business elite—that control power, and this increases the willingness of various groups to fight for power (Acemoglu and Robinson, 2001; Do, 2002). It also enables such groups to expropriate investors, sometimes with disastrous consequences, when they do come to power.

A struggle for power can manifest itself in "bad" macroeconomic policies. For example, weak governments often feel the need to print money in order to stay in power (see the cases of Chiang Kai-shek in China during the 1940s or the Bolshevik regime in its early days). From the point of view of politicians, of course, the choice is not between good and bad policies, but between defeat and victory.

UNBUNDLING INSTITUTIONS: POLITICS VERSUS CORPORATE GOVERNANCE

The institutions that appear to most affect growth and stability are political, that is, those institutions concerning the governance of the state. However, it is hard to separate state governance issues from the governance of elites—after all, it is usually some elite group that captures or fights for control of the state. To make this clearer, we need to distinguish between elites expropriating resources through either their political power or their economic power. The relevant issue is, therefore, the extent to which elites are constrained when they control the state and when they control big businesses.

In this context, corporate governance of firms may also matter for economic stability. By corporate governance we mean the effectiveness of mechanisms that minimize agency conflicts involving managers, particularly the legal rules that prevent managers from expropriating assets belonging to minority shareholders. Compared with the political dimension of institutions, these issues are more concerned with micro-level expropriation; that is, can a majority shareholder in one company "take the money and run" from outside minority shareholders, bondholders, and banks?

Corporate governance is clearly a political outcome that reflects the power of elites. When business elites are strong relative to the state and feel that their property rights are protected, they are encouraged to invest. At the same time, however, these elites may prefer to have limited investor protection and consequently weak corporate governance at the firm level. In contrast, when minority investors have some political power, we are more likely to see effective legal protection for investors and stronger corporate governance.

There is no robust, simple correlation between corporate governance and economic growth or instability in the broad sample of former colonies that allows us to measure the historically-determined component of institutions more precisely. This is partly because corporate governance and political governance are highly correlated, so it is hard to sort out their effects. For most developing countries, political institutions are so weak and the risk of expropriation by the state so high that firms cannot raise outside capital, so there is no incentive to adopt meaningful investor protection. Highly extractive political institutions lead to very weak corporate governance.

To find the effects of corporate governance *per se* we need to look at a narrower set of samples, where political governance does not vary much. For example, in a set of countries with some basic private property rights, Rajan and Zingales (1998) found that where investor protection is weak, external funds-intensive sectors are less likely to develop. Weak investor protection creates an effective barrier to entry for new business—if it is not possible to make a meaningful commitment to outside investors, then it is much harder to raise large amounts of capital.

Recent evidence also suggests that when investor protection is weak, sectors that make intensive use of external funds experience greater instability (Raddatz, 2002). The intuition here is that these sectors can attract funding during boom times, but when there is a downturn, no funding is available.

These effects are probably more important for middle-income countries today. Johnson et al. (2000) show that among emerging markets open to capital flows, those with weaker political and financial institutions experienced more severe crises during the late 1990s, suggesting an important interaction between global shocks and investor protection (see also Eichengreen and Bordo, 2002). Asian firms with weaker corporate governance also suffered larger stock-price declines during the 1997–1998 crisis (Mitton, 2002). For these countries, weak corporate governance interacts with portfolio flows of capital (by both domestic and foreign investors) to create instability.

There is a simple theoretical explanation for this phenomenon. If weak institutions mean that expropriation by managers increases when the expected rate of return on investment falls, then an adverse shock to investor confidence will lead to increased expropriation as well as lower capital inflow and greater attempted capital outflow from a country. These, in turn, will translate into lower stock prices and a depreciated exchange rate—a special case of the general link we find between economic instability and institutions. In the case of the Asian crisis, corporate governance provides at least as convincing an explanation for the extent of exchange rate depreciation and stock market decline as any or all of the usual macroeconomic arguments.

The Bangkok Bank of Commerce is a well-documented example of expropriation by managers that worsened as the bank's financial troubles deepened. "As the losses mounted, Thai authorities say, more and more money was moved offshore, much of it through a now-defunct Russian bank .... [It] came to look like straight siphoning" (*Wall Street Journal*, May 10, 1999, p. A-6). The experience of creditors in Hong Kong who lent to firms doing business in mainland China is similar—Hong Kong-based company liquidators were not able to recover assets of Chinese companies that defaulted on loans (*Wall Street Journal*, August 25, 1999, p. A-14). More generally, very few debt defaults from the Asian crisis of 1997–1998 resulted in investors receiving any liquidation value. *The Economist* (January 30, 1999, p. 59) reports that "despite the creation last year of a bankruptcy law in Indonesia where there had been none before, it is still virtually impossible to force a defaulted debtor into liquidation (the few creditors that have tried are still tangled up in legal appeals)." During the crisis, Korean minority shareholders protested the transfer of resources out of large firms, including Samsung Electronics and SK Telecom. Most collapses of banks and firms in Russia after the devaluation of August 1998 were associated with complete expropriation; creditors and minority shareholders got nothing (Troika Dialog, 1999).

In most of these instances, management was able to transfer cash and other assets out of a company with outside investors, perhaps to pay the management's personal debts, shore up another company with different shareholders, or deposit into a foreign bank account. The fact that management in most emerging markets is also the controlling shareholder makes these transfers easier to achieve. The downturns in these countries have been associated with significantly more expropriation of cash and tangible assets by management.

Weak corporate governance can prevent entry and growth by new entrepreneurs because it makes it harder for new entrepreneurs to attract capital. In addition, if there is a negative shock, with weaker corporate governance the powerful controlling shareholders—usually part of the elite—can protect themselves. Weak corporate governance can therefore affect both the distribution of losses in a crisis and, if investors anticipate these problems, make crises more intense.

The work of Mitton (2002) suggests that firms can, to some extent, help themselves by improving their corporate governance relative to the country average. Firms that have done well recently in Korea, for example, are those that have responded—at least to some extent—to shareholder pressure. However, it is hard for a firm to escape its home-country institutions. Even the best firm in Indonesia today is held back and made vulnerable by that country's weak political institutions and almost nonexistent protections for investors.

IMPLICATIONS

Research on the link between weak institutions and instability is still at a relatively early stage. However, there are already some important implications for policymakers and business.

The most important point is that there appears to be some "fundamental" institutions that determine both long-run economic prosperity and medium-run economic instability. These institutions are the rules and practices that protect the property rights of investors, including large and small entrepreneurs. The most important form of protection is probably against the risk of expropriation by government or—just as important—powerful large businesses. Corporate governance is therefore an important part of the institutions that matter.

However, it is possible to grow with weak institutions (e.g., China today). The mere fact of high growth (even around 10 percent per annum) for a number of years does not mean that institutions are not a problem. Looking at growth over a 20-year period is far too short a time frame to evaluate whether or not per capita income will really rise in a sustained way. Our work suggests that weak institutions have a greater impact periodically, rather than a great impact every year; it is the huge crisis every 20 or 40 years that really derails development. It is likely that the interaction between institutions and shocks produces crises.

If there is no growth in a country and all entrepreneurs fear the power of the state, then allowing strong business groups to form may help to encourage investment. If there are a relatively few large entrepreneurs, they may feel protected relative to the state. In effect, the state is constraining itself by allowing the development of a "countervailing power." This is one reasonable interpretation for what happened in Botswana after independence, and also in Korea when General Park encouraged the creation of chaebol (business groups) in the 1960s and 1970s. This is a risky strategy, however, because there is a danger that these powerful business groups will capture the state and engage in expropriation and rent-seeking rather than investing to increase productivity. If this happens early in development, as in the Philippines under Ferdinand E. Marcos, then it can produce just another version of "extractive" institutions that is not consistent with sustained growth. If the state capture happens later in the development process, as may have occurred in South Korea during the 1980s and 1990s, then the only way out is by weakening the power of the business groups through democratization and corporate governance reform.

Seen in this context, proposals for reforming corporate governance need to place effective constraints on the business and political elite. Such constraints may develop for two reasons. First, income growth can lead to the development of a broad middle class that demands limits on the power of the business elite. This is what happened recently in South Korea. Second, there may be a temporary period of domestic consensus in which everyone agrees to commit to outside institutions, as in eastern Europe with regard to European Union (EU) accession. If politicians in Poland or Hungary, for example, want to expropriate investors today, it is now much harder, as the costs of breaking with the EU are huge. This same mechanism obviously helped western Europe sustain steady growth from the 1950s, and is an important reason why Spain and Portugal have grown rapidly since the 1980s.

The future for Latin America, the former Soviet Union, and some parts of Asia looks much less promising. In countries such as Russia, Indonesia, and Argentina, there are no effective constraints on politicians and business elites. This does not prevent growth—in fact, the cases of Tsarist Russia, Argentina 1880 to 1920, and Indonesia under Suharto clearly demonstrate that growth over a 20 to 40 year period is quite possible with weak political institutions and almost nonexistent corporate governance. But the historical record indicates that long-term growth, over a period of 50 years or more, is quite unlikely when institutions are weak. Before too long, there is likely to be a major crisis that derails development.

APPENDIX

Our data on the mortality of European settlers come largely from the work of Philip Curtin. Systematic military medical record-keeping began only after 1815, an attempt to understand why so many soldiers were dying in some places. The first detailed studies were retrospective and dealt with British forces between 1817 and 1836. The US and French governments quickly adopted similar methods (Curtin, 1989, p. 3 and 5). Some early data are also available for the Dutch East Indies. By the 1870s, most European countries published regular reports on the health of their soldiers.

The standard measure is annualized deaths per thousand mean strength. This measure reports the death rate among 1,000 soldiers where each death is replaced with a new soldier. Curtin (1989 and 1998) reviews in detail the construction of these estimates for particular places and campaigns, and assesses which data should be considered reliable.

Curtin (1989) deals primarily with the mortality of European troops from 1817 to 1848. In that time period modern medicine was still in its infancy, and the European militaries did not yet understand how to control malaria and yellow fever. These mortality rates can therefore be interpreted as reasonable estimates of settler mortality. They are consistent with substantial evidence from other sources (see, for example, Curtin, 1964 and Curtin, 1968). Curtin (1998) provides similar data on the mortality of soldiers in the second half of the 19th century. These numbers have to be used with more care because there was a growing awareness of how to avoid epidemics of the worst tropical diseases, at least during short military campaigns.

The main gap in the Curtin data is for South America, since the Spanish and Portuguese militaries did not keep good records of mortality. Gutierrez (1986) used Vatican records to construct estimates for the mortality rates of bishops in Latin America from 1604 to 1876. Because these data overlap with the Curtin estimates for several countries, we were able to construct a data series for South America. Combining data from a variety of sources will introduce measurement error in our estimates of settler mortality. Nevertheless, since we are using settler mortality as an instrument, this measurement error does not lead to inconsistent estimates of the effect of institutions on performance.

REFERENCES

Acemoglu, D., and J. A. Robinson. 2001. "A Theory of Political Transitions," *American Economic Review* 91, pp. 938–963.

Acemoglu, D., S. Johnson, and J. A. Robinson. 2001. "Colonial Origins of Comparative Development: An Empirical Investigation," *American Economic Review* 91, pp. 1369–1401.

Acemoglu, D., S. Johnson, and J. A. Robinson. 2002. "Reversal of Fortune: Geography and Institutions in the Making of the Modern World Income Distribution," *Quarterly Journal of Economics* 117, pp. 1231–1294.

Acemoglu, D., S. Johnson, and J. A. Robinson. Forthcoming. "Institutions, Volatility, and Crises." In Takatoshi Ito and Andrew Rose, eds, *Productivity, East Asia Seminar on Economics, Vol. 13*. Chicago: University of Chicago Press (forthcoming).

Acemoglu, D., S. Johnson, J. A. Robinson, and Y. Thaicharoen. 2002. "Institutional Causes, Macroeconomic Symptoms: Volatility, Crises, and Growth," NBER Working Paper No. W9124. Cambridge, MA. National Bureau of Economic Research.

Bloom, D. E., and J. D. Sachs. 1998. "Geography, Demography, and Economic Growth in Africa," *Brookings Papers on Economic Activity*, no. 2, pp. 207–295.

Curtin, P. D. 1964. *The Image of Africa*. Madison, WI: University of Wisconsin Press.

Curtin, P. D. 1968. "Epidemiology and the Slave Trade," *Political Science Quarterly* 83, pp. 181–216.

Curtin, P. D. 1989. *Death by Migration: Europe's Encounter with the Tropical World in the 19th Century*. New York: Cambridge University Press.

Curtin, P. D. 1998. *Disease and Empire: The Health of European Troops in the Conquest of Africa*. New York: Cambridge University Press.

Do, Q.-T. 2002. "Institutions, Institutional Change, and the Distribution of Wealth." Unpublished Paper, Department of Economics, Massachusetts Institute of Technology.

Edwards, S. 1989. "The International Monetary Fund and the Developing Countries: A Critical Evaluation." In K. Brunner and A. H. Meltzer, eds., *IMF Policy Advice, Market Volatility, Commodity Price Rules and Other Essays*. Amsterdam: Elsevier Science Publishers.

Eichengreen, B., and M. D. Bordo. 2002. "Crises Then and Now: What Lessons from the Last Era of Financial Globalization?" NBER Working Paper 8716. Cambridge, MA: National Bureau of Economic Research.

Esty, D., et al. 1998. *State Failure Task Force Report: Phase II Findings. Woodrow Wilson Environmental Change and Security Project Report* no. 5, Summer, pp. 49–72.

Gallup, J. L., and J. D. Sachs, with A. D. Mellinger. 1999. "Geography and Economic Development," CID Working Paper No. 1. Cambridge, MA: Harvard University.

Gallup, J. L., and J. D. Sachs. 2000. "The Economic Burden of Malaria," CID Working Paper No. 52. Cambridge, MA: Harvard University.

Gurr, T. R. 1997. "Polity II: Political Structures and Regime Change, 1800–1986." Unpublished Paper, University of Colorado, Boulder.

Gutierrez, H. 1986. "La Mortalité des Eveques Latino-Americains aux XVIIe et XVIIIe Siecles," *Annales de Demographie Historique,* pp. 29–39.

Hall, R. E., and C. I. Jones. 1999. "Why Do Some Countries Produce So Much More Output per Worker than Others?" *Quarterly Journal of Economics* 114, pp. 83–116.

Johnson, S., P. Boone, A. Breach, and E. Friedman. 2000. "Corporate Governance in the Asian Financial Crisis," *Journal of Financial Economics* 58, pp. 141–186.

Johnson, S., J. McMillan, and C. Woodruff. 2002. "Property Rights and Finance," *American Economic Review* 92, pp. 1335–1356.

Jones, E. L. 1981. *The European Miracle: Environments, Economies, and Geopolitics in the History of Europe and Asia*. New York: Cambridge University Press.

Knack, S., and P. Keefer. 1995. "Institutions and Economic Performance: Cross-Country Tests Using Alternative Measures," *Economics and Politics* 7, pp. 207–227.

La Porta, R., F. Lopez-de-Silanes, A. Shleifer, and R. W. Vishny. 1998. "Law and Finance," *Journal of Political Economy* 106, pp. 1113–1155.

Mauro, P. 1995. "Corruption and Growth," *Quarterly Journal of Economics* 110, pp. 681–782.

Mitton, T. 2002. "A Cross-Firm Analysis of the Impact of Corporate Governance on the East Asian Financial Crisis," *Journal of Financial Economics* 64, pp. 215–241.

North, D. C. 1981. *Structure and Change in Economic History*. New York: W. W. Norton & Co.

North, D. C., and R. P. Thomas. 1973. *The Rise of the Western World: A New Economic History*. Cambridge: Cambridge University Press.

Olson, M. 1982. *The Rise and Decline of Nations: Economic Growth, Stagflation, and Economic Rigidities*. New Haven, CT: Yale University Press.

Raddatz, C. E. 2002. "Liquidity Needs and Vulnerability to Financial Underdevelopment." Unpublished Research Paper, Massachusetts Institute of Technology.

Rajan, R., and L. Zingales. 1998. "Financial Dependence and Growth," *American Economic Review* 88, pp. 559–586.

Troika Dialog. 1999. *Corporate Governance in Russia*. Moscow, May.

Chapter 14

Of Legal Transplants, Legal Irritants, and Economic Development

Katharina Pistor and Daniel Berkowitz

The collapse of the socialist system has given way to unprecedented economic and legal reforms in the former socialist countries. Over the past decade they have enacted new legislation in all areas of the law, drawing heavily on legal models from developed market economies, including common law and civil law countries. While the transplanted laws now on the books is largely consistent with Western practice, the enforcement of these new laws is often ineffective (Berkowitz, Pistor, and Richard, 2003).

As surprising as these results may be for advocates of legal reform projects, they only reflect similar experiences in many other parts of the world that received wholesale legal transplants (Watson, 1974) of Western-style laws in the 19th and early 20th centuries. In many such cases, legal transplantation was part of the colonization of a country or territories. In other cases, countries that had just become independent decided to modernize their legal systems using, again, Western models. This is particularly true in Latin America. Legal transplantation was also used as a means to fend off further Western intrusion and assure a country's sovereignty in legal matters (Kolesar, 1990; Means, 1980). The best example of this is Japan during the Meiji Restoration (Haley, 1991).

As we have shown in earlier work, most countries that received Western laws in this fashion have not succeeded in putting these laws into effect. Despite the fact that many countries frequently received laws only shortly after they had been put on the books in the "origin" countries, more than 100 years later we find that transplant countries, by and large, have less effective legal institutions than origin countries, even when controlling for the level of GDP in these countries (Berkowitz, Pistor, and Richard, 2002).

We suggest several, not necessarily mutually exclusive, explanations for these results.

First, the transplanted laws may not have been a good match for countries that were economically less developed and lacked the legal expertise to make the imported laws work. Rather than promoting economic development, the imported laws were ignored and became defunct.

Second, formal legal ordering in the law-receiving country may be discredited by a political regime that uses the law primarily as an instrument to entrench its own position, thereby undermining the credibility of the law and legal institutions as a "neutral arbiter" (North, 1990).

Third, social ordering in the law-receiving country may predominantly take forms other than formal legal ordering. The causes for this may lie in economic backwardness, the fact that the political system has discredited formal law, or in cultural preferences for informal over formal ordering.

Fourth, the transplanted formal law may conflict with existing norms, be they formal or informal. The transplanted law may not be rejected outright; instead, it may irritate the preexisting order (Teubner, 2001). Over time, frictions may be ironed out through a process of adjusting the legal import and modifying some preexisting rules. The end result of this process, however, is likely to differ from the intention of the law importers.

This chapter surveys existing literature for examples of each of the four explanations given above. We focus on the organization of economic activities, in particular on the organization and governance of firms. At first glance economic activities appear to be the least affected by politics or culture and thus are most susceptible to legal reform by way of legal transplantation. Nevertheless, even here, we find evidence for the "transplant effect"; that is, the imperfect implantation of formal legal norms.

The chapter is organized as follows. The following section surveys the experience of legal transplants in several countries, giving examples for each of the four explanations advanced above. We then analyze legal reform in transition economies. We suggest that the most important factors that lead to outcomes different from the intention and prediction of law reformers are political factors that undermine the credibility of formal law as a neutral ordering device on the one hand, and legal irritation that results from a bad fit between imported law and preexisting institutions on the other. The last part of the chapter sketches an agenda for legal reform in light of the experiences discussed in the previous sections.

EXPERIENCE WITH LEGAL TRANSPLANTATION: LESSONS FROM COMPARATIVE HISTORY

Over the past 200 years, countries' experiences with legal transplantation has been rather dismal. Legal transplantation has, by and large, not resulted in institutional borrowing of a kind that would have allowed less developed countries to catch up with more advanced countries. Put differently, convergence in formal law between origin countries and legal transplants has done little to bridge the gap between legal and economic development across countries (Berkowitz, Pistor, and Richard, 2002).

There are several telling exceptions to this disappointing outcome. Countries with a population that was familiar with the principles of the transplanted laws have been much more successful in making the law work than countries without that predisposition. These countries include the so-called British settlers' colonies: Australia, New Zealand, and Canada. Following settlement, the immigrants from the colonial empire, who effectively brought over and began to use laws from England, soon outnumbered the indigenous population. The official declaration by the crown that England's law would apply in these territories only confirmed that English law had been transplanted. Transplant countries that have substantially adapted the received legal code to their particular circumstances have also successfully developed effective legal systems. Rather than accepting the transplanted code without substantial change, these countries selectively and frequently made changes in the process of incorporating foreign laws into their own legal system. The prime example is Japan during the Meiji Restoration (Haley, 1991). We call countries with a population that is familiar with transplanted laws and/or that adapted transplanted laws "receptive transplants." Our regression results show that such countries are statistically indistinguishable from the origin countries, while legal and economic development is significantly lower in unreceptive transplants. More generally, these examples suggest that the process of legal transplantation is crucial for the future development of an effective legal system. The laws that were transplanted to New Zealand or Australia were not substantially different from the laws transplanted to the Indian subcontinent. In the former territories, laws were received by a population that was familiar, if not with the details of the laws, with the basic principle on which they relied, such as the recognition of the freedom of contract and private property rights. In contrast, on the Indian subcontinent, imported laws were superimposed on populations that had hitherto been governed by quite different norms and legal rules (Hooker, 1988). The imported laws thus did not meet a demand and often was at odds with preexisting norms of behavior.

There are a number of different reasons for the lack of demand or the problem of an ill-fit between imported and preexisting norms. In the following, we illustrate each of the four explanations listed at the outset. We do not suggest that the list is exhaustive or that any of the examples gives a full account of a particular country's experience.

Economic backwardness

The example of Colombia offers the most detailed account of the impact of legal transplantation in a country where the economic and legal conditions were not ripe at the time of transplantation. In a detailed study of the reception of western European and, later, Chilean law, in Colombia during the 19th century, Means (1980) documents how laws were enacted and changed without any impact on economic outcomes and without much apparent understanding by lawmakers as to what the introduction or change of a particular set of legal rules might entail.

Colombia enacted its first commercial code in 1853, copying extensively from Spain, which in turn had used the French Code de Commerce of 1807 as a model for its first independent commercial code, the Codigo de Comercio of 1829 (Frey, 1999). At the time, Colombia was economically underdeveloped. Only a few large companies were operating in the country, and most had been chartered under imperial Spanish rules that had applied in Latin America prior to the dissolution of the Spanish empire. The law that served as a model for Colombia in 1853 was the Spanish code of 1848. In fact, Colombia copied the Spanish code word for word, with one crucial exception. The lawmakers deleted the 1848 requirement that for a company to be registered it needed to obtain special approval, or a concession, from the state authorities. In effect, Colombia introduced free registration of corporations. In light of legal developments in Europe at the time, this was quite revolutionary. England had introduced free incorporation only in 1844, France would do so only in 1867 and Germany in 1870 (Horn, 1979). Spain had introduced free registration already in the 1829 code; in response, the country experienced a major boom and subsequent bust of the market (Pistor et al., 2002). Because of this, the 1848 code re-introduced the concession system.

Colombia ignored this change. In contrast to Spain, however, the liberalization of market entry and the availability of the corporate form for every company that complied with the provisions of the statutory law, had virtually no impact. Most firms continued to operate as unincorporated partnerships in apparent ignorance of the protection that incorporation could have afforded them (Means, 1980). Thus, the change in the law did not cause a boom in new entries, which could have been followed by a market crash. Nevertheless, Colombia changed its commercial code again in 1887, this time copying the revised Chilean commercial code of 1865. Apparently, the revision was more a matter of prestige than economic demand. The Chilean code required two separate presidential decrees for every company that wished to become incorporated. Again, Colombia copied the code almost verbatim, thereby reversing its liberal incorporation practice (Means, 1980) without much impact on its economy. This is in marked contrast to the Spanish experience, where the reversal of the free registration in 1848 derailed the incorporation market, which in turn created an economic slowdown. In response, Spain moved back to a free registration system in 1868.

Legal transplantation of corporate code in Colombia is a striking example of a total lack of impact of transplantation; however, it is by no means an exception. There is substantial evidence from other transplant countries that company laws were largely ignored many decades after these laws were transplanted. While it is difficult to obtain direct evidence of actual use of laws in commercial practice, an important indicator for the lack of domestic demand for law is the absence of legal change over long periods of time and especially during periods of substantial socioeconomic change. Pistor and Wellons (1999), for example, show that many of the fast growing east and Southeast Asian countries had received their laws often long before the economic takeover and did not change these laws much during the first decades of the economic boom. [1]

However, in a study that traces the evolution of corporate law in 10 jurisdictions, including four origins and six transplants, Pistor et al. (forthcoming; 2002c) find that countries that transplanted laws from other jurisdictions on average changed their laws much more frequently than countries that developed their laws largely internally. Table 14.1 below summarizes the rate of legal change in the 10 jurisdictions. Because of the small sample size, no distinction is drawn between receptive and unreceptive transplants in the summary statistics. As can be easily seen, the rate of legal change has been much higher in transplant than in origin countries both prior to and after 1980. Interestingly, in the period following 1980 the rate of change in most transplants dropped substantially. This could suggest that legal transplants have finally taken hold. Still, the trend has not affected all countries. Moreover, given the increasing pressure exerted by international lending institutions on borrowing countries to change their laws according to "best practice" standards, it is difficult to assert that the higher rate of change is a response to domestic demand. Finally, it is also the case that rapid changes observed in the unreceptive transplants (Spain and Malaysia pre-1980 and Colombia over the entire period) exhibit a cyclical dynamic that contrasts with the more progressive and gradual process of legal change observed in origin countries.

TABLE 14.1   **Rate of Change in Corporate Law in 10 Jurisdictions**

	PRIOR TO 1980	SINCE 1980	LEGAL TYPE
France	17.1	3.8	Origin
Germany	13.2	6.0	Origin
UK	10.5	4.0	Origin
US	8.9	10.0	Origin
Spain	18.9	2.4	Unreceptive transplant
Chile	15.9	9.5	Receptive transplant
Colombia	21.6	29.0	Unreceptive transplant
Japan	10.1	2.5	Receptive transplant
Israel	51.0	6.7	Receptive transplant
Malaysia	25.5	5.0	Unreceptive transplant
Mean Origin Countries	*12.4*	*5.95*	
Mean Transplant Countries	*23.6*	*9.18*	

Note: Rate of legal change refers to the average number of years between each major statutory legal change since the first enactment of a formal corporate law in any of these countries.

Source: Pistor et al. (2002c). Legal type taken from Berkowitz, Pistor, and Richard (2002).

Political regimes that discredit the rule of law

It has been observed in many historical studies of legal transplantation that formal laws designed to enhance entrepreneurial activity in fact deter it. As noted by the historian Professor William Kirby, one reason for this distortion of laws is that the state can commit itself neither to enforcing these particular laws or to the rule of law in general.

Kirby analyzed the market for medium-sized companies in Shanghai in the 1920s after the introduction of the first law for limited liability companies (LLCs)—closely held corporations—in China. To be legally recognized as an LLC, a company had to register with the official authorities. Only then could the company's owners benefit from the protection the law afforded them, namely that company creditors would have recourse against the company's assets, not, however, against the personal assets of the company's owners. The interesting feature of the market for medium-sized firms in Shanghai, Professor Kirby discovered, was that the majority of companies that called themselves limited liability companies and added the acronym to their names had in fact not registered and thus could not legally grant their owners limited liability protection. Kirby associated this phenomenon with the reluctance of Chinese entrepreneurs to have contact with government agencies that in the past had proved only too ready to use their power to the detriment of the entrepreneurs. In his own words, "it had become fashionable and modern to attach the term youxian gongsi (limited company) to almost any enterprise. But it was not in vogue to register with the government, even with the very weak central government of 1916–28" (Kirby 1995, p. 50).

As Bowen and Rose (1998) suggest, the "Kirby Puzzle" is not limited to China or to the question of incorporation. Many laws that might benefit investors, shareholders, creditors, and ultimately companies, such as disclosure requirements, but that would also reveal to the tax authorities the activities of the company in question, are frequently ignored in order to avoid contact with and possible intervention by a prerogative state or state agents that are not effectively constrained by law (Black, Kraakman, and Tarassova, 2000).

Put differently, introducing laws that are purportedly neutral in an environment where the rule of law does not apply to the state and its agents, will not produce the desired result—a finding that reflects the experience of the first law and development movement (Trubek and Galanter, 1974). Most economic actors are highly rational in the sense that they know the source of potential danger to their economic undertakings and they will avoid contact, even if this means foregoing some benefits this might hold for them.

This is not to suggest that entrepreneurial activities should not be governed by law and that the state should refrain from intervening in economic activities. The financial scandals that have plagued US financial markets over the past year or so provide ample evidence that lack of effective supervision and law enforcement may cause more harm than good. Indeed, markets reacted positively to the enactment of the

Sarbane/Oxley Act in July of 2002,[2] which sent a strong signal to directors, accountants, and lawyers that they may be held liable under criminal and civil law for similar
misconduct. This reaction indicates that there is substantial confidence not only in the
efficacy of the legal system, but also in the motives behind the harsher law enforcement mechanisms.

By contrast, in countries where the Kirby effect prevails, one would predict a
less sanguine market response to similar measures. The reason is that while stricter law
enforcement may not necessarily be used to support markets, it may also be used as a
pretext for government officials to suffocate potentially viable economic activities. In
fact, in China the announcement by the country's new chief regulator, Linda Chua, that
financial markets would be regulated more strictly in the future, has provoked rather
mixed reactions in China over the course of the last year,[3] indicating that the Chinese
government and its agencies still have problems signaling that their regulatory interventions are to support, rather than exploit, business activity.

Social ordering trumps legal ordering

The fact that different societies are governed by different sets of norms and
processes and that this may adversely affect the efficacy of legal transplantation has been
most famously stated by Montesquieu in 1748 (1748; and 1977). Because of cultural
differences across societies, it would be a *grand hasard*, a matter of luck or chance, for
norms that were developed in one society to hold in another.

There has been some debate about whether culture is indeed the factor that
prevents legal transplants from taking hold, or whether, at least in modern times, differences in the allocation of sociopolitical rights in society may be more important
(Kahn-Freund, 1974). However, the cultural argument still has much discursive power,
especially among scholars focusing on Asian societies. Many have argued that not only
do family or inheritance matter, but also how business affairs follow different rules in
these countries despite the extensive transplantation of Western law into the region.
The basic argument is that social relations in these countries are governed primarily
by informal norms, not by legal principles established in statutory or case law (Hamilton,
1998; Jones, 1994; Redding, 1990).

A well known example is the low litigation rates in Japan when compared with
Western countries at similar stages of economic development (Kawashima, 1963; Pistor
and Wellons, 1999). Other examples include the dominant role of the Japanese Ministry
of Finance during the high growth period after World War II and its use of administrative guidance rather than legal procedures (Upham, 1987); critically, however, (Weinstein
and Beason, 1994).

A difficult question in this debate has been whether the differences we observe
in the actual practice of law can be attributed to culture, or whether it is the result of
institutional design that may be justified by reference to culture but that, in fact, pro-

tects an entrenched political elite (Ramseyer, 1996). The decision to control the number of lawyers entering the attorneys' market (Haley, 1978) or to set court fees at a level that makes it difficult for small shareholders to bring action (West, 2001), may indeed reflect cultural preferences as well as political calculus.

For our purpose, the major point is that either way, the transplanted law will perform differently in the host environment. Cultural difference may directly influence the relevance of law and therefore make a society less receptive to formal law—be it imported or home grown. Alternatively, key actors may use actual, perceived, or made-up differences in culture to justify the creation of institutional barriers that undermine the effectiveness of the imported law and legal institutions. As a result, it may be quite dangerous to rely on the similarities in the law on the books, because as attorneys familiar with Japanese legal practices have pointed out, "looks can be deceiving" (Beller, Terai, and Levine, 1992).

Legal irritants

The transplant metaphor used for our analysis so far implies that the introduction of foreign law may result in either outright rejection, or in reception. In fact, there are many intermediate solutions. Teubner (1998) uses the term "legal irritant" to describe such intermediate responses of a law-importing jurisdiction. The receiving legal system will not necessarily reject the transplanted law, but frictions between preexisting norms and regulations will be revealed. Smoothing these frictions will take time. Case law must develop and courts must interpret the new law in the context of preexisting norms and institutions. They are more likely to interpret the new law from the perspective of these preexisting norms and thereby adapt the foreign element into the system they have helped create. As a result, the foreign law becomes assimilated. It may at the margin change the preexisting organism, but it will also change its character.

Teubner uses the transfer of the contractual bona fide principle from continental European civil law systems into English law as an example and predicts that the end result of the assimilation process will be quite different from legal practice on the Continent. He argues that "under present conditions it is inconceivable that British good faith will be the same as *Treu und Glauben* German style" which is highly principled and doctrinal (Teubner, 2001, p. 427). Instead, "the predictable result will be a judicial doctrine of good faith that is much more 'situational' in character" (Teubner, 2001, p. 429). If transplanting law from Germany to England results in such different outcomes, one can extrapolate the impact foreign law may have on social legal systems that are even further apart than England and Germany.

Indeed, what Teubner may call a legal irritant may develop into a serious inflammation of the local system—to return once more to medical metaphors. Take the example of the establishment of formal legal institutions for credit contracts in 19th century India (Kranton and Swamy, 1999). Observing the extraordinarily high interest rates that monopoly lenders charged Indian peasants, the British colonizers decided to introduce land titling systems and courts with the explicit goal of improving the peasants' livelihoods by broadening the market for lenders. The immediate response was that—as expected and desired—the number of lenders willing to lend to peasants increased. As lenders could readily use courts to evict peasants that failed to live up to their contractual commitments, they needed to invest less in information collection and long-term relationships. Lower entry barriers resulted in a greater supply of lenders who, in the increasingly competitive market, also lent at lower rates. Nevertheless, a backlash occurred. The mass eviction of peasants eventually resulted in a peasant revolt, the sources of which were investigated by British colonial officials.

Examining these official reports and analyzing the structure of credit contracts before and after the introduction of reform, Kranton and Swamy (1999) argue that the failure of the reform project resulted from a misunderstanding of the underlying economic rationale of the monopolist lending market and that this misunderstanding ultimately gave way to fatal piecemeal reforms. Prior to the introduction of formal legal institutions, the relation between lenders and peasants, they argue, was not simply one of extortion, the high interest rates notwithstanding. There was an important insurance mechanism built in. Lenders knew their borrowers and were able to distinguish between peasants who were unwilling to pay and those who were unable to pay. When peasants were unable to pay because of bad harvests or natural disaster, lenders would not enforce the contract, but extended it or provided additional finance based on the promise that the full amount would be paid back in the future.

Once formal institutions were introduced, lenders could enter the market and extend credits without investing in information or establishing long-term relationships. While this indeed broke the monopoly of the few lenders that controlled the market previously, it also destroyed the insurance aspect of the lending relationship. The hazards of piecemeal reforms introduced an element into the Indian peasant economy that not only irritated the system, but ultimately derailed it. The British colonizers recognized a problem—exorbitant interest rates charged by monopoly lenders—but they either failed to grasp the complexity of the lending relationship or underestimated the impact of the relationship.

This example serves as a caution against the assumption that in countries without well-developed formal legal systems legal reform should be easy, as one to design the law "from scratch" (Black, Kraakman, and Hay, 1996). Formal law does not operate in isolation from other parts of the legal system or from nonlegal ordering mechanisms. As a result, legal reforms may not only be rejected but, worse, the irritation caused by ill-conceived legal reform may develop into a full blown inflammation.

LEGAL TRANSPLANTS IN TRANSITION ECONOMIES

The former socialist countries of central and eastern Europe have undergone extensive legal reforms over the past 10 years. The scale and scope of these reforms is comparable to the wholesale transplantation of formal legal systems in the 19th century. There is hardly an area of the law that was not affected by the overhaul of these countries' legal systems, including constitutional, administrative, civil, criminal, commercial, and procedural law, and laws governing the organization and jurisdiction of courts, regulators, and so on. It is difficult to assess to what extent these reforms were driven by domestic reforms and to what extent they were encouraged, if not conditioned, by multinational lending institutions, including the International Monetary Fund, the World Bank, and the European Bank for Reconstruction and Development (EBRD), or by the European Union (EU), with its demand on acceding member states to comply with the acquis communautaire, the existing EU set of rules and guidelines.

Whatever the trigger for legal reforms, the contents of legal rules reveal the extent of foreign legal assistance (Pistor, 2000). Tracing the evolution of statutory corporate and bankruptcy law, it is possible to show that the central and eastern European countries, as well as the Baltic states (i.e., countries with historical links to western European legal systems), reestablished these links by borrowing once more from Germany, Austria, and France. This trend was reinforced by the desire to join the EU and the requirement to comply with existing harmonization requirements, which are strongly influenced by German and French law (Edwards, 1999). By contrast, in several former Soviet Union republics, strong US legal influence is apparent especially in areas such as corporate law and securities market regulation. The Russian corporate law of 1996, for example, was based on a draft law produced by Professors Black and Kraakman of Columbia and Harvard Law Schools, respectively (Black and Kraakman, 1996). From Russia the model traveled to Armenia and Uzbekistan, and several other republics.

The purpose of these extensive legal reforms was to build an institutional infrastructure for a market economy. The impact of these reforms on economic outcome, however, is questionable. In an empirical study, Pistor, Raiser, and Gelfer (2000) seek to establish a relation between the level of shareholder and creditor rights protection in statutory law on the one hand, and the development of stock and credit markets on the other. They use statutory legal provisions as proxies for legal indicators; standard measures for financial market development, in particular market capitalization and market liquidity for stock markets; and the volume of claims banks hold against the private sector for credit markets. Finding no statistically significant relation between either the level of legal protection on the books or the change in the level of protection over time with actual market development, they conclude that 10 years into the reform process, the impact of legal reforms on economic outcome (here financial market development) remains unclear.

These results contrast with studies of 49 mostly Organisation for Economic Co-operation and Development countries, for which La Porta et al. (1997; 1998) have established that there is a positive relationship between legal protection on the one hand and financial market development on the other. Similarly, Johnson et al. (2000) have found that, for Asian financial markets, the level of investor protection did make an empirically measurable difference with respect to how these countries were able to weather the storm of the east Asian financial crisis. By and large, countries with better legal protection on the books faired better than those with questionable protection.

In an attempt to explain the absence of a measurable empirical link between legal reform and economic outcome in transition economies, we turn once more to the four explanations for why transplants may not work.

Economic backwardness

Economic backwardness does not appear to be a powerful explanation for the lack of an empirical link between laws and financial market development in transition economies. International comparisons suggest that there is a strong relationship between the overall economic development of a country and its financial market development (Claessens, Klingebiel, and Schmukler, 2002). A comparison of financial market development in transition economies with countries at similar levels of GDP shows that relative to the overall level of economic development transition economies have achieved, their markets are remarkably underdeveloped (EBRD, 1998; Pistor, Raiser, and Gelfer, 2000). In other words, these economies are on average not economically backwards, but their financial markets are. If, as La Porta et al. (1997) suggest, law is an important determinant for financial market development, legal change should have helped bridge the gap in financial market development to countries at similar levels of GDP. A possible answer for the absence of a measurable impact of legal reforms on economic outcome is that legal and institutional reforms take time. Most countries had opened stock exchanges only in the early 1990s, and so had only a few years to develop these markets. Moreover, their legal systems were undergoing a major overhaul, with few areas of the law untouched. While legal reforms may have been necessary, the scale of these reforms did not promote legal certainty or the predictability of the legal system.

Weak institutions provide an alternative explanation. Indeed, the only legal indicator that shows a marginally (at the 10 percent level) significant positive relationship with financial market development in transition economies is a measure for the existence of—at least nominally—an independent financial market regulator (Pistor, Raiser, and Gelfer, 2000).

The Kirby effect

The Kirby effect may offer yet another explanation for the absence of an empirical link between the law and economic outcome. A simple prediction that follows from

Kirby's analysis is that in countries with low levels of rule of law, changes in the law on the books can be irrelevant or cause a deterioration in the regulatory environment.

Survey data that use indicators, such as the risk of expropriation or contract repudiation by the government, the level of corruption, the effectiveness of the judiciary, and the observance of legal rules when transferring power or enforcing rights, are widely used to measure the effectiveness of legal institutions (Knack and Keefer ,1994; Mauro, 1995; Rodrik, 2000). Most of these indicators explicitly refer to the willingness of the state and its agents to abide by legal rules. In other words, they seem to be picking up the "classic" notion of the rule of law, which refers to law as a constraint on the arbitrary exercise of power by the state (Craig, 1997).

There is substantial empirical support that respect for the rule of law has highly influenced financial market development in transition economies and the economic reform process more generally. In particular, Pistor, Raiser, and Gelfer (2000) find that whereas changes in the law on the books have had little impact on financial market development, the level of rule of law as measured by perception data is highly correlated with financial market development. The lower the rule of law ratings, the less developed financial markets.

These findings suggest that technical legal assistance is a very limited approach to legal and economic reforms. Legal reforms that are undertaken in isolation to address the problem of how to hold the state and its actors accountable may not only be ineffective, but also counterproductive. The strong quest to push through reform by almost any means has in practice often meant that undemocratic, if not outright unconstitutional, measures were favored by policy advisors and local politicians who supported economic reforms. The extensive use of decree power by the Russian president during the Yeltsin area is a good example of this policy (Shevtsova, 2000). Government flexibility, and thus freedom from too many legal constraints, was hailed as a necessary condition for achieving the desired economic outcome. With hindsight, it appears that the price paid for these policies has been not only the weakening of the rule of law, but also the lack of sustainable economic and financial development. Just as the Kirby effect predicts, uncertainty about the objectives of state action and the extent of government intervention results in side-stepping the law. Further support for this argument is found in the substantial growth of the informal sector in transition economies throughout the 1990s (Johnson, Kaufmann, and Shleifer, 1997).

Social ordering trumps legal ordering

The size of the informal sector in transition economies, which in some countries is estimated to amount to 50 percent of GDP or more, indicates that social ordering plays an important role in these countries. Failure to pay taxes, setting up companies without registering in accordance with often onerous legal requirements, hiring workforce on the black market, and so on, leads economic actors to also opt out of the legal system meant to order private relations, including contract enforcement and the protection of property rights. Other mechanisms have taken the place of law. There is strong evidence that racketeering and Mafia-like organizations do play an important role in several transition economies. By giving parties recourse to physical force, they make commitments credible and punish those that do not hold their side of the bargain (Frye and Zhuravskaya, 2000).

An alternative to employing rackets is to adjust economic activities so that they are in line with the fact that effective enforcement mechanisms are not available. Based on extensive surveys of small entrepreneurs in Vietnam, McMillan and Woodruff (1999; 2000) show that the lack of formal legal institutions restrains entrepreneurs' ability to expand. Repeat deals, mutual monitoring, and reputation bonds limit actors to members of the same network of entrepreneurs, but do not allow them to breach these established spheres of exchange (Greif, 2001; Landa, 1981). Thus, over the long run, the absence of legal institutions to enforce contracts among previously unrelated parties may create a ceiling for economic activities.

In contrast to the Asian experience, preference for nonlegal over legal ordering in transition economies appears to be less the result of cultural factors and more the result of political ones. A history of autocracy has undermined the credibility of law and legal institutions as neutral and trustworthy governance devices (Newcity, 1997). Put differently, the preference for social over formal legal ordering may be a response to the Kirby effect, not a genuine feature of eastern European or Eurasian cultures.

Legal irritants

The transition from centrally planned to some form of market economies; from single-party political systems to more pluralistic, perhaps even democratic regimes; and from law primarily as an instrument to support the central-planning system and the dictatorship of the proletariat to a general framework for social ordering, amounted to a major regime change in countries that were part of the former Soviet Union. Many of the newly introduced laws, especially in countries that were not constrained by presocialist bodies of law, were designed to further this regime change. Little effort was devoted to fitting new laws into preexisting bodies of law and to thereby minimize the irritation to the preexisting legal order.

At first glance this sweeping approach to legal reforms is plausible. After all, why, if everything else is changing, should laws remain stable? Still, many countries had begun to reform their legal systems prior to the collapse of the socialist system; they had introduced new laws that paved the way for economic and legal reforms. Examples of reform efforts that preceded the official collapse of the socialist regimes include the 1987 enterprise law in Hungary, or the 1991 general principles of civil law that had been adopted by the Soviet Union, but that were scheduled to enter into force only on January 1, 1992, a time when the Soviet Union no longer existed.[4] Granted, these reform efforts were less sweeping and more gradual in nature. As such they had less appeal as a device to shift countries on to a different path of socioeconomic development.

An argument in favor of a more gradual approach to legal reform is that radical change increases uncertainty about the meaning of the law. The law is not self-explanatory; all relevant parties will not agree on one interpretation of the law. Because laws are designed to address a large number of persons for a long period of time, laws are bound to be incomplete (Pistor and Xu, 2002). Case law may, over time, narrow the scope of possible interpretations of statutory law and offer guidance as to how it is to be applied to particular fact patterns. The closer the fit between a new law and the preexisting order, the more likely that the meaning of the law can be understood and new legal principles assimilated into the preexisting order. The poorer the fit, the greater the uncertainty about the meaning of the law and the outcome of a case. Uncertainty about the outcome of a court case is bound to discourage, rather than encourage, litigation. If plaintiffs face not only the uncertainty of whether they have the evidence necessary to hold a party liable (Priest and Klein, 1984), but also whether the application of the relevant law would actually result in liability because the law's scope and meaning has not yet been defined, they may be reluctant to incur the cost of litigation. The remarkable decline in commercial litigation in Russia during the first years of transition (Pistor, 1996) lends support to this proposition. While a general mistrust about the quality and independence of the courts may be an alternative explanation, uncertainty about the law is likely to have exacerbated such concerns.

In sum, the transition process by definition resulted in a major irritation of the preexisting legal order. In an attempt to make a clear cut with the past, many countries moved swiftly to replace old laws and enact new ones that were copied from abroad. Foreign technical assistance programs greatly influenced which models were chosen to reform existing legal systems. Relatively little effort was devoted to ensure that the imported law would stick. Few countries afforded a strategy of "wait and see and pick and choose" (Soltysinski, 1998).

The result has been 10 years of continuing legal reforms. Many countries have not only enacted a corporate, bankruptcy, and/or commercial code, they have extensively amended, revised and reenacted two to three versions of these laws within a decade. This is in marked contrast to the experience of earlier transplants, where law often stagnated for decades. Stagnation indicated a lack of demand. The constant reinvention of the legal system may or may not be an indicator of demand. In a number of cases legal change came in response to difficulties encountered with the law in legal practice, and this can be considered demand driven. An example is the recent revision of the Russian bankruptcy law. However, in many cases, repeated change was either externally prescribed (e.g., the adoption of the *acquis communautaire* by newly acceding member states to the EU) or indicative of a trial and error process in which the failure of earlier reforms gives rise to new ones.

In sum, legal reforms in transition economies went far beyond introducing legal irritants in an otherwise unchanged system. The entire system was changed repeatedly over the course of only a decade. While a call for a halt may go too far, it is time to realize that statutory legal change has largely run out of simple solutions. Lawmakers will not be able to anticipate all future contingencies and include them into statutory law. As a result, each new law will be found to be deficient in the near future. This is not a problem limited to transition economies, but it is particularly virulent there because of the pace of regional socioeconomic change. Still, the solution to these problems does not seem to lie in yet further statutory legal change. Instead, there is a need to empower law enforcement agencies, be they courts or regulators, to enable them to apply existing laws flexibly and to exert limited lawmaking powers in doing so.

REFORMING LEGAL REFORM

The major conclusion we have drawn from the above observations is that legal reform itself is in need of reform. The underlying assumption of most past and current reform projects is that there is something like "best practice" that could be captured in legal standards and exported to less advanced countries. Further, such projects imply that these standards, once put in place, will function as intended and indeed not much differently from they did in their home country.

Over 200 years of large scale legal transplantation should caution against such assumptions. The past decade of legal reforms in transition economies offer additional evidence that this type of law reform project is misguided. Most important, it underestimates the complexity of legal systems, and by implication, what it takes to create one. An effective legal system is not simply the result of a perfect design at one point in time. To be effective, legal systems must change; they must be able to respond to continuous challenges that arise from changing political, technological, and socioeconomic conditions. The most vivid recent example illustrating the need for this flexibility is the scandals that have affected US financial markets. Until only a year ago, the US laws were hailed as a model for superior financial market regulation. The fact that the system experienced a major crisis should not fundamentally alter this assessment. What counts is how the system responds to the problems the crisis revealed.

It should be self-evident that responses may, or rather, should, differ from country to country and from legal system to legal system. It is a sign that a legal system is mature when it is capable of assimilating foreign elements into its legal system and of enabling specific responses to be found to new challenges that are meaningful within the constraints of its own institutional setup. Viewed in this light, the prediction that English law will assimilate the contractual bona fide principle imported from the Continent in ways that may be difficult to swallow by civil law lawyers is not a defeat of legal transplantation, but demonstrates successful incorporation of foreign law.

By contrast, the legal systems in many emerging markets and developing countries lack similar absorption capacity. The history of wholesale legal transplantation has not furthered these countries' capacity to create conditions for a self-sustainable process of legal innovation and change. On the contrary, one may argue that wholesale transplantation has hindered such a process, as incremental learning processes were displaced by a series of sweeping legal reforms. Regulators may have sought to fix problems, but in fact problems were only exacerbated because the source of the problem lies not in a particular set of rules, but in the absence of conditions that encourage institutional change and adaptation.

Luckily, there are examples from which to learn. Take the case of the receptive transplants—in particular, adaptive transplants, that is, countries that adapted foreign law in the process of incorporating it into their home jurisdiction. This process of statutory assimilation seems to have facilitated the incorporation of important foreign concepts into domestic law. While this process has also changed the imported law, the net effect of that law is likely to have been greater than in countries that blindly adopted the law presented to them. The example of Colombia's development of corporate law in the 19th century is a case in point.

Reforming the process of law reform will slow down the pace of legal reforms; this, as argued above, is indeed desirable. It will give local actors a greater say in the process of picking and choosing laws. Obviously, this increases the chances that—at least in the eyes of policy advisors—a suboptimal solution may be chosen. But the tradeoff is that the optimal solution may fail because it is ignored or because it produces unintended side effects. Alternatively, entrenched political elites may use the law to further their position but traditional law reform projects have hardly avoided this outcome. Outsiders have limited leverage as to how laws are applied in practice. A viable solution to this dilemma is to halt legal reforms in countries where there are serious concerns about the abuse of law and the prevalence of the Kirby effect. Experience with economic development projects in general have shown that foreign aid works when there is local support and participation (World Bank, 1998). The same applies to legal reforms.

NOTES

1   Five of the economies included in this study (Hong Kong, India, Malaysia, Singapore, and South Korea) are coded as unreceptive transplants in Berkowitz, Pistor, and Richard, (2002). China, however, has not been coded.

2   See http://corporate.findlaw.com/industry/corporate/docs/publ107.204.html

3   *Caijiing* (trans: *Finance*). Interview with Shi Meilun, former deputy chair of Hong Kong's Securities and Futures Commission and deputy chairwoman of CSRC (in Chinese). January 20, 2002.

4   After going back and forth, the principles were enacted in the Russian Federation, as law-makers realized that abolishing all the laws of the Soviet Union effectively catapulted Russian law backward rather than forward, because it took some time to fill the legal vacuum left by the demise of the Soviet Empire.

REFERENCES

Beller, A. L., T. Terai, and R. M. Levine. 1992. "Looks Can Be Deceiving: A Comparison of Initial Public Offering Procedures under Japanese and U.S. Securities Laws," *Law and Contemporary Problems* 55, pp. 77–118.

Berkowitz, D., K. Pistor, and J.-F. Richard. 2002. "Economic Development, Legality, and the Transplant Effect," *European Economic Review* 47, pp. 165–195.

Berkowitz, D., K. Pistor, and J.-F. Richard. 2003. "The Transplant Effect," *American Journal of Comparative Law* (forthcoming).

Black, B., and R. Kraakman. 1996. "A Self-Enforcing Model of Corporate Law," *Harvard Law Review* 109, pp. 1911–1982.

Black, B., R. Kraakman, and J. Hay. 1996. "Corporate Law from Scratch." In R. Frydman, C. W. Gray and A. Rapaczynski, eds., *Corporate Governance in Eastern Europe and Russia*. Budapest: Central European University Press.

Black, B., R. Kraakman, and A. Tarassova. 2000. "Russian Privatization and Corporate Governance: What Went Wrong?" *Stanford Law Review* 52, pp. 1731–1803.

Bowen, R. J. II, and D. C. Rose. 1998. "On the Absence of Privately Owned, Publicly Traded Corporations in China: The Kirby Puzzle," *Journal of Asian Studies* 57, pp. 442–452.

Claessens, S., D. Klingebiel, and S. L. Schmukler. 2002. "The Future of Stock Exchanges: Determinants and Prospects," *European Business Organization Law Review* 3, no. 2.

Craig, P. 1997. "Formal and Substantive Conceptions of the Rule of law: An Analytical Framework," *Public Law*, pp. 467–487.

European Bank for Reconstruction and Development (EBRD). 1998. *Transition Report: Financial Sector in Transition*. London: European Bank for Reconstruction and Development.

Edwards, V. 1999. *EC Company Law*. Oxford: Oxford University Press.

Frey, M. 1999. *Die spanische Aktiengesellschaft im 18. Jahrhundert und unter dem Código de Comercio von 1829*. Frankfurt: Peter Lang.

Frye, T., and E. Zhuravskaya. 2000. "Rackets, Regulation, and the Rule of Law," *Journal of Law, Economics and Organization* 16, pp. 478–502.

Greif, A. 2001. "Impersonal Exchange and the Origins of Markets: From the Community Responsibility System to Individual Legal Responsibility in Pre-modern Europe." In M. Aoki and Y. Hayami, eds., *Communities and Markets in Economic Development*. Oxford: Oxford University Press.

Haley, J. O. 1978. "The Myth of the Reluctant Litigant," *Journal of Japanese Studies* 4, pp. 366–389.

Haley, J. O. 1991. *Authority Without Power*. New York: Oxford University Press.

Hamilton, G. G. 1998. "Culture and Organization in Taiwan's Market Economy." In R. W. Hefner, ed., *Market Cultures—Society and Morality in the New Asian Capitalism*. Boulder, Co: Westview Press.

Hooker, M. B. 1988. *Laws of South-East Asia: European Laws in South-East Asia*. 2 vols. Vol. II. Singapore: Butterworth.

Horn, N. 1979. "Aktienrechtliche Unternehmensorganisation in der Hochindustrialisierung (1860–1920), Deutschland, England, Frankreich und die USA im Vergleich." In N. Horn and J. Kocka, eds., *Recht und Entwicklung der Großunternehmen im neunzehnten und frühen zwanzigsten Jahrhundert (Law and the Formation of Big Enterprise in the 19th and Early 20th Century)*. Göttingen: Vandenhoeck & Ruprecht.

Johnson, S., P. Boone, A. Breach, and E. Friedman. 2000. "Corporate Governance in the Asian Financial Crisis 1997–98," *Journal of Financial Economics* 58, pp. 141–186.

Johnson, S., D. Kaufmann, and A. Shleifer. 1997. "The Unofficial Economy in Transition," *Brookings Papers on Economic Activity* pp. 159–221.

Jones, C. A. G. 1994. "Capitalism, Globalization and Rule of Law: An Alternative Trajectory of Legal Change in China," *Social & Legal Studies* 3, pp. 195–221.

Kahn-Freund, O. 1974. "On Uses and Misuses of Comparative Law," *The Modern Law Review* 37, pp. 1–27.

Kawashima, T. 1963. "Dispute Resolution in Contemporary Japan." In V. Mehren and A. Taylor, eds., *Law in Japan, The Legal Order in a Changing Society*. Cambridge, MA: Harvard University Press.

Kirby, W. 1995. "China Unincorporated: Company Law and Business Enterprise in Twentieth-Century China," *The Journal of Asian Studies* 54, pp. 43–63.

Knack, S., and P. Keefer. 1994. "Institutions and Economic Performance: Cross-Country Tests Using Alternative Institutional Measures," *Economics and Politics* 7, pp. 207–227.

Kolesar, R. J. 1990. "North American Constitutionalism and Spanish America: 'A Special Lock Ordered by Catalogue, Which Arrived With the Wrong Instructions and No Keys?'" In G. Athan Billias, ed., *American Constitutionalism Abroad*. New York: Greenwood Press.

Kranton, R., and A. Swamy. 1999. "The Hazards of Piecemeal Reform: British Civil Courts and the Credit Market in Colonial India," *Journal of Development Economics* 58, pp. 1–24.

La Porta, R., F. Lopez-de-Silanes, A. Shleifer, and R. W. Vishny. 1997. "Legal Determinants of External Finance," *Journal of Finance* 52, pp. 1131–1150.

La Porta, R., F. Lopez-de-Silanes, A. Shleifer, and R. W. Vishny. 1998. "Law and Finance," *Journal of Political Economy* 106, pp. 1113–1155.

Landa, J. T. 1981. "A Theory of The Ethnically Homogeneous Middleman Group: An Institutional Alternative to Contract Law," *Journal of Legal Studies* 10, pp. 349–362.

Mauro, P. 1995. "Corruption and Growth," *Quarterly Journal of Economics* 110, pp. 681–712.

McMillan, J., and C. Woodruff. 1999. "Interfirm Relationships and Informal Credit in Vietnam," *Quarterly Journal of Economics* 114, pp. 1285–1320.

McMillan, J., and C. Woodruff. 2000. "Private Order Under Dysfunctional Public Order," *Michigan Law Review* 98, pp. 2421–2458.

Means, R. C. 1980. *Underdevelopment and the Development of Law*. Chapel Hill, NC: University of North Carolina Press.

Montesquieu, C. L. 1748. *De L'Esprit des Lois*. Geneva: Barrilot & Fils.

Montesquieu, C. L. 1977. *The Spirit of Laws*. Berkeley: University of California Press.

Newcity, M. 1997. "Russian Legal Tradition and the Rule of Law." In J. Sachs and K. Pistor, eds., *The Rule of Law and Economic Reform in Russia*. Boulder, CO: Westview Press.

North, D. C. 1990. *Institutions, Institutional Change, and Economic Performance*. Cambridge: Cambridge University Press.

Pistor, K. 1996. "Supply and Demand for Contract Enforcement in Russia: Courts, Arbitration, and Private Enforcement," *Review of Central and East European Law* 22, pp. 55–87.

Pistor, K. 2000. "Patterns of Legal Change: Shareholder and Creditor Rights in Transition Economies," *European Business Organization Law Review* 1, pp. 59–110.

Pistor, K., Y. Keinan, J. Kleinheisterkamp, and M. West. Forthcoming. "Legal Evolution and the Transplant Effect." Online. http://www.law.columbia.edu/pistor/legal%20Evolution.pdf. *World Bank Research Observer*.

Pistor, K., Y. Keinan, J. Kleinheisterkamp, and M. West. 2002. "The Evolution of Corporate Law," *University of Pennsylvania Journal of International Economic Law* 23, no. 4.

Pistor, K., Y. Keinan, J. Kleinheisterkamp, and M. West. 2002c. "Innovation in Corporate Law: A Comparative Analysis of 10 Jurisdictions." (working draft)

Pistor, K., M. Raiser, and S. Gelfer. 2000. "Law and Finance in Transition Economies," *The Economics of Transition* 8, pp. 325–368.

Pistor, K., and P. Wellons. 1999. *The Role of Law and Legal Institutions in Asian Economic Development*. Hong Kong: Oxford University Press.

Pistor, K., and C. Xu. 2002. "Incomplete Law: A Conceptual and Analytical Framework and its Application to Financial Market Regulation," CLS Working Paper. New York: Columbia Law School.

Priest, G. L., and B. Klein. 1984. "The Selection of Disputes for Litigation," *Journal of Legal Studies* 13, pp. 1–55.

Ramseyer, J. M. 1996. "Odd Markets in Japanese History: Law and Economic Growth." In J. E. Alt and D. C. North, eds., *Political Economy of Institutions and Decisions*. Cambridge: Cambridge University Press.

Redding, S. G. 1990. *The Spirit of Chinese Capitalism*. De Gruyter Studies in Organization, 22. Berlin: Walter de Gruyter.

Rodrik, D. 2000. "Institutions for High-Quality Growth: What They Are and How to Acquire Them," *Studies in Comparative International Development* 35, pp. 3–31.

Shevtsova, L. 2000. "The Problem of Executive Power in Russia," *Journal of Democracy* 11, pp. 32–39.

Soltysinski, S. 1998. "Transfer of Legal Systems as Seen by the 'Import Countries': A View from Warsaw." In U. Drobnig, K. J. Hopt, H. Kötz and E.-J. Mestmäcker, eds., *Systemtransformation in Mittel- und Osteuropa und ihre Folgen für Banken, Börsen und Kreditsicherheiten.* Tübingen: Mohr Siebeck.

Teubner, G. 1998. "Rechtsirritationen: Der Transfer von Rechtsnormen in rechtssoziologischer Sicht." In J. Brand and D. Strempel, eds., *Soziologie des Rechts: Festschrift für Erhard Blankenburg zum 60. Geburtstag.* Baden-Baden: Nomos Verlag.

Teubner, G. 2001. "Legal Irritants: How Unifying Law Ends up in New Divergences." In P. A. Hall and D. Soskice, eds., *Varieties of Capitalism.* Oxford: Oxford University Press.

Trubek, D. M., and M. Galanter. 1974. "Scholars in Self-Estrangement: Some Reflections on the Crisis in Law and Development Studies in the United States," *Wisconsin Law Review,* pp. 1062–1102.

Upham, F. K. 1987. *Law and Social Change in Postwar Japan.* Cambridge, MA: Harvard University Press.

Watson, A. 1974. *Legal Transplants: An Approach to Comparative Law.* Edinburgh: Scottish Academic Press; London: distributed by Chatto and Windus.

Weinstein, D. E., and R. Beason. 1994. *Growth, Economies of Scale, and Targeting in Japan (1955–1990).* Cambridge, MA: Harvard Institute of Economic Research.

West, M. 2001. "Why Shareholders Sue: The Evidence from Japan," *Journal of Legal Studies* 30, p. 351.

World Bank. 1998. *Assessing Aid: What Works, What Doesn't, and Why.* New York: Oxford University Press for the World Bank.

Governance Seen by the Minority Shareholder

Chapter 15

Portfolio Investment in Emerging Markets:
An Investor's Perspective
Michael J. Johnston

The issue of corporate governance reform in emerging markets has recently become one of the most discussed topics in financial circles. It's understandable that today's academics, business people, investors, economists, and policymakers are eager to help emerging markets improve their standards of corporate governance. The most up-to-date research has shown that, particularly in emerging-market nations, improvements in corporate governance can lead to much greater equity valuation for individual countries. Since access to capital is a significant factor in growth, better corporate governance standards may play a significant role in helping the world's newest market economies realize their full economic potential.

Growth in emerging markets is especially crucial in light of the fact that such nations are home to most of the world's population. It is expected that over the next twenty years, these countries will constitute two thirds of the world's economic growth (see Figure 15.1). Given the fact that most of this growth will come from commercial enterprise not state-directed enterprise, corporate governance issues in emerging markets become critically important to this nexus of growth.

Corporate governance is the set of interlocking rules by which corporations, shareholders, and management govern their behavior. In any given country, the legal system helps set some corporate governance standards; others are determined by corporations themselves. The issue of corporate governance goes far beyond questions of the most effective management. A corporation's management may be deemed by shareholders to be doing an effective job, and yet the governance of the entity may be inadequate—this is the case, for example, where the management of a profitable and productive corporation is nevertheless siphoning off funds for their own purposes.

The question of appropriate standards of corporate governance is all the more important given the role of corporations in modern life. Corporations dominate the economies of market-driven countries. Corporations employ the majority of

I should like to thank Elizabeth A. Johnston for her able research and editing assistance.

FIGURE 15.1 **Expected GDP Growth by Region**

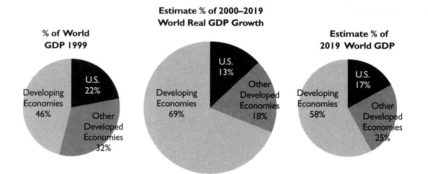

% of World
GDP 1999

Estimate % of 2000–2019
World Real GDP Growth

Estimate % of
2019 World GDP

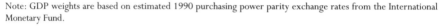

Note: GDP weights are based on estimated 1990 purchasing power parity exchange rates from the International Monetary Fund.

Source: Author's estimates

people, they provide most of the goods and services, and they utilize the second largest segment of resources (second to households). Since corporations are so vital to market-driven economies, the governance of corporations is a public issue as well as a private issue.

From an investor's perspective, corporate governance is a crucial factor in determining initially whether or not to invest in a country or company, and indeed in deciding whether to maintain investments over the years. The Capital Group Companies has been a major investor in emerging markets since 1979. We currently invest about USD 30 billion of our clients' assets in emerging markets. Our rich experience in the area has structured the way we think about corporate governance issues in what many experts believe will be the fastest-growing economies in the world.

WHY IS CORPORATE GOVERNANCE SO IMPORTANT TO AN INVESTOR IN EMERGING MARKETS?

Corporate governance is so essential to our investment decisions because it allows us to trust in our investment. A well-governed company has trustworthy and honest managers. Good corporate governance provides shareholders and the public with reliable reports and financial information. It makes sure that decisions will incorporate the best interests of all shareholders, including foreign or minority shareholders. It ensures that any restructuring, merger, or disposition of assets will treat all shareholders equally. It permits us to rest assured that rights, assets, or resources will not be siphoned away from shareholders unfairly or unequally.

Although some shareholders may use relatively short-term measures to evaluate management effectiveness—items such as share price (for public companies), earnings results, and market share within an industry—long-term investors such as the

Capital Group Companies need to think more deeply about the quality of a company. For this reason, we need to know the "hows" and "whys" of a corporation in order to understand its long-term prospects. This is where questions about corporate governance become critical: are the results credible over time? Are reports intended to edify shareholders, not mislead them? How does the corporation treat important stakeholders such as employees and communities? Does a management benefit disproportionately from good results without being penalized symmetrically for poor results? Does a corporation's governance structure provide effective, continuous oversight on these matters of results, fairness, and rewards? And in the event of any dispute, does the governance structure provide an environment to resolve disagreement? In the final analysis, effective corporate governance should provide a just and fair outcome to all the various stakeholders in a corporation's activities.

Such questions about corporate governance have been matters for debate in more-developed market economies for several decades. The issues become even more crucial, however, in the emerging-market context, because investing there has so many challenges beyond corporate governance that investors want to minimize all potential problem areas.

One significant challenge to investing in emerging markets is the system of government in the recipient country. Not all countries are constitutional democracies. Many lack the legal structure that undergirds a market economy, including well-developed, clear laws about contracts, bankruptcy, corporations, and the like. Many emerging markets lack proven or even trustworthy regulatory entities. The judiciary in many of these countries is less reliable than it is in developed countries, and in some cases it is corrupt. Resolving conflicts can be quite difficult.

Emerging markets also offer different cultures, many without the tradition of ownership by unaffiliated entities.[1] One example of this is in Asia, where family business groups control a large number of interlocking corporations.[2] Even where unaffiliated ownership exists, the traditions of modern day commercialism are not very long, nor are they necessarily deeply embedded. Even seemingly unrelated areas, such as the freedom of a country's press, have a role to play in corporate governance. Critical and independent media have often been a chief source of pressure on companies that are misbehaving as well as a strong voice for reforms; where there are no such independent media, this role remains unfilled.

Finally, emerging-market economies have, for the most part, a greater tendency for volatility, including but not limited to extreme swings in currencies, interest rates, and markets. Some of this volatility can be caused by economic volatility in some other emerging-market country, even if there is little or no direct economic linkage—a phenomenon called *contagion*. One of the best-known instances of the problem was the Asian financial crisis of 1997, during which financial problems in Asia soon proved contagious for eastern European and Latin American economies. Furthermore, many emerging-market countries have less predictability in the continuity of government and/or the consistency of policies, either of which can induce market volatility.

GIVEN THE PROBLEMS OF INVESTING IN EMERGING MARKETS, WHY SHOULD AN INVESTOR BE INTERESTED?

Emerging markets demand attention both for macroeconomic and demographic reasons, and also for several investment-specific reasons. At the macro level, most of the world's population lives in emerging-market countries. With economic growth rates for the next two decades expected to be very high for these countries as they play economic "catch-up," the size and scope for commercial development is huge.

In terms of specific investments, there are many attractions. Within emerging-market countries we regularly find exceptionally well managed, well financed companies. Often these companies have had to overcome challenges not experienced by companies in the developed world, and are better for it.

Furthermore, some emerging-market companies possess clear competitive advantages. Although developed-country multinationals such as Boeing, Coke, and Proctor & Gamble can serve many of the needs of emerging-market countries, they are unlikely to displace local enterprises fully. Local companies in many products and services have both a geographical and cultural advantage, for which there is no good substitute. Nations such as Russia have unique natural resources. Similarly, many emerging-market companies have unique cost advantages because of their location, particularly in labor costs. These companies, such as the software companies in India, prove themselves able to translate the cost advantages into doing competitive business in global markets.

Finally, often companies in emerging markets are simply better-value investments. The valuation of good companies in emerging markets is often cheaper than comparable companies in developed countries. Lower multiples, higher dividend yields, and lower stock price–to–book value ratios can discount much of the greater risk associated with investing in emerging markets. Investment results, consequently, can be better than those of developed markets, as they have been for the last three years (see Table 15.1).

There is also a growing pool of corporate debt issued by corporations in emerging-market countries, with interest rate spreads that can be very attractive. Not only can returns be attractive, but also the volatility of the debt security should be less than that of an equity. However, debt holders in some emerging-market countries can have difficulty claiming assets in the event of default; therefore, good corporate governance is also important to debt holders.

HOW DO WE, AS A LARGE INVESTOR IN EMERGING MARKETS, TRY TO IMPROVE THE ODDS OF NOT GETTING HURT BY A BAD CORPORATE GOVERNANCE ENVIRONMENT OR ACTION?

Our investing approach in emerging-market countries is well thought out and based on concrete research. We have approximately 35 investment analysts who specialize in emerging markets, and we invest about USD 30 billion of our clients' assets in these markets. Our investment analysts concentrate on specific geographical regions so that they are knowledgeable about both the companies and the countries of their responsibility. To

TABLE 15.1 **Rates of Return on Market Indices, US dollars**

Period Ending December 31, 2001
Annualized rates of return

INDEX[a]	CALENDAR				
	10 Years (%)	5 Years (%)	3 Years (%)	1 Year (%)	YTD 6/30/02 (%)
S&P 500 Index	12.90	10.70	−1.03	−11.88	−13.15
MSCI® EAFE Index[b]	4.66	1.09	−4.86	−21.28	−1.46
MSCI® World Index[c]	8.46	5.69	−3.09	−16.56	−8.63
MSCI® Emerging Markets Free Index[d]	3.05	−5.74	4.08	−2.37	2.07

Notes:

[a] All indices are unmanaged.

[b] MSCI® Europe, Australasia, and Far East Index with net dividends for US Pension Plans, Charitable Trusts, & Educational Institutions (calculated by Capital International S.A.)

[c] MSCI® World Index with net dividends for US Pension Plans, Charitable Trusts & Educational Institutions (calculated by Capital International S.A.)

[d] MSCI® Emerging Markets Free Index (gross dividends reinvested)

ensure that they are in touch with the most up-to-date information about the companies and countries of their responsibility, these analysts made more than 1,500 company visits to emerging markets during 2001. Our emerging-market specialists also rely on our approximately 175 developed-market industry investment analysts for specialized expertise on industry matters. In short, we exert every effort to be a "bottom-up" investment organization, an active manager as opposed to a passive or index manager.

To help promote good corporate governance in emerging markets, our organization has compiled a checklist of governance principles and best practices. The list is based in part on standards that other organizations, such as the Organisation for Economic Co-operation and Development (OECD), have published. We encourage our analysts to rely on this checklist when assessing a company's corporate governance.

In order to obtain the best information available about corporate governance practices, we of course talk to companies directly, but we also try to assess the level of corporate governance from the history of the company, from the reputation of its management and board by knowledgeable locals, and from any other relevant indications, such as a preponderance of "insiders" on the board. In very rare cases, we have litigated to correct illegal governance failures. However, we find this to be the least satisfactory protection, both because costs are prohibitive and because results are uncertain.

Finally, we try to exert pressure on a country or on a region for improvements in corporate governance. We stay in touch with country regulators and make suggestions on improvements in their practices. We also participate in several multilateral organizations whose goals include educating governments and corporations to the benefits of responsible corporate governance and helping to implement beneficial changes.

WHAT SEEMS TO BE WORKING, FROM OUR STANDPOINT, TO FURTHER BETTER CORPORATE GOVERNANCE?

Although of course much remains to be done, and each country is different, many countries are making great strides in the area of corporate governance reform on a variety of different fronts.

Major progress has been made in the area of disclosure, especially as corporations turn to the major, internationally recognized accounting firms. Korea is one of an increasing number of countries that have begun to require more and better disclosure; by law Korean companies are now required to produce quarterly results. In Russia, too, quarterly reports are now the norm. Chinese companies generally have very good reports, though they still have a great deal of work to do as they shift from "cash" to "accrual" accounting. A large part of this work requires training more financial officers who know accrual accounting, and this training is underway.

The culture of ethics required to support good governance is growing in emerging-market countries, though perhaps too slowly. For instance, a Korean company recently reduced the size of its board from 53 directors to 8, symbolizing that serving on a corporate board is now perceived not just as a reward or "perk," but as a serious job.

More and more, pressure for better corporate behavior is coming not just from the state or from foreign investors but also from domestic institutions such as NGOs and the press. In a recent incident in Korea, the press went public with information about a company whose board had acquired assets from an insider. The company's stock fell 20 percent in three days, forcing the company to disclose the details of the investment (which substantiated that the price paid was fair). The stock subsequently recovered. In Brazil, investment banks, rating agencies, and other independents (such as the media) have been able to exert a great deal of pressure for change. Recent research on corporate governance in India concludes that foreign institutional investors are in fact the best monitors, better than domestic financial institutions or family-run business groups (see Khanna and Palepu, 1999). The hand of the market is also at work: as stocks react negatively to bad behavior, corporate managers, who increasingly have stock ownership, are realizing the personal consequences of bad corporate behavior.

Some governments are finally recognizing that they must act to prevent what most academics perceive as the single greatest corporate governance problem in emerging markets: the potential for controlling shareholders to expropriate firm benefits from minority shareholders.[3] In Brazil, a new law has just gone into effect limiting the number of nonvoting shares a corporation can issue, thus preventing current insiders from disenfranchising new investors. Mexico has also recently passed new securities laws, including a provision that would prevent a holding company from acquiring a controlling share of a company and then forcing minority shareholders to sell at below-market prices.

Other moves are perhaps more tentative. Brazil has established a new stock exchange, the Novo Mercado, that lists only companies that agree to adhere to a checklist of good corporate governance practices. Korea has established a securities regulatory agency, the FSC. Both the FSC and the Novo Mercado are fledgling institutions that have yet to produce real change, but they are at least steps in the right direction. In general, the governments of most emerging-market countries now appreciate that better corporate governance standards not only improve the flow of portfolio capital to their countries, but also increase the chances of it remaining there.

Beyond improvements brought by governments, the marketplace itself is forcing better governance standards. There is no question that companies with high standards of corporate governance are more desirable to us than companies with lower standards. Because of this, we are willing to pay higher valuations for such companies. A well-known McKinsey (2002) study reported that investors were willing to pay premiums of up to 30 percent for companies with good corporate governance. Other studies have found that corporate governance practices that put minority shareholders in jeopardy lead to huge discounts on stock prices, as investors incorporate into stock prices the risks of purchasing a minority stake in the company.[4] For this reason, companies with higher standards of governance can expect lower costs of capital and more capital availability, both of which can improve their chances of success.

Beyond the marketplace itself, the formation of various coalitions to improve corporate governance in emerging markets is also having a beneficial effect. Two of these are the Asian Corporate Governance Forum and South Korea's Participatory Economy Committee – People's Solidarity for Participatory Democracy.

On the "bad news is good news" side of the ledger, the failure of governance in several high-profile US companies (Enron, WorldCom, and Dynegy) has drawn attention to the issue by a host of players, including emerging-market governments. This attention, by delineating the cost of bad behavior, is providing an urgency for reform that nothing else has yet accomplished.

In the final analysis, we will not consider investing in a company with a poor record of governance or a likelihood of bad behavior. Because other large investors have the same inclination, the markets themselves will continue to be a strong force for positive change.

WHAT ELSE NEEDS TO BE DONE TO PROMOTE BETTER CORPORATE GOVERNANCE PRACTICES IN EMERGING MARKETS?

We are generally pleased with the direction of changes, but think the pace is too slow. Companies themselves can take the initiative, and much can also be done by entities within emerging-market countries, with governments continuing to be a force and fulcrum for change.

Recent research shows that even in countries with extremely poor country-wide standards of corporate governance, companies that unilaterally adopt better corporate governance practices can see major improvement in their stock prices and thus in their access to capital (see, for example, Klapper and Love, 2002; La Porta et al., 1997). On the level of the individual corporation, companies can and should exert best efforts to ensure fairer treatment of minority shareholders. A persistent obstacle to ensuring that companies are widely held is the fact that in many Asian and Latin American countries, family ownership is the norm, as is interlocking control of several corporations. Yet in some Asian countries, such companies are facing a generational change that will make it difficult for them to remain closely held. In short, good corporate governance dictates that broadening the shareholder base is essential.

That being said, governments are crucial in acting as a force and a fulcrum for change. When contemplating reform, governments must bear in mind that quirky laws will not work. Argentina, for instance, has proposed a law that would hold liable for damages any shareholder who votes for a proposal that is enacted, but that subsequently creates a liability for the company. Obviously, this law means that deep-pocket shareholders are unlikely to hold shares or vote, which can only be to the detriment of the company. There are ample opportunities, however, for governments to lead the way for positive change.

A continuing problem in many places is the role of the government in the corporation. Most countries where state ownership was formerly the rule are moving very quickly in the direction of privatization. In China, for instance, better, more productive companies such as China Telecom are moving rapidly to list themselves on the Chinese and Hong Kong stock exchanges. However, in a number of countries, corporate governance is extremely politicized. For instance, in one former Eastern-bloc country, where the government owned a 30-percent share in a corporation, governmental elections produced a new government that installed a new corporate management, without any chance for other shareholders to vote. Too often, the state, as a majority or even minority shareholder in a previously state-owned but now privatized company, is abusive to minority shareholder rights. Such action not only reflects badly on the government, it also deters investors from future ownership in similar privatized entities.

Emerging markets must also become more aggressive about penalizing "insider trading," with commensurate penalties for violators, such as disgorgement of profits, fines, and jail time. A recent study in Mexico indicates that corporate news announcements have virtually no effect on share prices, in all probability because such announcements have been expected and thus have already been incorporated into share prices by market forces (see Bhattacharya, 2000). A better scenario would have all market participants receive significant information publicly and simultaneously.

Transparency still needs to be improved. In many cases, our analysts are unable to determine the background of a company's directors or the level of management compensation—including stock options. In some smaller markets, such as Italy and Mexico, members of the business community can offer first-hand knowledge about the reputation of corporate managers. But in point of fact, achieving greater transparency will probably require countrywide legal steps.

Many experts studying emerging markets are in favor of greater reliance on regulatory institutions rather than on courts to enforce securities laws.[5] As previously noted, a great number of emerging economies, such as South Korea, have imitated the United States or other developed countries in regulatory oversight. What seems to be lacking, however, is a fundamental philosophy for paying attention to the rights associated with other people's money.

Countries must also create additional venues of arbitration for resolution of conflicts over shareholder rights. Courts in many emerging-market countries have neither the time nor the background to handle such cases. Arbitration panels of legitimate, knowledgeable individuals backed by the legal system would be faster and fairer.

Others besides corporations and governments have roles to play. All emerging markets need better development of investment research and institutional ownership from domestic institutions. If there were more domestic institutions owning shares, and if such institutions took more care in their investing responsibilities, they could be the strongest force for positive governance changes.

Depository institutions can also do more. Proxy voting procedures for American Depository Receipts (ADR) or Global Depository Receipts (GDR) holders need to be faster and provide more complete information. Often with ADRs or GDRs that we own, we receive the proxy with insufficient time to vote; the disclosure information is likewise frequently incomplete. As a consequence, we often buy local shares with the attendant complex paperwork in order to receive faster, better proxies. Furthermore, depository institutions should consider penalties for those companies that engage in bad governance behavior. Depository institutions presumably could "de-list" the depository receipts, just as exchanges de-list companies for bad behavior.

WHO BENEFITS FROM IMPROVED CORPORATE GOVERNANCE IN EMERGING MARKETS?

The greatest benefit of improved corporate governance is that markets themselves become healthier: higher valuations, less volatility, more liquidity, less reliance on rumor, and a wider scope of investors—on balance, a more trustworthy marketplace.[6]

The beneficiaries of such healthy markets are numerous.

Foreign investors who have positions in emerging markets will benefit. If higher equity valuations are a result of corporate governance reform, then investment results will be higher than they would be otherwise. Improved governance also means fewer problems to anticipate and fewer conflicts to work through after the fact. Because foreign investors are more removed in both distance and in business connections, more trustworthy markets can have a very important attraction to this investor class.

Healthier emerging markets also benefit local investors. Better returns and fewer unexpected problems should help all investors. In addition, should future global financial crises occur, the "contagion" effect on markets would be far less severe if the fear of poor corporate governance were eliminated. Thus local investors have one less reason to worry about capital flight and the impact on the currency.

There are also many benefits to those companies whose stock is traded in emerging markets. As noted earlier, higher stock valuations, which usually accompany better governance, mean a lower cost of capital for the issuing company. Because more investors are willing to consider the stock of companies with better governance, it makes initial or secondary equity offerings easier. Because better governance removes an element of investor concern, a company's stock should be less volatile. This, in turn, should provide more financial continuity for the owners and managers of the company.

Eliminating governance problems also helps the companies' investors focus on the fundamental issues that management deems to be important. In the longer run, the emphasis on fundamentals lessens the impact of rumors and allows a company to avoid the "taint" of insider information.

More broadly, better corporate governance can have follow-on benefits for a country. It can assist in creating private pension funds, since future pension obligations can be more safely invested in local stocks. Emerging-market countries with higher standards of corporate governance also lessen the reality and image of corruption. Those thinking of investing can be more easily attracted to such countries.

Finally and most importantly, economic development is obviously fostered if companies enjoy freer access to growth capital at lower cost. To the extent that economic growth is faster, all sectors of society that benefit from faster growth can share in the rewards of improved corporate governance. Emerging-market countries that embrace a corporate governance reform agenda can expect significant improvements, from more and better jobs to increased standards of living for their citizens and enhanced opportunities for generating social programs.

CONCLUSION

As investors with decades of experience in emerging-market investing, we are well placed to observe progress across markets. Our experience has shown us that good corporate governance lays a foundation of trust, allowing us to have confidence in management of particular companies and eventually in the financial sector as a whole. With global attention increasingly turned toward the question of corporate governance in emerging markets, we think the time is ripe for positive change in terms of reporting, disclosure, minority shareholder rights, and increased policing of those rights by courts and regulators. Greater attention to corporate governance on the part of investors, companies, and governments will provide many benefits for emerging-market countries, including greater access to capital and improved economic growth, and, in a deeper sense, a culture of ethics and good business practices that will be the foundation for economic development for decades to come.

NOTES

1 The role that cultural differences play in corporate governance has been explored by a number of commentators. See, for example, Licht (2000).

2 Many studies have looked at the somewhat unique family-based structures of East Asian corporations. See, for example, Claessens, Djankov, and Lang (2000).

3 This was the conclusion reached by the acknowledged experts in the field—La Porta, Lopez-de-Silanes, Shleifer, and Vishny—in a 1999 World Bank discussion paper entitled "Investor Protections: Origins, Consequences, Reforms." Further scholarship has borne out their view, including especially studies of the East Asian financial crisis of 1997. See Mitton (2002), Claessens, Djankov, and Lang (2000), and Johnson et al. (2000). See also Gibson (2000) and Coffee (2001).

4 An excellent study by Nenova (2000) was one of the first to measure the value of corporate control rights: how much owning a majority stake in a corporation is worth. In countries with good corporate governance with minority shareholder protections, the value of control tends to be negligible—generally less than 10 percent of firm valuation. In countries such as Mexico, where protection for minority shareholders is poor, the value of control can be up to 50 percent of the firm valuation. Working with limited data, Stanford Law Professor Bernard Black has found similarly striking numbers about the value of good corporate governance. His survey of 16 large Russian firms finds that "a one-standard-deviation change in governance ranking predicts an 8-fold increase in firm value. A worst . . . .to best . . . change in governance ranking predicts a 600-fold increase in firm value!" (Black, 2001, p. 2131).

5 This is the recommendation of the World Bank, which has undertaken a project to help countries who request it to assess and improve their corporate governance standards. See Fremond and Capaul (2002).

6 In fact, La Porta et al. (1997) have demonstrated that countries with poor protection of shareholders and poor enforcement of law related to corporate governance also had less-developed markets for debt and equity.

REFERENCES

Bhattacharya, U., et al. 2000. "When an Event Is Not an Event: The Curious Case of an Emerging Market," *Journal of Financial Economics* 55, pp. 69–101.

Black, B. 2001. "Does Corporate Governance Matter? A Crude Test Using Russian Data," *University of Pennsylvania Law Review* 149.

Branson, D. 2001. "The Very Uncertain Prospect of "Global" Convergence in Corporate Governance," *Cornell International Law Journal* 34.

Claessens, S., S. Djankov, and L. Lang. 2000. "The Separation of Ownership and Control in East Asian Corporations," *Journal of Financial Economics* 58, pp. 81–112.

Claessens, S. et al. 1999. "Expropriation of Minority Shareholders: Evidence from East Asia," World Bank Policy Research Paper No. 2088. Washington, DC: World Bank.

Coffee, J. 2001. "Do Norms Matter? A Cross-Country Evaluation," *University of Pennsylvania Law Review* 149.

Doidge, C., G. Karolyi, and R. Stulz. 2001. "Why Are Foreign Firms Listed in the US Worth More?" NBER Working Paper No. 8538. Cambridge, MA: National Bureau of Economic Research.

Fremond, O., and M. Capaul. 2002. "The State of Corporate Governance: Experience from Country Assessments," World Bank Policy Research Working Paper No. 2858. Washington, DC: World Bank.

Gibson, M. 2000. "Is Corporate Governance Effective in Emerging Markets?" Federal Reserve Board Finance and Economics Discussion Series Paper 1999-63 (July). Washington, DC: The Federal Reserve Bank.

Johnson, S., P. Boone, A. Breach, and E. Friedman. 2000. "Corporate Governance in the Asian Financial Crisis, 1997–1998," *Journal of Financial Economics* 58, pp. 141–186.

Klapper, L. F., and I. Love. 2002. "Corporate Governance, Investor Protection, and Performance in Emerging Markets," World Bank Policy Research Working Paper No. 2818. Washington, DC: World Bank.

Khanna, T., and K. Palepu. 1999. "Emerging Market Business Groups, Foreign Investors, and Corporate Governance," National Bureau of Economic Research Working Paper No. 6955. Cambridge, MA: National Bureau of Economic Research.

La Porta, R., F. Lopez-de-Silanes, A. Shleifer, and R. Vishny. 1997. "Legal Determinants of External Finance," *The Journal of Finance* 52, pp. 1131–1150.

La Porta, R., F. Lopez-de-Silanes, A. Shleifer, and R. Vishny. 1998. "Law and Finance," *The Journal of Political Economy* 106, pp. 1113–1155.

La Porta, R., F. Lopez-de-Silanes, A. Shleifer, and R. Vishny. 1999. "Investor Protections: Origins, Consequences, Reforms," World Bank Financial Section Discussion Paper No. 1. Washington, DC: World Bank.

La Porta, R., F. Lopez-de-Silanes, A. Shleifer, and R. Vishny. 2000. "Investor Protection and Corporate Governance," *Journal of Financial Economics* 58, pp. 3–27.

Leuz, C., and R. Verecchia. 2000. "The Economic Consequences of Increased Disclosure," *Journal of Accounting Research* 38, pp. 91–124.

Licht, A. 2000. "The Mother of All Path Dependencies: Toward a Cross-Cultural Theory of Corporate Governance Systems," *Delaware Journal of Corporate Law* 26.

McKinsey & Company. 2002. *Global Investor Opinion Survey on Corporate Governance: Key Findings.* Online. http://www.gcgf.org.

Mitton, T. 2002. "A Cross-Firm Analysis of the Impact of Corporate Governance on the East Asian Financial Crisis," *Journal of Financial Economics* 64, pp. 215–241.

Nenova, T. 2000. "The Value of Corporate Votes and Control Benefits: A Cross-Country Analysis." On the Social Sciences Resource Network. Online. http://www.ssrn.com.

Pistor, K. 2002. "The Standardization and Law and Its Effect on Developing Economies," *American Journal of Comparative Law* 50.

Reese, W. Jr., and M. Weisbach. 2001. "Protection of Minority Shareholder Interests, Cross-listings in the United States, and Subsequent Equity Offerings," NBER Working Paper No. 8164. Cambridge, MA: National Bureau of Economic Research.

Tabalujan, B. 2001. "Why Indonesian Corporate Governance Failed: Conjectures Concerning Legal Culture," *Columbia Journal of Asian Law* 15.

Chapter 16

Corporate Governance, Public Policy, and Private Investment Decisions, 2002

William Dale Crist

CORPORATE GOVERNANCE 2002: ITS ROOTS

The fact that shareholders did not have any genuine say in the operation of US corporations, and that corporate management was accountable only to the board of directors, who, practically speaking, were accountable only to themselves, was pointed out by scholars as early as 1932 (Berle and Means, 1968). Nevertheless, by 1934, and again in 1940, Benjamin Graham and David Dodd, the founders of fundamental stock analysis, made the observation that an investor should take just as much care in *being* a stockholder as in *becoming* a stockholder (Graham and Dodd, 1940, p. 594). In the eyes of corporate management and the public in general, this academic plea for stockholder participation obviously was way before its time. Forty years later, the economic historian Alfred Chandler, Jr. made it very clear that US corporations were controlled by corporate management and not by stockholders, either directly or indirectly (Chandler, 1977). Although the ownership of corporate equity had become increasingly diverse and institutional investors had begun to proliferate and grow, the 1940 entreaty of Graham and Dodd still had no active champions by 1980.

Shareholder activism began in the United States only as a defensive strategy by a very few shareholders to protect against anti-takeover devices and self-serving policies designed to pay off executives to protect the corporate status quo rather than promote long-term interests of loyal shareholders. Institutional investors in general were accused of being transitory and interested only in short-term profits, and corporate executives argued that such shareholders had no right to participate in decisions concerning the long-term viability of the corporate entity.[1] However, the rapid growth of US pension funds during the period represented an impressive amount of truly patient capital, and many, such as the California Public Employees' Retirement System (CalPERS), quickly overcame their uncertainty regarding the appropriateness of being involved in corporate governance (see Hawley and Williams, 1994).

As corporate financial arrangements became increasingly complex during the 1980s, the relevance of corporate governance experienced a rather abrupt elevation in the informed investor's consciousness. CalPERS first adopted an active strategy to improve corporate governance in the United States in 1984 and became active in promoting improved corporate governance internationally in 1990. During this developmental phase of corporate governance policy, the CalPERS Board of Administration realized that, because of the system's size and heavy reliance on indexing as an investment strategy, it had a responsibility to behave as a permanent owner of corporate equity, not as a temporary investor. Further, recognizing a fiduciary duty to treat the proxy as an asset of the pension fund, CalPERS policy since 1984 has been to behave essentially like a permanent owner regardless of the amount of equity owned.[2] This policy has required a special kind of shareholder participation over the long term to improve the performance, and thus the capitalized value, of companies "owned." CalPERS' corporate governance strategy is based on the simple assumption that behaving like a permanent owner makes good investment sense for a large institutional investor with no short-term need for liquidity.

But even after all of the shareholder activism of the late 1980s and throughout the 1990s, 60 years after the work of Graham and Dodd, the involvement of shareholders in corporate governance—with the current focus being on institutional shareholders— remains a topic of controversy in much of the world. When shareholder activism began to attract the market's attention in the United States during the mid-1980s, investors and corporations in other nations were not yet participating. Now, with the inexorable development of a truly global economy, the corporate governance debate has widened. An increasing need for investors to diversify internationally, in both developed and emerging markets, has spread the concern regarding corporate governance to all corners of the world, where different laws, traditions and corporate cultures make the controversy even more challenging and more important. Disagreements over what are the best corporate governance practices and how can today's corporations be caused to adopt those practices finally has become a global debate.[3]

Recent examples of company failure and fraudulent financial reporting in the United States clearly are the result of bad corporate governance practices. So, although these business failures have brought considerable hardship to individuals owning the failed company's stock and bonds, the events have breathed new life into the debate over the nature and importance of good corporate governance. Public opinion and political attention finally have been raised to a level where the controversy regarding corporate governance clearly has shifted from whether or not institutional investors and government regulators should have a role determining corporate governance practices to how extensive and controlling should those roles be. Following an amazingly short period of legislative debate, the US Congress handed President George W. Bush new legislation that strengthened the ability of the federal government to investigate, regulate, and mandate behavior of corporate directors and managers. When President Bush signed the Sarbanes-Oxley Act of 2002 into law on July 30, 2002, 70 years of debate regarding the proper relationship between private corporations and the financial markets in which they flourish or flounder at last received the attention it deserved.

The continuing, and now public, debate regarding corporate governance appropriately centers on the critical nature of a corporate board's responsibility to hold management accountable and to be accountable itself to all of the company's owners and to the public in general. The new focus is also global, important to emerging markets as well as all developed economies. The evolving world of corporate governance now will appear to go even further into the daily operations of the company, and the concern of corporate management that too much board involvement will reduce management effectiveness will be a defensive battle cry. The new invigorated debate must therefore consider innovative approaches by which investors and public policymakers can influence or control the behavior of corporate directors and managers in a positive way without interfering with the company's day-to-day management. The appetite of informed institutional investors for stronger, more independent corporate boards, empowered by influential and organized shareholder activists voting their proxies, will almost certainly increase apace with the defensive appeals of corporate management all around the globe.[4]

THE CHANGE AGENTS AFFECTING INVESTMENT POLICY

Ten years ago, the chief executive officer of the Philips Pension Funds in the Netherlands listed several noteworthy observations regarding the nature and importance of institutional investors' involvement in corporate governance at that time (Snijders, 1992). These observations, 10 years later, retain their relevance and importance. The timelessness of the following observations enhances our ability to better understand current developments in institutional investor investment policy.

1. When corporate management does not take corrective action in a company that is clearly underperforming, the increasing difficulty of institutional investors to simply sell the shares (take the "Wall Street Walk") requires that greater attention be paid to watching and influencing the corporation's management. There definitely is a growing awareness of the fact that managers and directors are not as accountable to shareholders as they should be.

2. The increased patience of institutional investors, and the corresponding evolution of new long-term strategies, will inexorably spread to all of the world's economies as the globalization of the capital market continues to develop.

3. A combination of forces in today's capital markets works to ensure that a "supportive stable ownership" of producing corporations by institutional investors will continue to exist. This supportive stable ownership does not require that

shareholders "sit in the management's chair," and shareholders should not assume that they are competent to manage the business. Shareholder activism should be aimed at allowing [and assisting] management to act in the longer-term interest of the shareholder.

4. Corporate management should be totally accountable to the shareholders. This accountability is greatly enhanced by the presence of "independent outsiders" on the corporation's board of directors.

5. Continued evolution of institutional investor involvement in corporate governance will lead to an increasingly close relationship between the shareholder and the company's management.

Since that first sharp increase of investor interest during the mid 1980s, the perceived and actual importance of good corporate governance has continued to grow as a relevant variable in the decision-making process of institutional investors, as predicted by Dick Snijders in 1992. Now, in 2002, huge corporate failures and public discoveries of accounting fraud have caused another sharp increase in the attention being paid to the old problem of governing and managing a diversely owned corporate enterprise. It is wise to remember that today's increased focus on corporate governance is the product of evolution, not revolution. Contemporary news media reports of sensationalized business failures and business fraud notwithstanding, many leaders in the world of business and investment have warned for some time that bad corporate governance led to bad results.[5]

The agents for change that have had the most influence on corporate governance practices themselves during the past decade can be divided into two categories: (1) investor pressure affecting corporate attitude and behavior, and (2) government or institutional regulation of corporate behavior. Of these, the most important has been continuous increased pressure by institutional investors of all types on corporate leadership to improve governance. Regulatory bodies, stock exchanges, and, most recently, legislative and judicial bodies around the world have become more controlling of corporate governance practices than ever before, but many are still reluctant to exercise extensive authority.[6]

Because of the continued pressure of investors, and now the new pressure of changing public policy, the attitudes and behavior of the more enlightened corporate managers and corporate boards actually have changed for the better over the last decade. Possibly even more important, public policy makers are finally forced by political pressure to consider more seriously increased statutory and regulatory intrusion into the free enterprise options of corporations. As the courts continue to increase their involvement in enforcing the law and thereby writing new law, the pace of evolution in corporate governance practices will be increased and more consideration will be given by investment professionals to strategies that take a company's and a country's corporate governance record into account.

The continuing pressure from large segments of the public in the United States and in Europe to hold corporations more accountable in a social or environmental sense has also been an agent for change. However, these social pressures have caused confusion over what is meant by good corporate governance and what is meant by corporate social responsibility. This confusion has increased from the 1990s to the present time, and it needs to be honestly clarified if either agenda is to advance. Professional and academic conferences routinely have presenters who argue that good corporate governance pays more attention to the sustainability of business production activities as they affect conditions of workers, the environment, human rights in general, and even democratization of a nation. Although this observation is basically accurate, the primary objective of corporate governance is not good works, it is good business in a transparent and efficient market place.[7]

THE INVESTMENT DECISION

The importance of good corporate governance to the bottom line of a passively managed indexed equity portfolio has been recognized by most institutional investors for approximately 10 years. There has been no stronger advocate for improved corporate governance as a means of adding value to a stable indexed equity portfolio than CalPERS. CalPERS' emphasis on the importance of governance to investing has been narrowly focused on the responsibilities of the pension system as a long-term equity owner. Over time, CalPERS has gained a greater understanding of its natural competitive advantage as a pension system as it relates to governance investing. That advantage is the system's extremely long investment horizon. The theory is simple: companies that are well governed will, in the long term, out-perform competing companies that do not employ best practices of governance.[8]

All pension funds, public and private, and most indexed mutual funds as well, have an investment return horizon that allows them to be more patient. The nature of their liabilities does not require liquidity in the short term. Such funds have come to recognize that their fundamental exposure should be to broad equity markets over a long time period, and it does not make much investment sense to attempt to outsmart the market. Stock picking and market timing are costly activities that are not supported by historical evidence as strategies that will earn more on invested funds in the long run than can be earned by simply "owning the market." This is exactly the perspective that has led well-managed pension systems to embrace fully the notion that value can be added to a stable, passively managed index fund by encouraging corporations to hire management that manage for the long run. Further, short-term decision-making and accounting practices are being proven not to be in the best interest of corporate owners or of the market in general; this is especially so for rapidly growing pension funds with global investments.

Regardless of their relative importance to investment returns, there is little disagreement in the professional investor world that corporate governance improvements take a long time. It is therefore only natural that institutional investors with the greatest ability to hold assets for long periods of time would be most interested in passively managed indexed equity portfolios and in allocating resources to the business of improving corporate governance in general. The special nature of a governance strategy, as it relates to patient capital's perspective, is that a long-term owner will own positions in a large number of companies in public equity markets essentially forever. Such investors have an incentive as owners to take action that helps to protect that value over time, and potentially to enhance it. Some of the efforts to "take action" almost certainly add value in the long run, but are pursued year after year almost as an act of faith in the belief that incremental improvement in governance will make a difference. For example, pension systems have played an active role in a large number of proxy campaigns promoting specific shareholder resolutions intended to improve company performance by improving governance practices. However, evidence that shareholder resolutions and other proxy campaigns are effective in adding value to a portfolio is mixed (see del Guercio and Hawkins, 1999; Karpoff, Malatesta, and Walking, 1996).

For adding value to specific passively managed equity holdings, by far the most effective corporate governance strategy for CalPERS has been its "focus list" program. Begun in 1992, the program requires considerable research and analysis of companies in the indexed equity portfolio. Typically, more than 1,500 companies are screened for evidence of comparative underperformance and indications of poor corporate governance practices.[9] This screening activity generates an initial list of about 100 companies, and further screening reduces the number to approximately 20 companies that must be analyzed in depth. As part of the analysis, direct communication with each of these companies is initiated in order to discuss concerns and encourage change in governance practices. During the early 1990s, corporate reaction to CalPERS' governance questions and recommendations was often quite negative or nonexistent. During the past few years, however, many "targeted" companies, upon learning they had been selected as potential "focus" companies, voluntarily changed some of their governance practices (such as adding independent directors to their boards or separating the role of CEO and board chairman) or initiated share buybacks. The return on capital invested in each company under review is measured using Economic Value Added analysis. The final Focus List is normally published in the spring of each year and contains those companies that have not been responsive to CalPERS' recommendations. Companies that finally appear on the published Focus List generally appear only once because they ultimately do change their corporate governance practices. A few do repeat as targeted underperformers, and their continued poor comparative performance is evidence of their nonattention to constructive governance policy change. Over the past 10 years, the evidence that CalPERS' Focus List policy generates shareowner value is positive and CalPERS' investment policy will continue to include Focus List publication for US-based companies, and it may expand the practice to non–US companies (see Nesbitt, 1994; Anson et al., 2002).

The bottom-line value of promoting corporate governance principles and pressuring US corporations to adopt better corporate governance practices notwithstanding, the consideration of a corporation's governance practices as an important variable in the active investment decision-making process is a relatively new phenomenon for most institutional investors. The rapid rise of shareholder activism and the increasingly visible public market agitation for improved corporate governance practices during the 1990s created an active countervailing group of disbelievers and vocal critics. These critics generally discounted the corporate governance variable in making their active investment decisions, agreeing only that general principles of corporate governance were perhaps helpful in the aggregate, with most of the benefits going to "free riders."[10] These views are now changing as investment professionals have gained more experience and comfort with the notion that corporate governance practices can have an impact on the bottom line.

What are the implications of these changing views for the active investment strategies of patient institutional investors? It is now being realized that the long-term nature of a mature pension fund's liabilities not only justifies attempts to improve corporate governance practices, it also provides an advantage for certain active investment strategies. In fact, the critical nexus between corporate governance and active investment strategies in the public markets is the perspective of a long-term owner. As a long-term owner, a pension fund is naturally disposed to care about issues that realistically affect the company's long-term economic position. Thus, the variables that such investors care about most are the same variables that entrepreneurial owners care about over years and decades, not just quarters.

The important distinction that is being made here is the critical difference between "speculating owners" with a short-term perspective and "investing owners" with a long-term perspective. Technically, at any point in time, all stockholders are owners of the corporation. However, investors have many different criteria that drive their decisions and holding periods. Short-term "investors" are more accurately identified as speculators. Naturally, investors who speculate with a shorter time horizon demand greater liquidity and will not be willing to address longer-term issues. Hedge funds and most non-indexed mutual funds have a short-term view that does not permit strategies that require a long time for fulfillment. Consequently, their investment programs are all active and pay little attention to a corporation's governance practices. In fact, short-term investors/speculators often rely on limited transparency and even faulty disclosure to leverage what they believe to be legal "insider information" in the form of stock analysts' pronouncements. In contrast, a pension fund, by its very nature, can employ an active strategy characterized by a value-type selection process based on intense fundamental research, and incurs a subsequent addition of value through varying levels of direct company involvement acting with an owner's responsibility. This kind of active strategy must focus on corporate governance issues that affect a minority owner's ability to participate in corporate decision-making at the policy level. All of these strategy characteristics require time to effectuate—time that short-term, speculating shareholders do not have.

As the field of corporate governance–based investing has grown in recent years, several related strategies have emerged. Some strategies are, generally speaking, defined as screening methodologies designed to identify either well-governed or poorly governed companies. These strategies may be either negative decision–based, which underweight or eliminate poorly governed companies or markets, or positive decision–based, which overweight well-governed companies or markets. Many of the recently developed governance rating services are in part intended to support these strategies.[11] For example, CalPERS recently has placed an emphasis on corporate governance as an important variable in an active investment strategy. The strategy is to seek investment opportunities beginning with the identification of underperforming companies for which there is no discernable explanation for the company's performance other than weak management related to bad governance. Relying on past experience of communicating with poor performers in connection with the Focus List program within its passively managed equity portfolio, CalPERS has embraced the notion that increased returns with less risk are possible through an active investment strategy based on the corporate governance record of specific companies. CalPERS currently employs three external money managers using a governance strategy. One is a relational investment partner located in the United States, and two others are active governance-based investment funds located in the United Kingdom. In addition, CalPERS is implementing an active internal portfolio based on a governance strategy.[12]

There is solid proof that the evolution of CalPERS to its increased emphasis on active management based on governance factors has resulted in additional value to the fund, in the form of returns, and also in the form of validation that governance matters. In fact, CalPERS' new active strategies based on governance factors have added significant returns to the fund above and beyond relative benchmarks. Perhaps more importantly, many anecdotal cases have emphasized that long-term owners can play an important role at critical periods in a company's life by exercising their power. To facilitate this influence, corporate governance, whether examined at the company level or the market level, (domestically and internationally), must permit timely and reasonable involvement of shareowners.

One of the most important new governance-based investment strategies at CalPERS is the internally managed relational program. The strategic objective of this program is to broaden the opportunity set of CalPERS' investment portfolio for achieving investment returns not available in traditional public markets. The portfolio will take concentrated positions (up to 25 percent of capitalized value) in companies selected on the basis of fundamental analysis and corporate governance. This strategy will focus on unlocking intrinsic value in publicly traded US companies that are performing less well than their peers due to management- or governing board–related issues. CalPERS will work with the company's management, board of directors, and other shareowners to build a consensus identifying the deficiency and the means to correct it consistent with CalPERS' US Corporate Governance Core Principles and Guidelines. The primary source of potential investments will be through value and governance screens developed in the Focus List program.[13]

The increased emphasis on active management of equity assets based on corporate governance variables comes at the same time as an increased awareness of the importance of the global nature of investment return and the impact of emerging markets on the global economy. Economic globalization has made it necessary for very large institutional investors to consider investing some part of their portfolios into emerging markets both for diversification purposes and to take advantage of favorable risk-adjusted returns. To this end, CalPERS has established a new framework for evaluating emerging market countries. CalPERS' international investments are mostly managed by external managers selected on the basis of their investment strategy, geographic regions of expertise, and, of course, past performance. Once selected, the firms are delegated discretion for the assets under their control except that they are prohibited from investing in certain countries' markets as determined by the CalPERS "permissible country" policy.

Beginning with its initial investment in publicly traded equities of non–US companies, CalPERS has relied on an outside consultant to provide recommendations regarding countries in which investments were to be permitted without restriction and other countries in which investments were to be restricted or prohibited. Investments were made in various countries around the world on the basis of these restrictions.[14] In 1999, CalPERS decided to develop a specific policy for investing in emerging markets.[15] Developed global equity markets were deemed as a matter of policy to be permissible for future investment purposes, and investment in the emerging markets was to be limited to those determined through extensive analysis to be "permissible" (see Table 16.1).

TABLE 16.1   **CalPERS: Developed and Emerging Markets, 2002**

DEVELOPED MARKETS	EMERGING MARKETS
Australia	Argentina
Austria	Brazil
Belgium	Chile
Canada	China
Denmark	Columbia
Finland	Czech Republic
France	Egypt
Germany	Hungary
Greece	India
Hong Kong SAR	Indonesia
Ireland	Israel
Italy	Jordan
Japan	South Korea
Luxembourg	Mexico
Netherlands	Malaysia
New Zealand	Morocco
Norway	Pakistan
Portugal	Peru
Singapore	Philippines
Spain	Poland
Sweden	Russian Federation
Switzerland	South Africa
United Kingdom	Sri Lanka
United States	Taiwan
	Thailand
	Turkey
	Venezuela

The extensive analysis began with the recognition that many emerging markets already had undertaken many institutional reforms that increased their appeal to foreign investors. The reforms noted included stock exchange modernization, establishment of central clearing and settlement corporations and central depositories, establishment and empowerment of securities regulatory agencies, decreases in commission rates and other transaction charges, stricter accounting, auditing and information disclosure requirements, and establishment of insider trading rules. It was also assumed that reforms would be continued after the initial data were gathered for analysis from each of the countries.

CalPERS' permissible market analysis delineated two broad sources of risk in the emerging markets: country risk and market risk. Recognizing that without strong country infrastructures to support the capital markets, such markets could not be trusted to be viable in the long run, the selected country factors pertain to each country's stability, democracy, and openness in general. The market factors pertain to market-specific risks that are intended to determine whether the markets themselves, regardless of the reliability of the country's total infrastructure, can support institutional investment. The analysis considered three broad categories of factors relative to country risk: political stability, transparency, and productive labor practices. Five broad categories of factors were analyzed relative to market risk: market liquidity and volatility, market regulation and investor protection by law, capital market openness, settlement proficiency, and transaction costs.

The category of country risk was broken into three main country factors and several subfactors for analysis as follows:

1. *Political Stability.* This factor includes progress toward the development of basic democratic institutions and principles, such as guaranteed elimination of human rights violations and a strong and impartial legal system. The subfactors analyzed are: (a) civil liberties, (b) independent judiciary and legal protection, and (c) political risk.

2. *Transparency.* This factor includes financial transparency, including elements of a free press necessary for investors to have truthful, accurate, and relevant information. The subfactors analyzed are: (a) freedom of the press, (b) accounting standards, (c) monetary and fiscal transparency, and (d) stock exchange listing requirements.

3. *Productive Labor Practices.* This factor evaluates a country based on its ratification of and adherence to the International Labour Organization's (ILO) principles. The subfactors are: (a) ILO ratification; (b) the quality of enabling legislation to explicitly protect or prohibit the rights described in the ILO Convention; (c) the institutional capacity of governmental administrative bodies to enforce labor law at the national, regional, and local level; and (d) effectiveness of monitoring and enforcement of laws in the ILO Convention areas.

The category of market risk was broken into five main market factors and several subfactors for analysis as follows:

1. *Market Liquidity and Volatility.* This segment measures the ability to buy or sell assets in a country in a timely manner without adversely affecting security prices. The subfactors are: (a) market capitalization, the overall size of the country's stock market; (b) change in market capitalization, the growth of the country's stock market over the last five years; (c) average monthly trading volume rela-

tive to the size of the market; (d) growth in listed companies over the last five years; (e) market volatility as measured by standard deviation over the last five years attributable to both currency volatility and local market volatility; and (f) return/risk ratio in each market.

2. *Market Regulation/Legal System/Investor Protection.* This category analyzes the degree of legal protection for foreign investors as well as shareholder and creditors' rights. The subfactors analyzed are: (a) adequacy of financial regulation, (b) bankruptcy and creditors' rights, and (c) shareholders' rights.

3. *Capital Market Openness.* This category analyzes the level of restriction imposed on foreign investors. The subfactors analyzed are: (a) trade policy, measuring the degree to which there is oppressive government interference to free trade; (b) foreign investment, measuring governmental barriers to the free flow of capital from foreign sources including unequal treatment of foreigners and locals under the law; (c) banking and finance, measuring government control of banks and financial institutions and allocation of credit and the degree of freedom that financial institutions have to offer all types of financial services, securities, and insurance policies; and (d) stock market foreign ownership restrictions.

4. *Settlement Proficiency.* This category analyzes the country's trading and settlement practices to determine the degree of automation and the success of the market in settling transactions in a timely, efficient manner.

5. *Transaction Costs.* This category analyzes the costs associated with trading in a particular market and includes stamp taxes and duties, amount of dividends and income taxed, and capital gains taxes.

Once the basic research project had produced the best information available on each factor and subfactor at that point in time, all countries were compared as to the relative strength of each factor analyzed, and a quantitative value (a "score") was assigned to each factor for each country in an attempt to measure comparative strengths and weaknesses. Following discussions with investment managers, custodial banks, and brokerage firms, the quantitative scores assigned to the eight country and market factors and their subfactors were subjectively weighted to reflect the perceived relative importance of each factor. This methodology, all conducted by an outside consultant and independent subcontractors, generated a ranking of the emerging markets analyzed. The ranking was then discussed by the CalPERS Board, accepted as a matter of policy, and a decision was made as to which of the ranked countries would fall into the permissible category—that is, where the line would be drawn. This original ranking, which is unchanged at the time of this writing, is subject to change as the factors considered in each of the countries may change (see Table 16.2).

TABLE 16.2 **CalPERS: Permissible Markets, May 2002**

RANKING	COUNTRY	SCORE	MARKET CAPITALIZATION CUMULATIVE (%)
1	Argentina	2.63	0.95
2	South Korea	2.55	15.00
3	Taiwan	2.52	31.70
4	Hungary	2.50	32.67
5	Chile	2.44	36.07
6	Poland	2.39	38.02
7	Israel	2.36	41.85
8	Czech Republic	2.25	42.56
9	Peru	2.21	43.00
10	South Africa	2.17	49.80
11	Brazil	2.10	60.37
12	Mexico	2.10	69.07
13	Philippines	2.06	70.36
14	Turkey	2.02	72.54
15	Jordan	1.74	73.49
16	India	1.73	80.18
17	Thailand	1.64	81.81
18	Egypt	1.58	82.19
19	China	1.45	83.95
20	Malaysia	1.45	92.70
21	Colombia	1.42	93.00
22	Pakistan	1.40	93.25
23	Venezuela	1.32	93.53
24	Sri Lanka	1.31	93.53
25	Morocco	1.25	94.06
26	Indonesia	1.25	95.25
27	Russian Federation	1.15	100.00

As of September 2002, the first 14 of the ranked emerging market countries are assigned the status of "permissible countries" by CalPERS. These rankings apply only to publicly traded equity securities. CalPERS does own assets in some of the non-permissible countries, but will be purchasing no new corporate stock in these countries until such time as the ranking changes because of reevaluation, or the CalPERS Investment Committee determines to change the location of the dividing line. It is CalPERS' policy and intent to revisit the analysis at least annually, and more often for specific considerations brought to the attention of the system. The entire policy of designating some countries as not permitted for investment regardless of the qualities of specific companies in those countries is, itself, always subject to review and revision. One strong school of thought is that "country risk" is best evaluated on a continuum by the investment managers who are physically present in the various countries and who are therefore most competent to judge the risk to the shareowner. At the present time, however, it is hoped that the existence of the ranked list will give government and institutional policy leaders in the affected emerging-market countries both guidance and encouragement for improving the policy infrastructure that will attract increased investment from foreign patient capital sources.

The current emphasis on corporate governance as a variable that should be taken into consideration when investing in any company in any country is clear. The large number of new organizations that have been created to assist corporations worldwide in their efforts to improve governance practices is evidence of this new emphasis. More than 20 such organizations can be identified as newly active outside of the United States.[16] In Italy there is a new organization sponsored in part by the Italian stock exchange named *Governance Consulting* with the stated objective of providing counsel ". . . to stakeholders, boards of directors and management in creating business value through the transparent definition of roles and responsibilities,"—that is, better corporate governance.[17] In Asia there is the Asian Corporate Governance Association, ". . . dedicated to informing and assisting Asian corporations on improving their corporate governance practices."[18] As the newfound interest in corporate governance spreads around the globe, public policymakers in democratic countries are left little option but to take the matter seriously.

PUBLIC POLICY

Corporate failures and exposures of fraud in supposedly transparent business organizations during 2002 have so changed the business and political environment that public statements discounting the importance of corporate governance, or advising minority shareholders to mind their own business, are thought to be, at best, politically incorrect or, at worst, evidence of a weak mind protecting even weaker ethical standards.

Increased emphasis on proxy voting as an active investment strategy will continue into the future as institutional investors, labor unions, and small-stake individual shareowners become increasingly convinced that the voting of proxies can go to the shareowner's, and the worker's, bottom line. The establishment and promulgation of principles of good corporate governance and the active involvement of investors in their pursuit of improving corporate governance in general will continue to have influence in financial markets worldwide, separate from proxy voting practices.[19]

Organized labor in the United States has become much more involved in pressing for improvements in corporate governance as one method of increasing worker-owner influence away from the bargaining table. Major unions are very active in the Council of Institutional Investors, and the AFL-CIO is increasing its visible support of corporate governance reform. A recent headline in *The New York Times* reads "Labor to Press for Changes in Corporate Governance" (*The New York Times*, July 30, 2002, p. C-7).

It is important to remember that the increased accumulation of assets by very large institutional investors (primarily pension funds) led to the emphasis on corporate governance as a way to be active in an otherwise passively managed indexed equity portfolio. The documented importance of corporate governance over a 15-year developmental period now influences active investment decisions. The unfortunate short-term nature of most of the world's public equity markets in our high-tech telecommunication world has led to a level of price volatility that has proven harmful to all but a very few fortunate speculators. The increased focus on active advocacy for improved corporate governance as a means of adding value to investment portfolios over the longer period is one positive indicator that short-term speculation may be weakening as the major public equity market driver.

Public policy reform supporting many of the corporate governance principles advocated by patient capital for many years is currently gaining serious attention (even popularity) in both developed and emerging market countries. The continued willingness of institutional investors to pay a premium for equities bought from companies with sound corporate governance practices, operating in countries with protective shareholder laws and sound policy infrastructures, will make it easier for public policy–makers to reform the laws in favor of outside minority investors and more efficient markets. There is compelling evidence of a continuing focus on corporate governance as an important variable in making investment decisions.[20]

The rise of capitalism, the continued growth of pension funds and other patient institutional investors, and the increased attention paid to the value of well-established principles of good corporate governance bode well for the global economy in the 21st century. Investor pressure for reform will need to continue if corporations and the countries in which they are based are to improve the conditions under which more productive long-term investment can be made. The global demands for increased patient capital must be met if the world's developed economies are to continue in their leadership role, and if emerging economies are to be successful in their struggle to become part of an economically developed world supportive of democratic principles, free choice, and improved living conditions. The yet-underdeveloped economies around the globe are depending on such progress. It is the world's good fortune that apparently negative current events come on the foundation of positive experience with improving corporate governance globally. The long-run prospects seem very good indeed.

NOTES

1   Cf. Drucker (1988; 1991); *The Economist* (1994); Jacobs (1991, pp. 225–231; 1993, pp. 35–68); Johnson (1990); and Porter (1992).

2   Even very small minority ownership positions (less that one percent in large cap companies) are considered to be as important in the indexed equity portfolio, and deserving of corporate governance attention. See CalPERS (1995) and Pound (1995).

3   See *Business Week* (2002a; 2002b). For good examples of the extent of this debate, see the Organisation for Economic Co-operation and Development (OECD) web site at http://www.oecd.org/EN/home/0,EN-home-28-nodirectorate-no-no—28,00.html and the International Corporate Governance Network (ICGN) web site at http://www.icgn.org/documents/globalcorpgov.htm.

4   The immediate strengthening of objective research standards by securities analysts as represented by the global Association for Investment Management and Research (AIMR) is clear evidence of the increased level of debate. See AIMR press release at http://www.aimr.org/pressroom/02releases/02aimr-ros.html.

5   There is a rich body of literature available regarding the evolution of corporate governance and the contemporary scene, most easily located at http://www.thecorporatelibrary.com.

6   It is this writer's opinion that this balance is the most desirable for healthy development of the world economy. Pressure from investors in the financial markets backed up by increased regulation and statutory mandates is far superior to depending on regulation and statutory mandates as the primary agent of improving corporate governance.

7   The overlapping activities of shareowner value–oriented corporate governance advocacy and company stakeholder corporate governance advocacy is best studied by viewing the work of the Investor Responsibility Research Center and similar organizations. See http://www.irrc.org.

8   For a complete review of related research and the current policy considerations of CalPERS regarding alternative investments, see http://www:thecorporatelibrary.com and http://www:calpers.ca.gov/invest/invest.htm

9   CalPERS' "Corporate Governance Core Principles and Guidelines" are the standard a company's practices are measured against. See http://www.calpers-governance.org/forumhome.asp.

10   *Free riders* are all individual and institutional shareholders who benefit from rising market price of the shares they hold but have made no contribution to the costly work of identifying, analyzing, and communicating with the companies ultimately added to CalPERS Focus List.

11   For example, national rating agencies are establishing governance ratings, as are private organizations. In some cases, research analysts are also making a concerted effort to evaluate corporate governance as part of their research.

12   See http://www.calpers.ca.gov/invest/policies/pdfs/Active-International-Equities-Ext-Managed.pdf.

13   See http://www.calpers.ca.gov/invest/policies/pdfs/Internal-Relational-Program.pdf

14   As of June 30, 2002, CalPERS owned equity at a market value of USD 26.5 billion in approximately 2,400 companies in 40 countries outside of the United States.

15   The selected list of emerging markets is based on the World Bank definition and classification, and is drawn from the countries included in the emerging markets indices produced by the three major international equity market index publishers: Morgan Stanley Capital International, Standard & Poor's, and Financial Times.

16   See http://www.thecorporatelibrary.com

17   See http://www.governanceconsulting.com

18   For additional information contact jamie@acga-asia.org

19   As elaborated above, this includes such activities as CalPERS' annual Focus List, involvement in legislative and regulatory processes, and active support of external organizations focused on governance issues, such as the Council of Institutional Investors (CII) and the International Corporate Governance Network (ICGN).

20   See McKinsey & Company (2002).

REFERENCES

Anson, M., et al. 2002. "The Shareholder Wealth Effects of CalPERS' Focus List." Unpublished Paper, CalPERS Investment Office.

Association for Investment Management and Research (AIMR). 2002. Press release, July 17. Online. http://www.aimr.org/pressroom/02releases/02aimr-ros.html.

Berle, A., and G. Means. 1968. *The Modern Corporation and Private Property*, Revised Edition. New York: Harcourt, Brace & World.

BusinessWeek. 2002a. "Misreading the Enron Scandal," April 24.

BusinessWeek. 2002b. "The Corporate Cleanup Goes Global," May 6.

CalPERS. 1995. "Why Corporate Governance Today," CalPERS Policy Statement, August 14.

CalPERS. 2001. Statement of Investment Policy for Active International Equities—Externally Managed. May 14. Online. http://www.calpers.ca.gov/invest/policies/pdfs/Active-International-Equities-Ext-Managed.pdf.

CalPERS. 2002. *Statement of Investment Policy for Internal Relational Program*. April 15. Online. http://www.calpers.ca.gov/invest/policies/pdfs/Internal-Relational-Program.pdf.

CalPERS. 2002. *Corporate Governance Core Principles and Guidelines*. Online. http://www.calpers-governance.org/forumhome.asp.

CalPERS. 2002. Online. http://www:calpers.ca.gov/invest/invest.htm.

Chandler, Jr. A. D. 1977. *The Visible Hand: The Managerial Revolution in American Business*. Cambridge, MA: Harvard University Press.

The Corporate Library. Online. http://www.thecorporatelibrary.com.

del Guercio, D., and J. Hawkins. 1999. "The Motivation and Impact of Pension Fund Activism," *The Journal of Financial Economics* 52, pp. 293–340.

Drucker, P. 1988. "Management and the World's Work," *Harvard Business Review*, September–October.

Drucker, P. 1991. "Reckoning With the Pension Fund Revolution," *Harvard Business Review*, March.

The Economist. 1994. "Corporate Governance: Reluctant Owners," January 29.

Governance Consulting. Online. http://www.governanceconsulting.com

Graham, B., and D. Dodd. 1940. *Security Analysis*, 2nd Edition. New York: McGraw-Hill Book Co.

Hawley, J. P., A. T. Williams, and J. U. Miller. 1994. "Getting the Herd to Run: Shareholder Activism at the California Employees' Retirement System," *Business and the Contemporary World* 6, Fall.

International Corporate Governance Network (ICGN). 1999. *ICGN Statement on Global Corporate Governance Principles*. July 9. Online. http://www.icgn.org/documents/globalcorpgov.htm.

Investor Responsibility Research Center (IRRC). Online. http://www.irrc.org

Jacobs, M. T. 1991. *Short-Term America*. Cambridge, MA: Harvard Business School Press.

Jacobs, M. T. 1993. *Break the Wall Street Rule*. Reading, MA: Addison Wesley.

Johnson, E. 1990. "An Outsider's Call for Outside Direction," *Harvard Business Review*, March.

Karpoff, J., P. Malatesta, and R. Walking. 1996. "Corporate Governance and Shareholder Initiatives: Empirical Evidence," *Journal of Financial Economics* 42, pp. 365–395.

McKinsey & Company. 2002. "Global Investor Opinion Survey: Key Findings." Online. http://www.gcgf.org.

Nesbitt, S. 1994. "Long-Term Rewards from Shareholder Activism: A Study of the CalPERS Effect," *Journal of Applied Corporate Finance* 6, Winter.

The New York Times. 2002. "Labor to Press for Changes in Corporate Governance." July 30, p. C-7.

Organisation for Economic Co-operation and Development (OECD). Online. http://www.oecd.org/EN/home/0,,EN-home-28-nodirectorate-no-no—28,00.html

Porter, M. E. 1992. "Capital Choices: Changing the Way America Invests in Industry," *Journal of Applied Corporate Finance* 4.

Pound, J. 1995. "The Promise of the Governed Corporation," *Harvard Business Review*, March–April.

Snijders, R. 1992. "Shareholders' Activism and the Institutional Investor." Paper presented at Mees Pierson Seminar on Corporate Governance, Amsterdam, April 22.

Chapter 17

Corporate Governance
Responsibilities of Fund Managers and Institutional Investors

Mark Mobius

The term *corporate governance* has come to mean many things to many people. To some it concerns the behavior of corporations in their community regarding the environment, treatment of child labor in developing countries, and so on. To investors, fund managers, and investment managers, it has a very specific meaning: how companies treat shareholders, particularly minority shareholders. We, as investors, are less concerned about the relationship and interaction amongst managers, board directors, employees, clients, and the community at large and more interested in the relationship between the company and its shareholders. Once a fair treatment of the shareholder is in place, and once shareholders have their proper share in deciding the future of the company in which they are invested, other interests will fall into place since issues such as treatment of labor, care for the environment, and other social issues will take their rightful place as crucial issues that impinge on the company's success.

The premise of corporate governance is based on the answer to the question of whose interests a company should serve and how to ensure that managerial decisions do indeed further these interests.[1] The application of good corporate governance standards does not lie only with a company's management but also with shareholder groups such as fund managers and institutional investors. One critical form of such activism is participation on company boards.

The heightened awareness of the importance of the responsibilities of fund managers and institutional investors has increased recently as large companies such as Enron and WorldCom dissolved while shareholders stood by helplessly. As a result, independent members on boards as well as representatives of large investors have been reminded of their responsibilities. Although learning in the field of corporate governance has been rapid, only now has the world begun to understand that the boards can play a much more crucial role in sound corporate governance and the survival of a company.

What are the relevant roles of fund managers and institutional investors? Should they participate on company boards? Is this not logical in view of the large amounts of equity being held by fund managers and institutional investors? Is there a tendency toward greater control by fund managers in the corporate world? What are the advantages and disadvantages of fund managers and institutional investors becoming more active? What can be done to strengthen the role of fund managers and institutional investors?

ROLE OF THE BOARD

The board of director's role is to act as the main mechanism for effective monitoring of the management and for providing strategic guidance to the corporation. The principles (of corporate governance) make it clear that it is the duty of the board to act fairly with respect to all groups of shareholders and with stakeholders, and to ensure compliance with applicable laws. Board members should be able to exercise objective judgment on corporate affairs, independent of management (Nestor, 2000). These principles are good, but they cannot be implemented without the active participation and support of key major shareholders as well as minority shareholders.

Over the years, there has been an increasing tendency by companies, institutional investors, and fund managers to participate actively in improving board practices. Codes of conduct, more voluntary than formal, are being developed to improve key areas such as decision-making, disclosure, and candidature requirements for boards of directors. These "bottom-up" approaches are now fuelling the momentum for improving boardroom practices. Both at the levels of behavioral change and normative improvements, the push from within the corporations themselves as well as from investors has been defining the roles and responsibilities of boards.

The trend

Outside directorships by institutional investors is not a new phenomenon. Investment managers such as Capital International Research, Berkshire Hathaway, NCH Capital, and Soros Fund Management have been known to participate in boards.

Despite the growing importance of corporate governance practices, information in the areas of corporate ownership, structures, compositions, board practices, and compensation is still scarce. Mapping out the extent to which fund managers and institutional investors are part of corporate boards and discovering their respective compensations is hard to do. At best, in this situation, one can look at some global examples and attempt to put together a semblance of the situation.

In terms of the structure and balance of ownership, mutual funds and institutional investors are now increasingly controlling corporate equity. In the United States, mutual funds are one of the largest owners of corporations and control about USD 3 trillion in stock: as reported in August of 2002, "The 75 largest mutual fund companies control 44 percent of the voting power at US companies" (Salon.com, 2002).

In 1998, California Public Employees' Retirements System (CalPERS)—one of the largest pension funds in the United States—decided to put its representatives on the boards of companies in which it held investments (*San Francisco Business Times*,

1998). CalPERS believed that some of the companies were troubled and needed board-room reforms. At that time, CalPERS' approach seemed intrusive to spectators, but it clearly illustrated the importance of the responsibilities of institutional investors. Developing a basic definition of an ideal director, CalPERS concluded that board directors should be independent from management, maintain long-term commitment, have a large investment in the company, and also be "friendly" to shareholders' rights. At that time, CalPERS was investing in many of the Fortune 500 companies and was representing the interests of a large number of investors. Some of these companies had problems that could be resolved only through efficient boardroom practices, and to CalPERS, putting its own representatives on the board seemed the right thing to do. Being independent from the management, these representatives had the interest of the shareholders at heart and could introduce changes through proxy votes and boardroom lobbying.

In a recent study conducted by McKinsey & Co., investors indicated that they were willing to pay a premium ranging from 11 percent to 41 percent (depending on the country of investment) for companies that had good corporate governance standards (McKinsey & Co., 2002). This, they believed, meant that:

- There was a majority of outside directors on the board.

- The outside directors were truly independent of the management.

- The directors had significant shareholdings.

- A material proportion of the directors' compensation was related to their stockholdings.

- There were mechanisms for formal evaluation of directors.

- The boards were very responsive to investors' questions on governance issues.

The study results demonstrated that investors were willing to pay a premium for the shares of companies that they thought were practicing good governance. With large funds, such as CalPERS, taking a real interest in the companies in which they are investing, there is a great sense of relief amongst individual shareholders. The responsibilities of fund managers are now increasingly expanding to include ensuring good governance practices in companies that they recommend to their investors. After all, how can a manager invest its clients' funds in a company without being confident about its operations and without believing that the company will continue to operate to the best of its capabilities in the future and not be deceived by company executives? Although participation on the board does not guarantee this, it surely reduces the chances of deceptive behavior and thus results in greater confidence in the company.

Recent events in the corporate finance world have highlighted the importance of the role that fund managers play while they are on the boards of companies. Take as an example the Council for Institutional Investors,[2] a body set up in 1985 that aims to encourage its member funds, as major shareholders, to take an active role in protecting plan assets and to help members increase return on their investments as part of their fiduciary obligations. The Council has over 120 pension fund members with assets totaling more than USD 1 trillion. The Council, making effective use of Rule 14a-8 of the Securities Exchange Act of 1934, which permits shareholders in US companies to submit resolutions and requires companies to include them in proxy statements, tracks all companies reporting majority votes on shareholder-sponsored resolutions. Based on the results of such votes, the Council—according to its own rules of good governance— writes to the CEO of each of the companies and requests information on the board's processes for evaluating the results and the board's recommendations following the votes.

Relevance to emerging markets

In the wake of scandals such as the one surrounding Enron, the credibility of the systems and legislation in the developed markets is in question. Markets that were perceived to have had achieved a respectable model of corporate governance are now reeling. Although traditionally alarm bells really started ringing when one was confronted with the situation in emerging markets, this is no longer the case. The Enron and WorldCom fiascos have showed investors that developed markets are not necessarily safer than emerging markets. Emerging markets have come a long way in implementing sound corporate governance standards; with the growing importance of such practices, we expect efforts on this front to continue.

Admittedly, emerging markets still require assistance in terms of institution building. In these markets, majority/family ownerships are common, disclosure levels are low, shareholders' rights are sometimes ignored, and judicial recourse is uncertain. Board membership is one way of tackling these issues. A large number of companies face a lack of expertise in terms of human resources and experience. Poverty goes hand in hand with mismanagement, misappropriation, and corruption. As the principles of corporate governance are being introduced into the developing world, more and more companies are opening up to independent boards of directors who can curtail such problems. Fund managers who have a broader perspective of the financial world would be more useful on the boards of companies that are still looking for direction. Such individuals can help not only to improve boardroom practices, but also to lend credibility to a company. Companies have also been able to raise funds with greater ease as a result of having well-known and credible fund managers on their board. As iterated above, board representations may also minimize the chances of managements abusing the rights of minority investors.

Issues

While studying the context in which fund managers operate, there are several issues one must recognize. These issues cut across most of the managers' responsibilities and functions.

Lack of well-defined systems and procedures

Dipping back into the normative side of corporate governance, one does find that there is a lack of laws that articulate the responsibilities of fund managers and institutional investors. There are some codes that are being developed by individual companies, but there has been little progress in terms of policy-level intervention that defines relations and interactions. Individual companies or groups of investors may be able to devise their own strategies to deal with particular situations, but these measures may not be enough to improve the overall climate that supports sound corporate governance. Do these laws affect the larger community? CalPERS, when it saw that there was trouble, opted to go in and sort out the issues itself. This CalPERS could do, but can other institutional investors take up such an expensive exercise? In addition, will such measures help improve the legal requirements and compliance to the effect that boards exercise good corporate governance? The answers are probably that these might be short-term steps that one fund manager or institutional investor could take. They do not, however, formalize a general and internationally recognized practice. The need, therefore, is to have clear principles that guide fund managers and institutional investors in fulfilling their duties as board directors, portfolio managers, and representatives of a large number of shareholders.

Ownership

Who runs the company, the management or its shareholders? The question of ownership lies at the heart of the way in which loyalties are defined. Is the director loyal to the company, to the shareholders, or to the fund management institutions? Where are limits drawn? Are there controls that are set to delineate specific areas of interest for an individual? Ultimately, "governance is unlikely to improve much until the institutions that own large chunks of corporate America start acting as real owners, by keeping a sharper eye on their boards and their management" (*The Economist*, 2002). Being an owner allows the exercise of one's right over one's property. In Enron's case, no one owned that company. The directors abused their positions. The issue is that, if the shareholders see something wrong with the company in which they own stock, then what rights do they have to exercise their ownership?

Remuneration

According to a *BusinessWeek* executive compensation survey covering 365 public companies in the United States, the average CEO earned USD 13.1 million (the figures included salary, bonus, and long-term compensation) in 2000 (*BusinessWeek*, 2001). In comparison, the board chairman and CEO of Enron, Kenneth Lay, earned over USD 140 million, which included USD 123 million from exercising stock options. Enron's board of directors was fully aware of Lay's compensation package, approving it with "little debate or restraint" (US Senate Permanent Subcommittee, 2002). In early 2001, the company paid out a total of approximately USD 750 million in cash bonuses for 2000, when net income for the year totaled USD 975 million (US Senate Permanent Subcommittee, 2002). Despite knowledge of these bonuses, Enron's Compensation

Committee failed to realize this. This further highlights the need for independent directors who have the interests of the company and shareholders at the forefront of their decision-making.

Conflicts of interest

The Senate Subcommittee's report on the role of the board in the collapse of Enron (US Senate Permanent Subcommittee, 2002) states that one of the reasons behind Enron's collapse was the failure of the board, amongst other things, to address conflicts of interest. It allowed Enron's chief financial officer to set up and run LJM private equity funds, which transacted business with Enron and earned profits at Enron's expense. The board clearly overlooked this. In the report, the Senate Subcommittee recommended that "directors of publicly traded companies should take steps to prohibit conflicts of interest arrangements that allow company transactions with a business owned or operated by senior company personnel" (US Senate Permanent Subcommittee, 2002). The existence of a fund manager (who takes into account the interests of the shareholders) on the board might have prevented this conflict by asking the right questions and taking a tougher stand at board meetings.

Number of seats that a director can hold

In addition to his regular duties, a fund manager on the board of companies is required to attend board meetings and deal with other company-related issues, all of which requires time. In recent times, debates have emerged over the number of board seats that a board member can hold. As executives become senior in their professions and are in high demand, they tend to become more sought after. However, as their involvement in various boards expands, their representation on each respective board tends to become diluted and thus ineffective. The National Association of Pension Funds (UK) and the Association of British Insurers have recommended that executive directors hold only one non-executive seat in any other board, with non-executive directors holding up to five such seats (*Business Day (Johannesburg)*, 2002).

ADVANTAGES AND DISADVANTAGES OF HAVING FUND MANAGERS AND INSTITUTIONAL INVESTORS ON THE BOARD

Fund managers can bring a vast amount of resources to the companies that enlist them as board directors. On the other hand, their dual roles may also lead to various concerns.

Advantages

Enhancing the value of holdings

Templeton Asset Management, in its efforts for better corporate governance procedures and structures in emerging markets companies, has gained recognition, not just amongst institutional investors but with the invested companies as well. The managements of these companies have begun to understand the importance of good corporate governance and often sought Templeton's representations on these boards as a testimony of their stand. For example, the management of Lukoil recently invited me to join their board of directors. Having observed that they had indeed made much progress in providing transparency to the market, I agreed. Shortly after that, the market reacted and other institutional investors also begun to reevaluate Lukoil, as they believe that Templeton would not have agreed to become involved and put itself at risk if the level of transparency was not there. More importantly, Lukoil and Templeton's clients can rest assured that there is an independent voice and a pair of objective eyes at the board. As a result of this assurance, the efforts of the management are recognized and the value of companies such as Lukoil enhanced.

As mentioned earlier, names such as Franklin Templeton on a board may also indirectly increase the value of that company, especially when it is going public or seeking additional funding. For example, when Templeton's private equity fund decided to invest in Wimm-Bill-Dann, a Russian dairy producer, the management insisted that I take up a board seat as one of their conditions for the private placement. As our fund mandate allowed for board representation, I agreed. I have been told that my agreement to join the board of Wimm-Bill-Dann enhanced the attractiveness of the public offer of the shares of the company on the New York Stock Exchange. The IPO went exceptionally well for a Russian company.

Value can also be enhanced through improving the capacity of the company, by providing strategic guidance and sharing experiences. An expert in corporate finance would definitely be an asset to a newly established company.

Shareholder rights

Enron, which in a period of three months fell from being a respectable company to a corporate pariah, crossed all limits of shareholders rights and confidence. The company's board of directors failed to intervene in problems from accounting malpractice to misleading disclosures. "The Enron board of directors failed to safeguard Enron shareholders and contributed to the collapse of the seventh largest public company in the United States, by allowing Enron to engage in high risk accounting, inappropriate conflict of interest transactions, extensive undisclosed off-the-books activities, and excessive executive compensation. The Board witnessed numerous indications of questionable practices by Enron management over several years, but chose to ignore them to the detriment of Enron shareholders, employees and business associates" (US Senate Permanent Subcommittee, 2002). The board had ample warning. It was not a sudden collapse. Since 1999 many incidents occurred that should have prompted the directors to take some action. The first sign was when the accounting practices followed by Enron were deemed to be pushing the limits. In the next two years, the board approved several arrangements that amounted to considerable conflict of interest. By 2001, the company had pushed some of its activities off the books and had started misreporting on its financial statements. The board did not raise any questions. Its members, even during the Senate Subcommittee hearing, contended that they did as much as they could as board members.

The presence of representatives from shareholder groups such as fund managers or institutional investors on Enron's board might have resulted in fewer opportunities for malpractice in the boardroom. The issue is that shareholders' rights are not being safeguarded unless there is active interest by institutional investors. If the boards are left to their whims and fancies, in the way Enron's board was, then the rights of shareholders can be harmed. As a result of Enron's collapse, it was the shareholders who suffered the losses—not the management and certainly not the board. Should we really blindly trust people who have no investment in a company with overseeing its operations?

Investor confidence

As investors become more aware of how to protect their investments, they are also realizing that a well-run company is a better option than a company with little credibility. Investor confidence now hinges strongly on the level of comfort that the investors have with a certain board and the way it works. Investors are also looking for individuals on boards that have the experience and knowledge of running companies.

Protection of investors' interests

There are studies to suggest that, in general, companies with good corporate governance perform better. However, few institutional investors are willing to spend time and effort to promote corporate governance. More often than not, they would rather ride on the coattails of others. Active participation from fund managers and institutional investors could ensure that companies follow good corporate governance practices, the benefits of which could result in the form of higher stock prices. The results of a CLSA study show that there is a strong correlation between corporate governance and share-price performance. The data are analyzed by fitting groups of companies into quartiles of corporate governance ranking for various markets/sectors (495 companies and 25 markets). One of the key findings of the study was the presence of a strong correlation between corporate governance and the price performance of the largest stocks. In the three-year period covered by the study, the average total return of the 100 largest companies by market capitalization was 127 percent, with the top corporate governance quartile providing an average total return of 267 percent. Stocks in the bottom corporate governance quartile underperformed with an average return of 49 percent (CLSA, 2001).

Improved monitoring and oversight

Management competence is a very important decision-making factor when investing in companies, whether the companies are in developed or emerging markets. Being on the boards of these companies provides a certain level of scrutiny of the competence of the boards and the management that is not often available during routine company visits. The boards will now have to justify their decisions, as they know that their every step is being watched and their incompetence may be communicated to the investing public. The market will react unfavorably if reputable fund managers decide to sell out of the company or resign from the board because they do not believe in the ability of the board or the management of the company. This examination is in addition to the usual scrutiny of the accounts, appointment of auditors, compensation of the executives, related transactions, and transactions in which the directors have interests.

Access to information

Being on the boards of invested companies could allow fund managers to gain insight into the workings of the companies that may not be available at routine company visits. Additionally, these fund managers would be able to gain knowledge about the trends of the market and industry, the manufacturing process and its difficulties, the company's competitors and concerns, and the drive of the company. This is valuable information that may also contribute to the education of analysts and that will help them to value other companies in the same industry properly. The fund managers must, however, be careful not to make use of any material non-public information to benefit their clients or themselves.

Synergy

Investment managers—with their experience, their breadth of coverage, and their locations/coverage in markets—can help synergize the companies on whose boards they would serve by referring potential customers from other countries, by introducing additional capital to the company whether through their internal sources or their compatriots in the market, by linking potential partners that they might know or by merely sharing experiences.

Commitment

Many companies like to have institutional representatives on their boards as it signifies a certain commitment and belief in the management and company. In many ways, a refusal by the majority shareholders to support independent institutional investors as board members is a red flag that there is more than what is on the surface.

Disadvantages

The disadvantages to having fund managers and institutional investors on boards are few, but they should be discussed. From the point of view of an investment manager, there can be allegations of trading while pending the release of material information into the public domain. Also there can be allegations of trading on insider information where there is independence, as well as the possibility of lawsuits arising from duties as directors to the boards.

Trading restrictions pending release of information to public or on insider information

A fund manager, as a director of a company, needs to respect the periods during which disclosures cannot be made. As a director, the individual has the duty not to share any information; as a fund manager, there is a responsibility toward the company where he or she is employed. Hence, a conflict of interest may arise.

Independence

Are fund managers truly independent members of a company's board? When studying the concept of independence for board directors, one comes across definitions of directors who are independent from the management. The question is whether or not fund managers are also independent from being portfolio managers for that particular company. Most of the time it is not possible for the fund management company to nominate people who are not already dealing with investment decisions. In addition, as the market conditions and needs of the clients change, there might be times when the fund manager who is also a board director may start handling stocks of the same company. The issue is then of how to define *independence*. To whom is the fund manager loyal—the company where he or she is employed or the company on whose board he or she is?

Lawsuits

With growing corporate scandals such as those of Enron and WorldCom, board directors have been increasingly shying away from once-appealing jobs due to the growing possibilities of legal action. McKinsey & Co. reported that out of the nearly 200 board directors who were interviewed, over 25 percent had either stepped away from or turned down a seat because of personal legal liability issues (*USA Today*, 2002). In 2001, 485 class-action fraud lawsuits were filed in the United States, compared with just 109 in 1999 (*USA Today*, 2002).

RESPONSIBILITIES OF A FUND MANAGER AND INSTITUTIONAL INVESTOR

The responsibility of a fund manager or any director—or any person who is ever given a job—is toward the job itself. Although in an ideal world it would be possible to have only one role and fulfill it to the best of our abilities, practically in our lives we play a wide variety of roles. We strive to fulfill each role to the best of our capabilities; when one is a fund manager, one must give all to the position. However, when the fund manager takes the role of the director, he or she must also try to be the best director possible.

Good corporate governance is not a set of hard and fast rules and procedures. It is an attitude that brings a sense of responsibility into the corporate world. It says that there should be care taken in the way companies are run and there should be loyalty greater than pure self-interest. In the recent debacles, directors stood aside while management misled shareholders by fabricating the accounts, conducting shady deals, and disregarding corporate governance standards. The disinterest in the company or the idea of saving one's own self can only help corruption seep deeper into the corporate world.

Fund managers, despite their dual roles as investment managers and board directors, can ensure that they fulfill the following responsibilities as board directors by following two simple but important duties (*Delaware Corporate Litigation Reporter*, 2002).

Care

Fund managers must display care toward whatever they are supposed to do. If they are to review accounts, then that should be done carefully. Decisions that need to be made should be made with due diligence. Enron is a classic example of directors' indifference or malfeasance, where the company collapsed because there were instances where care was not taken. Any board director, in order to fulfill his or her fiduciary duty, must carefully gather data and study it in order to make appropriate decisions for the company.

Loyalty

The Delaware Surpreme Court stated that loyalty "as a public policy, existing through the years, and derived from a profound knowledge of human characteristics and motives, has established a rule that demands of a corporate officer or director, peremptorily or inexorably, the most scrupulous observance of his duty." The rule requires an undivided and unselfish loyalty to the corporation and demands that there shall be no conflict between duty and self interest" (*Delaware Corporate Litigation Reporter*, 2002).

Like the principles of corporate governance, these two parameters that define the responsibilities of fund managers and institutional investors are simple and straightforward. Forming the basis of any commitment, care and loyalty can help accomplish things in a just and fair manner.

RECOMMENDATIONS AND CONCLUSIONS

Corporate governance is an abstract idea that talks of things such as exercising care and being truthful as well as fair. In the hard world of corporate finance, such words may sometimes appear childish or naive. The truth is much farther from this. The following blocks of wisdom have helped many directors keep their companies afloat:

- Records of board meetings should be kept properly. Minutes should identify the decisions that were made, and should record the background discussions and rationales for decisions. Short and cursory notes can help create gaps in information, which can then be misused.

- Fund managers should not personally deal with a company's insolvency. They should keep track of a company's solvent status and make appropriate decisions if there are movements toward insolvency.

- Fund management companies may disperse the responsibilities amongst its employees, so that those individuals with direct trading decisions of the company are not also on its board. This would ensure decreased conflict of interest and unbiased trading by the fund manger.

- Setting down the written procedures for the approval of directorships, proper practice of his fiduciary duties, proper ring fence and sanitization of any material non-public information, keeping all transactions at arm's length, and providing training and education will also help reduce conflicts and ease the decision-making process.

As the corporate world strives to achieve maturity in terms of corporate governance issues, it also needs to delve into issues that need to be explored and solved. The importance of fund managers and institutional investors, as board members, is becoming increasingly evident. As a fund manager, I believe that only when we take an active role will our rights be respected.

It has been suggested that fund managers can also limit their exposure by recruiting independent third bodies to represent them on boards. Although this is a preferred option, it should be realized that it is often very difficult to find the right person for the job. The level of competence may be compromised or the representative may not be willing to devote sufficient time and/or effort to the same cause. Research undertaken by the National Association of Corporate Directors shows that the average outside director now spends between 175 and 200 hours (per directorship) a year preparing and attending meetings, compared with 100 hours in 1999 (*USA Today*, 2002). As such, there is a chance that an individual may not have the same motivation, and may decide to side with the management to avoid any confrontations or lengthy proceedings.

Thus, the question is not whether or not fund managers and institutional investors should participate on boards at all, but how the company and its investors can benefit from their participation.

NOTES

1   http://www.oecd.org/publications/observer/212/Article10_eng.htm

2   http://www.cii.org.

REFERENCES

Business Day (Johannesburg). 2002. "Corporate Activists Not Always Independent," July 5.

Business Week. 2001. "Annual Executive Compensation Survey 2000," April 16.

CLSA. 2001. "Corporate Governance in Emerging Markets: Saints and Sinners." CLSA Study, April.

Delaware Corporate Litigation Reporter. 2002. "Venture Capitalists as Directors: Avoiding Increased Liability From Serving on the Board of an Insolvent Company," April 1.

The Economist. 2002. "The Value of Trust," June 8–14, pp. 63–66.

Mc Kinsey & Company. 2002. *Global Investor Opinion Survey: Key Findings*. Online. http://www.gcgf.org.

Nestor, S. 2000. "International Efforts to Improve Corporate Governance: Why and How." Paris: Organisation of Economic Co-operation and Development, Corporate Affairs. Online. http://www.oecd.org/pdf/M000015000/M00015846.pdf

Salon.com. 2002. "The Feeling Is Mutual," August 27.

San Francisco Business Times. 1998. "Does CalPERS Really Want To Join the Board?" January 23.

USA Today. 2002. "Boards Find It Harder to Fill Hot Seats," July 31.

US Senate. 2002. Permanent Subcommittee on Investigations of the Committee on Governmental Affairs. *The Role of the Board of Directors in Enron's Collapse*. Washington, D.C., July 8.

Chapter 18

Corporate Governance and Private Equity Investments

Max Burger-Calderon, Philipp Gusinde, and Stefan Hoffmann

This chapter focuses on the interdependence between corporate governance and private equity investments. The chapter begins by outlining the difference between private equity investments and investments in public equity and bond markets and their impact on corporate governance structures. As private equity investments, in contrast to investments in public companies, are to a large extent negotiable and hence independent from the corporate governance rules provided by statutory law, the contractual design of efficient corporate governance structures is of predominant importance. Following this outline is a depiction of customary contractual provisions for the establishment of a corporate governance regime at the portfolio company level, and the pitfalls of such provisions. The chapter then deals with the corporate governance standards private equity companies apply to themselves as investees of the contributors to private equity funds.

THE DIFFERENCE BETWEEN PRIVATE EQUITY INVESTMENTS AND INVESTMENTS IN PUBLIC EQUITY AND BOND MARKETS AND ITS IMPACT ON CORPORATE GOVERNANCE STRUCTURES

The terms private equity and venture capital

Private equity and venture capital investments are equity investments in privately held (i.e., nonlisted) companies. Private equity/venture capital companies provide equity sources for smaller, often young and innovative, companies that do not (yet) have access to the public equity and bond markets. As private equity/venture capital investors take equity stakes in the portfolio companies they invest in, their investments not only improve the companies' liquidity through the cash contributions they make, but also strengthen the companies' debt-to-equity ratios and thus the companies' ability to attain further debt financing. Consequently, private equity/venture capital investments have a substantial impact on the portfolio companies' ability to finance their continued development and growth.

While the terms private equity and venture capital are widely used synonymously, there seems to be some trends toward using the term venture capital for investments in startups/early-stage companies, while the term private equity is applied to all other investments in privately-held companies. For the purposes of this chapter, the term private equity is to be used in the broader sense, encompassing all forms of equity investments in private companies.

A further distinction commonly made is the one between "informal" and "formal" private equity: informal private equity concerns direct investments made by so called "business angels," often wealthy individuals, in private companies; formal private equity is understood to be the investment of funds raised by private equity companies from institutional and individual investors in diversified portfolios of private companies selected by professional fund managers. This chapter exclusively deals with formal private equity.

The different occasions for private equity investments

There are various occasions for private equity investments. Every economically reasonable employment of equity funds in private companies can become a private equity project. In practice, private equity investments are distinguished according to the development stage of the investee company at the time of the investment. Early-stage, or "startup," financing covers the provision of funds for the development of a product idea through to market readiness and the preparation of marketing concepts. The next stage involves "growth financing" for companies wishing to expand their production facilities and their marketing network after a successful market launch, either through internal growth or through the acquisition of other companies in the same industry. Later-stage investments can be subdivided into "bridge financing" and "management buyouts" (MBO) or "management buy-ins" (MBI). Bridge financing is the provision of funds to enable a more mature company to overcome stagnating growth and prepare for a possible initial public offering (IPO). MBO and MBI transactions deal with the structuring and financing of solutions for the succession to company ownership and leadership, where a family-owned and family-run business can find no suitable successor within the family. In an MBO transaction the company is bought by the incumbent management, whereas an MBI concerns the acquisition by a new, external management team. As management hardly ever has the financial capability for acquisition, it regularly teams up with one or more private equity investors to finance the deal. For that purpose, the management and investor set up a new entity (NewCo) that purchases the company. In addition to the equity funds provided by the investor and the management's own capital contribution, NewCo typically raises a substantial amount of debt to finance the acquisition. The equity investors are thereby able to limit their equity exposure and increase their return on investment (the leverage effect). This, of course, goes hand in hand with an increased risk of losing the equity funds invested if the return of the borrowed moneys falls short of the interest costs.

A separate, and less significant, group in terms of investment volume are "turn-around financing" transactions, in which investors provide equity to support the reorganization of distressed companies.

The negotiation of investments

In contrast to purchases of securities issued by public companies, which usually take place anonymously, private equity investments are negotiated between the existing shareholders (often the founders/managers) and the private equity company. The private equity company's decision to invest and the existing shareholders' decision to accept a new investor are driven not only by the price offered or demanded, but also by the contractual conditions the parties are willing to adopt. This circumstance facilitates the contractual implementation of individual and sophisticated corporate governance frameworks, widely independent from the corporate governance standards provided by the rules of law applicable under the jurisdiction of the respective portfolio company's domicile. The detachment from generally applicable legal regulations and nonbinding corporate governance codes such as are promulgated by governments and organizations on a national level allows internationally active private equity investors to apply widely harmonized corporate governance standards to all their investments, no matter where these are located. However, rules of law can affect contractually-established corporate governance structures because they can restrict the enforceability of certain contractual provisions. As these rules differ between jurisdictions, each individual investment requires close cooperation between private equity companies and their lawyers in order to identify the relevant mandatory rules of law and adjust the contractual corporate governance scheme accordingly.

As corporate governance, in the private equity context, is based on a negotiated contractual framework within which the relationship between the financial investors and the management of the investee company is conducted, the current international corporate governance debate, which focuses on the role of independent directors and the protection of dispersed shareholders in public companies, is of limited relevance.

The contribution of business experience and know-how

In addition to the cash injections made into the portfolio companies, another substantial contribution of private equity investors is the provision of business experience and know-how. Especially in the early-stage financing of innovative companies with often young and inexperienced management, the project managers of private equity companies function as business advisers to the portfolio companies. In this type of investment, the private equity investors put their business reputation at stake with every acquisition. Thus it is essential for private equity companies to implement efficient corporate governance structures in order to be able to monitor and positively influence the portfolio companies' developments. This structure is important because it enables the private equity company to raise more funds from its investors in the future, as well as succeed against competing investors in future investment opportunities and ultimately fulfill its responsibility to the economy on the whole.

In an MBO/MBI context, private equity investors must be specifically experienced and skilled in the areas of financial engineering, tax, and corporate law. The existence of leverage financing requires the optimization of the company's tax situation and its corporate structure in order to maximize the generation of cash flows that are needed to discharge the ongoing obligations to pay interest and redeem debt; this optimization, in turn, requires efficient corporate governance structures. Accordingly, lender banks regularly seek to review investment documents prior to making a financing commitment, and they will demand that sufficient investor rights be included in the contractual arrangements.

The time limitation of private equity investments

Private equity investments have a time limit. Typically, private equity investors look for a return between five and eight years after the original investment so as to enable returns to be made within the time frame set out for the underlying funds. The return on investment is largely realized on exit, and not by the distribution of dividends. This explains why corporate governance structures in private equity investments focus not only on monitoring and controlling the current business operations, but also on securing a profitable exit for the investors.

CORPORATE GOVERNANCE AT THE PORTFOLIO COMPANY LEVEL

The contractual provisions for the establishment of a corporate governance structure at the portfolio company comprise board rights and information, voting and control issues, dilution protection rules, management incentive programs, and exit regulations. The basic scope and content of these provisions are set forth below.

Board rights and information

Private equity investors typically appoint directors to the board of directors of the investee company. In jurisdictions where the company has a supervisory board and a management board (e.g., in Germany), private equity investors usually appoint members to the supervisory board only, as the purpose of such supervisory boards is to monitor and control rather than to directly manage the investee company. The investor fulfills an advisory role through the (supervisory) board (via the investor-appointed board member), as the board is the body that discusses and evolves the future strategies for the company.

The number of directors that the private equity investor is entitled to appoint will depend on its relative bargaining power, and often reflects the relative shareholding proportions of the private equity investor and the other shareholders. Where the investor's share quota is likely to vary in the future, for example, because it intends to subscribe to further shares in future capital increases or syndicate its shares to other investors, it is possible to link the number of investor-appointed directors to the number of shares held by the investor.

Sometimes the private equity investor's right to appoint directors is extended to the boards of the investee company's subsidiaries, especially where the investee is merely a holding company. However, this procedure is not permissible in every jurisdiction.

On some occasions, a private equity investor will want to avoid appointing a director because, for example, of concerns regarding the legal responsibilities attached to board membership under the law of the relevant jurisdiction, or because the investor does not want third parties to view the investor as being involved in the management of the company. In these cases, the private equity investor will seek a right to appoint one or more observers who are entitled to receive information from management and to attend and speak (but not vote) at board meetings.

It is worth noting that in some jurisdictions, under certain circumstances, a private equity investor may risk liability (e.g., in the case of the insolvency or bankruptcy of the company) because the investor is a "shadow director." In such a jurisdiction, this risk is increased where the investor is considered to be actively managing the company or controlling the decisions of the boards.

In addition to receiving company information via their board members or observers, private equity investors often try to promote company undertakings entitling them to receive certain categories of information directly from the company. Such undertakings may cover, among other things, the provision of financial information including the preparation of annual and monthly accounts, budgets and cash flow reports, the right of investors to examine books and records of the company and to undertake due diligence on the company and its group, and the right to consult with the management. As the company information received by the investor or the board member/observer appointed by the investor is, by its nature, confidential, the distribution of such information is legally, and often contractually, restricted. However, private equity companies often seek certain easements of these restrictions, such as the right to share the information received with companies of its own group, in communications with their own investors, and sometimes even in communications with third parties, such as potential syndicates or purchasers of the investor's shares.

Voting and control

In the absence of express contractual regulations, a private equity investor's rights with respect to voting and control will depend on the corporate law of the particular jurisdiction within which the investee company is incorporated, the applicable provisions of which will, in turn, depend on the size of the investor's shareholding. In most jurisdictions, the investor will need to exceed 50 percent and in some cases 75 percent of the voting share capital in order to pass resolutions regarding significant corporate events, such as the amendment of the articles of association, the increase and decrease of the company's share capital, the repurchase of shares by the company, the declaration of dividends, the appointment of auditors, or the approval and adoption of the annual accounts of the company.

Where a private equity investor does not take a (qualified) majority position, it will seek contractual protection by veto rights over said corporate events. Even where an investor takes a majority stake, the investor will demand veto rights for management actions that do not require shareholder or board approval under statutory law, for example, capital expenditure or contractual commitments in excess of preagreed limits, major acquisitions or disposals, significant changes in the nature of the business of the company, changes of accounting methods or policies, or the appointment and dismissal of key personnel.

Once the scope of matters that are subject to a right of veto has been determined, the parties need to agree on whether these matters should be dealt with at the board or shareholder level; that is, whether the approval of the investor-appointed director(s) or the approval of the investor herself will be required. In this context the investor should consider that an investor-appointed director may face a conflict of interest between the interests of the company and the interests of the investor, as a nominee director is under a fiduciary duty to exercise his powers for the benefit of the company as a whole and not for the particular shareholder who appointed him. As opposed to the nominee director, in many jurisdictions, a shareholder is under no duty to take wider interests into account but can act solely in his or her own interests. Hence, in areas where conflicts of interest can arise it is preferable to ascribe the veto right to the shareholder level rather than to the board level. In practice, how the veto rights are split between the board level and shareholder level is often dependent on the propensity of the subject matter to create a potential conflict of interest.

Dilution protection

Especially in early-stage financing when company valuations are difficult to determine due to the lack of either a track record or sufficient financial data on the company, private equity investors face the risk that investors in future funding rounds will apply lower valuations and thereby economically dilute the initial investment. A further aspect of dilution is the reduction of influence in the company that results from the decrease of the shareholding percentage of the initial investor, which is triggered by the issuance of new voting shares.

One means to address both aspects of dilution involves preemption rights. In some jurisdictions these are provided by statutory law; in others, they have to be contractually agreed upon. Preemption rights entitle existing shareholders to subscribe to the number of shares necessary to maintain their existing percentage shareholding in the company each time new shares are issued. However, preemption rights as a form of dilution protection are often unattractive to private equity investors, since they require additional investment in the company.

Common methods to protect the initial investor from the economic effect of dilution include certain adjustment mechanisms, namely the so-called full ratchet adjustment and the weighted average adjustment.

A full ratchet provision is based on the understanding that if the company issues shares to a subsequent investor, the price per share of that later issuance shall be the price at which the earlier investor should have been entitled to invest in the first place. The full ratchet method can be backed up by the notion that the later valuation of the company is considered more accurate than the initial valuation, and that the initial investors should be treated as if they had invested at the latest, most accurate, valuation. Technically, the protected investor is granted the right to acquire as many additional shares at no cost as are necessary to make his average price per share equal to the price paid in the subsequent financing round. Full ratchet adjustments have frequently been used in the United Kingdom, especially in early-stage financing where valuations are difficult to support objectively.

As indicated by its name, the weighted average adjustment allows for the effect of the subsequent lower-priced investment relative to the aggregate price of shares issued in prior rounds. In contrast to the full ratchet mechanism, the weighted average approach leads to a proportionate adjustment that is less favorable for the protected investor, but often considered to be fairer than a full ratchet adjustment. The weighted average adjustment has been the most common form of antidilution protection for US private equity investors.

Management incentive schemes

Management incentive schemes used in the private equity context are primarily equity-based or equity-related. The general objective of such schemes is to equate the incentives of the management with those of the private equity investor, thereby creating a community of interests, which should assist not only with putting the deal together in the first place, but also to promote smooth management of the company in the future. In order to truly incentivize the management to strive for the creation of value for themselves and for the private equity investor, the scheme needs to be structured in such a way that the management shares in both the risks and the rewards of the venture.

The first decision to be made when structuring a management incentive scheme is between a real equity participation and an options solution. If the sharing of risks and rewards approach is taken seriously, options have to be discarded from the design of an efficient incentive program. Options might grant more flexibility to deal with changing circumstances (e.g., difficult market conditions or a delayed exit), as it is possible to rebase the exercise price that a manager must pay in order to subscribe to the underlying shares. However, options do not have the upsides and downsides of share ownership. From the downside perspective, the holder of options does not risk any own capital at the outset, while management equity requires a real financial commitment. From the upside perspective, ownership and a community of interests is more remote in an options program, as it requires that the options rest upon the achievement of certain performance criteria and other conditions, and that they are exercised.

The next issue to address concerns the conditions for the acquisition of management shares in comparison to those taken by the private equity investor. Almost invariably, the management will demand preferential treatment, so called "sweet equity," that is, participation in the form of a higher proportion of ordinary shares for each euro invested than the private equity investor gets. The incentive effect of sweet equity alone is questionable, as the benefit is granted to the management up front irrespective of its performance.

A preferable approach is to combine sweet equity with a performance ratchet mechanism, so that the amount of the "sweetened" management shares relative to that of the private equity investor increases (positive ratchet) or decreases (negative ratchet) depending on whether the company exceeds or falls short of certain targets, such as the private equity investor's target internal rate of return (IRR).

In any event, an efficient management incentive program has to account for the fact that different phases in the life of a company require different management skills. Therefore, every scheme has to consider the need to allow for a natural management turnover and to prevent the furtherance of rigidity. The instruments for providing the required amount of flexibility are so-called leaver rules. These rules provide for the compulsory sale of a manager's shares in the event that he leaves the company, with a distinction drawn between the circumstances of and reasons for the manager's departure. A "most favored leaver" is one who departs as a result of retirement, death or ill health, while "good leavers" have usually had their employment terminated by the company without cause. For both groups, the departing manager typically receives the higher of full fair market value or cost for his investment. The term "bad leaver" refers to the voluntary resignation of a manager, while "for cause leavers" are those who terminate the employment for cause. Bad leavers typically get the lower of fair market value or cost, while for cause leavers may be required to transfer for no consideration.

Exit

Exit methods and exit covenants

As mentioned earlier, securing a profitable exit is a primary focus of private equity investors. There are two principal types of exit route: the IPO of the investee company, and a trade sale to a strategic investor or secondary sale to another financial investor. In order to ensure that an exit is realized within the investment time frame of the private equity company, which in turn is determined by the duration of the private equity funds managed by it, private equity companies typically demand an exit covenant from the investee company in which it is acknowledged that the management will employ reasonable efforts to arranging an IPO, a trade sale, or a secondary sale prior to a certain date. However, because of its inevitable vagueness, such a clause is extremely difficult to enforce. In practice, it chiefly serves as a statement of intention and to focus minds on the anticipated exit strategy throughout the duration of the investment. Any such covenant will be made more effective by including arrangements as to how and by whom the exit will be controlled. Topics to be addressed include the questions of who has the right to force an IPO or trade sale, who is entitled to select the investment bank or other adviser organizing an IPO or trade sale, and who will pay the related fees. Further regulations may comprise the method of establishing the offer or trade sale price, the timing of the IPO or trade sale, the choice of stock exchange for an IPO, and the granting of lock-ups and warranties to underwriters (on an IPO) or purchasers (on a trade sale).

Management's motivation to work toward a profitable exit might be increased by equity-based incentive schemes, ideally in combination with performance ratchets.

The prospects of realizing the envisaged exit route and timing can be impaired by unwanted third parties entering the company with motivations and plans different from those of the private equity investor. This danger can be countered by restriction of transfer provisions that subject every transfer of shares to the investor's prior approval.

As a means of last resort to realize a timely exit, a private equity investor may try to negotiate buyback rights that require the management or the company to buy or redeem the investor's shares if no exit has been achieved within the defined period of time. However, this is only effective if the management is financially capable of funding the purchase of the shares or the company is legally able to do so. It should be noted that in several jurisdictions, buybacks or redemptions by a company of its own shares are usually only permitted if certain, fairly stringent, criteria are met. In addition, it will usually be the least profitable exit route, as a predetermined pricing formula will mean that the exit price is effectively capped and cannot be changed even if the business is worth more.

Initial public offering

Generally, an IPO is considered to be the most favorable exit route. In buoyant public capital markets, an IPO will generate a higher price than a trade sale or a secondary sale. An IPO is also often favored by the management as it allows them to remain in place and control, albeit with a range of institutional and private shareholders—this is often preferable to the personal risks of a trade sale to a single shareholder that brings its own management. The downside of an IPO is that it regularly does not provide a full exit, as statutory or contractual lock-up provisions, the negative price impact of block sales, and the lack of sufficient market liquidity usually require the investor to retain a significant portion of its investment for a certain period following the flotation. If the investor is able to sell only a small portion of its shares, a good flotation price will be of little value if the price in the market falls before the investor is able to sell the remainder.

If an exit by IPO on the US securities markets is envisaged, the private equity investor should insist on registration rights entitling it to demand that, if certain preset thresholds are met, the investee company register the sale of its securities with the Securities and Exchange Commission.

Trade sale/secondary sale

When stock markets are depressed, or if the private equity investor depends on a full exit, both trade sales and secondary sales become attractive. Many private equity investors actively consider the range of potential trade buyers before they make their initial investment. However, management is often opposed to trade sales because these regularly entail the loss of their independence. In case the management fails to realize a trade sale within a defined period, the private equity should have the contractual right to seek buyers and to disclose information about the company when soliciting offers from third parties. As a company is far more saleable when 100 percent of the shares are for sale, a private equity investor with a majority stake in the company will insist on a so-called drag along right, which enables the private equity investor to force the remaining shareholders to sell their shares to the chosen buyer on the same terms and conditions as did the investor. In most cases, a drag along right will only be accepted by the remaining shareholders if it is accompanied by so-called tag along rights for the minority shareholders, entitling them to sell their shares to the third party chosen by the private equity investor on the same terms and conditions as majority shareholders.

CORPORATE GOVERNANCE AT THE PRIVATE EQUITY COMPANY LEVEL

As opposed to informal private equity investors, such as business angels, private equity companies are not only investors. Private equity companies have to raise the moneys they invest in the portfolio companies from their investors, the contributors to the private equity funds. These investors are both wealthy private individuals and (to a much larger extent) institutional investors, including pension funds, insurance companies, and banks. As intermediaries of capital, the private equity companies' efforts to establish efficient corporate governance structures at their portfolio companies are not only vital for their own profits (which are, of course linked to the success of the funds they manage), such efforts are also a direct consequence of private equity companies' obligation toward their own investors.

Managers of private equity funds have to apply efficient corporate governance principles to themselves in order to allow their investors to monitor the administration of the funds entrusted to them. Typically, private equity firms today are characterized by a structure involving a general partner who manages the fund, investors, and an adviser to the fund. The general partner is responsible for making investment decisions and the ongoing operation of the fund. The adviser assists in implementing the fund's investment strategy by constantly looking for new investment opportunities, performing due diligence, preparing investment and divestment decisions, and monitoring portfolio companies.

It is therefore important to distinguish between corporate governance-related issues at the fund level and issues arising at the advisory company level. The life cycle of a fund usually comprises fundraising from investors, investment of the proceeds, management of investments, disposal of investments, distributions to investors and liquidation of the fund. Long before one fund is finally liquidated and all proceeds passed back to investors, a new fund is usually raised and invested.

The following paragraphs broadly follow these stages and highlight the corporate governance standards that private equity companies apply to themselves as investees of the contributors to private equity funds. As outlined in more detail below, the first four sections focus on corporate governance issues at the fund level, whereas the two sections that follow these four are viewed from the advisory company level.

Fundraising

The fundraising stage is where the basis of the general partner's relationship with the investors is established. Fundraising is usually restricted to certain potential investors who can reasonably be expected to be suitably experienced with investments involving a high degree of risk. To help in evaluating the risk associated with the investment, an offering memorandum that contains basic information on the scope of the fund (e.g., target economies), the investment policy and investment criteria, and other fund strategy-related information, is drafted. It is important that the document contains full and true information and that it is presented in a manner that is fair and not misleading.

As outlined in more detail further below, the decision to invest in the private equity fund usually constitute the only decision investors can (and should) take during the normal course of a fund's life. Ideally, investors should have the ability to choose between funds and their related strategies, but not to the ability to choose individual investments of a fund. If the offering memorandum has clearly stated that investments in, for example, biotechnology, are targeted, the investor should not be able to change his commitment simply because he thinks it might not be a good time to invest in this area right now.

Corporate governance issues can also arise when subsequent funds are raised. As described above, new funds are usually raised when an existing fund is almost fully invested. Raising subsequent funds is fundamentally important to every private equity company to ensure a going concern. However, conflicts of interest may arise when the investor base of the subsequent fund is different from its predecessor. Even if both funds pursue an identical investment strategy, it may become difficult to determine which fund will invest in a given opportunity. The same holds true if both funds are invested in one and the same portfolio company. Exit timing requirements will be fundamentally different, as the more mature fund may already be approaching the end of its life cycle. Again, the offering memorandum should disclose any parallel funds and properly define (subsequent) fundraising procedures.

Fund structure

As discussed above, the offering memorandum constitutes the basic document for the structure of a fund. In addition to a summary of the relevant risk factors, the following matters are usually addressed in this document:

- the investment strategy of the fund (targeted regions, targeted sectors), investment criteria, and investment restrictions;

- term, legal structure, and termination and liquidation procedures for the fund;

- a description of the management team, its powers, and the carried interest arrangements;

- the mechanism for the draw down of commitments, valuation principles, and co-investment rights; and

- default mechanisms and conflict of interest resolution procedures.

Of paramount importance to proper fund structuring is the definition of the terms of investment. Investors may be keen to acquire certain preferential rights or economic advantages (e.g., reduced management fees) in exchange, for example, for early or distinctively high commitments. However, as a general rule and whenever possible, all investors in a fund should be treated in the same way. Any preferential treatment or specific economic benefits to individual investors should be avoided, and, if unavoidable, made transparent to all other investors so that they at least know that certain other investors benefit from preferential treatment.

The extent to which specific investors are granted influence over the management of a fund should be considered with even greater care. If such influence alters the management structure of a fund it can compromise investors' limited liability. Substantial influence on the management of a fund and, in particular, the decisions to invest or divest, can subject the fund to merger regulations and notification requirements with undesirable consequences for the fund and the investor.

Therefore, as a general rule, investors should not have any influence on the day-to-day management of a fund. Investors as limited partners should not take a role that is explicitly reserved for the general partner, who is fully liable for his decisions. An advisory board with representatives from a few investors is a much more useful way of using the investor's experience and knowledge. A board of advisers can be consulted if certain portfolio developments arise or if a potential conflict of interest has to be managed.

Portfolio investments

In certain circumstances, investors may be inclined to invest alongside a fund, if a particularly interesting investment opportunity arises. If the fund structure does allow for parallel investments, these co-investment rights should always be granted to all investors in a fund. In all cases, the offering memorandum should disclose these facts. It should be noted that co-investments also trigger a fair amount of administrative processing.

As discussed earlier, the existence of two or more funds managed by the same general partner is common in the industry. Problems arise when these funds hold shares in the same investment. Depending on the age of the fund, return expectations might differ as newly-raised funds might favor an early exit to achieve favorable IRR statistics, whereas mature funds might have to exit because they have come to the end of their life cycle.

Exits from one fund to another should be considered with great care. While it might be the right time for one fund to exit (e.g., because of the life cycle of a fund), there may still be future value that can be created in the investment through a secondary buyout. However, clear conflict of interest issues can arise, such as price, and whether or not warranties are to be given, and what conditions are attached to the warranties. If the portfolio investment subsequently performs better than expected, the former shareholding fund could have done better by either holding on to the asset, by or requesting a higher valuation at exit. Whenever considering such a fund-to-fund transaction, the general partner should be able to demonstrate that it has been negotiated on an arms-length basis, and that no fund has been preferred at the expense of another. Investors in both funds should be made fully aware of the transaction.

Any potential acquirer of a portfolio investment up for sale will commonly seek a range of warranties and indemnities from the fund. The negotiation of warranties and indemnities will often be a key issue when disposing of an investment. In negotiating, one should consider the risks in giving such warranties and indemnities against any enhancement of return that they could bring. When deciding whether to give a warranty or indemnity, one should also take into account the remaining life of the fund, and the fact that in the future it may be difficult to draw down cash to meet liabilities in the event of a claim. Warranties and indemnities should normally only be given on a disposal where this is expected to produce an enhanced return for investors. In any case, the liability under such clauses should be capped in both quantum and time.

Investor relations

Reporting obligations are important for investors wishing to monitor the status of their investment. The nature of funds means that valuing an investment on an ongoing basis is difficult and, without information from the general partner, investors cannot effectively monitor the performance of the fund. The fund's constitutional documents should contain provisions regarding the general partners' obligations to provide reports to investors. These provisions should address the following issues:

- the frequency of reports to be made;

- the information to be contained in these reports;

- the manner in which the reports are to be made (e.g., in writing); and

- the basis of valuation that will be used for such reports.

The general partner should seek transparency in its relationship with investors by ensuring that all of them receive all significant information regarding the fund in a clear and timely manner. Certain investors may require different information, or information presented in a different way, to satisfy their own tax, regulatory, or commercial obligations. Where practicable, the general partner should comply with those requests.

To simplify the process of obtaining consents from investors and providing them with informal updates, particularly when there are many investors in a fund, it is possible to set up a representative advisory board or committee. It can also be a useful mechanism by which to obtain advice on managing conflicts of interest and agree on any changes to valuation principles. The Advisory Committee may be established to give consent on behalf of investors if a conflict of interest or duty has arisen concerning the fund, as well as to receive informal reports and provide feedback on other matters raised by the general partner. The powers of any such committee should be set out in the fund's constitutional documents, and the committee should not be able to influence the general partner's investment decisions, as this can compromise investors' limited liability and may give rise to issues relating to regulation of merger control.

Investment decisions

When making investments on behalf of a fund, the general partner must implement the fund's investment policy with due skill and diligence. The information acquired during the due diligence process, together with the general partners' own knowledge and expertise, will form the basis of any investment decision. The information required to make this decision will usually have been gathered and critically appraised during the due diligence phase. After due diligence, the information should be summarized for the investment committee that decides whether or not to make an investment. As outlined above, the individual investment decision should not be influenced by fund investors (as limited partners), but should always reside with the general partner.

Undertaking a successful due diligence exercise that confirms the validity of the underlying assumptions of a business plan will not generally be sufficient in itself. Investors look to the experience of the senior managers within a fund to add value to the due diligence exercise through the critical application of their business experience. Investment decisions should therefore be made by suitably senior and experienced personnel. It goes without saying that the investment decision should be made jointly (ideally by an investment committee). The persons responsible for proposing an investment should not be involved in making the investment decision, and, if they are, they should not have a deciding vote.

It is not only for investment decisions that proper standard procedures need to be in place. Internal processes that are directly or indirectly linked to investments should also adhere to high standards (e.g., human resource management, accounting, or record-keeping). There should be special attention to preventing insider trading, as some investment decisions may involve quoted companies. Especially in smaller private equity funds, investors may seek guidance with respect to key-man succession; that is, how the general partner avoids dependence on few key people in the firm.

It is common knowledge that an incentivized and motivated team is vital to the success of the general partner. By adopting appropriate policies to maintain a stable and motivated team, the general partner is likely to improve returns to investors. Therefore, suitable remuneration schemes should be implemented. It should be ensured that carried interest and similar arrangements are structured in a balanced manner to motivate and incentivize the team and its key members throughout the life of the fund. Carried interest arrangements should include provisions that prevent a bad leaver from participating in them. It should also be ensured that there are provisions delineating the extent to which good leavers are permitted to participate in carried interest arrangements. Valuation very often turns out to be a difficult task in this respect. Current methods include net asset value, market value, and third party valuations.

Portfolio work

It may be necessary or desirable to make further investments in an investee business (e.g., to fund future expansion plans or to refinance a poorly performing company). The opportunity to make a follow-on investment in a successful investee business may give rise to a conflict of interest, where the general partner is managing more than one fund in which she has invested, or where the general partner or its associates have invested directly in the investee business. The fund's constitution should make provision for further investments into an investee business after a fund's investment period, either through a "follow-on fund" or through provisions allowing the general partner to retain funds to make a follow-on investment. Decisions to make such follow-on investments should be done in the same manner as the original decision to invest, and should be supported by adequate written evidence that demonstrates that further investment is a clear benefit to the fund.

Unfortunately, not all investments will succeed, and while it may not be possible to save an investment made in a company that has a fundamental structural problem, it may be possible to turn around a poor performance record or preserve value in an investment through increased monitoring of the investment and meetings with management. When information received as part of the monitoring process reveals that an investment is not "performing," remedial action plans have to be implemented. However, conflicts of interest may arise if a quick exit is likely to preserve at least part of the original investment; some investors may be opposed to a long restructuring process during which the whole investment could be at stake.

CLOSING REMARKS

In private equity investments, efficient corporate governance structures are of predominant importance. As investments are negotiated, the parties set up contractual corporate governance schemes that are widely independent of the corporate governance rules of statutory law. Since private equity investors invest in companies in different industries and located in different jurisdictions, and that are in different stages of development, there is a particular need for the thorough design of appropriate corporate governance regimes.

In summary, the three-tier structure in formal private equity investments (comprising investors, a private equity company, and a portfolio company) requires strong active management on all three levels if it is to succeed.

Corporate Governance in Transition:
China, Russia, and Poland

Chapter 19

Corporate Governance in Mainland China
Where Do We Go From Here?

Anthony Neoh

THE ESSENTIAL QUESTION

The essential question facing corporate governance in developed economies is whether a board of directors can be expected to devise and operate a system of management of the affairs of a corporation so as to protect the interests of all internal actors (such as shareholders and employees) and external actors (such as creditors and the public interest). Implicit in this question is the concept of a separate corporate existence; in other words, the existence of a corporation as a separate body capable of acting in its own right, separate from the providers of capital, who enjoy equal protection under the law. This implicit assumption is one that has only recently arrived in mainland of China, which explains why ideas of corporate governance formed in developed economies do not readily find direct application in the mainland economy. Nearly two centuries of legal development have gone into the doctrines governing corporations in developed economies. But, as a developing country, China has developed its own legal system only since 1949, unlike most other developing countries, which have a legacy of legal systems inherited from former colonial rule or some other form of political dependency. To understand these implications, one must go back into history.

PREEMINENCE OF THE STATE-OWNED ECONOMY

When the People's Republic of China came into being, the first provisional constitution of 1949 abolished all previous laws. But this provisional constitution and the first constitution of 1954[1] both accepted diverse forms of property ownership, including ownership by providers of capital. Thus, although the laws of the old regime were abolished, economic relationships, particularly when it came to dispute resolution in

The views expressed here are completely personal and do not necessarily reflect the views of any institution the author has been associated with, including, but not limited to, the China Securities Regulatory Commission whose Chief Advisor the author has been.

courts or arbitral tribunals, had to be governed by principles borrowed from the former civil code. However, as time went on, and as capitalists and former landowners
were weeded out in increasingly tumultuous political developments, the forms of
ownership dwindled. In the 1975 and 1978 constitutions, now dubbed the Cultural
Revolution Constitutions, the recognized forms of property ownership came to two,
namely, state ownership and collective ownership.[2]

The 1982 constitution, enacted to replace the Cultural Revolution Constitutions,
did not open up the categories of ownership. In addition to adopting the two old forms
of property ownership, it emphasized that state ownership roots out exploitation and
promotes the concepts of full use of each person's skills and the (fair) distribution of
resources according to a person's contribution of labor.[3] Since 1982, however, individual enterprises have sprung up but they have been small businesses since the law only
allowed two forms of ownership. Therefore, as such enterprises grew, they had to
masquerade either as collectives or state-owned enterprises.[4] It was not until 1988,
in two constitutional amendments, that the private economy was recognized by law
and that land use rights could legally be held and transferred.[5] However, these amendments did little to encourage the private economy to emerge from its adopted hiding
places, namely, collectives and state-owned enterprises, because in 1993, another constitutional amendment dictated that the state-owned economy is the guiding force of
the people's economy and the state should consolidate and develop the state economy.[6] It was in this context that the Companies Law of December 1993[7] was enacted.

RECOGNITION OF PRIVATE RIGHTS AND THE PRIVATE ECONOMY

It was not until 1997, at the 15th Party Congress of the Chinese Communist
Party, that the legitimacy of private enterprises and the private economy was finally
and unequivocally written into official doctrine. The predominance of the state-owned
economy nonetheless remains part of official doctrine, although the Secretary General's
Report devoted substantial space to explaining Party Policy in this regard. In that
explanation, it was made clear that the predominance of the state-owned economy
means that the state should henceforth endeavor to restrict its holdings to industries
that are of strategic importance, namely, those industries that affect the defense of the
realm and the livelihood of the people. The 1999 constitutional amendments that
explicitly recognized the rule of law adopted this policy, and stated that individual
enterprises and the private economy are integral parts of the socialist economy and
should be protected by law.[8] Thus, the concept of equal protection for the providers
of capital only became a legal reality in 1999 and even then, it is attenuated by the
continuing acceptance of the predominance of the state-owned economy. The 16th
Party Congress, whilst accepting that all private providers of capital can join in the
political process of the Party,[9] did not deviate from the general doctrine of acceptance
of the predominance of the state-owned economy.

CORPORATE GOVERNANCE IN ITS INFANCY

Against the foregoing background, corporate governance, which relies on the equal protection of the providers of capital as an underpinning doctrine, can only be said to be in its infancy. Be that as it may, once we recognize this background, we should be in a better position to devise future policies. But first, let us look at the practical results of our legal and constitutional developments.

Although the concept of a separate corporate existence has been in our statute books since 1986[10] (and arguably earlier by way of legal analogy from the pre-1949 civil code), it was not until recently that most corporations became state-owned or began to masquerade as either state- or collective-owned. As a result, there has been little incentive to put speed behind the enactment of a comprehensive bankruptcy code despite the fact that one such code has been under consideration for nearly 10 years. At the same time, property rights have become obfuscated. Since state-owned enterprises are owned by the state, they receive their assets by state grant. These grants are not often formalized. To the extent that the grants are land or other user rights, the granting of these rights are contained in administrative decisions, records of which are either incomplete or sometimes lost or do not exist. Sometimes operational rights of businesses are dependent upon certain policies given to the enterprise as an expedient, but the rationale of that expedient has long since expired.

Since 1992, the State Council has tried to delineate property rights more clearly by forming a Bureau for State Assets. This Bureau has smaller versions of itself duplicated at the Provincial and City level, but was itself folded into the Ministry of Finance in 1995. The mission of this Bureau is to administer state assets and ensure that the state gets maximum value from these assets. Determining what value is, of course, a difficult thing, and a vexing question even in developed economies. The question of value can only be answered adequately when one has an efficient market where economic forces can compete relatively freely, and where the methods of accounting are well developed so that measured value is a reasonable reflection of economic reality. In the absence of efficient markets, it has not been possible to devise accounting methods which adequately reflect economic reality because as the markets become more efficient, historical methods of accounting lose their relevance. The mentality of the officials administering state assets is therefore one of conservatism, and one manifestation of this is that they hold fast to, and become imprisoned in, historical measures of value. In a fast changing economy, this holds the seeds to many future problems.

Still on the question of mentality, there is yet another changing scene being played out. At the central government level, it was not until 1992 that a movement to divest ministries of their commercial and industrial functions began. Between 1992 and 1995, the various ministries concerned with operating industry were closed and replaced by corporations wholly owned by the state. The movement was carried forward with greater energy when the 1995 administration of Premier Zhu Rongji came into power, and now, all commercial and industry activities previously operated by government ministries are in state-owned corporations. Former ministers were posted to the new corporate positions and government departments became nascent regulatory bodies. At the provincial level, the same drama is played out. Former government officials now head the various provincial state-owned corporations, and the former government units that headed these operations have either closed or incorporated into newly formed regulatory bodies. The government has worn these separate hats with much uneasiness. On the one hand, it has commercial and industrial enterprises to operate and responsibility for a vast army of employees. On the other, it has to play the role of regulator, and look after a wider, public interest. In many areas, the government has had to live an almost schizophrenic existence, being torn between these interests.

MANAGEMENT SUCCESSION

Furthermore, underneath this uneasy existence is the question of management succession. The current generation of managers have come from the ranks of government officials. Will the next generation come from the same ranks or should some other method of succession be found? This is both a management and political issue for China, as up to the present, management succession has been done by the Party Organization Department at various levels of government and not by a corporation itself. That is absolutely fine when the Party Organization Department has the clear mission of planning succession for public officials. Superimposing another mission on this function blurs the focus of the original mission. Political awareness and trustworthiness is clearly a highly important, and sometimes over-riding, attribute for a public official. But in a highly competitive commercial environment that is increasingly becoming globalized, another set of attributes will be more important than political attributes. This is a question to be pondered for the future, but the immediate result of the current system of management succession is that managers of state-owned corporations regard their political standing to be paramount. Where the state is not the only owner of the corporation, that mentality may have unpredictable consequences. Sometimes, the pursuit of political standing may well coincide with creating value for the minority owners, but sometimes there may be a deviation from that goal. What happens is a function of the direction of the political winds of the day. Managers under the current system of management succession will tend to not regard themselves as long-term players in the corporation, nor do they see their interests as identical to the pure economic interests of the corporation's owners. The majority owner has interests that are wider than pure economic interests, but the minority owners have pure economic interests. When the manager is appointed by the majority owner and sees his future being dictated by the majority owner, it is natural that he or she would side with the perceived interests of the majority owner. Thus, one of the underlying assumptions of corporate governance in developed economies, namely, that the mission of managers is to create shareholder value, do not figure as a pristine doctrine. There will continue to exist a degree of adulteration to the purity of the idea until the issues of management succession can be addressed.

In understanding the development of the capital markets and the concepts of corporate governance, one must therefore bear in mind the foregoing background. This background also explains to a certain extent why it is difficult to compare corporate governance in China to other developing economies. First let us look at the stock markets.

THE STOCK MARKETS SINCE 1992

Since 1992, the market capitalization of the stock markets have risen to over RMB 4 trillion, that is, USD 400 billion (see Figure 19.1). This market capitalization places China's stock markets in ninth place globally in market capitalization terms. However, there are two important differences to other comparable markets.

First, two thirds of the shares of the 1,200 listed companies are not listed, and are presently not allowed to be traded in the markets (see Figure 19.2). The state owns the preponderant share of the nonliquid stock of listed companies. This means that most companies listed in the stock market have the state as its majority owner. At the same time, the shares in listed companies are often held by holding companies wholly owned by the state, which have other less well-performing companies or businesses under their wings. As the state is the majority owner of listed companies, managers of these companies are appointed by the state. Since their future careers are determined by the state, these managers will not tend to see the improvement of

FIGURE 19.1 **Market Capitalization**

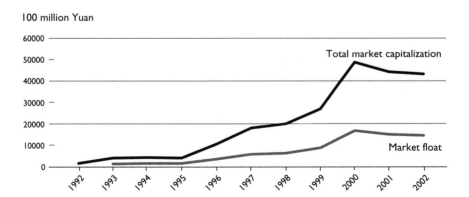

FIGURE 19.2 **Number of Listed Companies**

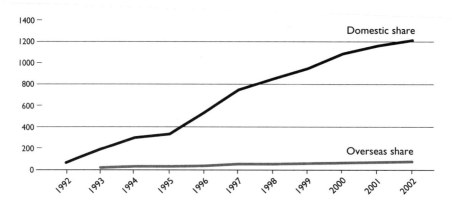

shareholder value as their only objective, nor do they tend to see their long-term future in these companies. The interests of the state and those of minority shareholders often intersect, but where they do not, the interest of the state would most probably, and is certainly expected to, prevail. This in turn leads to short-term behavioral patterns in the stock market.

The small stock of traded shares in the market are turned over far more frequently than shares in other markets and in fact, in the year 2000, which is the year the market had the highest historical turnover, each share in the market was traded five times. In other words, each share in the market changed hands once every two and a half months (see Table 19.1). This phenomenon illustrates that the investment horizon of traders in the stock market is very short-term, and an underlying assumption in the market is that value is maintained by scarcity. This mentality has created interesting consequences.

Since 1999, there has been an effort to improve standards of corporate governance in companies listed in the stock market.[11] In the past two years the effort has been stepped up vigorously in tandem with efforts to police the markets for manipulative activities and other misconduct. At the same time, there have been revelations of false accounting by a few listed companies and the culprits have been prosecuted. Whereas in other markets these efforts could be expected to improve investor confidence and thereby improve turnover and help businesses to raise more money in the markets, the reverse happened in China. Investor sentiment dropped to the lowest point in recent memory, and the market dropped to the lowest point since 1999 (see Figure 19.3). The China Securities Regulatory Commission has been criticized by the public for doing what its counterparts in other countries would be praised for. As the general economy has not contributed to the fall in the markets—listed companies continue to bring in expected performances and deposits in banks (see Figure 19.4) continue to grow as has the economy—there must be other causes.

TABLE 19.1 **Global Equity Markets 2000**

ORDER	MARKET	MARKET CAPITALIZATION USD BILLION	CONCENTRATION (%)	TURNOVER VELOCITY (%)
1	NYSE	11,535	57.1	87.7
2	Nasdaq	3,597	75.9	383.9
3	Tokyo	2,962	70.5	58.8
4	London	2,475	78.3	69.3
5	Paris	1350	86.2	268.8
6	Frankfurt	1186	45.3	128.6
7	Toronto	756	75.5	75.0
8	China (Hong Kong)	624	65.4	60.9
9	**China (domestic)**	**622**	**2.73**	**500.0**
10	China (Taiwan)	237	52.9	259.3

Notes:

All figures (except the figures relating to China's domestic exchanges are taken from http://www.fibv.com, the web site of the international organization of stock exchanges.

The figures relating to China's domestic exchanges are taken from CSRC's own database.

Concentration means the total turnover of the companies making up 5 percent of the total market capitalization expressed as a percentage of the total turnover of the whole market for the year. If liquid market capitalization is taken into account, concentration is about 5 percent in China's domestic markets.

Turnover velocity is the total turnover for the year expressed as a percentage of the total market capitalization. Turnover velocity has in fact climbed down from the 1996 high of 913 percent in Shanghai and 1350.3 percent in Shenzhen.

As the basic pattern of the stock market has been short-term trading, the liquidity created by market manipulation activities create an illusion of perceived wealth, and in some cases, where shares are sold in time, real wealth. When the actions of regulators stop or greatly reduce market manipulation activities, the liquidity evaporates, as does the wealth effect. In a market based on short-term trading, policy signals or perceived policy signals from the government also dictate market sentiment. When the government announced that it would sell its hitherto nonliquid shares of listed companies, the fear of an oversupply of shares further affected market sentiment. At the same time, when the market experienced high turnover, many listed companies took advantage of the opportunity to raise additional capital and thereby released more shares into the market. Intermediaries who rode the highs in the market were caught in the rapid downturn and incurred vast losses. The accumulation of unwelcome news and regulator activities in the markets created a massive overhang of unrealized losses, so that each time new investors were encouraged by new policy signals to come into the market, they were greeted by very eager sellers and market gains were immediately dissipated. The fund-raising capacity of the market remains at a low ebb, and new issues have found it difficult to find buyers (see Figure 19.5).

FIGURE 19.3 **Market Performance in China Stock Market**
(Share A/Share B Jan. 1992–Nov. 2002)

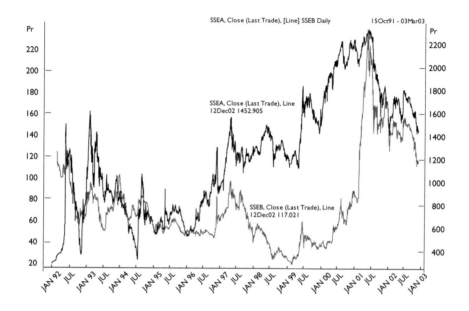

FIGURE 19.4 **Bank Deposits, 1952–2000 (Year-end)**

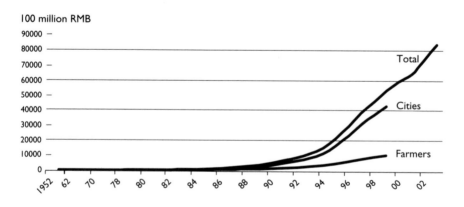

FIGURE 19.5 **Money Raised in the Market**

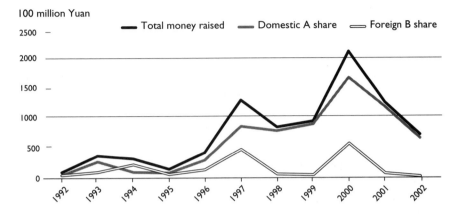

WHERE DO WE GO FROM HERE?

As can be seen, the present state of the markets is the result of "short termism" in managerial attitudes which in turn leads to short-term investment horizons. Yet in an economy that must look to solving the question of capital growth to mitigate the problems of an ageing population,[12] there is a need to inculcate "long termism" in managerial and investor attitudes. Only then can we expect the practices of good corporate governance to take root. Where do we go from here? There are at least two areas that we must address.

The introduction of Qualified Foreign Institutional Investors (QFII) will in time help bring in new capital into the stock markets and new investment patterns.[13] In Taiwan, which introduced the QFII system in the early 1990s, QFIIs have helped create the bell weather, blue chip stocks of the market by rewarding good management with substantial capital. As the successes of QFII investment became apparent in Taiwan, their investments have commanded a following among local retail as well as institutional investors. In time, the QFII system may well do the same for the Chinese stock market by introducing a longer-term investment horizon based on the performance of the management of the company. The market will respond to this evolving pattern by creating appropriate indices and derivative instruments (including nonleveraged passive investment funds), which will further help this pattern take root.

But the system of management succession must also addressed. There is a good case for separating management succession for public officials from management succession for managers of commercial enterprises, particularly for enterprises with minority shareholders. To achieve this, the state will have to tackle the fabled holy grail of separating politics from enterprise.[14] As such, we cannot expect an overnight solution. As a start, however, state enterprises could be managed according to commercial targets agreed between the state and the managers and a system of compensation set up based upon achieving of these targets. But so that these targets are realistically set and monitored, the state might consider appointing holding company boards with expert advisers from China and elsewhere.[15] As a start, autonomy could be given to the boards of listed companies to find their managers from the market. This could, of course, include recommendations from the majority shareholder who will continue to be advised by the Party Organization Department, but the board of a listed company will be given the responsibility to consider these candidates against the best available candidates in the market. The compensation of managers of listed companies can be designed to ensure that they must regard the creation of shareholder value as the primary objective not only in the short term, but also in the long term, so that option schemes, for example, could include exercise dates postdating the departure of the manager from the company.

Finally, the legal system must follow through with planned reforms. The bankruptcy code should see the light of day as soon as possible. The long-awaited reform of the Companies Law should also be introduced as soon as possible. The reforms under consideration include minority shareholders actions against directors and shareholders. With these reforms, the Investor Protection Association[16] now being studied by the China Securities Regulatory Commission will become meaningful.

Corporate governance will only have meaning when it is allowed to grow in fertile soil. The toils of the sower will come to naught if the seeds sown fall upon barren ground. Let us hope some of the issues raised here will be tackled in the future.

NOTES

1 Article 17 of the Common Program of the Political Consultative Congress of 1949 abolished all laws, regulations, and judicial systems established by the Kuomintang government that oppressed the people; all future laws must protect the people. In practice, in the early years of the People's Republic some of the commercial laws were adopted by reference to the Kuomintang Civil Code, even after the new constitution was adopted in 1954. In Article 5 of the 1954 constitution, the forms of property ownership were defined as: state ownership, that is, ownership by the whole people; collectives, that is ownership by collectives of those who contribute their labor; individual ownership; capitalist ownership.

2 Article 5 of the 1975 constitution states also that certain types of individual labor activities may be allowed by law but they must not be exploitative of others, and practitioners should be guided towards a socialist collective system.

3 Article 6. However, Article 11 allows the legal formation of personal enterprises and such personal enterprises will be protected by law.

4 For a more detailed discussion, see *The Private Sector in China,* a research study published by the International Finance Corporation of the World Bank, in 2000.

5 Articles 1 and 2 of the 1988 constitutional amendment.

6 Article 5 of the 1993 constitutional amendment.

7 The Companies Law became effective on July 1, 1994. The text of the Companies Law makes it plain that the Law was created with the state-owned economy as the centerpiece. For example, it has a special section dealing with companies wholly owned by the state and companies with majority ownership by the state—such companies have special privileges in terms of capital raising.

8 Article 16 of the 1999 constitutional amendment.

9 In its preamble the constitution establishes the leadership of the Chinese Communist Party, so participation in the Party political process means participation at the pinnacle of the political process.

10 See the Law establishing General Principles of Civil Law, 1986.

11 There has been a total of nine regulations and normative guides by the China Securities Regulatory Commission since 1999, seven of which were promulgated in the past two years:

1. Code of Corporate Governance for Listed Companies

2. Guidelines for Introducing Independent Directors to the Board of Directors of Listed Companies

3. Guidelines for the Holding of Shareholder's Meeting of Listed Companies

4. Guidelines for Article of Association of Listed Companies

5. Mandatory Provisions to be Incorporated into Article of Association of Companies Seeking Overseas listing

6. Guidelines for Responsibility of Director Secretary of Overseas Listed Companies

7. Notice Prohibiting Senior Management of Listed Companies from Holding Any Position in Controlling Shareholders of Listed Companies

8. Notice Regarding Provisions of Guarantee by Listed Companies

9. Guidelines for Overseas Listed Companies to Further Standardize and Reform Their Operations

12 By 2050, the number of old people in China will exceed the number of young people.

13 The QFII system was introduced on December 1, 2002.

14 This discussion has started during the time of the late Secretary General Hu Yaobang and of our late leader, Deng Xiaoping.

15 Models abound in the world. In Asia, we have the system of Tamasek in Singapore, and the French system of managing state-owned enterprises can also be studied.

16 This Association will most likely follow the Taiwan model whereby the Association will hold one share in each listed company and is able, if the Companies Law is amended, to take representative actions on behalf of all shareholders in the courts.

Chapter 20

Governance in an Emerging Financial Market
The Case of Russia

Igor Kostikov

How to become competitively stronger on the world market is a crucial problem for Russia, and its solution will secure the future of Russia as a state. The concept of competitiveness has several dimensions. One of the key ones is competitiveness on world financial markets. It implies (1) the ability to attract large investments and at the lowest possible price; and (2) the ability to use these investments efficiently, take the company to a new technological level by using them, increase output, and produce new goods and services.

THE NEED FOR IMPROVEMENT IN RUSSIAN CORPORATE GOVERNANCE
Poor corporate governance in Russian companies makes them much less attractive as investment objects. Investors, particularly foreign ones, require dramatic improvements in corporate governance as a condition *sine qua non* for any increased investment in Russian companies. The crisis of 1997–1998 in the emerging markets, especially in Russia, vividly showed that companies' surface well-being and glossy official reports might hide the absence of elementary sustainability and the lack of ability to respond to crisis situations. When managers face major problems, they try to solve them at the expense of investors. No wonder investors have been particularly insistent that they should receive full information about company affairs and take part in real control over the governance process. They want companies' assets to be used effectively, so that their own interests are served.

Experts say that Russian companies might expect a premium of 20 to 30 percent of their current share price for better corporate governance alone (some experts say it might be 50 percent or even higher). Over the last two years, the Russian stock market witnessed examples of Russian companies' value increased by hundreds of percent over a short time. For instance, the price of Yukos oil company stocks has grown over 900 percent from early 2000 to the middle of 2002; the price of Sibneft oil company stocks has grown over 850 percent over the same period; and telecommunications companies' stocks have grown from 250 to 400 percent over the same period. In February 2002, a major Russian food company—Wimm-Bill-Dann—made an initial public offer (IPO) (through American Depository Receipts) at the New York Stock Exchange. At the IPO, its shares were sold at USD 19.5, with a subsequent price rise at the secondary market. The capitalization/profit ratio for Wimm-Bill-Dann reached 21.3. By comparison, the same ratio of the world-famous French company Danone in 2001 amounted to 24.4. Thus we have witnessed the first case of foreign investors (mostly US investment funds) valuing a Russian company at a level close to that of a major Western company. Of course, not all companies have this potential, and phenomenal growth cannot be caused by improved corporate governance alone. Yet these examples clearly show the potential of the Russian corporate sector, or at least of a part of it, in terms of its value growth. We believe that this realization will fuel the enthusiasm of the most ambitious and advanced companies to improve their corporate governance practices as a way to attract more investment. Besides, improvement of corporate governance and higher credit rating would mean a better position on the credit markets and better quality of resources (a larger share of long-term and medium-term investors).

The pressure for better corporate governance practices in Russian companies does not come from foreign sources of capital alone. The domestic investment market is also changing. The developing pension reform promotes the gradual building of large Russian institutional investors—pension funds. As the funded pension schemes take root, Russian pension funds will accumulate large financial resources. Some of them will certainly be invested in corporate shares and other securities. We will therefore see increasingly strong interest in corporate governance as a factor that will affect investment decisions. We might also expect higher activity from other Russian institutional investors (insurance companies and unit investment trusts) in the medium term. For them, too, the corporate governance situation in Russian companies will become important.

LEGISLATIVE PROGRESS

The progress of legislation is an essential tool that will protect shareholders and other stakeholders from abuse by management. Russia has made good progress in this field over the years, and it continues to improve the legislative framework that governs corporate relations. Amendments and additions to the federal law On Joint-Stock Companies, which became effective on January 1, 2002, was another important step toward fine-tuning the regulations in order to make them consistent with developing practices. Amendments to the Criminal Code took effect on June 1, 2002. Under these amendments, managers and corporate officers who are guilty of nonprovision of information about company activities in due time, or who provide false information, will be penalized not only with fines but will also face the prospect of prison terms of up to two years.

Much is yet to be done to improve the legal framework of stockholder and stakeholder protection, including steps toward increasing the effectiveness of enactment and enforcement. At the same time, corporate governance is such a complex phenomenon that it could hardly be regulated by the legislative framework alone. First, we know that such a framework lags behind rapidly developing practices, while the multilevel procedures of amending it are lengthy and highly complicated. Second, the framework is very often inadequate for providing real, not token, protection of the shareholders' legal interests.

ROLE OF THE FEDERAL COMMISSION FOR SECURITIES MARKET

In this environment, the Federal Commission for Securities Market (FCSM) initiated a program targeted at substantial improvements to the corporate governance system. One of its components provides for the implementation of the best corporate governance practices that incorporate both foreign and Russian experience. To this end, FCSM administered the development of the Code of Corporate Governance, which, in April 2002, was presented to the Russian and international business communities. The development of the Code was initiated in the summer of 2000 and was carried out through regular consultations with companies, investors, and experts. The Coordination Council on Corporate Governance was established to serve as a policy forum through which to gather opinions and views of various interest groups and to integrate them in the process of the Code's development. This process was supported by a nationwide awareness campaign.

The Code of Corporate Governance

The Code is a summation of recommendations on all the main components of good corporate governance. Specifically, it contains chapters on each of the following elements governing corporate practice: shareholder general meeting, board of directors, management (executive) board, corporate secretary, major corporate actions, information disclosure, supervision of financial and business operations, dividend policy, and resolution of corporate conflicts. It is not a legislative or regulatory act, but it will be the basis for modalities of implementing its core principles. This will be done through the systems of regulations issued by the appropriate ministries and agencies, professional organizations' standards, amending the relevant laws, and rooting them in the business community practices.

The Code is intended to help shareholders have a clear idea of how one or another joint-stock company functions, who takes the key decisions and in whose interests, and how these decisions are consistent with the principles and procedures that provide for the best use of the shareholders' resources for increasing the value of their shares in the company. Thus, a shareholder will be able to learn:

- effective procedures of convening the shareholders' general meeting, which provides all shareholders with the opportunity to express their opinions;

- what functions the board of directors plays and how often it meets;

- whether the board discusses the problems that are truly important;

- whether there are board committees and what they do;

- what qualification and professional experience the board members have;

- what their results in previous (or full-time) positions are and, therefore, whether they are able to keep real control over the management's operation in the interests of all shareholders;

- what functions the corporate secretary should perform;

- what procedures should be observed while the board makes decisions on the most important corporate issues; and

- other issues of interest.

Principles of disclosure

The FCSM works on putting in place a mandatory information disclosure of companies' corporate governance practices and their consistency with the Code recommendations. The FCSM is now developing the principles of such disclosure. In our view, these principles should be focused on information revealing various aspects of the board's practices (composition of the board and of its committees, frequency of meetings, qualification of directors, and so on); the external auditor's practice, and the auditing (financial inspection) commission's practice. Companies will no longer manage to conceal the status of the main elements of their corporate governance, as occurred before. Accordingly, shareholders will have an opportunity to make much better weighted decisions.

To introduce the system of mandatory disclosure of company corporate governance against the recommendations of the best practices code is not an easy job. Despite the fact that now there are many national and company codes, no country has a system that would provide for the disclosure of information about companies' compliance with Code recommendations that would be full and clear enough to please the investors. The latter insist on the need to put such a system in place, but they are uncertain as to which of the many recommendations should be included and what might the improvement stages be. Therefore, the FCSM has to design an implementation modality for the Code recommendations, although even developed economies have not yet completed such modalities.

With material aspects of company corporate governance practice disclosed and compared with best practice recommendations, an investor will be able to make an informed decision on whether or not to trust his money to a given company. Clearly, there will always be a group of investors who are ready and willing to take high risks— that is, to invest certain amounts in companies with unclear corporate governance systems and low transparency. They will do so in the hope of receiving high profits driven by some other factors (the company owns unique technologies, benefits from monopoly positions on certain markets, and so on), but this strategy is a conscious choice for such investors. The FCSM's goal is the following: investors who do not tend to take high risks but want to invest in highly transparent companies, with a clear and understandable corporate governance system and sound protection for their legal interests, should have a broad choice.

Standards and ethics

In addition to ensuring greater disclosure, the FCSM seeks to introduce high professional standards and rules of ethics in the community of corporate directors. Boards of directors play a crucial role in overseeing company management and ensuring the protection of investor rights. As recent scandals have revealed, even in advanced economies much has still to be done to ensure that boards act in accordance with their mission and fiduciary duties. In Russia, we believe the need to introduce high professional standards is very important, bearing in mind the brief history of the Russian corporate sector and Russian businessmen's limited experience working under a market economy. To this end, the FCSM has encouraged the business community to establish the Russian Institute of Directors, a nongovernmental organization that will work on developing such standards and rules, offering training programs and prospectively acting as a self-regulatory organization for the corporate directors' community.

The FCSM seeks to introduce tighter rules for audit companies that audit firms whose shares are quoted on the open market. As the experience of advanced economies has shown, audit companies often enter into unjustified relations with their clientele of major corporations, helping them hide real facts and figures about their activities rather than disclose them for investors. Since major Russian companies are often audited by major Western audit companies, we believe that this problem should be tackled by joint efforts of the international community.

PROGRESS TOWARD GOOD CORPORATE GOVERNANCE PRINCIPLES

The FCSM expects that as the Russian economy advances along the way of reforms and the general economic situation improves, companies will themselves feel able to take practical steps to improve their governance. This will happen if companies want to attract current or future investments; to do this they will face the need to disclose their corporate governance practices.

The use of good corporate governance principles might be initiated either by companies' managers or shareholders. We think these steps are particularly important for large and rapidly growing companies. Such businesses, because of their nature, need to press managers and shareholders to expand the range of their external investors. This does not mean that companies with fewer shareholders do not feel the need to think about improving their corporate governance systems and taking appropriate measures, however. They too have many problems in this area. But these measures should be a priority for companies whose business scale is such that it generates risks for many investors.

Measures to put in place a good corporate governance system are also important for companies that are going through a merger or takeover. In 2001, Russia was rated first in eastern and central Europe by volume and number of takeovers, and most experts project further and more rapid development of this process. Building an effective and transparent corporate governance system is extremely important for those owners who want to retire from management or reduce their stock in the company as part of their investment diversification strategy, thus lowering the risks of their investments (which are higher if investments are concentrated in a few companies).

RECENT EXAMPLES

Since 1999, the FCSM has witnessed some progress in a number of Russian companies in terms of corporate governance.

In mid 2000, Tempest Consultants (UK) made a survey of investor relations in emerging markets (27 countries) to rate the issuers in terms of the quality of their investor relations policies. Of 13 categories—based on survey questions that asked, for example, about the clarity and depth of the information provided to investors, the quality of the information provided at one-on-one meetings or through a corporate web site, and the quality and transparency publicly disclosed information—the Russian oil companies (such as Sibneft, Surgutneftegaz, Lukoil, and TNK) won in 11.

Over the last two and half years, we have witnessed the formation of a group of Russian companies whose major shareholders and managers (these often coincide) arrived at the conclusion that their development prospects should be closely tied with the attraction of outside investment; securing such investment requires a breakthrough in corporate governance practices. These companies have taken serious steps to improve their corporate governance practices. These steps cover primarily such aspects as shareholder general meetings practice, keeping a registry with an independent registrar, general information disclosure, and investor relations. Very recently, some of these companies have taken dramatic steps in revealing their true ownership structure.

In 2002, the two largest Russian oil companies, Yukos and Lukoil (both on the Financial Times Top 500 of the largest world companies list and ranked 1 and 3 in terms of current market capitalization on the Russian stock market), revealed their ownership structure, identifying the exact number of shares owned by the top managers of these companies. The leading Russian food company, Wimm-Bill-Dann, has also revealed its ownership structure, thus setting an example for other companies in the industry.

Over the last two years, the number of companies that decided to pay substantial dividends to their shareholders has increased significantly.

At the its annual shareholder meeting held in 2002, Yukos oil company decided to pay USD 500 million as dividends, which comes to 16 percent of its net profits and is twice as much as the amount paid out in 2001 (see Table 20.1). Lukoil decided to pay USD 400 million as dividends (17.5 percent of its net profits). Sibneft oil company paid out USD 900 million as dividends in 2001. At its annual shareholders meetings, Sberbank and Gazprom decided to double the amount of dividends to be paid out; subsidiaries of Svyazinvest, the largest Russian telecommunications holding company, will pay out as dividends 22 percent of their net profits on average, with some subsidiaries paying up to 50 or even 89 percent of their net profits as dividends. Norilsk Nickel, the world's largest nickel and platinum producer, will pay 22 percent of its net profits as dividends and declared that in the future it will regularly pay from 20 to 25 percent of its net profits as dividends.

Of course, the percentage of net profits paid out as dividends by Russian companies in general is still far behind that of Western companies, yet progress as compared with all previous years is striking.

TABLE 20.1 **Dividends Paid as a Percentage of 2001 Net Profits**

COMPANY	DIVIDENDS AS PERCENTAGE OF NET PROFIT
Yukos	16
Lukoil	17.5
Norilsk Nickel	22
Svyazinvest	22
Sibneft	90
Mosenergo	15
Rostelekom	17
Gazprom	10

At the annual shareholder meetings held in 2002, outside (independent) directors were elected to boards of more than 60 leading Russian companies, 28 percent more than in the previous year. The United Machinery Plant has become the first Russian company whose board has a majority of independent directors (all are expatriates).

TRENDS AND GOVERNMENT SUPPORT

The FCSM considers that the above examples and trends should produce a positive effect on the Russian business community at large and lead to an extension of the group of Russian companies that espoused good corporate governance practices. The Commission believes that this process would take firmer roots and extend its scale if backed by the appreciation of foreign investors in the form of more investment coming to these companies, thus proving in the most practical way that good corporate governance pays off.

The program of corporate governance improvement initiated by the FCSM in 2002—which includes, among other features, the development of the Code—was supported by Russia's government. The draft Code was considered at the meetings of the government in November of 2000 and 2001. The resolutions taken at those meetings recommended that the state representatives in the governance bodies of joint-stock companies with public capital should actively promote the best corporate governance principles stated in the Code. The idea that any company with a large proportion of stock owned by the federal government could receive contracts or financial support from the federal government only if it follows best practices rules was also discussed. In early July 2002, Russian Prime Minister Mikhail Kasyanov met with the OECD general secretary Donald I. Johnston and confirmed that the Russian government considers corporate governance to be a high priority in its activities, and that it will continue to cooperate with the OECD and other international organizations on improving corporate governance practices in Russia.

REFERENCES

Brunswick UBS Warburg. Russia Equity Research. 2000a. *Corporate Governance Analyzer*. May. Online. http://bw.ru.

Brunswick UBS Warburg. Russia Equity Research. 2000b. *Corporate Governance Analyzer*. November. Online. http://bw.ru.

Federal Commission for the Securities Market. 2002. *Corporate Governance Code*. Moscow.

Kostikov, I., ed. 2002. *Board of Directors in the Corporate Governance System of Company*. Moscow: Flinta-Nauka publishers (in Russian).

Standard & Poor's. 1999. *Corporate Governance Scoring. OJSC Aeroflot-Russian International Airlines*. February. Online. http://www2.standardandpoors.com.

Standard & Poor's. 2001. *Corporate Governance Scoring. OJSC Petersburg Telephone System (PTN)*. August. Online. http://www2.standardandpoors.com.

Standard & Poor's. 2002a. *Corporate Governance Scoring. OJSC Lenenergo*. February. Online. http://www2.standardandpoors.com.

Standard & Poor's. 2002b. *Corporate Governance Scoring. OJSC Mobile Telesystems (MTS)*. May. Online. http://www2.standardandpoors.com.

Tempest Consultants. 2000. *Global Emerging Markets Survey*. London: Tempest Consultants.

Chapter 21

Governance in an Emerging Financial Market
The Case of Poland

Wieslaw Rozlucki

GENESIS OF THE CORPORATE GOVERNANCE MOVEMENT IN POLAND

General background

Progressive privatization of the Polish economy and an associated influx of foreign capital stimulating development of the capital market in Poland have necessitated the creation of professional corporate oversight in public companies. The idea of codifying and defining corporate governance best practices standards was also a response to the deteriorating state of corporate practices in Polish public companies.

It is also worth noting that, from an organizational standpoint, the Polish capital market does not differ from developed-world markets. Its dynamic growth has not, however, led to the development of sufficiently efficient forms of control exercised by means of instruments not originating directly in statutory law and related legal sanctions. This deficiency affects in equal measure actions taken by both professional managers and by investors themselves. Consequently, however, noncompliance with basic corporate governance standards affects, above all, shareholders in listed companies, as well as in those companies planning to go public in the near future. Poland's entry into an intensive period of acquisitions and mergers in the second half of the 1990s made this problem more acute.

Because of the above considerations, both theoreticians and practitioners from legal and economic circles have observed a need to reestablish an appropriate balance between the interests of investors providing capital and the companies managing it. This need to develop not only an effective control and oversight system, but also mechanisms to ensure "donors" of capital an influence on the manner of its use and on strategic decisions made by the companies, has been intensified by the progressive expansion of capital, both private and institutional (held by investment, pension, insurance, and other funds).

The emergence and development of the initiative to build Polish best practices of corporate governance was also influenced by progressive globalization of financial markets. It was also no doubt influenced by the corporate governance codes developed in several European countries, as well as the *Corporate Governance Principles* published in May 1999 by the Organisation for Economic Co-operation and Development (OECD).

Institutional background

At the end of 1998, a group of persons who had been involved in the transformation of the Polish economy since the beginning of the 1990s began to discuss the creation of a model for corporate governance in public companies that would be suited to the Polish capital market.

It was decided then that an institution, structure, or some other type of not only organizational but, above all, intellectual framework should be created to provide a platform for exchange of creative thoughts and opinions on this extraordinarily important issue from the viewpoint of the Polish capital market's direction of development.

Thus, an institutional platform for discussion of best practices, called the *Corporate Governance Forum*, was created at the beginning of 1999.

The following institutions have participated actively in the Corporate Governance Forum from the very beginning of its operation:

- The Polish Securities and Exchange Commission

- The Warsaw Stock Exchange

- The Polish Confederation of Private Employers

- The Polish Business Council

- The Business Development Institute—Privatization Centre Foundation

Since 2000, the Forum has operated with support from representatives of the World Bank, the OECD, and, since June 2002, the National Bank of Poland. Also joining in the efforts to create best practice principles were the Issuers Association, the Association of the Investment Fund Companies, and the Chamber of Pension Funds, who formed the Best Practices Board.

In bringing together all the major capital market institutions in Poland, therefore, the Forum had from the very beginning the legitimacy in the appropriate circles necessary for future implementation of the solutions and documents prepared by this group.

BEST PRACTICES COMMITTEE

The Best Practices Committee, which was to be comprised of a group of authorities in the area of capital markets and corporate governance—both practitioners and academics active on the Polish market—was created as a result of over two years of discussion and numerous meetings within the Forum. The main task and objective designated for the Committee was to develop corporate best practice standards for the Polish capital market and codify them as a set of guidelines that could be adopted by public companies.

The mission of forming the Best Practices Committee was entrusted to Professor Grzegorz Domanski (of the Domanski, Kawecki, Palinka Law Firm), co-author of the first Law on Public Trading in Securities and former president of the Exchange Supervisory Board. Professor Domanski proposed the following composition for the Committee:

- Ms Henryka Bochniarz—President of the Polish Confederation of Private Employers,

- Mr Krzysztof A. Lis—Chairman of the Business Development Institute,

- Mr Wieslaw Rozlucki—President of the Warsaw Stock Exchange,

- Mr Jacek Socha—Chairman of the Polish Securities and Exchange Commission, and

- Professor Stanislaw Soltysinski—Soltysinski, Kawecki & Slezak Legal Advisors

The Best Practices Committee was formally established in May 2001.

Apart from the above-mentioned members, other individuals also participate by invitation in the Committee's work, especially lawyers, economists, analysts, and scholars representing numerous institutions and companies active on the Polish capital market. Members of the Committee, as well as other invited participants, have not infrequently presented quite divergent positions on particular issues.

Therefore, many later entries incorporated into *Best Practices in Public Companies in 2002*, prepared by the Committee, are the expression of a compromise among the members.

BEST PRACTICE GUIDELINES

The Best Practices Committee has executed its main task (though it obviously has not finished its work) and presented to the industry the already-mentioned document, which was finally entitled *Best Practices in Public Companies in 2002*. The document was created in stages.

First, a decision was made concerning the methodology and structure of the document. Members of the Committee concluded that before starting the actual editorial work, a detailed analysis of the Polish market and the behavior of its participants would be necessary. This was to ensure that the document would be properly embedded in a corporate reality adapted to the needs of the Polish public market. It was decided to adopt a clear structure and system for the document, based directly on that contained in the Commercial Companies Code. The dualistic division of competencies among company authorities (supervisory and management boards)—characteristic for

the Polish legal system—was retained here as well. A certain didacticism was also introduced into individual paragraphs. The concept for the document's content is based on
a contrast of bad practices diagnosed on the Polish market with the best practices presented in the document.

Once editorial work was initiated, the first stage was the preparation of *Best
Practices in Public Companies*, "Chapter I: General Meetings of Shareholders." This was a
deliberate choice, for it was during general meetings that there was a particularly pal-
pable lack of corporate culture or guidelines that could constitute a reference point for
investors having difficulties in exercising their rights.

Next, the Committee prepared "Chapter II: Supervisory Boards," and "Chapter
III: Management Boards." In further work on the document, the Committee prepared
a uniform edition of the entire *Best Practices* in February 2002, which was then submitted for industry-wide consultation.

In the course of work on the document, Committee members drew inspiration from both the positive and the negative experiences of Polish public companies, as
well as from the codes of best practices used on foreign markets. The content of many
of the guidelines is a result of creative comparison of opinions and proposals from a
wide range of specialists.

The document *Best Practices in Public Companies in 2002* in its current form is
composed of both general and detailed rules assigned to particular bodies within the
company and entities associated with its activities.

The general rules concern the following issues: proper determination of the
company mission; introduction of the following principles: majority rule with simultaneous protection of the minority; honest intentions and non-abuse in exercise of
rights, and utilization of legal institutions by the company; court jurisdiction, i.e., non-
resolution by company organs of issues that should be the subject of court rulings; and
independence of expert opinions commissioned by the company.

The part containing detailed rules covers, on the other hand, the following:

- Best Practices of General Meetings,

- Best Practices of Supervisory Boards,

- Best Practices of Management Boards, and

- Best Practices in Relations with Third Parties and Third-Party Institutions.

In the course of work on the final form of the document, concluded on July 4,
2002, the editorial committee took into account opinions, requests, and critical comments presented during extensive consultations conducted in the second quarter of
2002 within Polish and international capital market communities, as well as among
representatives of academic circles and authorities in the area of law and economics.
Then the issue of corporate governance standards was subject to discussion by the

Exchange Supervisory Board (the Exchange's statutory oversight body), which was expected to make decisions concerning the mode and method of their implementation.

The Exchange Supervisory and Management Boards accepted the document in September 2002. At the same time, appropriate changes were introduced to the Exchange Rules. As far as implementation was concerned, as had been expected, the comply-or-explain approach was adopted.

By December 31, 2002, listed companies were obliged to submit statements of their intentions toward the observance of the guidelines contained in *Best Practices in Public Companies in 2002*. These were intention statements, with the detailed compliance statements to be submitted along with the companies' annual reports by July 2003.

THE ROLE OF THE WARSAW STOCK EXCHANGE

Mission of the Exchange

One of the main objectives of a market organizer should be a continuous attempt to create a trading platform attractive to both domestic and foreign investors, as well as to eliminate phenomena and behavior that damage the credibility of the capital market on which it operates.

Therefore, the Warsaw Stock Exchange, as one of the main institutions creating and shaping the Polish capital market, is vitally interested in establishing a proper corporate culture and, as means to achieve this goal, in introducing universal and commonly accepted standards of corporate governance in Poland. This is evidenced especially by the Exchange's involvement in the creation and, subsequently, in the work and operations of the Corporate Governance Forum, as well as the active participation of its representatives in the creation of *Best Practices in Public Companies in 2002*. The Warsaw Stock Exchange also carefully follows and analyses all current information, as well as European and worldwide trends, related to the development of the corporate governance concept.

Related to the basic mission mentioned above are more detailed objectives and tasks that the Exchange has designated for itself or that have been delegated to it. These include, among other things, functioning as the depository for the pact among the signatories of *Best Practices*. This function was entrusted to the Exchange by the Best Practices Board, whose creation and activity is closely linked to the corporate governance movement in Poland and to the Exchange's participation in it.

The aforementioned Corporate Governance Forum Best Practices Board is a pact among organizations active on the Polish capital market. It was created in February 2002 by the following institutions:

- the Chamber of Pension Funds,
- the Polish Chamber of Insurance,

- the Association of the Investment Fund Companies, and

- the Polish Bank Association.

Its mission is to propagate and foster the use of best corporate governance practices in public companies and, thereafter, in companies from the regulated market as well as in the economy as a whole. The Board declares its cooperation with the Best Practices Committee and support for its work, and will also participate in the process of dissemination of the publication *Best Practices in Public Companies in 2002*, initiating amendments and modifications to it when necessary. The Board also intends to represent circles comprised of professional entities active on the market in discussions concerning effective implementation of corporate governance principles.

Practical aspects: concepts and ideas concerning implementation of corporate governance

In Poland, corporate governance has become an additional and indispensable guarantee of system stability to the financial market, providing mechanisms and warning signals in difficult market situations. Of course, the mere presence of corporate governance in a given system and broad-scale adherence to its principles do not guarantee economic success or stabilization. Nevertheless, it does make the entire process of managing both company property and the associated ownership risk significantly more efficient.

Appreciating this fact, the Exchange strives to play a leading role among all entities in favor of propagating corporate governance on the Polish market. This institution has the necessary personnel, organizational capacity, and—also essential—technical potential to meet this challenge. In the process of promoting and improving corporate governance, new information technologies, particularly the Internet, are playing an increasingly important role.

The Warsaw Exchange, as an institution with sufficient numbers of qualified staff and efficient and already-proven internal structures, has important relevant experience in instituting its own corporate standards (suffice it to mention here, for example, the common position of the Exchange Management and Supervisory Board on managerial options plans, dividend payments, or share issue price). The Exchange is also perceived as an institution of public trust with strong influence on public opinion.

Moving on, however, from issues concerning the role and importance of corporate governance in stimulating successful and consistent development of the Polish capital market to the no less important issue of who should undertake the difficult task of propagating and consolidating the idea of corporate governance standards, and how this should be done, it should be stated that there is no longer any doubt that the Exchange has a key role to play in this process of popularizing and implementing best practices in corporate governance. In my opinion, this role should encompass not only the creation (and codification) of positive models to emulate, and the more difficult task of codifying rules already created in a spontaneous manner, but also the elimination of inappropriate behavior and habits.

Bearing this in mind, the Exchange has taken a series of actions aimed first at popularizing the idea of creating standards, and then at activating the whole capital market community in the consultation process, as well as reviewing subsequent drafts of best practices guidelines presented to the market by the Best Practices Committee. The Exchange has been, and will certainly continue to be, host, co-organizer, and sponsor of conferences, panels, and meetings during which issues related to the Polish corporate governance model have been discussed, including presentation of foreign experience in this field. Ensuring that a broad spectrum of voices could submit their comments on the project, on the other hand, provided the opportunity to create a document that takes into account the positions and arguments of all interested entities and groups. Of course, not all requests submitted could be incorporated; however, it was a worthwhile effort to get to know all those positions. Perhaps it will be possible to use them at a further stage of work and activities associated with the development of corporate governance in Poland. I consider the Exchange's active participation in all of these activities to be essential, since effective implementation of any standards can be guaranteed only by an institutional link between those who create these norms and simultaneously observe them.

Such a natural platform—linking the interests of investors who provide capital and of companies that manage and use the funds received—is the Exchange. The Exchange does not intend, however, to formally impose a document containing a set of corporate governance guidelines. This would be pointless at this stage of the concept's development; the document should rather find understanding within the companies and among their shareholders, as well as recognition among potential investors. Companies are confronted with a requirement to comply with the guidelines or explain why they do not follow them. The comply-or-explain rule is now part of the Rules of the Warsaw Stock Exchange. Listed companies were required to present their position regarding observance of best practices by the end of 2002. They met that obligation and the vast majority declared their intentions to respect the guidelines contained in the document *Best Practices in Public Companies in 2002*. Starting in 2003, companies have to include relevant statements in their annual reports. The Exchange expects detailed reports on the observance of corporate governance within companies by July 1, 2003.

The issue of embedding this requirement within the legal framework in force also figures in the scope of work currently being carried out in connection with amendments to the Law on Public Trading in Securities. It is not yet known, however, if this solution will find expression in the new legal regulations.

For effective enforcement of the guidelines, a body—preferably a nongovernment body—will be appointed to issue rulings cases related to the corporate governance code and to resolve any disputes and doubts that may arise. Such a role is to be fulfilled on the Polish market by the Capital Market Court. The initiative to appoint this Court enjoys the Exchange's broad-based support.

The Capital Market Court will be created by the Warsaw Exchange and the Central Table of Offers (CETO—a WSE subsidiary operating the regulated off-Exchange market). The Capital Market Court will function as a court of arbitration, acting only on motions by the parties involved—shareholders, investors, or companies themselves. On the motion of a concerned party, the Court will be able to reprimand an issuer that does not follow the disclosure standard concerning publication of the statement on observance or nonobservance of the corporate governance standards. In the future, competencies of the Court may also encompass issuing recommendations or opinions in matters concerning observance by public companies of corporate governance rules in force on the market.

FURTHER STEPS

The role of the Exchange is not limited only to actions related to the implementation and enforcement of corporate governance rules, for the guarantee of the whole project's success is continuous and broad-based promotion of the corporate governance concept, which should significantly facilitate the process of Polish companies' acceptance of the guidelines.

The activities of the Warsaw Stock Exchange described above relate to popularization of the creation and codification of best practices standards. Now, as work on the document has been finished, it is time for actions aimed at promoting their use. We would like companies' management and supervisory boards to understand that observance of best practices in corporate governance within their companies, increased transparency of their internal structures, and building of proper investor relations will, especially in the long run, work to their advantage. Domestic and foreign investors, on the other hand, should also accept the assessment of corporate governance as an additional yet important tool for the valuation of shares in Polish companies.

To achieve this, however, not only promotion is essential but also, and above all, education, which should lay the groundwork for common and conscious use of best practices. Therefore, the Exchange plans to be actively involved in educational activities. One of the ideas being considered is to establish in Poland an organization (e.g. Institute of Directors), modeled after similar institutions already existing in several developed European countries, focused on educating management circles in the field of corporate governance. By way of exchanging experiences during a conference organized by the Corporate Governance Forum, the first meeting of representatives from institutes of directors in central and eastern Europe took place in June 2002.

The Best Practices Committee has not finished its work. As its members declare, the guidelines contained in the document *Best Practices in Public Companies in 2002* do not constitute a closed catalogue and, as a collection of past experiences, will be constantly enriched with new content resulting from the changing needs of the market.

THE WARSAW STOCK EXCHANGE AS A MEMBER OF THE EUROPEAN CORPORATE GOVERNANCE INSTITUTE

For several years now, international organizations and movements have been emerging to popularize corporate governance and work toward reform of existing corporate law, as well as propagation of best practices codes. One of these organizations is the European Corporate Governance Institute (ECGI), whose mission is to integrate the international financial community around the idea of common and universal corporate governance rules and foster the exchange of views and experience in this field.

The Warsaw Stock Exchange has been an ECGI member since 2001. Membership in ECGI offers the Exchange an opportunity to participate in the international corporate governance movement, engage in direct exchange of opinions, and benefit from the experience of other Institute members. It also gives the Exchange a chance to present its own experience in this area—WSE has already forwarded a copy of *Best Practices in Public Companies in 2002* to the Institute.

REFERENCE

Organisation for Economic Co-operation and Development (OECD). 1999. *Principles of Corporate Governance*. Paris: Organisation for Economic Co-operation and Development.

APPENDIX Best Practices in Public Companies in 2002

Acting with integrity and respecting different interests in the right proportion is beneficial to stakeholders in a corporate environment. This requires compromise and moderation, which are necessary since a joint-stock company as such is the playground for various economic interests. Best corporate practices are strengthened by laying down customary rules of conduct, called nowadays *best practices*. These rules are usually general so as to avoid unnecessary restraints and to enable their flexible application in various situations and in companies of different profiles. However, some detailed rules may be used when drawing up statutes of companies and bylaws of their authorities. Thus, best practices constitute a set of detailed rules of conduct addressed both to authorities of companies and members of such authorities, as well as to majority and minority shareholders. This set of best practices, established for the needs of the Polish capital market, presents the core of corporate governance standards in a public joint-stock company. This is not a complete list. Built based on the Polish experience, it should be constantly developed in line with the changing needs of the market.

MEMBERS OF THE BEST PRACTICES COMMITTEE AT THE CORPORATE GOVERNANCE FORUM

Professor Grzegorz Domanski—Domanski, Zakrzewski, Palinka
Henryka Bochniarz—President of the Polish Confederation of Private Employers
Krzysztof A. Lis—President of the Business Development Institute
Wieslaw Rozlucki—President of the Warsaw Stock Exchange
Jacek Socha—Chairman of the Securities and Exchange Commission
Professor Stanislaw Soltysinski—Soltysinski, Kawecki & Szlezak

Warsaw, 4 July 2002

BEST PRACTICES IN PUBLIC COMPANIES IN 2002

GENERAL RULES
Objective of the Company
The basic objective of operations of a company's authorities is to further the interests of the company, i.e., to increase the value of the assets entrusted by its shareholders, with consideration of the rights and interests of entities other than shareholders, involved in the functioning of the company, including, in particular, the company's creditors and employees.

Majority Rule and Protection of Minority
A joint-stock company is a capital venture, and, therefore, it must respect the principle of capital majority rule and the primacy of majority over minority. A shareholder who contributed bigger capital also bears a higher economic risk. It is, therefore, justified that his interest be taken into consideration in proportion to the contributed capital. The minority must have a guarantee of proper protection of their rights, within limits set by the law and commercial integrity. While exercising its rights, the majority shareholder should take into account the interests of the minority.

Honest Intentions and No-Abuse of Rights
The exercise of rights and the reliance on legal institutions should be based on honest intentions (good faith) and cannot reach beyond the purpose and economic reasons for which these institutions have been established. No activities should be taken that exceed the limits so set and, thus, constitute an abuse of the law. The minority should be protected

against abuse of ownership rights by the majority and the interests of the majority should be protected against abuse by the minority of its rights, thus ensuring the best protection of equitable interests of the shareholders and other market participants.

Court Control

The company's authorities and persons chairing a general meeting cannot decide on issues that should be resolved by court judgments. This does not apply to activities that are within the powers of the company's authorities and persons chairing general meetings or that they are obliged to undertake by force of law.

Independent Opinions Ordered by the Company

When choosing an entity that is to provide expert services, including, in particular, the services of an expert auditor, financial and tax advisory services, as well as legal services, the company should consider whether there exist circumstances limiting the independence of this entity when performing the entrusted tasks.

BEST PRACTICES OF GENERAL MEETINGS

A general meeting should take place in a location and at a time to allow the participation of as many shareholders as possible.

A request for convening a general meeting and placing certain issues on its agenda, made by parties entitled to do that, should be justified. Draft resolutions proposed to be adopted by the general meeting and other key documents should be presented to the shareholders along with a justification and an opinion of the supervisory board prior to the general meeting, in advance so as to allow them to review and evaluate the same.

The general meeting convened at the request of shareholders should be held on a date given in the request, and if this date cannot be kept, on the closest date that will allow the general meeting to settle the issues placed on its agenda.

A general meeting whose agenda includes certain issues at the request of authorized entities or that has been convened at such request may be cancelled only upon consent of the requesting parties. In all other instances, a general meeting may be cancelled if its holding is hindered (*force majeure*) or is obviously groundless. The meeting is called off in the same manner as it has been convened, ensuring as little negative consequences for the company and its shareholders as possible, and in any case no later than three weeks prior to the original date of the meeting. A change in the date of the general meeting is made in the same manner as the cancellation, even if the proposed agenda does not change.

In order for a representative of a shareholder to participate in a general meeting, his right to act on behalf of the shareholder should be duly documented. It should be presumed that a written document confirming the right to represent a shareholder at a general meeting is in conformity with the law and does not require any additional confirmations and acknowledgment unless its authenticity or validity *prima facie* raises doubts of the company's management board (upon drawing-up the attendance list) or the chairman of the general meeting.

The general meeting should have regular bylaws setting forth the detailed principles of conducting the meetings and adopting resolutions. The bylaws should contain, in particular, provisions concerning elections, including elections to the supervisory board by voting in separate groups. The bylaws should not be subject to frequent changes; it is advisable that the changes enter into force as of the subsequent general meeting.

A person opening the general meeting should procure an immediate election of the chairman of the meeting and should refrain from any substantive or formal decisions.

The chairman of the general meeting ensures an efficient conduct of the meeting and observance of the rights and interests of all shareholders. The chairman should counteract, in particular, the abuse of rights by the participants of the meeting and should guarantee that the rights of minority shareholders are respected. The chairman should not, without sound reason, resign from his function, or put off the signing of the minutes of the meeting.

A general meeting should be attended by members of the supervisory board and the management board. An expert auditor should be present at an annual general meeting and at an extraordinary general meeting if financial matters of the company are to be discussed thereat.

Members of the supervisory board and the management board and the expert auditor of the company should, within their powers and to the extent necessary for the settlement of issues discussed by the general meeting, provide the participants of the meeting with explanations and information concerning the company.

All answers provided by the management board to the questions posed by the general meeting should take into account the fact that the reporting obligations are performed by a public company in a manner which follows from the Law on Public Trading in Securities, and certain information cannot be provided otherwise.

Short breaks in the session that do not defer the session, ordered by the chairman in justified cases, cannot be aimed at hindering the exercise of the rights by the shareholders.

Voting on issues placed on the agenda may be carried out only on issues related to the conduct of the meeting. This voting procedure cannot apply to resolutions that may have impact on the exercise by the shareholders of their rights.

A resolution not to consider an issue placed on the agenda may be adopted only if it is supported by sound reasons. A motion in this respect should be accompanied by a detailed justification. The general meeting cannot adopt resolutions to remove an item from the agenda or not to consider an issue placed on the agenda at the request of the shareholders.

A party objecting to a resolution must have an opportunity to concisely present the reasons for its objection.

Due to the fact that the Code of Commercial Companies does not provide for court control in the event where a resolution is not adopted by the general meeting, the management board or the chairman of the meeting should form the resolutions in such a way that each person who does not agree with a decision being the subject of the resolution has the possibility of challenging the same, provided that he is entitled to do so.

At the request of a participant in the general meeting, his written statement is recorded in the minutes.

BEST PRACTICES OF SUPERVISORY BOARDS

The supervisory board submits to the general meeting an annual concise evaluation of the company's standing. The evaluation should be part of the annual report of the company, made available to all shareholders early enough to allow them to become acquainted with the same before the annual general meeting.

A member of the supervisory board should have relevant education, professional and practical experience, be of high morals, and be able to devote all time required to properly perform the function on the supervisory board. Candidates for members of the supervisory board should be presented and supported by reasons in sufficient detail to allow an educated choice.

(a) At least one-half of members of the supervisory board should be independent members. Independent members of the supervisory board should not have any relations with the company and its shareholders or employees, which relations could have significant impact on the ability of the independent member to make impartial decisions.

(b) Detailed criteria of independence should be laid down in the statutes of the company.

(c) Without consent of at least one independent member of the supervisory board, no resolutions should be adopted on the following issues:

> performances of any kind by the company and any entities associated with the company in favor of members of the management board;

> consent to the execution by the company or its subsidiary of a key agreement with an entity associated with the company, member of the supervisory board or the management board, and with their associated entities; and

> appointment of an expert auditor to audit the financial statements of the company.

The above rule may be implemented by the company on a date different than that for the remaining rules of the set, but no later than by the end of 2004.

A supervisory board member should, most of all, bear in mind the interests of the company.

Members of the supervisory board should take relevant actions in order to receive from the management board regular and complete information on any and all significant issues concerning the company's operations and on the risk related to the carried out business and ways of managing such risk.

A supervisory board member should inform the remaining members of the board of any conflict of interest that arises, and should refrain from participating in discussions and from voting on passing a resolution on the issue in which the conflict of interest has arisen.

Information on personal, actual, and organizational connections of a supervisory board member with a given shareholder, and, in particular, with the majority shareholder, should be available to public. The company should have a procedure in place for obtaining information from members of the supervisory board and for making it available to the public.

Supervisory board meetings, save for issues that directly concern the management board or its members, and, in particular, removal, liability, and setting remuneration, should be accessible and open to members of the management board.

A supervisory board member should enable the management board to present publicly and in an appropriate manner information on the transfer or acquisition of the shares of the company or of its dominant company or a subsidiary, and of transactions with such companies, provided that such information is relevant to his financial standing.

Remuneration of members of the supervisory board should be fair, but should not constitute a significant cost item in the company's business or have material impact on its financial results. The remuneration should be in reasonable relation to the remuneration of members of the management board. The aggregate remuneration of all members of the supervisory board should be disclosed in the annual report.

The supervisory board should operate in accordance with its bylaws, which should be available to the public.

The agenda of a supervisory board meeting should not be amended or supplemented during the meeting that it concerns. This requirement does not apply if all members of the supervisory board are present and agree to the amendment or supplementation of the agenda, and in instances where the adoption of certain activities by the supervisory board is necessary in order to protect the company against damage and in the case of a resolution that concerns the determination whether there exists a conflict of interest between a supervisory board member and the company.

A supervisory board member delegated by a group of shareholders to permanently exercise supervision should submit to the supervisory board detailed reports on the performance of his task.

A supervisory board member should not resign from his function during a term of office if this could render the functioning of the board impossible, and, in particular, if it could hinder the timely adoption of an important resolution.

BEST PRACTICES OF MANAGEMENT BOARDS

Bearing in mind the interest of the company, the management board sets forth the strategy and the main objects of the company's operations, and submits them to the supervisory board. The management board is liable for the implementation and performance of the same. The management board cares for transparency and effectiveness of the company management system and the conduct of its business in accordance with the legal regulations and best practice.

While making decisions on corporate issues, members of the management board should act within the limits of justified economic risk, i.e., after consideration of all information, analyses and opinions, which, in the reasonable opinion of the management board, should be taken into account in a given case in view of the company's interest. While determining the interest of the company, one should keep in mind the justified in long-term perspective interests of the shareholders, creditors, employees of the company and other entities and persons cooperating with the company, as well as the interests of local community.

In transactions with shareholders and other persons whose interests have impact on the interest of the company, the management board should act with utmost care to ensure that the transactions are at arms' length.

A management board member should display full loyalty toward the company and avoid actions that could lead to implementing exclusively own material interest. If a management board member receives information on the possibility of making an investment or another advantageous transaction concerning the objects of the company, he should present such information immediately to the management board for the purpose of considering the possibility of the company taking advantage of it. Such information may be used by a management board member or be passed over to a third party only upon consent of the management board and only when this does not infringe the company's interest.

A management board member should treat his shares in the company and in its dominant companies and subsidiaries as a long-term investment.

Management board members should inform the supervisory board of each conflict of interest in connection with the performed function or of the risk of such conflict.

The remuneration of management board members should be set based on transparent procedures and principles, taking into account its incentive nature and ensuring effective and smooth management of the company. The remuneration should correspond to the size of the company's business enterprise, should be in reasonable relation to the economic results, and be related to the scope of liability resulting from a given function, taking into account the level of remuneration of members of management boards in similar companies in a similar market.

The aggregate remuneration of all members of the management board should be disclosed and itemized in the annual report. If the amount of remuneration of individual members of the management board significantly differs, it is recommended that a relevant explanation be published.

The management board should lay down the principles and procedure of operations and allocation of powers in the bylaws, which should be open and generally available.

BEST PRACTICES IN RELATIONS WITH THIRD PARTIES AND THIRD-PARTY INSTITUTIONS

The selection of an expert auditor for a company should guarantee impartiality of performance of the entrusted tasks.

In order to ensure proper impartiality of opinion, the company should change the expert auditor at least once every five years.

The expert auditor should be selected by the supervisory board or general meeting of the company, upon receiving recommendations from the supervisory board.

An auditor auditing annual accounts of a company or its subsidiaries cannot act as a special purpose auditor for the same company.

A company should acquire its own shares in such a way that no group of shareholders be privileged.

The statutes of the company, its basic internal regulations, information and documents related to general meetings, and financial statements should be made available in the registered office of the company and on its web site.

The company should have proper media relations procedures and regulations and an information policy, ensuring coherent and reliable information about the company. The company should, in compliance with the legal regulations and taking into account its interests, make available to mass media representatives information on its current operation and business, standing, and enable their presence at general meetings.

In its annual report, a company should make public its statement on the application of corporate governance standards. If the standards are not applied to any extent, the company should also publicly explain this fact.

Social Corporate Responsibility and the New Learning

Chapter 22

Corporate Values, Enterprise Risk, and the Board

Michael J. Phillips

THE CRISIS OF WORLD CAPITALISM IS ABOUT VALUES

When it comes to the state of world capitalism, something is rotten. Some assert that all the pistons in the economic engine are working; that this is all to do with the bursting of the tech bubble and the inevitable excesses associated with a long bull market. Others shout from the side streets that the global markets are keeping the small person down, catapulting the rich, the greedy, and the amoral to dizzier heights of wealth. Naturally, there is no easy answer. What can be said, however, is this: there is a well-reported crisis of world capitalism under way. We cannot hold a meeting of international business leaders without demonstrators in the streets outside. The leaders of some of our largest corporations are accused of abuse of their office for personal gain. The integrity of some of our largest financial intermediaries is questioned because of alleged abuse of conflicts of interest. Corporate financial statements, the structural foundation of our capital markets, are treated with suspicion.

There is a rattle in the transmission, a funny sound filtering up from beneath the hood as you shift gears, a mysterious puddle on the garage floor. The engine by which the West was won is cranking out black smoke. We need to swap our suits for overalls and, wrench in hand, examine the causes of this malfunction. This is what I intend to do in the course of this chapter: to review in a radical way the most basic building block of world capitalism, the joint stock company. I believe it is the evolved state of the modern company, in particular its values, that is at the core of the problem.

SUMMARY OF POSITION

Clearly there is a major problem with corporate governance. Better corporate governance really equates to stronger corporate values and better ethics. Companies have to become more like people, entities who in their daily lives aspire to multiple values, not all

I would like to acknowledge my daughter Kaz Phillips, Craig Ueland, Kathy Floyd, and John O'Neil, for their ideas and editing help. Also Andy Turner for going over the manuscript and helping me clarify some of my stranger economic conjectures, and Karl Ege and Dave Griswold for their help on the legal structure of companies.

of which are concerned with financial return. Leaders of companies need to take the main responsibility for this happening, with effective and independent boards providing checks and balances to ensure that the process does not go off track. A company that truly seeks to optimize a number of values, only some of which involve pure shareholder return considerations, is a different animal from the one we have today. To move to this situation will require some radical thinking and action. But it can be achieved with hugely positive results. In addition to being a more balanced and better governed organization, an ethical, value-oriented company (just like an ethical person) cannot ignore the great humanitarian issues that confront the world. This logic provides a "solve for both" solution. Reengineer the capitalist system to become more sensitive to ethical considerations, and we will address not only the concerns that we have lost our way and caused a crisis of public confidence, but we will also better tackle some of the global humanitarian and environmental problems that confront us all.

Do this effectively, and most of the popular opposition to "globalization" and "corporatism" will evaporate in time as corporations assume their rightful role, not just as well governed and ethical citizens in their parochial business environment, but also as proactive agents addressing with vigor, insight, and good humor the problems that confront our world.

PURE FINANCIAL RETURN MAXIMIZATION HAS TO GO

At the heart of the problem with current corporate values is the return-maximization orientation of companies. Of course it makes sense to prioritize shareholder financial return. As companies have evolved, this has been the one element in the structure of companies that has been unquestioned and unchanging. However, this has also given leaders of companies a legal and pseudo-ethical rationale for conduct that is, in some cases, much more self-serving. Management has become the most powerful stakeholder in the corporate equation. In many cases, without adequate checks and balances, management has subverted the return maximization requirement of companies to seek short-term rewards for shareholders and themselves.

So the corporation has to date been unquestionably regarded as an organization that seeks to *maximize return* on shareholders' funds. In this sense the corporation is a legal person with a single value. Real people have multiple values, they clearly require a return (compensation), but they live their lives taking into account other, non–return seeking values—like family, environment, sustainability, and their community. But many companies believe they cannot afford the luxury of being multiple value–centric. As company leaders view the world around them—the digital divide, the enormous health problems of the developing world, and many other humanitarian issues—the conventional corporate response is an abrogation of significant responsibility. They say simply; "Gee, I would like to help more, but I cannot reduce our shareholder return in any material way to alleviate these problems." So, *by definition*, the corporate resource allocation based on non–return seeking values is immaterial. To be cynical, management of companies may be more focused on their *own* return rather than that of the shareholders when they make those statements. That is why boards need to be more motivated to hold management accountable for their motives. For reasons we will consider later in this chapter, this is not working very well with many corporate board structures and board compensation.

THIS IS ABOUT GLOBAL RESPONSIBILITY, NOT JUST GOVERNANCE

The time has come for companies to show that they are good corporate citizens pursuing a value-centered approach. It will take courage and initiative on the part of boards and management to make it happen, but there is no doubt as to the eventual outcome. Companies must also take a share of the responsibility for attempting to redress some of the great humanitarian challenges. This is not about giving more money to charity (although money comes into the equation, as we will discuss later). Boards of directors need to hold management accountable for their value-centered approach. Companies are not configured this way at present, which creates risk for a corporate enterprise.

It is frequently argued that better corporate responsibility has resulted and will result in the long run in better shareholder returns. That may be the case, but we should not rely on the argument. Being a good corporate citizen—being eco friendly, creating a caring environment for our employees—may actually enhance return. But what about the larger, global issues? There may come a point where the cost of being a good *global* citizen cannot be rationalized on the basis of a multi-attribute utility function that still creates financial value maximization. If it costs a small measure of shareholders' return to do what is right for the company in terms of corporate ethics and for the world as a whole, that may be an optimal state in a broad sense. That is what the employees of the company may desire. As the main asset of companies is now people, who themselves have multiple values, this alignment of company and knowledge workers' values may be powerfully beneficial.

Leading companies attract the best knowledge workers because they have strong people centricity and demonstrable values. They care for their people, and they aspire to a set of values higher than those imposed by their regulators and the law. These are the companies that will be the pace-setters of this change. The CEOs of companies should be willing to look shareholders in the eye and tell them, "We are not seeking financial return maximization and mere compliance. We aspire to a higher, more complex set of values and, yes, there may be a small reduction in shareholder return as a result." Shareholders who do not respect that position will presumably sell their stock in favor of companies for which financial return maximization is the single objective. That is a price that value-centered companies should be cheerfully willing to pay. Management has to make this happen, as they have become by far the most powerful players in today's corporate environment.

MANAGEMENT POWER

Why is management so strong today? The answer is not that it has become greedy! Greed has a much richer and longer pedigree! This is about the changing power levels of corporate stakeholders. Nature abhors a vacuum. What has happened is that corporate leadership has been empowered by a reduction in strength in three areas: unions, shareholders, and independent board members.

The power and influence of unions in the corporate equation has been on the wane. They are collective bargainers, representing the individual. But many individuals today see a reducing utility in collective bargaining. They see themselves as seeking flexibility and control of their own destiny; they do not necessarily want to be bargained for collectively through a relatively rigid process. So, with individuals becoming more empowered in companies, the union's power has been declining. Think what a union is saying: "We will represent you; we will win you a 35-hour work week, four weeks' vacation, and retirement at 65 on a good pension." Increasingly the response from the younger knowledge worker is "No thanks! I may want to work 80 hours a week, have no vacation, and become wealthy so I can retire in my forties!" This is an oversimplification and probably unrealistic on the employee's part, but what is not at issue is the weakening state of the union as a stakeholder in today's company.

Shareholders are institutional and tend to be nonproprietary. This is one of the biggest issues in corporate governance today. In 1900, big shareholders saw themselves as proprietors, getting involved with the companies in which they had stakes. Today institutional shareholders of companies hold diversified portfolios. The overwhelming response of today's institutional shareholder to problems in a company in which it is a stakeholder is to vote with its feet—to sell the stock and not get involved. Besides, given the diversified nature of institutional portfolios, there are simply too many companies in which the institution is invested for it to get involved in the governance of individual companies.

Finally, CEOs have been empowered by a long and powerful bull market. An aura of invincibility has surrounded the management of many public companies. Boards simply have not had the fire power to hold them in check.

PROBLEMS WITH BOARDS

The board of directors of a company is the steward of a heavy fiduciary burden. It has a critical supervisory role, and should provide a check and balance for the CEO and other management. Boards are not as effective as they could be in this role. Here are the main problems:

- The long bull market has empowered CEOs and makes them hard to manage. Nothing succeeds like success, and it is tough for any board to keep in check a CEO who has delivered shareholder value, even if that has been created in a "high tide lifts all boats" environment of a big bull market.

- There is an issue of independence. "Friends and family" of senior management often find themselves on boards. CEOs love to put their CEO counterparts on their boards. These managers often run companies that have business relationships with the company concerned.

- And then there is compensation! Many board members are compensated almost exclusively with options and warrants. How can we expect independent board members to exercise restraint on management when they are compensated in a manner even more leveraged than the management themselves?

- In the United States in particular, the office of CEO and chairman of the board are frequently combined. It is not axiomatic that this linkage is a bad thing. But if the board is weak and/or nonindependent, it is a powerful disincentive to board members to challenge management behavior.

- Nominating and audit committees of boards are sometimes not made up exclusively of independent directors. Much has been discussed on the subject of audit committees. But the single biggest decision the board makes is the selection of CEO. Nonindependent nominating committees are a major impediment to strong board influence on management.

Recommendations on changes to board structure are made later in this chapter.

WHAT ABOUT THE WORKERS?

What about the employee as a stakeholder? Unlike unions and shareholders, individuals in companies are actually becoming *more* powerful. Why is this? The information and knowledge revolution has resulted in the empowerment of the individual. If we ask ourselves what the dominant institution in each millennium has been, we would probably suggest that the *religious order* was dominant in the first millennium, and the *nation state* was dominant in the second. What will be the dominant institution of the third millennium? I believe it will be the *individual*. People are more in command of their destiny than ever before. They are better educated, are more empowered, and are able to choose the organizations in which they work. The central "means of production" (in economic terms) today is people's brains, not plants and machinery! And unlike plants and equipment, brains cannot be owned. They only can be attracted, motivated, compensated, and inspired.

The labor/capital relationship that was the engine of the Industrial Revolution is being recast. What does this mean? I conjecture that it means that for any level of economic activity there will be more wealth in the hands of the individual and less in the balance sheet of the company for which he or she works. This makes sense if labor owns both itself and the means of production. (This has some interesting implications for stock valuation beyond the scope of this chapter.) It also means that individuals will be more attracted by organizations whose values are more closely aligned with their own. On the flip side, they will be less willing to have their values subsumed, made subordinate to the values of the company for which they work, if that company's values are very different from their own.

MARKET VALUE ISN'T THE SAME AS "WORTH" WHERE PEOPLE ARE CONCERNED

The most successful knowledge-based organizations are those that recognize that the critical interaction in the company is based on respect for each other's dignity as a human being. They acknowledge that employees have different compensation levels but recognize that this has to do with their *market value*, not their *worth as human beings*. Organizations that walk this walk, and demonstrably value and respect their people, find it easier to attract, motivate, inspire, and *retain* employees. But these organizations also have to be value-centric at the enterprise level. So there is a growing pressure from the ranks of the employees of companies to reflect the collective values of those individuals in the values of the enterprise itself. Knowledge workers now comprise the main asset of the company, yet this asset is nonproprietary and it can walk out of the door. Companies are at great risk if they have a culture that is heavily at variance with that of its people. So the company is slowly evolving to reflect the values of its employees, which requires it to consider family, community, environment, and sustainability as well as pure financial return. That is a multiple-value orientation rather than a single, return-focused one.

This does not happen overnight. So despite the increasing power of the individual employee in the company, management is empowered by default. And every now and again management abuses this power. I believe the vast majority of corporate management is straight and honest. But that fact, even if it is true, is basically irrelevant. Enough of management is compromised ethically to cause serious problems. That most of us are honest does not protect us from adverse consequences, or allow us to avoid responsibility to do something about the situation.

WHAT ABOUT INVESTMENT BANKERS AND SHAREHOLDERS?

There is a popular conception that corporate management's short-term focus is caused by market forces, by sell side analysts, and by shareholders. Again, at the risk of oversimplification, I do not think these are the significant drivers. Company leadership is responsible for this belief. In a powerful position, with few checks and balances, management can drive this agenda. Investment bankers do not call the shots, they just react. Shareholders also are not purely return-focused.

Today's shareholders, both institutional and individual, have demonstrated clearly in the market that they will not tolerate unethical corporate leadership. Put another way, they will forego the opportunity for superior return if they perceive a problem with a company's value orientation. This is partly return driven, but I believe it is also partly driven by the value sets of the investing institutions themselves. If so, this supports the notion that it is not demanding shareholders or short-term considerations that have driven otherwise innocent corporate leaders to compromise their ethical positions.

Most public pension funds have well developed social investing criteria, and corporate pension plans are significantly increasing their focus on corporate governance issues. The bottom line is that shareholders would not today shun a management committed to strong corporate values rather than pure return maximization. A company with strong value-centric leadership, attracting a powerful team of knowledge workers, can rise above this short-term condition. There is evidence that shareholders already recognize the worth of this cultural strength in the companies in which they invest.

ENTERPRISE RISK

We have considered some of the positive aspects of moving in this direction. But are there risks of proceeding in this way, and what enterprise risk is assumed if this course of action is not taken?

The risks of becoming more value centric are fairly easy to identify. The market will shun the company concerned because it is not explicitly pursuing a strategy of pure return maximization. Investors who feel this way will turn to companies that continue to maximize return, and these investors are presumably willing to assume the downside risk that the next company experiencing a problem related to its corporate ethics will be in this subset of the market.

Companies that do *not* follow this course of action to become more value centric will be increasingly exposed to the following types of enterprise risk. They will:

- Find it increasingly difficult to attract and retain the finest knowledge workers, as the divergence of personal and corporate values creates a damaging misalignment.

- Find it more difficult to attract top CEO and COO talent for the same reason.

- Find it more and more difficult to attract and retain top-level independent directors.

- Find themselves to be increasingly targets for protest, as more and more companies move to a more value-centric position.

- Find themselves likely to receive increased attention from regulators.

Even at this early stage, the enterprise risks associated with pursuing a pure return-seeking strategy outweighs the advantages. As time progresses, companies that do not follow a multi-value approach will be increasingly ostracized both by the market and by society as a whole.

WHAT DO WE DO?

The first thing is to recognize that this requires radical thinking and action. An incrementalist approach will not get us where we want to go.

We don't really have legal obstacles

Contrary to what we might think, there is no law that *requires* a corporation to maximize economic return. Corporate law is relatively flexible, and you could incorporate for a variety of reasons to maximize a number of different values. Most companies already devote some time and effort to ethical causes, even if these are not material. Most law on the subject concerns the division of the return created. This boils down to protection of minority rights, in effect ensuring that minority shareholders receive their fair share of the economic return.

The law also protects minority shareholders from being disadvantaged by management appropriating too great a share of the economic return. Envisage a company allocating a greater priority to being a good corporate citizen in all senses of the word. This makes the company more attractive to enlightened knowledge workers, and the company is viewed in the world community as responsive to pressing humanitarian and environmental issues. Under these circumstances, and bearing in mind the flexibility we already have, it seems unlikely there would be a big legal or legislative obstacle to evolving faster in this direction.

Board issues and culture

We have already considered the problems that reduce board power and independence. It is unnecessary to make a case for greater independence in boards and their committees—we can take that as a given.

In the area of compensation, we need to recognize that compensating board members with options and warrants only serves to align their interests with management. We need to take a closer look at compensation for board members. But, as a general rule, board compensation should be based on performance over time and built into a contract that differs from management in tone and responsibility.

A move toward greater value orientation is a cultural shift in a company. The board has its biggest potential influence here. What is the biggest influence in the promotion of a particular culture in a company? It is the leadership, of course! Who appoints the leader of the company? The board! A bad leader can destroy a good company's culture quickly. A good leader can remedy a poor culture much more slowly, but he or she still will be easily the biggest influence in the change of corporate culture. This is because the CEO and senior management of companies are the role models for behavior. If they behave badly, they legitimize the same behavior throughout the organization, and vice versa. Good management inspires good corporate behavior by setting an example and not tolerating unethical conduct. Boards have a huge part to play here. By nominating CEOs who will aspire to a value orientation, boards can effect a change in this direction quickly and effectively. Once they have the right CEO in place, they should support his or her position in this critical area.

As mentioned earlier in this chapter, the roles of chairman and CEO of a public corporation are often linked. Although this is not a bad thing in itself, the combination of this linkage with a weak board is a dangerous combination. We should consider separating the two roles as the norm, with provision to make exceptions where appropriate. If the default state is separation of the roles, boards will be more empowered than they are today. An independent board chairman would significantly increase the checks and balances to professional management. It would require purposeful action on the board's part to combine the roles, and as a result, in most public companies the two positions would be represented by different people.

GLOBAL RESPONSIBILITY FUND

The noncorporate world has some well-developed infrastructure for allocation of resources to the developing world. Supra government organizations, governments, NGOs, foundations, and other charities have a long history of organization and collaboration with one another. In the corporate sector, no comprehensive structure exists. Some organizations—such as the World Economic Forum (WEF)—have taken significant steps to increase business engagement in a whole range of corporate citizenship issues. In July 2001, the WEF launched its Global Corporate Citizenship Initiative, which has objectives broadly aligned with the sentiments of this chapter.

To take things to the next stage, we need to create an action-based organization that seeks to focus the corporate sector's contribution to global ethical causes and to interact with other similar organizations in the noncorporate world. Of course, companies are already concerned about the ethical issues we face today. For example, pharmaceutical companies *are* committing resources to solve medical problems in the developing world. So why propose a formal mechanism for collection and distribution of resources? It is because the current approach is not effective.

The same knowledge and information revolution that has empowered individuals and given them more control over their destiny has created the "digital divide" and an even bigger gap between rich and poor. In many countries, governments actually *inhibit* the distribution of aid. A fraction of the total resources allocated to global ethical causes actually reaches its target. It is this disconnect that has sabotaged "trickle down economics" and our aid programs. The concepts are valid, the motives sincere, but a trickle needs a stream bed down which to flow. We have a dam preventing that flow. We all have a responsibility to breach that dam.

My proposition is this: At the risk of proposing one more level of bureaucracy, I propose a global infrastructure to coordinate the allocation of resources from the corporate sector to ethical causes of all kinds. I have called this, for want of a better name, the *Global Responsibility Fund (GRF)*. The fund would do the following:

- Identify, collect, and distribute corporate resources to areas of need. It is hoped that a move to a more value-centric corporate environment will release *incremental* resources, but the fund should be involved with both existing and incremental resources, as well as contributions in-kind where corporate competency is relevant.

- Identify inefficiencies inherent in the current approach and take action to avoid duplication of effort and create synergies. Companies may not wish to lose an element of control over their donation programs. But the GRF could demonstrate the benefits of focusing effort and exercising the power of a concentrated program in those areas of greatest inefficiency (for example, dealing with bureaucracy and corruption.) This idea is not new. United Way is a living and breathing example of exactly this concept at work.

- Collaborate with other supranational organizations, governments, NGOs, and charitable organizations to aid efficiency here also.

- Provide public recognition to companies contributing to the GRF via an accreditation process. This process would be not only a "badge of honor" identifying the company as one making meaningful contributions to ethical causes, but also would be a seal of approval in terms of corporate governance, as no company with poor corporate governance would survive the screening to achieve accreditation.

The GRF needs a sponsor, of course, a credible structure of this nature requires significant resources. There are a number of candidates among supra-government organizations and even the bigger foundations. At this stage, I am floating the idea to discover how much acceptance this kind of concept has in the corporate sector. The presence of a high-profile organization of this nature could do much to address the criticisms of the anti-globalization movement and help to restore the dignity of the modern corporation as it sits alongside other institutions committed to addressing ethical issues on a global scale.

CONCLUSION

This chapter is an attempt to link the need for better corporate governance with the clear need for more and better organized resources to attack the major humanitarian problems that confront us globally. It is based on the idea that *a corporation, like a person, should have multiple values*. Companies following this approach will aspire to a number of values, some of which are not concerned with creating financial return for the company. These companies will have corporate values that are better aligned with the values of their employees, and this will strengthen the whole enterprise. It is inconceivable that a company that moves forward in this way will not review its role in addressing broader, global issues. This will result in an increase in resources being allocated to ethical causes. Companies that embrace this framework will be demonstrably superior corporate global citizens. This accreditation will far outweigh any cost associated with a multi-value culture. More effective deployment of existing and incremental resources will create a discernible change in the plight of billions of our fellow human beings. The kink in the machine is perhaps the fact that the machine should not be a machine after all, but instead an organic, sentient entity, trying, as we all try, to make the world a better place for generations to come.

Chapter 23

Redefining the Role and Content of Corporate Governance from the Perspective of Business in Society and Corporate Social Responsibility

Lutgart van den Berghe, in collaboration with Steven Carchon

The agenda of corporate governance has changed drastically in the last few years. If the 1990s was the decade of the shareholder, the first decade of the 21st century will broaden the claims on corporate governance to include other stakeholders. Faced with increasing pressure for corporate social responsibility and a broader role for business in society, it is no longer sufficient for a "responsible" firm to live by the law and focus on financial profit to create value for shareholders. At the same time, however, traditional approaches to corporate governance as well as traditional management tools and accounting principles do not allow for efficient and effective management of corporate social responsibility. This is the central thesis of the present chapter.

This discussion of potential new routes for redefining corporate governance begins with an outline for a hierarchical governance framework. The framework's different levels range from the role of the board of directors to the formulation of the company's fundamental raison d'être, which is central to the debate on corporate social responsibility. The framework alone does not generate concrete recommendations and principles that guide corporate governance with regard to a broader societal role of firms. Therefore, the chapter continues with a discussion of how financial corporate governance can be transformed into responsible corporate governance. This discussion is followed by one focusing on managing the triple bottom line of firms and on the broadening of monitoring mechanisms. The chapter ends with a presentation of the broader implications of an all-encompassing view of the firm.

BROADENING THE CORPORATE GOVERNANCE FRAMEWORK

Defining the company's reason for existence, that is, its mission and values, has primarily been the responsibility of top management, the board of directors, and the shareholders. Increasingly, market as well as nonmarket forces oblige these "governing" bodies to take a broader look at the corporation's role in society. The invisible hand of the market has been augmented by a new, invisible hand of critical global forces that includes the media and nongovernmental institutions. Faced with increasing pressure from these global forces for corporate social responsibility and a broader role for business in society, firms can no longer simply focus on financial profit and the creation of shareholder value.

Economic thinking on the theory of the firm has a long tradition and has produced a rather diverse set of views on the role of the corporation in society. Historically, corporate governance as well as traditional management tools and accounting principles have not explicitly been considered as involved with society. Although these new societal claims on firms have been integrated in economic and management theories, mainstream corporate governance thinking is still based upon the principles developed by the neoclassical theories of the firm. One explanation for the reliance on these more traditional theories can be found in the "dominant firm logic" paradigm.

According to this paradigm, all corporate governance systems are bound to converge toward one type of firm, where ownership is dispersed and disciplinary mechanisms are necessary to monitor managers so that they foster the interests of the shareholders. The dominant firm logic is often referred to as the "Berle and Means firm" (Berle and Means, 1932). This reliance on capital markets explains why the neoclassical theory forms the backbone of the corporate governance literature. However, these underlying paradigms do not allow for corporate social responsibility to be managed efficiently and effectively.

According to traditional governance discipline, the company primarily serves the interests of the shareholder. The main reference framework used to manage a firm financially is the optimal use of capital, and this is achieved by employing standard indicators such as the return on investment and equity and the risk-adjusted return on capital. Externalities are not taken into account, however. These externalities can be negative (e.g., because of a gap between social and private costs), but they can also be positive and welfare-improving.

Recently, the traditional view of shareholder primacy has become subject to increasing criticism by different groups, including the business community itself. The firm is more complex, it has been argued, with multiple types of principals and agents who are intertwined in a web of stakeholder relations. Conventional financial performance measurements are consequently now seen as limited in their ability to take into account the impact of corporate activity on all the stakeholders at the micro level. At the macro level, opposition to the negative effects of globalization is in fact a global and large-scale opposition against micro level-type environmental and social dysfunctions. Global opposition emphasizes the increased pressure being placed on the business world to be responsible for its actions, although such opposition is sometimes driven by the extreme and unrealistic expectation that the business community can and must solve all the problems of the world.

The increased expectations of the role of business in society and the urge to develop responsible firms have created the need to redefine the basic paradigms. The dominant firm logic is only relevant for a small subset of a wide range of firm types. The less relevant the Berle and Means firm typology is for a country, the less useful is the traditional firm paradigm. In particular, outside the Anglo-American area, Continental European, Asian, and less developed markets are characterized by numerous (and equally important) types of firms. This variety renders the approach of the dominant firm less relevant.

To embody the idea of the responsible firm, Van den Berghe et al. (2002) proposed a hierarchical governance framework. This framework is designed to allow a firm to take into consideration the potential components of modern corporate governance. In its simplest form, corporate governance focuses on the operation and composition of the board of directors (see level 1 in Figure 23.1). This is the central perspective used by most of the codes and recommendations on corporate governance.

FIGURE 23.1 **Hierarchical Corporate Governance Framework**

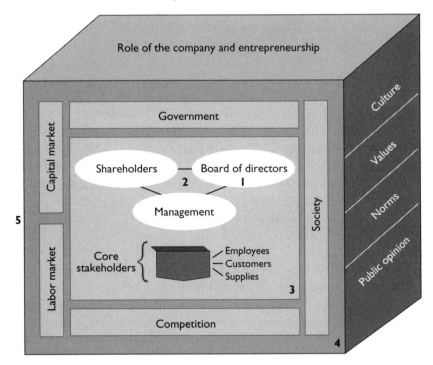

In a broader context, corporate governance can be viewed from the angle of the so-called corporate governance tripod (level 2), whereby particular attention is paid to the relationship between shareholders, directors, and management. The relationships in this tripod receive the greatest amount of attention both in the legal disciplines and in practice. The tripod is also the focus for much economic research; indeed, a great deal of this research concentrates on how the motives of management (the agent) can be aligned with the interests of shareholders (the principal). In this monitoring process, financial markets and external directors are assigned a major monitoring role.

From a modern management perspective, a more holistic approach at the corporate level is required (level 3, Figure 23.1). Companies are increasingly structured according to whether they are national or international. Moreover, global competition in a networked economy is giving rise to the embedding of companies in a cluster of networks with both suppliers and customers. Managing such networks therefore becomes a much more complex matter than managing a single company with one principal (the shareholder) and one agent (the management). In the new knowledge society, firms increasingly rely on networks and other long-term relationships. Consequently greater attention is being paid to employees and other stakeholders.

From a socioeconomic and political angle, the role of companies is increasingly being seen as that of a corporate citizen (level 4, Figure 23.1). Consequently, the mission of corporate governance has broadened to take into consideration the interests of all stakeholders. According to this approach, there is no distinction between levels 3 and 4; rather, the stakeholder model pays a great deal of attention to the sustainable or responsible enterprise.

At level 5, the corporate governance debate focuses on the question of the primary reason for a company's existence. The fundamental question is whether a company's raison d'être is to create shareholder value or prosperity for all stakeholders involved. This perspective is central to the discussion of corporate social responsibility and the responsible firm. Indeed, the debate on convergence of corporate governance models essentially boils down to this fundamental question.

FROM FINANCIAL CORPORATE GOVERNANCE
TOWARD RESPONSIBLE CORPORATE GOVERNANCE

The enlarged reference framework for corporate governance is insufficient for the development of a modern corporate governance toolbox; formulating a new toolbox requires more than reflecting upon the parties and interests involved. A broader societal role for the firm should also be included in the recommendations and principles that guide good corporate governance. Figure 23.2 gives an overview of the dimensions that corporate governance should cover.

FIGURE 23.2 **Governance Pyramid**

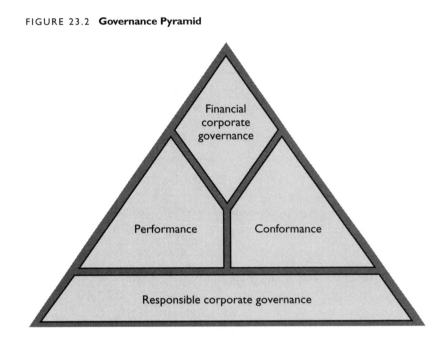

Financial corporate governance focuses on the structures and processes neces-sary for the pursuit of shareholder value. Important elements in this discussion are shareholder rights, protection of minority shareholders, and transparency and disclo-sure issues. This last issue remains by far the most important focus of the investment com-munity in general, and shareholder service firms more specifically.

Traditionally, attention has been focused on conformance issues in order to attain the goal of good financial corporate governance. The main reason behind the many codes and recommendations has been the development of a set of rules and principles to be respected by corporations. Living up to formal standards or bench-marks became the reference point that was used to judge the quality of corporate gov-ernance. However, many of these recommendations can easily lead to a kind of box-ticking exercise accompanied by a few superficial or cosmetic adaptations. The focus on compliance can, therefore, be a detriment to attending to the reality of gover-nance. Interesting examples where such box-ticking often occurs include disclosures of the composition of the board, having the minimal number of independent direc-tors, or establishing special board committees.

The great challenge, however, is to change the fundamentals related to the gov-ernance attitude and behavior of (business) leaders and directors. Only then will sub-stance reign over form. Numerous corporate governance codes, recommendations, and governance rating systems have been developed using this old perspective. The emphasis on conformance resulted in many recommendations to organize better control and supervision over management, such as to establish board committees (e.g., the audit committee), search for truly independent directors, oversee management, and so on. However, the failure of numerous firms that followed these recommendations, at least formally, has created much support for an enlarged governance approach.

The disproportionate emphasis on conformance drew attention away from the complementary issue of performance. We must not forget that corporate governance is not an aim in itself, but a mechanism of structures and processes that allows companies to realize their ambitions and goals and create welfare and economic well-being. The pursuit of shareholder value is hampered if the emphasis on processes and board structures is univocally oriented toward control and supervision. Attention must be given to the establishment of the necessary structures and processes to realize a firm's strategic objectives. Entrepreneurship and stewardship are instrumental in fostering business prosperity.

Directors have traditionally been sensitive to the demands of their shareholders. In the modern business environment, firms have increasingly had to cope with other critical stakeholders. The challenge for corporate governance in general and for board members more specifically, is to include the duty of balancing the interests of all stakeholders. In an information and knowledge society, a firm's reputation, intellectual capital and, finally, its license to operate, are largely dependent on this complex balance of interests. Therefore, the content of corporate governance has to be extended to include "responsible" corporate governance.

The essential difference between financial corporate governance and responsible corporate governance lies in the definition of the goal of the firm in general and of corporate governance more specifically. In both cases, corporate governance is about structures and processes that allow the firm to realize its strategic goals. Financial corporate governance defines the firm as the instrument of the shareholders and considers that the role of the firm and the duty of its directors is simply shareholder value maximization. Responsible corporate governance defines the firm as a long-term partnership of shareholders and other stakeholders. Therefore, corporate governance should aim at optimizing the (long-term) return to shareholders while satisfying the legitimate expectations of stakeholders. In fact, this supposes that shareholders become shared value holders. Understanding the issue of responsible corporate governance now lies at the heart of good corporate governance, and ignoring this broader scope could prove disastrous for corporate branding and financial performance. Responsible corporate governance transcends taking only the interests of employees into consideration. It is about balancing the legitimate interests of all stakeholders involved, with ethics and sustainable growth being of fundamental importance.

This enlarged corporate governance model, however, supposes not only a redefinition of the theory and role of the firm, but also necessitates rethinking the principal agent theory in order to include the concept of multiple principals and agents (i.e., stakeholder inclusiveness). Moreover, such a broadened role of the firm must lead to a reformulation of the role of the board of directors in general and of the duties of directors more specifically. The new company law in the United Kingdom as well as the duties included in the *Turnbull Report* (holistic risk management) can be illustrative in this matter.

It should be clear that a responsible firm is far more than a nice-to-have add-on such as charity and philanthropy. Corporate social responsibility is more than public relations or reputation management. The societal responsibilities of a firm must be fully integrated into corporate governance and management practice and theory. The modern view on the role of the firm in society should be translated into the firm's products, production process, treatment of stakeholders (including the environment), system of governance and accountability, and its codes of conduct (Wilson, 2000). The firm's new role should form an intrinsic part of modern business opportunities, threats, and risks. This role is so central to the success of the firm that corporate social responsibility cannot be completely delegated; it must become the final responsibility of senior management and the board of directors. Hence, a broader scope of firm performance is necessary.

THE TRIPLE BOTTOM LINE AND MONITORING MECHANISMS

For quite some time, the duties of a responsible firm have been approached in a rather fragmented way. A sustainable firm, it has been argued, has to be managed on the basis of a triple bottom line, focusing on financial, environmental, and social performance. Disclosure and public reporting has followed the same fragmented route; besides the traditional financial reporting, environmental and social reporting has also proliferated.

This fragmented approach has been criticized by numerous academics and business people because one loses sight of the magnitude of the interactions between each of these bottom lines. In fact, these different bottom lines do have to be addressed simultaneously because they interact with each other. A firm cannot meet its societal expectations if it is not competitive and profitable. On the other hand, profitability and competitiveness are not sustainable without sufficient attention to the needs of all stakeholders involved. Failure on one front necessarily entails failure on the other (Wilson, 2000). In fact, then, there is only one bottom line that needs to be redefined from an integrated performance management perspective (Jensen, 2001). However, the very diverse set of claims on companies today, the increasing impact of intangible assets, and the relevance of ownership principles all cause great problems in creating such an integrated performance management tool. Notwithstanding the important steps made with tools such as the balanced scorecard, the European Foundation for Quality Management, or the Global Reporting Initiative, academics still have a long way to go to develop a useful, integrated toolbox.

Enron, WorldCom, and other scandals show that companies' impact on society goes far beyond the loss of shareholder value. The social values that were damaged by these companies are numerous. In fact, the recent corporate scandals highlight the need for another kind of corporate monitoring, one that also concerns negative externalities.

Since the board of directors is the first instrument for monitoring the firm, the board should be aware of its enlarged duties. But in today's business environment it will mainly be the shareholder that has to be convinced of the new role for the firm in society. Although many family shareholders have been quite sensitive to societal needs, the movement of corporate social responsibility will probably be led by the larger international groups, most of which are listed on international stock exchanges. The overwhelming emphasis on corporate governance for listed companies (compare this with dominant firm logic) coupled with these companies' high visibility and international position places their shareholders in the spotlight for fostering responsible firms. Therefore, institutional shareholders could well become an important driving force.

Although shareholder activism attracts some attention in corporate governance circles, the term "shareholder" mainly relates to financial corporate governance and the fostering of shareholder value. More active monitoring by institutional investors to create the responsible firm is yet to be developed, but the sheer size of these companies will put institutional investors in the spotlight and encourage them to behave as responsible institutions. As trustees of the money of their members (pension funds) or customers (insurance companies, mutual funds), institutional investors have already come under increased scrutiny as the new invisible hand of the media and civil society. Combining institutional investor activism with the concept of the responsible firm leaves us with the possibility that these investors could well become the most important force in rethinking the corporate governance paradigms.

One possible route to stimulating the multiplier effect of shareholder activism could be to make institutional investors accountable for way business in society. Even in the absence of clear empirical evidence that corporate social responsibility leads to shareholder value maximization, just the belief by institutional investors that social responsibility is inevitable may prove to be a self-fulfilling prophecy. Similarly, most institutional investors today believe that corporate governance is a necessary precondition for good financial performance, although a clear causal relationship has yet to be established (Van den Berghe et al., 2002). Socially responsible investment funds could lead the way, as highlighted by Margolis and Walsh (2001): "While scholars continue to debate whether corporate social performance enhances corporate financial performance, companies continue to invest in social initiatives."

Institutional investors are crucial drivers behind the recent changes in corporate governance thinking. However, these investors are not immune to conflicts of interest and control-bias problems. To remedy these potential problems, corporate governance rules for institutional investors should be developed, or institutional investors will need to monitor their own corporate governance programs. The same holds for the numerous rule-setting bodies and semipublic institutions that perform a supervisory or monitoring function. In addition to the attention due to responsible corporate governance, therefore, more attention should be paid to societal governance (Van den Berghe et al., 2002).

Defining an optimal governance system is necessary in order to give the firm a better chance for success and foster the creation of shareholder value and economic wealth for all stakeholders. Optimal corporate governance can be developed along a double track: while basic corporate governance principles are universal, their translation and practical implementation needs to be differentiated according to firm type and the relevant governance challenges and problems associated with that type. (For a more detailed analysis of the synchronization between firm typology and relevant corporate governance challenges on the one hand and corporate governance rules and recommendations on the other hand, see Van den Berghe et al., 2002.)

CONCLUSION

While many continue to deny that the firm has a role to play in the sphere of social responsibility, others have attempted to integrate these corporate social responsibilities into mainstream shareholder-value thinking. Numerous arguments have been given for why such integration will finally be ineffective, but in our view these arguments still ignore the fact that the firm has a role to play in coping with its externalities. Moreover, these arguments still rely on the hypothesis that there is only one principal, the shareholder, while all other parties are "agents"; consequently, those who pursue such arguments do not accept the stakeholder model as a valid solution.

The solution we propose is to rethink corporate governance from the perspective of the newly-developed theories of the firm. This means broadening the corporate governance framework in two ways. One, going beyond the board of directors and the corporate governance tripod in order to include the interactions with and interests of all relevant stakeholders, and two, to broaden the emphasis on financial corporate governance to include performance as well as conformance issues. Important multiplier effects could be realized if the shareholder activism developed by large institutional investors were to be channeled toward promoting corporate social responsibility.

This enlarged role of the firm must be reflected not only in corporate governance duties, but also in a more holistic view of performance. However, this does not mean that corporate social responsibility has to lead to triple-bottom-line thinking. We make a plea to go beyond a fragmented approach and to develop a more integrated corporate performance and corporate reporting framework. It is here that the academic challenge is the most urgent but the least developed.

REFERENCES

Berle, A., and G. Means. 1932. *The Modern Corporation and Private Property*. New York: MacMillan.

Jensen, M.C. 2001. "Value Maximization, Stakeholder Theory, and the Corporate Objective Function," *Journal of Applied Corporate Finance* 14, pp. 8–21.

Margolis, J.D., and J.P. Walsh. 2001. *Misery Loves Companies: Whither Social Initiatives by Business?* New York: Aspen Institute Initiative for Social Innovation Through Business with Harvard Business School and the University of Michigan Business School.

Van den Berghe, L., S. Carchon, A. Levrau, and C. Van der Elst. 2002. *Corporate Governance in a Globalising World: Convergence or Divergence? A European Perspective*. Boston: Kluwer Academic Publishers.

Wilson, I. 2000. "Changing Societal Expectations: New Guidelines for Corporate Conduct," Keynote Speech delivered at the 3rd International Conference on Corporate Governance and Direction, Henley Management College, October 17.

Chapter 24

Corporate Governance Reform
Learning From Our Mistakes

Ira M. Millstein and Holly J. Gregory

Equity investors, no matter where they are situated or where they invest, share common expectations. Systematic failure to meet these expectations can result in a loss of investor confidence in entire markets. The challenge for all nations and corporations is to study these failures whenever they occur and apply their lessons to reform efforts. It is through shared learning from one another's experience that meaningful convergence in governance practices will come about—and not by efforts to simply mimic one system or another.

The United States in 2001 and 2002 and East Asia in 1997 and 1998 provide graphic illustrations of what happens to markets when investor expectations are not met. In the United States, recent revelations of management wrongdoing and financial reporting failures at leading companies caused investors to flee what had been considered—and likely still are—the deepest, most transparent, and most secure capital markets in the world. Between October 31, 2001 and October 31, 2002, the NASDAQ Composite Index fell by 21.33 percent, the S&P 500 by 16.42 percent, and the New York Stock Exchange (NYSE) by 13.44 percent. On the NYSE alone, this represents a loss in market capitalization of approximately USD 1.3 trillion. Between 1997 and 1998, Indonesia, Korea, Thailand, Malaysia, and the Philippines lost over USD 600 billion in market capitalization, approximately 60 percent of their combined precrisis GDP (Shirazi, 1998) when investors lost confidence in the East Asian markets due to the systemic failure of investor protection mechanisms and weak capital market regulation in systems that relied heavily on "crony capitalism" (Harvey and Roper, 1999; Pomerleano and Zhang, 1999; Claessens, Djankov, and Lang, 1999).

Market losses on the order of those in the United States in 2001 to 2002 and in Asia in 1997 to 1998 expose the fragility of investor confidence. Without adequate assurances and safeguards, including effective corporate governance, investor confidence can be quickly and seriously eroded. Corporate governance is designed to provide investors with assurances that the assets they have provided are being used for the purposes intended. The framework of laws and regulations that address corporate governance is continually evolving to provide greater protection and assurances for investors. This evolution is usually in reaction to failures in a system. By nature, positive reforms relating to corporate governance are reactive.

THE CORPORATE GOVERNANCE FRAMEWORK

Rules and norms of corporate governance are important components of the framework for successful market economies. Although corporate governance can be defined in a variety of ways, generally it involves the mechanisms by which a business enterprise, organised in a limited liability corporate form, is directed and controlled. It usually concerns mechanisms by which corporate managers are held accountable for corporate conduct and performance. Corporate governance is distinct from—and should not be confused with—the topics of business management and corporate responsibility, although they are related.

Weil, Gotshal & Manges LLP. 2002. *Comparative Study of Corporate Governance Codes Relevant to the European Union and Its Member States: Final Report & Annexes.* January 2002, p. 8.

The history of corporate governance in the United States provides an example of how reforms in securities statutes, listing requirements, and best practices take place in reaction to significant events. It is our belief that this sometimes painful progression can provide valuable insights—and perhaps some guidance—for all nations and companies as they seek to continually improve standards of governance.

Throughout the history of the US corporation, we have experienced outbreaks of corporate fraud, larceny, mismanagement, and outright abuse, but ultimately these outbreaks lead to legal reform and stricter regulation:

- In the late 1800s Congress enacted the Sherman Act and other antitrust laws to address the abusive monopoly power and related collusive and unfair practices of "the dreaded trusts" (as the economist Milton Friedman termed them) that had arisen in the late 19th century.

- In the early 1930s, federal securities laws were enacted in response to the infamous stock market collapse of 1929 and its exposure of some egregious examples of market manipulation, insider trading, and general abuse of investors. The Securities Act of 1933 and the Securities Exchange Act of 1934, which were adopted to remedy these problems, regulate primarily by mandating corporate financial disclosure. These laws and the related rules—which also imposed federal liability on officers and directors for fraud and abuse and established the Securities and Exchange Commission (SEC) to provide enforcement measures—emphasize disclosure as the primary tool for securities regulation, obviating the need for more detailed substantive regulation.

- In the 1970s, a series of corporate bribery scandals led not only to the passage of the Foreign Corrupt Practices Act—and its requirement that companies keep accurate books and records—but also caused the SEC to encourage the NYSE to require that listed companies have audit committees with a majority of independent directors.

- Significant performance failures in the late 1980s and early 1990s sparked US interest in shareholder activism—led by major public pension funds— and interested a number of corporations and business and investor associations in adopting codes of best practice.

- By the late 1990s, concerns about "creative accounting" led to additional audit committee requirements, primarily through listing rules. In 1999, a Blue-Ribbon Committee of corporate governance experts was formed at the behest of the NYSE and the National Association of Securities Dealers (NASD). Its mandate was to improve the effectiveness of corporate audit committees. The vast majority of the Committee's recommendations were adopted as listing requirements by both the NYSE and Nasdaq in December 1999.[1] Among other things, these included requirements that audit committees be comprised wholly of independent directors; that at least one audit committee member have financial expertise and that companies publish their audit committee charters.

The recent passage of the Sarbanes-Oxley Act, signed into law on July 30, 2002, and the proposed amendments to the listing rules for companies listed on the NYSE and Nasdaq are reactions to the most recent apparent failures of governance in the United States. However, instances of managerial self-dealing, financial reporting failures, and the related loss of market capitalization present a picture of conflict and imbalance that is not unique to the United States. In the early 1990s, financial scandals in the United Kingdom marked the beginning of the modern era of Europe's interest in corporate governance—and shareholder activism soon followed. Growing concern over the failure of a number of companies to reflect their true value in their financial reports, coupled with the collapse of a major bank and media empire led to the establishment of the Committee on the Financial Aspects of Corporate Governance and its subsequent publication of the seminal *Cadbury Report*. Concerns about corporate misconduct with regard to overstated income, improper accounting and questionable deal-making have arisen in France, Germany, and other European nations as well and have driven considerable interest in governance reform effort at both legislative and best practice levels. In the emerging markets of central and eastern Europe, Russia, and China, the move to a market system has also led to considerable interest in corporate governance with related legislative and best practice developments. And, in the late 1990s, the Asian crisis focused international attention on the importance of corporate governance.

In 1997, the Organisation for Economic Co-operation and Development (OECD) formed a Business Sector Advisory Group on Corporate Governance to provide guidance on policy relating to governance issues. The Advisory Group, composed of recognized business leaders from France, Germany, Japan, the United Kingdom and the United States, issued a report entitled "Corporate Governance: Improving Competitiveness and Access to Capital in Global Markets."[2] The report focused on "what is necessary by way of corporate governance to attract capital." The consensus was that corporate governance depends in large part on private sector action, with limited regulatory intervention, and that given the common goals of encouraging investment and efficient performance, common principles could be articulated. The Advisory Group identified four core standards of corporate governance—fairness, transparency, accountability, and responsibility.

THE OECD BUSINESS SECTOR ADVISORY GROUP ON CORPORATE GOVERNANCE

Regulatory intervention in the area of corporate governance is likely to be most effective if limited to:

- ensuring the protection of shareholder rights and the enforceability of contracts with resource providers (Fairness);

- requiring timely disclosure of adequate information concerning corporate financial performance (Transparency);

- clarifying governance roles and responsibilities, and supporting voluntary efforts to ensure the alignment of managerial and shareholder interests, as monitored by boards of directors—or in certain nations, boards of auditors—having some independent members (Accountability); and

- ensuring corporate compliance with the other laws and regulations that reflect the respective society's values (Responsibility).

Business Sector Advisory Group on Corporate Governance (1998, p. 20).

Upon the advice of the Advisory Group, the OECD organized an Ad-Hoc Task Force, with representatives from every OECD nation as well as a wide array of private sector institutions, to build upon the Advisory Group's core standards. In 1999, the

Task Force issued the OECD Principles of Corporate Governance, which, on ratification by the OECD ministers, became the first intergovernmental accord on the common elements of effective corporate governance (OECD, 1999). While the Principles are intended to be nonbinding, they have provided thoughtful guidance to nations seeking to improve corporate governance, and serve as the basis for numerous detailed corporate governance standards throughout the world.[3]

OECD PRINCIPLES OF CORPORATE GOVERNANCE

I. The Rights of Shareholders: the corporate governance framework should protect shareholders' rights.

II. The Equitable Treatment of Shareholders: the corporate governance framework should ensure the equitable treatment of all shareholders, including minority and foreign shareholders. All shareholders should have the opportunity to obtain effective redress for violation of their rights.

III. The Role of Stakeholders in Corporate Governance: the corporate governance framework should recognize the rights of stakeholders as established by law and encourage active cooperation between corporations and stakeholders in creating wealth, jobs, and the sustainability of financially sound enterprises.

IV. Disclosure and Transparency: the corporate governance framework should ensure that timely and accurate disclosure is made on all material matters regarding the corporation, including the financial situation, performance, ownership, and governance of the company.

V. The Responsibilities of the Board: the corporate governance framework should ensure the strategic guidance of the company, the effective monitoring of management by the board, and the board's accountability to the company and the shareholders.

OECD (1999, pp. 15–20).

What the Advisory Group and, later, the Task Force recognized was that capital is the essential factor in any growing economy: nations compete for investment capital, and the assurances investors seek as they decide whether to provide that capital are universal. Investors ultimately choose to place their capital where they can understand the risks and believe their investment is most likely to be protected from fraud or other misuse.

Recent research by La Porta et al. (1998, 2002) links strong investor protection laws with broader and deeper capital markets, a more dispersed shareholder base, and more efficient allocation of capital across firms. This research suggests that countries with poor investor protections have significantly smaller equity and debt markets. Companies in countries with weaker investor protection laws are more likely to have a large controlling shareholder—in other words, concentrated ownership. Concentrated ownership leads to less diversification and liquidity; weaker, less efficient markets mean a higher cost of capital. Without strong legal protections for minority shareholders, controlling shareholders may expropriate assets and engage in self-dealing practices to the detriment of the company and its other shareholders. Equity capital is more difficult to attract when minority investors fear expropriation—like transfer pricing, asset stripping, and dilution.

Corporate governance, whether expressed through laws, regulation or commonly accepted "best practices" and voluntary governance codes, is, in the end, about assuring investors that the assets of the companies they invest in will not be expropriated and that their investments will be protected. These assurances involve the tenets articulated by the OECD—transparency, fairness, responsibility and accountability of controlling shareholders, managers and supervisory bodies (the supervisory board in a two-tier system or the board of directors in a one-tier system) to the shareholding body at large—to achieve the ultimate goal: competitive corporate performance in the provision of goods and services.

Yet, corporate governance is not only important to investor confidence and market performance. It is also invaluable to the performance of individual firms. Research has shown that "a board that is active and independent of management...should be associated with higher returns to investors" (Millstein and MacAvoy, 1998).

Therefore, it should come as no surprise that investors make investment decisions, at least in part, on the quality of corporate governance. A survey by Russell Reynolds Associates (2001) of investors in Europe and the United States found that approximately half of European investors—and 61 percent of US investors—report that they have decided to reduce or divest an investment because of poor governance practices. Moreover, investors report that they understand the premium value of well-governed companies. According to a recent McKinsey survey of over 200 institutional investors in the United States, Western Europe, Asia, Latin America, and Eastern Europe/Africa, well over 70 percent in each region reported they would pay more for a well-governed company, all other things being equal.[4] The size of the premium varies by country and region—and, not surprisingly, appears to be inversely related to investor perceptions about the strength of legal protections and mandated disclosure. It was lowest in Canada and the United Kingdom (11 to 12 percent), marginally higher in France, Germany, and Sweden (13 percent), higher in South Korea (20 percent), Singapore (21 percent), and Japan (21 percent) and significantly higher in Russia (38 percent). This suggests that the quality of corporate governance at the company level is most valuable to investors where the disclosure and legal framework protecting shareholders is perceived as weakest. The study also indicates that investors' perceptions of the protections offered by the United States, relative to other countries, is lower than when the same questions were posed in 2000. This and, more graphically, the change in our markets underscore just how fragile and fleeting investor confidence can be.

DIVERSE LEGAL SYSTEMS AND COMMON PRACTICES

The near universal recognition of the need to preserve investor confidence through transparency, accountability, fairness, and responsibility reforms has driven and continues to drive convergence on notions of governance and of what constitutes best practice, despite differences in legal origins, regulatory systems, and governance models. As new reforms proliferate, this convergence will continue. However, absolute conformity is unnecessary and unlikely to be very healthy.

Last January our firm completed a study for the European Commission of corporate governance codes of best practice in European Union (EU) member states.[5] The goal was to determine whether the proliferation of governance codes creates a barrier to unification of European markets. Discussions with senior European private sector representatives revealed that code variation is not widely perceived to raise barriers to company efforts to attract investment capital. Rather, most European companies consider their domestic capital market as their primary source for equity capital. Thus, corporate decisions regarding which capital markets to access appear to be influenced primarily by liquidity and company law considerations, more than by the existence of corporate governance codes. Since the codes are flexible and nonbinding, a company is generally free to choose not to follow the code, as long as it discloses and explains such noncompliance.

The study revealed that even with the wide diversity in cultures, financing traditions, ownership structures, legal origins, and legal and regulatory frameworks among nations, investor expectations drive—and will continue to drive—similarities in corporate governance. For example, codes throughout the EU express a remarkable consensus on the kinds of items reserved for shareholder action or approval and issues relating to board structure, roles, and responsibilities; many suggest practices designed to enhance the distinction between the roles of the supervisory and managerial bodies, including supervisory body independence, separation of the chairman and CEO roles, and reliance on board committees. Given the formal structural differences between two-tier and unitary board systems, the similarities in actual board practices are significant. Under both types, there is usually a supervisory function and a managerial function, although this distinction may be more formalized in the two-tier structure. And both the unitary board and the supervisory board usually appoint the members of the managerial body—either the management board in the two-tier system, or a group of managers to whom the unitary board delegates authority in the unitary system. In addition, both bodies most often have responsibility for ensuring that financial reporting and control systems are functioning appropriately, and for ensuring that the corporation is in compliance with the law.

Notwithstanding the diversity in board structures among EU Member States, all codes place significant emphasis on the need for a supervisory body that is distinct from management in its decisional capacity for objectivity to ensure accountability and provide strategic guidance. As a result, codes that relate to unitary boards usually urge companies to appoint a majority of independent directors and frequently call for the positions of the chairman of the board and the CEO (or managing director) to be held by different individuals, or for a leader of the nonexecutive directors to be named.[6]

These are components of the proposed listing rule amendments filed by the NYSE and Nasdaq and expected to be adopted in 2003. The amendments call for boards to be comprised of a majority of independent directors and for the non-management and independent directors to hold regular sessions without members of management present. The NYSE's proposed amendments require that boards either name a "presiding" director to lead executive sessions or announce the method by which the presiding director is selected for these sessions. Although none of the US reforms actually go as far as to mandate the separation of the positions of chairman and CEO, many are beginning to recognize the advantages of doing so as a matter of best practices.

With heightened expectations about boards' monitoring and oversight responsibilities, questions arise concerning boards' actual ability to meet these expectations. For example, is it realistic to expect the board to be able to detect concerted fraud by managers if the board is made up primarily of outsiders? How does such a board ensure that it has sufficient information? We expect the next wave of governance reform efforts to focus on the information risks an outside board faces and how to control for such risks. As to board leadership, we have doubts about the extent to which a CEO is capable of leading the very board that is there to monitor him or her. (This is a concern that the senior author has expressed for well over a decade.) Moreover, the board's new responsibilities require that directors be better organized, trained, and informed. Such changes increase the need for independent leadership and the amount of time such a leader will have to devote to board duties. Since the CEO already is charged with running the company, it is hard to see how he or she will be able to spend the time and attention needed on board matters. If we, in the United States, move toward separating the positions, we will be borrowing and adapting what appears to be working well in most of the rest of the world. No matter the outcome of the reform effort, one message is clear—within a framework of suitable laws and regulations to protect investors, ideas about governance best practice have developed and will continue to develop over time by the business and investment communities, under the influence of market forces.

GOVERNANCE REFORM IN THE UNITED STATES

Although the current US reforms do not mandate the separation of the roles of chairman and CEO, they reflect a desire to shift the power center of the corporation away from the CEO to the board, in both subtle and not-so-subtle ways. Once again, the latest US corporate governance scandals did and should cause many to rethink how corporations are managed, what reforms are needed, and how they relate to the universally accepted fundamentals—transparency, ethical behavior, accountability, and governance. We can debate the merits of each of the many reform provisions, but the overall aim of shoring up confidence by focusing on the role of the CEO, the CFO, and the board and its committees in ensuring the integrity of financial reporting and other corporate conduct, is on target.

The Sarbanes-Oxley Act directly addresses issues of managerial and board integrity through a number of provisions.[7] In addition to requiring that all off-balance-sheet transactions that have or could have a material effect on the company's financials be disclosed in the Management Discussion and Analysis section of the company's reports, the Act requires that the company's CEO and CFO must certify in each annual and quarterly report that:

- they reviewed the report;

- to their knowledge the report does not contain a material misstatement or omission and the financial statements and other financial information in the report fairly present, in material respects, the financial condition of the company, results of operations, and cash flows for the periods covered in the report;

- they are primarily responsible for the company's controls and procedures governing the preparation of all SEC filings and submissions, not just the periodic reports subject to certification; and

- they regularly evaluate the "effectiveness" of these controls and procedures, and report to the audit committee any significant deficiencies or material weaknesses in the company's financial reporting controls, together with any corrective actions taken or to be taken. Their conclusions must be disclosed in the certified report.

Moreover, following any restatement of the company's financials due to material noncompliance with financial reporting requirements as a result of misconduct, these two corporate officers will have to reimburse their companies for any bonuses or incentive or equity-based compensation awarded.

Other provisions of the Sarbanes-Oxley Act give additional authority and responsibility to audit committees, and require that audit committees be comprised of directors who receive no remuneration from the Company other than for their service as directors. Under the Act, the audit committee must:

- preapprove all audit and nonaudit services (there is an exception for de minimus nonaudit services, however, even those services must be approved by the audit committee or authorized audit committee members before completion of the service);

- receive a report from the company's outside accounting firm which details: (1) all critical accounting policies and practices to be used; (2) all alternative treatments of financial information within GAAP that have been discussed with management and the ramifications of that treatment, as well as the accounting firm's recommendation; and (3) other material written communications between the accounting firm and the issuer's management.

Other provisions are directed toward creating a system of internal controls that ensures that outside directors have access to important information about the corporation. These provisions require that the audit committee establish procedures:

- for the receipt, retention, and treatment of complaints received by the company regarding accounting, internal accounting controls, or auditing matters; and

- for the confidential, anonymous submission by employees of concerns regarding questionable accounting or auditing matters. (The Act also protects "whistleblowers" by prohibiting companies from discharging, demoting, or otherwise discriminating against any employee who lawfully provides information regarding any conduct the employee reasonably believes constitutes a violation of the securities laws or financial fraud statutes.)[8]

The Act also requires companies to adopt and disclose a code of ethics for chief financial officers, or explain why they have not done so. In its implementing rules, the SEC has defined a "code of ethics" as a codification of standards reasonably designed to deter wrongdoing and promote honest and ethical conduct, avoid conflicts of interest, provide full and accurate disclosure, and prompt internal reporting of any code violations. In addition, the rule extends this code of ethics for chief financial officers to CEOs, controllers, principal accounting officers, and other persons performing similar functions. Any waivers or changes in the company code must be promptly disclosed.

Other current reform incentives—especially in the form of proposed new listing rules from the NYSE and Nasdaq—address board structures and processes designed to position the board to hold management accountable. For example, the proposed amendments to the NYSE Listing Rules would require that:

- independent directors comprise a majority of the board (with exceptions for "controlled companies," i.e., those companies having a shareholder or shareholding group in control of a majority of the voting shares);

- nonmanagement directors meet without management present in regular sessions;

- the name of the director who is to preside at the executive sessions (or the method of selecting that director if the presiding function rotates) be publicly disclosed in the company's annual proxy statement, along with a method for interested parties to communicate with the presiding director or with the nonmanagement directors as a group;

- boards have entirely independent nominating/governance committees and compensation committees (in addition to the current audit committee independence requirement);

- boards adopt and disclose a set of corporate governance guidelines covering topics such as director compensation, qualifications, and responsibilities;

- boards adopt and disclose a company code of ethics covering topics such as conflicts of interest and confidentiality.

Note that under the proposed amendments to the NYSE Listing Rules, a tighter definition of director independence would apply. For a director to be deemed "independent" under this new definition, the board must affirmatively determine that he or she has no material relationship with the company. A material relationship can include commercial, industrial, banking, consulting, legal, accounting, charitable, and familial relationships, among others. The company must disclose in its proxy statement the basis for determining that a relationship is not material. A board may adopt and disclose standards to help determine director independence, and may make a general disclosure if a director meets these standards. A determination that a director does not meet the independence standards must be explained. Current employees or immediate family members of current employees are automatically considered nonindependent. Former employees of the company, or of its independent auditor; directors who have been a part of an interlocking compensation committee arrangement; and immediate family members of the foregoing may be considered independent only after a five-year "cooling-off" period.

In sum, the new legislative and regulatory reforms emphasize the role of independent nonexecutive directors. An actively involved board comprised of a majority of independent directors—with wholly independent audit, nominating/governance, and compensation committees—is viewed as the key to ensuring that the management team will act in the best interests of the shareholders rather than in the best interests of the management or individual members of the team.

INTERNATIONAL IMPLICATIONS OF US REFORMS

The Sarbanes-Oxley Act—and to a lesser degree, the stock exchange rule proposals—will have an extraterritorial impact. Understandably, this is causing a good deal of debate in Europe and elsewhere. The act applies to all companies that have registered equity or debt securities with the SEC under the Securities Exchange Act of 1934, as amended. Thus, subject to any exemptions the SEC might grant, the Act applies to companies (whether organized within or outside the United States) that have registered a securities public offering in the United States, even if the securities were never sold or traded in US public markets.

To date, the SEC has provided little guidance on how, if at all, it may alter its rule making to accommodate non-US companies. The rules implementing the CEO and CFO certification requirements offered no accommodation to non-US companies and may enforce the view that "if you want access to our markets, you will have to play by some of our rules." The proposed amendments implementing the code of ethics requirement would also affect foreign companies, although some leeway is given. Although foreign companies, like US companies, would have to file a code of ethics as an exhibit to the company's annual report, and disclose changes to or waivers of any provision of it, they are not required to make the disclosure on their web sites or on a specific timetable. However, the SEC plans to strongly encourage them to make disclosures promptly.

In response to Sarbanes-Oxley, EU officials and others have voiced concerns about facing stricter—and potentially inconsistent—disclosure and governance standards in the US than in their home markets. This and related concerns about the costs associated with compliance may lead some European and Asian companies to reconsider registering or listing securities in the US markets, thereby avoiding the extraterritorial impact of the Sarbanes-Oxley Act and the proposed listing rule amendments.

Regardless of whether this occurs, the new requirements may lead European Union members to find common cause. A call for a unified response to the implications of the US reforms has already been made in the Bouton Report, a code of best practice issued in 2002 by French business associations.[9] The report states that:

> The recent adoption of new US legislation on corporate governance, the Sarbanes-Oxley Act, which has an impact on European companies listed in the US, illustrates just how much Europe needs to speak with a strong and single voice to avoid the risk that regulation be carried out unilaterally by the United States.
>
> Bouton (2002, p.25).

Despite concerns over the reforms' extraterritorial impact, EU Commissioner Fritz Bolkestein has noted that the EU and the United States "share a common vision" as to the need to restore investor confidence in capital markets and such a vision could further regulatory convergence on the main issues addressed in the Sarbanes-Oxley Act (Blum, 2002). After all, while the United States has had a number of highly visible apparent governance failures in 2001 and 2002, so have a number of EU member nations, including Germany, France, and the United Kingdom (as well as other non-EU nations, including Australia, Singapore, and Switzerland).

While it is arguable that the US problems have been more widespread and have had greater market impact, leading to the most sweeping reform efforts, one cannot overlook the reform efforts currently underway in Europe. Not only do these reforms reflect Europe's recognition of a need to restore investor confidence, but a comparison of their reforms with those passed in the United States demonstrates the continuing convergence on governance issues worldwide. For example, the recently released Winter (2002) Report, issued by the High Level Group of Company Law Experts set up by the European Commission, includes recommendations that are similar to those in the Sarbanes-Oxley Act and the proposed listing rule amendments. For example, like the NYSE, the Winter Report recommends that listed companies be required to include a statement in their annual reports about their corporate governance rules and practices. This statement should also be posted on the company's web site. The report also suggests that listed companies ensure that issues relating to governance, director compensation, and auditing be decided exclusively by nonexecutive or supervisory directors who are in the majority independent. By requiring that nominating/governance and compensation committees be entirely composed of independent directors (a requirement that already exists in listing rules for audit committees), the NYSE's listing rule proposals would guarantee that the same issues are decided only by independent directors.

Remuneration for directors is yet another issue on which the Winter Report and the proposed listing rule amendments converge. The report would require that stock option grants to directors receive shareholder approval. Both the NYSE and NASD listing proposals require shareholder approval of virtually all stock option grants. Like the Winter Report, the new US legislation and regulations also require detailed disclosure of director compensation. However, the report calls for more detail in the disclosure of individual pay for top executives and directors. Similar disclosure requirements are in place in Britain, France, Ireland, and the Netherlands, and the Cromme Commission may be on the verge of calling for it in Germany.

In addition, the Winter Report recommends that the responsibility for supervision of the audit of the company's financial statements lie with a committee of nonexecutive or supervisory directors who are at least in the majority independent. Under Sarbanes-Oxley, audit committees are given more power and responsibility in relation to the company's external and internal auditing, including the sole authority to hire and fire the company's outside auditor.

Finally, both Sarbanes-Oxley and the Winter Report address sanctioning directors for misleading financial and other key nonfinancial statements. However, the Winter Report does not propose specific penalties or sanctions for misleading financial statements by company officers. Instead, it suggests that decisions about the kinds of penalties and sanctions be left to the member states.

RENEWED EXPECTATIONS

Informed by the governance problems revealed in the past 18 months, reforms in the United States and elsewhere have led to new—or renewed—expectations of boards and CEOs:

- Investors expect directors to recognize that they are dealing with other people's money, which was entrusted to the board to be protected and, hopefully, rewarded (whether through increased share value over a period of time or dividends).

- Investors expect directors to maintain sufficient independence from managers in both appearance and fact to be capable of bringing objective judgment to bear on corporate strategy and management performance. The emphasis should be on arms-length relationships between directors and corporate managers.

- Investors expect directors to place far greater emphasis on avoiding conflicts of interest and insider transactions. And they expect directors to promptly address conflicts of interest when they arise.

- Investors expect directors to pay close attention to the board's oversight role, especially in regard to financial disclosure and legal compliance. They expect directors to devote more time and attention to the board and its committees, especially on audit committee functions.

- Investors expect directors to be wary of "imperial" CEOs, and those who may be more focused on their outsized compensation package than company performance. Investors expect directors to focus the CEO on building a strong management team and on encouraging long-term performance.

- Investors expect the CEO and the CFO to be candid about negative company performance. Directors should hear bad news directly from the CEO and make certain it is reported quickly to shareholders.

- Investors also would want CEOs—and CFOs and auditors—to adhere to higher than minimum standards on accounting and auditing practices, financial reporting practices and ethics. They expect financial disclosure to give a realistic view of the company's performance and prospects.

These expectations will determine the future of corporate governance practices and the general public discourse of the issue.

CONCLUSION

Around the world, legislative and regulatory efforts to reform corporate governance are building on the fundamental tenets of accountability, transparency, fairness, and responsibility. Reforms in the United States and elsewhere are emphasizing director independence and activation, clarifying board and audit committee oversight responsibilities, and highlighting managements' responsibility for accurate disclosure. Yet, by its very nature governance is exercised by managers and directors within the wide zone of ambiguity and discretion that is necessary to allow entrepreneurial activity. Ultimately, how managers and directors choose to act is not something that can be legislated or regulated, even though their responsible conduct is vital to the preservation of capital market systems around the world. In the final analysis, it remains to our leading businessmen and women to conduct themselves ethically and honestly so as to avoid the dishonorable practices of the past.

NOTES

1   The senior author of the chapter, Ira M. Millstein, co-chaired the Blue Ribbon Committee on Improving the Effectiveness of Corporate Audit Committees.

2   The senior author of this chapter, Ira M. Millstein, chaired the OECD's Business Sector Advisory Group on Corporate Governance.

3   For example, shortly after the Principles were ratified, the International Corporate Governance Network (ICGN) expanded on them from the point of view of investors. Euroshareholders, an organization of shareholder associations from eight European countries, adopted a set of corporate governance standards modeled both on the OECD Principles and the ICGN guidelines (Euroshareholders' Corporate Governance Guidelines 2000 are available at http://www.dcgn.dk).

4   See McKinsey & Company (2002). A "well-governed" company was defined as a company that was responsive to investors and had a board that was sufficiently independent of management to hold management accountable to shareholders. Id. at Exhibit 11.

5   See Weil, Gotshal & Manges LLP (2002).

6   This is already usually the case in two-tier board systems.

7   Sarbanes-Oxley Act of 2002, Pub. L. No. 107–204, 116 Stat. 745 (2002).

8   The Act provides for federal administrative and court proceedings, and remedies, to protect "whistle blower" employees. This is effective immediately. Id. at § 1107.

9   See Bouton (2002).

REFERENCES

Blum, P. 2002. "EU Warns on Sarbanes-Oxley Act." Sept. 6, 2002. Online. http://www.FinancialNews.com.

Bouton, D. 2002. Report of the Working Group Chaired by Daniel Bouton, "Promoting Better Corporate Governance in Listed Companies," Bouton Report. Sept. 23, 2002.

Business Sector Advisory Group on Corporate Governance. 1998. *Corporate Governance: Improving Competitiveness and Access to Capital in Global Markets: A Report to the OECD.* April 1998.

Claessens, S., S. Djankov, and L. H. P. Lang. 1999. "Corporate Ownership and Valuation: Evidence from East Asia." In A. Harwood, R. Litan, and M. Pomerleano, eds., *Financial Markets and Development: The Crisis in Emerging Markets.* Washington, D.C.: The Brookings Institution and World Bank.

Harvey, C. R., and A. H. Roper. 1999. "The Asian Bet." In A. Harwood, R. Litan, and M. Pomerleano, eds., *Financial Markets and Development: The Crisis in Emerging Markets.* Washington, D.C.: The Brookings Institution and World Bank.

La Porta, R., F. Lopez-de-Silanes, A. Shleifer, and R. Vishny. 1998. "Law and Finance," *Journal of Political Economy* 106, pp. 1113–1155.

La Porta, R., F. Lopez-de-Silanes, A. Shleifer, and R. Vishny. 2002. "Investor Protection and Corporate Valuation," *Journal of Finance* 57, pp. 1147–1171.

Millstein, I. M., and P. W. MacAvoy. 1998. "The Active Board of Directors and Performance of the Large Publicly Traded Corporation," *Columbia Law Review* 98.

McKinsey & Company. 2002. *Global Investor Opinion Survey: Key Findings.* July 2002

Organisation for Economic Co-operation and Development (OECD). 1999. *Principles of Corporate Governance.* Paris: Organisation for Economic Co-operation and Development.

Pomerleano, M., and X. Zhang. 1999. "Corporate Fundamentals and the Behavior of Capital Markets in Asia." In A. Harwood, R. Litan, and M. Pomerleano, eds., *Financial Markets and Development: The Crisis in Emerging Markets.* Washington, D.C.: The Brookings Institution and World Bank.

Russell Reynolds Associates. 2001. *CEO Turnover in a Global Economy: The 2001 International Survey of Institutional Investors.* June 2001.

Shirazi, J. K. 1998. "The East Asian Crisis: Origins, Policy Challenges, and Prospects." Presentation before the National Bureau of Asian Research and The Strategic Studies Institute Conference, *East Asia in Crisis,* June 1998. Online. http://www.worldbank.org/html/extdr/offrep/eap/jkssp061098.htm.

Weil, Gotshal & Manges LLP. 2002. *Comparative Study of Corporate Governance Codes Relevant to the European Union and its Member States,* on behalf of the European Commission, Internal Market Directorate General, January 2002.

Winter, J. 2002. *Report of the High Level Group of Company Law Experts on a Modern Regulatory Framework for Company Law in Europe* (Winter Report). November 4, 2002. Brussels.